D1106089

Handbook of Research on Cost–Benefit Analysis

Edited by

Robert J. Brent

Professor of Economics, Fordham University, USA

Edward Elgar

Cheltenham, UK • Northampton, MA, USA

© Robert J. Brent 2009

Published by
Edward Elgar Publishing Limited
The Lypiatts
15 Lansdown Road
Cheltenham
Glos GL50 2JA
UK

Edward Elgar Publishing, Inc.
William Pratt House
9 Dewey Court
Northampton
Massachusetts 01060
USA

A catalogue record for this book is available from the British Library

Library of Congress Control Number: 2009928595

Mixed Sources
Product group from well-managed
forests and other controlled sources
www.fsc.org Cert no. SA-COC-1565
© 1996 Forest Stewardship Council
FSC

ISBN 978 1 84720 069 3 (cased)

Printed and bound by MPG Books Group, UK

Contents

PART IV   DYNAMIC EVALUATIONS

Contributors

Parantap Basu, Professor of Economics, Durham University, UK.

Robert J. Brent, Professor of Economics, Fordham University, New York, USA.

Michele Campolieti, Associate Professor, Department of Management, University of Toronto, Canada.

William S. Cartwright, Assistant Professor, Department of Health Administration and Policy, George Mason University, Fairfax, VA, USA.

Frank Chaloupka, Distinguished Professor, Department of Economics, University of Illinois at Chicago, IL, USA.

Hans Fehr, Professor of Economics, University of Würzburg, Germany.

Rajeev K. Goel, Professor of Economics, Illinois State University, Normal, IL, USA.

Morley Gunderson, CIBC Professor of Youth Employment, University of Toronto, Canada and Fellow of the Royal Society of Canada.

Patrick Honohan, Professor of International Financial Economics and Development, Trinity College Dublin, Ireland.

Jyotsna Jalan, Professor of Economics, Center for Studies in Social Sciences, Kolkata, India.

Emmanuel Jimenez, Director, Human Development Sector, East Asia and Pacific Region, The World Bank, Washington, DC, USA.

James Laird, Senior Research Fellow, Institute of Transport Studies, University of Leeds, Leeds, UK.

J. Humberto Lopez, Lead Economist, Central American Department, The World Bank (PRMPR), Washington, DC, USA.

Bernhard Manzke, Senior Economist, Economics Department, Deutsche Bundesbank, Frankfurt am Main, Germany.

Peggy B. Musgrave, Emerita Professor of Economics, University of California, Santa Cruz, CA, USA.

Chris Nash, Research Professor, Institute for Transport Studies, University of Leeds, Leeds, UK.

Franco Papandrea, Professor and Director, Communication and Media Policy Institute, University of Canberra, Australia.

Harry Anthony Patrinos, Lead Education Economist, World Bank, Washington, DC, USA.

Richard M. Peck, Associate Professor, Department of Economics, University of Illinois at Chicago, IL, USA.

Rati Ram, Distinguished Professor, Department of Economics, Illinois State University, Normal, IL, USA.

Harry Telser, Senior Research Fellow, Socioeconomic Institute of the University of Zurich, Switzerland.

Booi Themeli, Assistant Clinical Professor of Economics, Fordham University, New York, USA.

Øystein Thøgersen, Professor of Economics, Norwegian School of Economics and Business Administration, Bergen, Norway.

Clem Tisdell, Professor Emeritus, School of Economics, University of Queensland, Brisbane, Australia.

Karl-Heinz Tödter, Deputy Head, Research Centre, Deutsche Bundesbank, Frankfurt am Main, Germany.

Peter Zweifel, Professor of Economics, Socioeconomic Institute of the University of Zurich, Switzerland.

Preface

The origin of this book was an invitation from Edward Elgar Publishing to construct a handbook on cost–benefit analysis (CBA) that would be a starting-point for those working on a PhD in this area. As someone who has spent his entire professional career writing, researching and advocating the use of CBA, and someone, in fact, whose own PhD was in this field, this was an invitation that was easy to accept. So this handbook provides an overview of the key areas of current research interest in the field of CBA and is designed as a starting-point for those interested in undertaking advanced research work.

The following guidelines were suggested to all potential contributors: choose an aspect of your subject area that you consider to be interesting and important to which you feel you have something that you want to add; identify the main policy choices and their impacts; address how the impacts have been, or could be, quantified in monetary terms; if specific impacts are hard to measure in monetary terms identify what types of study would inform the valuation process; choose whatever theoretical model or framework that you consider is the most appropriate for your purposes; leave it to the editor to relate your analysis to the general CBA field and to other contributions in the volume.

The end result, I am happy to report, was that not only did a very distinguished set of economists agree to contribute to the handbook, they also very much adhered to the guidelines. So the final selection consists of a set of newly commissioned studies which aim to be both comprehensive and innovative such that the current state of the art is covered and a suggested future agenda is indicated. The most important theoretical concepts are identified and the relevant matching empirical research is presented. In large measure, the chapters are surveys of their particular topics, and the introduction is simply a survey of their surveys.

The handbook is organized into four parts. Part I is the introduction, which provides a brief overview of CBA and then highlights how the various chapters have made contributions to the development of this field. Part II, which contains about a half of the chapters, involves the more standard microeconomic policy evaluations. Included are a series of surveys devoted to most of the main sectors in which CBA has been, or could be, applied. The main government areas, such as health, education and transport, are covered, but included also are policy concerns, such as financial regulation and labor markets, where CBA ideas have only more recently been applied. Part III shows how the relatively neglected area of macroeconomic policy can be integrated into a formal CBA framework. Policies for setting price stability, financing public debt, promoting economic growth and alleviating poverty can all be viewed with the lens of having associated costs and benefits and consequently higher or lower net benefit levels. Part IV, the final part, is devoted to dealing with dynamic considerations in CBA, whether it be in a microeconomic or macroeconomic setting. Benefits and costs change over time and this requires that a whole new set of considerations be included in CBA.

The success of the handbook will only be known by the extent to which there will be a new generation of research output adding to the cost–benefit literature.

Robert J. Brent

Acknowledgements

The editor and publisher wish to thank the authors and the following publishers who have kindly given permission for the use of copyright material.

American Enterprise Institute for excerpt: Hahn, R. and R. Litan (2006), An Analysis of the Ninth Government Report on the Costs and Benefits of Federal Regulations, Regulatory Analysis 06-05, Washington, DC: AEI–Brookings Joint Center for Regulatory Studies.

Association for European Transport for excerpt: Laird, J.J., K. Geurs and C.A. Nash (2007), 'Option and non-use values and rail project appraisal', *European Transport Conference, 17–19 October 2007, Leiden, Netherlands*, London: Association of European Transport.

Australian Communications and Media Authority for excerpt: ACIL Tasman (2005), 'Consumer Benefits Resulting from Australia's Telecommunications Sector', Sydney: ACMA.

Cambridge University Press for excerpt: Fehr, H., S. Jokisch and L.J. Kotlikoff (2005), 'The developed world's demographic transition – the roles of capital flows, immigration, and policy', in R. Brooks and A. Razin (eds), *Social Security Reform*, 11–43.

Commonwealth of Australia for excerpt: Papandrea, F. (1997), 'Cultural Regulation of Australian Television Programs', Occasional Paper 114, Bureau of Transport and Communications Economics: Canberra: AGPS.

Copyright Clearance Center for article: Parry, I. (2004), 'Are emissions permits regressive?', *Journal of Environmental Economics and Management*, **47**, 364–87.

Thomas Eisensee for excerpt: Eisensee, T. (2005) 'Essays on public finance: retirement behavior and disaster relief', Institute for International Economic Studies, Stockholm University: Monograph Series no. 54.

Elsevier for article: Henderson, R.A., S.J. Pocock, S.J. Sharp, K. Nanchahal, M.J. Sculpher, M.J. Buxton and J.R. Hampton (1998), 'Long-term results of RITA-1 trial: clinical and cost comparisons of coronary angioplasty and coronary-artery bypass grafting', *The Lancet*, **352**, 1419–25.

Her Majesty's Stationery Office for excerpts: Atkins (2006b), *High Speed Line Study*, Summary report; H.M. Treasury (2003), *The Green Book: Appraisal and Evaluation in Central Government*, London; Department for Transport (2007), 'Values of Time and Operating Costs', TAG Unit 3.5.6; Department for Transport (2007), 'Guidance on Rail Appraisal: External Costs of Car Use', TAG Unit 3.13.2.

International Monetary Fund for articles: Van Rijckeghem, C. and B. Weder (1997), 'Corruption and the rate of temptation: do low wages in the civil service cause corruption?', IMF Working Paper, WP/97/73, Washington, DC; Gupta, S., H. Davoodi and E. Tiongson, (2000) 'Corruption and the provision of health care and education services', IMF Working Paper, WP/00/116, Washington, DC.

MIT Press Journals for article: Nishiyama, S. and K. Smetters (2007), 'Does social security privatization produce efficiency gains?', *Quarterly Journal of Economics*, **122** (4), 1677–719.

Massachusetts Medical Society for article: Neuhauser, D. and A.M. Lewicki (1975), 'What do we gain from the sixth stool guaiac?', *New England Journal of Medicine*, **293**, 226–8.

OECD for excerpts: OECD (1995), 'Recommendations of the Council of the OECD on Improving the Quality of Government Regulation', OCDE/GD(95)95, Paris; Pearce, D., R. Atkinson, and S. Mourato (2006), *Cost–Benefit Analysis and the Environment: Recent Developments*, Paris; OECD (2007), Pensions at a Glance, Paris.

Springer Science and Business Media for article and excerpt: Santagata, W. and G. Signorello (2000), 'Contingent valuation of a cultural public good and policy design: the case of "Napoli Musei Aperti"', *Journal of Cultural Economics*, **24** (3), 181–204; Nocera, S., H. Telser and D. Bonato (2003), *The Contingent-Valuation Method in Health Care: An Economic Evaluation of Alzheimer's Disease*, Dordrecht, Boston, and London: Kluwer.

Sustainable Tourism CRC for excerpt: Choi, A., B. Ritchie and F. Papandrea (2008), 'The Economic Value of Australian National Cultural Institutions in the ACT', Gold Coast, Australia.

Taylor & Francis for article: Psacharopoulos G., and H.A. Patrinos (2004), 'Returns to investment in education: a further update', *Education Economics*, **12** (2), 111–34.

University of Chicago Press for excerpts: Feldstein, M. (1999), *The Costs and Benefits of Price Stability*, Chicago and London; Tödter, K.-H. and G. Ziebarth (1999), 'Price stability versus low inflation in Germany: an analysis of costs and benefits', in M. Feldstein (ed.), *The Costs and Benefits of Price Stability*, 47–94, Chicago and London.

University of Chicago Press via Copyright Clearance Center for article: Olken, B.A. (2007), 'Monitoring corruption: evidence from a field experiment in Indonesia', *Journal of Political Economy*, **115**, 200–39.

Wiley Blackwell for article: Echevarria, C.A. (2004) 'Life expectancy, schooling, retirement and growth', *Economic Inquiry*, **42**, 602–17.

World Bank for articles and excerpt: Belli, P. (1996) *Handbook on Economic Analysis of Investment Operations*, Washington, DC; Devarajan, S., K.E. Thierfelder and S. Suthiwart-Narueput (1999), 'The marginal cost of public funds in developing countries', Development Research Group; Devarajan, S., A.S. Rajkumar and V. Swaroop (1999), 'What does aid to Africa finance?', Development Research Group; Filmer, D. (2003), 'The incidence of public expenditures on health and education', Background Note for World Development Report 2004; Lopez, H. and L. Servén (2006), 'A normal relationship? Poverty, growth and inequality', Policy Research Working Paper 3814.

PART I

INTRODUCTION

1 Overview of the field and the contributions in the handbook
Robert J. Brent

1 Introduction

The basic principles of cost–benefit analysis (CBA) are not always well understood. An economist's training usually covers the difference between the net present value and internal rates of return rules for deciding whether a project is worthwhile, and includes a statement that issues such as measuring the benefits and costs, determining the social discount rate, and estimating distribution weights are controversial and very subjective. The would-be economist is left with the impression that his or her professional life can proceed quite nicely without having to bother with the niceties of CBA.

However, as is argued below, nothing is further from the truth than this false impression. CBA can be regarded as around half of economics, and possibly the more interesting part. This view can only be accepted if one first looks at what CBA is trying to do, examining what are the alternatives to undertaking a CBA, and then finding the alternative approaches lacking. This handbook is testimony to the fact that there is still a lot more work to do. But, CBA and public policy are inextricably linked. Public policy cannot progress without following the principles of CBA. Section 2 identifies those fundamental principles. Since there is much to do, the next step is to indicate what the contributors to this volume have identified as areas for further research. A guide to the rest of the chapters is given in Section 3. This section is built around an examination of some of the important themes in CBA. The summary and conclusions section points out the need for further research.

2 What is cost–benefit analysis?

A CBA is the best way of evaluating the desirability of a project. What makes it best is that it takes a wide view (considers all kinds of effects on all groups) and a long view (considers all time periods) – see Prest and Turvey (1968). The decision to approve or reject the project is made on the basis of a comparison of benefits with costs. If benefits are greater than costs, then the project is worthwhile. If costs are greater than benefits, the project is not worthwhile. And if the benefits equal the costs then society is indifferent between whether the project is approved or rejected. The benefit and cost categories and how they are to be measured are to be determined based on principles derived from welfare economics. Thus benefits are the maximum that consumers are willing to pay for the project, and costs are the minimum amounts that resources must receive to produce the project.

In practice, short-cuts are often taken. But welfare economics is still the benchmark to decide how valid are the short-cuts. Other ways of evaluating projects are simply partial CBAs. They either exclude some or all of the benefits, or exclude some or all of the costs. For example, cost-effectiveness analysis (CEA) seeks to achieve a given level of output at least cost. Cost minimization is, of course, a necessary component of a CBA. But, even if one is selecting the least-cost production method, to decide whether one should be producing the output at all depends on measuring the benefits, something excluded from CEA. So CEA does not do the full job of evaluating the desirability of a project.

With welfare economics as the base of CBA for both its theory and practice, it follows that CBA is not just an evaluation technique. An evaluation technique would be like a software program in a computer where, if you give it a set of numbers and use them to fill in selected boxes in the program, then the software will generate an outcome for you. Rather, CBA is a 'way of thinking'. One thing to think about is whether you have collected the right type of data to be inserted into the computer program. Some data are better than others from a welfare economic point of view.

To carry out a CBA there are a number of ingredients that need to be considered and estimated to form the benefit and cost estimates. Some or all of these will apply to a particular project to varying degrees. The ingredients are: shadow pricing of project inputs and outputs; allowing for externalities and public goods; employing a social discount rate to convert future benefits and costs to present-day values; estimating income distributional weights; allowing for risk and uncertainty; measuring intangible effects and the marginal cost of public funds; and incorporating user fees. Much of the CBA literature is devoted to an estimation of just one of these ingredients for general use rather than carrying out a full CBA. In this handbook, the chapters mainly deal with complete CBAs. When a specific ingredient is examined it is in the context of estimating it for a particular project.

Let us now clarify what is an evaluation, what is a project, and what is the alternative to the project.

What is an evaluation?

The economics literature uses the concept of an evaluation very loosely. However, for an evaluation to take place, the end result of the analysis must be a judgment or decision about the desirability of the project. Without this end result, the analysis can, of course, still be useful; but it cannot be an evaluation leading to an accept or reject decision.

A necessary condition for an evaluation is that an estimation of effectiveness be carried out. The project must have some positive impact on what it is trying to promote in order to start to justify the costs that are entailed in the project. If the project is not effective, then there are no benefits to offset the costs and the project can immediately be declared not worthwhile. For example, Smith (1981) in his evaluation of tax subsidies for housing in Canada, claimed that there was no conclusive evidence that social ills, such as crime, infectious disease, time lost from work, and alienation in the population, are caused by poor housing in Canada. So he concludes that there should be a substantial reduction in the amount of housing assistance.

But, what happens if the project is found to be effective? Does this render a CBA unnecessary? Not withstanding the common public policy practice of calling an effectiveness study of a project an 'evaluation', a CBA is still necessary because one has to establish whether the benefits that are derived from the effectiveness can outweigh the costs. Simply listing the benefit categories does not constitute an evaluation either. In his evaluation of rent supplements in the US, Dasso (1968) identifies no less than 11 categories of benefit, ranging from distributional advantages to gains in tax revenues (on this, see the role of transfers below). What is important is the monetary amount of any benefits not the size of the benefits list.

When projects do not directly involve the use of resources, as with changes in regulations, effectiveness studies are considered to be even more important. For it appears that one can receive benefits without incurring costs and so in this way pass a cost–benefit test automatically. In this so-called 'win–win' school of policy evaluation, one can focus exclusively on options that are effective in enhancing both efficiency and distribution.

Consider Datta's (2006) evaluation of joint titling in India. In India, as in many developing countries, the quality of housing in informal settlements is a problem. One solution is to give tenure regularization. If people are given property rights, then they are more likely to invest in the property and improve its quality. One weakness of the policy is that people once given property rights, have been selling their houses and moving to other areas as squatters and setting up new informal settlements elsewhere. To remedy this, Chandigarh in India introduced a joint-titling process for regularized settlements, whereby a wife's agreement had to be secured before property could be sold. Females were thought to be more likely to be attached to their home than males (who usually were the head of household who previously had control of sole property ownership rights) and so house sales would be reduced. This was in fact the case. So the policy was effective on efficiency grounds. At the same time, because females also felt more empowered, there was a gender equity benefit that was manifest in greater decision-making abilities for females. So both the efficiency and equity objectives were achieved simultaneously. With only minimal costs involved in changing property rights legislation, there were virtually no costs to offset the benefits and so no CBA methodology could turn down this policy change. In short, win–win was the result.

The reasoning behind win–win works in reverse with lose–lose interventions, that is, where no objectives are furthered. In this case projects can be rejected without further measurement. Chapter 9 points out that many regulations of financial markets that are identified in the chapter are lose–lose. They have evidence of little or no favorable effects, and adverse side-effects, so no further quantification is required to carry out the CBA. Chapter 12 on poverty reduction also concentrates on establishing the effectiveness of projects because there are a number of countries and regions, such as Egypt, Western Kenya and South Africa, where the overall level of poverty has increased, making effectiveness an issue.[1]

We shall be analyzing the win–win strategy further when the issue of how to include distributional considerations into CBA will be discussed. Here we just want to make the point that seeking win–win as an evaluation methodology is not a generally useful strategy. Typically programs involve costs. So even if all kinds of objectives are promoted, these achievements have to be measured in monetary terms (that is, converted into benefits) in order to see whether the win–win policy is in fact worthwhile. And what happens if both objectives are not improved together such that one objective is improved and the other is worsened? In this case there would be a policy impasse using the win–win strategy. 'Win–lose' could nonetheless be socially worthwhile if the size of the benefits from the objective that is improved would be so large that it exceeds both: (a) the loss of benefits from the objective that is worsened and (b) the project costs.

A good example of the win–win strategy, and what to do if it fails to materialize, involves the World Bank Poverty Group's policy of trying to achieve 'pro-poor growth'. The issue then is whether economic growth can be relied upon to bring about poverty reduction. The analysis in Chapter 18 on the trade-off between growth and inequality starts off with the win–win strategy, but ends up developing a new cost–benefit framework. The importance of changes in economic growth and changes in inequality can be judged in terms of their impact on poverty. Effectively then, poverty becomes the numeraire for the evaluation. If economic growth raises inequality (there is win–lose), which is found to result in the short run for a large number of countries over time, the issue is whether the resulting level of poverty will go up or not. It turns out that poverty does rise in the short run. But, in the long run, poverty falls with rising growth, irrespective of what happens to inequality. So we end up with a win–win policy in the long run in terms of growth and poverty reduction.

What is a project?

Many economists think that cost–benefit analysis relates only to the evaluation of projects that involve public expenditures. So as CBA is just one part of many in a public finance course, and public finance itself is just one part of many in the field of economics, CBA would seem to play a small role in the training of an economist. However, CBA is in fact half of economics. Half of economics is concerned with trying to understand how the economy works. The other half, the public policy part, is devoted to deciding the best ways to change how the economy works. This is where CBA comes into being. Policies should be introduced if the benefits exceed the costs, and not otherwise.

The practice of economics is to compartmentalize policies and treat them as parts of specialized fields. So labor economics policy is concerned with evaluating the minimum wage and employment subsidies; monetary policy is devoted to determining optimal interest and inflation rates; international trade alone explains how best to set foreign exchange rates and tariffs; and development economics covers policies for economic growth, inequality and poverty. The problem with this compartmentalization of public policy is that the commonality of the issues is obscured so that each policy is thought to be dealing with something unique. In reality, all the public policy fields are grappling mainly with the same set of problems, and existing CBA theory has already identified how to tackle many of them. Thus an optimal wage or wage subsidy, interest or inflation rate, foreign exchange or tariff rate, price of savings or investment, or income tax that redistributes income, are all values that in principle come under the heading of 'shadow pricing'. Shadow prices are determined by the objectives that are set and the constraints that exist. In CBA, efficiency and distribution are presumed to be the objectives; and the constraints are production functions and consumer budget lines. All of these considerations are in common and relevant in varying degrees to the setting of public policies no matter the particular field of economics in which they are housed. As we can see in Part II of the handbook, where the chapters present CBA as it is typically applied in most of the fields of economics, it is the practice that sets the fields apart and not the theoretical policy base, which is simply applied welfare economics.

To summarize: CBA can be applied to any type of policy change. If it involves changing what would otherwise go on in the economy then it involves CBA. Effectively this means that either by altering quantities directly, via a public expenditure or a government decree (a regulation), or by affecting quantities indirectly, by first influencing prices and wages, there will be a set of inputs and outputs that requires that a CBA be used to evaluate the changes. A project then is any type of policy intervention whether it is in the form of a public expenditure, a tax or subsidy change, or a government regulation. In fact, it is by thinking of monetary policy as regulation of reserve requirements and interest rates that one can immediately see the scope for expanding the realm of CBA from microeconomics to macroeconomics. In this handbook we present in detail all kinds of projects being evaluated, specifically projects involving: vocational training, public pensions, market extension (globalization), targeting Alzheimer's disease, drug abuse treatment, transport networks, project financing, alternative ways of building schools, adopting a pro-growth policy package, reducing the amount of bribes, supporting domestic TV programs, preventing financial crises, deciding to wait before one invests, reducing malnutrition, reducing inflation and poverty, reducing climate warming and providing information about smoking. Although every chapter contains a different project, there is inevitably some overlap in policy areas since education affects nutrition, transport affects health, and globalization affects almost everything.

What is the alternative to the project?
Strictly, for a project to be worthwhile, it is not sufficient just that the benefits be equal to the costs, as one has to know what is the alternative to undertaking the project that one is comparing it to. Denote the proposed project with the subscript 1 and the alternative with the subscript 0. Then the proposed project should be approved if: $B_1 - C_1 > B_0 - C_0$. Only if the alternative is to do nothing, with $B_0 = C_0 = 0$, will $B_1 - C_1 > 0$ be sufficient to decide the fate of the project. Often, as in the health-care field, one does not have the luxury of doing nothing as the disease may progress or, as with the case of alcoholism, the disease may get better on its own. Even when there is no explicit alternative project, there is always the implicit alternative project which is undertaking the exact same intervention, but after waiting one period. In this case, the next best alternative project 0 can be identical to project 1 except that it is undertaken a year later. As chapter 17 analyzes in detail, the option to wait may mean that having positive net benefits does not signify a desirable project.

When trying to estimate the net benefits of the project $B_1 - C_1$ relative to an alternative $B_0 - C_0$, the evaluator must be careful to ensure that the 1 relates to the effects with the project and the 0 refers to effects without the project, and it is not the case that 1 relates to the effects after the project and the 0 refers to effects before the project. The importance of estimating effects 'with and without' rather than 'before and after' has led to the widespread use of the 'difference-in-differences' estimator in policy evaluation work. If one looks at effects before and after, one may not just be looking at the contribution of the project, but also be including effects that are occurring over time unrelated to the project. The difference in net benefits after a policy change between the treatment group and the control group is one difference. But this difference should be subtracted from the difference in net benefits between the two groups prior to the project being implemented to form the difference-in-differences estimates.[2] Chapter 7 examines in greater detail how to estimate the contribution of a project in the context of labor market programs and Chapter 12 does the same for anti-poverty programs.

Given our definition of a project as anything that reallocates resources, then an alternative to the project can also be very broadly specified. In general one can identify two classes of alternatives. The first one, and this is often ignored, is to consider different levels of the original project. Thus if one is evaluating keeping open an unprofitable railroad line, with 10 stops between A and B, one can compare this with the net benefits of, say, providing half of the stations with full service or serving all 10 stations with half as many trains. There are many examples in this handbook of the evaluation of alternatives which are variations in the scale of the project. Chapter 2 considers the costs of having between one and six tests for the screening of colorectal cancer. Chapter 4 presents the rates of return for building schools with full and half maintenance. Chapter 10 compares the net benefits of zero inflation with rates of disinflation between 1 and 5 percent.

It is instructive to understand the difference between the consideration of alternative scales of operation and the consideration of alternative values for the key evaluation parameters (such as different values for the discount rate) as produced in a sensitivity analysis which accompanies the best estimates in many CBAs. In a sensitivity analysis, estimates of benefits can vary if one adopts different assumptions about the reliability of the data or the methods used to calculate the gains. One obtains different benefit outcomes for a given scale of operations and hence a given level of costs. But when the scale of operations alters, not only will the benefit estimates change, the cost estimates would also have to be different. Thus, in Chapter 3, the benefits of keeping open a line are attributed to those living within 2 km of the service, and these are compared to the alternatives where benefits go to those within 1 km and then within 5 km of the train service. The three sets of benefit estimates constitute a sensitivity analysis about what constitutes the appropriate catchment area for those who will benefit from the train service. If one is dealing with various sets of benefit figures due to alternative scales of operation being considered, as when additional bus services are to be added to take people to the train stations to ensure that larger numbers of potential train travelers can get benefits, then there will be different cost figures to accompany each one of the benefit figures because the cost to operate the additional bus services will also vary.

Apart from the scale of operations, the second set of alternatives to include in one's evaluation relate to different ways of achieving the main project outcome. Depending on the particular outcome, the alternative specified may be in very different sectors of the economy, or in the jurisdiction of very different government agencies. An example of the former in the handbook is Chapter 18, where six different policies for generating growth are being compared (including education, trade, infrastructures and finance); and an example of the latter is Chapter 12, where the four policy options for reducing poverty are workfare, conditional cash transfers, access to credit and targeting a poor region as a whole.

3   Some important cost–benefit themes

Textbooks are typically organized around analyzing and showing how to estimate the key ingredients of CBA. Hence there are chapters on shadow pricing, externalities and public goods, the social discount rate, income distributional weights and so on.[3] However rather than emphasizing these ingredients, the handbook can be viewed as being organized around certain themes which we introduce and discuss in this section. In this way one can obtain an appreciation of the history of CBA and the contributions made by individual chapters to the field.

The role of externalities in CBA

The existence of externalities is one of the main reasons on efficiency grounds why a CBA needs to be undertaken rather than relying on market forces to decide how to allocate resources. The private sector values outputs and inputs at market prices, which may either undervalue resources (if there are positive externalities) or overvalue them (if there are negative externalities) from the social point of view.

Strictly speaking, this argument in favor of CBA relates only to what used to be called in the CBA literature 'technological' externalities. This is where either the production or the utility function of one individual is affected by an activity generated by some other person (and there has been no compensating payment or other kind of adjustment to affect the scale of the activity).[4] However, there is a second category of externality identified in the early CBA literature, called 'pecuniary' externalities, which do not involve resource use and therefore do not require any addition or subtraction to market valuations.[5] An example of a pecuniary externality would involve an effect on the incomes of tradespeople who are located near a train station that is to be closed. If the station is no longer open, those who used to buy, say, cups of coffee and newspapers in the area close to the station now stop making these purchases. The local tradespeople experience a financial loss. This loss is not a cost involved with closing the station down because, presumably, the previous train travelers will make their journeys by some other mode using some other route and continue their purchases elsewhere. Tradespeople along those alternative routes would experience a financial gain from the 'new' purchases of their coffee and newspapers, and their profit would exactly offset the loss experienced by the local tradespeople. Pecuniary externalities then are to be excluded from cost–benefit calculations as they cancel out, unlike the technological ones.

Unfortunately, this distinction between technological and pecuniary externalities is often forgotten and misunderstood in the recent public policy literature, which uses the language of transfers or transfer payments to deal with financial exchanges. To take but one example, consider this alleged externality from a recent public finance text: 'An interesting twist on the measurement of smoking externalities is presented by the positive externalities for the taxpayer by the early death of smokers.' Taxpayers do not have to pay for the social security payments for people once they are dead. So, 'smokers benefit non-smokers by dying earlier.'[6] This so-called 'death benefit' is no benefit at all as it is just a pecuniary externality. If the smokers were not to die early, their income would go up by the amount that taxpayers have to pay for social security. Since they do die early, they 'lose' what the taxpayers now gain in tax savings. In either case there is a one for one gain and loss with no net difference related to resource use. Chapter 8 on regulation identifies two studies of proposed interventions aimed at reducing cigarette smoking that took very different approaches with respect to social security savings. One included them as benefits, the other excluded them. Obviously, evaluations cannot be compared if there is no agreement as to what to include or exclude. It is important that when evaluators exclude pecuniary externalities, as they should, that they then compare their results with others that also have their pecuniary externalities excluded.

Does this mean that redistribution has no role to play in CBA? Not at all, for CBA has developed since the early days when the technological/pecuniary distinction was first developed. Redistribution does not, with one exception, constitute a benefit category, but rather it requires that weights be attached to pre-existing efficiency benefit and cost categories. Instead of the CBA criterion being: $B - C$, the criterion becomes $a_B B - a_C C$, where a_B is the weight to the benefits B and a_C is the weight to the costs C. If the poor in the private sector are receiving the benefits and the rich finance the expenditures that the public sector make to undertake the project, then there are two weights embedded in the criterion. The first set of weights relates to income distribution. A dollar to the poor is worth more than a dollar to the rich from society's point of view. So a dollar's worth of benefits is worth more than a dollar's worth of costs. Second, since the finance for the project typically comes out of taxation, and this taxation causes an additional welfare cost in excess of the tax revenues collected (a 'deadweight loss' due to the existence of taxes that cause both consumers and firms to go for lower value options that they would not otherwise choose), the costs have a weight attached to them, called the marginal cost of public funds (MCF), that is a value in excess of 1. The combined effect of these two considerations is that benefits and costs have to be scaled up or scaled down according to their relative strengths. Chapter 15 on corruption uses and estimates such a criterion.

The exception to the rule that transfers have their impact just on the weights and do not affect the benefits and costs directly is when the transfers themselves generate real resource utilization. Chapter 3 on mental health refers to a very good example of what is entailed. An intervention to stop drug users from abusing themselves is an essential component in rehabilitation. But, just as important is the need to ensure that those treated successfully continue to be free from drug abuse. Supported housing can provide the environment in which a drug-free lifestyle is promoted. So supported housing in this context is not just a financial exchange where taxpayers who pay for the housing lose a sum equal to the subsidy amount that the person treated gains. This is because the full benefits of treatment would not be realized without the housing subsidy. Supported housing becomes an intervention in and of itself. For an example of a CBA in mental health that uses both sets of weights, and estimates the benefits with and without the transfers so that the real resource impact of the transfers can be seen separately, see Brent (2004).

To conclude this point: if a transfer (a) does not have a differential impact on income redistribution, and (b) has its effects that are within just one sector, whether intra-public or intra-private, and (c) is not instrumental in generating the benefits or costs, the traditional view that it should be excluded from the cost–benefit calculations is correct. When these three conditions hold, for example, smokers dying do not generate benefits that need to be incorporated into a CBA.

From microeconomic to macroeconomic CBA
It is also the existence of externalities that provides a possible justification for extending the reach of CBA from microeconomics to macroeconomics. The Keynesian multiplier theory is inherently an externality story. In the context of an economy with unemployed resources, the externality is technological. A firm that invests generates incomes for others and this

income increase leads to further spending that leads to the generation of even more income and subsequent spending. The final expenditure total is a multiple greater than one of the original investment that initiated the process. It is because the firm that makes the investment cannot appropriate all of the total gains that the externality created, overall investment is less that what is socially optimal. Public investment, or subsidies for private investment, can remedy this externality problem. In fact, monetary policy that lowers interest rates, and increases private investment in this way, can also be justified in these terms.

Note that when undertaking a microeconomic CBA, where one is trying to evaluate a particular localized investment (for example, a road, a school, a hospital), even in the context of nationally unemployed resources, one must be careful about attributing any of the multiplier effects to be benefits of the project. In general, any kind of expenditure would generate these macroeconomic benefits and so they are not specific to a particular project. So spending $10 million building a hospital on the east side of a city would produce approximately the same macroeconomic effects as building a hospital on the west side of the city, as would be the case if $10 million were spent on roads, or on schools in the city. Of course, if unemployment is localized, say in the north of a country rather than in the south, then the macroeconomic benefits would be an argument for siting a hospital in a northern city rather than a southern city. But, this still would not be an argument in favor of building the hospital as opposed to undertaking any other kind of investment in the northern city.

An exception would be if the particular investment is inextricably linked to mitigating the cause of the localized unemployment. If workers in one area without employment opportunities cannot commute to another area where there are employment opportunities, because of inadequate transport facilities, then improving the transport system would lead to employment benefits that investing in schools and hospitals could not have produced. This is one of the main insights that Chapter 5 on transport contributes.

In the context of full employment and price stability, which are the usual background assumptions of CBA, and where employment multiplier benefits do not exist, one role for CBA in a macroeconomic context is to evaluate the sources of finance for a project, whether loans, taxes or user fees. This is the framework for Chapter 14 on deficit finance. In macroeconomics, the consumption of a representative individual is often the unit of account, the numeraire. However, it is investment that is more important than consumption at any point in time because of its ability to generate higher levels of consumption in the future. One reason why investment starts off being suboptimal is due to the existence of taxes on capital that are widespread in developed economies. As different ways of financing a project impact on investment differently, the source of finance is not neutral, that is, different sources have varying opportunity costs and one should choose the source where the costs are least.

That investment should have a higher premium than consumption was the foundation stone for the CBA methodology for developing countries created in the 1970s by Squire and van der Tak (1975) for the World Bank, who undertake more public investment expenditures than many national governments. The tax distortion that was generating the higher premium was mainly on imports and sales. The premium on investment is even higher for developing countries than for developed ones as, in addition to tax distortions, the level of income per capita is so low that saving levels (the main source of funds for investment) are suboptimal. The Squire and van der Tak methodology was a natural bridge between microeconomic and macroeconomic CBA because it evaluated individual projects mainly from the point of view of their impact on the growth of per capita income. So emphasis was switched from contributions to income to one involving changes in the level of national income, a more dynamic perspective on economic efficiency.[7] Once a growth perspective is accepted there are many different ways that CBA can be co-opted to make evaluations of government policies. For example, Chapter 13 evaluates the growth effects of programs for malnutrition and education, and Chapter 18 examines whether a pro-growth policy is good for the poor. Chapter 15 on corruption uses both growth and household income to monitor policy changes.

In a microeconomic CBA, it is usual to measure all values in real terms, including the social discount rate, so that the effects of inflation on outcomes can be neutralized. However, from a macroeconomic perspective inflation is not neutral as it imposes a welfare cost on society just like any other distortion. It is the distortion of money demand that is relevant here. Chapter 10 on price stability argues that doing a CBA of lowering inflation involves combining macroeconomics with public finance as inflation magnifies tax-induced distortions as well as lowering the demand for money. Eliminating inflation can have large welfare effects as a percentage of national income.

The most obvious next question to ask is: when is GNP ever a good measure of the welfare impact from macroeconomic policy changes? Separate from the problem that GNP is constructed by applying equal weights to each group's income changes (see the section on distribution and CBA, below), there is the well-known difficulty that national income was never designed to be a measure of economic welfare as its main purpose is to record levels and changes in economic activity that passes through the market system. If there is no price charged then an activity is not recorded. A large part of the CBA of environmental projects is directed at measuring intangibles, and Chapter 5 explains the importance of option and non-use values for rail transport projects. However, even when prices are charged there could still be a valuation problem. At the microeconomic level the issue is one of pricing under monopoly and other forms of imperfect competition. At the macroeconomic level the issue could be one of speculation, which can cause GNP to go up without there necessarily being any welfare improvement.

For a clear example of the effects of speculation, consider the so-called 'Asian miracle' as it applied to South Korea from 1981 to 1991. A major reason why national income went up over this period was due to capital gains from land. Capital gains from land were 17 percent of GNP in 1981, rose to 36 percent by 1983, climbed again to 52 percent in 1988, before peaking at 73 percent in 1989. The percentage fell thereafter from 54 percent in 1990 to 29 percent in 1991, becoming small and negative in 1992.[8] Thus for a whole decade GNP was dominated by capital gains from land. Some of this reflects increased individual utility from residential use. But a large part of commercial use can be attributed to speculation without much welfare significance. It is important to note that from 1981 to 1988, the period when the capital gains from land was rising rapidly, the GNP growth rate at 9.9 percent was greater than the private consumption growth rate of 7.5 percent. Furthermore, the private consumption growth rate at 7.8 percent was higher in the prior 1965–80 period.[9] So consumption as a numeraire would give significantly different results from income as a numeraire in a macroeconomic assessment of welfare changes of policies undertaken over this period in South Korea. Since consumption has a closer link to a person's utility function than does income, the macroeconomist's use of consumption as the numeraire would seem to be more appropriate from a cost–benefit perspective.

Including distributional objectives with economic efficiency
A project is efficient if the sum of the willingness to pay of the gainers for the project outputs is larger than the minimum sum that the losers are willing to accept to give up the resources used to produce the project outputs. In this efficiency-only formulation of the CBA criterion, there are gainers and losers, so this is a win–lose situation. The existence of a number of losers resulting from a project is a welfare consideration in its own right.[10] But the literature has focused instead just on the possibility that the losers may be low income and so some projects could pass the efficiency test while making the poor poorer, that is, worsening the distribution of income.

Early welfare economists such as Hicks (1939) and Kaldor (1939), attempted to salvage the efficiency criterion by instituting the idea of compensation tests. If those who give up the resources are compensated, then there are no losers to consider and the project becomes a win–win strategy. However, it was almost immediately recognized that compensation could not usually take place in practice as there would be enormous administrative costs involved in identifying, locating and measuring the size of compensation when there are a large number of losers, as there would be by, say, siting an airport in an urban setting which would bring a lot of noise to the area. Instead, then, of giving actual compensation, hypothetical compensation was advocated. If the size of the gains were larger than the losses, then compensation could take place (if it were cost-less) and so there need be no losers. Note that although the criterion was packaged as a win–no lose strategy, it was still in practice win–lose as no compensation would actually take place.

What was ignored in all this discussion of compensation was that even if it did take place this would not make projects distributionally neutral. What the losers were willing to accept (as well as what the gainers were willing to pay) was a function not only of the intensity of their preferences, but also their ability to pay. If the existing distribution of income were not optimal, then basing compensation amounts on what the losers were willing to accept on the basis of the existing distribution of income is arbi-trary. For compensation might not be able to take place if the distribution of income were different. For example, a person living on $1 a day might be willing to put up with endless airport noise for a sum of $2 a day; while if that person were living on $1,000 a day the $2 would not appear to be so inviting to bear the airport noise.

What finally put the nail in the coffin of those advocating hypothetical compensation was the argument by Dasgupta and Pearce (1972). They invoked one of Kenneth Arrow's axioms that any social welfare function based on individual preferences should possess that of the 'independence of irrelevant alternatives'. If the choice is between building a school or a hospital, then the social decision should depend on the preferences just for these two options. Introducing an alternative that is not feasible at this time, say having a cure for cancer, should not affect the decision. If the hospital alternative is better when there is a choice between it and the school, then it should still be the chosen outcome if the choice is between it, the school and obtaining a cure for cancer. Given that compensation will not actually be taking place, it is an irrelevant alternative and should play no part in deciding the merits of a project.

That irrelevant alternatives cannot justify excluding distributional considerations from CBA is not well understood by economists. Instead there has been much theoretical work devoted to showing that *if* certain conditions hold, then efficiency-only can be used to guide CBA decisions.[11]

For example, in Harberger's (1978) classic article on why distribution should not be included in CBA, he makes the point that there are other government instruments than public expenditure decisions for achieving distributional objectives, such as the tax-transfer system.[12] Although other instruments can and have been used, there is no presumption that distributional objectives have been fully satisfied in practice such that the existing distribution can be viewed to be optimal even in an approximate sense. The potential use, but actual non-use, of other instruments is thus irrelevant to the fact that one should use distributional considerations in all instruments that impact on the economy. Thus our general definition of a project as anything that alters resource use in an economy means that distribution needs to be included in all instruments that affect the economy, whether they be taxes, transfers, regulations or public expenditures.

How then should CBA incorporate distributional considerations? The answer is by employing distribution weights. To see how this can take place, consider the following. To simplify matters, say there are two individuals or groups, the poor, P, and the rich, R, and represent the income of the poor as Y_P and the income of the rich as Y_R. The utilitarian base of welfare economics judges social welfare, W, according to: $W = Y_P + Y_R$, and changes in social welfare by: $\Delta W = \Delta Y_P + \Delta Y_R$. A project is something that changes incomes. Assume that the project raises the incomes of the poor (as they benefit from it) and lowers the incomes of the rich (as they pay for the project). This means that benefits $B = \Delta Y_P$ and costs $C = -\Delta Y_R$. The standard, efficiency-only cost–benefit criterion for projects then appears as:

$$\Delta W = \Delta Y_P + \Delta Y_R = B - C. \tag{1.1}$$

A dollar to a rich person does not have the same social significance as a dollar to a poor person. Denote the social marginal utility of income of an individual or group i by a_i. The a_i are the distribution weights. In our two-group, rich–poor world there are two weights a_R and a_P. These weights are attached to the income changes and hence the benefits and costs. The cost–benefit criterion becomes:

$$\Delta W = a_P \Delta Y_P + a_R \Delta Y_R = a_P B - a_R C. \tag{1.2}$$

Assume diminishing social marginal utility of income so that: $a_R < a_P$. It is useful to normalize distribution weights in terms of the weight for an average (or median) income earner being 1. So the assumption of diminishing social marginal utility of income implies $a_R < 1$ and $a_P > 1$. A comparison of equations (1.1) and (1.2) reveals that the standard cost–benefit criterion is the special case of income distribution weighting that sets $a_P = a_R = 1$, that is, each group is treated as if it were one of average income. This violates the assumption of diminishing social marginal utility of income. But, note that the standard approach does not avoid using distribution weights. It simply makes the untenable assumption that a dollar to all persons (or groups) is the same and equal to 1.

How can we be sure that assigning an equal weight to all group effects is an untenable assumption? The answer is in the same way that we can be sure about what the benefits and costs are in a CBA, that is, by reference to individual preferences. Individuals have preferences about goods and services that they receive or give up, but they also have preferences about goods and services that others receive or give up, particularly by the poor. Consider someone giving $1 to the poor via a private charity. They are not just saying that $1 provides the giver with some satisfaction. The donation provides the giver with more satisfaction than spending the dollar on him/herself and so is valued by the donor at greater than $1, say $1.1. Since the receiver can be assumed to value the dollar given as equal to $1, the $1 given has a total value of $2.1, which is clearly greater than the $1 of cost. Instead of just depicting the gain as $B = \$2.1$, we can represent it as a B of $1 being multiplied by 2.1. In which case $a_P B = \$2.1$ means that the dollar's worth of B attracts a distribution weight of 2.1, that is, $a_P = 2.1$.

Note that private and voluntary organizations in the US gave $13.4 billion to the developing world in 2005. Furthermore, the value of volunteer time was an additional $2.8 billion.[13] So the preference by donors to value dollars at greater than $1 when they go to the poor is very strong. But, strictly, private charitable giving does not directly have relevance for the CBA of public projects because such giving is a private project and thus can proceed without government involvement. However, it does confirm the hypothesis that individual utility functions do have the incomes of others included in them.

To justify public transfers we need to extend the analysis slightly. Consider the case where individual preferences for the incomes of others do exist, but are not strong enough to lead to private charitable giving. We shall see that public charitable giving using the tax system becomes worthwhile and that this can be justified in terms that use non-unit distribution weights for the poor.

Say $1 to the poor is valued by a rich person at 10 cents. The cost of giving for the rich is $1 and the benefit to them is only $0.10 and not $1.10 as before. So the rich individually (privately) would prefer not to give their dollars away. We have here a classic case of market failure and grounds for public involvement in the economy. For, as long as there were (at least) 11 rich persons for every one poor person, there would be 11 persons each getting $0.10 of satisfaction, producing total benefits of $1.1 and a cost of only $1. So net benefits would be positive at $0.10. Instead of treating the rich's preferences for income of the poor as part of the measurement of benefits, we can treat the income externality as determining the distribution weight to the poor as $a_p = 1.1$. We thus get the same net benefit $0.10 result as before via equation (1.2) and not equation (1.1) by considering a public charity that taxes the rich $1 and gives this to the poor (thus $B = \$1$ and $C = \$1$) and applying distribution weights $a_p = 1.1$ and $a_R = 1$.

It is important to emphasize that the CBA criterion given in equation (1.2) represents a two-objective social welfare function. The efficiency objective is reflected by the inclusion of B and C, and the equity objective by the distribution weights. The magnitudes of the distribution weights express the size of the trade-off between the two objectives. In response to the use of the efficiency-only criterion expressed in equation (1.1) being applied as standard practice, there has been a branch of the CBA literature that has overemphasized distribution in the form of an exclusive concern for poverty. We have already pointed out that Chapter 18 uses poverty as the numeraire in resolving the trade-off between growth and inequality in development projects. Chapter 12 effectively follows this same approach. One way to think of the poverty approach to evaluation is to consider it to be, like equation (1.1), just another special case of equation (1.2) where this time $a_R = 0$. It then becomes benefit maximization and not net-benefit maximization. So while it is useful and necessary to find out the changes in income and hence the benefits for the poor, this needs to be supplemented afterwards by the three other ingredients of equation (1.2), that is, C, a_p and a_R. One cannot avoid having to estimate and apply distribution weights, including one on a_p, just because one does not want the poverty effects to be ignored. One cannot judge whether any endeavors to end poverty in our lifetime are desirable, even if they should be feasible, unless one first specifies the distribution weights.[14]

The final issue, and the one that has been most neglected by the literature considering its importance, is how to determine the actual values for the distribution weights. One approach is to specify a function that has diminishing social marginal utility of income and present arguments why the rate of decline should take on particular values. This is the 'a priori' approach that appears in many studies of optimal taxation and other policies. Its use in CBA has been developed by Squire and van der Tak (1975) and a version of it appears in Chapters 6 and 15.[15] An alternative approach is based on the revealed preferences of government policy makers who make expenditure decisions on behalf of society that implicitly contain interpersonal or intergroup income comparisons. This approach was pioneered by Weisbrod (1968). Past weights may not be the 'right' weights, but they are a basis derived from actual experience on which to set the right weights.[16] More recently, in the health-care field, there is the use of questionnaires to extract individual preferences of interpersonal comparisons.[17]

While we wait for the literature to make more progress on determining the right set of distributional weights, the following suggestion might be useful particularly where poverty is a central concern. For those living on less than $1 a day, we could give changes in their income a social weight of 3. For those living on less than $2 a day, we could give their income changes a weight of 2. And for everybody else we could give their income changes the standard unit weight. These weights would be simple to apply, would respect the principle of diminishing marginal social utility of income and would not predetermine that public projects only consider the poor. What would be needed would be an analysis of the implications of these weights for a whole range of projects, say for a five-year period. One could then measure the extent to which poverty was affected and thereby fine tune the weights if the outcome was not in the desired direction or proceeded at too slow a pace.

One country that has recently decided to adopt distribution weights in its appraisals of projects is the UK as outlined in its *Green Book*.[18] Their suggested weights are based on the 'a priori' approach based on a formula that values a household's income inversely to median income. So if a household has twice the median income it gets a distribution weight of 0.5. What is particularly interesting about their approach is that they focus on weights across the five income quintiles. Chapter 15 explains the significance for weighting of using grouping of incomes rather than basing weights on individual income values in the context of the 'a priori' approach that uses the formula in the *Green Book*. Here we just want to report the quintile weights that they calculated for illustrative purposes and to compare and contrast these with the weights that we suggested in the previous paragraph. In the UK Treasury's *Green Book*, in Box 5.2, it lists two sets of weights, one for gross income and another for net income and they are presented as Table 1.1. They are expressed as ranges due to the uncertainty in knowing both the particular utility function and the measured quintile income levels.

The weights in Table 1.1 are in the range of 0 to 3 and of the same order of magnitude as our suggested poverty weights of 1–3. If poor is defined as being in the bottom quintile then the correspondence is even closer as both are in the range 2 to 3. The main difference between the two sets is that the poverty set is indifferent as to which income quintile is affected given that it is non-poor; each quintile except the bottom one gets a weight of 1; while the *Green Book's* weights are different according to whether the richest or next richest quintile group is affected. The research question then is to

Table 1.1   Illustrative distributional weights in the UK's Green Book

Quintile	Range (net)	Range (gross)
Bottom	1.9–2.0	2.2–2.3
2nd	1.3–1.4	1.4–1.5
3rd	0.9–1.0	1.0–1.1
4th	0.7–0.8	0.7–0.8
Top	0.4–0.5	0.4–0.5

Source: H.M.Treasury (2003, p. 94).

investigate whether society really cares about redistributions among quintiles that do not include the poorest and the richest.

One of the consequences of the relative lack of studies on how to actually determine the distribution weights is that there has been virtually no work on how the distribution weights should be set over time. To the extent that projects do finally reduce poverty, the social value of changes in income of the poor relative to the rich would also alter. Thus the path to the final set of weights, where everyone has equal weights, would need to be mapped out. This concern with the dynamic determination of weights takes us to the more general issue of the importance of allowing for the passage of time in our evaluations of projects, which is the subject matter of the next subsection.

Dynamic evaluations
Not only should every project be evaluated at least once using CBA, but every project should be evaluated more than once over time. This is because two of the central principles of all of economics are diminishing marginal utility on the consumption side and diminishing returns on the production side. Just because a highway project has a 30 percent rate of return when there are no paved roads around, while many schools exist earning 15 percent rates of return, this does not necessarily mean that priority should always be given to roads over schools. As roads are expanded, marginal benefits go down and (usually) marginal costs go up, so net benefits decline. There could then be a point at which schools have higher net benefits than roads.

A good example of the importance of the need to consider the timeframe in the evaluation of projects is presented in Chapter 13. An education project is not optimal when people are too hungry to read. Productivity will be low at this time and the consequential rate of economic growth will be low. So priority can be given to nutrition projects. Once nutrition has been built up and exceeds a certain threshold level, resources can be switched to education projects and this would now lead to a much faster rate of growth. A second good example of the importance of the time-frame is contained in Chapter 18. In the short run, poverty and inequality suffer when pro-growth policies are pursued. But, in the long run, this is not the case and an economic growth-enhancing strategy will be an anti-poverty project. Finally, we see in Chapter 12 that for temporary poverty alleviation, employment subsidies are helpful; while for persistent poverty alleviation, conditional cash transfers for education (or health) are more effective as future earnings and not just current earnings can be generated.

In many formal dynamic models in economics, the role of initial conditions can be all-important in fixing the future growth path. Although the analysis in Chapter 11 is not formal and more intuitive, the importance of initial conditions can easily be appreciated. Why is it that when one country gets exposed to globalization it gains, while another country encountering globalization loses, when it is the exact same globalization process that is being faced? The answer is that initial conditions can be different for some countries. Globalization brings more competition. When firms are in industries with falling costs, those countries that already operate on a large scale prior to globalization are better able to compete after globalization. Some developed countries have the advantages of these initial conditions, while many developing countries do not. As a result, just because one country does a CBA and finds that being open to globalization is worthwhile, it does not mean that other countries should necessarily follow suit. They need to do their own CBAs based on their particular initial conditions.

One area where a dynamic evaluation is essential involves poverty reduction as a primary objective rather than as a consequence of economic growth. As Krishna (2007) emphasizes, the level of poverty is a stock which consists of a large number of persons escaping from poverty occurring simultaneously with large numbers newly falling into poverty. Changes in poverty levels depend on the relative sizes of the additions and subtractions. If one just targets those currently in poverty and implements projects to help them escape from poverty then the projects can be successful, yet the overall numbers increase if those previously not in poverty now fall below the poverty line. Poverty projects should therefore not just be those aiming to take people out of poverty; they should include projects that prevent people falling into poverty, such as controlling heath-care costs and high interest private debt (what Krishna calls 'targeting the causes of poverty').

Chapter 12 makes the point that it is the poverty reduction that has occurred over and above that which would have occurred naturally due to economic growth that has to be estimated in order to judge the effectiveness of a particular poverty project. Effectively this means that, for poverty projects, the alternative project cannot be to do nothing. In this way, establishing whether there is a trade-off between growth and poverty, which is the subject matter of Chapter 18, is a precondition for being able to evaluate the effectiveness of an anti-poverty program.

4 Summary and conclusions

The subject matter of cost–benefit analysis is central to economics. Economics is about the allocation of resources. Since the current allocation is hardly ever optimal, decisions need to be made about reallocating resources. These decisions are to be made on the basis of a comparison of benefits or costs. For individuals, the measures of benefits and costs are private. For public decisions, the measures of benefits and costs are broader and longer.

Welfare economics is the basis of CBA because the measures of CBA are related to individual welfare, as reflected by their preferences, and these preferences have to be aggregated in some way to form societal preferences. These individual preferences are not restricted in form or content. They can not only refer to outcomes (for example, more goods and services), but can also refer to means to ends or processes (such as how goods and services are delivered). The possible outcomes can be in terms of goods and services received by others (and hence cover income redistribution) and include items not valued explicitly in markets (such as pain and suffering and noise). The means to ends can also be comprehensive, particularly in the heath-care field, ranging from giving a patient the choice about the gender of the doctor providing the gynecologist service, to allowing people to have a test for HIV at home rather than at a clinic. In all cases, individuals have a willingness to pay for something that they receive. If they value it, the item becomes a benefit. If they have to be compensated to give up something, the payment they are willing to accept becomes a cost.

Estimating benefits and costs on the basis of willingness to pay is, generally, best practice in CBA and, as made clear in Chapter 2, the health-care field is no exception even though, in any given application, short-cut or proxy measures are often used. This is usually because of the lack of data availability and the extent of aggregation involved with the specification of the outcome. For example, when a CBA is trying to value a person's life that is likely to be gained or lost from having a project, then evaluators have often used the present value of the stream of lifetime earnings to value the life (the so-called 'human capital approach'). Obviously this is a very crude measure, especially as people doing housework, and those unemployed or retired, may not be earning anything.[19] But, this widespread use of earnings to value a life should not conceal the fact that measuring willingness to pay is still the 'gold standard'. Strictly, economists do not value lives. Instead they value the *risk* of someone losing or regaining his/her life. Again, it is because individuals have preferences regarding risks that they are willing to bear, and the sums that compensate them for this risk addition or reduction, that CBA deals with valuing lives in the first place. Individuals also have preferences about goods received by others and, for this reason, income distribution cannot be ignored in CBA and has to be included with economic efficiency as a second social objective. Chapter 6, building on the work of others, provides a new argument for including distribution weights into CBA. Since including distributional issues is strongly resisted in the cost–benefit field, a new argument is important as one can never have too many of such arguments in order to combat this resistance.

Most of the main activities of a modern government are represented in the handbook, including general and mental health, transport, regulation, the environment, and labor and financial markets. Government activities are not restricted to just microeconomic sectors, so macroeconomic public policies that relate to social security, public debt, globalization, inflation, poverty, growth and malnutrition are also included. There is inevitably a lot of overlap in what constitutes an activity at the microeconomic level as, for example, education affects health, transport affects labor markets, and regulation affects every sector of the economy, which mean that preventing a financial crisis leads to many categories of benefit. Similarly, there will be a large overlap in activities at the macroeconomic level, as inflation affects growth, and growth can have enormous ramifications on poverty levels. Furthermore, the dividing line between macroeconomic and macroeconomic activities can often be blurred, as health affects growth (especially via its impact on malnutrition) and globalization leaves no part of the economy unaffected. For all these reasons then, when a project is being evaluated, one has to be flexible as to what to include as a benefit or a cost. Therefore the two headings in the handbook, microeconomic evaluations and macroeconomic evaluations, are suggestive only and not mutually exclusive categories.

The third and final heading in the handbook relates to dynamic evaluations. For microeconomic evaluations, dynamics are important because of the existence of diminishing return and diminishing marginal utility. In these circumstances, one should expect that the marginal benefit from extending output levels would be falling and that the marginal costs would be rising. Thus scaling up projects will probably lead to lower net benefits. This means that it is not sufficient just to establish that an existing level is socially worthwhile in order to justify extensions. Evaluation of the new levels are required in their own right. Undertaking a CBA is not a once and for all activity. It must be employed continually. For macroeconomic evaluations, dynamics are important as investment, growth, inflation and poverty rates are inherently variables that depend on rates of change over time and not just absolute levels. Output and input levels would therefore depend on time, and again should be expected to be changing. A static evaluation would not be decisive.

Apart from the data, measurement and estimation difficulties involved in carrying out CBA, it is important to be aware of a second fundamental problem with the practice of CBA. This involves the role of corruption. There is nothing that has plagued the public finance area in general, and the CBA field in particular, more than the existence of corruption. It is all very well to point out the many reasons why private markets fail and that this leads to a need for public policies to remedy these failings. But, what guarantee is there that getting the government involved will actually remedy the faults and not make matters even worse? In this handbook we have a chapter on corruption (Chapter 15) and provide evidence that public funds have been diverted from the designated project to other, and possibly private, uses. However, we also have evidence in this chapter of a CBA where reducing corruption was a project in itself that was not only effective, but also socially worthwhile. Nonetheless, until the time comes when we can control the extent of corruption, the duty of cost–benefit analysts is to ensure that the data they use for the benefits and costs reflects political realities and do not depend on an idealistic perspective. If the output of the project is lower than the level that would exist in the absence of corruption, it is the lower actual level that should appear in the evaluation, not the higher level. CBA is inherently a second-best evaluation method and existing constraints need to be recognized even if they are illegal distortions. As we shall see in the corruption chapter, bribes are not neutral transfer payments. They provide extra costs, but do not in themselves constitute benefits. Benefits arise only if output levels are greater than they would have otherwise been.

The corruption chapter is just the beginning of the analysis that is required for this area of CBA. By providing a general evaluation framework, it opens up the field for future research, which is, of course, the purpose of the whole handbook. With existing weaknesses and omissions exposed, it is hoped that a whole new generation of cost–benefit analyses will be forthcoming.

Notes

1. The evidence on countries and regions with increased poverty levels comes from Krishna (2007).
2. For a text on public finance that relies heavily on the difference-in-differences estimator when examining the effects of public policies, see Gruber (2007); and for an analysis of the strengths and weakness of the difference-in-differences estimator, see Bertrand et al. (2004).

3. See, for example, Brent (1998 and 2006).
4. See Buchanan and Stubblebine (1962).
5. For an early use of the distinction between technological and pecuniary externalities, see Marglin (1962).
6. See Gruber (2007, p. 167).
7. For a detailed examination of the Squire and van der Tak methodology, see Brent (1998).
8. See Table 5 of Park and Park (1998).
9. The growth figures in consumption and income come from the World Bank (1990).
10. For attempts to incorporate the number of losers in the social welfare function, see Brent (1984a, 1986, 1991b, 1992 and 1994).
11. See Hylland and Zeckhauser (1979), Christiansen (1981) and Boadway and Keen (1993).
12. For a discussion of the case for using distribution weights in CBA that addresses all of Harberger's concerns, see Brent (1984b).
13. The numbers related to US private giving to the developing world come from the Center for Global Prosperity (2007).
14. See, for example, the plan set out in Sachs (2005).
15. For a critique of the a priori approach see Brent (2006, pp. 336). To summarize: there are three major shortcomings: (a) there is no clear basis for selecting the income inequality parameter; (b) the weights are attached to income. Often a person is considered socially needy by a mixture of income and non-income criteria, such as age; and (c) the weighting function gives a complete specification of weights for all income groups, when not all income groups are of social concern, especially those in the middle of the distribution.
16. For an extension of the Weisbrod approach that incorporates a stochastic rather than a deterministic estimation methodology, see Brent (1979).
17. These comparisons have been framed in terms of different degrees of illness for different numbers of individuals; see, for example, the person trade-off approach associated with Nord (1995), but such surveys could easily be extended to relate to differences in income levels for different numbers of people.
18. See H.M. Treasury (2003, Annex 5).
19. For an alternative methodology to using earnings to value lives, that does not exclude those who are out of the workforce, but falls short of the 'willingness to pay' ideal, see Brent (1991a).

References

Bertrand, M., Duflo, E. and Mullainathan, S. (2004), 'How much should we trust differences-in-differences estimates?', *Quarterly Journal of Economics*, **119**, 249–75.
Boadway, R. and Keen, M. (1993), 'Public goods, self-selection and optimal income taxation', *International Economic Review*, **34**, 463–78.
Brent, R.J. (1979), 'Imputing weights behind railway closure decisions within a cost–benefit framework', *Applied Economics*, **9**, 157–70.
Brent, R.J. (1984a), 'A three objective social welfare function for cost–benefit analysis', *Applied Economics*, **16**, 369–78.
Brent, R.J. (1984b), 'On the use of distribution weights in cost–benefit analysis; a survey of schools', *Public Finance Quarterly*, **12**, 213–30.
Brent, R.J. (1986), 'An axiomatic basis for the three objective social welfare functions within a poverty context', *Economics Letters*, **20**, 89–94.
Brent, R.J. (1991a), 'A new approach to valuing a life', *Journal of Public Economics*, **44**, 165–71.
Brent, R.J. (1991b), 'The numbers effect and the shadow wage in project appraisal', *Public Finance*, **46**, 118–27.
Brent, R.J. (1992), 'The consumption rate of interest and the numbers effect', *Public Finance*, **47**, 367–77.

Brent, R.J. (1994), 'Counting and double-counting in project appraisal', *Project Appraisal*, **9**, 275–81.
Brent, R.J. (1998), *Cost–Benefit Analysis for Developing Countries*, Cheltenham, UK and Lyme, USA: Edward Elgar.
Brent, R.J. (2004), 'The role of public and private transfers in the cost–benefit analysis of mental health programs', *Health Economics*, **13**, 1125–36.
Brent, R.J. (2006), *Applied Cost–Benefit Analysis*, 2nd edn, Cheltenham, UK and Northampton, MA, USA: Edward Elgar.
Buchanan, J.M. and Stubblebine, C. (1962), 'Externality', *Economica*, **29**, 371–84.
Center for Global Prosperity (2007), *The Index of Global Philanthropy 2007*, Washington, DC.
Christiansen, V. (1981), 'Evaluation of public projects under optimal taxation', *Review of Economic Studies*, **48**, 447–57.
Dasgupta, A.K. and Pearce, D.W. (1972), *Cost–Benefit Analysis: Theory and Practice*, London: Macmillan.
Dasso, J. (1968), 'An evaluation of rent supplements', *Land Economics*, **44**, 441–9.
Datta, N. (2006), 'Joint titling – a win–win policy? Gender and property rights in urban informal settlements in Chandigarh, India', *Feminist Economics*, **12**, 271–98.
Gruber, J. (2007), *Public Finance and Public Policy*, 2nd edn, New York: Worth.
Harberger, A.C. (1978), 'On the use of distributional weights in social cost–benefit analysis', *Journal of Political Economy* (Supplement), **86**, 87–120.
Hicks, J.R. (1939), 'The foundations of welfare economics', *Economic Journal*, **49**, 696–712.
H.M. Treasury (2003), *The Green Book: Appraisal and Evaluation in Central Government*, London.
Hylland, A. and Zeckhauser, R. (1979), 'Distributional objectives should affect taxes but not program choice or design', *Scandinavian Journal of Economics*, **81**, 264–84.
Kaldor, N. (1939), 'Welfare propositions in economics and interpersonal comparisons of utility', *Economic Journal*, **49**, 549–52.
Krishna, A. (2007), '"For reducing poverty faster: target reasons before people', *World Development*, **35**, 1947–60.
Marglin S.A. (1962), 'Objectives of water resource development: a general statement', in A. Maas, M.M. Hufschmidt, K. Dorfman, H.H. Thomas Jr., S.A. Marglin and G.M. Fair (eds), *Design of Water Resource Systems*, Cambridge, MA: Harvard University Press, pp. 17–87.
Nord, E. (1995), 'The person-trade-off approach to valuing health care programs', *Medical Decision Making*, **15**, 201–8.
Park, Y.C. and Park, W.-A. (1998), 'Capital movements, real asset speculation, and macroeconomic adjustment in Korea', in Y.C. Park (ed.), *Financial Liberation and Opening in East Asia*, Seoul, Korea: Korea Institute of Finance, pp. 359–90.
Prest, A.R. and Turvey, R. (1968), 'Cost–benefit analysis: a survey', *Economic Journal*, **75**, 683–735.
Sachs, J. (2005), *The End of Poverty: Economic Possibilities for Our Time*, New York: Penguin.
Smith, L.B. (1981), 'Housing assistance: a re-evaluation', *Canadian Public Policy*, **7**, 454–63.
Squire, L. and van der Tak, H. (1975), *Economic Analysis of Projects*, Baltimore, MD: Johns Hopkins University Press.
Weisbrod, B.A. (1968), 'Income redistribution effects and benefit–cost analysis', in S.B. Chase (ed.), *Problems in Public Expenditure Analysis*, Washington, DC: Brookings Institution, pp. 172–222.
World Bank (1990), *World Development Report 1990: Poverty*, New York: Oxford University Press.

PART II

MICROECONOMIC EVALUATIONS

2 Cost–benefit analysis for health
Peter Zweifel and Harry Telser

1 Introduction and motivation

Many of the health-care services are transacted within the public sector, are financed by health insurance, or provided by members of professions where barriers to access are high. In these situations, observed prices are not informative in the same way as in open markets, where willingness to pay by consumers is at least equal to the market price and market prices reflect the value of the resources used in production (without externalities). Cost–benefit analysis (CBA) is an imperfect substitute for market valuations. It holds the promise of indicating to policy makers whether a health program is worth its cost.

However, CBA requires a measure of valuation by consumers, which is hard to come by. For this reason, alternatives to CBA have been developed in health economics, notably cost-effectiveness analysis (CEA) and cost-utility analysis (CUA). These alternatives are discussed in Section 2 and found deficient in important aspects. Section 3 is devoted to a particular challenge that health behavior seems to pose to the application of CBA, the often-heard quote being that consumers 'do not give a trifle for health when healthy but are willing to spend their fortune when sick'. It is shown that this does not necessarily reflect instability of preferences (which would render the application of CBA indeed difficult). Issues surrounding the measurement of true cost are discussed in Section 4, while Section 5 returns to the benefits side. The human capital approach is criticized for not being compatible with standard microeconomics. The alternatives are contingent valuation and discrete-choice experiments (DCEs). The latter are argued to be superior on several grounds. A rare empirical application of CBA is presented in Section 6 and conclusions are offered in Section 7.

2 Alternatives to CBA as applied to health

There are different approaches to evaluating health programs. They usually are distinguished by the units in which positive and negative effects of an intervention are measured. The simplest alternative is cost-effectiveness analysis. Here, the effects are measured by natural units on a one-dimensional scale. This can either be a clinical parameter such as the lowering of blood pressure in mm Hg or the lengthening of life in years. CEA allows us to evaluate and rank two or more mutually exclusive interventions, with the intervention having the lowest cost per unit of positive effect to be preferred. However, as soon as there is more than one health effect, CEA cannot be used. Furthermore, even if an intervention is cost-effective, it fails to answer the question of whether the program 'is worth the money', that is, whether it should be implemented at all.

Cost-utility analysis goes one step further by taking the multidimensionality of health into account. CUA reflects both lengthening of life and change in health status. It uses a cardinal utility function defined in terms of health (but no other goods), which maps these two dimensions of health into a scalar index, which then can be compared to the cost of the program. The best-known and most frequently used index is quality-adjusted life years (QALYs).[1]

To derive QALYs, all conceivable health states are evaluated on a scale from 0 (death) to 1 (perfect health). The other values are defined in such a way that for any number x between 0 and 1, a representative individual is indifferent between the following alternatives, 'survive one year in a health state with a utility index of x' and 'survive the fraction x of a year in a state of perfect health'. In this way, all health effects of an intervention are made comparable, permitting them to be aggregated into a single number, which can be interpreted as the 'gain in QALYs'.

The QALY concept is easy to apply. However, it has no sound decision-theoretic foundations since it is based on several restrictive assumptions. Preferences for health states and trade-offs against other objectives must be stable over the whole life cycle, there must be risk neutrality with respect to length of life, and preferences with respect to health states with durations of zero have to be equivalent (see Zweifel et al., 2009, ch. 2.3). There are several empirical studies suggesting that the requirements of the QALY concept are in general violated (see Dolan, 2000 for a survey).

If QALYs are used as a utility index in a CUA framework, the decision rule is to pick the intervention that maximizes the number of QALYs for a given budget. This rule is based on two fundamental value judgments:

1. the welfare of the affected person enters the collective decision rule exclusively through QALYs gained; and
2. it is irrelevant who experiences the increase in QALYs.

This makes CUA not compatible with the usual welfarist position adopted in economics, namely that collective decisions should be based on overall utility of the affected persons and not only health-related utility (see Boadway and Bruce, 1984). The use of QALYs and CUA in general may be justified if the health budget is fixed. However, there is empirical evidence suggesting that the distribution of QALYs matters, in the guise of a moderate or even strong preference in favor of the young rather than the old (see, for example, Johannesson and Johansson, 1997a, b for a specific case; or Schwappach, 2002 for an overview). In principle, it is possible to account for the distribution of QALYs in a generalized CUA framework. However, this requires considerably more information than a basic CUA.

Compared to CEA, CUA has the advantage of being applicable both to medical interventions of different types as well as non-medical interventions because it makes effects measured on different (for example, clinical) dimensions comparable by mapping them into a single utility index. It can be used to construct so-called 'league tables' of medical interventions, which have repeatedly shown that similar increases in QALYs can be achieved at very different costs. This type of information is useful to political decision makers who are responsible for allocating a fixed budget within the health-care sector.

However, CUA has its limitations, too. Besides weaknesses in its decision-theoretic foundations and its neglect of the distribution of QALYs among the members of society, CUA is conditional on whose utility function goes into the determination of QALYs. Furthermore, like CEA, CUA provides only a rank ordering of mutually exclusive interventions but fails to provide an answer as to the cutoff value of cost per QALY above which realization of a program cannot be justified. This is important as soon as the total amount of money to be allocated to health is not predetermined.

In CBA, both costs and benefits are measured in money, making it suitable to evaluate interventions occurring inside or outside the health-care sector and having any health and non-health consequences. If the money value of benefits exceeds that of cost, implementing the program is worthwhile. The application of this rule can be justified using the welfare economic criterion of 'potential Pareto-improvement' (also called the 'Kaldor–Hicks' criterion, see, for example, Zweifel et al., 2009, ch. 2.4).

3   A defense of the WTP approach

The crucial feature of health is that it does not constitute a tangible stock that can be held, controlled, and traded (see, however, the stock formulation by Grossman, 1972). This means that individuals cannot sacrifice 'health' in exchange for something else on a market – at least in a non-slave society. In addition, most laypeople would hesitate to say that they are consciously opting for a level of health that is below the maximum attainable. However, individuals do trade off a (small) reduction in the probability of being healthy in the future against other objectives (which will be called 'consumption' for simplicity). Let $(1 - \pi)$ denote this probability during a short period (a week, say). Accordingly, the probability of being in bad health is π. Let the individual use expected utility EU as the decision criterion, with utility derived from consumption depending on whether one is healthy (h) or sick (s). Therefore, expected utility is given by:

$$EU = \pi \cdot u_s[C_s] + (1 - \pi)u_h[C_h], \text{with } u_h[C] > u_s[C]. \quad (2.1)$$

Therefore, at a given level of consumption, utility in the healthy state exceeds utility in the sick state – a very natural assumption. Now an indifference curve in $[(1 - \pi), C]$-space can be constructed by varying π, C_s, and C_h while holding EU constant, resulting in the condition,

$$dEU = 0 = d\pi \cdot u_s[C_s] + \pi \frac{\partial u_s}{\partial C_s}dC_s + (1 - \pi)\frac{\partial u_h}{\partial C_h}dC_h + (-d\pi)u_h[C_h].$$
$$(2.2)$$

This can be solved for the slope of the indifference curve (setting $dC_s = dC_h := dC$) and writing u' for marginal utilities),

$$\frac{dC}{d(1 - \pi)} = -\frac{u_h[C_h] - u_s[C_s]}{\pi u'_s[C_s] + (1 - \pi)u'_h[C_h]}. \quad (2.3)$$

This slope (the marginal rate of substitution MRS) is negative since $u_h[C_h] > u_s[C_s]$, as stated above. Moreover, utility increases with consumption in both states ($u'_h, u'_s > 0$). Without further justification, assume MRS to be decreasing as usual, resulting in convex indifference curves (see Zweifel et al., 2009, ch. 2.4 for details). Now consider a sequence of periods, in each of which there is a probability of $(1 - \pi)$ of being in the healthy state and π of being in the sick state. If the initial state is 'healthy', it follows from the binary distribution that the expected number of periods in the healthy state (before a change to the sick state occurs) is $ET_h = 1/\pi$ (see, for example, Bhattacharyya and Johnson, 1977, p. 154). Since this is a monotonic transformation of $(1 - \pi)$, indifference curves can be drawn in a (C, ET_h)-space rather than in a $(C, 1 - \pi)$-space without loss of generality (see Figure 2.1). In the following, the argument will be couched in terms of consumption (C) and expected number of healthy periods (ET_h). Total time available is given by T, implying that the expected number of periods spent in the 'sick' state is

$$ET_s = T - ET_h.$$

Up to this point, the existence of an MRS between consumption and 'health' (more precisely, the expected number of healthy periods over a future comprising T periods, with $ET_h \leq T$) has been established. But

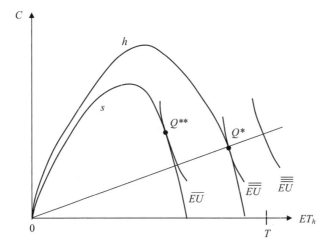

Figure 2.1   State dependence in the production of healthy time

this MRS is nothing but the individual's marginal willingness to pay (MWTP) for more time in good health because it indicates how much in terms of consumption (or income) he or she is prepared to give up for more time in good health. According to the model presented here, MWTP is predicted:

1. to depend on the initial endowment in terms of consumption and expected number of healthy periods (originally chances for good health $(1 - \pi)$);
2. to decrease when ET_h approaches its maximum value of T;
3. to increase but at a decreasing rate when a larger gain in ET_h is being considered.

It can also be shown that MWTP increases with initial consumption (or equivalently, wealth; see Zweifel et al., 2009, ch. 2.4 for details).

Now, members of the medical profession and many laypeople would doubt the existence of a stable preference field as displayed in Figure 2.1. Indeed, human behavior often is decried as, 'Not giving a trifle for health as long as one is healthy, but willing to spend one's entire fortune once one is sick'. This seems to be evidence in favor of unstable preferences, with MWTP strongly state dependent. If true, the argument would severely limit the usefulness of evidence with regard to WTP for policy purposes. However, it can be shown that the state dependence of *observed* MWTP may follow from a state dependence of the transformation curve between C and ET_h.

In Figure 2.1 consider the transformation curve with index h, holding for a current period in good health. From the origin, the curve starts with a positive slope because when $(1 - \pi)$ increases, the expected number of healthy periods ET_h increases as well, providing for healthy time that serves either to generate labor income (which can be used to finance consumption goods) or leisure time (which can be used to produce consumption services). Thus, for small values, healthy time has the character of an *investment good*, permitting consumption services to increase as well. The transformation curve reaches its maximum where the additional resources spent on increasing the chances of being in good health (and hence, expected healthy time) result in an equivalent gain in resources in terms of time available for work and investment in health (see ibid., ch. 3.3 for details). As is evident from Figure 2.1, at the optimum (symbolized by Q^*), health has turned into a *consumption good*, implying that more time spent in good health entails a sacrifice in terms of consumption.

Figure 2.1 contains a second transformation curve relating to sickness (s) during the current period. In bad health, one's productivity both in the labor market and in household production is reduced for at least part of the planning period T. Accordingly, this transformation curve runs lower and reaches its maximum value ET_h (and also C) sooner than its counterpart for good current health. In order to demonstrate that this difference rather than an instability in preference may be the source of observed state dependence of MWTP, two assumptions are made:

1. preferences are homothetic;
2. sickness in the current period affects the individual as a producer of future healthy time more strongly than as a producer of future consumption.

Given these assumptions, the two optima Q^* (good current health) and Q^{**} (bad current health) can be compared as follows. When moving towards the origin on the ray $0Q^*$, the slope of the indifference curve remains the same according to assumption (1). However, the slope of the transformation curve must become steeper on average for assumption (2) to be satisfied. This means that the optimum Q^{**} cannot possibly lie on the ray through the origin; indeed, it must lie above that ray, where the slope of the indifference curve is greater (in absolute value). However, this also implies that at Q^{**}, the marginal rates of transformation and substitution must be larger than at Q^*. In other words, the revealed MWTP for additional healthy time is greater if the current period is one of bad health than if it is one of good health. The observed MWTP thus turns out to be state dependent not because of any instability of preferences but because of the dependence of productive capabilities on current health status, which seems a very natural assumption.

> *Conclusion 1*: The observed instability of revealed MWTP for health (low when healthy, high when ill) need not be caused by an instability of underlying preferences but may well be caused by the dependence of individuals' productive capabilities on the current state of health.

Thus, the argument that individuals' preferences with regard to health and health care are too fickle to provide a basis for policy making need not be accepted. This is not to say that measuring true MWTP for health is without problems, quite the contrary. While in principle, it is possible to infer individuals' MWTP from the equality between the marginal rate of substitution and the marginal rate of transformation (and hence actual behavior) at the optimum points Q^* and Q^{**}, there are at least two reasons for important deviations. First, the rate of transformation is biased because of insurance coverage. With a coinsurance rate of 20 percent (say), the sacrifice of one dollar's worth of consumption in effect buys five times as much medical care as without insurance coverage. Thus, the transformation curve looks five times flatter than in Figure 2.1 to an insured individual who considers using medical care. The second reason is that as soon as individuals rely on medical care, they are not likely to actually reach the optimum Q^{**} (bad current health). This is due to the fact that they act under the influence of physicians, who pursue their own interests. To the extent that physicians are not perfect agents of their patients, they will misrepresent the trade-off between C and ET_h and/or influence their patients' MRS, both of which cause Q^{**} to be missed.

4 Issues with measuring true cost

In CBA, the costs of health-care programs fall into three categories. First, there are direct costs arising from the use of resources within the health-care sector, in other sectors and by patients and their families. Second, there are indirect costs due to productivity changes. Third, so-called intangible costs are caused by suffering or pain. It is both important and difficult to avoid double counting, taking into account only costs that are caused by the program and not incorporated in the benefit measures. If, for instance, an intervention reduces the pain of patients, the intangible cost of the disease is reduced. This would be accounted for separately in a CUA. However, in a CBA derived from experiments (see next section), these cost reductions are already incorporated into the WTP values. There are additional issues to bear in mind when measuring cost of health programs as part of a CBA.[2]

Vantage point of the analysis
A natural question to ask is, 'Whose costs, whose benefits?'. This may be society as a whole, a third-party payer, a physician, a hospital, or a patient. Clearly, costs and benefits differ between these vantage points. While, for example, travel to obtain care is clearly a cost component from the patient's and society's point of view, it does not have to be taken into account from a hospital's point of view. Since CBA may serve different kinds of decision makers, this is not a weakness but reflects the versatility of the tool.

Direct costs
Direct costs represent the value of all resources consumed by the intervention analyzed, including the neutralization of its side-effects and other current or future consequences. There are two different types of direct costs.

Direct health-care costs include physician services, hospital services, and drugs, used. Direct non-health-care costs accrue outside the health sector, such as care provided by family members and transportation costs to the hospital. In quantifying direct health-care costs, it may be problematic to use readily available hospital or physician charges, since the health-care market is not a competitive one, causing the charges to be a poor reflection of true (opportunity) cost (Finkler, 1982).

Different studies explored this issue in the context of hospital fees in the United States. While there were large differences in the magnitude of the cost estimates obtained from the various estimation methods, the ranking by cost was not affected (see, for example, Cohen et al., 1993; Taira et al., 2003). Therefore, failure to use true resource cost may not be too much of a problem in CEA and CUA (which are within health). This is not true of CBA, however (which pits health against other objectives).

Indirect costs
If the vantage point of society at large is adopted, indirect costs (that is, productivity losses) need to be accounted for. They include lost work hours due to absenteeism or early retirement, impaired productivity at work, lost or impaired leisure time, and premature mortality. Intangible costs of pain, suffering, and grief are real yet very difficult to measure. Depending on the scenario description (see below), they are incorporated into the benefits (WTP values) of a CBA and therefore should be neglected in the costs of a program.

Time horizon
Choice of time horizon can importantly affect the costs of a health-care intervention, which may accrue irregularly over time. For instance,

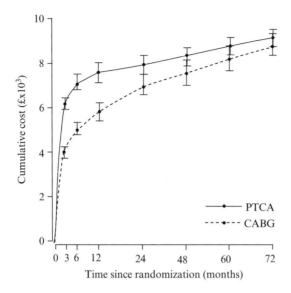

Source: Henderson et al. (1998, p. 1423).

Figure 2.2   *Cumulative costs of percutaneous transluminal coronary*
angioplasty (PCTA) and coronary artery bypass grafting
(CABG) over time (confidence intervals indicated by the bars)

Henderson et al. (1998) examined costs of percutaneous transluminal coronary angioplasty (PTCA) and coronary artery bypass grafting (CABG)
as a function of time. While after one year the costs of CABG were substantially higher than those of PTCA, this difference was not statistically
different any more after five years (see Figure 2.2). The time horizon
should be chosen in a way that does not bias the analysis in favor of or
against the intervention considered. It should be long enough to capture
important deferred effects (including unintended ones), amounting to
a disease episode, a patient's remaining life expectancy, or even several
cohorts of patients or individuals as in the case of HIV transmitted to children. Quantitative modeling approaches may be needed to estimate costs
and outcomes that are beyond those of officially available data. Of course,
the higher the discount rate used, the less important are future costs.

Average versus marginal cost
Economists stress the importance of using marginal cost in evaluation
because most decisions are not of the 'on/off' type but of the 'more/
less' type. In that situation, economic analysis may reveal that, beyond

Table 2.1   Cancer screening and detection costs with sequential guaiac tests

No. of tests	No. of cancers detected (in 000s)	Additional cancers detected (in 000s)	Total cost ($) of diagnosis	Additional ($) cost of diagnosis	Average cost ($) per cancer detected	Marginal cost ($) per cancer detected
1	65,947	65,947	77,511	77,511	1,175	1,175
2	71,442	5,496	107,690	30,179	1,507	5,492
3	71,900	0,458	130,199	22,509	1,810	49,150
4	71,939	0,038	148,116	17,917	2,059	469,534
5	71,942	0,003	163,141	15,024	2,268	4,724,695
6	71,942	0,000	176,331	13,190	2,451	47,107,214

Source: Neuhauser and Lewicki (1975, p. 227).

a certain level of spending, the additional benefits are no longer worth the additional (marginal) cost. For example, as shown in Table 2.1, the average cost per desired outcome of an iterative screening test may appear to be quite acceptable (for example, $2,451 per case of colorectal cancer detected at six tests per person), whereas the marginal cost of adding the sixth test would be an astronomical $47 million.

Discounting
Costs that occur in the future have less present value than costs that materialize today (since the money can be put into a bank, for example, to earn interest). Discounting therefore reflects the opportunity costs of capital, that is, the returns that could have been achieved elsewhere. Discounting makes flows of costs and benefits having different time profiles comparable in terms of their present value. The capital asset pricing model (CAPM) predicts that a project is competitive in the capital market if its expected rate of return Er_i satisfies the condition,

$$Er_i = r_f + \beta_i(Er_M - r_f). \qquad (2.4)$$

Thus, the benchmark is the so-called risk-free interest r_f, usually equated to the rate of return on government bonds. Since returns of shares on the capital market exceed the risk-free rate on expectation ($Er_M > r_f$), the (share of) firm i must achieve a higher rate of return than r_f if $\beta_i > 0$. Now β_i is the slope parameter in a regression of the firm's rates of return r_i on the market values r_M. Usual estimates hover around $\hat{\beta}_i = 1$. However, as soon as $\hat{\beta}_i < 1$, the (share of) firm i has a risk diversification effect. Now to the extent that the health intervention is sponsored by the government, $\beta_i = 0$ is the appropriate value, resulting in $Er_i = r_f$. Therefore, the rate of discount becomes equal to the interest rate on government bonds. However, the value of r_f should refer to bonds having about the same time horizon of the health-care intervention. A discount rate of 3 or 5 percent is typically used (Gold et al., 1996).

> *Conclusion 2*: In CBA, measuring the true resource cost poses several problems. Of particular importance are the choice of time horizon, the distinction between average and marginal cost, and the use of a rate of discount that is in accordance with capital market theory.

5   Alternatives for measuring benefits

To assign a money value to an improvement in length or quality of life, two entirely different concepts have been developed, the human-capital approach and the willingness-to-pay approach.

Human-capital approach

The human-capital approach (see, for example, Mushkin, 1978) places money weights on healthy time using market wage rates. Therefore, a life is valued in terms of the present value of the individual's contribution to the gross domestic product, which equals his or her labor income. There are several problems with this approach. First, wage rates should reflect marginal productivities of workers. However, there are often imperfections in labor markets, which cause wages to deviate from productivities due to discrimination by age or gender. Second, from a societal perspective, healthy time gained that is not sold for a wage has to be valued, too. This raises the question of how to place shadow prices on non-marketed resources.[3] Finally and as a matter of principle, the human-capital approach is not compatible with microeconomic theory (see, for example, Mishan, 1971). After all, it is the rest of society who (through the labor market and employers) value an individual, resulting in a zero value of life for pensioners and others who are unable to work, whereas in microeconomics, it is the individual who (subjectively) values consumer goods, jobs, risks, and life. Because of these economic and ethical flaws, we do not deem the human-capital approach an appropriate method for placing money weights on health benefits. The main focus will therefore be on the willingness-to-pay approach.

Willingness-to-pay approach

The willingness-to-pay (WTP) approach is based on the assumption that a person's utility depends both on disposable income and on length and quality of life. In contrast to CUA, it does not impose restrictions on the utility function. Length and quality of life are elements of the vector θ_i, while y_i denotes disposable income (or consumption). Thus, the utility of person i is given by:

$$U_i = U_i(\theta_i, y_i). \tag{2.5}$$

Suppose that an intervention causes θ to increase from θ_i^1 to θ_i^2. Then the willingness to pay Z_i for this intervention is defined by the maximum amount of money individual i would pay in order to obtain the intervention. This means that utility is the same in the two states,

$$U_i[\theta_i^1, y_i] = U_i[\theta_i^2, y_i - Z_i], \tag{2.6}$$

where [a] means 'evaluated at a'.

There are various ways to measure WTP. The main distinction is between revealed and stated preference methods. While revealed preference methods try to derive WTP values from actual behavior, stated preference methods elicit them by asking people more or less directly. In general, economists prefer to infer WTP from actual behavior. The market price provides a lower bound for WTP because consumers buy a product only if their WTP exceeds or equals the price paid. However, markets for medical care are both influenced by health insurance and heavily regulated, causing observed price to be too low and estimated WTP too high as a rule.

This leaves the possibility of measuring WTP by asking directly. On the one hand, contingent valuation confronts participants with one hypothetical scenario, reflecting the health-care intervention to be evaluated. The only attribute that varies is price. By way of contrast, discrete-choice experiments (DCEs) present participants with a series of yes/no choices between the status quo and an alternative that differs with regard to several attributes, not only price.

Revealed as well as stated preference methods have their specific pros and cons, which will be discussed in the following.

Revealed preference   Inferring WTP indirectly from market data has the important advantage of being based on actual consumer choices involving chances for health versus money, rather than hypothetical scenarios and choices. Risk preferences can be inferred from actions designed to avoid risks. A well-known example is the choice (or avoidance) of a job that is known for its risks to life and health (examples are truck drivers, miners, or electricians). The basic idea is to estimate the compensation required for accepting a higher risk of death from the difference in wage rates for occupations with and without an increased threat to life. However, everyday decisions such as putting on the safety belt also reveal risk preferences.

Yet, using revealed preference for measuring WTP has its problems as well. Wage–risk trade-offs are very context and job specific, and disentangling the many factors that confound the relationship between wage and health risk is difficult. One hardly finds two occupations that are identical except for their risk to life and health. Differences in wage rates also reflect differences in educational requirements, mental and physical demands experience, and many other characteristics of both workers and occupations.

Furthermore, there is a fundamental concern that risk–money trade-offs may not reflect the kind of rational choice revealing preferences that the WTP concept is based on. Notably, there are imperfections in labor markets (collectively negotiated wages) and limited rationality (biased estimates of occupational risk; for an overview, see Viscusi, 1992). As fatal accidents are relatively rare, it is questionable whether those affected know the frequencies, let alone use them as a basis for their subjective probability estimates. Surveys among drivers indicate that most underestimate their personal risk relative to the frequency of accidents observed in the driver population. Another question is whether observed behavior actually can be interpreted as the outcome of expected utility maximization as required by theory. Empirical evidence (presented already by Eisner and Strotz, 1961; see also Starmer, 2000) indicates that when dealing with relatively small risks, individuals systematically violate this rule. However, the known alternatives fare no better (Hey and Orme, 1994).

Finally, it can be questioned whether persons in risky occupations are representative of the total population. The fact that they chose such an occupation and no other presumably reflects a basic preference for it, implying that the wage differential could constitute the upper limit of their compensation asked for bearing the increased risk. Members of that particular profession thus may have a special preference for risky situations (perhaps for the thrill that comes with them) that is not shared by the rest of the population. Conversely, however, the observed wage differential marks the lower limit for the rest of the population because it would take a higher one to draw additional workers into their particular occupation. In conclusion, observed data may not be informative enough to permit estimation of WTP values.

Contingent valuation The traditional alternative to the method of revealed preference is contingent valuation (CV)[4]. The CV method measures the value of a non-market good by directly asking individuals how much the good (with attributes usually fixed) is worth to them. Typically the survey begins by giving some background information to respondents on the good in question. Next, they are told how the money would be collected to finance the good. Finally, respondents are asked about their WTP and possibly upper and lower bounds. Since the mid-1970s, CV has also been applied to health care, resulting in rapid growth of the number of CV studies published.[5]

Nevertheless, the CV method in health economics is still used reluctantly, for two main reasons. First, there are conceptual issues. The results of CV are criticized for lacking validity, since they depend heavily on the choice of the elicitation and estimation method. Indeed, both continuous and discrete CV formats are used, which vary in their familiarity to respondents and in their potential for biasing WTP values (Mitchell and Carson, 1989; Johannesson, 1996; Donaldson et al., 1998; Nocera et al., 2002).

The two main approaches to elicit WTP values by using a continuous CV format are open-ended questions and the payment card format. In the open-ended variant, individuals are directly asked to indicate their maximum WTP. As this may be too demanding (see, for example, Johannesson et al., 1991), the payment card variant confronts respondents with an ordered sequence of bids, with respondents indicating the maximum acceptable bid. In the discrete CV format, closed-ended techniques are prevalent. Here, respondents are asked only whether or not they would pay a single price out of a range. By varying the price in different subsamples, the proportion of respondents who are willing to pay the price can be calculated, and by multiplying this proportion by the number of respondents, a demand curve for the good can be estimated. Closed-ended techniques thus attempt to create a situation familiar to respondents by asking just yes-or-no questions.

The question of whether open-ended or closed-ended techniques should be preferred in CV studies is still an unsettled issue. More importantly, however, the CV approach suffers from its susceptibility to bias, in particular of the following types:[6]

- *Bias caused by reference values and the ordering of questions*   CV is prone to so-called 'anchoring' effects. Respondents indicate their WTP relative to some reference value rather than their own value. For example, in the payment card format, stated WTP frequently depends on the starting-point (*starting-point bias*). When several projects are presented at a time, the answer to the first question can influence all the following ones (*question-order bias*, see Boyle et al., 1996).

- *Sensitivity to wording of questions* The results of CV studies are very sensitive to the wording of the questions. For instance, the allocation of property rights (ownership bias) or the payment vehicle used can affect WTP values. At an even more basic level, there is the risk that respondents perceive the presented good or program quite differently from what investigators intended.
- *Attitude towards the object of investigation* When applying the closed-ended technique, there is the danger of 'yea-saying'. To express their general agreement with the object of investigation, respondents accept prices in excess of their true WTP (see Blamey et al., 1999).

Considering in addition the general problems associated with interview studies,[7] it seems doubtful that reliable WTP measurement can be obtained from CV studies. Nevertheless, this method has yielded theoretically plausible results when applied to health care (see, for example, Klose, 1999). Specifically, individuals with high incomes have been found to have a higher WTP than others. Moreover, measured WTP increases with the quantity of health services offered by a program.

However, external validity of stated WTP derived from CV studies in health care has not been established because WTP values differ substantially with regard to the elicitation technique and estimation method used. WTP values from discrete CV methods usually are much higher than those from PC formats (see, for example, Nocera et al., 2003, ch. 8.2, who noted differences in a magnitude of up to 500 percent). This is a problem since WTP values determine the absolute magnitude of welfare estimates and hence the outcome of a CBA (Boyle et al., 1996; Ready et al., 1996; Welsh and Poe, 1998).

Discrete-choice experiments DCEs are a variant of conjoint analysis, which was developed in psychology in the late 1960s (see Luce and Tukey, 1964). This method attempts to explain and predict consumers' behavior on the basis of their preferences for the attributes of a good. It is based on the new demand theory (see Lancaster, 1966), which defines preferences in terms of attributes rather than quantities of goods. Respondents in the survey then simply have to choose between programs differing in various attributes. In contradistinction to the CV approach, the status quo and the hypothetical alternative differ with regard to several or all attributes rather than price only.

Since the beginning of the 1980s, DCEs have been applied in transport economics and more recently to environmental economics (see, for example, Hensher, 1997; Bennet and Blamey, 2001). In the mid-1990s, the method was implemented in health economics as well (Ryan, 1995; Ryan and Hughes, 1997). In the meantime, quite a few DCE studies have been conducted (see Ryan and Gerard, 2003 for a first overview).

The behavioral assumption is that rational individuals will always choose the alternative with the higher level of (expected) utility. According to random utility theory (Manski, 1977; McFadden, 2001), the decision-making process within a DCE can thus be seen as a comparison of attained utilities after optimization, V_{ij},

$$V_{ij} = v(a_j, p_j, y_i, s_i, \varepsilon_{ij}).\qquad(2.7)$$

Here, $v(\cdot)$ represents the indirect utility function of individual i for a good j described by a vector of attributes a_j and a price denoted by p_j. The income of individual i is y_i, the socioeconomic characteristics are denoted by s_i, and the error term, by ε_{ij}. Given an additive error term, the individual will choose alternative j over alternative l if:

$$w(a_j, p_j, y_i, s_i) + \varepsilon_{ij} \geq w(a_l, p_l, y_i, s_i) + \varepsilon_{il}.\qquad(2.8)$$

Here, $w(\cdot)$ is the deterministic component of the utility that can be estimated, while the error terms reflect unobservable factors that vary between individuals and alternatives. The utility function $w(\cdot)$ can be inferred from observed choices by assuming that the probability P_{ij} of choosing alternative j over l, given the vector of attributes. The probability of this occurring is assumed to equal the difference in utilities, and therefore:

$$P_{ij} = \text{Prob} \left[\varepsilon_{il} - \varepsilon_{ij} \leq w(a_j, p_j, y_i, s_i) - w(a_l, p_l, y_i, s_i) \right].\qquad(2.9)$$

The assumption thus amounts to the probability of the noise $(\varepsilon_{il} - \varepsilon_{jl})$ being dominated by the systematic difference of utilities $[w(\cdot) - w(\cdot)]$. The MRS between two attributes k and m is given by the ratio of their marginal utilities,

$$MRS: = -\frac{\partial v/\partial a_k}{\partial v/\partial a_m}.\qquad(2.10)$$

The MRS shows the subjective importance of attribute k relative to attribute m. If the mth attribute is price (and hence the negative of disposable income net of price), MRS indicates the marginal WTP for attribute k. Therefore, relating back to equation (2.6), one has:

$$U_i[\theta_i^2, y_i - Z_i] \approx U_i[\theta_i^1, y_i] - (\theta_i^2 - \theta_i^1) \cdot \frac{\partial v/\partial \theta_i}{\partial v/\partial y_i}$$

$$= U_i[\theta_i^1, y_i] - (\theta_i^2 - \theta_i^1) \cdot MRS.\qquad(2.11)$$

The model defined by equations (2.7) to (2.10) is usually estimated by logit and probit techniques, depending on the assumption being made on the distribution of the error terms. For a more detailed explanation of discrete choice models and their application, see Louviere et al. (2000) or Train (2003).

A DCE therefore amounts to tracing out an indifference curve in attribute space, with the status quo defining the reference point. A preferred combination of attributes must lie above the indifference curve (or surface, respectively, in the case of more than two attributes), a rejected one, below. Through repeated choices, the indifference locus can be interpolated.

An important advantage of DCE over CV is due to the fact that respondents tend to evaluate all attributes of a program rather than focusing on price only. This makes DCE less susceptible to strategic behavior and other biases. Moreover, being based on an estimated utility function in attribute space, the results of a DCE can be used to determine WTP for any program that has the same set of attributes. However, being hypothetical, DCE are subject to the criticism that they may fail to elicit reliable and valid WTP values. Outside health, Louviere and Woodsworth (1983) have presented evidence suggesting that DCE can be used to explain modal choice in transportation, while Ghosh (1986) has found that they contribute to explaining the choice of a shopping mall. To this day, few studies have investigated the validity and reliability of DCE in the health-care field. However, first results obtained by Bryan et al. (2000), Ryan et al. (1998), Telser and Zweifel (2002, 2007), and Zweifel et al. (2006) indicate that DCE may be a valid and reliable approach to WTP measurement in the case of health as well.

Conclusion 3: The main alternatives are CV and DCEs when it comes to use stated rather than revealed preference for estimating benefits. The latter has important advantages, notably less susceptibility to a member of biases and greater similarity to actual decision-making situations.

6 Empirical example

Even if there are many papers in health care incorporating the term 'cost–benefit analysis' in their title, only a few CBAs have been conducted in this area until now. Indeed, the label 'CBA' is used in a very imprecise way in the health-care literature. Most of the published so-called CBAs are not full economic evaluations but rather costing studies where cost savings due to a health-care intervention are treated as benefits. However, these cost savings constitute a lower bound of a health program's benefits at best.

This misinterpretation leads to only programs that exhibit cost savings to be recommended whereas a true CBA may suggest even a program with higher costs to be worthwhile if it generates positive net benefits. According to Zarnke et al. (1997), only about 30 percent of all studies labeled CBAs valued health outcomes in money units. Since most of these used a human capital approach to value health outcomes, only about 10 percent of alleged CBA studies thus would meet the standards of cost–benefit analysis.

Moreover, even if outcomes of a program are valued in money units, usually they are not compared to cost. Most of the WTP studies are feasibility or pilot studies focusing on methodological issues but not on comparing cost to benefits (Drummond et al., 2005). Therefore, in the following we shall present one particular CBA as an example of a full economic evaluation.

Nocera et al. (2002 and 2003) conducted a CBA of three programs against Alzheimer's disease (AD) for Switzerland. First, the program 'care' tries to ease some of the strain on informal caregivers, who provide the bulk of long-term care to people suffering from AD. To elicit WTP for 'care', a scenario was built in which informal caregivers receive training in caring for demented patients. Additionally, they had the possibility to engage a professional nurse for a few weeks per year for free. Respondents were asked whether they would be willing to pay higher income taxes for such a care program to be implemented.

Second, the program 'diagnosis' focused on an early detection of AD. While no current therapy can reverse the progressive cognitive decline caused by AD, several pharmacological and psychosocial treatments exist which may delay the proceeding of the illness (Small et al., 1997; Mayeux and Sano, 1999). For these treatments to be effective, an early diagnosis of AD is important (Callahan et al., 1995). However, diagnosing AD is a relatively difficult task since there is still no validated test available. Currently, a first diagnostic tool is screening interviews, which inquire into personal details, family contact, and health state. Additionally, short quantified screenings of cognitive function such as the 'mini-mental state examination' (see Folstein et al., 1975) are used. If there are signs of dementia, a more comprehensive neuropsychological assessment conducted by specialists is needed (Small et al., 1997). To elicit WTP for 'diagnosis', Nocera et al. (2003, ch. 2) designed a scenario consisting of a routine dementia screening test, which is currently not reimbursed by Swiss sickness funds. Therefore, respondents were asked whether they would be willing to pay a higher health insurance premium for such a program to be included in the list of benefits.

Third, the program 'research' focused on research into curing AD.

Intensive research all over the world has led to an increasing understanding of the primary factors causing AD (see, for example, Vassar et al., 1999). But despite these advances, there exists no causal therapy for AD to date. The scenario asked respondents for their WTP to intensify research on AD at Swiss universities financed with tax money.

To elicit WTP values for these AD programs, different elicitation and estimation techniques were applied within a CV study. One aim was to analyze methodological problems in applying the CV method to measure people's values for the outcome of health programs. As expected, there were big differences in WTP values according to the elicitation technique used (see Table 2.2, column 3).

After eliciting WTP values, Nocera et al. (2003, ch. 6) additionally investigated whether the three programs against AD should be implemented from a societal point of view. Therefore, the costs of the three programs were estimated. In the case of the program 'care', the cost per AD patient (consisting of a two-day course for informal caregivers and the hiring of a professional nurse for four weeks) sum up to about CHF 9,300 per year (1 CHF equals some $0.84 at 2007 exchange rates). In Switzerland, 32,000 AD patients are cared for by informal caregivers at patients' homes. Therefore, if all of these patients were to take advantage of the care program, maximum possible costs of CHF 298 million would arise. These costs were then compared to estimated benefits, calculated by multiplying elicited WTP values with the number of the Swiss population of 18 years and older (see Table 2.2).

While the choice of the elicitation technique affects results in a substantial way, net benefits for the program 'care' are always positive. Therefore, from a societal point of view, the implementation of this program can be recommended since it generates more benefit than cost. The same is true for the program 'research', while the program 'diagnosis' can be

Table 2.2 CBA of the programs against Alzheimer's disease in Switzerland

Program	Maximum cost (millions CHF p.a.)	Total WTP (millions CHF p.a.)	Net Benefit (millions CHF p.a.)
Care	298	319–1568	21–1270
Diagnosis	175	17–919	−158–774
Research	561	561–1056	0–495

Source: Nocera et al. (2003).

recommended under some circumstances only. In a pessimistic scenario, it is possible that costs are higher than benefits resulting in a net benefit of CHF −158 million per year.

> *Conclusion 4*: In an empirical application of CBA, one finds programs 'care' and 'research' (but not 'diagnosis') to be worth the money for dealing with Alzheimer's disease.

7   Conclusion and outlook

Microeconomic theory predicts that consumers optimize the ratio of marginal utility to price or marginal cost. CBA is nothing but the attempt of implementing this rule for goods and services that are not marketable, such as public health programs. Since (marginal) utility is difficult to measure, health economists have developed cost-effectiveness and cost-utility analysis to skirt this difficulty. However, these alternatives to CBA have the disadvantage of failing to inform policy makers whether a public program is worth its money, possibly even at the price of an expansion of the budget devoted to health.

An important recent innovation in CBA is the experimental estimation of utility in the guise of marginal willingness to pay, which makes benefits commensurable with cost. This contribution argues that the conventional contingent valuation approach frequently is too prone to biases of several types to be worthwhile. Rather, it proposes discrete choice experiments as the tool of choice. In a discrete-choice experiment (DCE), all relevant attributes of the program are varied simultaneously, among them its price (usually in terms of a changed contribution to health insurance or to the public budget). Since an actual CBA using DCE evidence does not seem to have been performed by the time of writing (2007), the contribution presents a study based on CV in spite of the reservations stated above.

But even with all the recent progress in measuring the benefits side of CBA, there are at least two issues that need to be addressed in the future. The first concerns the modeling of the decision-making situation facing individuals in the experiment. Invariably, CBA (but also CEA and CUA) scenarios have been depicted as one-period, one-shot problems. However, individuals may be aware that their decisions today affect the range of choices open to them (and possibly even their preferences!) later on. If true, this would call for a dynamic modeling approach that spells out the restrictions defining an optimal control path over time. The second issue is distributional. Implicitly, CBA gives equal distributional weight to all individuals affected by a program. The problem of course is to weigh benefits (and possibly costs) according to some social welfare function. Fortunately, DCEs are able to provide estimates of these weights as well.

Mayeux, R. and M. Sano (1999), 'Drug therapy: treatment of Alzheimer's disease', *New England Journal of Medicine*, **341** (22), 1670–79.

McFadden, D. (2001), 'Economic choices', *American Economic Review*, **91** (3), 351–78.

Mehrez, A. and A. Gafni (1989), 'Quality-adjusted life-years, utility theory, and healthy-years equivalents', *Medical Decision Making*, **9** (2), 142–9.

Mishan, E.J. (1971), 'Evaluation of life and limb: a theoretical approach', *Journal of Political Economy*, **79**, 687–706.

Mitchell, R. and R. Carson (1989), *Using Surveys to Value Public Goods: The Contingent Valuation Method*, Washington, DC: Resources for the Future.

Murray, C.J. (1994), 'Quantifying the burden of disease: the technical basis for disability-adjusted life years', *Bulletin of the World Health Organization*, **72** (3), 429–45.

Mushkin, S. (1978), 'Cost of disease and illness in the United States in the YEAR 2000', *Public Health Reports*, **93**, 493.

Neuhauser, D. and A.M. Lewicki (1975), 'What do we gain from the sixth stool guaiac?', *New England Journal of Medicine*, **293**, 226–8.

Nocera, S., D. Bonato and H. Telser (2002), 'The contingency of contingent valuation', *International Journal of Health Care Finance and Economics*, **2** (3), 219–40.

Nocera, S., H. Telser and D. Bonato (2003), *The Contingent-Valuation Method in Health Care: An Economic Evaluation of Alzheimer's Disease*, Dordrecht, Boston and London: Kluwer.

Ready, R.C., J.C. Buzby and D. Hu (1996), 'Differences between continuous and discrete contingent value estimates', *Land Economics*, **72** (3), 397–411.

Ryan, M. (1995), 'Economics and the patient's utility function: an application to assisted reproductive techniques', PhD thesis, University of Aberdeen, Aberdeen.

Ryan, M. and K. Gerard (2003), 'Using choice experiments to value health care programmes: current practice and future research reflections', *Applied Health Economics and Health Policy*, **2**, 55–64.

Ryan, M. and J. Hughes (1997), 'Using conjoint analysis to assess women's preferences for miscarriage management', *Health Economics*, **6**, 261–73.

Ryan, M., E. McIntosh and P. Shackley (1998), 'Methodological issues in the application of conjoint analysis in health care', *Health Economics*, **7**, 373–8.

Schwappach, D.L.B. (2002), 'Resource allocation, social values and the QALY: a review of the debate and empirical evidence', *Health Expectations*, **5**, 210–22.

Shackley, P. and C. Donaldson (2002), 'Should we use willingness to pay to elicit community preferences for health care? New evidence from the "marginal" approach', *Journal of Health Economics*, **21**, 971–91.

Small, G.W., P.V. Rabins, and P.P. Barry et al. (1997), 'Diagnosis and treatment of Alzheimer's disease and related disorders – consensus statement of the American Association for Geriatric Psychiatry, the Alzheimer's Association and the American Geriatric Society', *Journal of the American Medical Association*, **278** (16), 1363–71.

Smith, R.D. (2003), 'Construction of the contingent valuation market in health care: a critical assessment', *Health Economics*, **12**, 609–28.

Starmer, C. (2000), 'Developments in non-expected utility theory: the hunt for a descriptive theory of choice under risk', *Journal of Economic Literature*, **38**, 332–82.

Taira, D.A., T.B. Seto, R. Siegrist, R. Cosgrove, R. Berezin and D.J. Cohen (2003), Comparison of analytic approaches for the economic evaluation of new technologies alongside multicenter clinical trials', *American Heart Journal*, **145**, 452–8.

Telser, H. and P. Zweifel (2002), 'Measuring willingness-to-pay for risk reduction: an application of conjoint analysis', *Health Economics*, **11**, 129–39.

Telser, H. and P. Zweifel (2007), 'Validity of discrete-choice experiments – evidence for health risk reduction', *Applied Economics*, **39** (1), 69–78.

Train, K.E. (2003), *Discrete Choice Methods with Simulation*, Cambridge: Cambridge University Press.

Vassar, R., B.D. Bennett and S. Babu-Khan et al. (1999), 'Beta-secretase cleavage of Alzheimer's amyloid precursor protein by the transmembrane aspartic protease BACE', *Science*, **286**, 735–41.

Viscusi, K.P. (1992), *Fatal Trade-Offs*, Oxford: Oxford University Press.

Weisbrod, B.A. (1964), 'Collective consumption services of individual consumption goods', *Quarterly Journal of Economics*, **78**, 471–7.

Welsh, M.P. and G.L. Poe (1998), 'Elicitation effects in contingent valuation: comparisons to a multiple bounded discrete choice approach', *Journal of Environmental Economics and Management*, **36**, 170–85.

World Bank (1993), *Investing in Health*, World Development Report 1993, Washington, DC: World Bank.

Zarnke, K.B., M.A.H. Levine and B.J. O'Brien (1997), 'Cost–benefit analysis in the health care literature. Don't judge a study by its label', *Journal of Clinical Epidemiology*, **50**, 813–22.

Zweifel, P., H. Telser and S. Vaterlaus (2006), 'Consumer resistance against regulation: the case of health care', *Journal of Regulatory Economics*, **29** (3), 319–32.

Zweifel, P., F. Breyer and M. Kifmann (2009), *Health Economics*, 2nd edn, Boston, MA: Springer.

3 Cost–benefit analysis of drug abuse treatment
*William S. Cartwright**

1 Introduction

In 2004, 19.1 million Americans, or 7.9 percent of the population aged 12 or older, were current illicit drug users (SAMHSA, 2005). Among these users, drug addiction becomes a serious problem for the individual, family, and society and requires treatment. Drug addiction is a serious mental health disease that involves cognitive, behavioral, and physiological factors that lead to misuse of a drug, although harmful consequences are observed for the individual. In chronic addiction, the brain also undergoes changes that are hypothesized to cause high relapse rates after abstinence. Drug abuse treatment requires the patient to participate in a therapeutic process over a varying length of time in order to learn how to maintain abstinence, and multiple episodes of treatment are often required. While in treatment, cognitive behavioral therapy is used to break old patterns of thinking and develop new skills to avoid drug use and criminal behavior. Drug abuse treatment involves assessment into the appropriate intensity of treatment which is then followed by a tailoring of services to fit individual need. Drug abuse treatment involves a number of specialty programs such as outpatient treatment, methadone maintenance, residential care, therapeutic communities, and after-care programs. Treatment programs will provide case management services to assist patients in negotiating medical services, other behavioral health services, and social services that are available in the community to assist in improving health and returning to normal social function. Effectiveness is usually measured in outcomes related to abstinence and to reduction in criminal behavior.

When government finances mental health services and drug abuse treatment in particular, are the citizens getting an adequate return on their investment? The answer to this question involves the use of considerable analytical techniques. With such information, governments may engage in rational budget decisions where incremental costs are explicitly tied to incremental benefits (or outcomes) in accordance with citizens' preferences and valuations (Cartwright and Solano, 2003). This is an application of cost–benefit analysis to the problems of allocating budgeted funds over several sectors: (i) private–public sector division; (ii) within public sectors (that is, public safety versus public health); and (iii) within public health (drug treatment services versus medical care). Primarily, the provision of financing indicates society's allocation of resources to the health services in question and would only be done if the cost–benefit analysis indicated a greater net social return or benefit to one program over another. Limiting this process is the information and human constraints that bound the number of studies that can be done on competing budget items.

Besides the basic investment question, cost–benefit analysis is also used to evaluate the value of regulatory controls imposed on public and private agents. Many financing options involve a trade-off between efficiency, administrative feasibility and costs, and equity. Cost–benefit analysis attempts to bring systematic quantitative measurement to alternatives rather than idiosyncratic subjective values of stakeholders whether producers, legislators, or government officials. Implementation and monitoring of the budget decision is critical after implementation of the rational budget decision, so *ex post* economic evaluation is also done to ensure adequate implementation of expenditures and programs.

There has been a long history of drug abuse treatment evaluation done by psychologists, sociologists, medical doctors, and occasionally economists. The past history of economic evaluations has been one of heterogeneous methods, but of continued positive findings for the economic contribution of drug abuse treatment. Of the various economic evaluations of drug abuse treatment undertaken, cost–benefit analysis was the most frequent. However, there is an expanding role for cost-effectiveness analysis that has picked up considerably in the 1990s with the availability of high-quality clinical trials and real-world, effectiveness studies. So far, evaluation using a utility analysis (cost-utility analysis), as usually conducted in medical intervention cost-effectiveness analysis, has only recently been done (Daley et al., 2005). Economic evaluation is undergoing steady progress in methodological development for drug abuse treatment as detailed in this chapter.

Some states are finding the use of cost–benefit analysis critical to their budget planning for mental health services where there are large external costs to society. Under state legislative direction, the Washington State Institute for Public Policy (Aos et al., 2001) has attempted to examine the comparative costs and benefits of program interventions to reduce crime. They evaluated numerous research studies, conducted over a 25-year period, and it was indeed possible to draw some conclusions on what worked and did not work. Some 41 interventions were examined with a meta-analysis of effect sizes and an assessment of both benefits and costs for just crime reduction. Drug abuse treatments fared well in this evaluation even though the criminal domain is only a partial net benefit valuation because interventions have multidimensional joint outputs. In the State of Washington, there is a research infrastructure to evaluate programs in the real world, and there is an analysis that weighs the evidence from the various studies. For example, the study found for juvenile offenders that multi-systemic therapy, functional family therapy, aggression replacement training, and coordinated services were interventions with significant economic returns in distinct contrast to criminal justice interventions that offered little economic advantage. Further, drug abuse treatment programs and drug courts in prisons were found to have positive returns, especially when aftercare was added. Such evaluations and conclusions of basic services research and economic studies are critical to developing science-based knowledge and technology transfer.

2   Perspective for mental health and drug abuse treatment interventions

The US Public Health Service's Panel on Cost-Effectiveness in Health and Medicine (Gold et al., 1996) specifically recommended that an economic evaluation should start with the 'social perspective'. Because drug use, abuse, and dependency are a broad public health problem, a social evaluation must account for effects across the *entire population.* Treatment units, insurance companies, governments and taxpayers are subsumed in a social perspective, but only in their roles as agents for individual citizens and consumers. Drug abuse treatment and prevention affects everyone through all of the significant health, public safety, and social outcomes that flow from interaction with the treated person. Because of these external costs and spillover effects, social costs must be carefully enumerated and include both 'private costs' and 'social costs'. Private costs include not only the treatment program costs of the intervention, but also patient time costs (often ignored). Benefits accrue to the individual and society through increases in productive employment and also from the cost savings generated by improvements in beneficial behavior, which society will enjoy.

The social perspective does not represent the interest of any particular group or agent in society. It denotes the broadest view of the consumers in that society and the potential willingness to pay for such health and safety improvements. This leads to some confusion over the utility of the perspective in presenting results to the real world. For example, managed care companies may be deemed to be an important agent in society for establishing treatment systems or paying for them, but incentives may lead them to allocate their resources inefficiently from the social point of view. State agencies may seem to be the natural stakeholder as they seek to show that their budget is utilized in a 'cost-effective' manner, which may enhance their political standing. For some evaluations a narrow interest may be entirely appropriate, but most likely the economic analysis involves the interest of other groups in society besides an immediate bureaucratic one. Conflict over budgets and resource allocation is generated when public health officials who finance the public treatment system must interact with those who are responsible for managing the jails and prisons for incarcerated drug users. For example, doing a study of treatment effects on prisoners may have different implications to society if released prisoners do not receive aftercare in the public health system. Problems also arise when considering the role of social services in the effectiveness of treatment as observed at the clinic. For example, two clinics may be equally skilled and effective, but the provision of housing services to women may have a substantial impact on health and drug abuse outcomes for that group.

Perspective approaches have varied. For example, Alterman et al. (1994) established no specific perspective, but helpfully estimated both provider costs and patient costs that could be useful for Veteran Administration decision makers. Avants et al. (1999) recognized the social perspective, but the study included only a subset of costs. Fals-Stewart et al. (1997) measured social costs, but included support from public assistance that was a part of the treatment process. Usually such transfer payments are excluded as they redistribute resources rather than use them up. In this case fewer patients received public assistance in the behavioral therapy's treatment group. As represented in this study, there is the realistic pull of the 'taxpayer perspective' that is discussed further below. In a new study, French et al. (1999) studied a therapeutic community that was modified for mentally ill, chemical abusers and explicitly adopted the social point of view for the cost–benefit study. Here, a rather complete set of benefits was estimated for criminal activity, employment, and other health services, but correctly not transfer payments. This study highlighted a problem that many economic evaluations share in that the economic investigators did not participate in the original instrumentation of the research design, and this limited the valuation of benefits (for example, no HIV/AIDS).

The 'taxpayer' point of view has certain face validity to evaluation practice. Usually this is operationalized by estimating the cost savings to society with the inclusion of transfer payments of welfare programs that are funded by governments. While this perspective has no theoretical standing in economic terms, it perhaps is relevant in 'political' terms. But just what goal the taxpayer is maximizing for society is usually left unspecified. Any reduction in utilization and costs of social programs is regarded as 'beneficial'. Furthermore, the studies generally avoid a specific statement on the budgetary impact of whether an actual reduction in the budget is expected or perhaps at best, it is budget neutrality. Where budget reduction is anticipated, the decrease in the 'deadweight loss' of the reduced tax effort should be factored into the benefits of drug treatment (Cartwright, 1998).

Technically, the deadweight loss is the loss in consumer surplus with no offsetting benefit to some other part of society, and so it meets a social perspective viewpoint. This would tend to increase the importance of such cost savings when valued at the correct taxpayer's margin (Boardman et al., 1996; Brent, 2003). Because social programs with 'wrap-around' services (social services added to treatment services) are financed out of a complex of state, local and federal taxes of the services, the deadweight loss becomes a more complicated weighted average of funding streams. The analysis proceeds with the saved expenditures multiplied times a deadweight factor to compute the value of the services saved, if it is assumed that government would not simply spend the budget dollars.

3 Benefits

The number of potential incremental benefits complicates the evaluation problem for drug abuse treatment (Cartwright, 1998). Even detailing the impact of cost savings from reduced criminality requires a large effort because of the complexities of the criminal justice system. In Box 3.1, six benefit domains from drug abuse treatment for a standard incremental analysis are illustrated. For an individual treatment study, evaluations with high policy significance would qualify for the expenditure of extensive research inputs needed to address these domains.

BOX 3.1   BENEFITS OF DRUG ABUSE TREATMENT: DOMAIN OF RESOURCE SAVINGS

Private protection resources
Victim resource losses
Criminal justice resources
Addict labor income and legal employment
Illegal drug production resources
Medical savings

People who are in treatment or have completed treatment generate incremental 'cost savings' attributable to the change in behavior, and economists have developed several guidelines for estimation. First, cost savings are from the point of view of domestic product or income in the overall economy. Therefore, cost-of-illness studies are an excellent guide to identifying and evaluating these benefits since these studies estimate the burden on the economy. Second, resources must be used up, not simply transferred. For example, destruction of property would be estimated, but not the transfer of property or the redistribution of government transfer programs. Therefore, one measures the reduction in administrative burden as transfers are reduced by drug abuse treatment, rather than the expenditures on the social program. Finally, double counting is to be avoided. For example, one would avoid counting both the reduction in the value of illegal drug consumption and illegal earnings since consumption would have been financed out of the earnings.

While the criminal justice benefit is often paramount, it is also difficult to estimate. For the most part, some reduction in criminal behavior is measured, but considerable modeling must be done to translate this into the cost saving in the complex, criminal justice system. The impact on policing, courts, parole, probation, and corrections must be handled and each of these is a system in its own right. Analysts usually seek to achieve some simplifications so that they infer a reduction in system expenditures due to changes in specific criminal acts and arrests, that is, a kind of opportunity cost pricing. From available evaluations, criminal justice domain estimates are widely available. Even restricting benefits to criminality outcomes, drug abuse treatment for youths and adults continue to be found to make a net social contribution to society.

A benefit often neglected is the consumption expenditures on illegal drugs. For the most part, it is assumed that at the margin the consumer would experience a marginal benefit for the marginal cost of the consumption, and reductions in consumption are simultaneously offset by the consumer reductions, so there is a net washout. No inclusion would be appropriate. Of course, reduction in drug use and hence expenditures are explicit goals of prevention and drug abuse treatment programs and for the national drug control effort. For example, cocaine consumption was explicitly evaluated as an outcome by the RAND study of Rydell and Everingham (1994) in which they estimated the potential reductions for supply versus demand strategies in a cost-effectiveness approach. Here, it is the policy outcome that is evaluated for various program costs. Alternatively, the consumption side of the market may be used as an approximation for the resources devoted to the production and distribution of the illegal drugs. Productive resources are devoted to this activity and represent an opportunity cost to the economy that should be valued. Since accounting records of illegal activities are clandestine, one may roughly approximate the value of such resources utilizing consumption value and some notion of market structure and production costs (Hannan, 1975; Cartwright, 1998). Since drug distribution may represent a local monopoly, a decrease in the percentage of the mark-up would be appropriate. However, the value of risk for engaging in illegal activities may be difficult to estimate and infer as an economic input into the legitimate economy. In using the consumption approach, double counting must be avoided for the various supply-side and income factors.

4 Costs

Box 3.2 identifies costs of drug abuse treatment programs. These costs are generated in the treatment program as part of the therapeutic intervention adopted by the program or, in economic parlance, the production function. Some ambiguity exists because treatment services also include services to address the whole problem of rehabilitating the person. Housing, medical care, legal assistance, childcare, transportation, employment services and other ancillary services are offered as 'wrap-around' services to the drug abuse treatment intervention. Treatment researchers often consider 'wrap-around' services an effective component of treatment, and this would complicate the role of these services, because other analysts consider such goods redistribution of goods and services. Care must be taken to distinguish between the transfer (welfare) of these services and the actual treatment program expenditures. For example, supported housing is an intervention that can offer an individual a drug-free lifestyle so that the housing becomes an intervention in and of itself. But of course, individuals have to live somewhere and so how should one treat the costs of such an approach? Usually, one asks what the patient would have done in the absence of the program.

BOX 3.2   COSTS OF DRUG ABUSE TREATMENT: DOMAINS OF RESOURCE COSTS

Treatment program operating expenses
Treatment program overhead expenses
Medical care
Ancillary or wrap-around social services
Criminal justice supervision
Medical care costs
Time costs: employment income forgone while in treatment and travel time
Transportation cost

In examining costs, the first problem is to sort out the difference between economic costs and accounting costs. Economic costs are the opportunity costs of the resources used in the treatment of patients and are equal to the best alternatives foregone. While this is somewhat easy to say, most of cost–benefit analysis is devoted to getting these measurements correctly done. However, in the real world, plenty of financial data is available on specific drug abuse treatment units that are obviously using resources to open their doors for business and utilizing principles of financial management in order to measure their performance. A distinction must be made between the notion of financial viability and economic efficiency. The financial viability of an organization is independent of the economic analysis of its efficiency, since an economically inefficient organization can exist with a rich set of financial resources. The American medical establishment has been criticized for having achieved this.

Financial performance is evaluated from accounting reports embodied in the statement of operations (revenues and costs), the balance sheet (asset and liabilities of the firm), and statement of cash flows (actual money received and spent over a time period). It is tempting to take such statements and uncritically use them to evaluate economic costs, and indeed, this is often done. While not explicitly stated, such analysis often involves the additional assumption that social opportunity cost is identical to private opportunity cost. This is not the case in public health policy analysis, where a social perspective is required. The skilled analyst utilizes the financial information of the treatment unit and also independent measures of actual resource use in order to determine economic costs. For example, if a public treatment unit receives a free building to house its unit, it need not consider rent as a transaction in its financial statements, but society would view the building as having alternative uses, and so the economist imputes a rental value to the building in use. Fortunately, there is a growing body of scientific work to provide adequate guidance on issues of costs (Drummond et al., 1997; French et al., 2002c).

In drug abuse treatment research, standard instruments have been developed to collect economic costs by valuing all the resources in a drug treatment program (French et al., 2002c). In governmental agencies with drug abuse services responsibility, there has been a move to establish standardized accounts to aid in monitoring performance and to establish fair prices to treatment units. Such costing development is critical to the enhancement of the treatment field since individual interventions must be priced; programs must manage their cost structure; and public treatment systems must manage costs and quality as well provide accountability. Unit service costs, the disaggregated services that are bundled into treatment episodes, are an important complement (Anderson et al., 1998).

5 Cost–benefit analysis studies

At the outset, it would seem futile to pursue cost–benefit studies if drug abuse treatment did not have efficacy and/or effectiveness (Cartwright, 1998, 2000a). Fortunately, drug abuse treatment has been shown in a number of studies to have effectiveness. Prendergast et al. (2002) present a meta-analysis for drug abuse treatment effectiveness, and Marsch (1998) similarly did a meta-analysis for methadone maintenance. As shown in the Prendergast et al. study, measured effectiveness is higher in evaluation studies with a pre-post measure of individual behavioral change versus a pre-post study with a comparison group. The pre-post measure of individual behavioral change is by far the most frequent evaluation done of drug abuse treatment, and yet it is considered the weakest design because of the lack of a comparison group. Stronger designs are now being emphasized in treatment evaluations with adequate statistical power and randomization into control groups.

Traditional cost–benefit analysis is grounded in the economic assumption of consumer sovereignty. This would imply a simple measure of the demand for drug abuse treatment would be sufficient for the analysis. However, drug abuse treatment has major public good aspects related to the promotion of public safety, a traditional concern of the criminal justice system. Thus, a major part of the value of drug abuse treatment is imparted through reduction of the external costs that are inflicted on society by the criminality of drug abuse users, abusers, and addicts. There are also other intangible values related to family, culture and the general demand for a drug-free culture for infants, children and adolescents. The demand for a drug-free culture may also be viewed as important for the functioning of the economy since labor productivity is still a major source of income and wealth. As a result of the perceived value of these benefits, drug abuse prevention and treatment is subsidized by governments as a 'merit good'. Such drug abuse treatment services can be consumed directly by individuals, and ordinarily economic efficiency would be driven by the free interplay of supply and demand forces, but the high level of external benefits make subsidization an excellent vehicle for increasing consumption to capture social benefits.

Early economic evaluations estimated a broad base of benefits. The first two evaluations of Holahan (1970) and Leslie (1971) were grounded in responses to the heroin epidemics in Washington, DC and New York City, respectively. Both typically had to rely on perceived benefits of treatment rather than solid estimates in order to proceed with their analysis. At the national level, Maidlow and Berman (1972) conducted a cost–benefit study, but used a limited formulation of treatment benefit that was defined as the $30,000 per year that the heroin addict steals to support his/her addiction. However, the calculations were a model of clarity. McGlothlin et al. (1972) also did a national study and utilized theft income of addicts. They found that a hypothetical combination of civil commitment and out-patient treatment provided the most net social benefit. Fujii (1974) used an economic model to guide his investigation and introduced the relapse rate as part of the natural history of treatment in order to adjust benefits. In a California case study, Sirotnick and Bailey (1975) found positive net benefits where they utilized illegal drug spending as a proxy for crime cost to society. Hannan (1975, 1976) in his dissertation, later published as a book, developed a utility theory of addict behavior in which a choice is made between legitimate and illegitimate labor time. He estimates a simple equation that finds an increase in arrests as a result of higher heroin prices. Levine et al. (1976) found a similar direction of change between heroin price and property crime in a study of methadone treatment expansion in Detroit, where the decrease in victim losses (the benefit) was greater than the cost of treatment.

Finally, closing out the 1970s, Rufener et al. (1977) conducted a cost–benefit and cost–effectiveness analysis of The National Institute on Drug Abuse (NIDA) supported drug abuse programs for five different modalities of treatment. The underlying data came from the Drug Abuse Reporting Program (DARP) that had effectiveness measures for 'before and after' comparisons of behavior change. Utilizing 'cost of illness' methods based on human capital models, the cost–benefit analysis was grounded in iden-tified cost savings to society. A cost of illness study estimates costs such as drug abuse treatment, hospitalization, and pharmaceuticals. Costs in lost time for treatment or labor productivity costs are included along with criminal justice and other incremental governmental costs.

Rufener et al. were able to estimate four separate cost-effectiveness ratios for each modality and noted the difficulty of comparing across dif-ferent outcomes. Their benefit analysis built on methods first presented by Fujii (1974) and the estimates of Levine et al. (1976) on property crime reduction. They found a net social benefit for all modalities, and a rather high benefit–cost ratio of 12.8 to 1 for outpatient drug-free treatment.

In the 1980s, Griffin (1983) published a therapeutic program study without an economic framework, while Tabbush (1986) provided an economic analysis of the efficiency of the California system. At the end of the 1980s, Harwood et al. (1988, 1989) published a study consistent with Rufener et al.'s (1977) methods and with 'cost of illness' methods. Here the effectiveness data came from the Treatment Outcome Prospective Study (TOPS) and property crime was treated as a transfer (but later included in a measure of cost to 'law-abiding citizens'). In an economic approach, property destroyed as a result of drug-related crime is included in the opportunity cost to society. Outpatient drug-free treatment had a higher benefit–cost ratio than outpatient methadone or residential treatment. What is remarkable for this decade is how little work was being done while the epidemic raged, but stronger economic frameworks were being developed.

In the 1990s, Gerstein et al. (1994) conducted a widely quoted study, 'Evaluating Recovery Services: The California Drug and Alcohol Treatment Assessment (CALDATA)'. This study utilized state databases, provider records, and a follow-up interview with participants in treatment in a 'before and after' evaluation. The analysts looked at residential programs, 'social model' programs, outpatient programs, and outpatient methadone. Such studies suffer from the methodological problem of 'regression to the mean' whereby some improvement may have occurred without treatment, and hence the importance of using a comparison group, which was absent for this evaluation. Reported benefit–cost ratios varied from 4/1 to 12/1, and these have often been quoted in policy discussions. In addition to the societal perspective, the 'taxpayer' prospective was estimated as consisting of criminal justice costs, victim losses, health-care utilization, lost legitimate earnings, and the additions of theft losses (stolen property or money) and income transfers (public assistance, disability insurance). This study shows the feasibility of actually doing this type of study, but one wonders why it is always a one-shot approach and not continuously produced to affect policies for continuous improvement of the state system.

Recently, California has embarked on a new policy with a commitment to treatment with the Substance Abuse and Crime Prevention Act, also known as 'Proposition 36', which was passed by 61 percent of California voters on November 7, 2000. First- and second-time, non-violent, simple drug possession offenders would be given the opportunity to receive substance abuse treatment instead of incarceration. Proposition 36 was funded with $120 million annually for five and a half years, and there are fears that this is insufficient. While one cannot claim 'cause and effect' between the CALDATA study and Proposition 36, the timing of evaluation followed by the new treatment initiative and financing gives the appearance of rational budgeting. There is a six-year lag between the study and the new policy, which of course means that other considerations were at play in this period. In a subsequent analysis of this data, Harwood et al. (1998) found treatment beneficial for women although with lower cost savings than the men, but the women had lower costs to begin with. Flynn et al. (2003b) found higher benefits for women in their study using Drug Abuse Treatment Outcome Study data from 1992.

Oregon commissioned a similar type of study to CALDATA (Finigan, 1996) which remains an unpublished state report. A statistical sample of treatment completers was compared to a group who received little or no treatment, which is an improvement over the CALDATA methodology. Treatment completers did better by reducing their criminality, increasing their legitimate incomes, reducing child welfare cases, and reducing medical expenses. Using basically the same categories of CALDATA, once again the taxpayer perspective was adopted. Overall, it was estimated that every tax dollar spent on treatment completers in 1991–92 produced $5.60 of avoided social cost. Oregon rationally included substance abuse coverage in its publicly sponsored health plans, but in the state budget crunch of 2003 it eliminated such coverage. Establishing financing streams less vulnerable to economic downturns would be critical to maintaining human capital in states where major allocation decisions are being made over public health services.

Fals-Stewart et al. (1997) reported on a small clinical trial that compared the outcomes of randomly assigning married male patients to either behavioral couples therapy or individual-based treatment. They find behavioral couples therapy to have nine times more net benefit than individual therapy. As is common, they defined social costs in terms of public assistance expenditures, rather than the increase in administrative burden. Flynn et al. (1999) utilize the data collected in the Drug Abuse Treatment Outcome Study and focus only on the reduction of crime costs for residential and outpatient drug-free treatment. Benefit–cost ratios were from 1.33 to 3.26 for outpatient drug-free and 1.68 to 2.73 for residential treatment, where residential treatment did quite well as compared to other studies. Mauser et al. (1994) conducted a small study of 259 persons assigned to a treatment diversion program without a comparison group in a 'before and after' evaluation. The study found criminal justice cost savings, a decline in productivity and an increase in medical care costs. Overall, net benefits were positive for this program. Hartz el al. (1999) looked at the impact of adding contingency contracting to standard treatment and found a 4.87 benefit–cost ratio although the sample was too small for a statistical significance.

In the start of the new decade beginning in 2000, there was greater interest in cost–benefit studies. First, Daley et al. (2000) utilized the Massachusetts treatment data for 439 women to examine the impact of treatment on crime cost savings for substance-abusing pregnant women. A regression equation was used to control for program and client characteristics. Residential treatment for women was found to have the largest net benefit and the highest benefit–cost ratio at 2.11 to 1. In a randomized trial, Robertson et al (2001) studied juvenile offenders who received either behavioral cognitive therapy or intensive supervision. A comparison group was also established which received standard probation or parole. Regression equations were utilized to control for differences among the groups and self-selection bias. The only measured benefit was the short-run cost savings in the criminal justice system, and the cognitive behavioral therapy (2 to 1 benefit–cost ratio) beat both intense supervision and usual treatment. Thus, this paper explored criminal justice theories based on levels of supervision as the primary means to affect outcomes. Utilizing 1992 DATAOS, Flynn et al. (2003a and b) also examined criminal justice benefits in methadone maintenance and found positive net benefits for women and men. Flynn also finds that longer-stay patients generate larger net benefits. Drug abuse treatment can have a beneficial effect for some women and adolescents involved in crime.

French and his colleagues at the University of Miami have published a steady stream of cost–benefit analysis results and methodological improvements for the field. French has pioneered the development of the Drug Abuse Treatment Cost Analysis Program (DATCAP), a consistent costing interview procedure for developing treatment program and patient costs. He has also pioneered the utilization of the Addiction Severity Index, a prevalent screening tool in treatment, to measure economic benefit for the outcomes in a variety of clinical and effectiveness studies. The societal perspective is always used. These studies have found a positive net benefit for: a modified therapeutic community for mentally ill chemical abusers in New York City (French et al. 2002b); public residential treatment in the State of Washington (French et al., 2000); and specialty residential treatment for pregnant and parenting women in Arkansas that exceeded standard residential treatment (French et al., 2002a). These studies all had some drawbacks in the effectiveness component of the original design, but the economic evaluation was well done with the focus on careful methodological development. In a quasi-experimental study of addiction treatment in Chicago, Salome et al. (2003) found an overall benefit–cost ratio of 4.26 for a sample of 2,862 patients.

Studies have broadened the focus to populations of pregnant women, juveniles and homeless persons. For pregnant, substance abusing women, treatment is seen as particularly relevant for improving the health of the women and the fetus. Residential treatment seems to have strong benefits that overcome the higher costs incurred in such treatment. This shows in the Daley et al. (2000) study in Washington and the French (2002a) study in Arkansas. A study of a modified therapeutic community for homeless and mentally ill chemical abusers also found strong benefits even though costs were particularly high for this very needy population. In Washington, outpatient and residential treatment had robust benefits over costs and were similar in their economic impact.

Moving beyond the concept of a single treatment episode, Zarkin et al. (2005) introduced the use of a lifetime simulation model to estimate

Table 3.1   A summary of benefit–cost ratios for drug abuse treatment
            programs

Treatment program	Average	Std dev.	N
Methadone	5.73	4.67	19
Residential/therapeutic	6.48	6.34	16
Outpatient	6.11	6.82	14
State	5.70	1.23	3

Source: Author's Calculation.

the benefits and costs of methadone maintenance treatment. With the dynamic model, the benefit–cost ratio was a robust 38 as compared to the typical one-treatment static model of 4. Examining drug abuse treatment in the criminal justice system, a randomized clinical trial compared treatment with a co-located probation officer versus the standard client's choice. Given the small size of the sample and the nature of the intervention, one could not conclude that the new intervention was better than the old. In California, Ettner et al. (2006) found that the state was obtaining about a 7 to 1 benefit–cost ratio, but here the design was a before and after comparison of clients.

Appendix Table 3A.1 summarizes the available cost–benefit studies in drug abuse treatment. Extracting from this table, Table 3.1 illustrates raw means of benefit–cost ratios that indicate robust net social benefits for treatment. By illustrating the benefit–cost ratio, the effect of inflation does not have to be taken into account, and the ratio is interpreted as the current or real dollars that invested in treatment will generate cost savings to society of around six dollars. Of course, the quality of the various studies has not been evaluated and used to weight the various study results as would be done in a meta-analysis such as in the Prendergast et al. study of effectiveness.

6   Future directions

Evaluation has a long history in the field of drug abuse treatment and has sustained a conclusion that such treatment has a positive economic contribution. While cost savings and human capital methods are now being consistently applied, other approaches are ready to be explored. Furthermore, the correlations between clinical and economic measures are so small that economic evaluation must be done (Dismuke et al. 2004). Perhaps, willingness to pay for drug abuse treatment will receive more attention. This would neatly combine with financing questions of coverage for such treatment and begin to answer the question of how society values treatment and why institutions are not moving towards complete coverage and parity. Broadly, health insurance that provides the same benefits and cost sharing for treatment of substance abuse dependence as other diseases such as diabetes or hypertension would be providing parity. With the current lack of funding for treatment, more taxpayer-oriented studies do not seem to be on the cutting edge of science nor what will be useful information for public policy. It is not possible to escape from the complexity of drug policy by focusing on a so-called practical perspective.

Cost–benefit analysis will continue to be applicable to clinical studies of innovative treatment interventions. Even with small effects, innovations appear to have an incremental impact on treatment outcomes and are economically worthwhile (Cartwright, 2000b) compared to the incremental cost, but small effects come with a cost of higher sample sizes in clinical studies. At some point a breakthrough innovation may have a revolutionary impact on the treatment system, but such innovations are unusual. The research community recognizes that at minimum an intervention should be 'costed out' in an economic fashion in order to provide basic information to health-care decision makers. Finally, emphasis must be placed on bringing the economic evaluator into the clinical study at the beginning of the research design so that sufficient consideration can be given to methods, instrumentation, and databases.

Cost-utility studies may be the next movement in economic evaluation of treatment, but this would be a move toward cost-effectiveness of medical evaluation. Feasibility has been shown in one small study (Daley et al., 2005). Cost utility at least promises to form a consistent aggregation for outcomes that are valued by members of society. There is of course the ongoing question of whose preferences will be measured. Here the reference case should focus on the general population as recommended in the US Public Health Service report (Gold et al., 1996). Of course, cost-utility studies have their own limitations as compared to a cost–benefit study, but doing them brings drug abuse treatment into consistency with the worldwide extensive interest in evaluation of medical interventions.

So far, some comprehensive state evaluations have been conducted. Such studies have been one-shot affairs with weaker evaluation designs. Expansion along this line would seem to provide system decision makers with useful information on the efficiency and effectiveness of their current system operations. Decision makers need timely information and such sophisticated studies of system performance in order to assist in rational budget allocations. This would require further health services research and database developments in the state information systems. Aligning the state information systems with an analytical and evaluative component would help to rationalize the investment in human services at all levels of government. Furthermore, links between drug abuse treatment and other public medical services must receive additional analysis. Only through consistent and persistent analysis can the information systems be improved so that they are useful for real decision-making studies.

New populations are now being targeted in order to reach public health goals as found in the US Department of Health and Human Services *Healthy People 2010* (2000, Ch 26: 'Substance abuse'). Much more work is needed to expand economic evaluations on substance abusing women, juveniles and adolescents, patients with comorbidities, and other groups suffering health disparities. Criminal justice populations are of considerable interest as convicted users are coming out of prison in increasing numbers and concerns arise as to the state of their rehabilitation and ability to remain drug free and to avoid criminal activity. A number of treatment options need to be explored in the complicated criminal justice system that involves populations in pre-adjudication status, jail, prison, probation, and parole. Right now, major interest is focused on such initiatives as drug courts and California's Proposition 13 diversion program to treatment.

An ongoing question for state system financing and delivery is the right balance of residential and outpatient treatment. However, there is no balance when coverage is drastically cut for drug abuse treatment with severe budgetary shortfalls. These two issues are illustrative of the interaction of financing issues and cost–benefit analysis. While they are logically separated, in practice one is involved in both simultaneously when making decisions a treatment system. Maintaining drug abuse treatment funding in the face of budgetary shortfalls is a critical public health policy need in the near future.

A specific evaluation issue for drug abuse treatment is still being researched. Since drug abuse is related to criminal activity, the standing of the patient continues to be an issue of importance. Costs and benefits are driven by the perspective of the evaluation and the standing of the participants. Criminals may be given standing in the sense that their preferences are counted in the evaluation. However, their preferences may be eliminated completely in the Anglo-Saxon tradition of declaring individuals outlaws with no rights in society. Declared an outlaw, property theft would be counted as a social cost. Where preferences exist for the addict, property theft would be considered a transfer and not counted. To count or not to count, that is the question.

Note

*   Please do not quote without permission. The views expressed are solely those of the author and are not the responsibility of his organizational affiliation. Funding was not provided by any outside source, and there are no perceived conflicts of interest.

References

Alemi, F., Taxman, F., Baghi, H., Vang, J., Thanner, M. and Doyon, V. (2006), 'Costs and benefits of combining probation and substance abuse treatment', *Journal of Mental Health Policy and Economics*, **9**, 57–70.

Alterman, A.I., O'Brien, C.P., McLellan, A.T., August, D.S., Snider, E.C., Droba, M., Cornish, J.W., Hall, C.P., Raphelson, A.H. and Schrade, F.X. (1994), 'Effectiveness and costs of inpatient versus day hospital cocaine rehabilitation', *Journal of Nervous and Mental Diseases*, **182** (3), 157–63.

Anderson, D.W., Bowland, B.J., Cartwright, W.S. and Bassin, G. (1998), 'Service-level costing of drug abuse treatment', *Journal of Substance Abuse Treatment*, **15**, 201–11.

Aos, S., Phipps, P., Barnoski, R. and Leib, R. (2001), 'The comparative costs and benefits of programs to reduce crime', Olympia: Washington State Institute for Public Policy, www.wsipp.wa.gov/crime/pdf/costbenefit.pdf.

Avants, S.K., Margolin, A., Sindelar, J.L., Rounsaville, B.J., Schottenfeld, R., Stine, S., Cooney, N.L., Rosenheck, R.A., Li, S.H. and Kosten, T.R. (1999), 'Day treatment versus enhanced standard methadone services for opiod-dependent patients: a comparison of clinical efficacy and cost', *American Journal of Psychiatry*, **156** (1), 27–33.

Boardman, A.E., Greenberg, D.H., Vining, A.R. and Weimer, D.L. (1996), *Cost–Benefit Analysis: Concepts and Practice*, Upper Saddle River, NJ: Prentice Hall.

Brent, R. (2003), 'The tax implications of cost shifting in cost–benefit analysis in mental health', *Applied Economics*, **35** (8), 943–50.

Cartwright, W.S. (1998), 'Cost–benefit and cost-effectiveness analysis of drug abuse treatment services', *Evaluation Review*, **22** (5), 609–36.

Cartwright, W.S. (2000a), 'Cost–benefit analysis of drug treatment services: review of the literature', *Journal of Mental Health Policy and Economics*, **3** (200), 11–26.

Cartwright, W.S. (2000b), 'Cocaine medications, cocaine consumption and societal cost', *Pharmacoeconomics*, **18** (4), 405–13.

Cartwright, W.S. and Solano, P.L. (2003), 'The economics of public health: financing drug abuse treatment services', *Health Policy*, **66**, 247–60.

Daley, M., Argeriou, M., McCarty, D., Callahan, Jr., J.J., Shepard, D.S. and Williams, C.N. (2000), 'The costs of crime and the benefits of substance abuse treatment for pregnant women', *Journal of Substance Abuse Treatment*, **19** (4), 445–58.

Daley, M., Shepard, D.S. and Bury-Maynard, D. (2005), 'Changes in quality of life for pregnant women in substance user treatment: developing a quality of life index for the addictions', *Substance Use and Misuse*, **40** (3), 375–94.

Dismuke, C.E., French, M.T., Salome, H.J., Foss, M.A., Scott, C.K. and Dennis, M.L. (2004), 'Out of touch or on the money: do the clinical objectives of addiction treatment coincide with economic evaluation results?', *Journal of Substance Abuse Treatment*, **27**, 253–63.

Drummond, M.F., O'Brien, B.O., Stoddart, G.L. and Torrance, G.W. (1997), *Methods for the Economic Evaluation of Health Programs*, Oxford: Oxford University, Press.

Ettner, S.L., Huang, D., Evans, E., Ash, D.R., Hardy, M., Jourabchi, M. and Yih-Ing, H. (2006), 'Benefit–cost in the California treatment outcome project: does substance abuse treatment 'pay for itself?', *Health Services Research*, **41**, 192–213.

Fals-Stewart, W., O'Farrel, T.J. and Birchier, G.R. (1997), 'Behavioral couples therapy for male substance-abusing patients: a cost outcomes analysis', *Journal of Consulting and Clinical Psychology*, **65** (5), 789–802.

Finigan, M. (1996), 'Societal Outcomes and Cost Savings of Drug and Alcohol Treatment in the State of Oregon', Office of Alcohol and Drug Abuse Programs, Oregon Department of Human Services and Governor's Council on Alcohol and Drug Abuse Programs.

Flynn, P.M., Kristiansen, P.L., Porto, J.V. and Hubbard, R.L. (1999), 'Costs and benefits of treatment for cocaine addiction in DATOS', *Drug and Alcohol Dependence*, **57**, 167–74.

Flynn, P.M., Porto, J.V., Rounds-Bryant, J.L. and Kristiansen, P.L. (2003a), 'Costs and benefits of methadone treatment in DATOS – Part 1: Discharged versus continuing patients', *Journal of Maintenance in the Addictions*, **2**, 129–49.

Flynn, P.M., Porto, J.V., Rounds-Bryant, J.L. and Kristiansen, P.L. (2003b), 'Cost and benefit of methadone treatment in DATOS–Part 2: Gender differences for discharged and continuing patients', *Journal of Maintenance in the Addictions*, **2**, 151–68.

French, M.T., Sacks, S., De Leon, G., Staines, G. and McKendrick, K. (1999), 'Modified therapeutic community for mentally ill chemical abusers: outcomes and costs', *Evaluation and the Health Professions*, **22** (1), 60–85. Erratum **22** (3), 399.

French, M.T., Salome, H.J., Krupski, A., McKay, J.R., Donovan, D.M., McLellan, A.T. and Durell, J. (2000), 'Benefit–cost analysis of residential and outpatient addiction treatment in the State of Washington', *Evaluation Review*, **24** (6), 609–34.

French, M.T., McCollister, K.E., Cacciola, J., Durell, J. and Stephens, R.L. (2002a), 'Benefit–cost analysis of addiction treatment in Arkansas: specialty and standard residential programs for pregnant and parenting women', *Substance Abuse*, **23** (1), 31–51.

French, M.T., McCollister, K.E., Sacks, S., McKendrick, K. and Deleon, G. (2002b), 'Benefit–cost analysis of a modified therapeutic community for mentally ill chemical abusers', *Evaluation and Program Planning*, **25** (2), 137–48.

French, M.T., Salome, H.J. and Carney, M. (2002c), 'Using the DATCAP and ASI to estimate the costs and benefits of residential addiction treatment in the State of Washington', *Social Science and Medicine*, **55**, 2267–82.

French, M.T., Salome, H.J., Sindelar, J.L. and McLellan, A.T. (2002d), 'Benefit–cost analysis of addiction treatment: methodological guidelines and empirical application using the DATACAP and ASI', *Health Services Research*, **37** (2), 433–55.

Fujii, E.T. (1974), 'Public investment in the rehabilitation of heroin addicts', *Social Science Quarterly*, **55**, 39–50.

Gerstein, D.R., Johnson, R.A., Harwood, H.J., Fountain, K., Suter, N. and Malloy, K. (1994), 'Evaluating Recovery Services: The California Drug and Alcohol Treatment Assessment (CALDATA)', General Report, Sacramento, CA: California Department of Alcohol and Drug Programs.

Gold, M.E., Siegel, J.E., Russell, L.B. and Weisnstein, M.C. (1996), *Cost-Effectiveness in Health and Medicine*, New York: Oxford University Press.

Griffin, K.S. (1983), 'The therapeutic community: a cost–benefit analysis', *International Journal of Therapeutic Communities*, **4**, 3–10.

Hannan, T.H. (1975), *The Economics of Methadone Maintenance*, Lexington, MA: Lexington Books.

Hannan, T.H. (1976), 'The benefits and costs of methadone maintenance', *Public Policy*, **24** (2), 197–226.

Hartz, D.T., Meek, P., Piotrowski, N.A., Tusel, D.J., Henke, C.J., Delucchi, K., Sees, K. and Hall, S.M. (1999), 'A cost-effectiveness and cost–benefit analysis of contingency contracting-enhanced methadone detoxification treatment', *American Journal of Drug and Alcohol Abuse*, **25** (2), 207–18.

Harwood, H., Fountain, D., Carothers, S., Gerstein, D. and Johnson, R. (1998), 'Gender differences in the economic impacts of clients before, during, and after substance abuse treatment', *Drugs and Society*, **13** (1/2), 251–69.

Harwood, H.J., Hubbard, R.L., Collins, J.J. and Rachal, J.V. (1988), 'The costs of crime and the benefits of drug abuse treatment: a cost–benefit analysis using TOPS data', in Leukfeld, C.G. and Tims, H.M. (eds), *Compulsory Treatment of Drug Abuse: Research and Clinical Practice*, NIDA Research Monographs 86, Rockville, MD: National Institute on Drug Abuse.

Harwood, H., Hubbard, R., Collins, J.J. and Rachal, J.V. (1989), *A Cost–Benefit Analysis of Drug Abuse Treatment*, Research Annual on Law and Policy Studies, Greenwich, CT; JAI Press.

Holahan, J. (1970), 'The Economics of Drug Addiction and Control in Washington, DC: A Model for Estimation of Costs and Benefits of Rehabilitation', A Report for the Office of Planning and Research, Washington, DC: US Department of Corrections.

Hubbard, R.L., Marsden, M.E., Rachal, J.V., Harwood, H.J., Cavanaugh, E.R. and

Ginzburg, H.M. (1989), *Drug Abuse Treatment: A National Study of Effectiveness*, Chapel Hill, NC: University of North Carolina Press.

Leslie, A.C. (1971), *A Benefit/Cost Analysis of New York City's Heroin Addiction Problems and Programs*, New York: Health Services Program.

Levine, D., Stoloff, P. and Spruill, N. (1976), 'Public drug treatment and addict crime', *Journal of Legal Studies*, **5** (2), 435–62.

Logan, T.K., Hoyt, W.H., McCollister, K.E., French, M.T., Leukefeld, C. and Minton, L. (2004), 'Economic evaluation of drug court: methodology, results, and policy implications', *Evaluation and Planning* Review, **27** (4). 381–96

Maidlow, S.T. and Berman, H. (1972), 'The economics of heroin treatment', *American Journal of Public Health*, **62** (10), 1397–406.

Marsch, L.A. (1998), 'The efficacy of methadone maintenance interventions in reducing illicit opiate use, HIV risk behavior and criminality: a meta-analysis', *Addiction*, **93** (4), 515–32.

Mauser, E., Van-Stelle, K.R. and Moberg, D.P. (1994), 'The economic impact of diverting substance-abusing offenders into treatment', *Crime and Delinquency*, **40** (4), 568–88.

McGlothlin, W.H., Tabbush, V.C., Chambers, C.D. and Jamison, K. (1972), *Alternative Approaches to Opiate Addiction Control: Costs, Benefits, and Potential*, Washington, DC: US Department of Justice.

Prendergast, M.L., Podus, D., Chang, E. and Urada, D. (2002), 'The effectiveness of drug abuse treatment: a meta-analysis of comparison group studies', *Drug and Alcohol Dependence*, **67** (1), 53–72.

Robertson, A.A., Grimes, P.W. and Rogers, K.E. (2001), 'A short-run cost–benefit analysis of community-based interventions for juvenile offenders', *Crime and Delinquency*, **47** (2), 265–84.

Rufener, B.L., Rachal, J.V. and Cruze, A.M. (1977), *Management Effectiveness Measures for NIDA Drug Abuse Treatment Programs: Vol. I. Cost Benefit Analysis*, Rockville, MD: National Institute on Drug Abuse.

Rydell, C.P. and Everingham, S.S. (1994), *Controlling Cocaine: Supply versus Demand Programs*, Santa Monica: Rand Corporation.

Salome, H.J., French, M.T., Scott, C., Foss, M. and Dennis, M. (2003), 'Investigating variation in the costs and benefits of addiction treatment: econometric analysis of the Chicago target cities project', *Evaluation and Program Planning*, **26**, 325–38.

Sirotnik, K.A. and Bailey, R.C. (1975), 'A cost–benefit analysis for a multimodality heroin treatment project', *International Journal of the Addictions*, **10** (3), 443–51.

Substance Abuse and Mental Health Services Administration (SAMHSA) (2005), 'Results from the 2004 National Survey on Drug Use and Health: National Findings', Office of Applied Studies, NSDUH Series H-28, DHHS Publication No. SMA 05-4062), Rockville, MD.

Tabbush, V. (1986), 'The effectiveness and efficiency of publicly funded drug abuse treatment and prevention programs in California: a benefit–cost analysis', California Association of County Drug Program Administrators.

US Department of Health and Human Services (2000), *Healthy People 2010*, 2nd edn with 'Understanding and improving health' and 'Objectives for improving health', 2 vols, Washington, DC: US Government Printing Office.

Zarkin, G.A., Dunlap, L.J., Hicks, K.A. and Mamo, D. (2005), 'Benefits and costs of methadone treatment: results from a lifetime simulation model', *Health Economics*, **14** (11), 1133–50.

Table 3A.1 *Cost–benefit analysis of drug abuse treatment*

Author(s)	Study	Programs under evaluation	Design	Sample	Cost–benefit analysis
Holahan, 1970	The Economics of Drug Addiction and Control in Washington, DC: A Model for Estimation of Costs and Benefits of Rehabilitation (DC Gov)	Narcotic Treatment Administration (short-term commitment, methadone maintenance plus additional services)	Cost-benefit planning model	None, based on judgment	Cost $1,400,000 Benefit $5,750,770 B/C 4
Leslie, 1971	A Benefit/Cost Analysis of New York City's Heroin Addiction Problem and Programs, 1971 (New York City)	Detoxification Antagonists Methadone Odyssey House Increased enforcement Phoenix House Heroin maintenance State NACC Involuntary incarceration Heroin legalization	Cost-benefit planning model for New York City	None, based on literature review and author's judgment	Methadone 7.9 Odyssey House 6.5 Phoenix House 3.1 Involuntary incarceration 1.7
Maidlow and Berman, 1972	The Economics of Heroin Treatment (none)	Methadone maintenance Therapeutic community	Cost-benefit planning model for US	None, based on literature review and author's judgment	Therapeutic community Cost $14,704 Benefit $213,836 B/C 14.5 Methadone maintenance Cost $13,231 Benefit $247,967 B/C 18.7

Study	Title (evaluation)	Programs	Method	Sample	Results
McGlothlin et al. 1972	Alternative Approaches to Opiate Addiction Control: Costs, Benefits, and Potential (Dept of Justice)	Methadone maintenance – strict control / Methadone maintenance – dispensing only / Heroin maintenance / Therapeutic community / Civil commitment / Civil commitment and other program	Benefit–cost planning model for US	None, based on literature review and author's judgment	Civil commitment Cost $2,400 Benefit $11,750 B/C 4.90 Methadone maintenance Cost $875 Benefit $12,735 B/C 14.55
Fujii, 1974	Public Investment in the Rehabilitation of Heroin Addicts (none)	Detoxification / Civil commitment / Imprisonment and parole / Methadone maintenance / Heroin maintenance / Heroin legalization	Benefit–cost planning model for US	None, based on literature review and author's judgment	No B/C ratio Net benefit is reported for: Methadone maint. $10,639 Imprisonment & parole $8,271 Civil commitment $4,030 Detoxification $1,378
Hannan, 1975	The Economics of Methadone Maintenance (none)	Methadone maintenance treatment programs	Pre–post treatment program data from New York City	931 male patients	Methadone maintenance Cost $1,784,000 Benefit $8,164,00 B/C 4.58

Table 3A.1 (continued)

Author(s)	Study	Programs under evaluation	Design	Sample	Cost–benefit analysis
Sirotnik and Bailey, 1975	A Cost–Benefit Analysis for a Multimodality Heroin Treatment Project (California)	Central intake Therapeutic community Halfway house Detoxification Methadone maintenance	Pre–post outcome, no control	N=285 heroin addicts who were treated for at least one day from July 1, 1971 to December 31, 1972. Only 25 in follow-up	Community heroin treatment Cost $1,272,041 Benefit $4,631,960 B/C 3.64
Levine et al., 1976	Public Drug Treatment and Addict Crime (NIDA)	Public treatment programs Methadone	Natural experiment of four-year expansion of Detroit programs	Monthly public patient enrollment from 1970 to 1974	Methadone maintenance Cost $67,680 Benefit $129,430 B/C 1.91
Rufener et al., 1977	Management Effectiveness Measures for NIDA Drug Treatment Abuse Programs (NIDA)	Outpatient drug free Outpatient detoxification Inpatient detoxification Methadone maintenance Therapeutic community	Cost–benefit and cost-effectiveness with pre- and post-comparison using DARP data. One-year calculation	Used DARP and economic cost study of drug abuse	Outpatient B/C = 12.82 Methadone maint. B/C = 4.39 Therapeutic community B/C = 2.23

Author/Year	Title	Treatment types	Data source	Design/Method	Results
Griffin, 1983	The Therapeutic Community: A Cost–Benefit Analysis (Gaudenzia House)	Therapeutic community	Literature review, local data, Pennsylvania State data	Hypothetical five-year program data	Therapeutic community Cost $1,391,625 Benefit $9,116,086 B/C 6.55
Tabbush, 1986	The Effectiveness and Efficiency of Publicly Funded Drug Abuse Treatment and Prevention Programs in California: A Benefit–Cost Analysis (California County)	Residential Methadone Outpatient	Literature review, California criminal justice and program data	Cost–benefit planning model of California data during and post-treatment benefits	Heroin treatment Residential B/C = 26.3 Methadone maint. B/C = 13.8 Outpatient B/C = 24.7 Cocaine Residential B/C = 5.6 Outpatient B/C = 23.0
Harwood et al., 1988	The Costs of Crime and the Benefits of Drug Abuse Treatment: A Cost–Benefit Analysis Using TOPS Data (NIDA)	Residential treatment Outpatient methadone Outpatient drug free	Prospective study of 11,000 drug users, from 41 programs and 10 cities. Nonrandom sample	Comparison of individual pre-, during, and post-treatment using TOPS data and regression adjustment of after treatment crime benefits	Residential B/C = 2.01 Methadone maint. B/C = 0.92 Outpatient B/C = 4.28
Hubbard et al., 1989	Drug Abuse Treatment: A National Study of Effectiveness (NIDA)				
Gerstein et al., 1994	Evaluating Recovery Services: The California Drug and Alcohol Treatment Assessment (California)	Residential programs Social model Outpatient programs Outpatient methadone	3 stage random sampling: 16 counties, 110 providers, 3055 patients, 1859 interviewed	Pre-post treatment comparison of patients. Follow-up survey conducted on average 15 months after treatment	Residential B/C = 2.44 Social model B/C = 2.40 Outpatient B/C = 2.88 Methadone maint. B/C = 2.44

Table 3A.1 (continued)

Author(s)	Study	Programs under evaluation	Design	Sample	Cost–benefit analysis		
Mauser et al., 1994	The Economic Impact of Diverting Substance-Abusing Offenders into Treatment (Wisconsin)	Treatment alternatives program consisting of case management assessment and referrals, coordinate care, monitor compliance. Mainly outpatient and day treatment	Pre–post outcome, no control	N = 76, clients admitted to program from June 1990 through May 1991	Cost	Benefit	B/C
					$6,291	$11,314	1.80
Finigan, 1996	Societal Outcomes and Cost Savings of Drug and Alcohol Treatment in the State of Oregon (Oregon)	State substance abuse programs	Pre–post with nonrandom comparison group	Random sample drawn from 1991–1992 fiscal year from outpatient and residential patients. All methadone patients were included	Cost	Benefit	B/C
					$14,879,128	$83,147,187	5.59
Fals-Stewart et al., 1997	Behavioral couples therapy for male substance abusing patients: a cost outcomes analysis (VA/NIAAA)	Behavioral couple therapy (BCT) Individual behavioral therapy (IBT)	Randomized clinical trial Husband effects Health care Criminal justice Illegal income Public assistance	Married or cohabiting males N = 80	BCT Benefit Cost B/C IBT Benefit Cost B/C		$6,629 $1,373 4.83 $1,904 $1,360 1.4

Harwood et al., 1998	Gender Differences in the Economic Impacts of Clients Before, During, and After Substance Abuse Treatment (None)	Residential programs Social model Outpatient programs Outpatient methadone	Pre–post treatment comparison of patients. Follow-up survey conducted on average 15 months after treatment	3 stage random sampling: 16 counties, 110 providers, 3055 patients, 1859 interviewed	Residential Men B/C = 6.2 Women B/C = 2.4 Outpatient Men B/C = 13.9 Women B/C = 7.4 Methadone maint. Men B/C = 5.5 Women B/C = 5.3 Social Model Men B/C = 4.5 Women B/C = 4.0
Flynn et al., 1999	Costs and Benefits of Treatment for Cocaine Addiction in DATOS (NIDA)	Long-term residential Outpatient drug free	Pre–post comparison of patients. Follow-up survey at 12 months after discharge	Naturalistic and nonexperimental sample of 502 patients in 19 programs	Long term residential Cost $11,016 Benefit $21360 B/C 1.94 Outpatient Cost $1,422 Benefit $2,217 B/C 1.56
Hartz et al., 1999	A Cost-Effectiveness and Cost–Benefit Analysis of Contingency Contracting-Enhanced Methadone Detoxification Treatment (NIDA)	Methadone detoxification and treatment	Comparison of standard treatment to contingency contracting enhancement	Randomization of 102 opioid addicted patients into two arms of trial	Methadone maint. Cost $191.37 Benefit $ $932.18 B/C 4.87

Table 3A.1 (continued)

Author(s)	Study	Programs under evaluation	Design	Sample	Cost–benefit analysis
Daley et al., 2000	The Costs of Crime and the Benefits of Substance Abuse Treatment for Pregnant Women (HCFA)	Publicly funded treatment (five treatment modalities)	Pre–post comparison of pregnant women before and after treatment Taxpayer	Sample of 672 women	Methadone B/C = 1.54 Residential B/C = 2.11 Outpatient B/C = 1.72 Res/outpatient B/C = 2.10 Average B/C = 1.54

French et al., 2000	Benefit–Cost Analysis of Residential and Outpatient Addiction Treatment in the State of Washington (NIDA)	Full continuum of care (residential + outpatient) versus partial continuum (outpatient alone)	Pre–post comparison of persons in two arms	Natural intent to treat consecutively recruited Medicaid-funded patients (N = 263)	Full continuum
					  Cost $2,530
					  Benefit $20,363
					  B/C 8.05
					Partial continuum
					  Cost 1,137
					  Benefit $12,310
					  B/C 10.83

Robertson et al., 2001	A Short-Run Cost–Benefit Analysis of Community-Based Interventions for Juvenile Offenders (NIDA)	Intensive supervision versus cognitive behavioral	Quasi-experimental with control group in standard probation or parole, regression model	293 youth offenders on parole or probation (ages 11–17)	Cost $ 1,493 Benefit $2928 B/C 1.96

Study	Title	Program	Design	Sample	Results
French et al., 2002a	Benefit–Cost Analysis of Addiction Treatment in Arkansas: Specialty and Standard Residential Programs for Pregnant and Parenting Women (NIDA/CSAT)	Specialty residential treatment (pregnant and parenting women's living centers versus standard residential treatment versus standard detox and rehabilitation in a residential setting	Naturalistic intent to treat, recruitment at entry, before and after	N = 85, pregnant women over the age of 18	Specialty treatment Cost $8,035 Benefit $25,178 B/C 3.13 Standard treatment Cost $1,467 Benefit $9,557 B/C 6.52
French et al., 2002b	Benefit–Cost Analysis of a Modified Therapeutic Community for Mentally Ill Chemical Abusers (NIDA)	Modified therapeutic community compared to treatment as usual	Pre–post comparison for homeless persons with co-occurring problems	Sequential assignment in a naturalistic setting	Cost $20,361 Benefit $273,698 B/C 13,44
French et al, 2002c	Using the DATCAP and ASI to Estimate the Costs and Benefits of Residential Addiction Treatment in the State of Washington (NIDA/CSAT)	Publicly funded adult residential programs (intensive inpatient, extended care, long-term care programs)	Pre–post comparison in a natural setting	Naturalistic intent to treat N = 75	Residential treatment Mid range Cost $4,912 Benefit $21,329 B/C 4.34
French et al., 2002d	Benefit–Cost Analysis of Addiction Treatment: Methodological Guidelines and Empirical Application Using the DATCAP and ASI (NIDA)	Publicly funded outpatient drug-free programs	Case study Pre- and post-comparison in a natural setting	N = 178; ASI at 7 months past post-admission	Outpatient mid-range Cost $258 Benefit $4,643 B/C 18.00

Table 3A.1 (continued)

Author(s)	Study	Programs under evaluation	Design	Sample	Cost–benefit analysis		
Flynn et al, 2003a	Costs and Benefits of Methadone Treatment in DATOS—Part 1: Discharged versus Continuing Patients (NIDA)	Outpatient methadone treatment	Patients completing a 3-month in-treatment and 12-month follow-up, year 1992	Patients discharged before completing a year versus continuing patients N = 394	Benefit	$10,288	
					Cost	$ 3,429	
					BC ratio:	3.00	
					Net benefit for continuing patients: $7,168, higher than discharged		
Flynn et al, 2003b	Costs and Benefits of Methadone Treatment in DATOS—Part 2: Gender Differences for Discharged and Continuing Patients (NIDA)	Outpatient methadone treatment	Men and women patients completing a 3-month in-treatment and 12-month follow-up, year 1992	Patients discharged before completing a year versus continuing patients N = 394	Women B/C	3.62	
					Male B/C	2.60	
Salome et al., 2003	Investigating Variation in the Costs and Benefits of Addiction Treatment: Econometric Analysis of the Chicago Target Cities Project (NIDA, SAMHSA)	Target cities improvement program Outpatient methadone Intensive outpatient Halfway house Inpatient	Quasi-experimental	N = 2672; Intakes	Cost	$1,943	
					Benefit	$8,268	
					B/C	4.26	

Study	Title	Intervention	Design	Sample	Measure	Value
Logan et al., 2004	Economic Evaluation of Drug Court: Methodology, Results, and Policy Implications (NIDA)	Drug court	Quasi-experimental	Entrants versus assessed, but did not enter Total N = 745 Graduated, 222 Terminated, 371 Assessed, 152	Cost per participant 12-month benefit net savings B/C	$3,178 $8,624 $5,446 2.71
Zarkin et al., 2005	Benefits and Costs of Methadone Treatment: Results from a Lifetime Simulation Model (NIDA)	Methadone	Monte Carlo simulation	Population Aged 16–18	ΔCost ΔBenefit ΔB/ΔC ratio	$ 1,958 $148,852 76
Alemi et al., 2006	Costs and Benefits of Combining Probation and Substance Abuse Treatment(NIDA)	Seamless probation Probation officer collocated with treatment Traditional probation Client's choice	Randomized clinical trial	Probation (N = 272)	Δcost seamless vs traditional = $38.84 per day ΔBenefit B/C	$2.31 0.06
Ettner et al., 2006	Benefit–Cost in the California Treatment Outcome Project: Does Substance Abuse Treatment 'Pay for itself' (CA Dept of Alcohol and Drug Programs, CSAT, RWJ)	Methadone Outpatient Residential	Pre-post treatment 9-month follow-up	Patients in 45 (N = 2,567)	Cost Benefit B/C	$1,583 $11,487 7.26

Notes: Sources are in reference list. Acknowledged support is indicated in parentheses in study entry.

83

4   Can cost–benefit analysis guide education policy in developing countries?

Emmanuel Jimenez and Harry Anthony Patrinos

1   Introduction

If the true test of the value of an economic theory is longevity, the human capital model passes with flying colors. Its basics are simple and empirically testable (and generally validated). An individual will invest in his or her human capital – an additional year of schooling or on-the-job training – as long as the marginal gain from that investment exceeds its added cost. The gains extend over a lifetime and are discounted to the present. If some of these gains accrue to others, governments need to stimulate individuals to take them into account in making decisions. Public action may also be needed if poor individuals cannot mobilize the resources to finance the investment now, despite a promise of big gains in the future.

This human capital framework has been a driving force for the huge investments in education in developing countries in the past 40 years. In addition to education's social benefits, the recognition of its long-term economic benefits has spurred finance and budget ministries to action. In global terms, education spending has mushroomed from 3.7 percent in 1970 to 4.5 percent of GDP in 2002 (see Figure 4.1). This has led, by some accounts, to profound increases in the number of young people going to school, particularly at primary levels. There were more than 688 million children enrolled in primary schools globally in 2005, up 6 percent from 1999 alone. Worldwide average schooling level for the population was 5.0 years of schooling in 1970 attained across 103 countries (based on calculations from Barro and Lee's (2000) database). There was a 31 percent increase by 1999, when average schooling went up 1.5 years of schooling to above 6.5 years.

Because the framework is one of an economic investment, cost–benefit analysis (CBA) should be an important tool in making key decisions about the amount and types of investments. As reviewed in the next section, the methods to apply this tool are well-established. And, as described in Section 3, the applications of these methods have played a strong role in advocating for greater overall spending on education as a national priority.

But CBA has been less successful as a guide to set priorities for public policy. Section 4 shows that using such analysis, and specifically quantified

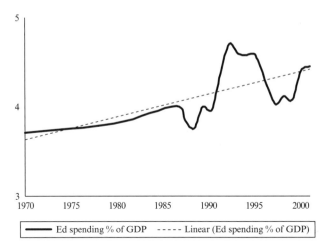

Figure 4.1 Worldwide education spending as % of GDP

analysis of rate of return (ROR), net present value (NPV) or even cost-effectiveness (CE), to guide aggregate government spending has not been widespread. And at the micro level, CBA has also not been used extensively in justifying specific education projects. Why not? We argue that some key methodological shortcomings have been responsible: specifically, the difficulty of estimating social, as opposed to private, benefits; the complexity of measuring the costs and benefits of other dimensions of education other than access to a year of attending an educational institution; and attribution of outcomes to actual interventions. Addressing these issues are the key research challenges for the future.

While research on the computation of more robust quantifications of costs and benefits continues, CBA should still be used to guide public investment. We argue in Section 5 that the discipline of describing the costs and benefits of a project does help decision making – far more than the practice of simply saying that such investments are 'socially' justified. Combined with sound overall sectoral analysis, CBA is crucial to providing the rigorous framework that allows public authorities to make tough choices among competing investment projects. Section 6 concludes.

2 Applying cost–benefit analysis to education: principles
The application of CBA to education is straightforward and is well treated in some of the most recent textbooks in development economics (see Perkins et al. 2006). A schematic of the benefits and costs of investing in an additional year of education beyond the primary level is shown in Figure 4.2. The private benefit (B) of investing in another year of

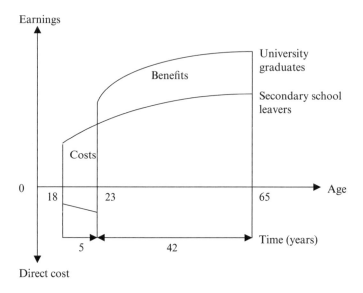

Figure 4.2   Stylized age–earnings profile

education is the gain in earnings for the rest of a person's working life. The private cost (C) will include any fees or direct cost that the individual pays plus the opportunity cost in terms of forgone income. Because these values occur over time, they must be discounted to the present to be comparable. The NPV is the difference between the discounted values of the net present streams of benefits and costs.

A rational investor – in this case a student or his/her family – will undertake the investment (such as an additional level of schooling) if the NPV is positive. Another criterion would be to calculate the internal ROR and compare it with the returns from alternative investments. From this schematic, if t represents a unit of time, the private ROR to education (r) is computed straightforwardly from the following formula:

$$\Sigma B_t/(1 + r)^t = \Sigma C_t/(1 + r)^t$$

The social benefit (SB) is the monetized value of the gains to others in society, such as the positive effects of having educated people interact with each other, greater social cohesion, and so on. The social cost (SC) is the monetized value of the cost to others in society, such as the fiscal cost if the education is subsidized, including the deadweight cost of mobilizing public resources. The social return is computed by replacing B and C by SB and SC in the equation above.

Estimating these returns has led to a mini-cottage industry of scholarship (for a review, see Psacharopoulos and Patrinos 2004). One method is to compare earnings profiles for people with different educational levels. In the case of university education, for example, the formula to compute the private ROR is:

$$\sum_{t=1}^{42} \frac{(W_u - W_s)_t}{(1 + r)^t} = \sum_{t=1}^{5} (W_s + C_u)(1 + r)^t,$$

where $(W_u - W_s)$ is the earnings differential between a university graduate (subscript u) and a secondary school graduate (subscript s, the control group). C_u represents the direct costs of university education (tuition and fees, books), and W_s denotes the student's forgone earnings or indirect costs. A similar calculation can be made for the other levels of education. However, there is an important asymmetry between computing the returns to primary education and those to the other levels. Primary school children, mostly aged 6 to 12 years, do not forgo earnings during the entire length of their studies. On the assumption that children aged 11 and 12 help in agricultural labor, two or three years of forgone earnings while in primary schooling have been used in the empirical literature (Psacharopoulos 1995).

To compute the social RORs to education, which are the appropriate guide for public investment, one must make adjustments. On the cost side, the costs would need to include society's spending on education. Hence, in the above example, C_u would include the rental of buildings and professorial salaries. Gross earnings (that is, before taxes and other deductions) should be used in a social ROR calculation, and such earnings should also include income in-kind where this information is available. A key assumption in a social ROR calculation is that observed wages are a good proxy for the marginal product of labor, especially in a competitive economy using data from the private sector of the economy. Civil service pay scales are irrelevant for a social ROR calculation, although they may be used in a private one. The *social* attribute of the estimated ROR refers to the inclusion of the full resource cost of the investment (direct cost and forgone earnings).

Ideally, the social benefits should include non-monetary or external effects of education (for example, lower fertility or lives saved because of improved sanitation conditions followed by a more-educated woman who never participates in the formal labor market). Given the scant empirical evidence on the external effects of education, social ROR estimates are usually based on directly observable monetary costs and benefits of education. Since the costs are higher in a social ROR calculation relative to the one from the private point of view, estimated social returns are typically lower than a private ROR. The difference between the private and the social ROR reflects the degree of public subsidization of education.

The discounting of actual net age–earnings profiles is the most appropriate method of estimating the returns to education because it takes into account the most important part of the early earning history of the individual. However, this method requires comprehensive data – one must have a sufficient number of observations in a given age–educational level cell for constructing 'well-behaved' age–earnings profiles (that is, not intersecting with each other).

The earnings function method, also known as the Mincerian method (see Mincer 1974), involves the fitting of a function of log-wages ($\ln W$) – usually hourly or weekly, using years of schooling (S), years of labor market experience (X) and its square (X^2) as independent variables. Thus, the basic earnings function is:

$$\ln W_i = \alpha + \beta S_i + \gamma_1 X_i + \gamma_2 X_i^2 + \varepsilon_i.$$

In this semi-log specification, the coefficient on years of schooling (β) can be interpreted as the average private ROR to one additional year of schooling, regardless of the educational level this year of schooling refers to. Also, the earnings function method can be used to estimate returns to education at different levels by converting the continuous years of schooling variable (S) into a series of dummy variables, say D_p, D_s and D_u, to denote the fact that a person has completed the corresponding level of education (primary, secondary, university), and that, of course, there are also people in the sample with no education in order to avoid matrix singularity. Then, after fitting an extended earnings function using the above dummies instead of years of schooling in the earnings function, the private ROR to different levels of education can be derived. Again, care has to be taken regarding the forgone earnings of primary school-aged children. Although convenient because it requires less data, this method is slightly inferior to the previous one as it assumes flat age–earnings profiles for different levels of education (see Psacharopoulos and Layard 1979).

3   Applying cost–benefit analysis to education: practice

The analysis described in the preceding section to estimate the rate of return to education has been applied often to argue why nations ought to invest more national resources to education. The latest results indicate that the average private ROR to another year of schooling averaged over 100 countries is 10 percent (Psacharopoulos and Patrinos 2004). The returns are higher in lower-income areas. The same diminishing returns

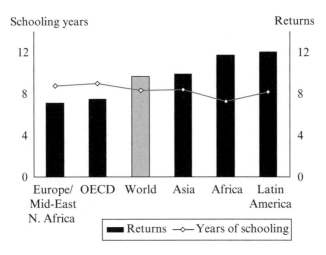

Schooling years

Returns

Source: Psacharopoulos and Patrinos (2004, p. 114).

Figure 4.3 Returns to schooling by region (%)

apply across countries: the more developed the country, the lower the returns to education at all levels. The high returns to education in low-income countries must be attributed to the relative scarcity of human capital. The average private returns to another year of schooling by region are presented in Figure 4.3. The highest overall returns are found in Latin America, followed by sub-Saharan Africa. The lowest returns are in the educationally advanced Organisation for Economic Co-operation and Development (OECD) and non-OECD Europe/Middle East/North Africa. Overall, women receive higher returns on their schooling investments; but for other reasons, in most countries, women receive less pay, regardless of occupation.

For a long time the returns on educational investment were higher at lower levels of schooling. The scarcity of human capital in low-income countries provided a significant premium to investing in education. The high returns on primary education provide an added justification for making education a priority in developing countries. Over time, on average, the ROR to education has fallen. This decline coincides with a significant increase in average years of schooling for the population as a whole. During the last 12 years, average returns on schooling have declined by 0.6 percentage points (Psacharopoulos and Patrinos 2004). At the same time, average schooling levels have increased. Therefore, and according to theory, everything else being the same, an increase in the supply of education has led to a slight decrease in the returns on schooling. That is, if there are no 'shocks' – such as changes in technology – that increase the demand for schooling, then an increase in overall schooling levels should lead to a decrease in the returns to schooling.

Over recent decades, we have seen the returns to schooling decline in many low-income countries, while the technological revolution has increased demand for skilled labor in some developed countries and the returns to schooling have increased. Amidst the fluctuations, there has been a downward trend in the returns to schooling since the 1980s. The proportion of the population with secondary schooling and above has risen markedly over the decades while the proportion of the population with only primary education has declined. This means that primary education has become almost universal; subsequently the returns to primary schooling have declined the most over time. For secondary education, both RORs and the proportion of population have risen together until the 1980s when the proportion of the secondary education population appears to be inversely related to the private ROR to secondary education.

Estimates such as these have been used extensively in policy fora to argue that more needed to be invested in education, especially basic education. For example, in the campaigns for 'Education for All', analysts have used these RORs as a call to action. While education is seen by many as a basic human right, these economic arguments are seen as essential to releasing the national resources to invest in schools and universities. In the *Education for All Global Monitoring Report 2002* it is stated that 'available estimates of rates of return for developing countries consistently show that both private and social returns to primary schooling are higher than at secondary and tertiary levels. Their magnitudes are generally greater than typical returns to capital in other economic sectors' (UNESCO 2002: 34). The Global Campaign for Education (2005: 3) argues:

> [E]ducation, especially for girls, empowers families to break the cycle of poverty for good. Young women with a primary education are twice as likely to stay safe from AIDS, and their earnings will be 10–20 per cent higher for every year of schooling completed. Evidence gathered over 30 years shows that educating women is the single most powerful weapon against malnutrition – more effective even than improving food supply. Without universal primary education, the other Millennium Development Goals – stopping AIDS, halving the number of people living in poverty, ending unnecessary hunger and child death, amongst others – are not going to be achieved.

4   Limits to applying cost–benefit analysis to guide public investments
While compelling for advocacy nationally and even globally, the ROR estimates have proven to be less useful as a guide for setting government spending priorities at the aggregate level. For example, the World Bank's Public Expenditure Reviews (PERs) are undertaken:

to assist the borrowers in understanding their development problems and potential solutions as well as help illuminate the World Bank's own country assistance strategy. One of the major factors contributing to the success of the ensuing country lending program is therefore the quality of analysis undertaken in the PER. In an effort to improve the treatment in PERs of human development issues in general, and education sector issues in particular, the Human Development Network of the World Bank has formulated guidance notes for analyzing public expenditure in the human development sectors. (http://go.worldbank.org/6837YTCIR0)

When one looks at these guidance notes for education, including the section helpfully labeled 'Bottom line: How much is enough? Is public spending adequate and sustainable?', there is no mention of CBA.

At the micro level, the record is also, at best, mixed. CBA was originally developed to guide public investments, especially in infrastructure, that are packaged as individual 'projects' which have well-defined time-bound objectives. While a great deal of education recurrent spending goes towards salaries, much public investment for capital, including that funded by international donors, is 'projectized'.

Has CBA been used to justify these projects? The short answer is 'not really'. The World Bank, as the world's premier investor in such projects, shows that while most have some sort of economic justification, only 39 percent were judged 'good', and a further 35 percent were judged acceptable; the remaining 26 percent were judged marginal. Only 39 percent had a good CBA.

So, why has CBA, despite being so 'naturally' suited to guide educational investments, not been used to inform choices? The main reason is that, while it has been relatively straightforward to obtain estimates of the private returns to education, credible estimates of the social returns, which are necessary for public investment analysis, remain elusive. Indeed, until recently, education projects in developing countries were 'exempt' from CBA because the benefits of such projects were 'social' and were considered inherently unmeasurable. The World Bank's Operational Policy – part of the procedures and policies defining lending and supervision activities of the World Bank for World Bank credits – 10.04, Economic Evaluation of Investment Operations (April 1994), states:

> [I]f the project is expected to generate benefits that cannot be measured in monetary terms, the analysis (a) clearly defines and justifies the project objectives, reviewing broader sectoral or economywide programs to ensure that the objectives have been appropriately chosen, and (b) shows that the project represents the least-cost way of attaining the stated objectives.

Besides a lack of formal CBA in education projects, this exemption also meant that education projects did not specify outcomes; it was also extremely rare to find any unit costs or quantitative analysis of alternatives. It also led some economists to consider the sector as 'soft' and to reluctance among some finance ministers to borrow for education. While we would agree that the true benefits are difficult to measure, it is nevertheless possible to measure them.

Aside from the inability to obtain credible and robust estimates of social returns, two other critical constraints have prevented CBA from being a truly practical tool in public decision making. One is the CBA's shortcomings in accounting for the diverse nature of the outcomes of educational investments – beyond a year spent in school. And the other is the lack of evidence in attributing outcomes to investments. We discuss the need for more progress to be made in research in these areas.

Estimating social returns

Getting the counterfactual right   Traditional CBA assumes that the public sector is the sole financier and provider of education. The alternative to public investment is often assumed to be no education at all. Therefore, the cost of the project is simply the cost of alternative investments to education (and the cost of mobilizing public funds, although that is often overlooked as well – see Devarajan et al. 1997).

This simplistic assumption leads to problems in the analysis and could lead to an overestimate of the returns to the investment. In many countries, especially beyond basic education, the public sector is no longer a monopolist. What does this imply for CBA? At the very least, the counterfactual needs to take into account the effect on the private sector. When there is an active private sector, the expansion of public schools could simply draw students away from private schools. For example, in the Philippines, the share of the public sector has shifted from one-third of all secondary school students to two-thirds. A study estimates that a project to expand public secondary schools would lead to an increase in enrollment that was 40 to 50 percent less than might be expected because of the substitution effect away from private schools (Jimenez and Sawada 2001). This phenomenon has spread to primary schools (see Table 4.1). In Pakistan, private schools at the primary level now account for 30 percent of total enrollment (Andrabi et al. 2007). In India, almost 20 percent of rural students are enrolled in private schools, and almost 30 percent are in private schools in urban areas (Kingdon 2007).

CBA also needs to estimate the 'social' benefits and costs of the intervention by accounting for externalities, redistribution and correcting for other market failures.

Table 4.1   Private enrollment share, selected countries (%)

Country	Primary			Secondary		
	1990	2005	Δ	1990	2005	Δ
Benin	3	12	300	8	25	213
Bolivia	10	9	−14	26	16	−39
Brazil	14	10	−28	35	12	−65
Burkina Faso	9	14	56	41	39	−5
Chile	39	51	31	49	52	6
Colombia	15	19	27	39	24	−38
Eritrea	31	8	−74	11	6	−45
Indonesia	18	17	−6	49	44	−10
Jordan	23	30	30	6	16	167
Netherlands	69	69	0	83	83	0
Peru	13	16	23	15	22	47
Senegal	9	12	33	24	23	−3
South Africa	1	2	100	2	3	50
Thailand	10	16	60	16	13	−19
Togo	25	42	68	17	28	65
Tunisia	1	1	0	12	5	−58
United States	10	10	0	10	9	−10
Venezuela	14	14	0	26	25	−4

Sources: UNESCO, OECD, EDSTATS.

Accounting for externalities   The benefits of education may extend to others beyond the individual student. So, the true benefit from a year of education cannot be captured by the difference in earnings as a result of that year. According to Lucas (1988), for example, a worker's schooling enhances his or her own productivity as well as those of co-workers, thereby giving rise to classic *externalities* or spillover effects. The general level of education in the workforce also expands production possibilities, by facilitating the discovery, adaptation and use of more economically rewarding, albeit technologically more demanding and knowledge-intensive, production processes.

Besides its direct impact on economic production, education can yield other, community-level benefits. These non-market effects include the possible contribution of education to improving social equity, strengthening national cohesiveness, reducing environmental stress through its effect on fertility and population growth, reducing crime rates, and so on (see Table 4.2 for a partial list).

Some studies have succeeded in identifying positive externalities, and have quantified them (see Weisbrod 1964; Haveman and Wolfe 1984; Wolfe and

Table 4.2   Non-market and external benefits of education

Benefit type	Findings
Child education	Parental education affects child's educational level & achievement
Child health	Child's health positively related to parental education
Fertility	Mother's education lowers daughter's births
Own health	More education increases life expectancy
Spouse's health	More schooling improves spouse's health & lowers mortality
Job search efficiency	More schooling reduces cost of search, increases mobility
Desired family size	More schooling improves contraceptive efficiency
Technological change	Schooling helps R&D, diffusion
Social cohesion	Schooling increases voting & reduces alienation
Crime	Education reduces criminal activity

Source: Based on and adapted from Wolfe and Zuvekas (1997).

Zuvekas 1997). If one could include externalities to typical estimates, then social RORs might well be higher than private RORs on education, perhaps more than double (Haveman and Wolfe 1984; Wolfe and Zuvekas 1997). Rauch (1993) finds higher social returns (at 8.1 percent), compared to private returns (4.8 percent), by comparing workers' educational level and increases in wages with average educational level attained in US metropolitan statistical areas. Acemoglu and Angrist (2000) also find higher social returns (9.1 percent versus 7.4 percent) by instrumenting a quarter of birth dummies for individual education, and compulsory school attendance laws and child labor laws in states of birth for average education (see also Moretti 2002).

Externalities may be generated at all levels of education, but their magnitude may differ, implying different levels of subsidies. Many analysts would agree that lower levels of education produce more externalities than higher levels. Literacy and other knowledge imparted at the lower levels of education are generally seen as an effective means for achieving national identity and cohesiveness. Unfortunately, there is very little empirical evidence on the magnitude of externalities across education levels, though there are some intriguing new results. A one-year rise in the average primary schooling of neighboring farmers is associated with a 4.3 percent rise in output, compared to a 2.8 percent effect of one's own primary education in Uganda (Appleton 2000). Another study found that neighboring farmers' education raises productivity by 56 percent, while one's own education raises productivity by only 2 percent in Ethiopia (Appleton 2000); however, the 56 percent figure seems rather high. Overall, the results are inconclusive. In India, researchers have argued that, because other members of a household benefit from having even just one literate member who can read and write for them, the 'true' literacy rate is underestimated (Basu and Foster 1998).

Not having information about the magnitude of externalities can lead to inconclusive policy analysis. For example, for purely measurement reasons, most ROR computations obtain estimates of social RORs that are lower than those for private returns: social and private benefits are assumed to be the same because the former are almost impossible to estimate; and while the private costs include only the opportunity costs of children, the social costs are assumed to include the costs to the government as well. Taken at face value, this would imply that education should be privately provided and, in fact, need not be subsidized at all. The fact that the projects went ahead anyway with public funding may have been the right policy conclusion. Nevertheless, clearly the decision did not arise from the quantitative analysis.

Estimating distributional objectives   Income redistribution and poverty reduction are by now well-accepted social benefits (see World Bank 2006). Because it is so difficult in developing countries to use taxes and other revenues to redistribute income, societies must use spending to do so. Investment in education can be an important tool because it not only redistributes present income, but also redistributes the opportunity to earn over the long term.

It is difficult to capture the redistribution objective in standard CBA, as shown elsewhere in this volume. The theory of how to do so has been well established for many years. Squire and van der Tak's (1975) pioneering work showed how the standard ROR formula could be adjusted with the proper distribution weights to come up with the right magnitude. In practice, however, it has been difficult to define such weights.

Recent analyses of the incidence of public spending indicate that the extent to which the social deviates from private benefits will vary by level of education. In fact, when one takes redistribution into account, the social benefit to primary education would be boosted relative to that of other levels of education. This point is illustrated in Table 4.3, which shows that the poorest quintile in several countries do not benefit from public subsidies to tertiary education.

Correcting for market failures   Another reason why wage differentials fail to capture the true returns to education is because of imperfect labor

Table 4.3   Proportion of public subsidy received by the poorest quintile by education level

Country	Primary	Secondary	Tertiary
Colombia, 1992	39	21	5
Kenya, 1992/93	22	7	2
Ghana, 1991/92	22	15	6
Mexico, 1996	30	19[a]	1
Morocco, 1998/99	17	4	2

Note: [a] For junior secondary education; for senior secondary education, the proportion is 5%.

Source: Filmer (2003).

markets. The screening literature, for example, argues that the estimated earnings gains may overestimate the value of education because these gains are not necessarily due to the added productivity of the young student but because the labor market values the sorting that schooling does between the highly and lowly skilled. If so, then, correcting for such information failures may be a better investment than the large capital and recurrent costs needed to expand a school system. This would argue for a social benefit curve that is lower than the private one depicted in Figure 4.2. However, we know of no studies in developing countries that can provide evidence of this.

Accounting for diverse educational outcomes
Most education projects no longer just aim to expand the number of years of education, which has been the only outcome used in most CBA. As stated earlier, many countries have made exceptional progress in their goal of access to primary education. As projects expand their objectives to include quality improvements and more efficient management, CBA that measures only the returns to staying another year in school is no longer adequate.

Present techniques are ill-equipped to contend with a more diverse set of project outcomes. In the World Bank's assessment, only 64 percent of all project appraisal documents included provision for testing for learning performance which was judged good. Two others (9 percent) were judged acceptable. Six projects (27 percent) were judged to be only marginal in their arrangements for testing for learning performance. (One project financed only technical assistance and so testing was not applicable.)

One issue is how to estimate the ROR, not to inducing another child to stay in school one more year, but to having that child learn more than he or she would have otherwise. The literature on what affects learning outcomes has been fraught with many pitfalls. The role of improved schooling, a central part of most development strategies, has become controversial because expansion of school attainment has not guaranteed improved economic conditions. The evidence is just beginning to be gathered. Hanushek and Woessmann (2007) review the role of education in promoting economic well-being, focusing on the role of educational quality. They conclude that there is strong evidence that the cognitive skills of the population – rather than mere school attainment – are powerfully related to individual earnings, to the distribution of income, and to economic growth. New empirical results show the importance of both minimal and high-level skills, the complementarity of skills and the quality of economic institutions, and the robustness of the relationship between skills and growth. International comparisons incorporating expanded data on cognitive skills reveal much larger skill deficits in developing countries than generally derived from just school enrollment and attainment. The magnitude of change needed makes it clear that closing the economic gap with industrial countries will require major structural changes in schooling institutions.

Glewwe and Kremer (2006) argue that schools in developing countries face significant challenges. These include distortions in educational budgets often leading to inefficient allocation and spending of funds; weak teacher incentives leading to problems such as high rates of teacher absenteeism; and curricula often focused excessively on the strongest students and not well-matched with the typical student, especially considering the high rates of teacher and student absenteeism. Numerous school reform initiatives have been proposed, ranging from programs designed to strengthen links between teacher pay and performance, to reforms to decentralize budget authority, to voucher and school choice programs. Although the evidence is scarce on teacher incentive programs in developing countries, results from Israel suggest that teacher incentives positively and significantly affected student education outcomes (and mainly for weaker students). Results from Kenya suggest that teacher incentives increased teachers' efforts on short-run outcomes (test scores) but not on stimulating long-run learning (through changes in teacher attendance, student dropout rates, or pedagogy) (Glewwe et al. 2003). Decentralization programs appear promising, but the results of decentralization policies appear to be very heavily dependent on the details of implementation. Finally, a school choice program in Colombia yielded dramatic benefits for participants (Angrist et al. 2002, 2006), but evidence from voucher programs in Chile (Hsieh and Urquiola 2006) and developed countries suggests that more research is needed to gauge the generalizability of such program impacts.

In short, more research is needed on the effects of such initiatives, which are often the components of education projects, on what students learn.

Attribution
Many projects seek to expand the educational system of a country. One problem is attributing any change in outcomes to the project, as opposed to the myriad of other factors which could lead to an expansion of enrollment. This could in principle be corrected for by comparing expected educational outcomes in a project site with those places not included in the project. However, it could be that the population in a project site is not strictly comparable with those outside the project. Educational authorities, for example, could target disadvantaged areas and this could lead to an underestimate of project benefits because the expected gain in the project areas would be less due to the characteristics of people there.

The attribution problem can be addressed when proper impact evaluations of earlier projects are used for prospective evaluations. This is still a work in progress. At the World Bank, for example, only 26 percent of all education projects approved in the 2006 fiscal year contained evidence from, or a plan for, an impact evaluation.

Impact evaluations of projects and programs provide important information for decision makers in determining how to prioritize and fund interventions (Cook 2003; Barrow and Rouse 2005). Sometimes the additional cost of doing a thorough impact evaluation is actually quite small. When projects are results oriented and require baseline data, an intelligently designed initial collection of data can determine whether an impact evaluation will be feasible – sometimes without any additional data collection. The main cost of a random assignment study is the cost of collecting data, and the cost of collecting data for a bad study is just as high as collecting data for a good one (Angrist 2004).

Critics sometimes claim that impact evaluations only tell us whether something has an impact without telling us why and how. But a good impact evaluation can provide reliable evidence about how the outcome is achieved when it simultaneously collects information on processes and intermediate outcomes. Impact evaluations are not a replacement for theories, models, needs assessments, and monitoring, all of which are needed to complement the analysis of impact. However, it is equally true that the knowledge gained from impact evaluations is a necessary complement to these other kinds of analyses (Savedoff et al. 2005).

While policy makers are keen to know the likely impacts on student academic achievement of various policy interventions, retrospective studies offer only limited guidance. Even the best retrospective studies suffer from serious estimation problems, the most serious being omitted variable bias with respect to school and teacher characteristics, unobserved child and household characteristics that are correlated with observed school and teacher variables, and measurement error in school and teacher data.

This has turned attention in recent years to many studies based on natural experiments and randomized trials.

Evidence from recent natural experiments in middle-income countries suggests that increases in school resources (as measured by the student–teacher ratio) raise academic achievement on reading tests (but not math tests) among black students in South Africa (Case and Deaton 1999). Case and Deaton examined education outcomes in South Africa using data collected in 1993, when government funding for schools was highly centralized and blacks had virtually no political representation of any kind. The authors argue that blacks did not control the funds provided to their children's schools and that tight migration controls limited their ability to migrate to areas with better schools. Studies using Israeli data indicate that reducing class size raises reading scores and (less often) math scores (Angrist and Lavy 1999) and that providing computers has no effect on academic performance (Angrist and Lavy 2002).

Randomized trials offer evidence from some relatively poorer developing countries as well. In Nicaragua, workbooks and radio instruction had significant impacts on pupils' math scores, and the impact of radio education was particularly high (Jamison et al. 1981). Provision of textbooks raised performance on academic tests in the Philippines (Tan et al. 1997), but in Kenya the only effect of textbooks was among the better students (most likely because the textbooks were too difficult for many students) (Glewwe et al. 2006). Evidence from Kenya also suggests little impact on test scores of reductions in class size (ibid.), flip charts (Glewwe et al. 2004) and deworming medicine (Miguel and Kremer 2004), although school meals were found to have positive impacts on test scores as long as teachers were well trained (Vermeersch and Kremer 2004). A remedial education program in urban India, focused on improving the learning environment in public schools, appears to have increased test scores at a low cost (Banerjee et al. 2000).

While these natural experiments and randomized trials are beginning to build a database of results that are less likely to suffer from the estimation problems that plague retrospective studies, a much larger set of results is needed before they can be used in CBA and general conclusions can be drawn for policy makers. But even so, some results are evident. One interpretation of these results is that in many developing countries, the most effective means of improving school quality may be through addressing the problem of weak teaching. The remedial education program in urban India, the radio mathematics program in Nicaragua, and the computer instruction program in India all provided inputs which addressed the problem of weak teaching, whereas programs which provided inputs that were dependent on use by the teachers themselves (such as the flipcharts and, to some extent, the textbook program in Kenya) were less effective.

5   Can cost–benefit analysis still be a useful guide for education policy?

Given the difficulties of calculating social RORs in education, one might be tempted to eschew CBA all together. In fact, as noted earlier, some agencies have done exactly that, by exempting education projects, say, from undergoing CBA, which infrastructure projects go through. The argument simply is that education investments are worthwhile to do for non-economic reasons and in that case, policy analysts need only ensure that it is provided at least cost.

If CBA is narrowly construed to be ROR or NPV calculation, then, we believe that, for the reasons outlined earlier, it will continue to have limited applicability in real-world policy settings for education. The empirical literature to date is simply too limited for analysts to obtain robust estimates of social benefits. However, if CBA is defined less as an exercise to calculate one figure, such as an internal rate of return (IRR) or NPV that is the go or no-go decision criterion, and more as a rigorous argumentation that the benefits of an investment outweigh the costs, even if not all of them are quantified, then they can greatly improve policy making.

Such an analysis will be necessary to convince policy makers, especially core economic ministries such as finance, budget or planning, to allocate the appropriate budget for education, especially as developing countries make crucial decisions that go well beyond expanding primary education, where the social benefits are uncontroversial. Almost all countries recognize the need to provide basic education for all as a *sine qua non* of nationhood. But the trade-offs become more obvious as countries decide how much to invest in improving what goes on in schools, in expanding access to secondary- and even tertiary-level institutions, and in rationalizing the technical and vocational education curriculum with an academic one. In these decisions, CBA, even if it does not produce the 'classic' IRR, is crucial in informing the tough choices that policy makers need to make.

Research shows that good project economic analysis, including CBA, is strongly associated with better project outcomes. In fact the quality of the CBA is associated with higher quality of project outcomes. The probability of less than satisfactory project outcomes given a poor economic analysis rating at the design stage is four times higher than that for a project with good quality economic analysis (Vawda et al. 2003). Moreover, from a political economy point of view, simply arguing that it is worthwhile to invest in education because it is a social responsibility may not carry much weight in hard-nosed discussions with finance and budget ministries that must make hard choices across all sectors.

Such results have prompted large institutions that finance much of education spending in developing countries, such as the World Bank, to re-evaluate the earlier exemptions against CBA and to begin go re-emphasize

CBA as part of its economic analysis of projects. The economic analysis of a project is supposed to help select and design projects that contribute to the welfare of a country. Various tools of economic analysis help determine the economic and fiscal impact of the project, including the impact on society and the major stakeholders involved, as well as the project's risks and sustainability (see Box 4.1).

Even if one cannot do a CBA that produces an IRR for an entire project, it is often very useful to do such calculations on a subset of project components where quantification is more feasible. This type of CBA, limited though it may be, can still produce very useful practical guidance, as shown in the Ethiopian example below. In other cases, it may be better to simply limit oneself to cost-effective analysis, as shown in the example from the Philippines which follows the discussion on Ethiopia.

BOX 4.1   A GOOD ECONOMIC ANALYSIS ANSWERS THE QUESTIONS

1. What is the objective of the project? This helps identify tools for the analysis. A clearly defined objective also helps in identifying the possible alternatives to the project.
2. What will be the impact of the project? This question concerns a counterfactual as the difference between the situation with or without the project is crucial for assessing the incremental costs and benefits of the project.
3. Are there any alternatives to the project? If so, how would costs and benefits of the alternatives to achieve the same goal compare to the project in question?
4. Is there economic justification of each separable component of the project?
5. Who gains and who loses if the project is implemented? The analysis has to make sure that the most benefit accrues to the poor.
6. What is the fiscal impact of the project?
7. Is the project financially sustainable and what are the risks involved?
8. Are there any other externalities? What is the environmental impact of the project?

Source: Belli (1998, p. xx).

CBA on a project component: Ethiopia
The World Bank's Ethiopia Education Sector Development Program (ESDP) is noteworthy for its complexity. The ESDP, an expenditure program to restructure and expand Ethiopia's educational system, aims to improve overall educational attainment while achieving greater social equity. Its longer-term objective is to achieve universal basic education by 2015. The project to support it has many components, including the building, upgrading and renovation of primary schools, curricular reform, teacher upgrading, and book provision at the basic education level. At the secondary level, the program contributes to the expansion of secondary school facilities, curriculum revision, teacher upgrading, and instructional materials and equipment. For technical and vocational education and training, the program supports employer and market surveys and the encouragement of private participation. For teacher training the program contributes to upgrading and expansion of teacher training facilities, curriculum revision, distance education, head teacher training, and establishment of national standards. The fifth component assists in the expansion of the tertiary sector. Finally, an institutional development component supports planning, financial management, implementation, and monitoring and evaluation capacities of the Ministry of Education. A comprehensive CBA of such a program would not be feasible given issues pointed out in the earlier sections of estimating social returns, the distributive effects and attribution. Moreover, the data in Ethiopia are sparse and of low quality.

The economic analysis of this project was guided by the questions listed in Box 4.1. The work included fiscal impact analysis, institutional risk analysis, analysis of alternatives, and poverty analysis, all supported by broader country and economic work. A crucial part of the work also includes CBA of one part of the project – which could have led to different design alternatives had it not been undertaken.

One of the main activities is the building, upgrading and renovation of primary schools. In fact, there will be 2,423 new first-cycle primary schools built within walking distance of communities. The massive civil works campaign requires the coordinated effort of planners, educators, communities and contractors. New primary school construction alone is a costly exercise (912 million Ethiopian birrs or US$325 million), representing 25 percent of the capital expenditure of ESDP. These schools will need to accommodate the students required to enroll in order for the project to attain the enrollment targets set in the ESDP.

To make it a good investment, the schools will have to last beyond the period of the ESDP, so that Ethiopia can attain the goal of universal primary education by the year 2015, as set in the government plan. In order for schools to last, maintenance becomes an issue. Historically, schools in

Ethiopia have been built with a variety of materials, depending on local conditions, donor involvement and community participation. During the previous regime, enrollment drives necessitated the construction of *chika* – mud and thatch – schools, which are quick and cheap to construct, but require heavy maintenance and in any case do not last many years. In more recent years a variety of cheap techniques have been used in order to increase enrollments, including open-air schools. Parents and communities do not value the *chika* schools, which do not resist termites and which wash away in the rain. The building of *chika* schools also contributes to the depletion of forests. Routine maintenance of school buildings is not a tradition in Ethiopia. Very little maintenance and repair activities have been performed over the years. However, it is demonstrated that communities are more interested in maintaining the 'element' (constructed of hollow concrete block, stone or concrete element) schools because they value them more than the *chika* schools. Nevertheless, school committees are not interested in maintaining schools, regardless of government proclamation. It is necessary, therefore, that the government makes routine maintenance a priority and takes appropriate policy decisions. Any kind of *chika* structure requires more maintenance than element schools.

Under ESDP, schools will be built using something other than *chika*, unless there are no local alternatives. *Chika* schools are considered uneconomical and should be abandoned. But does this make economic sense? CBA was employed to answer this question.

Household survey data were used to estimate the returns to schooling. In 1996, in Ethiopia the returns to schooling were high. Overall, another year of schooling is associated with a 23 percent gain in earnings. Returns are high for both males and females, at 23 and 22 percent; in rural and urban areas, at 21 and 15 percent; and by level, that is, primary, secondary and university, at 25, 24 and 27 percent, respectively. So while these estimates might tell us that education overall is a good investment, they offer no guidance on what level is more appropriate, nor do they give any guidance about the main investment objective, getting more children into school, or more specifically what sort of buildings should be constructed.

Chika schools certainly are a cheap initial investment (Table 4.4). However, the maintenance requirements are heavy and even a fully maintained *chika* school will not last much longer than ten years.

The question of which technology to adopt for school buildings depends on crossover discount rates (Hirshleifer 1958). The lower the discount rate the more attractive are materials other than *chika*. Using information on construction, transportation and maintenance costs, a CBA was carried out to determine which building material would be the best choice for ESDP, assuming a 30-year time profile, so that concrete and stone were

Table 4.4   Cost comparison of school buildings, 1992 birr*

Material	Capital (investment)	Recurrent (maintenance)	Lifetime (years)	Cost/year lifetime
Concrete element	213,000	2,130	40	7,455
Stone	189,284	1,893	40	6,625
Brick	170,400	5,000	30	10,680
Hollow concrete block	127,800	1,278	30	5,538
Chika	85,200	6,000	10	14,520
Corrugated iron sheet	31,950	5,000	10	8,195

Note: * Ethiopian currency; 1 birr = $0.10.

used in one project, brick and hollow concrete block in 1.33 projects, and *chika* and corrugated iron sheet in four projects. The results of the analysis are summarized in Table 4.5. Fully maintained, hollow concrete block is a much better alternative. Assuming a discount rate of 12 percent, then the preferred investment option is hollow concrete block.

However, maintenance is an issue in Ethiopia. Experience shows that school buildings are not well maintained. *Chika* requires heavy maintenance; there is no indication that this will take place and so the assumption of full maintenance is not realistic. For this reason, a sensitivity analysis considers the more realistic case that maintenance will be less than adequate. For simplicity's sake, half of the required maintenance is assumed to take place. Effectively, this makes all alternative technologies preferable to *chika* construction. Given the fact that parents and communities are more likely to get involved in the maintenance of element schools, then the returns to switching to an alternative technology are likely underestimated here. With the more realistic assumption of half maintenance, brick and stone, and possibly concrete element, are good investments.

The choice of technology of course also depends on the availability of local materials. It may simply not be possible to transport certain materials to remote areas. For many rural areas there will be impossible transportation problems. In such cases there is no alternative other than building with *chika*. In less extreme cases there may be roads, but the cost of transporting materials may be prohibitive. To examine this problem, sensitivity analysis was carried out assuming scenarios of cost escalation due to transportation difficulties using orders of magnitude of 10 to 30 percent. The results show that even in the case of hollow concrete block there are instances when it is not a good investment. All of the alternatives to *chika* have a lower present value. However, the total undiscounted cost of using the different alternatives is different and they have differing

Table 4.5 Summary cost–benefit analysis of school buildings (IRR*)

Material	Full maintenance (%)	Half maintenance (%)	Transportation difficulties: cost escalation (%)		
			10	20	30
Concrete element	6	9	7	5	2
Stone	8	11	10	8	6
Brick	5	12	10	6	3
Hollow concrete block	17	23	19	14	8
Chika	(base case)	(base case)	(base)	(base)	(base)

Note: Since the estimates of the life span of school buildings is arbitrary, then it is assumed that concrete, stone, brick and concrete block buildings last for 40 years. Since stone is not transported, but only the concrete necessary, the transportation cost increases are reduced to 5, 10 and 15 percent.
* Internal rate of return calculations based on savings due to selection of material versus *chika*.

time profiles. Therefore, the alternative one chooses may depend on the opportunity cost of capital. In the cases examined here, the higher the opportunity cost of capital assumed, the greater the likelihood of choosing *chika* over the alternative. This is because with the *chika* model one is postponing investment. In other words, there is a discount rate at which *chika* becomes the preferred option, despite higher undiscounted total cost or lower present value of the alternatives. To illustrate this example, the case of *chika* versus hollow concrete block (HCB) is used. The present value of the two methods, assuming half maintenance costs, is plotted along with the associated discount rate (Figure 4.4). As is shown in the graph, there is a discount rate at which building *chika* schools is preferred to HCB. This is known as the crossover discount rate (Gittinger 1995), which is 23 percent in the case highlighted. This is the same as the IRR calculated for the benefits (cost-savings) stream presented above for the case of half maintenance, which is (hopefully) the realistic scenario.

Lose the social benefits: cost-effectiveness analysis in the Philippines
Another practical method that can be used when social benefits are not estimable is to use cost-effective analysis. Cost-effectiveness is appropriate whenever the project has a single goal that is not measurable in monetary terms: for example, to provide education to as many children as possible but through several interventions that simultaneously increase reading speed, comprehension, and vocabulary, but that are not equally effective in achieving each of the goals. Comparing among methods to achieve

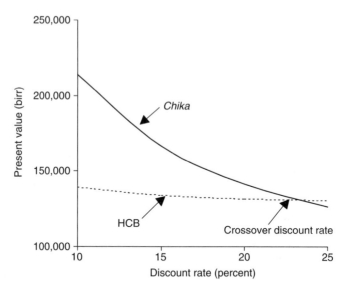

Figure 4.4   Graphic derivation of crossover discount rate, choice between chika *and hollow concrete block alternatives in Ethiopia*

these aims requires that we reduce the three goals to a single measure, for which we need some weighting scheme.

An example of how to apply this technique is a project in the Philippines. Concern about high dropout rates and poor student performance in elementary schools led the Philippine government to embark on a long-term plan for improvement. Under the 10-year Program for Comprehensive Elementary Education Development launched in 1982, the government invested an estimated $800 million (in 1981 prices), with support from the World Bank, in such inputs as textbooks, equipment, resource materials, staff training and classroom facilities. In 1990, a follow-up World Bank-financed project continued support for investments totaling $410 million (1990 prices) over a four-year period. To inform the design of the future investments, Tan et al. (1995) used data generated under the previous two World Bank operations to assess the cost-effectiveness of alternative inputs to improve student learning. The authors first estimated the relation between selected school inputs and student learning using regression analysis, and then estimated the costs of the relevant input. The available data permitted an evaluation of the individual effects on student learning of workbooks, classroom furniture, class size, teacher qualifications, and preschool education, controlling for variations in students' initial levels of learning and their family background, as well as for differences in classroom and school management practices. Simple division of the costs by the corresponding regression coefficients gave the desired cost-effectiveness ratios.

The results showed that in this particular case smaller classes and higher teacher qualifications had no effect on student performance, and therefore could be ruled out as priorities for policy intervention. Three school inputs – workbooks, classroom furniture, and preschool education – had unambiguously positive effects on learning. Because in this case preschool education was costly, it was less cost-effective than the other two inputs.

6   Conclusions

We have argued that CBA is still a potentially important tool in the economists' arsenal. But it is essential that research, especially on the social benefits of education, makes further progress if it is to be used on a day-to-day basis to calculate credible ROR quantitatively. To make CBA a more useful tool, we have also called for more research on the effects of policy interventions on outcomes beyond access to a year in school and what children earn as a result, such as on what children actually learn. Such research should focus on ensuring that the interventions can actually be attributed to observed outcomes. This is now being done with the push for more impact evaluation (Duflo 2004; Duflo and Kremer 2004).

In the meantime, we think that it is still worthwhile to go through the discipline of noting the benefits and costs even if social IRR or NPVs of comprehensive education projects cannot be calculated robustly. Research shows that projects that have some form of competently done CBA have better outcomes than those which do not. We have given examples where CBA on individual project components, where it is feasible to estimate benefits and costs or cost-effective analysis, has made significant contributions to project design.

References

Acemoglu, D. and J. Angrist (2000), 'How large are human capital externalities? Evidence from compulsory schooling laws', *NBER Macroannual, 2000*, Cambridge, MA, pp. 9–59.

Andrabi, T., J. Das and A.I. Khwaja (2007), 'Religious school enrollment in Pakistan: a look at the data', *Comparative Education Review*, **51** (4): 446–77.

Angrist, J.D. (2004), 'American education research changes tack', *Oxford Review of Economic Policy*, **20** (2): 198–212.

Angrist, J. and V. Lavy (1999), 'Using Maimonides' rule to estimate the effect of class size on children's academic achievement', *Quarterly Journal of Economics*, **114** (2): 533–76.

Angrist, J. and V. Lavy (2002), 'New evidence on classroom computers and pupil learning', *Economic Journal*, **112** (482): 735–86.

Angrist, J., E. Bettinger, E. Bloom, E. King and M. Kremer (2002), 'Vouchers for private schooling in Colombia: evidence from a randomized natural experiment', *American Economic Review*, **92** (5): 1535–58.

Angrist, J., E. Bettinger and M. Kremer (2006), 'Long-term educational consequences of secondary school vouchers: evidence from administrative records in Colombia', *American Economic Review*, **96** (3): 847–62.
Appleton, S. (2000), 'Education and health at the household level in Sub-Saharan Africa', Center for International Development Working Paper No. 33, Cambridge, MA: Harvard University.
Banerjee, A., S. Jacob, M. Kremer, J. Lanjouw and P. Lanjouw (2000), 'Promoting school participation in rural Rajasthan: results from some prospective trials', mimeo, MIT, Cambridge, MA.
Barro, R.J. and J.-W. Lee (2000), 'International data on educational attainment: updates and implications', Center for International Development Working Paper No. 42, Harvard University.
Barrow, L. and C. Rouse (2005), 'Causality, causality, causality: the view of education inputs and outputs from economics', Working Paper 2005-15, Federal Reserve Bank of Chicago.
Basu, K. and J.E. Foster (1998), 'On measuring literacy', World Bank Policy Research Working Paper No. 1997, Washington, DC.
Belli, P. (1998), *Handbook on Economic Analysis of Investment Operations*, Washington, DC: World Bank.
Case, A. and A. Deaton (1999), 'School inputs and educational outcomes in South Africa', *Quarterly Journal of Economics*, **114** (3): 1047–85.
Cook, T.D. (2003), 'Why have educational evaluators chosen not to do randomized experiments?', *Annals of American Academy of Political and Social Science*, **589**: 114–49.
Devarajan, S., L. Squire and S. Suthiwart-Narueput (1997), 'Beyond rate of return: reorienting project appraisal', *World Bank Research Observer*, **12** (1): 35–46.
Duflo, E. (2004), 'Scaling Up and Evaluation', in F. Bourguignon and B. Pleskovic (eds), *Accelerating Development*, Washington, DC: World Bank and Oxford: Oxford University Press, pp. 341–69.
Duflo, E. and M. Kremer (2004), 'Use of randomization in the evaluation of development effectiveness', in O. Feinstein, G.K. Ingram and G.K. Pitman (eds), *Evaluating Development Effectiveness* (World Bank Series on Evaluation and Development, Vol. 7), New Brunswick, NJ: Transaction, pp. 205–31.
Filmer, D. (2003), 'The incidence of public expenditures on health and education', Background Note for World Development Report 2004, World Bank, Washington, DC.
Gittinger, J.P. (1995), *Economic Analysis of Agricultural Projects*, 2nd edn, Baltimore, MD: Johns Hopkins University Press.
Glewwe, P. and M. Kremer (2006), 'Schools, teachers, and education outcomes in developing countries', in E.A. Hanushek and F. Welch (eds), *Handbook of the Economics of Education*, Vol. 2, Amsterdam: Elsevier, pp. 946–1017.
Glewwe, P., N. Ilias and M. Kremer (2003), 'Teacher incentives', Poverty Action Lab Paper No. 11, Cambridge, MA.
Glewwe, P., M. Kremer, S. Moulin and E. Zitzewitz (2004), 'Retrospective vs. prospective analyses of school inputs: the case of flip charts in Kenya', *Journal of Development Economics*, **74**: 251–68.
Glewwe, P., M. Kremer and S. Moulin (2006), 'Textbooks and test scores: evidence from a randomized evaluation in Kenya', mimeo, University of Minnesota and Harvard University.
Global Campaign for Education (2005), *Missing the Mark: A School Report on Rich Countries' Contribution to Universal Primary Education by 2015*, Johannesburg.
Hanushek, E. and L. Woessmann (2007), *Education Quality and Economics Growth*, Washington, DC: The World Bank.
Haveman, R.H. and B. Wolfe (1984), 'Schooling and economic well-being: the role of non-market effects', *Journal of Human Resources*, **19** (3): 128–40.
Hirshleifer, J. (1958), 'On the theory of optimal investment decision', *Journal of Political Economy*, **66** (4): 329–52.

Hsieh, C.-T. and M. Urquiola (2006), 'The effects of generalized school choice on achievement and stratification: evidence from Chile's voucher program', *Journal of Public Economics*, **90** (8–9): 1477–503.

Jamison, D., B. Searle, K. Galda and H. Stephen (1981), 'Improving elementary mathematics education in Nicaragua: an experimental study of the impact of textbooks and radio on achievement', *Journal of Educational Psychology*, **73** (4): 556–67.

Jimenez, E. and Y. Sawada (2001), 'Public for private: the relationship between public and private school enrollment in the Philippines', *Economics of Education Review*, **20** (4): 389–99.

Kingdon, G. (2007), 'The progress of school education in India', *Oxford Review of Economic Policy*, **23** (2): 168–95.

Lucas, R. (1988), 'On the mechanics of economic development', *Journal of Monetary Economics*, **22** (1): 3–42.

Miguel, E. and M. Kremer (2004), 'Worms: identifying impacts on education and health in the presence of treatment externalities', *Econometrica*, **72** (1): 159–217.

Mincer, J. (1974), *Schooling, Experience and Earnings*, New York: Columbia University Press.

Moretti, E. (2002), 'Estimating the social return to higher education: evidence from longitudinal and repeated cross-section data', NBER Working Paper 9108, Cambridge, MA.

Perkins, D.R., S. Radelet and D.L. Lindauer (2006), *Economics of Development*, 6th edn, New York: W.W. Norton.

Psacharopoulos, G. (1995), 'The profitability of investment in education: concepts and methods', Human Capital Development and Operations Policy Working Paper 63, World Bank, Washington, DC.

Psacharopoulos, G. and R. Layard (1979), 'Human capital and earnings: British evidence and a critique', *Review of Economic Studies*, **46** (3): 485–503.

Psacharopoulos, G. and H.A. Patrinos (2004), 'Returns to investment in education: a further update', *Education Economics*, **12** (2): 111–34.

Rauch, J. (1993), 'Productivity gains from geographic concentration of human capital: evidence from the cities', *Journal of Urban Economics*, **34**: 384–400.

Savedoff, W.D., R. Levine and N. Birdsall (2005), 'When will we ever learn? Recommendations to improve social development through enhanced impact evaluation', Consultation Draft, Center for Global Development, Washington, DC.

Squire, L. and H.G. van der Tak (1975), *Economic Analysis of Projects*, Washington, DC: World Bank and Johns Hopkins University Press.

Tan, J.-P., J. Lane and P. Coustere (1997), 'Putting inputs to work in elementary schools: what can be done in the Philippines?', *Economic Development and Cultural Change*, **45** (4): 857–79.

UNESCO (2002), *EFA Global Monitoring Report 2002*, Paris: UNESCO.

Vawda, A.Y., P. Moock, J.P. Gittinger and H.A. Patrinos (2003), 'Economic analysis of World Bank education projects and project outcomes', *International Journal of Educational Development*, **23**: 645–60.

Vermeersch, C. and M. Kremer (2004), 'School meals, educational attainment, and school competition: evidence from a randomized evaluation', World Bank Policy Research Working Paper WPS3523, Washington, DC.

Weisbrod, B.A. (1964), *External Benefits of Education*, Princeton, NJ: Princeton University, Industrial Relations Section.

Wolfe, B. and S. Zuvekas (1997), 'Non-market effects of education', *International Journal of Education Research*, **27**(6): 491–502.

World Bank (2006), *World Development Report 2006: Equity and Development*, Washington, DC: World Bank.

5 Cost–benefit analysis in transport: recent developments in rail project appraisal in Britain

Chris Nash and James Laird

1 Introduction

The transport sector was one of the first in which the technique of social cost–benefit analysis became widely applied. In Britain, following the appraisals of the M1 motorway (Coburn et al. 1960) and of the Victoria line underground railway in London (Foster and Beesley, 1963), social cost–benefit analysis rapidly established itself as a routine part of the appraisal of government spending on transport. While one of the first applications of cost–benefit analysis in transport was to an underground railway, its application as a technique to rail investment was slower to develop, because although the rail system in Britain, and indeed in most countries outside North America, was publicly owned, it was run as a separate commercial organisation. Paradoxically it has been with the privatisation of the railway in Britain that cost–benefit analysis has become the norm. The reason is that passenger services in Britain are run under franchises, with service levels specified by government, creating a need to appraise alternative service levels both at the franchise specification stage and in considering alternative bids. Moreover, the government directly or indirectly finances rail infrastructure, creating a need to appraise alternatives in terms of quality, capacity and cost.

There would, however, be no need for cost–benefit analysis (except perhaps to consider the distributive implications of schemes) if all goods in an economy, including transport, were produced under conditions of perfect competition and zero externalities. Economic efficiency would be ensured by simply leaving the private sector to produce what was profitable. That these conditions do not hold good in the transport sector is no doubt a major reason why transport has been an extensive user of the techniques of social cost–benefit analysis. Transport infrastructure and public transport services are produced under conditions of increasing returns to scale and significant environmental and safety externalities. However, it has been shown that, provided we are willing to assume that the rest of the economy is operating under perfect competition and zero externalities (or that all externalities are appropriately charged for) then we may confine our cost–benefit analysis to the transport sector as detailed in equation 5.1 (Dodgson, 1973; Jara-Diaz, 1986):

Economic benefit = Transport users' benefit (consumers' surplus)
+ Change in transport operators' profits (producers' surplus)
+ Changes in government grants and indirect tax revenue
+ Change in external costs (e.g. accidents, pollution, etc.)   (5.1)

All grant and indirect tax transfers between government, the private sector and transport users are included in equation (5.1). This allows the full economic impact on each group of actors to be assessed within the cost–benefit analysis while ensuring that transfers between the actors, with no welfare impact, net out. Government impacts should also be weighted by the marginal cost of public funds (MCPF) due to the fact that transfers between the government and other actors impose a welfare burden on society. In UK transport appraisal practice the MCPF is not considered, although in England the fact that projects are generally only considered good value for money if they have a ratio of net benefit to cost to public funds in excess of 1.5 does indirectly allow for this. Changes in indirect taxation also appear in (5.1) as the presence of indirect taxation distorts the transport market and the wider economy, resulting in a welfare impact when the demand for transport services change. This impact is equivalent to the change in indirect tax revenue.

For a road scheme, the process developed basically as a comparison of the costs of construction and maintenance with the value of the savings in time, accidents and operating costs brought about by the scheme; the computer program used to perform this comparison was called COBA (DoT, 1981). In support of this process an enormous number of studies have been used to examine the willingness to pay of the public to save time (Wardman, 2001) and to reduce risks of death or injury (Blaeij et al., 2003). However, there has been growing debate over many years on the extent to which a simple partial equilibrium approach such as this truly captures all the costs and benefits of a transport project. Moreover, increasing stress has been placed on the environmental implications of road schemes and therefore the environmental benefits of transferring car trips to rail. Initially the reaction to these criticisms was to nest the cost–benefit analysis within a multicriterion framework in which environmental and wider economic effects were assessed on a qualitative, or quantitative but non-monetised basis (DETR, 1998). However, increasingly, research has led to these items being valued in money terms.

If the assumption of perfect competition elsewhere in the economy does not – at least approximately – hold, then this partial equilibrium approach is inadequate. If reductions in transport costs lead to an expansion in the output of particular goods, there will be further benefits to the extent that the price of these goods exceeds the marginal cost of production. If, however, production of these goods entails uncorrected externalities, then there may be disbenefits as well. There may be further benefits in labour markets if reduced transport costs lead to a reduction in involuntary unemployment or increased agglomeration economies. These issues have been long debated in the literature, but in terms of practical introduction into standard cost–benefit analysis have only just come to the fore.

For many decades, a further issue has been the source of controversy regarding public transport appraisal. This is the fact that for public transport users, the introduction or removal of services may lead to changes in the destinations to which they can travel at all unless they can get access to a car or use a taxi. For car users in a Western economy, this tends not to be the case, as the road network allows them to reach anywhere they choose, although big changes in speeds may change the practicality of regularly travelling to another specific location, for instance as a place of work. The issue that has therefore arisen is whether the public is willing to pay something in order to have available public transport services to a wider range of destinations than would otherwise be the case. A possible explanation for this lies in the existence of 'option values' for public transport.

In the next section we introduce the basic approach regarding the application of cost–benefit analysis to rail transport projects, illustrating the approach with an example of the appraisal of high speed rail (HSR) investment. We then consider in turn wider economic effects and option values before reaching our conclusions.

2   Appraisal of rail schemes

Introduction
As stated above, one of the pioneering cost–benefit analyses was a public transport application in which it was found that benefits from reduced congestion both elsewhere on the underground rail system and on the roads would justify subsidising the project. However, already this study has drawn attention to an important component of public transport appraisals – the need to make assumptions about the fares that would be charged on the new line and elsewhere in the network. If the project were to be financed by a general increase in fares, then the disbenefits of this and the resulting transfer of traffic to roads would make the project not worthwhile (Beesley and Foster, 1965). Of course, the growth in toll roads and in other forms of road pricing makes similar assumptions necessary in road investment appraisal.

Experience has suggested that this is not the only reason why public transport appraisal tends to be more complex than that for roads. A further reason is the complication of the measurement of public transport service quality. While for roads, there is evidence that driving conditions may modify the value of time (for instance, driving in heavily congested conditions may lead to a higher value of time) and that reliability is very important, journey time and safety have remained the main quality measures. For public transport, quality embraces such factors as crowding, frequency of service, the need to change vehicles and the quality of the environment in which this takes place, information availability and quality and the comfort and on-board facilities of the vehicle in which the journey takes place. This in turn leads to the need to appraise a wide range of options in terms of all these characteristics; the fact that complementary investments may also be desirable (for instance, new rolling stock may require investment in track and signalling to make the most of its capabilities) also tends to lead to a multiplicity of options. Although there is some evidence on how to value these quality impacts, it is less extensive and less robust than for simple time savings (Wardman, 2001). Moreover, public transport is often (in Britain usually) provided by private companies under some sort of franchise or contract or as a purely commercial venture, so it is necessary to identify the funding gap in socially desirable investments and find ways of making the investment financially attractive to the private sector. Finally, the benefits of public transport often include benefits of diverting traffic from private transport resulting from distortions in charging for the use of roads, so a multimodal appraisal is necessary.

Options to consider

Appraisal requires comparison of a base case with a series of 'do-something' alternatives. It is necessary to be clear what the base case is and to ensure that a realistic range of options is examined. A base case that literally assumes a 'do-nothing' situation may be very unfavourable, particularly in the face of growing traffic; on the other hand, the base case should not be padded out with unnecessary investments. In general, the base case should be a 'do minimum', and other likely investments should be examined as alternative 'do-something' options. These alternatives should be compared on an incremental basis to see whether the additional cost of moving to a more expensive option is justified.

In the case of rail schemes, the base case should therefore include such investment as is necessary to keep the existing service running, and consideration should be given to how to deal with any exogenous growth in traffic. This might mean investing in additional rolling stock or revising fare structures and levels. More major changes should be considered as 'do-something' alternatives. These might include upgrading existing infrastructure, or indeed construction of additional road or airport capacity. There will also be options regarding the investment option – how far to extend a new line; to which alternative points to run new trains; and what service frequency and pricing policy to adopt. It is essential to examine sufficient alternatives to be confident that the best alternative has been identified.

It is also necessary to consider the timing of investment. The new proposal might turn out to have the highest net present value (NPV), but if the demand and the other benefits from it are forecast to grow over time then it might still be better to postpone the investment.

Costs

Rail projects typically involve construction of new lines, stations and so on and purchase of new rolling stock, and additional train operating costs and externalities. Both construction of rail infrastructure and the operation of trains lead to environmental costs in terms of land take, visual intrusion, noise, air pollution and contribution to global warming. The first three of these impacts are likely to be much stronger where trains go through heavily populated areas. Considerable progress has been made in valuations of such environmental impacts in recent years. For local and regional air pollution, the impact pathway method (Friedrich and Bickel, 2001) has been developed, which traces through the emission, transformation and deposition of these pollutants, and their impact of the receptor in terms of people's health and damage to buildings or crops. The latter is generally valued at cost in market prices, while the former requires values of a statistical life or of life years lost. In the case of noise nuisance, it is necessary to examine the population affected and the level of the increase of noise nuisance; valuation typically makes use of house price studies as a basis for estimating willingness to pay to avoid noise nuisance (Soguel, 1994). Global warming is the most difficult environmental externality to value, but many studies have been undertaken – for a review and the basis of current British valuations, see Stern (2006). Environmental externalities also depend on whether trains are electrically powered, and air pollution and global warming impacts depend on the primary fuel used to generate the electricity; in countries with extensive hydro or nuclear electricity these will be negligible, whereas where coal, oil and gas are used they will be more significant, as will other forms of air pollution.

Benefits

The principal benefits from rail schemes are:

- time savings;
- additional capacity;

Table 5.1   Value of time savings for rail passengers in the UK

Standard valuations	(£ per hour, 2002 market prices)
Leisure	4.46
Commuting	5.04
Business	36.96

Source: DfT (2007a, p.4), www.webtag.org.uk.

- reduced externalities from other modes;
- generated traffic; and
- wider economic benefits.

Each of these elements will be discussed in turn.

When it comes to valuation, time savings are generally split into business, commuter and leisure. There is extensive research on the valuation of time savings; the current valuations used in rail schemes in Britain are as shown in Table 5.1. The high value for business time is based on the fact that much business travel takes place during working hours and directly reduces labour productivity, although questions have been raised on whether the full business value of time should be applied in this case on two grounds (Hensher, 1977):

- many long-distance business trips start and end outside normal working hours; and
- when travelling by train it is possible to work on the way.

However, research has shown that firms are willing to pay the sort of rate implied by current valuations even in these circumstances, presumably because of the benefits they perceive in shortening long working days and having staff less tired (Marks et al., 1986).

The most recent review of evidence on values of time undertaken for the British government (ITS, 2003) and which led to the adoption of the values shown in Table 5.1, gave careful consideration to what was likely to happen to the value of time over time. The advice given by the British Department for Transport is that working-time values, which are based on the wage rate, should rise in proportion to GDP, while non-working-time values have an elasticity of 0.8 to GDP. Thus long-term growth of values of time is assumed to be in the range of 1.5–2 per cent per annum.

Additional capacity is obviously only of value if demand is exceeding the capacity of the existing route. But in those circumstances additional capacity may be of value not just in allowing for growth between the cities served by the new line, but also, by relieving existing lines of traffic, for other types of service such as suburban passenger or freight. Where the effect is to allow rail to carry traffic which would otherwise use other modes, the benefits may be quantified as the net user benefits plus net reduction in externalities minus the net cost of the change of mode. There is also clear evidence (Gibson et al., 2002) that running rail infrastructure less close to capacity benefits reliability; it may also lead to less overcrowding on trains. Both of these features are highly valued by rail travellers and especially business travellers (Wardman, 2001). It should be noted that capacity constraints also make the alternative of upgrading existing infrastructure more problematic; for instance, running higher-speed tilting trains on infrastructure shared with slower traffic may not be feasible.

Typically a substantial proportion, but not all, of the new traffic attracted to rail will be diverted from other modes – mainly car and, in the context of long-distance trips, air (British studies such as Atkins, 2003, suggest that this may be of the order of 50 percent, with the remainder being totally new travel). To the extent that infrastructure charging on these modes does not cover the marginal social cost of the traffic concerned, there will be benefits from such diversion. Estimation of these benefits requires valuation of marginal costs of congestion, noise, air pollution, global warming and external costs of accidents and their comparison with taxes and charges on the other modes.

For road transport, there may be a benefit or a cost from diverting traffic to rail depending on whether marginal external cost is greater or less than taxes and other charges on road transport (see Table 5.2).

In the case of air, the absence of fuel tax means that there is normally no charge for environmental externalities, although this is crudely allowed for in some countries (including Britain) by a departure tax. (Value-added tax (VAT) at the standard rate should not be seen as an externality charge since it does not influence relative prices except when charged on some modes and not others; in some cases in Europe VAT is charged on domestic rail and air fares, in some on rail but not air and in some on neither.) The other key issue for air is charging for slots at congested airports. The allocation of slots by grandfather rights, and charging structures based on average costs of running the airport (or less where there are subsidies) means that charges may not reflect congestion costs imposed on other planes, the opportunity cost of slots or the costs of expanding capacity. A further benefit of rail projects may therefore be the release of capacity at airports for use by other, typically longer-distance flights. Regarding accidents, there has never yet been a fatality on a purpose-built high-speed conventional rail system (there has on a maglev track), and the record of

Table 5.2 Marginal external costs of car (p/km 2002 prices and values)

Cost type	Congestion band	Conurbations			Other urban			Rural			Weighted average
		Motor-ways	A roads	Other roads	Motor-ways	A roads	Other roads	Motor-ways	A roads	Other roads	
Congestion	Average	3.8	40.4	20.1	n/a	16.2	4.2	2.5	1.6	4.0	9.9
Infrastructure	All	0.0	0.1	0.1	n/a	0.1	0.1	0.0	0.1	0.1	0.1
Accidents	All	0.0	2.4	2.4	n/a	2.4	2.4	0.0	0.5	0.5	1.3
Local air quality	All	0.7	1.0	1.1	n/a	0.5	0.5	0.3	0.3	0.2	0.5
Noise	All	0.2	0.2	0.2	n/a	0.2	0.2	0.0	0.0	0.0	0.1
Greenhouse gases	All	0.3	0.4	0.4	n/a	0.3	0.3	0.4	0.3	0.3	0.3
Indirect taxation	All	-4.2	-4.4	-5.2	n/a	-3.6	-4.7	-4.5	-3.5	-3.4	-4.1
Total	All	0.7	40.0	19.0	n/a	16.1	3.1	-1.3	-0.7	1.8	8.0

Note: Indirect taxation calculation is based on fuel duty at 47p in 2003 (2003 prices) staying constant in real terms thereafter. The indirect taxation figures are not likely to be correct before 2003.

Source: DfT (2007b, p.5), www.webtag.org.uk.

conventional rail is much better than car, though not bus or particularly air (Evans, 2003).

Generated traffic leads directly to benefits to users, which are generally valued at half the benefit to existing users, on the basis of a linear approximation to the demand curve. But as commented above there has been much debate as to whether these generated trips reflect wider economic benefits that are not captured in a traditional cost–benefit analysis. This issue is considered further in the next section.

Another key factor influencing the outcome of an appraisal is the choice of discount rate. Low discount rates favour capital-intensive investments such as rail projects. Practice varies substantially within the European Union. In Britain the current practice is to discount at a pure time preference rate of discount of 3.5 per cent, reducing to 3 per cent after 30 years, but to allow for capital shortages by requiring a benefit/cost ratio of at least 1.5 and preferring projects where it is at least 2.

British HSR proposals
In 2003, the consultants Atkins completed a study for the Strategic Rail Authority of the potential for the introduction of high speed rail in Britain between London and the north (Atkins, 2003). This study took place in a context of rapid growth in rail passenger and freight traffic in recent years, leading to severe overcrowding on both long-distance passenger services and London commuter services, and a lack of capacity for further growth in freight. Thus a major objective of the scheme was to relieve existing routes, as well as providing faster more competitive services between the major cities. This rather general remit led to the need to generate and study a wide range of options. Altogether, some 14 options were studied in depth, the main issues being whether to have a single route north from London which might split further north to serve cities up the east and west sides of the country, or to have two separate routes, and how far north to go. The obvious starting-point would be a new route from London to the heavily populated West Midlands. The further north the line was extended, the less heavily used the new sections would be, but this effect might be offset by the fact that these extensions attract additional traffic on to the core part of the network. It is a characteristic of British geography that a single line could serve the major cities of London, Birmingham, Leeds, Newcastle, Edinburgh and Glasgow, while a conventional or high-speed branch could serve Manchester.

It was forecast that the new line if built to its extremities would attract nearly 50 million passenger trips per year in 2015, although most of these would use only part of the route. This high figure reflects the high population density of Britain and the large number of origin–destination pairs

Table 5.3   Appraisal of options 1 and 2 (£bn PV)

	Option 1	Option 2
Net revenue	4.9	20.6
Non-financial benefits	22.7	64.4
Released capacity	2.0	4.8
Total benefits	29.6	89.8
Capital costs	8.6	27.7
Net operating costs	5.7	20.5
Total costs	14.3	48.2
NPV	15.3	41.6
B/C	2.07	1.86

Source: Atkins (2006b, p.61) Appendix B, Table 2.1 with errors in totals corrected.

that the line would serve. Of these, around two-thirds would be diverted from existing rail routes and the remainder split almost equally between diversion from other modes and newly generated trips. Most of the forecast diversion occurred from car – the forecast of diversion from air was surprisingly low given experience of the impact of HSR on air traffic elsewhere. However, this outcome reflects the assumption that typically rail fares would be more expensive than air.

Results of the appraisal of two options are shown in Table 5.3. Option 1 is the line from London to the West Midlands, which is the obvious first phase of any HSR programme in Great Britain, and is seen to be well justified in its own right. But option 2, the extension through to both Manchester on the West Coast route and right through to Scotland via the East Coast, is also shown to be justified, with an incremental benefit–cost ratio representing good value for money. It is obviously important, however, to examine the issue of timing and phasing. The study showed that, if feasible, immediate construction of the whole line was the best option.

Although net revenue more or less covers operating costs for both options, the capital cost can only be justified by non-financial benefits and released capacity. A breakdown of the composition of costs and benefits for option 1 is given in Table 5.4. Some 78 per cent of benefits take the form of time savings and reduced overcrowding, with 19 per cent due to increased net revenue and only 3 per cent taking the form of reduced road congestion and accidents. The value of the released capacity was not included in this analysis, but adds some 7 per cent to the overall benefits.

On balance it was thought that the non-quantified environmental benefits were slight, with the benefits of diverting traffic from more environmentally damaging modes being largely offset by the construction

Table 5.4   Cost–benefit analysis results, option 1

	% of total benefits or costs
Benefits – revenue	
High speed line revenue	64
Classic rail revenue	−45
Net rail revenue	19
Benefits – users	
Journey time/reduced overcrowding	76
Accidents	2
Total user benefits	78
Benefits – non-users	
Journey time/vehicle operating costs	3
Total non-user benefits	3
Present value benefits	100
Costs	
Capital	69
High speed line operating	41
Classic operating	−9
Present value costs	100

Source: Atkins (2006b), unpublished additional information.

and operation of the new line. It is an interesting question whether more of the user benefits could be captured as revenue by more sophisticated yield management techniques than the simple fare structure modelled. Such yield management methods are already in use on other high-speed services, including Eurostar services between London, Paris and Brussels. They might also boost benefits by increasing diversion from air.

In summary, then, this study found a strong case for HSR, based on the high patronage that could be attracted by a single line linking most of the major conurbations of Britain, in the context of growing demand leading to severe overcrowding and shortages of capacity on the existing infra-structure. This case rested solely on conventional benefit measures. In the next section we consider whether such schemes may have wider economic impacts that should be taken into account.

3   Wider economic benefits of transport schemes

Additionality
Invariably transport projects are promoted on the basis that they are expected to deliver, as one of their objectives, regional or national

economic growth, job creation or improvements in living standards. Politically, at least, transport projects are expected therefore to have some effect on the wider economy. The controversy commented on earlier, however, arises as a conventional appraisal does not take such effects into account. This is not because these effects are considered irrelevant, but because they are not considered additional to the benefits already included within a conventional appraisal.

As transport is an intermediate good, the linkages between it and other sectors of the economy are numerous and varied. With perfectly functioning markets, changes in transport cost affect business operating costs, as the cost of transporting factor inputs to the production process, the costs of distributing finished goods and the productivity of employees travelling on company business are altered. Transport cost changes also affect the labour market, as the reservation wage includes a component to compensate for commuting costs incurred. The land market is affected by transport cost changes as well, with rents adjusting to reflect changes in accessibility and associated changes in real income. These price and wage changes affect demand for goods, services and labour – all of which affect welfare. Demand is abstracted from competing goods and further rounds of price and output adjustments occur – all as a consequence of a transport investment. None of this is disputed; the important question from the perspective of a transport cost–benefit analysis is whether these effects have additional welfare impacts to those experienced by users, transport operators and the government (as set out in equation 5.1).

As stated in the introduction, if markets are competitive (that is, price equals marginal social cost), then a transport cost–benefit analysis is sufficient to capture the total economic impact of a transport project. That is, the welfare impacts in the final economic markets – product and services, labour and land – exactly equal the directly measured effects in the transport market. However, key market failures in the product and services market and in the labour market as well as the fact that transport is a network good (Economides, 1996; Shy, 2001) can imply that prices do not equal marginal social cost in all transport-using sectors of the economy, and as such additional welfare impacts can be felt (van Exel et al., 2002; Laird et al., 2005). All network goods exhibit characteristics that can include sunk costs and significant economies of scale, scope or density (that is, subadditivity in production), as well as positive consumption externalities (whereby an individual's valuation of a good is dependent on the number of other users attached to the network) (Economides, 1996; Shy, 2001). At the outset it is important to realise that these additional welfare impacts can be negative as well as positive and therefore may work in the opposite direction to that signalled by the change in transport user benefits.

Market failure in the product, services and labour markets
If imperfect competition in the product and services market exists then a transport induced expansion of output will give rise to an additional welfare impact stemming from this market. This is because in the presence of imperfect competition, output is restricted below its socially optimum level. Imperfect competition may arise through incidence of market power as firms engage in product differentiation[1] or firms become large relative to their market. The latter is particularly true in geographically isolated areas, where, as a consequence of geography, firms can act as local monopolists. Transport improvements by bringing regions closer together can increase the intensity of competition between firms, eroding dominant market positions and reducing price–cost mark-ups. Specifically, if the product and services markets were competitive then a transport-induced price reduction (from P_0 to P_1 in Figure 5.1a below) would result in a welfare gain of Area A plus Area B. This is equivalent to the result that would be obtained by a conventional transport cost–benefit analysis. However, as output is suppressed under imperfect competition and prices are marked up above marginal social cost by $P_0 - MC_0$, an additional welfare gain, from output expanding from X_0 to X_1, will occur under imperfect competition – Figure 5.1b. This is equivalent to Area C. The transport improvement may also erode any geographically induced source of market power (that is, $P_1 - MC_1$ could tend to zero). At the limit, that is when all market power is eliminated, this implies that X_1 is the socially optimum level of output.

Two potential sources of market failure in the labour market can also occur, giving rise to additional welfare impacts to those contained in a transport cost–benefit analysis. The first derives from the presence of a labour tax that distorts the supply of labour from the social optimum and the second can occur in the presence of involuntary unemployment.

As the supply of labour depends on commuting costs, a transport improvement that lowers commuting costs will increase labour supply at the national level. In the presence of a labour tax (for example, income tax) the supply of labour is, however, restricted below its social optimum. Therefore the increase in labour supply gives rise to an additional welfare impact. This is analogous to the situation depicted in Figure 5.1b. In this situation, however, the additional welfare impact, Area C, falls to the government in the form of additional income tax revenue.

Typically, transport projects are not of a sufficient scale to increase labour supply at a national level. In the main, the impacts of the majority of transport projects are redistributive with respect to employment,

(a) Perfect competition

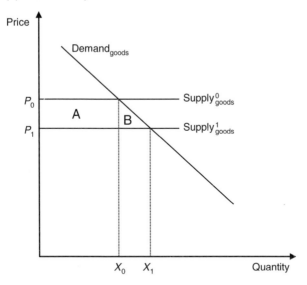

(b) Imperfect competition

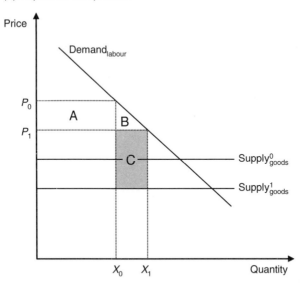

Figure 5.1   Impact of transport improvement in the goods and services market

encouraging employment growth in one region at the expense of reduced growth in another region. If, however, involuntary unemployment exists and a transport project both reduces commuting costs and increases the demand for labour, a calculation of the welfare impact in the transport market (using the rule of a half) will incorrectly estimate the benefit attributed to the generated traffic. This can be illustrated by drawing from an example in which wages in the labour market exceed the market clearing wage – that is wages are sticky in a downwards direction and a labour supply surplus exists. With reference to Figure 5.2 involuntary unemployment exists ($E_0^* - E_0$) as the wage (W_0) is higher than the equilibrium wage (W_0^*). A labour supply surplus therefore exists. A transport project that lowers commuting costs results in a downward shift in the labour supply curve. With sticky wages however employment levels and wages remain unaffected (that is, $E_1 = E_0$ and $W_1 = W_0$). The welfare impact of the transport improvement equals Area A. This is the benefit felt by existing workers travelling to work more easily and can be correctly measured in the transport market. The level of involuntary unemployment ($E_1^* - E_1$) has also increased as a result of the downward shift in the labour supply curve. Now if the general improvement in transport supply redistributes employment to the region, this is akin to a rightward shift in the labour demand curve. The final level of employment becomes E_2 and the level of involuntary unemployment is reduced to ($E_2^* - E_2$). A welfare gain equivalent to Area B is therefore felt by workers, no longer involuntarily

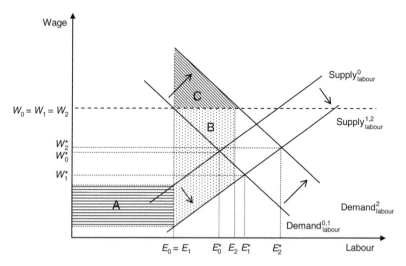

*Figure 5.2   Welfare impact of transport induced shift in labour demand
under labour supply surplus*

unemployed, in the form of wages paid over and above the reservation wage. A welfare gain is also felt by employers, equivalent to Area C, as they enjoy an increase in consumer surplus – their willingness to pay for the additional labour exceeds the wage they pay. A conventional transport user benefit analysis that correctly estimated the increase in commuting trips would, however, using the rule of half, incorrectly assign half the economic benefit of existing trips to these generated trips – when in fact the benefit is given by the sum of areas B and C. The total welfare impact of the transport cost reduction and the associated increase in employment is given by the sum of Areas A, B and C of which only Area A can be measured in the transport market.

Transport/economy network effects
While the characteristics of a network good without government intervention leads to price departing from marginal social cost (that is, a market failure) (Economides, 1996), a well-specified transport cost–benefit analysis, as set out in equation 5.1 and discussed in the previous section, should capture the additional welfare impacts that the first two points give rise to. That is, and returning to the rail theme of the chapter, a well-specified analysis would consider the extent to which train operating costs are subject to economies of density, and that rail network performance varies with the level of demand. Recent research and policy interest has therefore focused on the third bullet point in Section 2 – positive consumption externalities.

Positive consumption externalities arise within transport using sectors of the economy as transport improvements bring economic agents – the consumers, producers and suppliers – closer together and, in doing so, raise labour productivity above and beyond what would be expected from the transport efficiency saving alone. The numerous microeconomic linkages between economic agents, brought closer together by the transport improvement, generate the externalities which, collectively and at a localised level, give rise to aggregate increasing returns or agglomeration economies. While Marshall (1890) is credited with the first description of the sources of agglomeration, the literature describing the exact microeconomic linkages and evidence for them is, almost 120 years on, still fresh – see Duranton and Puga (2004) and Rosenthal and Strange (2004) for reviews.

Three key sources of localised aggregate increasing returns or agglomeration economies were identified by Marshall: input sharing, labour market pooling and knowledge spillovers. Duranton and Puga (2004) categorise the microeconomic mechanisms underpinning these sources as either sharing, matching or learning:

- *Sharing*   When firms are grouped together, increasing external returns can exist as a consequence of both final producers sharing the same supplier of intermediate goods and the productive advantages of sharing a wider variety of differentiated intermediate inputs. Furthermore, in an environment where demand for finished goods and for labour may be subject to, at the firm level, random shocks, expected profits increase with labour market pooling or sharing. This arises as a consequence of the sharing of risk between firms, though it requires no assumption associated with risk aversion.
- *Matching*   Increasing labour market size, for example through labour market pooling, can also improve the quality of each firm–employee match. Quality in this sense relates to the productivity of the workers in their job. That is, an increase in the number of economic agents trying to match improves the expected productivity of each job–employee match. Furthermore, an increase in the number of people and firms trying to match improves the chances of matching, that is, equilibrium levels of frictional unemployment are expected to be lower, the larger the labour market.
- *Learning*   The microeconomic foundations of knowledge generation, diffusion and accumulation, that is learning, have received less attention than those of sharing and matching (ibid.). There is, however, a substantial body of evidence on the advantages of cities for learning (see Rosenthal and Strange, 2004, for a review). As learning involves 'face-to-face' interactions, environments which bring large numbers of people in contact with one another can facilitate knowledge generation, diffusion and accumulation. Furthermore, diversity and cross-fertilisation between industrial sectors, as occurs in large agglomerations, is considered an important mechanism for stimulating innovations (Jacobs, 1969). Industrial diversity is, however, not a necessary condition for innovation as for example the competitive forces in the nineteenth-century Lancashire cotton industry agglomeration ensured new ideas and manufacturing methods were continuously developed (Crafts and Leunig, 2006). More recently, foreign direct investment is viewed as a source of knowledge generation and diffusion within a national or local economy (for example, Eddington, 2006).

While many aspects of agglomeration economies are well described, our understanding of the microeconomic foundations to agglomeration economies is, however, still incomplete. This is particularly true with respect to knowledge spillovers, but even with respect to matching and sharing there exist competing theories. On the positive side, the existence of competing theories underpinning agglomeration economies suggests that the concept of agglomeration economies is robust to various specifications and assumptions. On the negative side, however, it is difficult to make firm policy recommendations regarding economic development policy, and the role of transport policy within that, as the recommendations may well vary with the microeconomic foundations. What, however, is clear is that the nature and scale of the externality will vary by industry type. One would expect significant effects for industries where specialist inputs are required (for example, skilled labour and dedicated intermediate goods). Similarly we would expect significant effects in industrial sectors where research and development is high or face-to-face contact is needed between employees.

Where consumption externalities exist and where as a consequence of a transport intervention employment increases, Venables (2007) shows that two additional measures, to those described earlier, are needed to capture the full welfare impact of the improvement.[2] The first of the two additional measures relates to the manner in which an expansion of city employment raises productivity and therefore output of not just new city workers but also of existing workers via the microeconomic linkages previously described. The second arises as a consequence of the distorting effects of taxation. The transport improvement induces a shift of employment from outside of the city into the city. The decisions of the new city workers are, however, based on the wage increment (between city and out of city wages) net of tax. The value of output to society exceeds this with the difference accruing to government as tax revenues. This is similar to the argument expressed in Figure 5.2, however, it relates specifically to a redistribution of employment from the less productive area outside the city to the more productive city, rather than an increase in employment at the national level.

Measuring wider economic benefits in practice
There are typically two approaches to the inclusion of wider economic benefits in an appraisal, which we have categorised as top down and bottom up. The bottom-up approach uses spatial computable general equilibrium (SCGE) models of the economy to explicitly represent imperfect competition, imperfect labour markets and the microfoundations to agglomeration effects. This approach measures the welfare gain at the level of the household. The top-down approach, on the other hand, takes as its starting-point a transport cost–benefit analysis and adds in additional elements of welfare for each market failure. Such an approach is epitomised by the UK's approach (DfT, 2006a) to measuring wider economic benefits.

The principal advantage of the SCGE bottom-up approach is that it contains an explicit representation of the microfoundations of market imperfections, allowing the model to be sensitive to variations in the underlying economic characteristics of the region. SCGE models are, however, only in the infancy of their development and as such, these models are not widely available, with the few in existence typically having been developed in universities (Gunn, 2004). Furthermore simplifications in the representation of labour markets, labour migration, household behaviour, the product market, the land market and the level of industrial disaggregation have to be made, and to properly model the economic impacts of a transport improvement such models need to be interacted with a transport model to ensure that the feedback linkages between the transport and the economy are captured. The application of an SCGE model to the appraisal of a transport improvement is therefore a far from trivial task (Laird et al., 2005).

While there are a number of theoretical applications of SCGE to transport improvements (for example, Venables and Gasiorek, 1998; Venables, 2007), there are very few examples in the literature of applications of SCGE models to real transport infrastructure. The two principal examples of applications are the RAEM model in the Netherlands, which has been applied to the assessment of a maglev[3] high speed rail project (Oosterhaven and Elhorst, 2003; Elhorst et al., 2004), and the CGEurope model which has been applied in a variety of European Commission (EC) research projects examining the economic impact of the Trans-European Transport Network (TEN-T) most notably in IASON[4] (Bröcker et al., 2004). With respect to the TEN-T network, the IASON research indicated that completion of all of the TEN-T priority infrastructure projects may generate between 20 and 30 per cent more economic benefit than would be measured in a normal transport cost–benefit analysis. Elhorst et al. (2004) show in their appraisal of four variants of a maglev line that inclusion of wider economic benefits may change benefits as measured in a conventional transport cost–benefit analysis by between −1 and +38 per cent.[5] Their results are very interesting in a number of ways. First, they demonstrate that including wider economic effects into an appraisal can lower as well as increase economic welfare, and second they indicate that for what appear to be very similar projects (each project variant is a maglev line), very different levels of additionality can be obtained. The differences between the project variants arise as a result of the different impacts they each have on the labour market. The two variants that provide a high-speed link between the four cities of the Randstad, that is the variants that re-enforce the Randstad agglomeration, have positive impacts for overall productivity of the Randstad region (a welfare gain) but have a negative welfare impact on the regions from which labour is abstracted (which have a labour supply surplus). The opposite is the case for the variants that link the periphery (Groningen) to the core (the Randstad)[6] and, as the welfare gain from improving the efficiency of the labour market exceeds the productivity decrease from shifting employment from the core to the periphery, the core–periphery projects, in this situation, have more net positive additionality than the projects that re-enforce the core. It is important to note that this core–periphery versus core re-enforcement is not a general result and is a consequence of: the characteristics of the regional labour markets; the manner that the project variants redistribute employment between regions; but also, and importantly, the manner that national wages by industry prevail in the Netherlands.

The UK approach to measuring wider economic benefits (DfT, 2006a) is top down, and probably represents the only formalised national appraisal methodology for incorporating such impacts. Typically, three measures are added to a conventional transport cost–benefit analysis. These relate to the welfare gain from increased output in an imperfect product and services market (see Figure 5.1) and the productivity gain from increases in agglomeration size plus the tax windfall to the government from redistribution of employment to more productive jobs as set out in Venables (2007). In terms of the details of the recommended methodology, a further 10 per cent of business time and reliability savings is added to cost–benefit analysis to represent the welfare gain from expanding output in imperfectly competitive product and services markets. This is based on evidence of price–cost margins in UK industries and the theoretical work undertaken by Venables and Gasiorek (1998). The productivity gain from increases in the size of the agglomeration is captured, not through a detailed analysis of the underlying microeconomic linkages, but through an aggregate relationship between agglomeration size and productivity. Rice et al. (2006) and Graham (2007) present recent UK evidence on such relationships[7] and these, particularly Graham's, form the basis of the calculation of the productivity effect in UK scheme appraisal. The evidence that both Rice et al. and Graham have presented is related to urbanisation economies – that is where the agglomeration economies are driven by pure economic mass (for example, city size). Localisation economies occur when agglomeration economies are driven by proximity to firms in the same sector or related sectors. Rice et al. found that moving a mass of population 30 minutes away reduces its impact on productivity by three-quarters. Once the mass of population is 80 minutes away it has a negligible effect on productivity. Overall they find an elasticity of productivity with respect to distance-weighted working-age population of 0.053. Graham derives elasticities of productivity to distance-weighted employment for 28 industry groupings. He finds an average elasticity for the service sector of 0.197, for the manufacturing sector of 0.07 and an

Table 5.5   Wider economic benefits for rail projects in the UK

Scheme	Description	Wider economic benefits as proportion of user benefits
London Crossrail – urban rail	The project links the west of London (Heathrow/Maidenhead) with areas east of London (Essex and Kent). Estimated to provide 40% of the extra rail capacity London needs by 2015	56%
Midland Mainline – inter-city	Journey time improvement between Derby, intermediate stations and London	22%
East Coast Mainline – inter-city	Increased frequency between London and Leeds (from 4 to 5 trains per hour)	10%
East Coast Mainline – commuter	Between 25% and 40% increase in capacity (service dependent) for commuter services between East Anglia and London	32%

Sources: Atkins (2006); DfT (2006a).

elasticity that is not statistically significant for the primary sector. These average elasticities, however, disguise considerable variation, with specific industry values ranging from zero to 0.33 for the service sector, and from −0.19 to 0.38 for the manufacturing sector.

While the UK wider economic benefit calculation guidance has been applied to many projects since it was first published in 2005, not least by the Eddington study team (Eddington, 2006), few of the results are in the public domain. Four of the projects that are, are summarised in Table 5.5. As can be seen from this table, a wide variation in the relationship between wider economic benefits and user benefits is found. Wider economic benefits form a substantial 56 per cent of user benefits for the London Crossrail project. There are two main drivers to this: First, improved accessibility to Central London increases its economic mass and raises average productivity of all workers in Central London, and second, 33,000 jobs are expected to be redistributed to Central London – the most highly productive part of the UK – by 2027 (DfT, 2006a). The redistribution of jobs occurs as Central London becomes a more attractive place for workers to commute to (lower commuting costs), but also a more attractive place for businesses to locate to. In contrast, the improved inter-city train frequencies on the East Coast Mainline (ECML) are expected to generate wider economic benefits that form only 10 per cent of user benefits. The difference between the Crossrail and the ECML inter-city projects arises as the inter-city services do not have a strong impact on the labour market, whereas Crossrail does. The inter-city Midland Mainline (MML) journey time improvement has, given the strategic function of the service, a similar minimal impact on the labour market as the inter-city ECML project. However, it differs from the ECML inter-city project in that the MML route links together a series of large urban areas, and by reducing journey times between these areas it delivers significant agglomeration benefits. The final project, improving capacity on commuter routes between East Anglia and London, is similar to Crossrail in that it increases the size of the London labour market and therefore has both agglomeration and labour market impacts – though not of Crossrail's size. For this project we therefore find that wider economic benefits form 32 per cent of user benefits – somewhere between the inter-city projects and Crossrail's.

The Department for Transport's approach to the inclusion of the wider economic benefits of transport projects represents an important step forward in appraisal methodology. While it is quite mechanistic compared to the bottom-up SCGE modelling approach, it does represent a pragmatic methodology that can be readily applied – notwithstanding that it is important to be aware of its limitations. First, the approach hinges on the robustness of the elasticities of productivity to agglomeration. However, the current evidence base is restricted to elasticities of productivity to urbanisation, and therefore is incomplete with respect to all productivity gains from transport improvements, as we would also expect that localisation economies would be elastic to transport improvements. To an extent this limitation can be seen in that Graham found two industries with negative urbanisation elasticities – the manufacture of rubber and rubber products, and the manufacture of medical and precision equipment. Second, the approach assumes that the labour market operates efficiently (aside from the market failures that generate the urbanisation economies), thus there are no regions with a surplus supply of labour and no regions with a labour shortage. As the Netherlands example shows, redistributing employment between regions with a surplus supply of labour and those with a shortage of labour can dominate the welfare gains from a change in productivity – albeit this result may well depend on the particular legislative framework in the Netherlands, where national industry wages are fixed by statute.

A final, but important comment, on both the top-down and the bottom-up approaches is that they both assume that the transport efficiency savings can be frictionlessly translated into the wider economy. There is, however, a large body of evidence to suggest that while transport is a necessary condition for economic growth, it is not the only condition (SACTRA, 1999;

McQuaid et al., 2001). Unless the other conditions to economic growth are satisfied, we would expect some dampening of the wider economic effect of a transport improvement. Specifically, given that the microeconomic foundations to agglomeration economies emphasise the role of labour matching, knowledge generation and knowledge diffusion, we would expect that for the agglomeration gains from a transport improvement to be realised, transport policy must form only one element of a complete cross-sectoral policy package. Frictions in any element of the microeconomic linkages underlying agglomeration economies, including in land-use policy, will ultimately dampen the scale of the wider economic benefits – see Laird (2007) for an example of labour market frictions dampening the impact of transport policy on wages. This combined with limitations to both the top-down and bottom-up approaches and the fact that we would expect wider economic effects to lag (in time) behind the opening of new infrastructure would suggest that estimates of the welfare impacts of wider economic effects should be treated, for the moment at least, as an upper bound to a conventional transport cost–benefit analysis appraisal.

4 Option values and non-use values

While the issue of wider economic benefits is raised most often in the context of major new urban or inter-urban rail projects, that of option and non-use values is more often raised when considering whether unprofitable lines should be closed. In this section, we consider in turn the principles of option and non-use values, and evidence on their magnitude and on their possible impact on appraisals.

Principles
That there might be an option value for the availability of transport services was suggested in the paper which first put forward the idea of option values (Weisbrod, 1964), but most of the subsequent literature on option values has concentrated on environmental goods (for example, Carson et al. (1995) noted some 2,000 papers or studies where empirical estimates of option and non-use values for environmental goods have been made). Whether option values exist over and above expected use values and whether other non-use values might also exist has continued to be a source of controversy.

The idea underlying option values can be explained using the following example. Consider a strategy or plan which includes the reopening of a closed railway line linking a series of rural towns and villages to a major town or city that already has a railway service. Even if particular individuals living in one of the villages along the route do not intend to use the rail service, they may still value having the option to use the service if they need it. For example, car-owners may value the ability to use the service when for whatever reason they cannot drive or their car is unavailable. Non-car-owning residents who generally do not travel beyond the village may value the knowledge that, should they need to reach the town or city, the facilities exist for them to do so, at reasonable cost and with a reasonable level of convenience. In addition, those who do intend to use the service on a regular basis may also have an option value, over and above the value of their intended use of the service, since they too may value the options offered for rail travel other than those already taken account of in their individual plans and expectations. While a full analysis of user benefits will include the expected value of any such occasional use, theory suggests that in circumstances where the lack of the transport facility would cause inconvenience, people may be willing to pay a premium over and above their expected use value to ensure that the service exists.

From this example, it can be seen that:

- option values are associated with uncertainty about use of the transport facility;
- option values may exist even if the option of using the transport service is never taken up;
- option values are related to the individual's attitude to uncertainty – in practice, a range of option values is likely to be found within the population; and
- when surveying option values there is a real risk of double counting, particularly when trying to separate individuals' willingness to pay to have the option of using the service (the option value) from their willingness to pay for their expected actual use of the service (the use value).

If we further ask when option values might be significant, we need to consider how serious the absence of the service would be. For very occasional short journeys, including short journeys to a railhead to continue a longer journey, some sort of upper limit might be imposed by the possibility of using taxi. Where there is a possibility of becoming dependent on the service for more frequent or longer journeys for which taxis would be prohibitively expensive, then the possibility of a significant option value becomes more real. For instance, someone who might become dependent on rail for commuting to a major town or city for which congestion and parking problems make a car unattractive, or who is unable to drive, might be expected to particularly value the availability of a public transport service. Similarly, for an elderly person the possibility of needing to regularly visit hospital as an outpatient or visitor might lead to a significant willingness to pay.

Non-use values on the other hand differ from use values and option values in that a value may be placed on the continued existence of a good regardless of any possibility of future use by the individual in question. The motivation for the desire for the good to continue to exist may, however, vary from one circumstance to another. For example, individuals may value a good for altruistic reasons, reasons of indirect use or because the good has some existence, bequest or intrinsic value. Examples of situations where non-use values may exist in a transport environment include:

- a resident knowing that neighbouring pensioners are able to make essential journeys (this may be because of genuine altruism or because it means they will not be called upon to act as chauffeur!);
- a householder living on a busy road experiencing less noise, and a car commuter experiencing less congestion as a consequence of other commuters using a rail service; and
- where the vitality of a community may depend on the transport link – for example, where a substantial proportion of the economic activity in the community stems from either passing trade or from business associated with the provision of transport services.

In the context of a scheme appraisal, the option value is always additional to user benefits and environmental and safety externalities. Non-use values on the other hand may double count some elements of benefit already included in an appraisal. For example, non-use values of a new rail line stemming from road noise reduction are already included in the appraisal as a noise benefit. In contrast, a non-use value that a resident may hold because pensioners are able to use the service is additional.

It is important to note that two possibly substantial contributors to non-use values represent a double counting of benefits. The first is that associated with land values and the second is that associated with the profitability of businesses. Changes in land values generally represent a capitalisation of the user benefits already in the appraisal, so their inclusion would be double counting. Under the partial equilibrium assumption, a change in business profitability is expected to cancel out with changes elsewhere in the economy giving a net welfare effect of zero.

Empirical evidence
The field of measuring transport option values and non-use values is far from developed. To date we are aware of only six exploratory studies that have attempted this measurement, with the results from five of them publicly available. Additionally only two of the empirical studies have attempted to separate option values from consumer surplus and non-use

benefit categories. All applications of the option value and non-use value concepts in the transport field are related only to bus or rail services. Also, existing studies have not included potential users from other parts of the country. Although residents in outlying areas outside the service area of the rail links are generally unlikely to use the train under any circumstances, a small proportion (possibly with an option value) may be possible future visitors to the case study areas or have other non-use values.

The approach taken to valuation has been based on survey methods and used a combination of contingent valuation and stated preference methods. There are a number of particular difficulties in such surveys. The first is the obvious one of strategic bias, that respondents who stand to gain from the preservation of a public transport service but do not think that they will bear the costs will have an incentive to bias their answers upwards, and vice versa. Studies have tried to guard against this by setting the questions in the context of a realistic trade-off between public transport spending and taxes. The second problem is that of double counting, as referred to above. The approach to this problem has generally been to seek to derive an aggregate value of willingness to pay for the service and then to deduct separate estimates of the benefits other than option or non-use values.

The best evidence at present for Britain comprises Humphreys and Fowkes's (2006) research for train services, which found a value of £190 per household (2002 prices and values) and Bristow et al.'s (1991) research for bus services (£104 per household at 2002 prices and values) (see Laird et al., 2007 for a review). These figures represent an aggregation of both option and non-use values and are an average of users' and non-users' values. It should be noted that these values relate to small communities and local rail stations. They do not relate to communities adjacent to mainline stations or stations that serve a predominantly long-distance market. Additionally, these values represent household values for personal travel only and do not reflect the values that businesses may hold.

As mentioned earlier, the non-use value may double count benefits already included in a transport cost–benefit analysis. To avoid double counting, one ideally just excludes the element of the non-use value that is not altruistic. Drawing from Humphreys and Fowkes, this would appear to be approximately 14 per cent of the sum of the option and non-use value. A much more conservative approach to avoid double counting would be to exclude all of the non-use value from the appraisal. However, there is uncertainty regarding the split between option and non-use value with Humphreys and Fowkes (2006) suggesting a low non-use proportion, and Geurs et al. (2006) suggesting a much higher value, making this a more uncertain proposition than may have first been thought.

The values set out above reflect the absolute level of option and non-use values for a particular mode and level of service. Transport appraisal on the other hand is concerned with incremental changes in service provision. Therefore it is the difference between the option and non-use values before and after the transport policy has been implemented that is important to an appraisal.

Possible implications of option values – a worked example
The importance of option and non-use values in rail appraisal varies with the characteristics of the rail service and the type of proposal. This can be seen in Table 5.6, where summary indicators for four rural rail schemes are presented (Highland Rail Developments, 2000; Highland Rail Partnership, 2003; Halcrow, 2006; DfT, 2006b). Three of the rail schemes are in lightly trafficked areas of the rail network in the north of Scotland, while the fourth scheme is situated near reasonably large conurbations, and importantly has a reasonably frequent rail service (at least hourly over a 16-hour day). Consequently, this line is much more heavily trafficked than the north of Scotland lines. Option and non-use values are attributed to each household within the catchment area of the station from which the project makes it possible to commute to a reasonably large conurbation. From the perspective of the cost–benefit analysis, it is the change in option and non-use value that is important. Therefore for the projects where commuting opportunities are created it is the difference between the option and non-use value of bus (£90) and rail (£170)[8] that drives the benefits. The user benefits and present value of benefits (PVB) have been calculated in accordance with standard UK practice.

There exists a large variation in the relationship between user benefits and option and non-use value benefits. This reflects the different characteristics of the schemes. Where user benefits are high, as in the rail closure example, option and non-use values form a low proportion of the PVB. This is typified by the line closure appraisal. Here we can see that while several communities lose their rail service, the strength of the user benefits (from those services) dominates the option and non-use values. Where user benefits are low, option and non-use values can form a substantial element of the welfare impact of the scheme. An extreme example is the Cononbridge station reopening, where option and non-use values are almost six times the level of user benefits. Primarily this occurs because user benefits are low due to the disbenefits to existing users (caused by the extra stop) almost cancelling out benefits to new users. Table 5.7 shows that option and non-use values can contribute anything between 9 and 117 per cent of the PVB.

Table 5.6 Size of option and non-use values relative to user benefits and the present value of benefits

Scheme	Area type	No. of households affected	Annual patronage on line (single trips in opening year)		Option and non-use values as percentage of:	
			Do minimum	Do something	Transport user benefits	PVB
Beauly station reopening (opened 2002)	Remote community in North Scotland	550	125,000	148,000	87	84
Cononbridge station reopening (proposal)	Remote community in North Scotland	1,000	250,000	270,000	561	117
Invernet – provision of services within the Inverness travel to work area. Increase in frequency of approximately 50% north of Inverness and provision of commuting opportunities to 6 communities (opened 2005)	Remote communities in North Scotland	2,600	485,000	557,000	64	57
Anonymised example (rail closure) (hypothetical proposal)	Rural communities in a part of southern England near to some moderately sized conurbations	3,700	3,798,000	0	9	9

Note: Transport appraisals have been undertaken in accordance with UK standard practice (www.webtag.org.uk). The option and non-use values used are £170 for rail and £90 for bus (2002 prices and values).

Source: Laird et al. (2007, p.16), Table 6.

Table 5.7   Sensitivity of option and non-use values

Scenario	60-year present value of option and non-use value (£)	Percentage difference (from central estimate)
Central estimate for anonymised rail closure example	18.1	–
Sensitivity tests (All sensitivity tests based on the central estimate with the following differences)		
Only households within 1km of a station attributed an OV and NUV	9.4	−48
All households within 5km hold an OV and NUV	45.2	+150
The OV and NUV of rail is additional to that of bus	26.2	+44
All of the NUV double counts user benefits	10.9	−40
No change in unit values over time	11.5	−37

Note: Central estimate is based on households within 2km of station holding an option and non-use value; the option and non-use value of a bus service in the presence of a rail service is negligible; 14 per cent of the sum of the option and non-use value represents double counting of user benefits; and the real value of option and non-use values increases in line with GDP/capita.

Source: Laird et al. (2007, p. 18), Table 6.

A consequence of the lack of development in the field of transport-related option and non-use values means that a number of difficulties arise in applying them in a transport appraisal. Uncertainties in the catchment area of stations and whether option and non-use values are held by households outside those catchment areas, the real growth in values over time, the potential for double counting in the non-use value and the option and the non-use value of a mixed mode (bus and train) package can all significantly affect the present value of option and non-use values in an appraisal (see Table 5.7). Furthermore, the limited data on option and non-use values means that variations in frequency of service and connectivity to different-sized employment centres are not reflected in the appraisal. For example, one might expect the option and non-use values associated with the new stations and train services in the north of Scotland case studies to be less than those derived by Humphreys and Fowkes, as the frequency of train services is lower in the north of Scotland compared to the North Berwick to Edinburgh service surveyed by Humphreys and Fowkes, and Inverness does not offer as many employment and social opportunities as does Edinburgh.

Conclusions

Application of cost–benefit analysis to transport projects is now long established. We have examined the traditional approach, which is built around enormous amounts of research into values of time and of accident risk as the two key ingredients, supplemented now by increasing evidence on environmental valuation. We have seen that its application to rail projects tends to be more complex than to road, because of the range of options available, the choices that need to be examined regarding service level, quality and fares and the interdependance of projects. However, there is no intrinsic reason why this method should not be applied to rail schemes as well as roads.

However, two issues have arisen of particular importance for rail schemes in recent years. The first is the issue of wider economic benefits, where the argument that the impact of rail schemes on the labour market may lead to substantial wider benefits has now passed into standard British transport appraisal practice. Obviously this impact is most likely to be significant for schemes which generate substantial changes in commuter traffic in areas with high productivity, where estimates suggest that up to 60 per cent may be added to conventional economic benefits. Obviously this benefit may also apply to road schemes.

The second issue concerns the existence and size of option values and other indirect benefits – the willingness by the community to pay to maintain services even when the directly estimated user benefits do not justify the cost. Obviously these benefits are of particular relevance to investment in new stations or closure decisions on lesser used parts of the network, where again empirical evidence suggests that they could have a significant impact on the recommendations of cost–benefit analysis. This benefit would only apply to road schemes if they really opened up opportunities that would not otherwise exist.

While methods to take account of both these factors are now a part of standard British appraisal advice, the evidence on which they are based is far from conclusive. Thus these issues remain at the top of the agenda for future research on the application of cost–benefit analysis in the transport sector.

Notes

1. Market power derived from product differentiation will be weak where goods are close substitutes.

2. Venables sets this within the context of an urban transport improvement.
3. Magnetic levitation train.
4. IASON was an EC fifth framework research project with the objective of improving the understanding of transportation policies on short- and long-term spatial developments in the EU.
5. Oosterhaven and Elhorst (2003) report a wider range (−15 per cent to +83 per cent) derived from earlier versions of the model.
6. The distance between Groningen and the Randstad is 190 kilometres which, for context with the HSR proposals discussed earlier in this chapter, is equivalent to the first stage of the north–south line – the section between London and Birmingham in the UK.
7. Rosenthal and Strange (2004) give an international review of the empirical evidence on the relationship between productivity and agglomeration.
8. The option and non-use values used are £170 for rail and £90 for bus (2002 prices and values). These have been derived from Humphreys and Fowkes (2006) for rail and Bristow et al. (1991) for bus, converted to a 2002 price base and deflated by 14 per cent (and rounded to nearest £10) to account for double counting in the non-use value.

References

Atkins (2006a), 'Inter-urban rail forecasts', in Eddington (ed.), pp. 203–380.
Atkins (2006b), *High Speed Line Study*, Summary report, London: Atkins.
Beesley, M.F. and C.D. Foster (1965), 'The Victoria Line: social benefits and finances', *Journal of the Royal Statistical Society*, Series A (General), 128.
Blaeij, A. de, Florax, R.J.G.M., Rietveld, P. and Verhoef, E. (2003), 'The value of statistical life in road safety: a meta-analysis', *Accident Analysis and Prevention*, **35** (4), 973–86.
Bristow, A.L., Hopkinson, P.G., Nash, C.A. and Wardman, M. (1991), 'Evaluation of the use and non-use benefits of public transport', Report No. 2, Application of the method, ITS Working Paper 310, Leeds: Institute for Transport Studies, University of Leeds.
Bröcker, J., Meyer, R., Schneekloth, N., Schürmann, C., Spiekermann, K. and Wegener, M. (2004), *Modelling the Socio-economic and Spatial Impacts of EU Transport Policy. IASON (Integrated Appraisal of Spatial economic and Network effects of transport investments and policies) Deliverable 6*, Funded by 5th Framework RTD Programme, Delft: TNO Inro.
Carson, R.T., Wright, J., Carson, N., Alberni, A. and Flores, N. (1995), *A Bibliography of Contingent Valuation Studies and Papers*, La Jolla, CA: Natural Resource Damage Assessment, Inc.
Coburn, T.M., Beesley, M.E. and Reynolds, D.J. (1960), 'The London–Birmingham motorway', *Road Research Technical Paper 46*, Crowthorne: Road Research Laboratory.
Crafts, N. and Leunig, T. (2006), 'The historical significance of transport for economic growth and productivity', in Eddington (ed.), pp. 4–70.
Department for the Environment, Transport and the Regions (DETR) (1998), *Guidance on the New Approach to Appraisal*, London: Her Majesty's Stationery Office.
Department of Transport (DOT) (1981), *The COBA 9 Manual*, London: Department of Transport.
Department for Transport (DFT) (2006a), *Transport, Wider Economic Benefits and Impacts on GDP*, London: Department for Transport.
Department for Transport (DFT) (2006b), *Consultation on the Implementation of the Railways Act 2005 provisions on closures and minor modifications*, London: Department for Transport.
Department for Transport (DFT) (2007a), 'Values of Time and Operating Costs', TAG Unit 3.5.6, London: Department for Transport.
Department for Transport (DFT) (2007b), 'Guidance on Rail Appraisal: External Costs of Car Use', TAG Unit 3.13.2, London: Department for Transport.
Dodgson, J.S. (1973), 'External effects and secondary benefits in road investment appraisal', *Journal of Transport Economics and Policy*, **7** (2), 169–85.
Duranton, G. and Puga, D. (2004), 'Microfoundations of urban agglomeration economies',

in Henderson, J.V. and Thisse, J.F. (eds), *Handbook on Urban and Regional Economics Volume 4 Cities and Geography*, Oxford: Elsevier, pp. 2063–117.

Economides, N. (1996), 'The economics of networks', *International Journal of Industrial Organization*, **14**, 673–99.

Eddington, R. (ed.) (2006), *The Eddington Transport Study*, Annex A: Research, Norwich: Her Majesty's Stationery Office.

Elhorst, J.P., Oosterhaven, J. and Romp, W.E. (2004), 'Integral Cost–Benefit Analysis of MAGLEV Technology under Market Imperfections', Research Report 04C22, Groningen: Groningen Research School SOM, University of Groningen.

Evans, A.W. (2003), 'Accidental fatalities in transport', *Journal of the Royal Statistical Society*, Series A, **162** (2), 253–60.

Foster, C.D. and Beesley, M.E. (1963), 'Estimating the benefits of constructing an underground railway in London', *Journal of the Royal Statistical Society*, Series A (General), **126** (1), 46–93.

Friedrich, R. and Bickel, P. (eds) (2001), *Environmental External Costs of Transport*, Heidelberg: Springer Verlag.

Geurs, K.T., Haaijer, R. and van Wee, B. (2006), 'The option value of public transport: methodology for measurement and case study for regional rail links in the Netherlands', *Transport Reviews*, **26** (5), 613–43.

Gibson, S., Cooper, G. and Bell, B. (2002), 'Capacity charges on the UK rail network' *Journal of Transport Economics and Policy*, **36** (2), 341–54.

Graham, D.J. (2007), 'Agglomeration, productivity and transport investment', *Journal of Transport Economics and Policy*, **41** (3), 317–43.

Gunn, H. (2004), *SCGE Models: Relevance and Accessibility for Use in the UK, with Emphasis on Implications for Evaluation of Transport Investments*, Cambridge: RAND Europe.

Halcrow (2006), *Appraisal of Proposed Re-opening of Station at Conon Bridge: Transport Economic Efficiency Analysis*, Report to the Highland Rail Partnership and HITRANS, December.

Hensher, D.A. (1977), *Value of Business Travel Time*, Oxford: Pergamon.

Highland Rail Developments (2000), *Beauly Station Re-opening Rail Passenger Partnership Funding Bid*, Lairg, Scotland, May.

Highland Rail Partnership (2003), 'Invernet revenue and cost projections', Excel spreadsheet.

Humphreys, R.M. and Fowkes, A.S. (2006), 'The significance of indirect use and non-use values in transport appraisal', *International Journal of Transport Economics*, **33** (1), 17–35.

Institute for Transport Studies (ITS) (2003), *Values of Travel Time Saving in the UK*, Leeds: Institute for Transport Studies, University of Leeds.

Jacobs, J. (1969), *The Economy of Cities*, New York: Random House.

Jara Diaz, S. (1986), 'On the relation between users' benefits and the economic effects of transportation activities', *Journal of Regional Science*, **26**, 379–91.

Laird, J.J. (2007), 'Commuting costs and their wider economic impact', paper presented at 39th Universities' Transport Study Group Conference, 3–5 January, Harrogate, UK.

Laird, J.J., Nellthorp, J. and Mackie, P.J. (2005), 'Network effects and total economic impact in transport appraisal', *Transport Policy*, **12**, 537–44.

Laird, J.J., Geurs, K. and Nash, C.A. (2007), 'Option and non-use values and rail project appraisal', European Transport Conference, Leiden, Netherlands, 17–19 October, London: Association of European Transport.

Marks, P., Fowkes, A.S. and Nash, C.A. (1986), 'Valuing long distance business travel time savings for evaluation: a methodological review and application', PTRC Summer Annual Meeting, University of Sussex, 14–17 July, London: PTRC, pp. 87–98.

Marshall, A. (1890), *Principles of Economics*, London: Macmillan (8th edn published in 1920).

McQuaid, R.W., Greig, M., Smyth. A. and Cooper, A. (2004), 'The Importance of Transport in Business', Location Decisions', Report to the Department for Transport, Edinburgh: Napier University.

Oosterhaven, J. and Elhorst, J.P. (2003), 'Indirect economic benefits of transport infrastructure investments', in Dullaert, W., Jourquin, B. and Polak, J.B. (eds), *Across the Border: Building upon a Quarter Century of Transport Research in the Benelux*, Antwerp: De Boeck, pp. 143–62.

Rice, P., Venables, A.J. and Patacchinni, E. (2006), 'Spatial determinants of productivity: analysis for the regions of Great Britain', *Regional Science and Urban Economics*, **36**, 727–52.

Rosenthal, S.S. and Strange, W.C. (2004), 'Evidence on the nature and sources of agglomeration economies', in Henderson, J.V. and Thisse, J.F. (eds), *Handbook on Urban and Regional Economics. Volume 4: Cities and Geography*, Oxford: Elsevier, pp. 2119–71.

Shy, O. (2001) *The Economics of Network Industries,* Cambridge: Cambridge University Press.

Soguel, N. (1994), *Évaluation monétaire des atteinties a l'environment: Une étude hédoniste et contingente sur l'impact des transports* (Monetary evaluation of environmental costs – a hedonic and contingent valuation study of the impact of transport), Neuchatel: Imprimerie de L'evolve SA.

Standing Advisory Committee on Trunk Road Assessment (SACTRA) (1999), *Transport and the Economy*, Norwich: Her Majesty's Stationery Office.

Stern, N. (2006), *The Economics of Climate Change,* London: Stationery Office, www.sternreview.org.uk.

van Exel, J., Rienstra, S., Gommers, M., Pearman, A.D. and Tsamboulas, D. (2002), 'EU involvement in TEN development: network effects and European value added', *Transport Policy*, 9, 299–311.

Venables, A.J. (2007), 'Evaluating urban transport improvements: cost–benefit analysis in the presence of agglomeration and income taxation', *Journal of Transport Economics and Policy*, **41** (2), 173–88.

Venables, A.J. and Gasiorek, M. (1998), *The Welfare Implications of Transport Improvements in the Presence of Market Failure*, Report to SACTRA, Norwich: Her Majesty's Stationery Office.

Wardman, M. (2001), 'A review of British evidence on time and service quality', *Transportation Research E*, **37** (2), 107–28.

Weisbrod, B.A. (1964), 'Collective-consumption services of individual-consumption goods', *Quarterly Journal of Economics*, **78**, 471–77.

6 Cost–benefit analysis of environmental projects and the role of distributional weights

Robert J. Brent and Booi Themeli

1 Introduction

Does the standard cost–benefit framework break down when one is dealing with projects that impact the environment? A recent contribution by Brekke (1997) suggested that the standard framework does have inherent weaknesses. The numeraire matters in that a positive evaluation using income as the numeraire could easily be reversed when environmental goods are used as the numeraire. The outcome for environmental projects would then seem to be indeterminate. Johansson (1998, p. 489) responded by arguing that Brekke's conclusion follows only 'due to a very unusual interpretation of the meaning of a social cost–benefit analysis'. He therefore proceeds to demonstrate that the numeraire does not matter. Finally, Drèze (1998, p. 484) agrees 'that Johansson's rejoinder is undoubtedly correct', yet he claims that the numeraire does matter if a distributionally unweighted cost–benefit analysis (CBA) is undertaken. The unresolved issue is, how can Johansson's and Drèze's analyses both be correct?

Apart from this unresolved issue, there is the difficulty that the intuition that motivated Brekke's contribution was lost in the debate. He argued that it was the fact that environmental goods are of the nature of pure public goods that causes the choice of numeraire to be an issue. Unfortunately the implication of this feature of environmental goods did not appear in his analysis even though the assumption of equal consumption of environmental goods was present in his calculations. Drèze recognized that there was something important in Brekke's analysis that has received insufficient attention so far in the literature. But, he did not exactly deal with Brekke's intuition. Rather, Drèze focused on the role of distribution weights in CBA. While it is true, as we show below, that much of the debate on the choice of the numeraire does resolve around precisely what assumptions one is willing to make concerning distribution weights, it is still the case that the real point that Brekke wished to introduce has so far been left out of the analysis.

Thus our main purpose in this chapter is to: (a) reformulate the cost–benefit framework underlying Brekke's and Johansson's analyses in order that one can clearly see under what circumstances the numeraire matters in CBA, and (b) extend the framework to cover Brekke's insight related to the pure public good nature of environmental outputs. The end result should be a better understanding of any special conceptual difficulties of undertaking a CBA of environmental projects.

Once we have resolved the Brekke–Johansson–Drèze debate, and have explained that for environmental goods the need to make a choice for the numeraire means that distribution weights are required to carry out a CBA, which is the subject matter for Section 2, the next step, contained in Section 3, is to review the literature as to how distribution weights were employed for environmental projects and with what effects. Section 4 presents a complete CBA of a pollution-reducing intervention that incorporates distribution weights. The final section summarizes and concludes.

2   The choice of numeraire in CBA and the role of distribution weights

We start by establishing the proposition that for most CBAs the choice of numeraire is not decisive to determining whether a project is worthwhile. Then we highlight the environmental literature which is based on the premise that a particular numeraire is required to allow for distributional considerations to be accommodated. From there we go to our main analysis of the role of the numeraire for environmental projects to demonstrate that for these projects: (a) the numeraire matters, and (b) the choice of numeraire is tied up with the choice of distributional weights. We close by explaining that it is because environmental outputs are of the nature of pure public goods that distribution weights are required for environmental projects.

Background

Historically, distributional weights were a central component of the project appraisal manuals of the 1970s (for instance, UNIDO 1972; Little and Mirrlees 1974; and Squire and van der Tak 1975).[1] In these manuals these was a choice between expressing the units of benefits and costs in terms of domestic prices or in terms of world prices, that is, there was a choice of numeraire. The main reason why domestic prices differed from world prices was because domestic prices added tariffs to the world prices. Since tariffs were not opportunity costs, they should be excluded. Note that tariffs related largely to international traded goods. Many goods and services, such as health, education, and labor, were not internationally traded. So tariffs distorted the relative prices of traded and non-traded goods and services.

To negate the impact of the tariffs in a CBA, either one could keep the traded goods valued in world prices and scale down the domestic prices by the amount of the tariffs to their world price equivalent (which is the world price numeraire approach used by Little and Mirrlees, and Squire and van der Tak) or one could keep the non-traded valued in domestic prices and scale up the traded goods by the amount of the tariffs to their domestic price equivalent (which is the domestic price numeraire approach adopted by UNIDO). In principle, there was a one-for-one correspondence between the outcomes expressed in domestic prices and in world prices. Thus, if domestic prices were $1 + t$ higher than world prices (where t is the average tariff rate), then world prices could be multiplied by $1 + t$ to produce their domestic price equivalent, or domestic prices could be divided by $1 + t$ to form their world price equivalent. The choice of numeraire did not alter the decisions made. If S is the social net benefits, then its sign determines whether the project is worthwhile. Multiplying S by $1 + t$ makes the magnitudes appear larger, and dividing S by $1 + t$ makes the magnitudes appear smaller. But the sign of the outcome does not depend on whether S is scaled up or down. All that happens with the alternative numeraire is that positive outcomes become more or less positive, and negative outcomes appear more or less negative.

In practice there was a difference between the two numeraires, because UNIDO used a single, aggregate estimate of $1 + t$, while Little and Mirrlees, and Squire and van der Tak, used individual commodity estimates of $1 + t$. So the world price approach would be more precise. But, the choice of numeraire came down to the costs and feasibility of collecting more precise data rather than one of establishing the relative theoretical advantage of one approach over the other. So the convention in CBA was that the choice of numeraire was not important. But, note that this result was basically derived from a situation where the numeraire was considered of the nature of a pure private good (where the consumption by one person reduces the consumption of others).

Choice of numeraire for environmental projects
A number of recent papers and textbooks, including Londero (1996a), Potts (1999), Freeman (2003), Yitzhaki (2003), Johansson-Stenman (2005) and Azqueta and Sotelsek (2007), have argued for the use of a *domestic price numeraire* to define and identify income effects of a project on specific target groups for environmental investments. Potts (1999) used this approach with the example of a district heating project in the Republic of Latvia. In his study, direct measurements of income effects were adjusted using shadow price estimates to determine indirect income effects. In another paper that focused on the employment generation impact of many environmental investments, Azqueta and Sotelsek (2007) suggest the use of efficiency wages in the economy when appraising the impact of environmental investments. And in his case study on the environmental benefits

and costs of a Kunda cement factory in Estonia, Karmokolias (1996) used domestic price estimates to value the following impacts: soiling and material damage, real estate values, health, forestry and agriculture, tourism, raw materials and personnel turnover at the cement company, and global effects of SO_2 and NOx emissions. According to Potts (1999), this approach has two major advantages. First, the distributional impact is transparent and therefore its desirability or otherwise can be subjected to debate. Second, the approach allows for the specification of target groups in whatever way happens to be appropriate for the project under consideration. Accordingly, it is thus easier to integrate the analysis with other forms of analysis such as stakeholder analysis, where the target groups may be defined by characteristics specific to the project or project area.

It is clear that the focus on a domestic price numeraire in the latest analysis in the literature is in order to accommodate distributional effects in the CBA of environmental investments. This is because one needs to calculate incomes in order to incorporate income distribution effects, and for incomes it is domestic and not shadow prices that are the determinant. However, as we shall now see, the numeraire can be divorced from the issue of what weights to set only when one numeraire is chosen, that is, with social utility as the numeraire.

Alternative cost–benefit frameworks
An explicit social welfare function W will be used to help clarify the cost–benefit calculations made in the Brekke–Johansson–Drèze numeraire debate. Following Brekke, benefits are in environmental units E and costs are in income units Y. The problem is how to evaluate outcomes when benefits and costs are in these two different units. Two individuals are involved, individual 1 who is the materialist and individual 2 who is the environmentalist. The welfare function can be written as:

$$W = W(Y_1, Y_2, E_1, E_2). \tag{6.1}$$

A public project leads to simultaneous changes in costs and benefits:

$$dW = W_{Y1}dY_1 + W_{Y2}dY_2 + W_{E1}dE_1 + W_{E2}dE_2, \tag{6.2}$$

where $W_{.i}$ is the social marginal utility of a change in a project unit to individual i, which is given by the product of the marginal social significance of the utility of individual i, W_i, and the individual's marginal utility from any unit, U_i. Johansson assumes explicitly, and Brekke assumes implicitly, a utilitarian social welfare function, where $W_{.i} = 1$. This sets $W_{.i} = U_{.i}$. Equation (6.2) then reduces to:

$$dW = U_{y1}dY_1 + U_{y2}dY_2 + U_{E1}dE_1 + U_{E2}dE_2. \tag{6.3}$$

Brekke's analysis starts with a distribution of income that is equal. He then assumes a project that produces environmental benefits that are of the nature of a pure public good (where consumption by one can lead to consumption by all) such that $dE_1 = dE_2 = 1$ which is financed in equal amounts by the two individuals according to: $dY_1 = dY_2 = -1$. Taking the partial derivatives from $U_1 = 4Y_1 + E_1$ and $U_2 = Y_1 + 4E_2$, and substituting them in equation (6.3), we obtain the resulting change in social welfare as $dW = 0$.

It is important to understand that the calculation just presented has *social utility* as the numeraire. One can alternatively work with either income or environmental units as the numeraire. Let U_{YA} represent the marginal utility of income of someone at the average level of income and U_{EA} represent the marginal utility of environmental output of someone at the average level of environmental 'consumption' (appreciation). Since U_{EA} and U_{EA} can be regarded as constants,[2] carrying out a CBA in income units, dividing equation (6.3) by U_{YA}, or environmental units, dividing equation (6.3) by U_{YA}, will not alter the evaluation outcome. In either case, the change in social welfare will be zero. This is essentially the Johansson contribution. The choice of numeraire does not matter, contrary to Brekke's claim.

If the numeraire does not matter, what then are we to make of the Brekke calculations? The answer is that his results are obtained by particular abstractions from the general framework given by equation (6.3). Take first the case of working with income units. Divide equation (6.3) by U_{YA} to obtain:

$$dW/U_{YA} = (U_{y1}/U_{YA})dY_1 + (U_{y2}/U_{YA})dY_2 + (U_{E1}/U_{YA})dE_1$$
$$+ (U_{E2}/U_{YA})dE_2. \tag{6.4}$$

If one sets the distribution weights $(U_{y1}/U_{YA}) = (U_{y2}/U_{YA}) = 1$, then equation (6.4) reduces to:

$$dW/U_{YA} = dY_1 + dY_2 + (U_{E1}/U_{YA})dE_1 + (U_{E2}/U_{YA})dE_2. \tag{6.5}$$

Now applying the partial derivatives from the postulated utility functions, and the assumed values for the project costs and benefits, we obtain the outcome that $dW/U_{YA} = +2.25$.

Next take E units as the numeraire. Dividing equation (6.3) by U_{EA} leads to:

$$dW/U_{EA} = (U_{Y1}/U_{EA})dY_1 + (U_{Y2}/U_{EA})dY_2 + (U_{E1}/U_{EA})dE_1$$

$$+ (U_{E2}/U_{EA})dE_2.$$

(6.6)

Assigning the distribution weights $(U_{E1}/U_{EA}) = (U_{E2}/U_{EA}) = 1$ means that equation (6.6) becomes:

$$dW/U_{EA} = (U_{Y1}/U_{EA})dY_1 + (U_{Y2}/U_{EA})dY_2 + dE_1 + dE_2. \qquad (6.7)$$

Proceeding as before, with the derived individual marginal utilities and the given project cost and benefits, we find that $dW/U_{EA} = -2.25$.

Clearly, as correctly conjectured by Drèze, understood by Johansson, and just demonstrated above, whether Brekke obtained $+2.25$ or -2.25 as an outcome was simply a product of his using different sets of distribution weights with the alternative numeraire. The different sets of weights correspond to assuming unweighted (that is, unity) weights when aggregating income effects (and weighting environmental effects by individual marginal utilities when aggregating environmental effects) with income as the numeraire, and assuming unweighted weights when aggregating E effects (and weighting income effects by individual marginal utilities when aggregating income effects) with environmental units as numeraire.

It is true, therefore, that Brekke's analysis suffers from a consistency problem. The weights he used with either income or environmental units as numeraire were not consistent with the weights that were behind those in the general framework where utility was the numeraire. This is what the analysis tells us. But, it ignores the practical problem posed by Brekke's work that Drèze wished to emphasize, as to what weights are actually employed when carrying out CBAs. If unity weights are going to be used for some benefits and costs, but not for others, then the choice of numeraire *will* in fact help determine the outcome.

This conclusion very much mirrors that from the 1970s' debate between Little and Mirrlees (1974) and UNIDO (1972) over the choice of numeraire in project appraisal (whether to make the calculation using domestic or foreign prices) summarized above. In theory one could show that outcomes would be equivalent using either methodology, yet when it came to the estimation of parameters, different approaches were adopted and thus outcomes would be different in practice (see Lal, 1974; Brent, 1998).

Environmental units as pure public goods
All the analysis and conclusions so far have missed Brekke's intuition. That is, the results have not really depended on environmental outputs

having the property of a pure public good. A pure public good is one that is equally consumed by all. It is true that Brekke assumed $dE_1 = dE_2 = 1$, but he also had $dY_1 = dY_2 = -1$. What played no part in the analysis was that for a pure public good, $dE_1 = dE_2 = E$, while for a private good, $dY_1 + dY_2 = Y$. The equal consumption property of public goods ensures that marginal rates of substitution will be different across individuals. Thus, it is not just the fact that the distribution weights behind the income numeraire were different from those with the environmental units that should concern us. The assumption of $(U_{E1}/U_{EA}) = (U_{E2}/U_{EA}) = 1$ behind the E numeraire was actually *impossible* (if individuals have different tastes). The implications of this can best be understood by extending the cost–benefit framework a little from that used in Section 2.

On close inspection of the Brekke analysis, we can see that E units have not been included in Y units. This explains the fact that although incomes are assumed equal both pre- and post-project, the marginal utilities of income for the two individuals are not equal. Individual 1's marginal utility of income is four times that of individual 2 because s/he values income more relative to environmental units. This means that the traditional approach of using equal income weights cannot be correct even if there is an optimal income tax that equalizes income (in the context of an equal marginal sacrifice rule).

It might seem that matters would be a lot easier if environmental accounting were added to national income accounting. But this would not be the case, as we now explain. Define X as a proxy for private goods and let E be environmental units as before. Suppressing prices, we can measure income by: $Y = X + E$. The counterpart to equation (6.3) would be:

$$dW = U_{X1}dY_1 + U_{X2}dY_2 + U_{E1}dE_1 + U_{E2}dE_2 \qquad (6.8)$$

and the cost–benefit framework with income as the numeraire would become:

$$dW/U_{YA} = (U_{X1}/U_{YA})dY_1 + (U_{X2}/U_{YA})dY_2 + (U_{E1}/U_{YA})dE_1$$
$$+ (U_{E2}/U_{YA})dE_2. \qquad (6.9)$$

A competitive market price for X would bring about $(U_{X1}/U_{YA}) = (U_{X2}/U_{YA})$. On the other hand, no uniform pricing for E could enable $(U_{E1}/U_{EA}) = (U_{E2}/U_{EA})$ to be satisfied. This seems to be the important insight that Brekke wished to convey. Without the ability to equalize marginal rates of substitution for environmental goods, we must agree with Drèze that equal weighting schemes that are the current practice of the World Bank are not viable. There is no alternative to trying to estimate the requisite weights in equation (6.3) directly.

To summarize: the conclusion from Section 2 that the choice of numeraire need not be important for CBA would only be the case under one particular set of social weights for benefits and costs. Weights that give equal values for E units and unequal values for Y units, or equal values for E units and unequal values for Y units, not only violate the equivalence between Y and E numeraires, they also ensure that *neither* of them will lead to outcomes that would be obtained with social utility as the numeraire. If environmental goods were involved, even equal incomes would not justify using equal income weights. In addition, the public good nature of environmental goods would preclude equal weights assumptions for E units. So using environmental goods as the numeraire would not be feasible. This last result holds even if environmental accounting takes place and a value is put on E goods as a part of a measure of national income Y.

3   The use of distribution weights in environmental projects

Using distribution weights means that the value of a dollar of benefits or costs is allowed to vary based on who receives the benefits or bears the costs. There are two main methods for deriving the distribution weights. One is the 'a priori' approach which involves specifying a social welfare function and imposing restrictions on that function that allow for distributional concerns. The second method is to use the imputational approach, which is to derive estimates of the weights from the revealed preferences of public decision makers. Since there are no revealed preference estimates of distribution weights in the environmental field, and the a priori approach has been used extensively for environmental projects, we shall concentrate solely on this latter approach.

Deriving distribution weights from a specification of the social welfare function

Parry (2004) and Parry et al. (2005) have utilized the methodology developed by Squire and van der Tak (1975) for deriving distribution weights from a specification of the social welfare function. Social welfare is to be a function of the utility of each individual, which for simplicity is just a function of their income Y_i relative to someone at the average $\overline{Y}$:

$$W = W[U_1(Y_1/\overline{Y}),\ U_2(Y_2/\overline{Y}),\ldots,\ U_i(Y_i/\overline{Y}),\ldots,\ U_n(Y_n/\overline{Y})],\quad (6.10)$$

where U_i represents the utility for individual i. Assuming concavity with respect to income in either the individual utility functions (that is, decreasing marginal utility per dollar of income), or in the social welfare function (that is, decreasing marginal social welfare per util[3]) will cause the marginal social welfare per dollar for any given individual to decline in that individual's income. To this end, an iso-elastic welfare function was adopted:

$$W = (1 - \eta)^{-1} \sum \frac{Y_i^{1-\eta}}{\overline{Y}^{-\eta}} \qquad (6.11)$$

where η is society's aversion to relative inequality. An individual i's income distribution weight relative to the average, a_i, is defined as the derivative of the social welfare function with respect to the individual's income. Differentiating (6.11) we obtain:

$$a_i = \frac{\partial W}{\partial Y_i} = \frac{Y_i^{-\eta}}{\overline{Y}^{-\eta}} = \left(\frac{\overline{Y}}{Y_i}\right)^{\eta}. \qquad (6.12)$$

At one extreme, for $\eta = 0$, $a_i = 1$. Weights are constant and equal to unity for all. This is the standard, efficiency-only set of distribution weights that dominates CBA and public policy practice. For $\eta = 1$, recommended by Squire and van der Tak, distributional weights are inversely proportional to average income:

$$a_i = \frac{Y_i}{\overline{Y}}. \qquad (6.13)$$

On the basis of equation (6.13), if individuals have one-tenth the income of the average, a dollar of benefits or costs is worth 10 dollars to them, while for those with incomes 10 times the average, their dollars of benefits and costs are valued at 10 cents. At the other extreme, $\eta = \infty$ means that weights are zero on all but the very poorest individual.

How to set the range for the inequality aversion parameter
Environmental applications of the social welfare function method to setting distribution weights include work by Parry (2004) on the social costs of emission permits, Mayeres (2001) on various transportation policies and both Fankhauser et al. (1997) and Pearce et al (2006) on the distributional aspects of climate change damages across rich and poor nations. We shall first discuss the implications of fixing the inequality aversion parameter η in the context of the Pearce et al. (2006) application, which has one of the widest set of distribution weights, and then go on to discuss the Parry (2004) set of weights, since this application will be covered in detail in Section 4 of this chapter.

Pearce et al. (2006) estimated the damage from a doubling of CO_2 concentrations from pre-industrial levels for the world in total, and for poor

Table 6.1   Estimates of weighted climate change damages ($US bn)

	$\eta = 0$	$\eta = 0.5$	$\eta = 1.0$	$\eta = 2.0$
Poor countries	106	184	318	954
Rich countries	216	125	72	24
Total	322	309	390	978

Source: Pearce et al. (2006, p. 232).

and rich countries shown separately. These damage estimates were then weighted based on magnitudes of η varying between 0 and 2. Their results are shown in Table 6.1. In the table, the second column ($\eta = 0$) presents equally weighted damage estimates, and the remaining columns show damage estimates weighted with different positive values for η.

From the table we see that the magnitude of η strongly affects the estimated climate damages for rich and poor nations. As the inequality aversion parameter η increases in size, the relative size of damage shifts from mainly being a problem for rich nations towards mainly being a problem for poor nations. Based on the findings, Pearce et al. point to the importance of considering the justifiable range for the parameter η.

How does one know what is a reasonable range of values for the inequality aversion parameter? First, we can eliminate the two extremes $\eta = 0$ and $\eta = \infty$. The equal weights case ($\eta = 0$) must be wrong even if it is standard practice in CBA. How can a dollar to a person living in extreme poverty be worth the same as a dollar to a person who is a multi-billionaire? The other extreme ($\eta = \infty$) is just as objectionable even though it is consistent with the maximin principle associated with Rawls (1971). In this case only the effect on the worst-off individual in society matters. This has serious difficulties as part of a social criterion for CBA because if a project benefits the worst-off individual and makes *everyone else worse off*, then this weighting scheme would approve the project. What is *social* about a social CBA when one is focusing on the impact on just one individual in a society when making a CBA? A dictatorship is still a dictatorship even if the dictator is the poorest of the poor.

It is reasonable to suggest therefore that the appropriate set of values for the aversion parameter must be in the intermediate range: $0 < \eta < \infty$. So Pearce et al.'s upper-bound range of 2 would seem to be admissible. But note what it implies. Using equation (6.12), we see that if individuals have one-tenth the income of the average, a dollar of benefits or costs is worth 100 dollars to them, while for those with incomes 10 times the average, their dollars of benefits and costs are valued at only one cent. Opponents of non-unity distribution weights argue that if distributional weights differ too much between people, then they could be used to justify excessively inefficient projects. As an argument for equal weights it is clearly invalid, since a social CBA has two objectives (efficiency and distribution) not just one (efficiency). So having a very inefficient project that saves the lives of the poor may very well be socially worthwhile.

However, as an argument for putting limits on the magnitudes by which weights can vary, and suggesting that $\eta = 2$ could be too high, there could be some validity in examining arguments seeking limits for η. To illustrate the point, Harberger (1978) and Layard (1980) use an example where R is richer than P and it costs c dollars deadweight efficiency loss at the margin to transfer one dollar from R to P (c being endogenous). Now if we again use the notation a_i to represent the weight for an individual i (so that a_P is the weight for the poor person and a_R is the weight for the rich individual), then the argument is that one should continue to transfer dollars from R to P so long as:

$$- a_R + a_P (1 - c) > 0. \tag{6.14}$$

The conclusion is that, at an optimum, one would never observe a_P greater than a_R by more than the factor c:

$$- a_P/a_R > 1/(1 - c). \tag{6.15}$$

So, with $c = 0.20$, if $a_P/a_R > 1.25$ then transfers to the poor should continue. When transfers stop, and projects are used to redistribute income to the poor, 1.25 is the largest relative weight to the poor that can be used in a project evaluation.

What should one make of this argument? As a principle of CBA it has a serious weakness as CBA is inherently a 'second-best' evaluation method. It takes existing constraints as given, and it tries to evaluate outcomes in the presence of the constraints. It does not assume that other policies are optimal and that the constraints (other than production feasibility, which is the first-best's only constraint) do not exist. So, in practice, optimality using equation (6.15) has not taken place, and many tax-transfer programs that could reduce income inequality and increase social welfare do not take place. However, let us use the logic behind this analysis to make the reverse case for a minimum value for distribution weights. Given that optimality in transfers has not taken place, the weight on the poor relative to the rich should never be *less than* $1/(1 - c)$.

To see how weights were determined in practice, we shall use the income numbers presented by Parry (2004) in his evaluation of emission permits which we will be examining in detail in the case study at the end of this

Table 6.2   Distribution weights used by Parry (2004)

Income quintile	Income per quintile	Distribution weights		
		$\eta = 0$	$\eta = 0.5$	$\eta = 1$
1	$10,294	1.00	1.73	2.98
2	$18,404	1.00	1.29	1.67
3	$25,856	1.00	1.09	1.19
4	$36,462	1.00	0.91	0.84
5	$62,453	1.00	0.70	0.49
Mean	$30,694	1.00	1.00	1.00

Source: Constructed by the authors based on data in Parry (2004).

chapter. He grouped incomes by quintiles. The incomes by quintile and the weights attached to these incomes based on equation (6.12) are shown in Table 6.2 (based on the data in Parry 2004, table 6.1).

The inequality aversion parameter was limited to the range 0 to 1. We can see that the lower the aversion to inequality, the nearer the weights get to unity, which is the traditional CBA set of weights that correspond to an efficiency-only social welfare function. Given the income levels and the particular values for the inequality aversion parameters, we see that the range of estimates for the weights is very modest, in all cases within the interval 0.7 to 3.

Let us summarize this discussion on the appropriate range of values for the inequality aversion parameter η by reviewing the suggested results in the literature. Squire and van der Tak recommend 1 as the best estimate, and taking 0 to 2 as values for use in a sensitivity analysis (undertaking the evaluation with the next-best alternative estimates). Brent (2006) recommends 0.5 as the best estimate as this gives the poor importance, but the poor do not dominate completely the outcomes. He then suggests 0 and 1 as the alternative values. Parry's (2004) η estimates arc those in the Brent range. Although Pearce et al. use values for the inequality aversion parameter in the range 0 to 2, they argue in Pearce (2003) and Pearce et al. (2006) that a magnitude of 0.5 to 1.2 is defensible for further use in CBA to evaluate climate change.

4   A cost–benefit analysis of emission permits
Parry (2004) included distribution weights as a part of his evaluation of emission permits in the US. The project he focused on was government-issued tradable emission permits to control power plant emissions of sulfur dioxide (SO_2) at the national level, and nitrogen oxides (NO_x) at

the regional level (the Los Angeles Basin and for a group of states in the Northeast). The permits were given out free of charge by the regulators to those electricity firms in existence, that is, 'grandfathered'.

There were four alternatives to the grandfathered permits. One was for the government to auction the emission permits instead of giving them to the firms free. In this case the government receives the revenue and then subsequently shares it out to individuals. This is equivalent to a 100 percent profits tax. Parry calls this alternative an 'emissions tax'. The second alternative is to impose a performance standard. This involves requiring firms to reduce emissions by a specified level, not necessarily corresponding to the emissions level that the firm would choose for maximizing profits (equating marginal abatement costs to the market price of the permits). The third alternative is by way of a technology mandate. Firms are required to reduce emissions, but only by using a specified technology (end-of-pipe abatement). Again this alternative need not lead to the profit-maximizing level of abatement as the firm cannot choose the cost-minimizing method for responding to the emission reduction. The final alternative is to charge an input tax (a tax in proportion to the sulfur content of the coal used). The emission reduction here (per unit of output) is smaller than for the technology mandate as the policy does not give a differential advantage to end-of-pipe abatement.

For each of the five projects, the grandfathered and the four alternative projects, Parry estimated the income change ΔY (by quintile of the US income distribution) that resulted from the emissions and hence output reduction of electricity. These quintile income changes (1 to 5, with 1 the lowest quintile and 5 the highest) were then to be multiplied by their distribution weight to form the aggregate welfare change, which Parry called the 'social cost of emission control policies' or the weighted 'net burdens' and this can be represented as:

$$\Delta W = a_1 \Delta Y_1 + a_2 \Delta Y_2 + a_3 \Delta Y_3 + a_4 \Delta Y_4 + a_5 \Delta Y_5, \qquad (6.16)$$

where a_1 to a_2 are the quintile distribution weights. The a priori approach was used to calculate the weights. Table 6.2, presented earlier, gives the estimates of the five quintile weights that Parry used for each of the three inequality aversion parameters (0, 0.5 and 1).

As Parry did not estimate the benefits of the reduction in pollution caused by the reductions in emissions, the evaluation could be considered to be a partial CBA of pollution reduction, that is, considering only the costs. Alternatively we can treat the emission permits and their alternatives as a tax-transfer project, with those whose incomes are going up, the beneficiaries, receiving positive transfers (subsidies) and those whose incomes have declined, the losers, paying taxes. In this case we can regard the income changes as a complete CBA of the tax-transfer project. However, because outputs are changing as well as the incomes being redistributed, the income changes strictly correspond to a joint electricity output reduction and transfer project.

Therefore, there are two main reasons why incomes change from the emission permits system. First, the abatement reduction leads to a decline in output of electricity and this reduction causes the price of electricity to rise. This price rise will cause a reduction in income for all five quintile groups. To the extent that quintiles consume differing amounts of electricity, and the lower quintiles consume more as a share of their income, the emission reduction will cause quintile-varying income reductions.[4] Second, the permits themselves redistribute incomes. Initially, with the permits being given away free, the electricity firms benefit. Firm profits rise and all the quintiles gain to the extent that they are shareholders in the firm. The higher quintiles own the larger percentage of the stocks, so they gain the most.[5] The income losses and profit gains for emission permits are depicted in Figure 6.1. Note that the consumption losses are not just the higher expenditure amount but include also the loss of consumer surplus

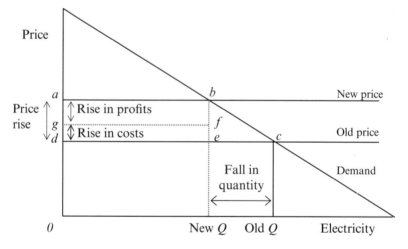

Note: The permits lead to a reduction in output, from the old to the new Q of electricity. This lower quantity leads to a rise in price generating an increase of revenues equal to *adeb*. Reducing pollution involves higher costs and this is equal to area *gdef*. So of the increase in revenues, *agfb* constitutes profits and this produces income gains for the owners of the stocks in the firm. Because of the rise in price, consumers lose income equal to the extra expenditure they have to pay, area *adeb*, and the consumer surplus triangle given as *bec*.

Figure 6.1   The income effects of emission projects

(the excess of willingness to pay over the amount that consumers have to pay).

Subsequently, the government taxes some share of the profits. Parry takes 35 percent as the tax for four of the alternatives, and 100 percent for the alternative that is the emissions tax since, by definition, all of the profits are taxed for this alternative. The government then redistributes the tax revenues it receives in one of two ways. The first is to return the revenues to the quintiles (called 'recycling' the revenues) in a distribution-ally neutral way, that is, in proportion to their pre-project shares of total income. The second way is progressive, which involves giving each quintile the same lump-sum amount which is, of course, a larger share the lower is the income of the quintile.

The income changes for the five alternatives are shown in Table 6.3 (Parry's table 6).[6] Separate results are given for: (a) a 44 percent reduction in SO_2, a 10 percent reduction in carbon, and a 30 percent reduction in NO_x; (b) for the three sets of distribution weights that correspond to differ-ent values for the inequality aversion parameter; and (c) for the two ways of returning the tax revenues.

In Table 6.3, the positive numbers indicate that there is an income loss from the alternative (there is a positive cost or burden) while the negative numbers mean that incomes have increased from the alternative. The case where $\eta = 0$ corresponds to a pure efficiency evaluation. Any recycling of revenues is irrelevant in this case as, like the classical case of transfers in CBA, gains and losses cancel out. For SO_2, the three alternatives, emissions permits, the emission tax, and performance standards are approximately equally efficient, while the costs (income losses) of the technology mandate and the input tax are about double the size of the other three alternatives. When distribution issues are incorporated into the evaluations, the perform-ance standard is the most efficient under proportional recycling and it is the emissions tax that becomes the least costly under lump-sum recycling. For carbon and NO_x, the first three alternatives are again the most efficient (that is, with outcomes using weights given by $\eta = 0$). When $\eta > 0$, we see that emissions controls can generate negative losses (income gains), especially when there is lump-sum recycling. With lump-sum recycling, the emissions tax and the input tax are equally beneficial in the case of carbon emissions, but the input tax is by far the most beneficial alternative for NO_x.

Overall then, we see that whether emission controls are a burden or a blessing depends on the size of the distribution weights one uses to calcu-late outcomes in the CBA. Grandfathered permits, the performance stand-ard and the technology mandate always generate income losses; while the two emission reduction alternatives involving taxes can be positive or negative according to one's aversion to inequality.

Table 6.3   Total social costs of pollution control policies ($ m)

	$\eta = 0$	$\eta = 0.5$		$\eta = 1$	
		Proportional Recycling	Lump-sum Recycling	Proportional Recycling	Lump-sum Recycling
SO$_2$					
Grandfathered permits	1,018	1,255	1,084	1,636	1,241
Emissions tax	1,018	1,138	650	1,390	262
Performance standard	1,026	1,030	1,030	1,133	1,133
Technology mandate	2,041	2,048	2,048	2,253	2,253
Input tax	2,013	2,248	1,277	2,741	496
Carbon					
Grandfathered permits	1,310	3,262	1,766	5,702	2,244
Emissions tax	1,310	2,240	−2,035	3,549	−6,333
Performance standard	1,943	1,949	1,949	2,144	2,144
Technology mandate	na	na	na	na	na
Input tax	1,310	2,240	−2,035	3,549	−6,333
NO$_x$					
Grandfathered permits	562	801	626	1,140	736
Emissions tax	562	682	183	889	−264
Performance standard	564	565	565	622	622
Technology mandate	805	807	807	888	888
Input tax	1,777	2,142	437	2,777	−1,163

Source: Parry (2004, p. 234).

5   Conclusions

The main focus of this chapter has been on the Brekke–Johansson–Drèze debate over the choice of numeraire for the CBA of environmental projects. We saw that, for most project evaluations, the choice of numeraire need not be important for cost–benefit analysis. However, for environmental projects, this would only be the case under one particular set of social weights for benefits and costs. Weights that give equal values for E units and unequal values for Y units, or equal values for E units and unequal values for Y units, not only violate the equivalence between Y and E numeraires, they also ensure that *neither* of them will lead to outcomes that would be obtained with social utility as the numeraire. If environmental goods were involved, even equal incomes would not justify using equal income weights. In addition, the public good nature of environmental goods would preclude equal weight assumptions for E units. So using environmental goods as the numeraire could not be feasible. This last result holds even if environmental accounting takes place and a value is put on E goods as a part of a measure of national income Y.

Apart from recognizing the fact that it is because environmental goods are of the nature of pure public goods, and through this fact that we have a new argument for the inclusion of distribution weights into CBA, especially for environmental projects, this chapter has also been concerned with how distribution weights have been applied in practice in the environmental field. The main applications have relied on assuming an isoelastic social welfare function where the slope of the social marginal utility of income was given by the inequality aversion parameter. Values for η in the range of 0 to 1 were mainly used. For these values, the distribution weights applied to quintiles in the evaluation of a wide variety of emission controls in the US did not vary excessively, such that distribution would be the only determinant of CBA outcomes and efficiency would not matter at all, as some of the opponents of distribution weights have feared. The value η = 2 would seem to be excessive in this regard. However, one did not need values this high to demonstrate that climate change has burdened the poor countries to a greater extent than the rich countries. As we saw, the value η = 0.5, which has been advocated as the best estimate for this parameter, was sufficient to change the verdict on climate change from being a problem for rich countries towards being a problem for poor nations.

Notes

1. 'Project appraisal' is the term applied to CBA for evaluations that relate to projects in less-developed countries.
2. Note that U_{EA} and U_{EA} will be set equal to 1 in the calculations below.
3. 'Per util' is shorthand for 'per any individual's utility change'.
4. Parry uses estimates that have the 1 to 5 quintiles consuming electricity with 3.5, 11.1, 9.1, 23.4 and 53 percent, respectively, of their budgets.
5. Parry uses estimates that have the 1 to 5 quintiles owning 3.5, 11.1, 9.1, 23.4 and 53 percent, respectively, of the stocks.
6. For consistency with the notation used throughout this chapter we have changed Parry's inequality aversion parameter β to Squire and van der Tak's η.

References

Azqueta, D. and Sotelsek, D. (2007), 'Valuing nature: from environmental impacts to natural capital', *Ecological Economics*, **63**, 22–30.

Brekke, K.A (1997), 'The numéraire matters in cost–benefit analysis', *Journal of Public Economics*, **64**, 117–23.

Brent, R.J. (1998), *Cost–Benefit Analysis for Developing Countries*, Cheltenham, UK and Lyme, USA: Edward Elgar.

Brent, R.J. (2006), *Applied Cost–Benefit Analysis*, 2nd edn, Cheltenham, UK and Northampton, MA, USA: Edward Elgar.

Drèze, J (1998), 'Distribution matters in cost–benefit analysis', *Journal of Public Economics*, **70**, 485–8.

Fankhauser, S., Tol, R. and Pearce, D. (1997), 'The aggregation of climate change damages: a welfare theoretic approach', *Environmental and Resource Economics*, **10**, 249–66.

Freeman A.M.I. (2003), *The Measurement of Environmental and Resource Values: Theory and Methods*, Washington DC: Resources for the Future.

Harberger, A. (1978), 'On the use of distributional weights in social cost–benefit analysis', *The Journal of Political Economy*, **86**, 87–120.

Johansson, P.-O. (1998), 'Does the choice of numéraire matter in cost–benefit analysis?', *Journal of Public Economics*, **64**, 489–93.

Johansson-Stenman, O. (2005), 'Distributional weights in cost–benefit analysis – should we forget about them? How to bring a poverty focus to the economic analysis of projects', *Land Economics*, **81**, 337–52.

Karmokolias, Y. (1996), 'Cost benefit analysis of private sector environmental investments', IFC Discussion Paper 30, International Finance Corporation, Washington, DC.

Lal, D. (1974), 'Methods of project analysis: a review', World Bank Staff Occasional Papers 16, World Bank, Washington, DC.

Layard, R. (1980), 'On the use of distributional weights in social cost–benefit analysis', *Journal of Political Economy*, **88**, 1041–7.

Little, I.M.D. and Mirrlees, J.A. (1974), *Project Appraisal and Planning for Developing Countries*, London: Heinemann.

Londero, E. (1996a), 'Reflections on estimating distributional effects', in Kirkpatrick, C and Weiss, J (eds), *Cost–Benefit Analysis and Project Appraisal in Developing Countries*, Cheltenham, UK and Brookfield, USA: Edward Elgar, pp. 54–74.

Londero, E. (1996b), *Benefits and Beneficiaries: An Introduction to Estimating Distributional Effects in Cost–Benefit Analysis*, Washington, DC: Inter-American Development Bank.

Mayeres, I. (2001), 'Equity and transport policy reform', Discussion Paper, Center for Economic Studies, Brussels, Belgium.

Parry, I. (2004), 'Are emissions permits regressive?', *Journal of Environmental Economics and Management*, **47**, 364–87.

Parry, I., Sigman, H., Walls, M. and Williams, R. (2005). 'The incidence of pollution control policies', Discussion Paper, Resources for the Future, Washington, DC, June.

Pearce, D. (2003), Conceptual framework for analyzing the distributive impacts of environmental policies's paper prepared for the OCED Environment Directorate Workshop on the Distribution of Benefits and Costs of Environmental Policies, Paris.

Pearce, D., Atkinson, R. and Mourato, S. (2006), *Cost–Benefit Analysis and the Environment: Recent Developments*, Paris: OECD.

Potts, D. (1999), 'Forget the weights, who gets the benefits? How to bring a poverty focus to the economic analysis of projects', *Journal of International Development*, **11**, 581–95.

Rawls, J. (1971), *A Theory of Justice*, Cambridge, MA: Harvard University Press.

Squire, L. and van der Tak, H. (1975), *Economic Analysis of Projects*, Baltimore, MD: Johns Hopkins University Press.

UNIDO (1972), *Guidelines for Project Evaluation*, New York: United Nations Industrial Development Organization.

Yitzhaki, S. (2003), 'Cost–benefit analysis and distributional consequences of government projects', *National Tax Journal*, **56**, 319–25.

7 Cost–benefit analysis applied to labour market programmes
Michele Campolieti and Morley Gunderson

1 Introduction

The evaluation of labour market programmes has been a 'growth industry' in recent years.[1] This has been especially the case with respect to government-supported training programmes for unemployed or disadvantaged workers, but also for programmes such as wage subsidies, vocational rehabilitation, and work requirements under welfare. This literature has also been a 'growth industry' in the application of econometric techniques in various areas: sample-selection bias correction procedures; instrumental variable procedures; propensity score and other matching techniques; difference-in-difference estimates; longitudinal or panel data analysis; and hazard estimates of duration analysis. As detailed subsequently, these procedures have generally been used to obtain *causal* estimates of the *incremental* impact or benefit of a particular labour market programme. While the estimates of such incremental benefits have involved sophisticated procedures, it generally stops there, without it being incorporated into a more a more full-blown cost–benefit evaluation.

Cost–benefit evaluation as applied to labour market programmes has the same advantages as cost–benefit evaluation applied to other areas. As indicated subsequently, it facilitates comparisons across different programmes by evaluating them by a common metric – the dollar costs and benefits. It facilitates decisions as to whether programmes should be discontinued or contracted or expanded, depending upon whether they meet the cost–benefit test, or whether they can be justified on other grounds (for example, equity or distributional grounds). Cost–benefit analysis provides a template for ensuring or cataloguing that all costs and benefits are considered in an evaluation, and to quantify the intangibles where feasible. It explicitly sets out the assumptions and components that are used in the analysis and shows how the results can be sensitive to such assumptions; in effect, it puts 'all cards on the table'. In evaluating labour market programmes especially, it enables us to incorporate important concepts such as opportunity cost, time cost, the value of leisure, willingness to pay, discounting, deflating, and externalities or social benefits. And it emphasizes important distinctions such as between transfer costs and real resource costs.

161

As with cost–benefit evaluation in general, its application in the evaluation of labour market programmes can be fraught with hazards and misuse – perhaps unintentionally given the complexities that can be involved, or perhaps intentionally to support particular agendas. As detailed subsequently, examples include double counting of benefits as when pure transfer benefits are not also included as a cost, and the inappropriate inclusion of multiplier effects. As well, there is a danger that simply because the results of an evaluation are quantified, they will be regarded as sacrosanct, without recognizing that the analysis is only as good as the data and methodology – 'garbage in, garbage out'.

With cost–benefit analysis, however, the calculations and assumptions are (or at least should be) explicitly laid out, so it is possible to detect such misuse and to illustrate how the results would change if alternative procedures were used. Even with its potential problems, cost–benefit analysis must be judged relative to its alternatives – and such alternatives are more likely to involve subjective judgements that are not explicitly set out. To modify Winston Churchill's dictum that democracy is the worst possible system – except for all others: cost–benefit analysis may be the worst of all evaluation methods, except for all others.

In the labour market area, programme evaluation often involves multiple lines of evidence. Such multiple lines often include:

- econometric evaluation of incremental programme impacts, although rarely with those incremental impacts forming the benefit component of a formal cost–benefit evaluation;
- focus groups;
- key informant interviews;
- case studies; and
- surveys, often assessing the attitudes and perceptions of programme participants and programme administrators.

If the data that are used in the econometric evaluation are adequate to enable estimation of causal incremental impacts, then the econometric evaluation is generally regarded as the most important aspect of the multiple lines of evidence. The more qualitative information is generally regarded as supplementary, or used if the econometric evaluation is considered weak. Hence, the econometric evaluation of incremental impacts forms a key aspect of the evaluation of labour market programmes, and those issues will receive particular attention in this study.

The purpose of this chapter is to outline how cost–benefit analysis is used in the evaluation of labour market programmes. The analysis begins with a discussion of the benefit side, dealing with a range of issues: typical outcome or benefit measures; econometric procedures for estimating causal incremental impacts; the counterfactual and the importance of comparison groups; intermediate benefits linked to ultimate benefits; non-tangible benefits; external spillovers and social benefits; real and transfer benefits and benefits to whom; incorporating distributional issues; and multiplier and community effects. The analysis then shifts to the cost side, dealing with a range of issues: direct and opportunity cost; the valuation of leisure; real resource and transfer costs; and cost shifting. Issues associated with indexing and discounting are then discussed, followed by the techniques for doing the cost–benefit calculations once the costs and benefits are enumerated. The chapter concludes with examples of the application of cost–benefit evaluation to labour market programmes that illustrate the various issues.

At the outset, it should be emphasized that the chapter deals with cost–benefit analysis and not cost-effectiveness analysis. The latter, which is also done in the evaluation of labour market programmes, deals with the most cost-effective way of achieving certain targets that are quantified in physical rather than monetary units. The target, for example, could be obtaining employment for individuals, or having them leave welfare.

2   Estimating benefits

Typical outcome or benefit measures
The outcomes that are typically used as benefit measures in the evaluation of labour market programmes are invariably measures of wages, earnings (wages times hours worked) and/or employment. Ideally, they would be measures of total compensation to also include fringe benefits. Total compensation represents the additional output to society from the programme as reflected by what employers are willing and able to pay for that additional output. Wages and earnings are gross of taxes – the appropriate measure since this reflects what employers are willing to pay and hence the value they place on the productivity of the labour (Commonwealth of Australia 2006b, p. 39). In a competitive economy, wages reflect the social value of output produced by labour.

Intangibles
Intangible outputs that cannot generally be measured or assigned a dollar metric are not included as part of the formal cost–benefit analysis of labour market programmes. These are often obtained from focus groups, key informant interviews, case studies and surveys. They include such factors as confidence, self-esteem, reliability and enhanced skills (HRDC 1999, p. 2). The intangible benefits can be especially important to document for

programmes that have such benefits as intermediate outcomes as part of their mandate. Sometimes they can be regarded as ends in themselves, but more often as intermediate outcomes that would lead to improved ultimate outcomes pertaining to wages and employability.

In such cases, the intermediate outcomes could be connected to ultimate outcomes such as wages and employment through the results from external literature and dollar values attached. For example, a programme that reduced absenteeism by 5 days per year could have that outcome converted to a benefit figure by simply multiplying by the daily wage rate (which assumes that the absent days have no value to employees). Or a programme that resulted in a youth not dropping out of school could evaluate the additional schooling based on the evidence of the monetary value of completing high school. For intangibles that cannot be converted to a monetary figure (for example, self-esteem) any change in self-esteem would simply be reported as an intangible outcome.

External or spillover benefits

The literature on the returns to education is replete with estimates of external or spillover benefits to society in general where the recipients do not pay for the spillovers but nevertheless benefit from them. Examples include: reduced crime (Grogger 1998; Lochner and Moretti 2004); increased participation in voting, volunteering and civic activities (Acemoglu and Angrist 2000; Dee 2004; Milligan et al. 2004); and increased educational opportunities for children (Oreopoulos et al. 2006).

While such externalities or spillover benefits have been documented in the education area (and are relevant considerations in estimating the social returns to education), this has not been common in the area of labour market programmes such as training. Perhaps the labour market programmes are more geared to private returns such as getting a job, while more general education is conducive to generating such social spillovers.

Real versus transfer costs and benefits

Savings in transfer payments such as welfare or unemployment insurance or disability payments are often regarded as a benefit to governments or taxpayers from labour market programmes that result in recipients becoming employed. Such savings are often an explicit goal of certain labour market programmes and hence are legitimate outcomes to measure and to estimate.

They are, however, a transfer payment and involve a reduction in transfers from taxpayers to recipients; what taxpayers gain, the former recipients lose. They should not be added to any real benefits such as enhanced wages and employment that result in increases in real resources to society.

The same applies to benefits that may accrue to a particular level of government because the costs are simply shifted to another level of government. These are not social benefits in the sense of saving of real resource costs. Rather, they simply involve the transfer of costs in that what one party gains, another loses.

Distributional issues

As is common in cost–benefit evaluations, distributional issues in the evaluation of labour market programmes are usually dealt with separately from the efficiency issues associated with estimating incremental net benefits of a programme. The analysis is often done separately for different groups with different degrees of disadvantage or vulnerability. Comparisons of net benefits are then made across the different groups, with the notion that the programmes may be viable for the more disadvantaged groups even though they do have as large net benefits (or even positive net benefits) when compared to more advantaged groups.

Distributional issues could be incorporated more formally by explicitly weighting the benefits more heavily for the more disadvantaged groups (Brent 1984, 1991). Weights could be based, for example, on the progressive income tax rates, which implicitly reveal that society puts more weight on a dollar to a low-income person than to a high-income person by taxing the low-income person at a lower rate. Or weights could be based on the implicit weights from past projects which were undertaken by governments to assist disadvantaged groups even though they yielded lower net benefits than projects for more advantaged groups. Such explicit weighting is not common in the evaluation of labour market programmes. Rather, the distributional issues are discussed separately, if raised at all.

Costs and benefits to whom

The previous discussion highlighted the importance of keeping track of the costs and benefits *to whom*. A reduction in welfare payments is a benefit to taxpayers but a cost or lost benefit to former recipients. An increase in taxes paid by recipients who now have a job is a benefit to other citizens, but a cost to those who now pay taxes.

These may be legitimate factors to keep track of so as to ascertain the costs and benefits to whom. But they do not directly contribute to the net social benefits to society since they involve largely offsetting costs and benefits (see Table 7.1, below).

Multiplier effects

Usually as an advocacy position to make a programme look more favourable, some evaluations of labour market programmes multiply the benefits by some multiple to account for the fact that the additional earnings from the recipients generate additional jobs as the earnings get spent. This in turn generates additional earnings which further generate jobs when they get spent, and so forth.

The inclusion of such multiplier effects are generally inappropriate since they assume that the funds used to pay for the programmes would not have alternative uses that would also generate multiplier effects throughout a community. But such multiplier effects would also occur from foregone expenditures and investments elsewhere, or from the tax reductions if the funds were not spent on any programmes.

3   Estimating causal incremental benefits

As indicated previously, the main advances in the evaluation of labour market programmes have been made in estimating the *causal incremental* benefits of a programme such as a training programme. Such causal estimates try to deal with two main problems that otherwise occur in evaluating such programmes. Selection bias occurs when programme participants are selected into the treatment group (for example, a training programme) on the basis of unobservable characteristics such as motivation or ability or organizational skills, and these characteristics also affect the outcome. The selection or creaming[2] can be done by programme administrators (for example, if they are paid on the basis of placements) or by the participants themselves or both. Endogeneity of the treatment occurs when the treatment (for example, the training) is a function of the expected outcome rather than an exogenous cause of the outcome. Much of the recent literature on evaluating the causal incremental benefits of a labour market intervention essentially deals with ways of controlling for such biases.

Education returns
The literature on estimating the returns to education has been very successful in controlling for selection bias and obtaining exogenous variation in education so as to estimate causal returns (Card 1999). Examples include using:

- IQ or test scores to control for ability bias (for example, Griliches 1977).
- Same-sex identical twins, one of whom obtains more education than the other (for example, Miller et al. 1995; Ashenfelter and Rouse 1998).
- Geographic proximity to an educational institution that facilitates acquiring more education (for example, Card 1995; Cameron and Taber 2004).

- Tuition changes that can influence education acquired (for example, Kane and Rouse 1995; Chen 2008).
- The Vietnam draft lottery that encouraged people to stay in school to defer military service (Angrist and Krueger 1994).
- Job opportunities in the local labour market that can affect schooling decisions (for example, Cameron and Taber 2004).
- Compulsory schooling laws that can compel some to acquire more education (for example, Angrist and Krueger 1991; Oreopoulos 2006a, 2006b).

Unfortunately in the evaluation of labour market programmes, such 'natural experiments' that give rise to (arguably) exogenous variation in education or ways of controlling for selection bias, are not readily available. For labour market programmes such as training, information is not available on measures such as IQ, or identical twins, or training tuition, or draft lotteries, or compulsory training ages, or additions or subtractions to years of training. The amount of training acquired could be affected by distance from a training centre or by local labour market conditions, but these also reflect other confounding influences.

As such, the literature on evaluating the incremental benefits of labour market programmes such as training has tended to rely on other procedures to control for selection bias and the possible endogeneity of the intervention such as training.

Experimental designs
Experimental designs rely on the random assignment[3] of individuals to a treatment group (for example, training) and a control or comparison group (that is, no training). This approach is preferred because there are fewer problems (for example, internal validity or sample selection or endogeneity) with this sort of research design when estimating causal incremental effects of a programme. With random assignment, simple differences in mean outcomes yield an estimate of the *causal* effect of the *treatment* or labour market initiative. In most cases there is no need to use regression or other analysis to include controls for observable covariates when estimating the impact of a treatment.

However, if the experiment becomes 'contaminated' so that assignment is not truly random or there is some crossover, this might not be the case. This could occur, for example, if the easiest or most difficult cases become assigned to the treatment group, or if recipients are able to get reallocated across the programmes. Random assignment experiments can also be very expensive and take considerable time to be conducted and the results to emerge. As well, they can give rise to concerns over fairness since some groups receive a treatment and others do not (albeit they are *ex ante* fair as long as the assignment is truly random, even though they may not be *ex post* fair).

Quasi-experimental methods

Quasi-experimental research designs refer to situations in which there might not necessarily be an experiment with random assignment, but there has been some change in legislation or policy that would be similar in spirit to an experiment in that it creates a treatment group, which is affected by the policy, and a comparison group, which is unaffected by the policy. There are a large number of alternative quasi-experimental designs, which are summarized in detail in Cook and Campbell (1979). Our discussion will focus on two approaches which have found many applications in economics: regression discontinuity and difference-in-differences. Both of these cases rely on a treatment and comparison group as well as data before and after an intervention.

The regression discontinuity design is based on the following structure. Suppose that individuals can be classified according to a score with a specified cut-off point. Individuals above the cut-off receive a treatment, while those below the cut-off do not. In the simplest case, if assignment to the programme had an effect on outcomes (for example, wages) then there would be a discontinuity in the plot of wages against the score at the discontinuity point. Imbens and Lemieux (2008) provide a discussion of the recent developments in the economics literature and also provide a practical guide for researchers applying this methodology. Imbens and Lemieux (2008), and Cook (2008) also provide brief reviews of recent applications in economics.

Black et al. (2003) use a variant of the regression discontinuity approach to evaluate a labour market programme in Kentucky where job search assistance and training are provided to unemployed clients. Their expected duration of unemployment is first estimated, and then transformed into a score. They are then allocated into the programme on the basis of the score in descending order of their expected unemployment duration. The allocation is stopped once the 'treatment' slots are allocated. Those who were marginally in the programme (treatment group) are then compared to those who marginally missed out on being in the programme (control groups). This research design is referred to as a 'tie-breaker experiment'.

Another popular non-experimental approach to obtaining estimates of the impact of programme interventions is the difference-in-difference approach (Meyer 1995). The difference-in-difference methodology makes use of a treatment and comparison group and has observations on both groups before and after the intervention administered to the treatment group. While it is possible to also estimate the effect of an intervention without a comparison group or without pre-intervention data, the advantage of the difference-in-difference approach is that it can reduce some of the threats to internal validity that will be present with those alternative approaches (ibid.).

The key identification assumption underlying the difference-in-difference methodology is that the time trend in the comparison group is an adequate proxy for the time trend that would have been present in the treatment group had there been no intervention (Athey and Imbens 2004). This means that the identification of the treatment effect in any difference-in-difference analysis will depend on the appropriateness of the comparison group for the treatment group. In order to ensure a proper comparison group there are a number of different approaches that could be taken. Dean and Dolan (1991a, 1991b) look at the effects of vocational rehabilitation on the labour market outcomes of participants in the programme and use dropouts from the programme as a comparison group.[4] Their rationale for this choice is that the participants and dropouts could be similar on the basis of observed characteristics or in the reasons they were enrolled in the programme. Another approach that has been used in the literature is to weight observations so as to make the treatment and comparison groups more similar (for example, Abadie and Gardeazabal 2003; Campolieti 2006). The weighting can ensure that groups are more similar because individuals from the comparison and treatment groups that are most similar can be attached higher weights, while individuals from the groups that are not similar could be attached lower weights.

Matching and inverse probability weighting
Matching procedures can also be used to estimate the effect of an intervention on outcomes. In this framework the outcomes of the treated group are compared with those from the matched comparison group. The individuals are matched on the basis of some observed characteristics. There are two variants to these procedures. The first matches individuals on the basis of some group of individual characteristics (for example, age, gender, educational attainment, and so on) (for example, Abadie and Imbens 2002). The second matches individuals on the basis of the propensity score or the conditional probability of receiving the intervention, where this probability is a function of observed individual characteristics. The propensity score approaches compute the treatment effect as the difference between the outcomes for the treated and a weighted average of matched individuals from the comparison group (Todd 2006). Todd discusses some of the alternative weighting schemes that could be used with these estimators. One of the main advantages of the matching estimators is that they do

not require specifying a functional form for the outcome equation, so they do not lead to that sort of misspecification bias (ibid.). Consequently, the incremental benefit of a programme is simply the difference in their mean outcomes (Heckman et al. 1998; O'Leary et al. 2001) between the treatment and suitably weighted comparison groups.

Inverse probability weighting is often used to deal with survey non-response and attrition (Robbins et al. 1995). In particular, the observed sample may not be a random sample of the population, so observations are weighted by the inverse probability of being sampled. This concept can also be applied to the estimation of treatment effects in the potential outcome framework that underlies matching estimators (Rubin 1974). In this case, the counterfactuals could be a non-random sample of the population. The inverse probability weighting can correct for the 'unrepresentativeness' by reweighting observations and make it possible to get consistent estimates of the treatment effect (Hogan and Lancaster 2004). Like the matching estimators, the treatment effect can then be computed as the difference in the outcomes between the treatment and comparison groups. Also, like the matching estimators they estimate a propensity score and use it to weight the observations.

Selection correction procedures
Corrections for selection bias can be done through the Heckman (1979) two-step procedure. In the first stage, a probit equation is estimated on the probability of being in the select subsample of those who receive the labour market intervention or treatment (for example, training). This is then used to construct a sample-selection correction term (the inverse Mill's ratio) which is included in the second-stage outcome equation (for example, wages, employment) along with a measure of the treatment. One issue that frequently arises in applications using this approach is the identification of the model. While the model is nominally identified because of its functional form, many researchers have also tended to have exclusion restrictions on the selection and outcome equations in the model. However, it is sometimes difficult to find these exclusion restrictions because variables that influence the selection process often influence the outcome of interest. Consequently, many researchers have relied on using polynomials of different variables to generate the exclusion restrictions to assist with the identification of the model (for example, among others, Mroz 1987).

Summary of estimating causal incremental benefits
Clearly there are various methodologies for estimating the causal incremental benefits of a labour market programme to provide the benefit component for a cost–benefit evaluation. Most involve non-experimental

ways of approximating a random assignment experiment so as to control for any selection bias and endogeneity of the programme intervention.

We should note that these procedures generally involve different ways of estimating treatment effects (that is, training). For example, the propensity score and inverse probability weighting approaches differ in how they weight observations from the treatment and comparison groups, while the difference-in-difference estimators do not necessarily weight observations differently. Since these estimators all differ in how they approach the estimation of the treatment effect there can be differences in the size of the estimates they produce. However, the differences in the magnitude of the estimates (if any) will generally depend on the data that are being analysed. As such, it is not possible, for example, to rank the expected incremental benefits that will result from the different procedures such as random assignment, or regression discontinuity, or difference-in-difference estimates with a comparison group, or pre–post treatment differences without a comparison group, or Heckman selection-correction procedures, or propensity score matching estimates (with its variants). All that can be said is that true random assignment should give the best estimates of a true causal incremental impact of a programme such as training, and that the other procedures approach that gold standard to the extent that they approximate random assignment.

4 Estimating costs, indexing and discounting

Labour market programmes typically involve a variety of costs: costs of personnel associated with providing the intervention such as counselling or training; capital cost for such factors as buildings and equipment; wastage of material used in training (less the value of output produced); an imputed value of the time of any volunteers since such time involves a use of resources with an opportunity cost; and the opportunity cost of the time of participants while receiving the intervention. The last may be very low or non-existent if, for example, they otherwise would be unemployed.

As is the case with benefits, care must be taken to distinguish between transfer costs where what one party gains and another loses, and real resource costs which involve the using up of real resources that therefore are not available for other uses. Transfer costs are relevant for calculating the costs and benefits to different parties (for example, programme participants or the rest of society) but they are not relevant for calculating the total social costs and benefits because they are offsetting.

If they do not already have a market value, the market value of the resources used for the activity should be used to impute a cost. This would be the case, for example, if there were wastage of output as a result of training programme participants or if supervisors spent time providing on-the-job training in which case their market wage could be used to impute the cost of their time.

The loss of leisure time while participants are in the programme or employed afterwards could also be imputed and treated as a cost. Such imputations have led to valuations of leisure at around 40 per cent of wages (Greenberg 1992, 1997; HRDC 1999, p. 8). As a practical matter this is generally not done in the evaluation of labour market programmes since the value of 'leisure' is generally not regarded as substantial for persons who are often otherwise unemployed. The purpose of labour market programmes is to enhance employment and wages; forgoing leisure is regarded more as giving up being unemployed.

As with all cost–benefit analysis, the appropriate concept of cost is marginal costs to compare with the marginal or incremental benefits of the programme. Fixed or sunk costs are not relevant since they will be incurred irrespective of the number of participants in the programme. Average costs are typically greater than marginal cost because some fixed costs do not vary with the number of participants. As such, the use of average cost would likely overstate costs and hence provide a conservative estimate of the net benefits of the programme.

Costs and benefits should be converted to real terms to adjust for inflation. Future costs and benefits are obviously discounted although there is considerable debate over the appropriate discount rate that should be used. Brent (1989), for example, highlights that rates ranging from 3–25 per cent have been justified in the literature, and he estimates an implied rate of around 70 per cent based on the actions of a government agency. As indicated by Boardman et al. (2001, pp. 249–50), the rates used in practice and endorsed by various agencies typically range from 0–10 per cent. They suggest rates between 1 and 7 per cent as appropriate and that 'using 4 percent would not be unreasonable' (p. 250). Sensitivity analysis to a range of rates is obviously appropriate.

5   Illustrative presentation format

Many of the issues discussed previously can be illustrated in Table 7.1 based on the stylized suggested format as set out in Boardman et al. (2001, p. 275) and largely followed in McConnell and Glazerman (2001, p. xvi).

Costs and benefits are illustrated for programme participants and the rest of society, with total social costs and benefits being the sum of the two. Benefits in the form of increased total compensation go to programme participants and hence are also a benefit to society. The output produced while in the programme and reduced crime are benefits to the rest of society and therefore also to total society. Reduced transfers to, and increased taxes from, participants are a benefit to the rest of society who

Table 7.1 Stylized presentation of costs and benefits

Costs and benefits	Programme participants (A)	Rest of Society (B)	Total society (C = A + B)
Benefits from increased output			
Increased gross earnings and fringe benefits	+	0	+
Output produced while in programme	0	+	+
Spillover benefits from reduced crime	0	+	+
Reduced transfers to participants	–	+	0
Increased taxes paid by participants	–	+	0
Costs of programme			
Cost of counsellors and trainers	0	–	–
Operating cost	0	–	–
Capital and building costs, amortized	0	–	–
Imputed value of volunteer labour	0	–	–
Wastage of output during training	0	–	–
Increased childcare costs	–	0	–
Allowances received by programme participants	+	–	0

otherwise have to pay those transfers and forgo the taxes, but they are an equivalent loss to programme participants and hence net out as no effect on total society. Costs of counsellors and trainers, operating expenditures, amortized capital costs and the imputed cost of volunteer labour are all real resource costs used up in the programme and hence are a component of total social costs. Wastage of output and material during training is a cost to the rest of society and hence a component of total cost. Increased childcare expenses are a cost to programme participants and hence a component of total cost. Allowances received by programme participants are a transfer benefit to them but an equivalent cost to the rest of society and hence net out as there is no effect on total society.

6   Some detailed applications

The effect of vocational rehabilitation on disability insurance beneficiaries
Campolieti et al. (2007) estimate the effect of vocational rehabilitation (VR) on the labour market outcomes of disability insurance beneficiaries using administrative data from Canada. They did not have a natural comparison group for the programme participants so they drew their comparison group from the administrative records on disability beneficiaries who

were reassessed for the ability to return to the labour market or may have returned to the labour market. Campolieti et al. (2007) estimate the effect of VR with both propensity score matching estimators as well as inverse probability weighting. They conduct their analysis separately by gender because there can be differences in the attachment to the labour market by gender.

Their estimates indicate that VR increases the probability of leaving the disability rolls and finding employment. The magnitude of the incremental benefits vary somewhat by the type of estimating procedure but generalizations cannot be made as to whether one procedure will produce a larger or smaller estimate than any other procedure. The estimates also indicate that VR has a bigger impact on the labour market outcomes of women (that is, their probability of leaving the disability rolls and finding employment). Their analysis also reveals some of the differences that can occur with the inverse probability and matching approaches. Campolieti et al. found that the inverse probability weighting approach produced larger treatment effects for women and smaller treatment effects for men, relative to the treatment effects obtained with the propensity score matching estimates. Consequently, they found that the gender differences in the impact of VR between women and men were much larger when the inverse probability weighting approach was used.

Campolieti et al. also look at the potential net benefits of VR by looking at the benefit savings that would accrue to the programme after individuals leave the disability rolls. They incorporated the much higher probability that the treatment group (50 percentage points) leaves the disability rolls in their calculations by computing an expected net benefit. They found in their base case (a discount rate of 3.9 per cent) that the expected net benefits for the treatment group exceeded those of the comparison group by about $80,000 per person. In spite of the fact that the VR programme had a larger impact on the probability of leaving the disability roles for women than for men, the benefit savings were larger for men than women. This reflects the larger benefit payments that men receive compared to women because of higher pre-disability earnings. They also conduct a sensitivity analysis (discount rate of 1.9 per cent for the lower bound and 5.9 per cent for the upper bound). The smaller discount rate increased the size of the difference in the net benefits between the treatment and comparison groups to about $100,000 per person. The larger discount rate narrows the difference of the net benefits between the two groups to about $60,000 per person. The sensitivity analysis clearly indicates the potential impact of the selection of the discount rate on the discounted net benefits. They also confirm that there could be substantial cost savings generated by VR programmes.

The lower benefit savings for women compared to men gives rise to an interesting methodological issue in the evaluation of training or other labour market programmes. As indicated, the lower benefit savings for women occurred because they tended to receive lower disability payments because of their generally lower wages prior to their disability. To the extent that the lower wages for women arise in part because of discrimination, then their lower disability payments will also reflect discrimination. In theory, it is possible to adjust for this in the cost–benefit evaluation by adjusting female wages to a non-discriminatory norm (for example, wages of an otherwise comparable male). In practice, this will be made difficult by the fact that there is not a consensus as to the precise extent to which female wages (or the wages of any potentially discriminated against group) reflect discrimination. As well, such adjustments would have to be made to all wages (indeed all prices) that could be distorted by such factors as unions or wage fixing laws or wage setting by monopsonistic employers. To our knowledge, this is not done in any of the cost–benefit evaluations of labour market programmes.

As a practical matter it is likely best to estimate the costs and benefits separately for different groups and then comment on how the different net benefits may reflect discrimination or other distorted market prices. Certainly this should be done whether or not any refinements are also made to apply distributional weights to groups that may be subject to discrimination, or attempts are made to correct for distortions in market wages that may reflect discrimination (or any other source of distortion for any prices).

Illustrative application through Job Corps evaluations
Many of the issues discussed previously can also be illustrated by the cost–benefit evaluations that have been done on the Job Corps (JC) programme – the largest training programme for disadvantaged youths in the US.

Job Corps participants and control group   In the JC analysis described in McConnell and Glazerman (2001), and continuing an earlier evaluation by Long et al. (1991), eligible youths were randomly assigned to a treatment or programme group (who could enrol in JC) or a control group (who could not enrol). The control group were allowed to enrol in other programmes just as JC participants would have been allowed to enrol in them if they had not taken JC. As such, the impact estimates are of the incremental impact of JC relative to the counterfactual of no JC. The evaluators carefully monitored the random assignment to ensure it did not become contaminated. Of those who could enrol in the programme, 73 per cent did enrol and 27 per cent did not, the latter being 'no shows', (McConnell and Glazerman 2001, p. 9). In the subsequent calculations, the benefits are calculated only for those who enrolled and hence received the treatment (p. 13) although they indicate that the results are similar if they were based on all eligible applicants to also include the 'no shows' (p. 25).

Benefits   Three categories of benefits were calculated:

- benefits of increased output from the additional productivity of JC recipients as measured by their increased earnings and fringe benefits in the post-programme period, as well as the value of any output they produced during the training period;
- benefits from increased taxes and the reduced use of other support programmes; and
- benefits from reduced crime.

As in the format set out in Boardman et al. (2001, p. 275) and outlined in Table 7.1, McConnell and Glazerman calculated benefits separately for participants and the rest of society and were careful to distinguish transfer benefits, treating them as a positive benefit to the rest of society that benefited by the increased taxes and reduced transfer payments, but subtracting those benefits from the participants since they paid the taxes and no longer received the transfer payments. They then summed the benefits to participants and the rest of society to get total social benefits. The incremental programme benefits were simply the differences in average outcomes between programme and control group members, as is appropriate for true random assignment.

They used the difference in average outcomes even if that difference was not statistically different from zero on the grounds that it is still an unbiased estimate of the programme impact and is therefore preferable to using the alternative of zero (p. 25). This could be a contentious decision since an alternative perspective could have assigned zero to an insignificant coefficient, based on the principle of hypothesis testing that one gives the benefit of the doubt to the null hypothesis so that insignificantly different from zero should be treated as zero. In that vein it may be appropriate to perform sensitivity analysis by treating insignificant coefficients as zero as well as their estimated value. Alternatively, one could take different estimates (some of which are statistically significant and others that are not) and take a weighted average with the weights given by the standard errors (Leamer 1978, p. 76). This weighted or pooled estimate would give the most weight to the more precisely estimated point estimates and less weight to the imprecise estimates. With this pooled estimate the insignificant estimates are not treated as zero, they are just weighted less.

All impacts were valued at market prices. For example, the additional output of participants is valued at their total compensation (wages plus fringe benefits) since this reflects what employers are willing and able to pay for that output. Where market prices are not available for a cost or benefit, McConnell and Glazerman used the market value of the resources used for the activity associated with the benefit or cost. For example, the benefits from a reduction in the use of the criminal justice system were based on the value of the resources used for investigations, bookings and arrest, prosecutions and trials and sanctions based on information from other studies (p. 26).

The incremental earnings benefits were estimated from self-reported survey data for treatment and control group participants conducted 12, 30 and 48 months after the start of the intervention.

With respect to the predicted longevity or decay of the benefits, they assumed that if the benefits did not decline in the (approximately) three-year observation window after they left the programme, then the benefits (appropriately discounted) would continue for the rest of their working lives. But if the benefits declined during the post-programme observation window, then they were truncated at the end of that three-year period.

Costs   Costs included programme operating cost and staff cost (counselling, training) as well as capital cost for land, buildings, furniture and equipment. Costs were also imputed for donations of food, medical supplies and volunteer time, since these represent a use of resources with an opportunity cost. Student pay, food and clothing were treated as a transfer cost from the rest of society to participants because they were regarded as having an intrinsic value to recipients, regardless of their value as an investment; it would be the equivalent of giving them a cash transfer. As such, they were treated as a cost to the rest of society but an equivalent benefit to participants so they offset each other in the calculation of total social costs. They did not include an imputed value for the cost of the leisure forgone (for example, as outlined by Greenberg 1997) while participants were in the programme or employed afterwards. For such unemployed, disadvantaged youths the value of 'leisure' was not regarded as substantial. They imputed a value for the additional costs associated with the additional childcare required while participants were training or working subsequently. The cost figures were obtained mainly from financial reporting forms.

While they were aware that marginal costs would be the appropriate measure, they used average costs because marginal costs were not available and because the difference would not be that great in the long run when fixed costs could be amortized over a longer period (p. 27). As well, since average costs are typically greater than marginal cost because some fixed costs do not vary with the number of trainees, this means that their cost figures may be at the higher end and hence would yield a conservative estimate of the impact of JC.

Indexing and discounting
All costs and benefits were converted to real terms using a GDP price index on the grounds that it includes all goods and services and hence is appropriate for the many different types of costs and benefits of the programme (p. 28).

McConnell and Glazerman cite much of the considerable literature that deals with the appropriate discount rate to use to calculate the net present value of benefits and costs. They use a discount rate of 4 per cent to approximate the real rate of return on 30-year Treasury bonds and they cite a number of studies that recommend its use (p. 29) including Hartman (1990) and Lyon (1990). Rationales for that rate are that it is readily available, it reflects the opportunity cost of government borrowing and it generally gives similar results to other conceptually appropriate measures. It is also a rate recommended by both the Congressional Budget Office and the General Accounting Office. McConnell and Glazerman appropriately do sensitivity analysis to see how their results differ by alternative rates and find that their results are somewhat sensitive since the benefits are long term; however, benefits exceed costs for discounts rate of 10.5 per cent or less.

They also test the sensitivity of their results to other assumptions used in their analysis. For example, they estimated upper and lower bounds of the estimated programme impact by using end-points of the confidence intervals around those estimates. In general, their results were robust across alternative assumptions.

Results   McConnell and Glazerman found that in the first year after the programme, the earnings of participants were lower than those of the control group, but in the next two years they were considerably higher. As such, when projected over the remaining work life of participants the incremental earnings benefits of the programme were substantial. The higher earnings were a result of both a higher probability of being employed and higher wages and fringe benefits if employed. Overall, they estimate that JC yielded incremental benefits to society of about $31,000 ($27,300 from increased earnings) compared to costs of about $14,000, yielding net benefits to *society* of about $17,000 or a benefit/cost ratio of slightly over 2. The net benefits to *participants* were about $20,000, mainly from their increased earnings net of taxes and the fact that they did not pay programme costs. While the *rest of society* pays for the programme cost of about $16,500, most of this is offset by increased taxes paid by participants as well as reductions in other transfer costs, so that the net cost to society is only about $3,200 per participant.

They tested the sensitivity of their results to alternative assumptions, especially those pertaining to the projected longevity of the benefits after the observation period for which they had data, and concluded that for reasonable alternative assumptions, the results were fairly robust. They indicated, however, that more accurate estimates of the future benefits could be obtained in future years when administrative data on earnings become available.

In a subsequent study of that programme using the *administrative* data that ultimately became available, Schochet et al. (2003) indeed found that the long-term earnings gains did not persist. The administrative data were based on employer reports of earnings to the Internal Revenue Service for Social Security purposes and on wage records reported to Unemployment Insurance offices, and is regarded as much more accurate than the self-reported survey data of the earlier study. Schochet et al. found that estimated earnings impacts were negative in the first and second years after the programme, positive and statistically significant in the third and fourth years post-programme, and essentially zero in years 5–7 after the programme. Overall, they find 'no beneficial earnings impacts that are statistically significant for any subgroup' (p. xvi). As such, they conclude that 'The revised benefit–cost estimates suggest that the benefits to society of Job Corps are smaller than the substantial programme cost' (p. xvi). For *programme participants*, however, they still find that benefits exceed costs, and since these are otherwise disadvantaged groups, this finding has important distributional implications. They also found that there was some heterogeneity in the benefits with older youths benefiting more than younger youths, suggesting that reallocation of resources may be merited.

7   Concluding observations

Clearly, cost–benefit evaluations of labour market programmes are feasible and could provide the information that could facilitate decision making with respect to what programmes to expand or contract, and where to reallocate resources within programmes. Even if the calculations were not used for these purposes, the very process of doing the cost–benefit evaluation would highlight important factors to consider in an evaluation. These include: opportunity cost and forgone income, equity and distributional considerations, willingness to pay, discounting, deflating, externalities, and the importance of distinctions between transfer costs and real resource costs.

Care has to be taken, however, in the use of cost–benefit analysis when applied to labour market programmes since there is a danger that because an item is quantified it may be given a degree of sanctity that is not merited by the nature of the data and the procedures especially for estimating the incremental benefits of the programme. Rounding a wrong number to 10 decimal points does not make it a more accurate number even though it may foster the appearance of accuracy.

Nevertheless, great strides have been made in the methodologies for evaluating the incremental causal benefits of many labour market programmes. Taking the next step of more often incorporating this information into more formal cost–benefit calculations is likely itself to yield benefits that exceed the costs.

Notes

1. Summaries of that literature include: Barnow (1987, 2000), OECD (1993, Chapter 2), Heckman et al. (1999), Lalonde (1995), Leigh (1995), Riddell (1995), Friedlander et al. (1997), Stromsdorfer (1987), Barnow and King (2000), and Warburton and Warburton (2002).
2. Evidence of cream skimming is discussed in Heckman et al. (1994, 1999).
3. Random assignment was used, for example, in Orr et al. (1996) for the JTPA program in the US, and McConnell and Glazerman (2001) and Schochet et al. (2003) for the Jobs Corp in the US.
4. Other examples of internal comparison groups include Hollenbeck and Huang (2003) who used applicants to the state's employment service as a comparison group for a treatment group that received training, and Holzer et al. (1993) who used firms that applied for funds for training but did not receive them as a comparison group for firms that applied for and received funds for training.

Bibliography

Abadie, Alberto and Guido Imbens (2002), 'Simple and bias-corrected matching estimators for average treatment effects', NBER Technical Working Paper, Cambridge, MA.

Abadie, Alberto and Javier Gardeazabal (2003), 'The economic costs of conflict: a case study of the Basque country', *American Economic Review*, **93**, 113–32.

Acemoglu, Daron and Joshua Angrist (2000), 'How large are human capital externalities? Evidence from compulsory schooling laws', *NBER Macroeconomics Annual 2000*, Cambridge, MA, 9–59.

Angrist, J. and A. Krueger (1991), 'Does compulsory school attendance affect schooling and earnings?', *Quarterly Journal of Economics*, **106**, 979–1014.

Angrist, J. and A. Krueger (1994), 'Why do World War II veterans earn more than non-veterans?', *Journal of Labour Economics*, **12**, 74–97.

Ashenfelter, Orley (1978), 'Estimating the effects of training programmes on earnings', *Review of Economics and Statistics*, **60** (1), 47–57.

Ashenfelter, Orley and David Card (1985), 'Using the longitudinal structure of earnings to estimate the effect of training programmes', *Review of Economics and Statistics*, **67**, 648–60.

Ashenfelter, Orley and Alan Krueger (1994), 'Estimates of the economic return to schooling from a new sample of twins', *American Economic Review*, **84** (December), 1157–73.

Ashenfelter, Orley and Cecilia Rouse (1998), 'Income, schooling and ability: evidence from a new sample of identical twins', *Quarterly Journal of Economics*, **113** (February), 253–84.

Athey, Susan and Guido Imbens (2004), 'Identification and inference in non-linear difference-in-difference models', unpublished manuscript, Berkeley, CA: University of California, Department of Economics.

Barnow, Burt S. (1987), 'The impact of CETA programs on earnings: a review of the literature', *Journal of Human Resources*, **22** (Spring), 157–93.

Barnow, Burt S. (2000), 'Exploring the relationship between performance management and programe impact: a case study of the job training partnership act', *Journal of Policy Analysis and Management*, **19** (Winter), 118–41.

Barnow, Burt S. and Christopher T. King (2000), *Improving the Odds: Increasing the Effectiveness of Publicly Funded Training*, Washington, DC: Urban Institute.

Black, Dan, Jeffrey Smith, Mark Berger and Brett Noel (2003), 'Is the threat of reemployment services more effective than the services themselves? Evidence from random assignment in the UI system', *American Economic Review*, **93**, 1313–27.

Boardman, Anthony, David Greenberg, Aidan Vining and David Weimer (2001), *Cost–Benefit Analysis: Concepts and Practice*, 2nd edn, Englewood Cliff, NJ: Prentice Hall.

Brent, Robert J. (1984), 'The use of distributional weights in cost–benefit analysis: a survey of schools', *Public Finance Quarterly*, **12** (April), 213–30.

Brent, Robert J. (1989), 'The Farmers Home Administration's social discount rate', *Applied Economics*, **21**, 1247–56.

Brent, Robert J. (1991), 'On the estimation technique to reveal government distributional weights', *Applied Economics*, **23**, 985–92.

Cameron, Stephen V. and Christopher Taber (2004), 'Estimation of educational borrowing constraints using returns to schooling', *Journal of Political Economy*, **112**, 132–82.

Campolieti, Michele (2006), 'Disability insurance denial rates and the incidence of hard-to-diagnose medical conditions', *Contributions to Economic Analysis and Policy*, **5** (1), Article 15, (23 pages).

Campolieti, Michele, Morley Gunderson and Jeffrey Smith (2007), 'The effect of vocational rehabilitation on the employment outcomes of disability insurance beneficiaries: new evidence from Canada', University of Toronto, Centre for Industrial Relations and Human Resources, Working Paper.

Card, David (1995), 'Using geographic variation in college proximity to estimate the return to schooling', in L. Christofides, K. Grant and R. Swidinsky (eds), *Aspects of Labour Market Behaviour: Essays in Honour of John Vanderkamp*, Toronto: University of Toronto Press, pp. 201–22.

Card, David (1999), 'The causal effect of education on earnings', in Orley Ashenfelter and David Card (eds), *Handbook of Labor Economics, Vol. 3A*, Amsterdam: Elsevier Science, pp. 1801–63.

Chen, S. (2008), 'Estimating the variance of wages in the presence of selection and unobservable heterogeneity', *Review of Economics and Statistics*, **90** (May), 275–89.

Cobb-Clark, Deborah A. and Thomas Crossley (2002), 'Econometrics for Summative Evaluations: An Introduction to Recent Developments', Australian National University: Centre for Economic Policy Research, Discussion Paper No. 454, December.

Commonwealth of Australia (2006a), *Introduction to Cost–Benefit Analysis and Alternative Evaluation Methodologies*, Canberra: Commonwealth of Australia, Department of Finance and Administration.

Commonwealth of Australia (2006b), *Handbook of Cost–Benefit Analysis*, Canberra: Commonwealth of Australia, Department of Finance and Administration.

Cook, Thomas D. (2008), '"Waiting for life to arrive": a history of the regression discontinuity design in psychology, statistics and economics', *Journal of Econometrics*, **142**, 636–54.

Cook, Thomas D. and Donald T. Campbell (1979), *Quasi-Experimentation: Design and Analysis Issues for Field Settings*. Boston, MA: Houghton Mifflin.

Dean, David H. and Robert C. Dolan (1991a), 'Fixed effects estimates of earnings impacts for the vocational rehabilitation program,' *Journal of Human Resources*, **26** (Spring), 380–91.

Dean, David H. and Robert C. Dolan (1991b), 'Assessing the role of vocational rehabilitation in disability policy', *Journal of Policy Analysis and Management*, **10** (Fall), 568–87.

Dee, Thomas S. (2004), 'Are there civic returns to education?', *Journal of Public Economics*, **88** (August), 1697–720.

Friedlander, Daniel, David H. Greenberg and Philip K. Robins (1997), 'Evaluating government training programmes for the economically disadvantaged', *Journal of Economic Literature*, **35** (December), 1809–55.

Greenberg, David (1992), 'Conceptual issues in cost–benefit analysis of welfare-to-work programs,' *Contemporary Policy Issues*, **10** (October), 51–64.

Greenberg, David (1997), 'The leisure bias in cost–benefit analysis of employment and training programs', *Journal of Human Resources*, **32** (Spring), 413–39.

Griliches, Zvi (1977), 'Estimating the returns to schooling: some econometric problems', *Econometrica*, **45**, 1–22.

Grogger, Jeff (1998), 'Market wages and youth crime', *Journal of Labour Economics*, **16** (October), 756–91.

Hartman, Robert (1990), 'One thousand points of light seeking a number: a case study of CBO's search for a discount rate policy', *Journal of Environmental Economics and Management*, **18**, S3–S7.

Heckman, James (1979), 'Sample selection bias as a specification error', *Econometrica*, **47**, 153–61.

Heckman, James J., Rebecca L. Roselius and Jeffrey A. Smith (1994), 'US education and training policy: a re-evaluation of the underlying assumptions behind the "New Consensus"', in L.S. Soloman and A. Levenson (eds), *Labour Markets, Employment Policy and Job Creation*, Boulder, CO: Westview Press for the Milken Institute, pp. 83–121.

Heckman, James J., Hidehiko Ichimura, Jeffrey A. Smith and Petra Todd (1998), 'Characterizing selection bias using experimental data', *Econometrica*, **66** (September), 1017–98.

Heckman, James, Robert LaLonde and Jeffrey Smith (1999), 'The economics and econometrics of active labour market programs', in Orley Ashenfelter and David Card (eds), *Handbook of Labor Economics*, Vol. 3A, Amsterdam: North-Holland, pp. 1865–2097.

Hogan, Joseph W. and T. Lancaster (2004), 'Instrumental variables and inverse probability weighting for causal inference from longitudinal observational studies', *Statistical Methods in Medical Research*, **13**, 17–48.

Hollenbeck, Kevin M. and Wei-Jang Huang (2003), 'Net Impact and Benefit–Cost Estimates of the Workforce Development System in Washington State', Kalamazoo, MI: Upjohn Institute for Employment Research, Upjohn Institute Technical Report No. TR03-018, July.

Holzer, Harry, Richard Block, Marcus Cheatham and Jack Knott (1993), 'Are training subsidies for firms effective? The Michigan experience', *Industrial and Labor Relations Review*, **46** (July), 625–36.

HRDC (1998), *Quasi-Experimental Evaluation*, Ottawa: Human Resources Development Canada.

HRDC (1999), *Cost–Benefit Analysis of Labour Market Programmes*. Ottawa: Human Resources Development Canada.

Hui, Shek-wai and Jeffrey Smith (2002), *The Labour Market Impacts of Adult Education and Training in Canada*, Human Resources Development Canada.

Imbens, Guido W. and Thomas Lemieux (2008), 'Regression discontinuity designs: a guide to practice', *Journal of Econometrics*, **142**, 613–35.

Kane, Tom, and Cecilia Rouse (1995), 'Labour market returns to two-year and four-year college', *American Economic Review*, **85**, 600–614.

Kemper, Peter, David Long and Craig Thornton (1994), 'A benefit–cost analysis of the supported work experience', in R. Hollister, P. Kemper and R. Maynard (eds), *The National Supported Work Demonstration*, Madison, WI: University of Wisconsin Press, pp. 239–85.

LaLonde, Robert J. (1995), 'The promise of public sector sponsored training programs', *Journal of Economic Perspectives*, **9** (Spring), 149–68.

Leamer, Edward E. (1978), *Specification Searches: Ad Hoc Inference with Nonexperimental Data*, New York: John Wiley.

Leigh, Duane E. (1995), *Assisting Workers Displaced by Structural Change: An International Perspective*, Kalamazoo, MI: W.E. Upjohn Institute for Employment Research.

Lochner, Lance and Enrico Moretti (2004), 'The effect of education on crime: evidence from prison inmates, arrests and self-reports', *American Economic Review*, **94** (March), 155–89.

Long, David A., Charles D. Mallar and Craig V. D. Thornton (1991), 'Evaluating the benefits and costs of the Job Corps', *Journal of Policy Analysis and Management*, **1** (Autumn), 55–76.

Lynch, Lisa M. (1992), 'Private-sector training and the earnings of young workers', *American Economic Review*, **82** (March), 299–312.

Lyon, Randolph (1990), 'Federal discount rate policy, the shadow price of capital, and challenges for reforms', *Journal of Environmental Economics and Management*, **18**, S29–S50.

Magnum, S., G. Magnum and G. Hansen (1990), 'Assessing the returns to training', in L. Ferman, M. Hoyman, J. Cutcher-Gershefeld and R. Savoie (eds), *New Developments in Worker Training: A Legacy for the 1990s*, Madison, WI: Industrial Relations Research Association, pp. 55–90.

McConnell, Sheena and Steven Glazerman (2001), *National Job Corps Study: The Benefits and Costs of Job Corps*, Washington, DC: Mathematica Policy Research.

Meyer, Bruce D. (1995), 'Natural and quasi-experiments in economics', *Journal of Business and Economic Statistics*, **13**, 151–61.

Miller, Paul, Charles Mulvey and Nick Martin (1995), 'What do twins studies reveal about the economic returns to education? A comparison of Australian and U.S. findings', *American Economic Review*, **85**, 586–99.

Milligan, Kevin, Enrico Moretti and Philip Oreopoulos (2004), 'Does education improve citizenship? Evidence from the U.S. and the U.K.', *Journal of Public Economics*, **88**, 1667–95.

Moffitt, Robert (1991), 'Programme evaluation with non-experimental data', *Evaluation Review*, **15**, 291–314.

Mroz, Thomas (1987), 'The sensitivity of an empirical model of married women's hours of work to economic and statistical assumptions', *Econometrica*, **55**, 765–99.

Nicholson, Walter (2001), 'The Design of Summative Evaluations for the Employment Benefits and Support Measures (EBSM)', Human Resources Development Canada, September.

O'Leary, Christopher, Alena Nesporova and Alexander Samorodov (2001), *Manual on Evaluation of Labour Market Policies in Transition Economies*, Geneva: International Labour Office.

OECD (1993), *Employment Outlook*, Paris: Organisation for Economic Co-operation and Development.

Oreopoulos, Philip (2006a), 'The compelling effects of compulsory schooling: evidence from Canada', *Canadian Journal of Economics*, **39**, 22–52.

Oreopoulos, Philip (2006b), 'Estimating average and local average treatment effects of education when compulsory schooling laws really matter', *American Economic Review*, **96**, 152–75.

Oreopoulos, Philip, Marianne Page and Ann Stevens (2006), 'The intergenerational effects of compulsory schooling', *Journal of Labor Economics*, **24** (4), 729–60.

Orr, Larry, Howard Bloom, Stephen Bell, Fred Doolittle, Winston Lin and George Cave (1996), *Does Training for the Disadvantaged Work? Evidence from the National JTPA Study*, Washington, DC: Urban Institute Press.

Riddell, W. Craig (1995), 'Human capital formation in Canada: recent developments and policy responses', in Keith Banting and Charles Beach (eds), *Labour Market Polarization and Social Policy Reform*, Kingston: Queen's University School of Policy Studies, pp. 125–72.

Robbins, James P., Andrea Rotnitsky and Lue Ping Zhao (1995), 'Analysis of semiparametric regression models in the presence of missing data', *Journal of the American Statistical Association*, **90**, 106–21.

Rubin, Donald B. (1974), 'Estimating causal effects of treatments in randomized and non-randomized studies', *Journal of Educational Psychology*, **66**, 688–701.

Schochet, Peter, Sheena McConnell and John Burghardt (2003), *National Job Corps Study: Findings Using Administrative Earnings Records Data*, Princeton, NJ: Mathematica Policy Research.

Sianesi, Barbara (2004), 'An evaluation of the Swedish system of active labour market programs in the 1990s', *The Review of Economics and Statistics*, **86** (February), 133–55.

Stromsdorfer, Ernst (1987), 'Economic evaluation of the Comprehensive Employment and Training Act: an overview of recent findings and advances in evaluation methods', *Evaluation Review*, **11** (August), 387–94.

Thomas, Brinley, John Maxham and J.A.G. Jones (1969), 'A cost–benefit analysis of industrial training', *British Journal of Industrial Relations*, **7** (July), 231–64.

Todd, Petra E. (2006), 'Matching estimators', University of Pennsvlania, Department of Economics, unpublished manuscript.

Warburton, William P. and Rebecca N. Warburton (2002), *Measuring the Performance of Government Training Programs*. Toronto: CD Howe Institute Commentary, No. 165, June.

Woodbury, S. and R. Spiegelman (1987), 'Bonuses to workers and employers to reduce employment: randomized trials in Illinois', *American Economic Review*, **77**, 513–30.

8 Regulation and cost–benefit analysis
Franco Papandrea

1 Introduction

Regulation refers to rules, ordinances, orders, standards, conditions or principles promulgated by governments or delegated authorities to prescribe or proscribe the behaviour or conduct of private sector agents with the goal of promoting and enhancing the economic and social well-being of society. Regulations are generally binding instruments enforceable by law and breaches are typically subject to penalties. All levels of government (federal, state and local) as well as delegated non-government organisations, such as standard-setting bodies, and industry and professional associations engage in regulatory activities that affect a very wide range of economic and social pursuits.

All societies are governed by rules and conventions of behaviour that seek to promote the common good or public interest. The coverage of rules expands as societies become more complex and members engage in an increasing range of activities. But with increased complexity comes an increased risk that some regulations, although based on good intentions, will fail to deliver all or part of the sought-after benefits, and might even result in outcomes that worsen society's well-being. Faced with such a problem, scholars and legislators have been devoting considerable attention to the development of criteria and tools to help assess the desirability and efficiency of regulatory instruments.

Economists in particular were drawn to the study of regulatory issues in the period after the Second World War when governments in the Western developed world increasingly enacted interventionist economic policies in the pursuit of full employment and prevention of severe macroeconomic fluctuations such as those experienced in the pre-war period. In the postwar period many countries experienced rapid economic growth and prosperity, and regulation was partly credited for the success. But in the 1970s, when many industries in the Western developed world were unable to withstand the challenge of competition from producers in then developing countries, the policy focus shifted to free market principles and regulation was subjected to increasing scrutiny. A restructuring of economies and industries followed as more and more countries sought to dismantle their regulatory frameworks and deregulate their markets. As a result, the need for both existing and proposed regulations is being increasingly scrutinised and cost–benefit analysis (CBA) has became a key tool for regulatory policy evaluation.

Notwithstanding the greater scrutiny of regulatory proposals, regulation is affecting an increasing proportion of economic activities in most developed countries. Regulation, itself, is big business. According to some estimates, costs associated with federal regulation in the US in 2006 exceeded one trillion dollars (Crews, 2007), a figure almost as large as the total GDP of Canada and larger than Australia's GDP. While much regulation will undoubtedly produce benefits in excess of costs, some regulatory interventions do not sufficiently deliver the desired benefits. Costly regulatory mistakes are not unknown.

Better analysis of regulatory proposals might not only help avoid costly regulatory mistakes, but should also assist the development of more efficient instruments. Both the pervasiveness of regulation and the sheer magnitude of regulatory costs suggest that, with better evaluation and assessment of regulatory proposals, there would be ample scope for significant improvements in social welfare. In many countries, governments faced with concerns about increasing regulatory burdens on economic activities have established formal regulatory oversight procedures and mechanisms that include mandatory evaluation of the costs and benefits of regulatory proposals. The growing interest in reducing the cost of regulation is also evident in international agencies such as the Organisation for Economic Co-operation and Development (OECD) and the World Bank, which have been promoting the adoption of better regulatory practices.

2   Economic rationale for regulation

Goods and services produced by a society are generally allocated to its members through some combination of individual and collective choice. Individual choice is commonly expressed through the exercise of voluntary exchange in markets. Collective choice is exercised mainly through government action or other collective choice mechanisms.

Social welfare is defined as the aggregate welfare of all members of a society. A basic assumption in welfare analysis is that individuals are the best judges of their own welfare and will use their endowments to maximise their welfare. Because individuals have unique preferences, different distributions of a given set of endowments will produce different levels of social welfare. However, because of the uniqueness of individual preferences, gains and losses of social welfare accruing to different individuals are incommensurate with each other. Consequently, without resorting to some form of value judgement it is not possible to determine whether a change in the distribution of endowments leads to a net improvement in overall social welfare. The specification of a social welfare function would be one way of converting individual gains and losses into an index or some other scale capable of being aggregated into a measure of welfare for society as a whole. But a universally accepted welfare function has been elusive. As a result, the concept of Pareto efficiency, which offers a way out of the dilemma of individual welfare comparisons, has become the most widely used value judgement in modern welfare economics.

Pareto optimality
The Pareto criterion deliberately rules out any attempt to add up or otherwise make commensurable the welfare measures of different individuals. The criterion states that a change in the economy making at least one individual better off without making anyone else worse off is an unambiguous improvement in social welfare. On the basis of this criterion, change should continue to be pursued until it is no longer possible to make someone better off without making someone else commensurably worse off; that is, until a Pareto-optimal or Pareto-efficient allocation of resources is achieved. In practical terms, however, because a policy change invariably makes some individuals better off and others worse off, and because those changes are incommensurate, the Pareto criterion is incapable of determining whether the change is desirable.

A useful solution to this problem was independently developed by both Nicholas Kaldor and John R. Hicks. They proposed a modification to the Pareto criterion based on the concept of compensation between gainers and losers resulting from a policy change. Essentially the modified Pareto criterion would judge a policy change to be a social improvement if the gainers could fully compensate the losers and still be better off (Kaldor), or conversely, if the losers could not profitably oppose the change by paying off the gainers (Hicks). In other words, a policy change would be desirable if the sum of the welfare gains and losses generated by the change is greater than zero. Compensation need not actually occur for the policy change to be desirable, all that is required is that there be a 'potential' to ensure that at least one person is made better off without anyone else being worse off (that is, potential Pareto improvement exists).

Under the standard restrictive assumptions, a fully competitive market has the special property of being able to automatically attain an efficient allocation of resources in the Pareto-optimal sense. The market equilibrium thus attained, however, is not unique. There are many Pareto-optimal possibilities and a competitive market can attain each one provided it starts with the correct initial distribution of resources. Consequently, the fact that a resource allocation attained by a competitive market is efficient does not necessarily mean that the distribution of resources is the most desirable from the viewpoint of society as a whole. From a regulatory perspective this implies that, while a competitive market left to its devices can be relied upon to work towards achieving economic efficiency, an external intervention guided by a value judgement might be required to achieve a desirable distribution of resources.

There are many situations where markets fail to achieve efficient outcomes. In the real world the attributes assumed for a perfectly competitive economy are often violated and there are many instances when an efficient equilibrium is unattainable through the effects of market forces alone. Perfect information is unlikely to ever be a reality; buyers and sellers are not price takers in all markets; products and factors are not homogeneous; decreasing returns to scale do not always pertain; entry into all markets is not free; and consumption and production may have external effects. The presence of these or other market imperfections inhibits the production of optimal social welfare outcomes. Consequently, if we accept that competitive markets are efficient, then it follows that regulatory intervention in the operations of a market should be entertained only in instances of market failure. A second potential reason for consideration of regulatory intervention is the pursuit of a more desirable distribution of resources, which the market is unable to achieve without some external intervention. Thus, we could say that a necessary precondition for regulation must be the necessity either to correct for market failure or to attain a 'social objective'.

The existence of such a precondition, however, is not a sufficient justification for regulatory intervention. Although fully competitive markets are a theoretical ideal, many less than fully competitive markets perform well enough to be considered efficient and may outperform regulated markets. Regulation is not costless to implement and intervention is justified only if the benefits of the intervention outweigh the costs. The overarching justification for regulation must be an improvement in social welfare. Consequently, a second precondition for regulation is that the related benefits exceed the related costs. In other words, the regulation must generate a net benefit to society. A further consideration is that typically more than one option is available to policy makers considering regulation. To maximize social welfare, the option that should be chosen is the one that maximizes the resultant net benefits to society.

It is not always easy to determine whether a regulation will improve society's welfare. The fundamental tenet of the Pareto-improvement criterion is that, other things being equal, an intervention that leads to an increase in economic efficiency is a good thing. But similarly, the achievement of desirable social objectives such as a more equitable redistribution of resources, would also improve society's well-being. The interaction of these two aspects of social welfare can pose a considerable problem in determining whether a policy intervention leads to an improvement.

If social welfare is thought of as having two components, economic effi-ciency and distributional justice, an increase in economic efficiency which does not impact adversely on distributional justice would be an indisput-able gain in social welfare. Similarly, an improvement in distributional justice which does not decrease economic efficiency is also an indisputable gain in social welfare. A problem arises, however, when an improvement in either economic efficiency or distributional justice is accompanied by a decrease in the other.

Regulatory decisions often impinge on both economic efficiency and social considerations. Under those circumstances, policy makers have no objective rules or criteria at their disposal to assess whether the trade-off between the two competing outcomes results in an overall gain in social welfare. Consequently, they are called upon to make subjective assess-ments guided by their perception or understanding of the social values held by their society. Ultimately, as they are accountable to society for their choices, any such choice should be transparent and quantified to the fullest extent possible.

Types of regulation

Regulation may be used for a variety of reasons and may take many differ-ent forms depending on its purpose. Regulatory measures tend to fall into two main categories reflecting the broad objective they seek to address, namely *economic* and *social* regulation.

Economic regulation refers to regulatory interventions applied to economic markets that are generally motivated by a desire to redress the effects of a market failure and thus encourage conduct and outcomes that mimic those of a fully competitive market. The main focus is on improv-ing economic efficiency and strengthening the functioning of markets rather than displacing market operations. Economic regulation generally affects both demand and supply decisions that are likely to have an impact on production, consumption and distribution of products and services. Consequently, economic regulation is likely to alter the relationship between buyers and sellers as well as the economic costs and economic benefits that accrue to them. The deregulatory movement of recent times is primarily concerned with a reconsideration of traditional economic regulation of industries.

Social regulation refers to regulatory interventions whose primary purpose is to safeguard or enhance social well-being in areas such as safety, health, environment, protection of disadvantaged and vulnerable people, and promotion of social and cultural values. The objective of much safety, health and environmental regulation is to reduce the risk of harm occurring. This requires policy makers to make judgements about acceptable levels of risk as part of a trade-off between risk reduction and increased economic costs. While the focus of social regulation is primarily on securing social benefits, the regulatory instruments will necessarily have an economic effect that is likely to impact on both producers and consumer groups and on the functioning of economic markets.

Regulatory instruments also may be grouped into broad categories. Spulber (1989: 37) notes that regulation generally might take three different forms:

- instruments such as price regulation, property rights and contract rules that interfere directly with the market allocation mechanism;
- instruments that impact on consumer decisions including taxes, subsidies or other transfer and controls on what products or services may be consumed; and
- instruments that impact on firm supply decisions, including production taxes and subsidies, restrictions on entry, production inputs or outputs, production technologies, or product characteristics.

3   Appraisal of regulatory policies

The function of regulatory appraisals is to assess whether proposed or existing regulations pass the 'net benefit to society' test. Although regulation may be necessary and beneficial to the functioning of markets or for the attainment of a social objective, there is a widely held view that regulatory instruments are often misguided or inefficient. Hahn and Litan (2006), for example, point to a substantial number of US federal regulations failing the net benefit to society test. Inefficiencies can also be a problem. The Report of the Australian Government's Taskforce on Reducing Regulatory Burdens on Business (Regulation Taskforce, 2006: 7) noted that 'the nature and design of regulation, and how it is administered and enforced' can be a considerable cause of complexity and cost. The Taskforce highlighted the following as being among features that are problematic in the design of regulations:

- unclear or questionable objectives;
- a failure to target the regulation sufficiently – for example, regulation that is too blunt or disproportionate to the problem;
- undue prescription;
- excessive reporting or other paperwork requirements;
- overlap, duplication or inconsistency with other regulation, either within jurisdictions or between jurisdictions;
- poorly expressed and confusing use of terms, including the use of inconsistent definitions in different regulations; and
- unwarranted differentiation of local regulation from international standards.

Most of these and similar problems can be averted by more attentive consideration and analysis.

Appraisal of proposals using the perfectly competitive market model typically implies that economic value dominates all other influences on behaviour. While such an assumption can be useful in predicting behavioural differences in a market context, it should be recognised that in a government policy context, other factors, including traditional concepts of equity and public service, are often significant influences on the role and behaviour of politicians and bureaucrats. In other words, economic value is only one of several arguments, and not necessarily the critical factor, influencing government operations.

In a less than perfect world, government actions are not always consistent with maximisation of social welfare. Just as competitive markets fail to work efficiently in certain conditions, regulation too is prone to failure. Regulators are not omniscient and may often be less well informed about market conditions than those they seek to regulate, and may consequently face difficulties in choosing efficient regulatory instruments to address particular problems. Political considerations are also at play and can influence government decisions. In all regulatory interventions there are winners and losers, and powerful vested interests can often influence outcomes in their own favour. Politicians, also, may place their own self-interest above the public interest and sometimes their actions may be motivated by political gains rather than a desire to correct market failures or secure socially desirable goals.

Regulators are frequently called upon to make decisions based on limited information and are often under considerable political pressure to address issues or problems quickly – conditions not conducive to ideal or efficient outcomes. But even when not under pressure, information on likely effects of proposed regulations is difficult to obtain and outcomes are often dependent on assumptions about the likely impact.

In terms of efficiency, markets generally perform better than government mechanisms. Government intervention, however, can contribute to improvements in the functioning of markets by, for example, removing or reducing barriers to competition and improving the flow of information between producers and consumers. Similarly, market forces can improve the functioning of government agencies by providing incentives that reward lower costs and higher quality performance. Privatisation and other measures that increase the contestability of products or services supplied by government agencies, for example, have been shown to be capable of substantial improvements in efficiency (for example, airline deregulation, and competition in the supply of telecommunication services).

Inappropriate or less than fully effective regulations reduce social well-being generally and can impose substantial additional costs and other inefficiencies on affected industries, with consequential harmful impact on national productivity. Inappropriate regulations can increase costs and misallocate resources by:

- altering the incentives of firms to use the most efficient combination of resources;
- altering the distribution of economic rents between capital and labour;
- reducing the incentives of firms for technological or product innovation; and
- reducing the responsiveness of firms to consumer needs.

Determining whether an existing or proposed regulation is both effective and efficient, and is the best solution to the problem being addressed, requires systematic analysis and evaluation of all the associated cost and benefits. CBA lends itself to such a purpose and has become a widely used technique in the assessment of regulation.

4   Cost–benefit analysis

CBA was initially developed as a tool for the assessment of the economic value of large construction projects. Although the genesis of the underlying principles can be traced to earlier periods, the earliest applications of CBA-like techniques are associated with evaluations of large water-management projects under the US Flood Control Act 1936, which conditioned federal participation to projects whose 'benefits to whomsoever they accrue are in excess of the estimated costs'. By the 1960s, the fundamental framework for the use of CBA had been firmly established and the technique was increasingly applied to the evaluation of a wide range of policies and projects. In 1981 with Executive Order 12291, President Ronald Reagan mandated the systematic application of CBA to government regulatory initiatives. Subsequent presidents have continued to require its mandatory application in the assessment of all major regulatory initiatives proposed by federal agencies. Outside the USA, many countries, including the United Kingdom, Australia, Canada and members of the European Union are increasingly requiring CBA of policy proposals as an input to decision making.

CBA seeks to identify and measure the economic effects of a policy intervention on the individual welfare of all members of society. It uses 'willingness to pay' for a benefit, or 'willingness to accept compensation' for a cost, as a convenient metric to measure changes in the welfare of affected individuals. Benefits and costs include all tangible and intangible effects that a policy has on the social and economic well-being of individuals in society. In valuing benefits and costs, CBA makes no attempt to distinguish between the utility that different individuals derive from the changes. Colloquially, 'a dollar is a dollar is a dollar' no matter where it occurs.

The main underlying principles and features of CBA are:

- individual welfare is derived from satisfaction of individual preferences;
- benefits and costs are defined, respectively, as gains and losses in well-being;
- willingness to pay (WTP) to secure a gain or to avoid a loss is used as a monetary measure of individual preferences;
- individual preferences, expressed in WTP amounts, are aggregated to determine society's preferences;
- discounted present values are used to compare aggregate costs and benefits accruing in different time periods; and
- different options for a policy or project are compared in terms of their net benefits or are ranked on the basis of their cost–benefit ratio.

CBA of a regulatory policy can be an extensive and challenging process involving a series of potentially complex steps. The basic steps in the use of CBA to evaluate regulatory policies may be summarised as follows:

- definition of the objectives of the regulatory policy;
- identification of feasible options for the policy intervention;
- identification of the relevant scope and the impacts of the intervention;
- estimation of the monetary value of the impacts;
- adjustment for uncertainty and time effects;
- determination of net cost/benefit of the feasible options; and
- comparison of options.

Assessing desirability of regulation
While relatively straightforward in principle, the application of CBA can pose considerable difficulties in practice. First and foremost, the objectives that policy makers are seeking to pursue with a regulatory intervention must be clearly defined. To evaluate the desirability of intervention an analyst needs to know what the regulation is intended to achieve. In many cases the objectives of regulatory policies are stated in broad general terms that are not conducive to testing of the likely effectiveness of the proposed

regulation, or indeed whether the regulation is needed to achieve desired outcomes. The objectives should be logically connected with the proposed regulatory instruments and should be amenable to empirical measurement against expected outcomes.

Typically, the desired outcomes can be achieved by several different courses of action, all of which may need to be carefully considered and evaluated. Focusing on the problem that regulatory intervention is intended to address should help identify potentially feasible options. Non-regulatory solutions, if available, should be given careful consideration, ahead of regulatory options. Theoretically, an infinite number of options are available. Consequently, analysts need to be pragmatic to identify a most likely set of distinct feasible options. Consultation with policy makers and other stakeholders should assist considerably in identifying potentially feasible options and rejecting those unlikely to be feasible or acceptable to the policy makers.

Some of the potential options can be discarded at this stage with simple tests about their consistency with policy constraints or because of their significantly greater cost relative to other options (assuming that the options generate similar benefits). Others are less easily dismissed without at least some qualitative and quantitative analysis of their effects. In all cases, dismissal of further analysis of a potentially feasible option should be demonstrably justified.

Key issues for consideration in the identification of feasible options include:

- consistency with objectives and strategies of policy makers;
- availability of different instruments to achieve an objective (for example, possibilities include information campaigns, education, taxes, licensing, and prohibition and associated penalties);
- degree to which objectives of the regulation can be met. Often, for example, setting a different permissible threshold for an undesirable activity (for example, level of permissible lead emissions for motor vehicles) may achieve most of the desirable benefits at a much lower cost; and
- risk of an option producing outcomes that diverge from those expected.

For each feasible course of action, it is necessary to identify the relevant effects as costs or benefits. The analysis should include details of how the costs and benefits are distributed to affected groups. For a strict application of the potential Pareto-improvement criterion, all direct and indirect effects on all members of the community that arise from a policy change must be taken into account. Where significant, the analysis should include compliance costs incurred by those affected as well as costs incurred by regulators in administering and monitoring the regulation.

Determining what is the relevant market and what costs and benefits have standing in the analysis is an area of primary concern in CBA. Usually CBA is applied to limited and tightly defined problems in the primary market with the assumption that other markets are not affected. The assumption that other markets are given enables costs and benefits to be estimated from the effects of the identified changes in the relevant market. Unless there is clear evidence of distortion in secondary markets or that the effect in the primary market produces a change in relevant prices in the secondary markets, the impact on secondary markets can often be ignored. A good practice is to initially identify and list all possible effects and classify them as costs or benefits to various affected groups. Objective reasoning can then be used to determine what is included in the analysis. Pragmatically, effects with relatively minor impact on the overall cost of the regulation may be omitted if they are unlikely to influence significantly the outcome of the analysis (but their identity and the reasons justifying their omission should be noted). Nonetheless, determining what should be included can be a difficult decision and choices can have a major impact on the cost–benefit outcome. Two studies of proposed regulatory interventions aimed at reducing cigarette smoking illustrate this effect.

The health consequences and related costs is a common feature of concern in policies designed to reduce consumption of cigarettes and were key elements of the two studies considered here. The first study by Viscusi (1994) estimated the costs and benefits of using higher taxes on cigarettes to reduce smoking in the United States. The effects of premature death arising from smoke-related lung cancer, and heart and other diseases were a crucial component of the analysis in this study. Higher health-related costs associated with smoking were offset against cost savings arising from reduced social security and pension payments to smokers because of the incidence of premature death. On this basis, the study concluded that 'not only is there not a rationale for imposing a tax due to these insurance-related externalities, but rather on balance there is a net cost saving to society even excluding consideration of the current cigarette taxes paid by smokers' (p.47).

The second study was conducted in Australia (Applied Economics, 2003) and assessed the costs and benefits of proposed health warnings to be displayed on packaging of tobacco products. As for the US study, mortality and health-related costs were major considerations. In contrast with the US study, however, this study estimated that substantial net benefits would accrue from reduced mortality and related improvement in health.

The main difference in the range of costs and benefits considered in the two studies seems to be the exclusion of social security and pension payments as costs of increased longevity in the Australian study and the exclusion of benefits accruing from longer and healthier productive life likely to be associated with a lower incidence of smoking in the US study.

Much of the regulatory effort of governments, particularly in relation to social regulation, is directed at reducing both the risk or likelihood of occurrence of hazardous events and the consequences of hazardous events when they do occur. When considering regulation, policy makers will need to make judgements about the *real* nature of the risk and its likely consequences and determine the extent to which risk reduction is both possible and cost-effective.

Risk assessment should provide a reasoned, evidence-based analysis of:

- the likely frequency that the hazardous event will occur without regulatory intervention;
- who is likely to suffer from adversity from the event;
- the severity of the harm or injury likely to be sustained (both temporary and permanent); and
- likely consequential outcomes or behaviour that may change the nature and extent of the risk.

Risk assessment often faces significant information difficulties, particularly in relation to effects of exposure to potential health hazards. In some instances, considerable costs may be involved in ascertaining the potential health effects of exposure to the hazard, identifying the population at risk, and the distribution of compounding factors that may increase or reduce the health impact on the affected population. There may be a need, therefore, to balance the value of additional information against the cost of obtaining it and to make judgements about the extent to which a detailed assessment is likely to be a cost-effective addition to better-informed decisions.

Estimation of monetary values

The primary function of CBA is to estimate changes in social welfare likely to be produced by a regulatory instrument. Thus, in a regulatory context, CBA always involves a comparison of what would be likely to happen in the absence of the regulatory intervention (the reference case) with the expected outcomes resulting from the intervention. Establishing the reference case or counterfactual is therefore a critical element in assessing whether the regulatory change is likely to produce a net benefit. For both the reference case and the intervention case, the estimates of costs and benefits relate to prospective rather than actual outcomes and will be dependent on the assumptions used to define the outcomes.

Existing market conditions are likely to provide the best starting-point for the specification of counterfactual outcomes. This is particularly so for economic regulation designed to alter market conditions and related behaviour of economic agents. Generally, the expectation is that existing market conditions tend to reflect historical developments as well as anticipated developments in the market. They are also likely to reflect any moderating effects on market behaviour if players perceive a risk that the behaviour may induce a regulatory intervention. As a starting-point, in the absence of any evidence to the contrary (for example, implementation of major technological changes), it would be reasonable to assume that existing conditions and trends will be likely to persist and can be used to construct the counterfactual case.

In a competitive market, market prices carry information about marginal cost of production and marginal value to consumers, and are reliable measures of individual valuations of changes in consumption of goods and services. But care should be exercised in using market prices as measures of social cost and social values in situations where markets are constrained from reaching an equilibrium, and particularly when demand or supply are constrained and not everyone can buy and sell goods as they choose. These are instances of market inefficiency, and other mechanisms may need to be used to estimate relevant prices and costs.

All regulatory interventions have a cost in the form of resources that are drawn away from other uses. In other words, they impose an opportunity cost equal to the value that the required resources would have in their best alternative use. In an efficient market, the marginal value of resource is equal to its opportunity cost. Provided that the additional demand for the resource arising from the regulatory intervention is relatively small, the price effect of the additional demand can be assumed to be negligible and opportunity cost for the required resource can be taken to approximate market price. However, when additional demand for the resource is substantial and is likely to induce a price change in the resource market, the estimation of opportunity cost needs to take account of the changes in social surplus resulting from the price change. In such a situation, opportunity cost equals expenditure plus (minus) the decrease (increase) in social surplus. Similarly, estimation of opportunity cost in the presence of market failure or inefficient markets must take careful account of changes in social surplus.

Outcomes of a regulatory intervention are usually valued on the basis of willingness to pay for the benefits received from, or to avoid the costs imposed by, the regulation. For traded commodities, the required information is obtained directly from market transactions. When the relevant commodities are not traded in markets, determination of their value becomes more complex because of the need to employ alternative mechanisms to obtain the necessary data.

Some would argue that certain intangible commodities such as cultural heritage, species preservation, human life and environmental degradation are priceless (see, for example, Ackerman and Heinzerling, 2001–02). But even if such arguments were accepted, policy makers would still ultimately be left with making a judgement on the amount of resources allocated to the preservation of those commodities and thus implicitly determine their value. A more helpful approach to valuation of intangible commodities relies on distilling relevant information from consumers' actions.

Consumers regularly make observable decisions which can provide measurable quantitative evidence of the value they place on a range of intangible costs and benefits. People in hazardous jobs, for example, are prepared to take increased risks to their personal safety in return for higher pecuniary rewards. Similarly, differences in the prices of houses under noisy flight-paths near airports and similar houses in similar but less noisy locations provide information about how much people value noise pollution. The willingness to pay for many other types of intangible benefits can be inferred from similarly related market data that include a component reflecting the value of the cost or benefit of interest. Procedures using related market data to estimate the value of non-marketed goods are known as 'revealed preference methods'.

The use of indirect methods to estimate values can be prone to identification and specification problems. There is a considerable chance that people may not be well-informed about the extent of the risk to their health or safety in the context of where they work or live or may have limited alternative choices available and estimates derived from these techniques will suffer accordingly. Econometric estimates may also suffer because of the omission of important determinants in the specification of supply and demand functions for the item of interest. The existence of such problems and their likely impact on the derived estimates should be noted whenever these techniques are used in CBA. Nonetheless, such methodologies do provide useful estimates in certain circumstances.

Another commonly used approach to determining willingness to pay for non-traded goods is to obtain the information by asking people directly in specially commissioned surveys. Valuation techniques based on such an approach are referred to as 'stated preference methods'. There are two main methods in current usage: contingent valuation, and choice modelling.

The contingent valuation method (CVM) was initially developed by environmental economists to estimate economic values of environmental benefits and damages to the environment (Mitchell and Carson, 1989 provide a comprehensive introduction to the methodology). CVM employs survey methods to collect information on willingness to pay for a marginal change in the supply of intangible benefit in a hypothetical market setting. Its use is not without controversy and its estimates are prone to various types of bias. The use of CVM received an important endorsement from a panel of experts convened by the National Oceanic and Atmospheric Administration and co-chaired by economics Nobel laureates Kenneth Arrow and Robert Solow. The panel concluded that CVM studies using a set of recommended good practices were capable of producing 'estimates reliable enough to be the starting point of a judicial process for damage assessment' (Arrow et al., 1993, p. 43). In more recent times it has been increasingly applied to estimate values of other intangible benefits, particularly in the fields of culture and heritage (for a survey of cultural and heritage applications, see Noonan, 2003).

Santagata and Signorello (2000), for example, used CVM to estimate the value of total benefits accruing to residents of Naples from a city government cultural programme providing free access to 46 cultural heritage sites (churches, palaces, historical squares and a museum). The cost of the program of 4.3 billion Italian lire was equivalent to a cost of 4,800 Italian lire per each adult (18 or more years) resident of Naples. They used an open-ended question to collect WTP data in a face-to-face survey of 500 adult residents of Naples, and found that 66 per cent of respondents were prepared to contribute greater than the per capita average cost to maintain the programme. Users had a substantially greater WTP than non-users to maintain the programme. Details are provided in Table 8.1.

Choice modelling (CM) is an analytical framework used to analyse the influence that different levels and combinations of attributes have on individual choices. It is based on the Lancastrian notion that any product may be defined in terms of its attributes which in turn provide the basis for how much consumers value the product. Changes in the levels of the

Table 8.1   Willingness to pay to maintain free access to cultural heritage sites in Naples

	Citizens	Users	Non-users
WTP = 0 (%)	48.3	34.1	67.2
WTP > cost per capita (%)	51.5	65.9	32.8
Average WTP (Italian lire)	16,995	23,797	7,960
No. of observations	468	267	201

Source: Santagata and Signorello (2000, p. 195).

Table 8.2   Estimated total economic values for Old Parliament House and the National Museum of Australia

	Old Parliament House	National Museum of Australia
WTP (A$ million)	86.1	73.4
Public Funding in 2006 (A$ million)	15.6	40.1
WTP/public funding	5.5	1.8
No. of observations	785	796

Source: Choi et al. (2008, compiled from pp. 12, 15 and 19).

attributes are reflected in commensurate changes in consumer valuations. In a CM survey, respondents are offered choices of hypothetical alternative scenarios with several component attributes, including a monetary component, and are asked to select the preferred alternative from each choice. The choices implicitly reveal the respondent's marginal value for the components and the information is used in logit type models to estimate the value of the non-traded components of interest (for a detailed introduction, see Hensher et al., 2005).

CM lends itself to application in a wide range of regulatory situations, particularly where relevant benefits are embedded in a commodity with several of attributes. For example, CM was used in a recent study of the cultural benefits accruing to Australian society from two publicly funded national institutions in Australia: Old Parliament House (a political history museum) and the National Museum of Australia (Choi et al., 2008). Two separate national mail surveys, one for each institution, were conducted to collect WTP data for hypothetical marginal changes in a number of the institutions' attributes including a monetary component (tax or entry fee). The hypothetical changes were used to construct several choice sets, each with four options, and respondents were asked to identify their preferred choice in each set. The estimated total economic value of Old Parliament House derived from the data collected in the study was considerably higher (5.5 times) than the amount of annual public funding received from the government; that for the National Museum of Australia was 1.8 times its annual public funding (see Table 8. 2 for details).

Regulatory instruments typically have ongoing effects generating costs and benefits for as long as the instruments remain in force. In CBA analysis the full stream of future costs and benefits is relevant. However, because of difficulties in estimating realistic costs and benefits far into the future, it may be prudent to exclude estimated costs and benefits beyond a pragmatically determined cutoff point (strong justification might be necessary to include anything beyond 20 years).

When comparing costs and benefits that accrue in different time periods it is necessary that they are valued commensurately. First, to allow for the effects of inflation over time, the costs and benefits should be measured in real rather than nominal terms. Second, the analysis must take account of the fact that accruals in future periods are normally valued less than present accruals and consequently need to be appropriately discounted to account for the time difference. The concept of 'present value' which applies an appropriate discount to convert streams of future cost and benefits to a commensurate value basis is the standard methodology used to address this problem.

General equilibrium models
The partial equilibrium assumption that other markets are not affected works reasonably well in most cases because indirect impacts are typically small. When the effects beyond the primary market are substantial, the assumption is not tenable and the effects need to be included in the analysis. This can be done with the use of a general equilibrium model.

General equilibrium models simulate the key interrelationships among the production sectors of an economy and are useful tools for economy-wide assessment of major changes. Use of such models enables analysts to estimate the main effects of exogenous changes, including policy changes, on the various sectors of the economy and overall on GDP. Unfortunately, it is not easy to determine a priori whether a change will lead to significant economy-wide effects requiring the application of a general equilibrium model. Some rules of thumb suggest that regulations affecting intermediate products used widely throughout the economy (such as telecommunications, transport or energy) or policies generating large costs would be likely candidates for analysis with a general equilibrium model.

ACIL Tasman (2005) employed a computable general equilibrium model in a cost–benefit study of telecommunications reforms commissioned by the Australian Communications and Media Authority. The model included all sectors of the economy and captured direct and indirect effects. Benefits to consumers were represented by increases in private consumption while those to small business were estimated from increases in payments to capital. Economic welfare benefits were measured as increases in GDP due to price competition and innovation. The report noted the difficulty in isolating the role of the liberalisation reforms in the observed changes and stressed that the estimates were dependent on the reference case and model assumptions. The study concluded that

Table 8.3   Estimated benefits of Australian telecommunication changes: 2003/04–2004/05

Category of benefit	Increase generated by the reform
GDP	0.24%
Household consumption	0.28%
Employment	0.24%
Investment	0.24%
Consumer benefits	A$1.3 billion
Small business benefits	A$216 million

Source: ACIL Tasman (2005, compiled from pp. 56 and 58).

the reforms had benefited nearly all economic sectors and had produced significant increases in GDP, household consumption, employment and investment. The results are summarised in Table 8.3.

Another interesting example of the application of a general equilibrium model to estimate the social cost of environmental quality regulations in the USA is provided in Hazilla and Kopp (1990). The application of their model indicated that although pollution controls were required only in some sectors of the economy, production costs increased, and output and labour productivity decreased, in all sectors. Pezzey and Lambie (2001) provide a comparative review of four general equilibrium models that have been used to assess economy-wide impacts of greenhouse emission controls.

Comparison of options

The sum of the present value of the risk-adjusted stream of costs and benefits generated by a regulatory option represents its net present value. Any option with a positive net present value (that is, one with a net benefit) satisfies the potential Pareto-improvement criterion. A negative net present value indicates that the economic costs exceed the economic benefits of an option. However, a net negative present value does not necessarily condemn an option from adoption, provided that there are unmeasured social benefits or that the option pursues a desirable redistribution of resources. But in such a case, policy makers will have the onus of demonstrating that the unmeasured social benefits or those accruing from the redistribution of resources are at least commensurate with the estimated economic costs.

Net present value is commonly used to rank and compare regulatory options on the basis of their absolute net benefits to society. Another commonly used comparison ranks the options on the basis of their cost–benefit ratio which provides a measure of the 'benefit' return per unit of cost of implementing an option. The two rankings reflect different measures and thus serve different purposes. It may or may not be the case that the option with the greatest net benefits will also have the greatest cost–benefit ratio. Generally, benefit maximisation is the more-relevant measure in the appraisal of regulatory proposals and benefit–cost ratio the more appropriate measure in the appraisals of policies subject to a budget constraint. But this may not always be the case. There are often occasions when policy makers may be concerned about the weight of the burden that a regulatory proposal may impose on groups bearing the cost of the regulation. In such cases, implementation of a regulation may be conditional on costs not exceeding a particular limit and a combination of both measures might be appropriate for the ranking of options.

5   Criticisms and limitations

The application of CBA to the assessment of regulation, particularly in areas such environmental, health and safety regulation, has generated considerable, sometimes strident, debate among proponents and opponents of the methodology. Examples from the established literature include: Ackerman and Heinzerling (2001–02); Kelman (1981); Adler and Posner (1999); Frank (2000); Kornhauser (2000); Sunstein (2002); Viscusi and Gayer (2002); Hahn (2004) and Shapiro (2005).

The criticisms range from moral justifiability of the formal theory to the appropriateness of particular applications. The more common criticisms include:

- CBA creates artificial prices for benefits that cannot be quantified;
- CBA is biased against regulation because costs are easier to quantify than benefits;
- CBA ignores issues of social inequality;
- CBA inappropriately puts a price on life, the environment and other irreplaceable unique resources and assets;
- CBA makes inappropriate use of discounting;
- because of the many underlying assumptions the methodology produces meaningless numbers; and
- CBA does not produces better outcomes than other decision analysis tools.

The focus of the preceding discussion has been on the application of CBA to the analysis of regulatory policies. The usefulness of CBA in this respect has been amply demonstrated in recent decades and, as noted, governments around the world are increasingly demanding its use in policy evaluation. Consequently, while the criticisms are acknowledged, the discussion here is limited to some broad observations. Those wishing to follow the debate in more detail are referred to the cited literature.

CBA should be seen for what it is: an analytical tool to assist the evaluation of proposals by policy makers, and not a mechanistic decision-making instrument. CBA is not without limitations. As noted above, while CBA is focused on economic efficiency considerations, society does place considerable value on distributional equity and other social objectives that cannot be judged by economic efficiency alone. Policy makers, as representatives of the collective will of society, are called upon to make value judgements about acceptable trade-offs between efficiency and other goals. In other words, CBA is a valuable and important element of policy consideration but should not be elevated to the status of an exclusive test for policy action. Implementation of a regulation with estimated net costs may well be acceptable, provided that offsetting social benefits are objectively and justifiably given greater weight than the estimated shortfall in economic benefits. In such a situation, CBA plays another very important role in holding policy makers accountable for their decisions and promoting a greater transparency in decision making.

Although the CBA bottom line is 'net benefit' which abstracts away from distributional concerns it does not mean that those concerns should not and cannot be accommodated. Policy makers are often concerned about the distributional impact of policies. It is good CBA practice to identify and list all possible effects of a regulatory change and classify them as costs or benefits to various affected groups. If the relevant data are available, the impacts on the affected groups can be assessed and can be used to inform policy makers.

Similarly, the fact that some of the costs and benefits of a regulation may be very difficult to quantify does not mean that CBA is inappropriate or of little value. A key principle of CBA is that all relevant costs and benefits should be taken into account. An inability to quantify certain costs or benefits in particular circumstances does not mean that they should be ignored in the decision making. Rather, it is important that the unquantified costs and benefits are noted and described as fully as possible. The description should include supporting scientific and other evidence and, where possible, reasoned and justified indications of the likely maximum and minimum order of magnitude of their value. CBA can then be used to estimate the net value of all the other measurable costs and benefits. By being presented with an estimate of quantifiable net value side by side with detailed descriptions and likely effects of the unquantified cost and benefits, decision makers will be better placed to make informed decisions.

Kornhauser (2000) makes the important distinction that cost–benefit analysis does not price life, the environment or any other irreplaceable commodity. Rather, cost–benefit analysis places a value on specific policies offered in specific contexts. In most cases, regulatory policies seek to alter the level of risk associated with a deleterious event and not eliminate the event altogether. The crucial consideration of policies in this context is to achieve a socially acceptable balance between the amount of reduction and the associated cost. Individually and collectively people make similar trade-offs in everyday life. Government decisions on the allocation of resources to mortality reduction or other risk-reduction programmes routinely imply a finite value to the saving of lives, and suggest that such a value is acceptable to society. Similarly, decisions on environmental protection also imply that society places a finite value for particular environmental damage. The use of WTP measures to estimate benefits associated with reduced risk to irreplaceable commodities, by extension, should be no less acceptable.

Some critics (for example, Ackerman and Heinzerling, 2001–02) argue that placing a value on life is morally wrong and that in any event the value of life is a constant and thus should not be subject to discounting. They also argue that discounting improperly trivialises future harms and the irreversibility of some environmental problems. Discounting has been a controversial issue in environmental economics. Much of the perceived problem arises from considerations far into the future for periods much longer than usually encountered in other economic policy evaluations. In typical economic analyses over standard time periods, efficient use of money is a key issue, whereas other issues such as equity and sustainability may become more dominant in long-term environmental policies. What needs to be resolved is what the proper balance between them should be when considerations move from standard time periods to the long-term future. Determining the proper balance involves a value judgement and hence disagreements should not be surprising. However, this should not detract from the principle of using discounting to ensure that the cost of capital is taken into account when comparing streams of costs and benefits that occur in different time periods. Heal (1997) and Nordhaus (1997) provide detailed commentaries on the use of discounting in the context of long-term environmental policies.

All estimating methodologies are based on a variety of assumptions and CBA is no different in this respect. Not everyone will agree with the assumptions, but that does not mean that the use of the assumptions is inappropriate. It simply means that the results are conditional upon those assumptions and should be interpreted accordingly. Any methodology based on assumptions must be used judiciously, taking account of the circumstances in which it is applied. When used judiciously, CBA does provide useful and worthwhile information likely to improve the efficiency of regulatory decision making. Of course, other methodologies can also assist efficient decision making and should be used in appropriate circumstances. The key issue is what is best in the prevailing circumstances in which the methodology is used. The answer need not necessarily be CBA. Also, it does not necessarily mean that when CBA is employed, other methodologies should be excluded. For any methodology, the test of appropriate use should be whether the application is likely to result in a cost-effective improvement in the quality of decision making.

CBA is primarily concerned with allocative efficiency issues. In the standard format it does not take account of intertemporal consequences that may arise from technological change and other productivity-improving activities. Regulatory policies, however, may impact on dynamic efficiency. The impact can be positive or negative depending on whether the regulatory change encourages or discourages productivity-improving investment and activities. The magnitude of the impact can be substantial, but difficult to predict. While it would be desirable to take account of prospective technology and productivity changes in CBA, because of the considerable uncertainty associated with predictions of future changes it is imperative that all assumptions and alternative scenarios used in the analysis are clearly defined and reported.

6   A specific application

Many countries outside the US often employ empirically untested 'public interest' claims to justify regulation to increase consumption of domestic cultural outputs. Australian domestic content quotas for television programming are an example. The quotas apply to free-to-air commercial television services and mandate that 55 per cent of all transmission time is to be devoted to domestic programming including subquotas for drama, documentaries and children's programmes. Initially introduced as minor quotas to safeguard domestic employment opportunities when television transmissions started in Australia in 1956, the regulatory obligations have since been reviewed and expanded on several occasions in pursuit of cultural identity objectives. None of the reviews has sought to quantify the costs and benefits of the regulation. Dominated by activists, interest groups, television proprietors and production industry lobbyists, the reviews have generally resulted in compromises which attempted to balance the claims of the competing interests groups rather than maximise net benefits to society.

Approach to assessment of Australian television content regulation
An empirical assessment of the costs and benefits of the Australian domestic television programming regulation was undertaken by Papandrea

(1997). The study followed standard welfare economics criteria to assess whether government intervention was justified and whether the adopted policy instruments were efficient and produced optimal results. The following is a summary of that assessment.

The assessment involved four separate steps, namely:

- establishing the likely existence of market failure;
- assessing whether the intervention generated a net benefit to society;
- assessing the likely efficiency of the regulatory instruments; and
- assessing potential improvements to the regulatory instruments.

The likely existence of the 'market failure' precondition for regulation typically relies on examination of the attributes of the market and of the regulated activity. Television programmes have both 'information' and cultural characteristics. In common with other information goods, all production costs are incurred in making the first copy of the programme. The marginal cost of subsequent copies is very close to zero. Consequently, domestic production of television programmes is unable to compete with similar imported programmes initially produced for other markets. But not all domestic programmes are so affected. Some genres such as local news, current affairs and sports programmes enjoy substantial measures of natural protection from imported substitutes. The cultural attributes of television programmes are a byproduct of production in the sense that they reflect and reinforce the cultural characteristics of the market for which the programmes are first produced. Thus consumption of domestic programmes is seen as producing external benefits that act to enhance national culture and identity, while consumption of imported substitutes is seen as having the opposite effect. These and other culturally related attributes of television programming imply prima facie justification for some form of policy intervention.

Establishing whether the regulation produced a net benefit to society was the most critical aspect of the study. Estimates of both the additional cultural benefits produced by the regulation and the additional costs it imposed were not easily derivable. First, it was not possible to determine accurately what level of domestic programming was due exclusively to the regulation. Second, television viewing generates private as well as external cultural benefits that occur jointly and are thus not separable. Third, potential imported substitutes for domestic programmes also confer private and external benefits (or disbenefits) to viewers, further complicating the estimation of incremental benefits from domestic programmes. Fourth, compliance with the domestic programming quotas, other than those mandating first release programmes of particular genres, could be achieved with many different combinations of programmes broadcast in different timeslots of varying opportunity costs (in terms of advertising revenue forgone). And fifth, unavailability of relevant data necessitated indirect estimation of both costs and benefits.

On the cost side, aggregate operational cost data, including aggregate cost of Australian and imported programming, were available from the broadcasting regulator. In addition, estimates of average production costs per hour of programming could be sourced from industry experts. However, there was very little information that could be used to derive realistic estimates of the quantity of domestic programmes attributable to the regulation. The use of different scenarios for this purpose was considered but not adopted because of concerns that it would add undesirable complexity to the analysis. Similarly, differentiation between private and external benefits of viewing domestic programming was a major constraint to the estimation of cultural benefits. To minimise the impact of these constraints, the study sought to derive an approximate value of net benefits by comparing estimates of total programming costs with estimates of total benefits. The underlying assumption was that competition between commercial television operators would ensure that the cost of supplying non-regulated programming was commensurate with the benefits the operators derived from advertising. Thus any difference between total domestic programming costs and total (private plus external) benefits derived from such programmes by the Australian public would be likely to approximate the net benefit or cost of the regulation.[1] Contingent valuation was used to estimate total benefits.

The Australian Bureau of Statistics was commissioned to collect the contingent valuation data as part of one of its quarterly national surveys of Australian households. In addition to standard demographic characteristics of respondents, the survey collected information on:

- perceptions on whether consumption of domestic television programmes generated cultural benefits to Australian society;
- willingness to pay for the *existing* mandated level of domestic programming on free-to-air television services;
- willingness to pay for a *10 per cent increase* in the existing mandated level of domestic programming on free-to-air television services; and
- relative valuation of the main categories of domestic programming that are regularly broadcast by free-to-air television services.

The most critical aspect of CVM is the formulation and presentation of a realistic hypothetical market for the elicitation of WTP data in a way that minimises the scope for responses prone to strategic or other bias. An incentive-compatible referendum format was used to pose the valuation questions relating to the mandated level of domestic programming and for a proposed incremental increase in the mandated level.[2] In relation to the existing level of programming, respondents were first informed of the annual average cost per household associated with the supply of Australian programmes and were then asked whether, in the light of the perceived benefits, the amount should be changed as follows:

> On average each household pays about $120 a year in taxes and increased prices for advertised goods to finance Australian TV programs.
>
> Considering the benefits your household and the community get from Australian programs, do you think this amount should be increased, decreased or stay the same?

Those supporting increased or decreased expenditure were then asked to state their maximum willingness to pay 'to retain the current amount of Australian programs on TV'.

A similar approach was used to elicit WTP information for an incremental increase in domestic television content. Respondents were first asked a dichotomous choice question on their household's willingness to pay 'an extra $12 each year in increased prices and taxes for a 10% increase in Australian programs'. Depending on their answer, respondents were asked one of two different nested follow-up questions. Those who answered 'yes' to the initial question were asked whether they were prepared to pay more than A$12, and those with an affirmative response were further asked to state the maximum amount that they were prepared to pay each year. Those who answered 'no' to the initial question were asked whether they would be prepared to pay an amount less than A$12 each year, and those with an affirmative response were further asked to state the maximum amount that they were prepared to pay each year.

Assessment of the regulation's efficiency also included an evaluation of how effective the domestic programme quotas were in achieving the desired objective. Both empirical and qualitative assessments were used to determine compliance with the quotas. To test whether the support provided by the regulation was consistent with community preferences and thus potentially effective in its objective, the survey elicited information on the viewing preferences of respondents. It also posed separate questions on respondents' opinion as to whether the quantity of, and the support for, various categories of domestic programmes should be increased or decreased. Respondents were also asked to indicate their preferred allocation of a notional mandated funding increase to the various categories of domestic programming.

From the analysis of the relevant data, it was evident that the overall transmission quota contributed the least to the objectives of the regulation because many of the domestic programmes were highly likely to continue to be broadcast in the absence of the quota. These included programmes such as news, current affairs and sports which enjoyed a large element of natural protection from imports and were popular with audiences. In contrast, the specific subquotas for children's programmes and adult drama were a significant influence on the market behaviour of television stations. However, these subquotas did not appear to be well-targeted in promoting desired programming.

Results and conclusion

At a general level, the survey found widespread acknowledgement of the cultural benefits of domestic television programmes, implying considerable public support for the regulation. Some 72.5 per cent of respondents, for example, were of the view that domestic programmes are 'important for the preservation of the Australian way of life' and over 62 per cent believed that Australian programmes benefited all Australians.

Consistent with general support for regulation, only 15 per cent of all respondents wanted a decrease in expenditure on Australian programming. An additional 7.7 per cent were indifferent to, or unable to, give a response (don't know/don't care) to the question. An increase was supported by 12 per cent. Details are provided in Figure 8.1.

The distribution of responses to the willingness to pay for an incremental expansion of domestic content are illustrated in Figure 8.2. The proposed payment of an extra A$12 per year for the suggested 10 per cent increase in Australian programming was acceptable to 48 per cent of respondents. A further 7.1 per cent indicated that they would be prepared to pay an amount less than A$12 per year. Thus a total of 55 per cent of respondents indicated a positive valuation for the proposed increase.

The survey found considerable dissatisfaction with the existing distribution of support among the various programme categories. Less than one-third (31.2 per cent) of the large majority of respondents who supported at least the prevailing level of expenditure on Australian television programming were satisfied with its distribution among the various programme categories. Of those indicating that the expenditure should be increased, only 14.6 per cent were happy with the existing allocations. Overall, a change in the distribution of expenditure was supported by 65.6 per cent of respondents.

Additional questions in the survey collected both qualitative and

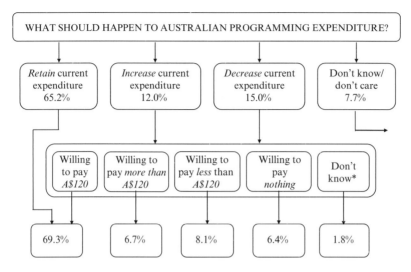

Note: * willing to pay an unspecified amount less than A$120.

Source: Papandrea (1997, p.137).

Figure 8.1 Valuation of Australian TV programmes

quantitative information on respondents' support for increased or decreased expenditure on individual domestic programme categories. Using two separate opinion questions, respondents were asked to first indicate which categories of domestic programming should receive increased or decreased support. In both cases, respondents were free to choose one or more categories. The programme categories most often nominated for increased support were documentaries (41.9 per cent of respondents) and children's programmes (36.1 per cent). The categories nominated for reduced support were sports (29.4 per cent); drama (series/serials) (19.4 per cent); light entertainment (17.4 per cent); and news and current affairs (16.3 per cent). Details are provided in Table 8.4.

To further explore support for particular types of programmes, respondents were also asked to distribute a notionally mandated amount approximately equivalent to a 10 per cent increase in expenditure on domestic programmes among the various programme categories. Consistent with the general opinions findings, half of the total proposed increase in expenditure was allocated in almost equal shares to documentaries and children's programmes (see Figure 8.3 for details).

Overall, the study revealed widespread acceptance of the community benefits that are likely to accrue from the provision of Australian films and

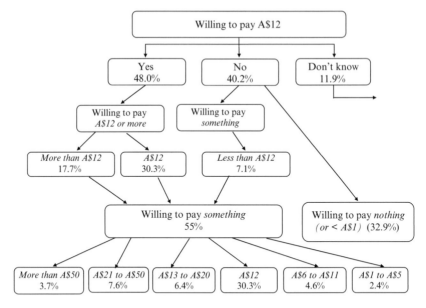

Note: Minor discrepancies due to routing.

Source: Papandrea (1997, p. 143).

Figure 8.2   Willingness to pay for a 10% increase in Australian programmes

Table 8.4   Opinions on changes to level of support for domestic programmes

Programme category	Increase expenditure (%)	Decrease expenditure (%)
News, current affairs	4.4	16.3
Documentaries	41.9	0.7
Sports	4.2	29.4
Series/serials	8.1	19.4
Light entertainment	6.6	17.4
Children's programmes	36.1	0.5
Other	13.2	1.6
None of the above	0.8	4.8

Source: Papandrea (1997, p. 152).

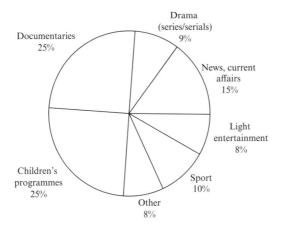

Source: Papandrea (1997, p. 154).

*Figure 8.3   Distribution of additional expenditure on Australian
programmes*

television programmes. Generally, Australians appear to have been satisfied with the policy in support of domestic television programmes. For a large majority, the current level of expenditure associated with Australian programmes is at least commensurate with the value of the benefits. A moderate level of demand for some increased expenditure on domestic programmes was also revealed.

While regulatory assistance for domestic programming was widely supported, its distribution was not. Demand for additional domestic programming was strongly influenced by genre. Children's programmes attracted the strongest support for additional expenditure followed by documentaries. Support for additional expenditure on drama, one of the main categories promoted by the regulation, was relatively weak. The only category attracting less support was light entertainment.

These results suggest that the benefits from the regulation could be increased by encouraging a different mix of domestic programmes. The most desirable shift in regulatory support was the promotion of increased expenditure on children's programmes and documentaries, with a commensurate decrease in other categories.

The analysis also found that the overall transmission quota was largely redundant as virtually all commercial television stations consistently broadcast more than the mandated level of domestic programmes. Better targeting of the specific subquotas was also likely to increase their efficiency.

7   Regulatory oversight

The rapidly changing economic environment of recent decades has cast a spotlight on structural rigidities and other impediments to economic adjustment and growth resulting from unwarranted or inefficient regulation. Consequently, regulatory reform became a key element of structural change policies adopted by many governments to address the challenges emerging from the changing economic environment. Existing regulations came under increasing scrutiny as many advanced economies embarked on reform of major sectors such as telecommunications, transport, energy and financial services. New proposals for regulation were also increasingly subjected to stringent scrutiny. The positive early experiences highlighted the importance of coordinated management of regulatory processes and review of regulation.

Seeking to improve regulatory efficiency, governments in many countries have established formal processes and mechanisms to limit the use of regulation and minimise the deleterious effects that poorly planned and inefficient regulations can have on economic growth and national well-being. The aims of these processes and mechanisms are broadly consistent and generally tend towards ensuring that regulation is introduced only when other less intrusive mechanisms are demonstrably unsuitable and that the proposed regulatory instruments generate the greatest possible net benefits to society. For example, the policy principles and procedures to be followed in the development of regulation in the United States are detailed in Executive Order 12866 of 30 September 1993 (see Box 8.1). Other developed countries have adopted similar procedural frameworks.

Responsibility for the oversight of federal regulatory activity in the United States in accordance with Executive Order 12866 has been assigned to the Office of Management and Budget (OMB). The function is performed by OMB's Office of Information and Regulatory Affairs (OIRA). Before recommending regulatory intervention, agencies have the onus to demonstrate the necessity for the proposed action. In particular, all 'economically significant' regulatory action (proposals with an annual effect on the economy of US$100 million or more) by federal agencies is subject to review by OIRA before they are proposed for public comment and again before they are issued in final form. OIRA reviews draft proposals for consistency with the regulatory principles enunciated in Executive Order 12866 and determines whether the proposed agency has assessed the costs and benefits of regulatory alternatives. In addition, a principal requirement of the review process is that agencies must prepare and submit to OIRA a regulatory impact analysis (RIA) providing an assessment of the costs and benefits of reasonably feasible alternative action.

BOX 8.1   EXECUTIVE ORDER 12866 OF SEPTEMBER 30, 1993

Statement of Regulatory Philosophy and Principles

Regulatory Philosophy
Federal agencies should promulgate only such regulations as are required by law, are necessary to interpret the law, or are made necessary by compelling public need, such as material failures of private markets to protect or improve the health and safety of the public, the environment, or the wellbeing of the American people. In deciding whether and how to regulate, agencies should assess all costs and benefits of available regulatory alternatives, including the alternative of not regulating. Costs and benefits shall be understood to include both quantifiable measures (to the fullest extent that these can be usefully estimated) and qualitative measures of costs and benefits that are difficult to quantify, but nevertheless essential to consider. Further, in choosing among alternative regulatory approaches, agencies should select those approaches that maximize net benefits (including potential economic, environmental, public health and safety, and other advantages; distributive impacts; and equity), unless a statute requires another regulatory approach.

Principles of Regulation
To ensure that the agencies' regulatory programs are consistent with the philosophy set forth above, agencies should adhere to the following principles, to the extent permitted by law and where applicable:

1. Each agency shall identify the problem that it intends to address (including, where applicable, the failures of private markets or public institutions that warrant new agency action) as well as assess the significance of that problem.
2. Each agency shall examine whether existing regulations (or other law) have created, or contributed to, the problem that a new regulation is intended to correct and whether those regulations (or other law) should be modified to achieve the intended goal of regulation more effectively.

3. Each agency shall identify and assess available alternatives to direct regulation, including providing economic incentives to encourage the desired behavior, such as user fees or marketable permits, or providing information upon which choices can be made by the public.
4. In setting regulatory priorities, each agency shall consider, to the extent reasonable, the degree and nature of the risks posed by various substances or activities within its jurisdiction.
5. When an agency determines that a regulation is the best available method of achieving the regulatory objective, it shall design its regulations in the most cost-effective manner to achieve the regulatory objective. In doing so, each agency shall consider incentives for innovation, consistency, predictability, the costs of enforcement and compliance (to the government, regulated entities, and the public), flexibility, distributive impacts, and equity.
6. Each agency shall assess both the costs and the benefits of the intended regulation and, recognizing that some costs and benefits are difficult to quantify, propose or adopt a regulation only upon a reasoned determination that the benefits of the intended regulation justify its costs.
7. Each agency shall base its decisions on the best reasonably obtainable scientific, technical, economic, and other information concerning the need for, and consequence of, the intended regulation.
8. Each agency shall identify and assess alternative forms of regulation and shall, to the extent feasible, specify performance objectives, rather than specifying the behavior or manner of compliance that regulated entities must adopt.
9. Wherever feasible, agencies shall seek views of appropriate State, local, and tribal officials before imposing regulatory requirements that might significantly or uniquely affect those governmental entities. Each agency shall assess the effects of Federal regulations on state, local, and tribal governments, including specifically the availability of resources to carry out those mandates, and seek to minimize those burdens that uniquely or significantly affect such governmental entities, consistent with achieving regulatory objectives. In addition, as appropriate, agencies shall seek to harmonize Federal regulatory actions with related state, local, and tribal regulatory and other governmental functions.

10. Each agency shall avoid regulations that are inconsistent, incompatible, or duplicative with its other regulations or those of other Federal agencies.
11. Each agency shall tailor its regulations to impose the least burden on society, including individuals, businesses of differing sizes, and other entities (including small communities and governmental entities), consistent with obtaining the regulatory objectives taking into account, among other things, and to the extent practicable, the costs of cumulative regulations.
12. Each agency shall draft its regulations to be simple and easy to understand, with, the goal of minimizing the potential for uncertainty and litigation arising from such uncertainty.

According to the relevant OMB circular (OMB, 2003), there are three key elements of regulatory analysis, namely:

1. a statement setting out the need for the proposed regulatory action,
2. an examination of the alternative approaches that may be used to address the identified need, and
3. a quantitative and qualitative evaluation of the benefits and costs of the proposed action and the main alternatives identified by the analysis.

In addition, the circular states that a proper evaluation of benefits and costs requires:

- an explanation of how the actions required by the proposed rule, and by each of the alternatives, are linked to the expected benefits;
- identification of a 'no action' baseline against which the costs and benefits of the proposed rule and alternatives are measured; and
- identification of expected undesirable side-effects and ancillary benefits of the proposed rule and alternatives, which should be added as appropriate to the direct benefits and costs.

OMB is required to report annually to Congress on the costs and benefits of major federal regulation. Only rules generating costs or benefits of at least $100 million in any one year for which an agency quantified a substantial portion of their costs and benefits are included in the estimates. It is also noted that in many instances agencies were unable to quantify

Table 8.5   Estimates of the total annual benefits and costs of major federal rules, October 1, 1995 to September 30, 2005 (millions of 2001 dollars)

Agency	Number of rules	Benefits	Costs
Department of Agriculture	7	3,530–6,747	2,215–2,346
Department of Education	1	633–786	349–589
Department of Energy	6	5,194–5,260	2,958
Department of Health and Human Services	19	21,313–33,268	3,853–4,029
Department of Homeland Security (Coast Guard)	1	44	305
Department of Housing and Urban Development	1	190	150
Department of Justice	1	275	108–118
Department of Labor	4	1,138–3,440	349
Department of Transportation	13	2,913–4,948	3,212–6,622
Environmental Protection Agency	42	58,670–394,454	23,572–26,200
Total	95	93,899–449,412	37,071–43,665

Source: OMB (2007: Table 1-1).

all benefits and costs. The 2006 report (OMB, 2007) states that the estimated annual benefits of major Federal regulations reviewed by OMB from October 1, 1995, to September 30, 2005, range from $94 billion to $449 billion, while the estimated annual costs range from $37 billion to $44 billion. Environmental Protection Agency rules are responsible for the majority of the reported costs and benefits. A summary is provided in Table 8.5.

These aggregate figures suggest that regulation is generating a substantial net benefit to American society and is thus consistent with the public interest. However, although the figures clearly indicate an overall net benefit from regulation, it does not follow that each individual regulation produces a net benefit. In their analysis and comments on the draft version of OMB's 2006 report, Hahn and Litan (2006, p. 3) note that many of the individual rules do not pass a strict cost–benefit test defined as one that '*quantified* benefit and cost estimates and *excludes* unquantified benefits and costs' (emphasis in original). They apply such a test to 124 rules for which OMB had provided some information on both costs and benefits between October 1, 1992 and September 30, 2005. On this basis they

Table 8.6   Major rules passing a strict cost–benefit test (1992–2005)[a]

	Number of rules passing	Percentage passing	Total annualized net benefits[e]
Best estimate[b]	99	80%	$332 billion
Best-case scenario[c]	108	87%	$536 billion
Worst-case scenario[d]	77	62%	$127 billion
(No. of rules examined = 124)			

Notes
a. This cost–benefit test subtracts quantified costs from quantified benefits. The analysis includes 126 non-transfer rules described in the OMB's reports that were finalized between October 1, 1992 and September 30, 2005. Two regulations of the 126, 'Child Restraint System' and 'Roadway Worker Protection', had net benefits of zero. We excluded them from the pass/fail test analysis because they neither pass nor fail.
b. When the OMB presents a single estimate, we take that as the best estimate. When only a range is provided, we take the midpoint for costs or benefits as the best estimate.
c. When a range is provided, this scenario uses the maximum benefits and minimum costs.
d. When a range is provided, this scenario uses minimum benefits and maximum costs.
e. Total annualized net benefits are the sum of annualized net benefits for all 124. Annualized net benefits for each regulation equal the annualized benefits of the regulation minus the annualized costs, as reported by the OMB. Numbers are rounded to the nearest billion 2001 dollars. These calculations do not adjust for the fact that regulations are implemented in different years.

Source: Hahn and Litan (2006: Table 1).

concluded that '80 per cent (99 of 124) of the major non-transfer rules with quantified costs and benefits would pass a benefit–cost test using best estimates based on OMB's numbers. The other 20 per cent would fail'.[3] Table 8.6 provides details of the number of rules passing the test under 'best-case' and 'worst-case' scenarios.

Similar analysis of previous OMB reports to Congress come to similar conclusions. For example, an examination by Hahn and Layburn (2003) of the data on new 'non-transfer' regulations published in the 2003 OMB report concluded that for the previous several years less than half of the new transfer rules considered would have unambiguously passed 'a cost–benefit test based on quantified estimates of benefits and costs', the implication being that better oversight of regulatory proposals could have produced significant additional benefits to society.

8   Regulatory governance
In many developed countries the level of regulatory activity has been rapidly increasing in recent decades as governments respond to an

expanding range of economic, social and environmental issues. In Australia, for example, according to a government-appointed taskforce, the Australian Parliament had passed more pages of legislation in the 15 years from 1990 than it had in the nine preceding decades (Regulation Taskforce, 2006). In the United States, approximately 4,000 final rules are issued annually by federal agencies and more than 48,000 final rules were issued from 1995 to 2006 (Crews, 2007). Similar patterns of regulatory activity are evident in other developed countries and governments have been under some pressure to ease the increasing burden of regulation on economic activity.

At government levels, there has been considerable action and interest in ensuring better or more stringent scrutiny of the effects of regulatory proposals. Many governments require the preparation of regulatory impact statements as an integral part of proposals for the introduction of new regulation as well as of proposals to reform existing regulatory arrangements. But even with a high level of scrutiny there is no guarantee that regulation will always produce outcomes that will increase the well-being of society (Hahn and Malik, 2004). The pervasiveness of regulation clearly implies that considerable gains can be achieved with improved regulatory processes and both governments and international organisations have been giving increasing attention to the issue.

The OECD (1995, p. 11), noting the 'far-reaching and complex regulatory systems' developed by member countries in recent decades, stresses that 'quality regulation is crucial for government effectiveness'. In seeking to improve regulatory performance, 'member countries have increased their attention to the quality of regulatory instruments' including an increased focus 'on the functioning of the administrative processes through which regulations are developed, implemented, adjudicated and revised'. But the OECD also noted that member countries were nonetheless experiencing 'similar and troublesome problems with their use of regulation' including concerns about its 'growing quantity and costs . . . the quality of individual regulations [and] the legitimacy and openness of regulatory decision processes'.

Drawing on principles for good regulatory practices developed by several countries, the OECD has framed a checklist to promote improved governance of regulatory decision making (see Box 8.2). In particular, the checklist stresses the need for a clear and precise definition of the problem, and of its scope and effects, so as to identify those aspects of the problem which can be addressed by regulation and those which can not be so addressed. It also stresses the need to ascertain that no alternative non-regulatory mechanisms exist to address the problem and to ensure that the benefits of regulation justify the costs.

BOX 8.2   THE OECD REFERENCE CHECKLIST FOR REGULATORY DECISION MAKING

1. *Is the problem correctly defined?*
    The problem to be solved should be precisely stated, giving evidence of its nature and magnitude, and explaining why it has arisen (identifying the incentives of affected entities).
2. *Is government action justified?*
    Government intervention should be based on explicit evidence that government action is justified, given the nature of the problem, the likely benefits and costs of action (based on a realistic assessment of government effectiveness), and alternative mechanisms for addressing the problem.
3. *Is regulation the best form of government action?*
    Regulators should carry out, early in the regulatory process, an informed comparison of a variety of regulatory and non-regulatory policy instruments, considering relevant issues such as costs, benefits, distributional effects and administrative requirements.
4. *Is there a legal basis for regulation?*
    Regulatory processes should be structured so that all regulatory decisions rigorously respect the 'rule of law'; that is, responsibility should be explicit for ensuring that all regulations are authorised by higher-level regulations and consistent with treaty obligations, and comply with relevant legal principles such as certainty, proportionality and applicable procedural requirements.
5. *What is the appropriate level (or levels) of government for this action?*
    Regulators should choose the most appropriate level of government to take action, or if multiple levels are involved, should design effective systems of co-ordination between levels of government.
6. *Do the benefits of regulation justify the costs?*
    Regulators should estimate the total expected costs and benefits of each regulatory proposal and of feasible alternatives, and should make the estimates available in accessible format to decision-makers. The costs of government action should be justified by its benefits before action is taken.

7. *Is the distribution of effects across society transparent?*
    To the extent that distributive and equity values are affected by government intervention, regulators should make transparent the distribution of regulatory costs and benefits across social groups.

8. *Is the regulation clear, consistent, comprehensible and accessible to users?*
    Regulators should assess whether rules will be understood by likely users, and to that end should take steps to ensure that the text and structure of rules are as clear as possible.

9. *Have all interested parties had the opportunity to present their views?*
    Regulations should be developed in an open and transparent fashion, with appropriate procedures for effective and timely input from interested parties such as affected businesses and trade unions, other interest groups, or other levels of government.

10. *How will compliance be achieved?*
    Regulators should assess the incentives and institutions through which the regulation will take effect, and should design responsive implementation strategies that make the best use of them.

Source: OECD (1995, pp. 9–10).

9   Prospective issues

Although governments in many countries routinely require the use of CBA in the evaluation of regulatory proposals, there is considerable debate about the role of the methodology in regulatory decision making. Much of the debate concerns the need for policy makers to give due weight to equity, ethical and moral considerations when making regulatory decisions. The ongoing growth of social regulation will continue to provide fuel to this debate, with particular focus on the limitations of CBA.

That CBA has limitations is widely acknowledged, but as yet other methodologies capable of outperforming CBA as an evaluative tool for policy decisions have not emerged. As Sunstein (1996) notes, regulation is not only about economic efficiency but has diverse legitimate purposes. Acknowledgement of other purposes is not an argument against CBA, but does have important implications for its use and methodological limits. Addressing and exploring these implications and limits offers fertile ground for future research and scholarship.

Several scholars have offered suggestions for possible improvement to the use of CBA in regulatory evaluation generally. Among them, Sunstein (1996) provides suggestions on better integration or balancing of CBA with other considerations in decision making. Kopp et al. (1997) also offer several suggestions for improvement in the analysis of regulatory activity. Adler and Posner (1999) review some of the limitations of CBA and make several suggestions for considerations of non-economic criteria when applying the methodology to analysis of regulation. Hahn and Sunstein (2001–02) also propose ways for greater integration of CBA in regulatory evaluation.

Increasing attention to social regulation in areas such as health and safety, and the environment also highlights some of the limitations in current practices. Issues such as the appropriate value of life in CBA, risk measurement, assessment of acute and chronic health effects, and valuation of ecosystems remain unresolved. So too does the appropriate discount rate for use in climate change related regulation whose effects are very long term and well beyond those typically encountered in business and financial analysis. These are complex issues that would benefit greatly from the attention of researchers and scholars.

Notes

1. This assumed that advertising revenue derived from the supply of the programmes was approximately equal to the private benefits accruing to viewers.
2. For a detailed discussion of the CVM study, including the development of the questionnaire, see Papandrea (1997) – the questionnaire and a summary of the CVM survey are also available in Papandrea (1999).
3. Broadly, non-transfer rules are environmental, health and safety regulations not involving a transfer of wealth among individuals.

References

ACIL Tasman (2005), 'Consumer Benefits Resulting from Australia's Telecommunications Sector', Report prepared for the Australian Communications and Media Authority, ACMA, Sydney.

Ackerman, F. and L. Heinzerling (2001–02), 'Pricing the priceless: cost–benefit analysis of environmental protection', *University of Pennsylvania Law Review*, **150**: 1553–84.

Adler, M. and E. Posner (1999), 'Rethinking cost–benefit analysis', *Yale Law Journal*, **99** (2): 165–247.

Applied Economics (2003), 'Cost–Benefit Analysis of Proposed New Health Warnings on Tobacco Products', Report Prepared for Commonwealth Department of Health and Ageing, December, www.treasury.gov.au/documents/836/PDF/Cost_Benefit_Analysis. pdf, accessed 18 December 2007.

Arrow, K., R. Solow, P. Portney, E. Leamer, R. Radner and H. Schuman (1993), *NOAA Panel on Contingent Valuation*, National Oceanic and Atmospheric Administration, Department of Commerce, Washington DC.

Choi, A., B. Ritchie and F. Papandrea (2008), 'The Economic Value of Australian National Cultural Institutions in the ACT', Sustainable Tourism CRC, Gold Coast, Australia.

Crews, C. (2007), *Ten Thousand Commandments*, Competitive Enterprise Institute, Washington, DC, www.cei.org/pdf/6018.pdf.

Frank, R.H. (2000), 'Why is cost–benefit analysis so controversial?', *Journal of Legal Studies*, **29** (June): 913–30.

Hahn, R (2004), 'The economic analysis of regulation: a response to the critics', *University of Chicago Law Review*, **71**: 1021–54.

Hahn, R. and E. Layburn (2003), 'Tracking the value of regulation', *Regulation*, Fall: 16–21.

Hahn, R. and R. Litan (2006), 'An Analysis of the Ninth Government Report on the Costs and Benefits of Federal Regulations', Regulatory Analysis 06-05, AEI–Brookings Joint Center for Regulatory Studies, June, www.aei-brookings.org, accessed 2 June 2007.

Hahn, R. and R. Malik (2004), 'Is regulation good for you?', *Harvard Journal of Law and Public Policy*, **27** (3): 893–916.

Hahn, R. and C. Sunstein (2001–02), 'A new executive order for improving federal regulation? Deeper and wider cost–benefit analysis', *University of Pennsylvania Law Review*, **150**: 1489–552.

Hazilla, M. and R. J. Kopp (1990), 'Social cost of environmental quality regulations: a general equilibrium analysis', *Journal of Political Economy*, **98** (4): 853–73.

Heal, G. (1997), 'Discounting and climate change: an editorial comment', *Climatic Change*, **37**: 335–43.

Hensher, D., J. Rose and W. Greene (2005), *Applied Choice Analysis*, Cambridge University Press, Cambridge.

Kelman, S. (1981), 'Cost benefit analysis: an ethical critique', *AEI Journal on Government and Society Regulation* (January/February): 33–40.

Kopp, R., A. Krupnick and M. Toman (1997), 'Cost benefit analysis and regulatory reform: an assessment of the science and the art', Discussion Paper 97-19, Resources for the Future, Washington, DC.

Kornhauser, L.A. (2000), 'On justifying cost–benefit analysis', *Journal of Legal Studies*, **29** (June): 1037–57.

Mitchell, R. and R. Carson (1989), *Using Surveys to Value Public Goods: The Contingent Valuation Method*, Johns Hopkins University Press, Baltimore, MD.

Noonan, D.S. (2003), 'Contingent valuation and cultural resources: a meta-analytical review of the literature', *Journal of Cultural Economics*, **27** (3–4): 159–76.

Nordhaus, W.D. (1997), 'Discounting in economics and climate change: an editorial comment', *Climatic Change*, **37**: 315–28.

OECD (1995), 'Recommendations of the Council of the OECD on Improving the Quality of Government Regulation', OCDE/GD(95)95, OECD, Paris, www.olis.oecd.org/olis/1995doc.nsf/LinkTo/OCDE-GD(95)95, accessed 23 August 2007.

Office of Management and Budget (OMB) (2003), 'OMB Circular A-4, Regulatory Analysis', Appendix D in 'Informing Regulatory Decisions: 2003 Report to Congress on the Costs and Benefits of Federal Regulations and Unfunded Mandates on State, Local, and Tribal Entities', www.whitehouse.gov/omb/inforeg/2003_cost-ben_final_rpt.pdf, accessed 15 May 2007.

Office of Management and Budget (OMB) (2007), '2006 Report to Congress on the Costs and Benefits of Federal Regulation and Unfunded Mandates on State, Local, and Tribal Entities', www.whitehouse.gov/omb/inforeg/2006_cb/2006_cb_final_report.pdf, accessed 23 January 2008.

Papandrea, F. (1997), 'Cultural Regulation of Australian Television Program', Occasional Paper 114, Bureau of Transport and Communications Economics, AGPS, Canberra.

Papandrea, F. (1999), 'Willingness to pay for domestic television programming', *Journal of Cultural Economics*, **23** (3): 147–64.

Pezzey, J. and R. Lambie (2001), 'Computable General Equilibrium Models for Evaluating Domestic Greenhouse Policies in Australia: A Comparative Analysis', Report to the Productivity Commission, AusInfo, Canberra.

Regulation Taskforce (2006), 'Rethinking Regulation: Report of the Taskforce on Reducing

Regulatory Burdens on Business', Report to the Prime Minister and the Treasurer, Canberra, Australia, January, www.regulationtaskforce.gov.au/finalreport/regulation taskforce.pdf, accessed 9 August 2007.

Santagata, W. and G. Signorello (2000), 'Contingent valuation of a cultural public good and policy design: the case of "Napoli Musei Aperti"', *Journal of Cultural Economics*, **24** (3): 181–204.

Shapiro, S. (2005), 'Unequal partners: cost–benefit analysis and executive review of regulations', *Environmental Law Reporter*, **35** (July): 10433–46.

Spulber, D. (1989), *Regulation and Markets*, MIT Press, Cambridge, MA.

Sunstein, C. (1996), 'The cost–benefit state', Chicago Working Papers in Law and Economics (Second Series) No. 39, University of Chicago.

Sunstein, C. (2002), *Risk and Reason*, Cambridge University Press, Cambridge.

Viscusi, K. (1994), 'Cigarette taxation and the social consequences of smoking', NBER Working Paper No. 4891, www.nber.org/papers/W4891.

Viscusi, K. and T. Gayer (2002), 'Safety at any price?', *Regulation*, **25** (Fall): 54–63.

9 Can cost–benefit analysis of financial regulation be made credible?
Patrick Honohan

1 Introduction

Finance has long been a relatively highly regulated sector of the economy. Safety and soundness of banks, avoiding fraud and abuses of information and power, and guarding against the use of the financial system to launder the proceeds of crime, have been the primary concerns of regulators. Yet, even if most of the financial system works well, there are still banks that fail, bankers that commit frauds sometimes on a massive scale, stock prices are manipulated and the gullible cheated. Every failure that comes to public notice gives rise to a clamor for additional regulation. But can more regulation really be justified, and if so of what type? Indeed, can current regulations be justified either by the scale of damage avoided or the success in avoiding it?

Increasingly, appeal is being made to the methodology of cost–benefit analysis to resolve issues of this type. The trend towards requiring regulatory impact assessments (RIAs) for new regulations is firmly established, and these assessments are effectively applications of cost-benefit analysis[1] – though the degree of rigor and thoroughness of the assessments varies widely. In particular, the new enthusiasm for regulatory assessment has not yet been matched by a comparable expansion in the collection and use of quantified information. All too often the effectiveness of any given regulation in achieving its objective is either taken for granted or justified by an external mandate (for example, a statute enacted by parliament or the result of adherence to international practice). Where quantification is attempted, it is often confined to the cost side of the equation,[2] perhaps a response to the lobbying capacity of the regulated industry. While direct and compliance costs are easier to measure than the beneficial outcomes and impacts, it is in the latter areas that most uncertainty lies. Indeed, there seems to be little hard evidence of sizable, or indeed any, benefits from some of the most far-reaching regulations and regulatory structures. This is especially so for developing countries when there has been inappropriate transplantation of regulatory models developed for a different and more sophisticated environment. Sizable adverse side-effects are often neglected in RIAs.

Much of current financial regulatory practice traces its origins to the era of the Great Depression in the United States when thousands of banks failed, imposing heavy losses on depositors and deepening the economic recession. This led to the establishment of deposit insurance and to an accompanying regime of banking supervision more systematic and rigorous than had existed anywhere before designed to reduce the incidence of fraud, mismanagement or excessive risk taking that could result in losses to depositors (and hence to the deposit insurer). The collapse of New York stock market prices which marked the early stages of the crisis also triggered a reassessment of market practices and the codification and enforcement of regulations around mutual funds and against the manipulation of stock market prices. Concentrations of economic and financial power were also the target of US legislation and regulation in the 1930s.

Other countries with more heavily concentrated banking and financial systems with restrictive entry of new service providers continued to rely on informal or self-regulation late into the century, but the opening up of competition in the 1980s and 1990s, together with the growing incidence of bank failures and deepening of stock markets was accompanied by a shift towards greater formality of official regulation in all countries by the turn of the century. The US model was everywhere influential in the regulatory designs adopted, but national market conditions, legal structures and administrative and political practice mean that there are considerable differences between the way in which regulation is conducted in different countries. A degree of harmonization was sought particularly in the prudential regulation of banking where regulatory arbitrage between internationally active banks became significant by the 1980s. The successive Basel Committee agreements in this area, especially in regard to the establishment of regulatory minimum capital requirements, have been designed to help provide a level regulatory playing field and thus reduce the pressures from international regulatory arbitrage. Focus on prudential regulation has greatly increased as a result of the regulatory failures observed during the great banking crisis which begun in August 2007 and deepened during 2008.

At the same time, the increasing complexity of financial instruments and modes of delivery and the greater access of retail customers to a wide range of service providers gave rise on the one hand to a demand for greater consumer protection against abuses and on the other to a perception that de facto exclusion of low-income and other groups from financial services represented a policy problem calling for regulation. These pressures tended to expand the range of regulations and the responsibility of regulatory agencies. Use of the financial system by drug-dealers and other beneficiaries of illicit earnings to launder money, and by terrorists, also triggered international pressures on legislators and regulators to take countermeasures.

The accumulation of responsibilities and mandates results in a broad, demanding and complex set of regulatory arrangements in most countries. The design of these regulations is under constant review not least because of demand from the industry for a reduction in the regulatory burden under which they labor. But, in addition, the continuous flow of financial innovation, together with recurrent regulatory failure, gives rise to the need for additions and refinements to current regulations in order to ensure that they are fit for purpose. The need for cost–benefit analysis is thus not a one-off matter, but one which is likely to continue for the foreseeable future.

All of these reasons for regulation can be rationalized in terms of standard market failure theory (market power, externalities, information asymmetries). From that perspective, the task of the regulator is to address multiple market failures in what is a highly complex information-intensive industry subject to pervasive scale economies. In practice, though, it is totally impractical to try to embed an analysis of regulatory impact in a comprehensive model of the sector. For one thing, regulation cannot seek to correct fully the effects of information asymmetry and scale economies. After all, the acquisition and exploitation of information is at the heart of some of the most profitable lines of activity. Scale economies, both in information acquisition and processing, and from risk pooling, are inherent in most financial business. As long as there is a financial industry to be regulated, information asymmetries and scale-driven market power will remain key forces defining the sector, and they interact in ways that defy any regulatory attempt to completely nullify their effect.

Instead, regulatory innovation today still in practice responds to pressure points rather than attempting a holistic correction of underlying sources of market failure. At least five categories of pressure point continue to generate pressure for regulatory innovation. First, fraud and intermediary failure. Second, securities market manipulation. Third, misselling, including overlending or overcharging abuses. Fourth, access for excluded groups (including 'redlining'[3]). Fifth, money laundering and terrorism financing. The examples to be discussed in this chapter range across these categories.

Because of the variety of issues that arise, there is no set methodology for RIAs except in the broadest terms.[4] In practice, such analyses must make use of diverse approaches. This chapter will review some of this diversity, noting in particular the temptation to focus on what is easiest to measure even though this is in almost all cases much less important than aspects that are harder to measure. We distinguish between measurement of direct and indirect (compliance) costs of regulation on the one hand, and direct (sought-for) benefits and indirect side-effects, positive and negative.

We shall conclude that, although the actual and potential costs of bank failures are large, the effectiveness of current regulatory policies in reducing the frequency or size of failures has proved impossible to measure with any precision. Furthermore, the direct and compliance costs of prudential regulation[5] may often be outweighed by adverse side-effects (such as unintended reductions in the range or quality of products or restricting competition), which may be appreciable.

Many applications of cost–benefit analysis in the sector hinge on the application of shadow or social prices – as distinct from market prices – to input and output quantities that are measured relatively easily. In contrast, the constraining problem in applying cost–benefit to financial regulation is more typically discovering the quantities. Therefore acquisition of quantitative information concerning details of the impact of regulations is key. But because financial markets are subject to high cross-elasticities and driven by information flows and asymmetries inherently hard for analysts to assess, obtaining credible impact estimates is challenging.

Section 2 looks at what is typically the easiest part of this search for quantification, namely the measurement of direct and indirect (compliance) costs. This part is relatively well developed, and numerous quantifications have been provided in the literature.

More difficult to answer is the question: how effective will the regulation be in achieving the benefits towards which it is aimed? Sometimes in regulatory impact analyses, this is not even attempted. Indeed, the practice in US regulatory agencies is often to take the statutory mandate underlying the regulation as given (regardless of whether this mandate is likely to achieve a sizable social benefit) and to assess the cost-effectiveness of the regulation in meeting this mandate. Again, RIAs conducted in the UK of the transposition of EU legislative directives into British law and regulations now generally take the transposition as a given, and proceed to discuss the least-cost and most effective way of doing so, without second-guessing the likely benefits of the regulation as a whole.

Section 3 presents some examples of the benefits of well-functioning financial systems and the social damage of systemic failures. These may serve to establish upper bounds on the benefits to be obtained from successful regulation. Drilling down on a particular example, Section 4 looks in more detail at methodological issues in measuring the benefits of preventing or mitigating banking failures.

Regulations may not, however, be successful. Section 5 considers some evidence of the degree to which regulations are effective in achieving stated goals. Section 6 concludes.

2   Looking under the lamppost: measuring direct and compliance costs of regulation

Enforcing financial regulations entails resource costs for the official regulator, who needs to collect, audit and evaluate relevant data, often including making on-site visits to the regulated financial service provider. Although it would be cheaper to apply *ex post* enforcement by waiting until violations become conspicuous, the danger that considerable social harm will have been incurred by the time compliance failures have become evident mean that this is not the favored enforcement approach for many financial regulations, notably those relating to prudential issues. These resource costs can be appreciable and must of course be factored into any cost–benefit analysis even if they have been covered by an industry levy.

The financial services industry is well positioned to complain about the costs of regulation, and it does. Industry's costs are not confined to the payment of levies that may be imposed by the regulator to defray its expenses.[6] Considerable administrative costs arise for service providers in ensuring and documenting compliance. This would include the costs of providing retail customers with the detailed information and guidance which is typically required nowadays in the interest of avoiding mis-selling. In the case of regulations for anti-money laundering and countering the financing of terrorism (AML–CFT), reporting suspicious or large transactions to official financial crimes investigative bodies entails sizable costs.

The creation of the single financial regulator, the Financial Services Authority (FSA) in the United Kingdom, and the greater formalization of regulation that ensued, led to considerable debate about the administrative compliance costs of regulation in that country. A recent analysis commissioned by the FSA of the administrative compliance cost of 158 regulations identified as imposing such costs on financial firms arrived at a total figure of £600 million, or about 0.05 percent of UK GDP (see Table 9.1).[7]

Interestingly, there appear to be appreciable economies of scale at least in prudential regulation of banks, at least if scale is measured by such indicators as the number of banks, or balance sheet size. Based on data from European banking regulators, Schüler and Heinemann (2005) estimate that a 2 percent increase in the size of the regulated market can be supervised with only a 1 percent increase in the regulator's budget or staffing. They conclude that considerable social gains can be made by moving to a pan-European banking regulator.[8]

To be useful for policy decisions, estimates of administrative cost, whether of the regulator or the regulated, should refer to the incremental cost of the particular regulation being examined: sometimes the systems created to allow compliance for one set of regulations can make compliance with subsequent regulations cheap and easy.[9] Even if the exercise is

Table 9.1   Top 20 regulatory costs for financial firms in the UK

Regulatory compliance activity	£m	% of total
Money laundering – records of evidence customer identity	99.2	16.7
Money laundering – records of transactions	70.3	11.8
Money laundering – staff training	46.3	7.8
Training and competence record requirements	38.7	6.5
Money laundering – reporting to National Criminal Intelligence Service	38.5	6.5
Claims information to be kept for three years	29.9	5.0
Records of policy summaries and policy documents provided to customers	24.9	4.2
Life insurers annual returns	21.3	3.6
Retail mediation activities returns – general insurance	16.0	2.7
Application for authorization	14.8	2.5
Making and retaining records of complaints	14.4	2.4
Half-yearly complaints report	13.9	2.3
General insurers annual returns	13.8	2.3
Retail mediation activities returns – financial advisors	12.7	2.1
Client asset records	11.8	2.0
Application for approval of approved persons in controlled functions	9.1	1.5
Securities and futures firms regular returns	8.6	1.5
Application for variation of permission (VOP)	8.2	1.4
Client money audit	7.7	1.3
Records of non-real time financial promotions	6.9	1.2

Source: Real Assurance (2006).

designed to estimate the total impact of all regulations, the cost of complying with these regulations must be explicitly referred to a baseline of costs that would be incurred by the financial firm even in the absence of regulation as the consequence of good business practice in its own interest. Unfortunately, such counterfactuals can be difficult to quantify in practice.

The main approaches that can be used to obtain estimates of an industry's compliance costs may be grouped into case studies, surveys, econometric models and analogies (Elliehausen, 1998). Case studies involving an in-depth exploration of processes and procedures offer considerable advantages to the researcher not least because of the interactive nature of the exercise allowing researchers to revise the exact formulation of questions as they come to understand the provider's business better. Although it might seem that asking the regulated about their own costs would necessarily impart an upward bias to the estimates, Elliehausen points out that the respondents in case studies may owe their job within the financial firm to the existence of regulation. Besides, the regulated firms are in a continuing relationship with the regulator, including the potential for negotiating cost-reducing reforms to unnecessarily burdensome regulations; therefore they will not wish to compromise their credibility with the regulator in these matters. For these and other reasons, Elliehausen argues in his careful analysis of the various likely sources of error in case study and survey-based calculations that, given careful and detailed interview design, case studies are easier to get right.

But the experience of different firms may differ greatly, depending in particular on their mix of products as well as on the way in which they deliver these products. If so, a handful of case studies may not be representative of the costs of the industry as a whole. A detailed study by DeLoitte (2006) of UK regulations found a very wide range of estimated regulatory costs from well under 1 percent of other operating costs in some financial firms to over 30 percent in others, even when the comparison was restricted to firms conducting investment and pension fund advice. This consideration points to the merits of using larger surveys, which necessarily compromise on the level of detail and tailoring of the questionnaires. Some recent studies adopt a hybrid approach in which a relatively large number of firms are surveyed, but each firm is asked only about a restricted set of the regulations most relevant to its business (an example is in Real Assurance, 2006).

In contexts where case studies and surveys are not available, for example where the goal is to predict the likely impact of a regulation which is not yet in place, econometric methods and calculations by analogy can be useful. Econometric techniques would depend on the availability of cost data from a range of settings with different regulatory arrangements. Calculation by analogy (that is, estimating a cost by modeling the supposed compliance process as a combination of activities with known unit costs) is something which can be attempted nearly always, and is a staple of *ex ante* assessments, even if its reliability may be uncertain. It likely generates an upper bound on the costs, in that the ingenuity of the regulated firms will likely improve on the modeled process.

Apart from administrative costs, regulated firms often incur material opportunity costs from having to comply with such regulations as minimum capital requirements (which may raise the cost of funds) and minimum liquidity requirements (especially where the class of qualifying liquidity instruments is very constrained, as it sometimes is even to non-interest-bearing deposits at the central bank). While these certainly affect the distribution of regulatory costs, care must be taken in the overall calculation not to mistake quasi-taxes or transfer payments as resource costs. Thus, the opportunity cost of unremunerated liquidity reserve requirements is best thought of as an implicit or quasi-tax (Honohan, 2003), and not as an economic cost *per se* – though its distorting effects will have economic costs, best treated in the present context as side-effects.

Just as the drunk man favored looking for his lost carkeys under the lamppost where it was bright, and not where he had dropped them, the empirical literature on regulatory impact has concentrated mostly on the direct costs of enforcing and complying with regulations, rather than on benefits and side-effects. Yet in many cases these are in quantitative terms at least potentially much more important.

3   Quantification of potential benefits

To the extent that some underlying law and regulation is critical to the emergence of efficient financial systems, the econometric literature linking financial sector development with national economic growth points to very considerable long-term gains from good regulation, especially for countries starting from relatively low levels of financial development.[10] From this literature, it appears that having a strong financial system is crucial not only in mobilizing savings, but especially for improving the productivity of national investment, as financial markets and intermediaries select the most creditworthy or promising outlets for their investable funds. Other econometric findings point to the role of investor protection, and more generally of national legal systems in promoting financial depth,[11] and depositor confidence is also crucial. Thus regulation has a role in achieving these substantial benefits. The finance and growth literature thus seems to provide little constraint on regulatory cost–benefit. The size of the long-term benefits from financial development are too large to constrain the justifiable costs of effective regulation. The problem is in pinpointing the regulations that do actually contribute to financial development, whether measured by financial deepening, or by the performance and liquidity of securities markets.[12]

The maximum potential benefits of some of the other goals of financial regulation could be approached in a similar way, though here the evidence is less strong.[13] For example, the overall economic benefits of broader financial access have not been as thoroughly documented as have those of financial deepening. Access is largely a distributional issue: even in poor countries the benefits of access to the poor will not add up to a high percentage of GDP, but it will affect the well-being of the beneficiaries *relative to their starting income*.[14] Thus only welfare analysis employing an inequality-averse criterion function welfare analysis will generate a large overall national benefit from improvements in access. Note, however, that in poor countries, reduction of absolute poverty (to which better financial access can contribute) may be a prerequisite for the conditions that allow sustainable rapid medium-term growth.

The economic costs of financial crises can also be very large, thereby potentially justifying large costs of prudential regulation. Hoggarth et al. (2002) estimate the costs of systemic banking crises from the subsequent dip in national GDP. This approach has the merit of concentrating on resource costs rather than transfers, but is rendered problematic by the consideration that exogenous economic downturns also trigger crises and reveal hidden bank insolvencies: thus causality between banking crises and the contemporaneous economic downturns is bidirectional. An alternative approach is to measure the costs of banking crises from the total fiscal cost of recapitalizing failed banks or compensating depositors. Interestingly, in respect of 39 systemic banking crises for which both estimates are available, the two methods arrive at quite a similar average (12.5 percent of GDP for the fiscal costs and 14.6 percent for the economic costs), though, as is evident in Figure 9.1, the cross-crisis correlation between the two estimates, at less than 0.5, is not especially close (Honohan and Klingebiel, 2003). Thus, although precise estimates cannot be hoped for, even after the event, the potential cost of a systemic banking crisis is very high. Once again, therefore, even costly prudential regulations can be justified if they can be shown to reduce markedly the probability of a systemic crisis.

As a further illustration of the kinds of issues that arise in measuring benefits, we take a closer look at the challenges to obtaining good measures of the benefits of preventing or mitigating banking crises.

4   Measurement challenges: a closer look at the benefits of preventing or mitigating banking crises

One important practical example of the methodological measurement challenges facing the cost–benefit analyst of financial sector regulation relates to the social damage caused by large or systemic banking crises. It is important to get an appropriate measure of this damage inasmuch as prudential regulations can be justified only to the extent that they prevent or mitigate such damage.

As already mentioned (Section 3, above), two main approaches have been adopted in the literature to estimating the total economic damage resulting from systemic banking crises. One seeks to evaluate the overall loss of national output resulting from the crisis, whereas the other attempts to compute the total fiscal outlay. Apart from the two practical difficulties of (i) judging what the counterfactual path of national output would have

Compare costs.xls

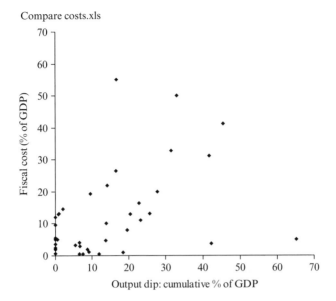

Note: The figure shows, for each of 39 banking crises around the world, estimates of (a) the fiscal cost and (b) the dip in GDP associated with the crisis.

Source: Honohan and Klingebiel (2003).

Figure 9.1 Two measures of the damage caused by systemic banking crises

been without the crisis and (ii) obtaining reliable information on the scale of initial fiscal outlays, each is some distance from an ideal measure of welfare losses.

For instance, there are practical and conceptual difficulties in deciding how to map fiscal outlays onto a welfare loss attributable to regulatory failure. One relates to timing. There may be an important difference between the initial outlay made by official agencies – such as the central bank, the deposit insurer or a bank restructuring agency – when one or more banks get into trouble and the final bill that has to be absorbed by the taxpayer. For example, the Swedish banking crisis of 1991–94 entailed initial fiscal outlays totaling 4 percent of GDP, but a subsequent rebound in the Swedish property market eventually allowed the debt recovery agency to sell the portfolio of distressed assets that it had acquired at relatively favorable prices, so that when everything had been disposed of, the net fiscal outlay was 2 percent of GDP or even lower (see Englund, 1999). Likewise, the difficulties in 2007 of the British bank Northern Rock forced it to make exceptional borrowings amounting to the equivalent of about

US$50 billion from the Bank of England, and to receive in addition an even larger special depositor guarantee from the UK Treasury. Although most commentators assumed that the vast bulk of these borrowings – if not all – would eventually be repaid, no private sector purchaser was willing to assume the liability on terms deemed acceptable to the UK authorities, and the bank was nationalized. In both of these cases, it is rather unclear what number should be taken as the fiscal cost. Should the post-crisis upturn in the Swedish property market be seen as a windfall gain, and as such not to be netted out in calculating the fiscal outlay properly attributable to the crisis? On the other hand, given the assurances officially provided as to the solvency of Northern Rock at the time of the policy intervention, is it reasonable to take the loans and guarantee provided to that bank as merely a financing transaction entailing no real transfer of resources?

The other major difficulty with the fiscal outlay approach is in distinguishing between transfer costs and true economic costs. Even a major loss such as that (amounting to the equivalent of about US$7 billion) incurred by the French bank Société Générale in 2008, as the result of reckless activity by a rogue trader, could be seen as entailing zero social costs. The counterparties of Société Générale in the loss-making trades were other banks and institutional investors. If the loss was an idiosyncratic negative shock to the shareholders of Société Générale, it was a corresponding positive shock for the shareholders of the counterparties. If each of the shareholders held well-diversified portfolios it is plausible that the event may have even had negligible distributional effects. In the case of Société Générale, the loss-making bank had large enough capitalization to absorb the loss, in contrast to Barings, which failed in similar circumstances in 1993 imposing losses on some creditors, despite the scale of the losses from rogue trading in that case being little more than US$1 billion. Should banking losses attributable to management deficiencies and failure of the regulatory authorities to detect and prevent such events be included in a cost–benefit calculation even if the bank's shareholders are willing and able to absorb the losses? Presumably no, if the transactions involved amounted to a zero-sum game between market participants, as in some of the rogue trader cases. But the question is still applicable even if the losses reflected real resource costs such as ill-advised lending to finance projects with a negative net present value.

Even though no large international bank had failed by early 2008, actual and feared losses resulting, for example, from the mispricing of risk in the US sub-prime[15] mortgage market were contributing to a credit crunch which was beginning to slow output growth in the major industrial countries; this reflected the pattern observed in 1990–91. Banking weakness thus caused economic damage in many countries even where there were no fiscal outlays. Yet developing a credible methodology for judging what fraction of the macroeconomic slowdown should be attributed to the banking weaknesses remained elusive.

Finally there are distributional aspects to the damage caused by banking crises which have not often been considered in detail. These may be crucial in a calculation of the social benefits of prudential regulation to limit crises. There can be no presumption that the damage is spread evenly across the income distribution. In some cases, the poorest seem to have escaped the worst of the crisis, as have the richest, though the distinct characteristics of each crisis mean that no uniform distributional pattern has been detected (Honohan, 2005).

A comprehensive analysis of the damage caused by the US sub-prime crisis will certainly have to take account of a complex set of additional elements, including distributional aspects. Soaring defaults on residential mortgages which had been underwritten overoptimistically reflected falling house prices that threatened to place many of the borrowers in a situation of negative equity and rising interest rates that made servicing the debt unaffordable for the low-income borrowers involved. Already in 2007, US lenders initiated 50 percent more foreclosures on residential mortgages than in previous years. The sizable transactions costs of the foreclosure proceedings looked set to represent a considerable part of the lenders' losses (Bernanke, 2008). But in addition, the hardship imposed on the borrowers concerned who would have to move home, and also lose their credit rating, are important factors for a cost–benefit analysis of policy interventions to mitigate or prevent this kind of problem. This last element is especially important if the cost–benefit analysis is distribution weighted (for example, as discussed in Brent, 2006) as it surely needs to be in the case of sub-prime lending. To do this we would need a lot of microdata, such as estimates of the amounts borrowed by individuals at different income levels, and the incidence of foreclosures at each income level. While some microdata exist, such as those employed by Dell'Ariccia et al. (2008) to describe the relaxation of underwriting standards in the US mortgage industry, detailed distributional data on financial assets and liabilities are collected only twice a decade or so, even in the United States.

This catalog of practical difficulties clearly illustrates the potential and need for detailed methodological and practical work to get a better grip on how to measure damage due to banking crises for the purpose of social cost–benefit analysis. This would apply as much to the analysis of policy measures such as extension of deposit insurance, or government debt-relief programs, as to regulations such as capital adequacy.

5   But does it work? Estimating the effectiveness of regulatory policy
Although the potential benefits may thus be large, it does not follow that
regulations established with the intention of achieving these benefits do
well in achieving the goals set for them. Worse, because of the complexity
and fluidity of financial systems, some regulations may be counterproductive. Any cost–benefit analysis in financial regulation thus has to pay
particular attention to the mechanism. Even if we have a good measure of
the costs and the hoped-for benefits of a particular regulation, comparing
these will be merely misleading if the regulation's supposed mechanism
does not work.

This is especially true, perhaps, for the vast array of prudential regulations designed to guard against low-frequency events such as systemic
crises. Ineffective or counterproductive regulations can persist because of
the difficulty of detection or proof. The failure of even the most prudential
regime of the most advanced economies to prevent the great financial crisis
is a case in point. But the occurrence or not of such a rare event as a systemic
crisis provides only limited evidence in favor of or against the regulation.[16]

Cross-country studies broaden the range of evidence, though the very
different institutional environments that exist in different financial systems
across the world mean that such studies need to work hard to convince
the reader that sufficient controls have been included to ensure that the
true effect of financial regulations have been isolated. Coding the different
forms of financial regulation also needs to be done with some delicacy, or
else dissimilar regulations will be treated the same, blurring their estimated
effect. Several examples of the cross-country approach may be mentioned,
including those relating to prudential regulation, crisis management and
usury laws. In each case, the wider evidence seems to reveal ineffectiveness
or even counterproductivity of important parts of widely used regulatory
approaches.

Cross-country evidence has recently been used to throw light on the
effectiveness of the large and onerous regime of bank regulation that has
been put in place worldwide because of the history of bank failures. Using
a large database coding numerous characteristics of the regulatory system
across some 150 countries, Barth et al. (2006) sought evidence of the
impact of different regulatory approaches on the performance of national
financial systems. The measurement of regulatory practice in this field
is complicated by formalism. Thus, for example, it is often low-income
countries known to have weak governance structures whose formal and
explicit rules for capital adequacy in banking are the toughest; however,
when it comes to less conspicuous and more qualitative aspects of regulation (for example, the detailed methods for calculating capital adequacy),
these countries fall behind.

Bearing these cautions in mind, it is nonetheless interesting to find that enhanced regulatory power, including discretionary power, of bank regulators – often seen by practitioners as a prerequisite for achieving safe-and-sound banking – proves not to be significantly correlated with any favorable dimensions of financial sector outcome, whether in terms of financial depth or stability. Instead, the one sizable effect that emerges consistently from the econometric analysis of Barth et al. indicates that regulatory power contributes to a banking environment in which corruption is frequently reported by users of banking services. More spending on a prudential regime that relies on official discretion would, according to these results, never pass a cost–benefit test. However, other features of a modern regulatory structure, notably those, such as accounting and disclosure requirements, that enhance the ability of large private market participants to exercise market discipline, do show up as having favorable effects.

The effectiveness of crisis management policies has also been evaluated on cross-country data, specifically on a sample of 39 systemic crises in the last two decades of the twentieth century. Honohan and Klingebiel (2003) find that accommodating policies such as blanket deposit insurance, temporary forbearance on the enforcement of capital adequacy and open-ended liquidity assistance to distressed banks, although adopted to soften the impact and reduce the costs of crises, were systematically associated with higher crisis costs.

The econometric findings of Barth et al. and of Honohan and Klingebiel on effectiveness of different elements of prudential regulation and crisis management rely on samples including a very wide range of country types. They do not so much cast doubt on established regulatory and crisis management practice in advanced economies as question the unthinking transplantation of that practice to weaker institutional environments. Of course, if the effectiveness of regulations varies widely in this way across countries at different levels of development, that in itself makes it problematic to use cross-country evidence in inferring the likely effectiveness of particular policies in a given country.

With regard to usury ceilings, a more limited cross-country study, lacking formal econometrics, also suggests that these may be counterproductive in limiting the actual cost of credit and the level of overindebtedness of poor households. Tighter interest ceilings (and other rules for lenders) in France and Germany may have had quite significant effects on restricting the range and availability of legally provided credit, compared with credit in the United Kingdom, and seem to have been associated with a higher incidence of overborrowing as more of the destitute in those countries borrow in the illegal market (Policis, 2006). The fraction of borrowers who have defaulted on high-cost, sub-prime credit cards is much higher in US states with binding usury laws than in states without such laws, pointing to the lack of other more suitable sources of credit for low-income borrowers (Policis, 2004).

Regional variations in regulation within large countries such as the United States can offer a similar basis for cross-sectoral econometric analysis, or at least to a useful control group. For example, in their analysis of a law introduced in North Carolina in 1999 to reduce the incidence of predatory lending (tougher than the US Federal Statute, the so-called Home Ownership and Equity Protection Act, HOEPA, of 1994), Elliehausen and Staten (2004) were able to show, using a nationwide survey of over 1.4 million mortgage loans, that while lending to high-risk customers in North Carolina fell sharply after the law was enacted, this did not happen to customers in neighboring states.[17]

Interregional regulatory variation is sometimes induced by a deliberate policy experiment, for example in China, which has exploited its vast population and land area, and limited interregional integration, to pilot many of its numerous policy reforms in selected regions.

Before and after studies are less convincing if there are no control groups, because of the numerous other causal factors which may have changed over time; but they can be useful when the relevant data is very specific. For example, the recent study by Monteiro and Zaidi (2007) looks at mortgage product prices in the UK following the imposition of a regulation designed to improve transparency of the market. Despite the regulation, the dispersion of mortgage prices offered by different suppliers did not decline. The study also found an increase in the average mortgage product price (which the authors interpret as possibly reflecting a passing-on of the additional costs of the regulation). Intuitively, the relevance of the first finding on price dispersion is more plausible, as any of a variety of other factors could have altered average product prices, which tend to be volatile.

Apart from cross-country, cross-regional or before-and-after studies, it may be possible to carry out a controlled experiment by modifying the regulation in respect of some segment of the regulated market. This may of course be impractical for any of a variety of reasons, not least the potential for boundary effects, as the close competitors of firms experiencing modified regulation could be strongly affected. An interesting example is provided by the Office of Economic Analysis (2007) describing the removal of short-selling restrictions on a large pilot sample of some one thousand US stocks (about one-third of the components of the Russell 3000 index). The short-sale restrictions, introduced into US stock markets in 1938 and designed to ensure orderly market conditions, had been criticized for possible side-effects in distorting price discovery by limiting the extent to which pessimistic investors could influence market prices. The study examined distributional characteristics of the prices for the pilot equities and found little evidence either of a beneficial or a distorting effect of the regulations. For example, the pilot stocks displayed no return skewness, as might be observed if bear speculators were trying to manipulate market prices. And the pattern of returns on the pilot stocks was statistically the same as for the remaining stocks, apart from a statistically significant 24 basis point excess return for the pilot stocks on the first day of the experiment.

In estimating benefits, econometric methods clearly come into their own, and are needed to obtain parameter estimates even if the overall calculation of benefits requires the use of a model or analogy. But direct survey evidence can sometimes be relevant. In the case of regulations that reduce customer risk, it is, for example, possible to use a hedonic approach, for example, by surveying customers and asking them what premium they would be prepared to pay for assurance that intermediaries with which they were dealing were subject to a certain rule.

These examples illustrate the wide variety of types of evidence that can be brought to bear in estimating regulatory benefits. Not all of the bits of evidence actually measure the desired outcomes or the ultimate impact of the regulation. For example, the ultimate goal of transparent product pricing is not a narrowing of price differentials across different suppliers. Mapping evidence of such a reduction onto a metric that is commensurate with the cost side of the equation would be by no means straightforward, and would involve the use of models that are neither widely accepted nor robustly calibrated.

Of course when, as in most of the examples selected here, the evidence is for little or no favorable effects, and some adverse side-effects, then policy advice based on the cost–benefit analysis requires no further quantification.

Side-effects of regulatory policy in finance can be more subtle and far-reaching than those already hinted at above. Two examples may be provided.

The US Community Reinvestment Act (CRA), which calls on banks to lend equally to all communities, is designed to reduce 'redlining' of geographic districts and other forms of discrimination in loan markets. It is often cited as a program that has had few side-effects on the functioning of the financial system, and studies suggest that it may have resulted in some impact on lending and perhaps a favorable knock-on effect on economic activity in the targeted geographic areas (Litan et al., 2001; Zinman, 2002). But Hylton (2006) has suggested that CRA compliance costs are much higher for small banks, and that this paradoxically discourages the entry of small community 'development-oriented' banks which are exactly those with the capacity and motivation to solve asymmetric information problems which act as barriers to effective finance in the low-income urban areas which are the target of the Act.

As an even more elaborate and important example of indirect effects, consider the political dynamic which has been unleashed on low-income countries by the Basel 2 process.[18] The complexity of the internal ratings systems used in Basel 2, and the fact that they need extensive historic data in the local market, make the use of these systems problematic in most low-income countries.[19] Yet foreign-owned banks in many countries are urging local regulators to allow them to apply the internal ratings system adopted by their head office. If regulators make such a concession, they will find it very difficult to resist political and other pressure from locally controlled banks to allow them also to adopt internal ratings in order to 'level the playing field' even though the systems they introduce will be largely unproven and hard to supervise. In this way, introduction of Basel 2 could seriously damage the ability of regulators in low-income countries to enforce a substantive regime of capital adequacy.

6   Bolting the door: reactions to failure

Regulatory failure is a powerful driver of regulatory reform. Yet evidence of failure is not necessarily evidence that the reforms will work. The pendulum of regulatory fashion swings in a wide arc. Although 2006 marked the publication of several officially sponsored studies into the cost of regulation to the regulated entities, by late 2007 the credit crisis of that year had triggered reconsideration of a number of regulations. Anti-predatory lending legislation and regulations were being tightened and consideration given to the reintroduction or enhancement of liquidity requirements for banks. Were the correct lessons learnt? Tighter US Truth-in-Lending regulations seemed to move in the right direction to reduce predatory lending, but what was being done to correct the perverse incentives of brokers originating unaffordable sub-prime mortgages and their interaction with the credit rating industry? And as for the way in which interbank markets seized up in 2007, was this really the consequence of inadequate liquidity requirements on individual banks, or did it reflect a generalized scramble for liquidity against which individual liquidity requirements could never have provided adequate or least-cost protection?

Despite the new wave of regulatory impact assessments, cost–benefit analysis in financial regulation is in its infancy. Estimating the benefits of financial regulation requires an opportunistic approach to information collection. The potential sources of data are varied but the actual sources are in practice rare. Much of the evidence on benefits of some of the most important regulatory measures is quantitatively blurred, but it often points to several of the actual measures currently in place being misdirected. The importance of getting the regulations right is undoubted, considering the huge growth benefits of a well-developed financial system and the costs of systemic failure. Improved quantification of benefits as well as costs can yield sizable social dividends.

Notes

1. The Lamfalussy Committees (2008) use the term 'cost–benefit analysis' to refer specifically to *quantitative* evaluation of the impact of a regulatory policy, whereas the goal of 'regulatory impact assessment' is (for them) the broader one of submitting policy-making to a systematic and structured approach. But regulatory impact assessment and cost–benefit analysis are increasingly interchangeable terms in this context.
2. For example, of 25 cost–benefit analyses of major financial sector rules reviewed by the Office of Information and Regulatory Affairs of the US Office of Management and Budget, 2001–07, 20 contained monetized estimates of the costs of the rule, whereas only six contained monetized estimates of benefits (www.whitehouse.gov/omb/inforeg/regpol-reports_congress.html).
3. The US term 'redlining' refers to the practice of discriminating against borrowers from certain geographical districts. It evokes maps marked to indicate areas not favored by the lender.
4. Thus, for example, the EU Lamfalussy Committee's *Guidelines* (2008) describe the impact assessment process as going through successive stages: identification of problem, development of main policy options, definition of policy objectives ('linking a proposed policy to regulatory objectives helps justify regulatory interventions'), analysis of impacts, comparison of options, consultation, publication and review.
5. Prudential regulation is the term given to measures employed to ensure that financial institutions are operated in a safe-and-sound manner, limiting the risk of failure or default.
6. Indeed, such levies do not represent a resource cost in themselves: if they exceed the regulatory resource costs, the excess should not be counted as part of the social costs of regulation.
7. Real Assurance (2006). Most of the regulations imposed very small costs: the top 20 regulations accounted for about 85 percent of the total (see Table 9.1), and about half of this related to just four AML regulations. In order to obtain these estimates, the authors of the study surveyed, for each regulation, a handful of firms affected by it, asking them for an estimate of how many hours of work for each grade of staff were required for compliance. Standard hourly wage estimates were applied to the reported hours, and the estimates scaled up to industry size.
8. Schüler and Heinemann based their estimates on data on the number of regulatory staff and the regulatory budget for 113 countries for 1999 and 2002, sourced from the Barth et al. (2006) database mentioned below. They regressed these dependent variables on measures of financial sector size to obtain the estimates of economies of scale. Of course this begs the question of quality and whether the loss of local knowledge induced by centralization would result in poorer regulatory outcomes. The US persists in having multiple financial regulators with overlapping remits.
9. On the other hand, coping with new regulations often involves appreciable set-up costs, which often exceed the annual running costs of compliance. An excellent example is provided by Elliehausen and Lowery (2000) in their analysis of the costs of compliance with changes in Truth-in-Lending regulations in the US. This argues against repeated regulatory change.
10. Levine (2005). The proposition that only countries starting with low financial depth benefit from deepening is evidenced by Aghion et al. (2005). The estimated causal effects from cross-country regressions are substantial. For example doubling financial depth

from 20 percent of GDP to the world mean of around 40 percent is estimated to result in a 2 percentage point permanent increase in economic *growth* (World Bank, 2001). Even costly policies are worthwhile if they can be shown to deliver such an improvement.

11. The term 'financial depth' refers to any of a variety of measures of the scale of the financial system, for example, total monetary liabilities of the banking system as a percentage of GDP. Financial depth is a convenient though crude summary measure of the state of development of finance in a country.

12. For example, improving the integrity of securities markets by reducing price manipulation and by increasing the protection of minority shareholders can lower the cost of capital and increase the liquidity of securities markets, as has been shown by numerous studies. These intermediate gains can be mapped through to gains to economic growth by using the results of the cross-country econometric studies.

13. In their overview of the benefits of regulation, Ozera (2006) lay out a taxonomy of the various detriments (to the consumer, to the producer and to the wider economy) of market failure attributable to market power, externalities and information asymmetries as well as to avoidable risks and incentive problems. For Ozera, consumer detriments come in six forms: suboptimal (from poor information) or reduced (because of discouraged suppliers) choice; or higher costs from: operational risks; financial risks (default of your supplier); systemic risks; or market power of firms.

14. Actually, if confined to rigorous econometric analyses making plausible corrections for the inferential problems posed by sample selection bias, the evidence for large welfare improvements from microfinance access is surprisingly weak (Honohan, 2004; World Bank, 2008). A stronger effect on poverty is found for financial deepening.

15. A wave of financial innovation in the US in recent years has resulted in a great increase in the number and size of loans being made to borrowers who do not satisfy the creditworthiness criteria traditionally used by lenders. This lending is termed 'sub-prime'. From 2006 it became clear that the underwriting standards used in the sub-prime market were overoptimistic and the inevitability of heavy loan-losses became increasingly evident.

16. For a discussion of the potential application of a 'precautionary principle' to systemic financial risks precisely because of this measurement difficulty, see Schwarcz (2007).

17. Although the reduction in the volume of loans was considered an adverse side-effect when the study was published, subsequent experience with mis-sold sub-prime mortgages in the US made it clear that the federal regulations were not sufficient to prevent brokers from originating mis-sold mortgages to repackage and sell on in securitized bundles. By end-2007, new regulations tightening the impact of the HOEPA (and of the Truth-in-Lending Act) were proposed by the Federal Reserve Board.

   To this rather negative catalog of evidence relating to the effectiveness of some of the most significant dimensions of financial regulation may be added the skeptical conclusions of Truman and Reuter (2004) on AML–CFT regulation.

18. The Basel Committee on Banking Supervision, representing prudential regulators from 13 countries has defined a common international approach to bank regulation. The current version of this approach, termed Basel 2, was agreed in 2004 and was to come into effect at different dates in different countries from January 2008 (www.bis.org/publ/bcbsca.htm).

19. The credit rating industry assumed by Basel 2 to be in place as a substitute for internal ratings is also problematic. Few low-income countries have such an industry today, and there is good reason to believe that any *de novo* credit rating industry would be fatally weakened by the distorted incentive structure created by Basel 2 (Honohan, 2001).

References

Aghion, Philippe, Peter Howitt and David Mayer-Foulkes (2005), 'The effect of financial development on convergence: theory and evidence', *Quarterly Journal of Economics*, **120** (1): 173–222.

Barth, James R., Gerard Caprio, Jr. and Ross Levine (2006), *Rethinking Bank Regulation: Till Angels Govern*, New York: Cambridge University Press.

Bernanke, Ben S. (2008), 'Reducing preventable mortgage foreclosures', Speech on March 4, www.federalreserve.gov/newsevents/speech/bernanke20080304a.htm, accessed 22 December 2008.

Brent, Robert J. (2006), *Applied Cost–benefit Analysis*, 2nd edn, Cheltenham, UK and Northampton, MA, USA: Edward Elgar.

DeLoitte (2006), *The Cost of Regulation Study*, London: Financial Services Authority.

Dell'Ariccia, Giovanni, Deniz Igan and Luc Laeven (2008), 'Credit booms and lending standards: evidence from the subprime mortgage market', CEPR Discussion Paper No. 6683, London: Centre for Economic Policy Research.

Elliehausen, Gregory (1998), 'The cost of bank regulation: a review of the evidence', Staff Studies 171, Washington, DC: Board of Governors of the Federal Reserve System.

Elliehausen, Gregory and Barbara R. Lowery (2000), 'The costs of implementing regulatory changes: the truth in savings act', *Journal of Financial Services Research*, **17** (2): 165–79.

Elliehausen, Gregory and Michael Staten (2004), 'Regulation of subprime mortgage products: an analysis of North Carolina's predatory lending law', *Journal of Real Estate Finance and Economics*, **29** (4): 411–33.

Englund, Peter (1999), 'The Swedish banking crisis: roots and consequences', *Oxford Review of Economic Policy*, **15** (3): 80–97.

Hoggarth, Glen, Ricardo Reis and Victoria Saporta (2002), 'Cost of bank instability: some empirical evidence', *Journal of Banking and Finance*, **26** (5): 825–55.

Honohan, Patrick (2001), 'Perverse effects of an external ratings-related capital adequacy system', *Economic Notes*, **30** (3): 359–72.

Honohan, Patrick (2003), 'The accidental tax: inflation and the financial sector', in Honohan (ed.), *Taxation of Financial Intermediation: Theory and Practice for Emerging Economies*, New York: Oxford University Press, pp. 381–420.

Honohan, Patrick (2004), *Financial Sector Policy and the Poor: Selected Issues and Evidence*, Washington, DC: World Bank.

Honohan, Patrick (2005), 'Banking sector crises and inequality', World Bank Policy Research Working Paper WPS 3659, July.

Honohan, Patrick and Daniela Klingebiel (2003), "The fiscal cost implications of an accommodating approach to banking crises', *Journal of Banking and Finance*, **27**: 1539–60.

Hylton, Keith N. (2006), 'Development lending and the community reinvestment act', Boston University School of Law Working Paper Series, Law and Economics Working Paper No. 06-07, Boston, MA.

Lamfalussy Committees (CESR Committee of European Securities Supervisors, CEBS Committee of European Banking Supervisors, CEIOPS Committee of European and Occupational Pensions Supervisors) (2008), *Impact Assessment Guidelines for EU Level 3 Committees*, Paris, London and Frankfurt.

Levine, Ross (2005), 'Finance and growth: theory and evidence', in Philippe Aghion and Steven Durlauf (eds), *Handbook of Economic Growth*, Vol. IA, Amsterdam: Elsevier Science, pp. 865–934.

Litan, Robert E., Nicolas P. Retsinas, Eric S. Belsky, Gary Fauth, Maureen Kennedy and Paul Leonard (2001), 'The Community Reinvestment Act after Financial Modernization: A Final Report', Washington, DC: US Department of the Treasury.

Monteiro, Nuno and Rida Zaidi (2007), 'Market impacts of MCOB', Occasional Paper 27, London: Financial Services Authority.

Office of Economic Analysis (2007), 'Economic Analysis of the Short Sale Price Restrictions Under the Regulation SHO Pilot,' Washington, DC: US Securities and Exchange Commission.

Ozera Consulting Ltd (2006), 'A framework for assessing the benefits of financial regulation', London: Financial Services Authority.

Policis (2004), 'The Effect of Interest Rate Controls in Other Countries', London: UK Department of Trade and Industry.

Policis (2006), 'Economic and Social Risks of Consumer Credit Market Regulation: A Comparative Analysis of the Regulatory and Consumer Protection Frameworks for

Consumer Credit in France, Germany and the UK', London, www.policis.com/pdf/ Economic_and_Social_Risks_of_Consumer_Credit_Market_Regulation.pdf, accessed 22 December 2008.

Real Assurance Risk Management (2006), 'Estimation of FSA administrative burdens', London: Financial Services Authority.

Schüler, Martin and Friedrich Heinemann (2005), 'The costs of supervisory fragmentation in Europe', ZEW Discussion Paper No. 05-01, Mannheim: Center for European Economic Research, ftp://ftp.zew.de/pub/zew-docs/dp/dp0501.pdf.

Schwarcz, Stephen L. (2007), 'Systemic risk', Washington, DC: AEI-Brookings Joint Center for Regulatory Studies, Related Publication 07-25.

World Bank (2001), *Finance for Growth: Policy Choices in a Volatile World*, New York: Oxford University Press.

World Bank (2008), *Finance for All? Policies and Pitfalls in Expanding Access*, Washington, DC.

Zinman, Jonathan (2002), 'The efficacy and efficiency of credit market interventions: evidence from the Community Reinvestment Act', Cambridge, MA: Harvard University Joint Center for Housing Studies Working Paper No. CRA02-2.

PART III

MACROECONOMIC EVALUATIONS

10 The welfare effects of inflation: a cost–benefit perspective

Karl-Heinz Tödter and Bernhard Manzke*

If there is anything in the world which ought to be stable it is money, the measure of everything which enters the channels of trade. What confusion would there not be in a state where weights and measures frequently changed? On what basis and with what assurance would one person deal with another, and which nations would come to deal with people who lived in such disorder? (François LeBlanc 1690 in Einaudi, 1953, 233)

1 Introduction

This chapter provides a theoretical and empirical overview of the welfare effects of inflation from a cost–benefit perspective. Cost–benefit analysis is a technique of applied welfare analysis which is widely used to judge the social desirability of an economic project or a policy change.[1]

In a modern society, inflation creates or amplifies distortions in many areas of economic activity and influences virtually all decisions of economic agents. Inflation has a similar effect on the value of money and savings as the sun on a cube of ice, it simply melts it away. Moving the ice cube into the shadow, like moderate and even low inflation, just slows the melting process. In contrast, price stability – potentially – freezes the value of money indefinitely.[2]

People decidedly dislike inflation (Shiller 1997, 14), but 'opinions differ across countries, between generations in both the US and Germany, and, even more strikingly, between the general public and economists'. For a long time there have been conflicting views among economists concerning the costs and benefits of inflation (Dowd 1994, 305). While many economists agreed that inflation is undesirable – without having a clear idea how bad it is – others argued that eliminating inflation would impair output and employment. Still others said that inflation could be dealt with by other means, for example, indexing the tax code (Aiyagari 1991). Today, price stability is widely accepted as the overriding objective of monetary policy, with a view to keeping inflation low and stable and to avoid deflation (Wood 2005, 1; Weber 2007). However, despite this broad consensus and concerted action, Romer and Romer (1997, 1) remark that 'the economic rationale and policy implications of low inflation are only partly understood'.

Understanding the welfare gains of reducing inflation requires a combination of the traditional subjects of macroeconomics and public finance. Economic research has uncovered a number of channels through which inflation affects output and welfare. In assessing the welfare implications of inflation, starting with Bailey (1956), the distortions to money demand played a prominent role. Later, Darby (1975) and Feldstein (1976) focused attention on distortions created by interactions of inflation and taxation.

In this chapter, we embark on a journey through theory and evidence of the welfare effects of reducing inflation. We stop at some important places, but we shall also miss many interesting vistas. We concentrate on simple, stripped-down models and selected empirical results.[3] Partial as well as general equilibrium approaches are discussed. As regards empirical evidence, Feldstein (1999a) is stressed for two reasons: the Feldstein report covers a wider range of inflation cost channels than most other studies and it provides comparable evidence for four large Organisation for Economic Co-operation and Development (OECD) countries, based on a common analytical framework.

The benefits of reducing inflation are discussed in Section 2. Inflation-induced distortions of money demand and tax-inflation distortions of intertemporal saving and consumption allocation are reviewed, followed by brief discussions of the effects of inflation on growth, the welfare effects of unanticipated inflation and of inflation uncertainty. Section 3 addresses the costs of disinflation. The sacrifice ratio is analyzed within a New Keynesian model and some empirical evidence is presented. Finally, the trade-off between the benefits of reducing inflation and the costs of disinflation is discussed. Section 4 concludes.

2 Benefits of reducing inflation
The benefits of reducing inflation or – expressed differently – the costs of inflation depend on two major factors: the institutional structure of an economy and the extent to which inflation is fully anticipated or not. Fischer and Modigliani (1978, 812) present a 'long and surprisingly pervasive' list of the real effects of inflation. They divide the costs of inflation into six categories, those that would

1. persist in a fully indexed economy; and those due to
2. nominal government institutions,
3. nominal private institutions and habits,
4. unanticipated inflation through existing nominal contracts,
5. uncertainty of future inflation, and
6. government attempts to suppress symptoms of inflation.

First, even in an economy that has fully adapted to inflation,[4] there are inflation costs because money holdings pay no interest and menu costs rise because firms have to change price lists more frequently. Second, nominal government institutions create inflation costs because the tax system was largely designed for non-inflationary times. Asset holders are taxed on nominal interest income, which can have dramatic negative effects on the after-tax real return. Inflation also tends to increase the cost of capital. Moreover, progressive tax brackets and nominal accounting methods accentuate these effects. Third, the private sector continues to rely on nominal institutions and practices such as nominal mortgage repayment contracts in the face of ongoing inflation (frontloading effect). Nominal accounting methods reflect a type of money illusion that results from the convenience of using money as a unit of account. Fourth, if contracts for goods or services are fixed in money terms or otherwise sticky, unanticipated inflation leads to arbitrary redistributions between buyers and sellers and nominal debt contracts lead to redistributions between debtors and creditors. Fifth, inflation uncertainty creates or increases the reluctance to make future commitments and leads to a shortening of nominal contracts, thereby increasing transaction costs. The final, sixth point becomes relevant in times of high inflation, as public annoyance over inflation may lead to costly wage and price controls and concern over fiscal losses through bankruptcies, and instability of the financial system may trigger control of interest rates and intervention in bond and equity markets.

Distortion of money demand
Economic theory has had difficulty establishing the welfare costs of inflation. For a long time the Classical dictum of monetary neutrality ('money is a veil') hampered a profound analysis.[5] Economic theory suggests (McCallum 1989, 124) that the 'pace of a steady, anticipated inflation has little effect on the values of most real variables including per capita income, consumption, and the real rate of interest'. We may then ask whether the rate of inflation is of any consequence at all in terms of the welfare of the individuals of a society. If economic agents care only about real magnitudes, why should inflation be a problem, provided it is steady and anticipated?

Even in a fully indexed economy there is one real variable that is not invariant to inflation: real money balances. Since money earns no interest, the nominal interest rate is the opportunity cost of holding it. Thus, inflation raises interest rates and renders holding money more costly. More time and energy is required for trips to the bank and shopping activities, giving rise to the proverbial 'shoe leather costs' of inflation. Since individuals are induced to hold lower real money balances than in times of price stability, their attainable utility level is lowered. Moreover, inflation either induces firms to change their prices more often, increasing their 'menu costs', or causes variability in relative prices, leading to misallocation and microeconomic inefficiency. In addition, in order to accommodate the increased number of currency transactions by households, more economic resources are allocated to the financial sector and diverted away from potentially more productive uses (overdevelopment of the financial system).[6]

Quantitative analysis of the welfare cost of inflation was started by Bailey (1956). In his classic article he treats the welfare cost of inflation as analogous to an excise tax on a commodity or productive service, and measures its quantitative importance by an appropriate area underneath a money demand function. Assuming fully anticipated and stable inflation, the following discussion focuses on two central questions (Walsh 2003, 59): how large is the welfare cost of inflation and what is the optimal inflation rate?

A partial equilibrium framework

<u>Money demand</u>   To review Bailey's approach, it is convenient to start with a simple money demand function:[7]

$$\frac{M}{P} = k(i)\, Y, \quad \frac{\partial k}{\partial i} \equiv k_i < 0. \tag{10.1}$$

Real money demand (M/P) is proportional to real income (Y). The cash ratio ($k = M/PY$), that is the ratio of money demand to GDP, is decreasing in the nominal interest rate. The nominal (i) and the real (r) interest rates are related through the Fisher equation:[8]

$$i = (1 + r)(1 + \pi) - 1 = r + \pi(1 + r), \tag{10.2}$$

where π denotes the rate of inflation. Under price stability ($\pi = 0$) money demand becomes $k(r) \equiv k_0$. The absolute interest rate elasticity (η) and semi-elasticity (ξ) are:

$$\eta(i) = -\frac{\partial M}{\partial i}\frac{i}{M} = -\frac{\partial k}{\partial i}\frac{i}{k}, \quad \xi(i) = \frac{\eta(i)}{i}. \tag{10.3}$$

<u>The welfare triangle</u>   Whenever market prices are distorted by taxes, monopolistic practices, or other forms of inefficiency, Harberger triangles appear (Harberger 1954).[9] Figure 10.1 depicts money demand (expressed as cash ratio) as a function of the interest rate. Consumer surplus (CS), as a ratio to income (PY), corresponds to the area $A + B + C$. Inflation reduces CS to the area C and inflation tax revenue (TR) is raised (area B). A deadweight loss (DWL) or excess burden of inflation (area A) is created, which is the loss of CS not compensated by TR.

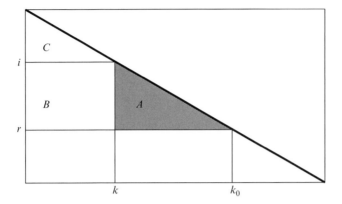

Figure 10.1   Money demand

The Harberger welfare triangle is a linear approximation of the DWL:

$$A = \frac{(i - r)}{2}[k_0 - k(i)]. \tag{10.4}$$

A Taylor expansion of $k(i)$ at $\pi = 0$,

$$A = \frac{(i - r)^2}{2} \frac{\eta k(i)}{i}, \tag{10.4'}$$

shows that the elasticity of money demand (η or ξ) is key to DWL measurement. If money demand is nonlinear, the integral:

$$A = \int_r^i k(x)\,dx - B \tag{10.5}$$

can be used to calculate the DWL more accurately.[10] The TR of the inflation tax is:

$$B = \pi(1 + r)\,k(i). \tag{10.6}$$

Since lump-sum taxes leave no room for evasion, they are welfare neutral and create no DWL. Thus, the ratio of DWL to TR is a measure of the (average) inefficiency of the inflation tax:

$$\lambda_{\text{inf}} = \frac{A}{B}. \tag{10.7}$$

Table 10.1   Welfare accounting I

Scenario	CS	TR	DWL
No inflation	A+B+C	0	0
Inflation	C	B	A

Table 10.1 summarizes the welfare accounting.

<u>Indirect welfare effects</u>   Phelps (1973) pointed out that the Harberger triangle overstates inflation cost if there is no lump-sum tax available. Collecting the inflation tax (10.6) enables the government to reduce other taxes, which creates indirect welfare gains.[11] Accepting that logic, the overall welfare loss of inflation can be defined as:

$$W = A - \lambda B, \qquad \lambda \geq 0, \tag{10.8}$$

where λ denotes the inefficiency of the tax system. Since (10.8) can be written as $W = (\lambda_{inf} - \lambda) B$, inflation is costly if $\lambda_{inf} > \lambda$.

<u>Illustration</u>   Consider the linear money demand function,

$$k(i) = \gamma - \delta i, \quad \gamma > \delta i, \quad \eta = \delta i/k, \tag{10.9}$$

where γ is the satiation level which applies at zero interest. From (10.9) both the Harberger triangle (10.4) and integration (10.5) yield:

$$A = \pi^2 \frac{\delta(1 + r)^2}{2}. \tag{10.10}$$

Inflation cost is small at low inflation rates but increases rapidly. Setting ($r = 0.04$, $\gamma = 0.3$, $\delta = 2$) implies a cash ratio of 14 percent of GDP at 4 percent inflation, which is close to the average ratio of M1 to GDP in the US between 1991 and 2006. Table 10.2 suggests that the direct welfare cost of 1 or 2 percent inflation is less than 0.1 percent of GDP. At 10 percent inflation it reaches 1 percent of GDP, even net of indirect revenue effects.

A general equilibrium framework   More recently, neoclassical general equilibrium models have been applied to quantify inflation cost. In these models of a non-monetary economy there is no money as a medium of transactions, and money as a store of wealth is dominated by interest-bearing assets.[12] To use this framework, a role must be assigned to money. Three main approaches have been followed in the literature (Walsh 2003,

Table 10.2   Inflation cost for linear money demand (% of GDP)

Inflation (%)	1	2	3	4	5	10
Direct welfare effect (A)	0.01	0.04	0.10	0.17	0.27	1.08
Indirect revenue effect ($-\lambda B$)	-0.06	-0.11	-0.15	-0.17	-0.18	-0.04
Overall welfare effect (W)	-0.05	-0.07	-0.05	0.00	0.09	1.04
Inflation tax inefficiency	0.05	0.12	0.20	0.30	0.45	8.67

Note: $r = 0.04$, $\gamma = 0.3$, $\delta = 2$, $\lambda = 0.3$.

43): (i) impose transactions or illiquidity costs of some form that create a demand for money,[13] (ii) put money directly into the utility function (MIU or Sidrauski approach)[14] or (iii) assume that money is used to transfer wealth intertemporally in an overlapping generations (OLG) model.[15]

<u>A Sidrauski model</u>   Following Lucas (2000), consider a simple version of a MIU-type model. The representative household faces the budget constraint: $P_t Y_t + M_t = P_t C_t + H_t + M_{t+1}$. Nominal income ($P_t Y_t$) and the stock of money (M_t) are used to finance consumption ($P_t C_t$), to pay or receive lump-sum taxes (H_t), and to transfer money to the next period (M_{t+1}). The household solves the dynamic optimization problem:

$$\text{Max} \sum_{t=0}^{\infty} \beta^t U(C_t, M_t/P_t)$$

$$\text{s.t.} \quad Y_t + M_t/P_t = C_t + H_t/P_t + (M_{t+1}/P_{t+1})(1 + \pi_{t+1}), \tag{10.11}$$

where U denotes utility, β ($0 < \beta < 1$) is the discount factor and $\pi_t = P_t/P_{t-1} - 1$ inflation. The budget constraint in (10.11) is rewritten in real terms. The first-order conditions (f.o.c.) imply that the marginal rate of substitution between money and consumption equals the opportunity cost of holding money (i), neglecting time subscripts:[16]

$$\frac{U_m(C, M/P)}{U_c(C, M/P)} = i, \tag{10.12}$$

where i is given in (10.2) and r is the real return on capital. With logarithmic utility:

$$U(C, M/P) = \ln(C) + \alpha \ln(M/P), \tag{10.13}$$

(10.12) becomes $\alpha PC/M = i$. In equilibrium $(C = Y)$ the following relationship between real money and real income holds:

$$\frac{M}{P} = \frac{\alpha Y}{i},$$ (10.12')

or, equivalently, $k(i) = \alpha/i$. To measure the welfare cost of inflation, Lucas (2000) employs the 'compensating variation' approach. He calculates the percentage income compensation (ω) needed to leave the household indifferent by solving the condition:

$$U\left[Y_0, \frac{\alpha Y_0}{r}\right] = U\left[(1 + \omega) Y_0, \frac{\alpha(1 + \omega) Y_0}{i}\right].$$ (10.14)

Conceptually, ω corresponds to the area $A + B$ in Figure 10.1. Correcting the private welfare loss for changes in tax revenues (B) yields (10.15a). Integrating (10.5) and the Harberger triangle (10.4) yield (10.15b) and (10.15c):

$$A_{Comp} = \left(\frac{i}{r}\right)^{\frac{\alpha}{1+\alpha}} - 1 - \alpha(1 + r)\frac{\pi}{i}$$ (10.15a)

$$A_{Int} = \alpha\ln\left(\frac{i}{r}\right) - \alpha(1 + r)\frac{\pi}{i}$$ (10.15b)

$$A_{Harb} = \pi^2\frac{(1 + r)^2\alpha}{2ri}$$ (10.15c)

Table 10.3 shows that for inflation rates up to 10 percent, (10.15a) and (10.15b) yield almost identical results, while the Harberger triangle increasingly overstates inflation costs.

Table 10.3   Deadweight loss of inflation in partial and general equilibrium (% of GDP)

Inflation (%)	1	2	3	4	5	10
Compensation	0.03	0.08	0.15	0.22	0.29	0.62
Integration	0.03	0.09	0.16	0.23	0.30	0.63
Harberger triangle	0.03	0.10	0.19	0.30	0.41	1.05

Note: $r = 0.04$; to be broadly consistent with the linear money demand function (10.9) used in Table 10.2, the parameter α is calibrated such that $\gamma - \delta i = \alpha/i$ holds at $i = r + 0.03$, giving $\alpha = 0.0112$.

What is the optimal rate of inflation?

Zero inflation   Money is the yardstick with which economic transactions are measured. Inflation changes that yardstick and undermines all three roles of money, as a unit of account, as a means of transactions, and as a store of value. The rationale of zero inflation was nicely expressed by LeBlanc (1690) more than 300 years ago, cited at the beginning of the chapter. In particular, money is most useful as a unit of account if people think and calculate in nominal rather than in real terms (Akerlof 2007, 30). Moreover, price stability improves the transparency of the price mechanism. People can recognize changes in relative prices without being confused by changes in the overall price level. Such considerations (Konieczny 1994) suggest that the optimal inflation rate is zero:

$$\pi^* = 0. \tag{10.16a}$$

Friedman rule   Money demand reflects the marginal utility of economic agents from cash holding (Tower 1971, 850). Money can be printed (almost) costless but individuals incur positive costs of holding money balances.[17] Thus, inflation induces them to hold less cash than would be socially optimal. Friedman (1969, 34) stated the famous rule: 'Our final rule for the optimum quantity of money is that it will be attained by a rate of price deflation that makes the nominal rate of interest equal to zero'. This implies:[18]

$$\pi^* = -r. \tag{10.16b}$$

Seigniorage maximization   Seigniorage (s) is the government revenue from its monopoly to print money. A frequently used definition, expressed as a fraction of GDP, is: $s = i\,M/PY = i\,k(i)$.[19] Lower private money stocks (M) induce the government to issue more interest-bearing bonds. Seigniorage is maximized if condition $\partial s/\partial i = k + i\partial k/\partial i = 0$ holds, which can be expressed as $\eta(i) = 1$. Linear money demand (10.9) gives:

$$\pi^* = \left(\frac{\gamma}{2\delta} - r\right)\frac{1}{1+r}. \tag{10.16c}$$

Welfare loss minimization   Viewing the overall welfare loss in (10.8) as a function of the inflation rate, and assuming that λ is a constant, loss minimization yields the f.o.c.:

$$A_\pi(\pi) - \lambda B_\pi(\pi) = 0. \tag{10.17}$$

Table 10.4   Optimal inflation (%)

	Friedman rule	Zero inflation	Loss minimization	Seigniorage maximization
Optimal inflation	−4	0	2.0	3.4

Note: Money demand (10.9) with $\gamma = 0.30$, $\delta = 2$, $r = 0.04$, $\lambda = 0.3$.

Hence, at the optimum the (marginal) inefficiency of the inflation tax (A_π/B_π) equals that of the alternative tax (λ) (Marty 1976). Money demand (10.9) implies optimal inflation:

$$\pi^* = \frac{\lambda}{1 + 2\lambda}\left(\frac{\gamma}{\delta} - r\right)\frac{1}{1 + r}. \qquad (10.16d)$$

Unless $\lambda = 0$, positive inflation is optimal. As Table 10.4 illustrates, there is no unique optimal rate of inflation. Moreover, it should be noted that only the money demand channel of inflation cost is taken into account so far.

Empirical evidence   Recently, Lucas (2000) reviewed the state of knowledge in the line of research started by Bailey (1956). He considered two alternative money demand specifications: a double-log version originated by Meltzer (1963) with constant elasticity η and a semi-log version originated by Cagan (1956) with constant semi-elasticity ξ:

$$k(i) = A\,i^{-\eta}, \qquad (10.18a)$$

$$k(i) = B\,e^{-\xi i}. \qquad (10.18b)$$

If the interest rate approaches zero, money demand in (10.18a) rises without bound, whereas it converges to a fixed satiation level (B) in (10.18b). Thus, at low interest rates, both functions behave very differently. Integration (10.5) yields inflation cost:

$$A_{LogLog} = \frac{\eta}{1 - \eta}A\,i^{1-\eta}\left[1 + \frac{(1 - \eta)}{\eta}\frac{r}{i} - \frac{1}{\eta}\left(\frac{r}{i}\right)^{1-\eta}\right], \qquad (10.19a)$$

$$A_{SemiLog} = \frac{B}{\xi}[e^{-\xi r} - (1 + \xi(i - r))\,e^{-\xi i}]. \qquad (10.19b)$$

Table 10.5   *Inflation cost with log-log and semi-log money demand (as %*
              of GDP)

Inflation (%)	1	2	3	4	5	10
Lucas, log-log (1)	0.01	0.04	0.08	0.13	0.18	0.42
Lucas, semi-log (2)	0.01	0.04	0.08	0.13	0.20	0.63
Serletis & Yavari, log-log (3)	0.01	0.02	0.04	0.06	0.08	0.22
Ireland, semi-log (4)	0.00	0.01	0.01	0.02	0.04	0.14

Note: $r = 0.04$; (1) $A = 0.05$, $\eta = 0.5$; (2) $B = 0.35$, $\xi = 7$; (3) $A = [0.12]$, $\eta = 0.21$; (4) $B = 0.17$, $\xi = 1.79$

Sources: Lucas (2000), Ireland (2007), Serletis and Yavari (2004), and own calculations.

Based on US data for 1900–1994, Lucas (2000) estimated: $\eta = 0.5$, $\xi = 7$. Serletis and Yavari (2004) as well as Ireland (2007) updated Lucas's data up to 2001 and 2006, respectively. Cointegration tests led Ireland to prefer the semi-log form ($\xi = 1.79$) while Serletis and Yavari chose a log-log function ($\eta = 0.21$).

As Table 10.5 confirms, the interest rate elasticity is very important in determining inflation cost. Thus, Gillman (1995, 60) rightly noted: 'trustworthy welfare cost estimates require trustworthy money demand functions'. Unfortunately, empirical estimates of money demand elasticities are uncertain. Knell and Stix (2005) report a wide range of estimates. The median estimate for US narrow money ($\eta = 0.26$) suggests that inflation-caused distortions of money demand are small.

Checking robustness, Lucas generalized the Sidrauski MIU model (10.11) by including the labor–leisure choice and a proportional income tax, similar to Chari et al. (1996). Apart from very low interest rates, similar inflation costs are obtained. Moreover, Lucas applied a version of the transaction cost model developed by McCallum and Goodfriend (1987, 263). In this model, the use of cash is motivated by an explicit transactions technology, rather than by the MIU approach. Again, only small differences in the estimated inflation costs result.

Search-theoretic models   Monetary macromodels typically assign some role for money that is not made explicit, such as putting money in the utility function or imposing cash-in-advance constraints. Search-theoretic models of monetary exchange explicitly model the frictions that render money essential. Lagos and Wright (2005) developed a model, refined by Craig and Rocheteau (2007), that allows agents to interact periodically in centralized and decentralized markets. Under competitive pricing (sellers receive no economic profit), this model comes up with welfare costs of 10 percent inflation of about 1 percent of GDP, which is only slightly higher than in most previous studies. However, if sellers have market power such that the gains from trade are divided between buyers and sellers, the welfare cost of 10 percent inflation can be as high as 5 percent of GDP, depending on the trading frictions assumed, which lead Craig and Rocheteau (2005, 4) to conclude: 'Overall, the search approach of monetary exchange seems to suggest that inflation may be significantly more costly than previously thought'. Chiu and Molico (2007) also present a search-theoretic model along the lines of Lagos and Wright (2005) in which the welfare cost of increasing inflation from zero to 10 percent is only 0.62 (0.20) percent of income for the US (Canada).

Hyperinflation   In extreme cases of hyperinflation the welfare losses of inflation can be dramatic (Bernholz 2003). Under such conditions people stop using money and return to inefficient barter transactions. Evaluating evidence from seven historical hyperinflations in Europe between 1920 and 1946, Bailey (1956, 110) found that the welfare cost was about a third of income, the largest reaching half of income.

Moderate inflation   Gillman (1995) reports partial equilibrium evidence of the welfare gains of reducing inflation from 10 percent to zero in the range from 0.22 percent (Eckstein and Leiderman 1992) to 0.45 percent of GDP (Lucas 1981) with Fischer's (1981) estimate of 0.3 percent in between. Wolman (1997), using a transactions-time approach to money demand, estimated the welfare gain from reducing inflation from 5 percent to zero at 0.6 percent of output, the additional benefit achieved by optimal deflation being small. More recently, Attanasio et al. (2002) arrive at estimates less than 0.1 percent of GDP.

General equilibrium models, summarized by Gillman (1995), have been employed more recently to estimate inflation costs through the money demand channel. Making use of a cash-in-advance constraint, Cooley and Hansen (1989) were among the first to try to evaluate the costs of inflation in such a framework. They found that an inflation rate of 10 percent (relative to an optimal inflation rate of –4 percent in their model) resulted in a welfare cost of 0.4 percent of income. This result is, however, rather sensitive to the assumption on the relevant period over which individuals are constrained (which is closely related to the definition of money).

The general equilibrium model of Dotsey and Ireland (1996) features an explicit transactions technology that produces a money demand function similar to those estimated for the US economy. In this model, inflation

*Table 10.6   Money demand (welfare effect of reducing inflation from 2
percent to zero as % of GDP)*

	US	Germany	UK	Spain
Direct welfare effect	0.02	0.03	0.02	0.04
Indirect revenue effect	−0.05	−0.06	−0.05	−0.10
Overall welfare effect	−0.03	−0.04	−0.02	−0.07

Source: Feldstein (1999a, compiled from pp.12, 73, 123 and 137).

induces agents to inefficiently substitute market activity for leisure and to devote productive time to economizing their cash holdings. Solving the model with exogenous growth yields welfare losses of 10 percent inflation of 0.20 (0.92) percent of output if money is measured as currency (M1).

Zee (2000) estimates the welfare effects of lowering inflation from 4 to 2 percent in an OLG model with money as a factor of production. Modifying the Fisher equation so that the after-tax real interest rate is held constant, the welfare gain he calculates is rather modest, amounting to less than 0.2 percent of GDP annually.

Low inflation   Table 10.6 reports results for the welfare effect of permanently reducing inflation from 2 percent to zero through the money demand channel in four countries (Feldstein 1999a). As Table 10.6 shows, the benefits of reducing money demand distortions are small. If indirect tax effects are taken into account, the overall welfare effect of eliminating 2 percent inflation becomes negative.

Summing up, empirical evidence from partial and general equilibrium approaches suggests that the welfare effects of low inflation through the money demand channel are relatively small, net of revenue changes even negative. Thus, in view of the high degree of inflation aversion among the population (Shiller 1997; Di Tella et al. 2001), there must be other and possibly more powerful channels through which low inflation causes welfare losses, as will be explored in the next subsection.

Distortion of savings and consumption allocation
Tax laws in most countries are written for an economy without inflation. The interaction of inflation with existing tax rules (and social security systems) is complex and exerts powerful effects on the economy. Inflation affects decisions of households about savings and of firms about investment.[20] Tax-inflation distortions arise in many areas of economic activity, for example, in the taxation of wages, profits, interest incomes, and capital gains. One of the

most important channels through which inflation affects real economic activity is a nominal-based capital income tax structure. In particular, taxation of nominal capital income directs savings away from fixed non-residential investment and causes increases in the effective tax rates. On the other hand, in many countries nominal interest expenses for residential investment can be deducted. This encourages the expansion of consumer debt and stimulates the demand for owner-occupied housing. The likely result is a reduction of productive capital formation (Feldstein 1983, 1).

A general equilibrium framework

Money as the only store of value   In a basic OLG model,[21] individuals live for two periods (generations). They derive utility (U) from consumption in their youth ($C_{young} \equiv C_y$) and from consumption in retirement, when old ($C_{old} \equiv C$). Young individuals receive labor income (Y), consume (C_y) and save for retirement ($S = Y - C_y$). Since for now it is assumed that money is the sole store of value, financing retirement consumption creates money demand ($M = S$). The representative agent solves:

$$Max\ U = U(C_y, C), \qquad (10.20a)$$

$$s.t.\ C_y + M = Y, \qquad (10.20b)$$

$$C = M/P. \qquad (10.20c)$$

Both constraints combine to give the intertemporal restriction $C_y + PC = Y$, where P is the price of retirement consumption, which is normalized to 1 in the first period. The following intertemporal relationship holds between savings of the young generation (S) and their retirement consumption (C):

$$C = S/P. \qquad (10.21)$$

With annual inflation π and generation length of T years, the price level in the second period is $P = (1 + \pi)^T$. From the f.o.c. one sees that in the optimum the ratio of marginal utilities is equal to the (relative) price of retirement consumption ($U_C/U_{C_y} = P$). With a logarithmic utility function

$$U = \ln(C_y) + \alpha\ln(C), \qquad (10.22)$$

where α measures the preference for retirement consumption, the following solution is obtained:

$$C_y = \frac{1}{1 + \alpha} Y, \qquad (10.23a)$$

$$C = \frac{M}{P} = \left[\frac{\alpha}{1 + \alpha} \frac{Y}{P} \right]. \qquad (10.23b)$$

The Harberger triangle (10.4) underneath the demand curve for retirement consumption (area A) measures the DWL of inflation (as a ratio to income Y):

$$A = \frac{1}{2}(P - P_0)[C(P_0) - C(P)] = \left[\frac{\alpha}{1 + \alpha} \frac{(P - P_0)^2}{2 P_0 P} \right] \qquad (10.24)$$

where $P_0 = 1$ is the price for retirement consumption under price stability. The DWL of inflation implied by (10.24) is large because inflation erodes total savings. Assuming ($\pi = 2\%$ p.a., $T = 30$ years) yields $P = 1.81$. Thus, each dollar saved at youth has a purchasing power of only 55 cents when old. With $\alpha = 0.25$, the DWL of 2 percent inflation is 3.63 percent of income.[22]

<u>Interest-bearing money</u>   If the government pays interest π on money holdings, ignoring technical problems, constraint (10.20c) changes to $C = (1 + \pi)^T M / (1 + \pi)^T = M$. Thus, the price of retirement consumption remains constant ($P = P_0 = 1$), agents are immune to inflation and the DWL vanishes ($A = 0$).

<u>Interest-bearing bonds, untaxed</u>   Now assume that an interest-bearing bond (B), paying nominal interest (i), is available to transfer savings across time in the OLG economy. The budget constraints change to:

$$C_y + B = Y, \qquad (10.20b')$$

$$C = \frac{(1 + i)^T}{(1 + \pi)^T} B. \qquad (10.20c')$$

The price of retirement consumption becomes $P = (1 + \pi)^T (1 + i)^{-T}$. Using (10.2) gives $P = (1 + r)^{-T}$, which is independent of inflation. Again, the DWL of inflation vanishes ($A = 0$).

<u>Interest-bearing bonds, taxed</u>   Things change dramatically if nominal capital income (iB) is taxed. With a tax rate τ ($0 \le \tau \le 1$), nominal after-tax return of bonds (net return) becomes:

$$i_n = [(1 + r)(1 + \pi) - 1](1 - \tau), \qquad (10.2')$$

and constraint (10.20c) changes to:

$$C = \frac{(1 + i_n)^T}{(1 + \pi)^T}B. \qquad (10.20c'')$$

Thus, taxation changes the price of retirement consumption to $P = (1 + \pi)^T(1 + i_n)^{-T}$. Because there is an interaction between inflation and (capital income) taxation, the welfare loss can no longer be approximated by the Harberger triangle. As will be shown in the next subsection, the welfare cost of 2 percent inflation amounts to 1.54 percent of income.

Indexing the tax system   Trivially, the welfare loss of inflation can be eliminated if either capital income taxation is abolished ($\tau = 0$) or price stability rules ($\pi = 0$). A third way is indexation of the capital income tax. To do this, the price of retirement consumption under inflation $P(\tau_{ind})$ must be the same as under price stability, which is $P_0 = (1 + r(1 - \tau))^{-T}$. Solving yields the indexation formula:

$$\tau_{ind} = \tau\frac{r(1 + \pi)}{r(1 + \pi) + \pi}. \qquad (10.25)$$

Thus, indexation requires a downward adjustment of the tax rate in line with inflation. In principle, indexation can eliminate the welfare cost of inflation ($A = 0$). However, indexation of tax codes has not been used by major industrial countries.[23] Table 10.7 summarizes the preceding discussion.

A partial equilibrium framework   Partial equilibrium approaches do not formulate a fully developed general equilibrium model. However, usually

Table 10.7   *Welfare cost in the OLG model (cost of 2% inflation as % of GDP)*

Money only		Bonds		
No interest	Interest	Untaxed	Taxed	
			Indexed	Non-indexed
3.63	0	0	0	1.54*

Note: $\alpha = 0.25$, $T = 30$, $\tau = 0.3$, $r = 0.04$, $\pi = 0.02$; * See Table 10.9.

there is a theoretical framework in the background, as for example an OLG model in the Feldstein report, where the intertemporal relationship (10.21), linking savings of the young generation and their retirement consumption, is exploited. In the simple benchmark OLG model (10.20) this does not imply any loss of information.

<u>Welfare trapezoid</u> To determine the welfare loss of inflation when there are interactions of two distortions, inflation and taxation, three scenarios with different interest rates, prices and consumption levels (R, P, C) need to be distinguished:

No tax, no inflation: R_0 $\qquad$ $P_0 = (1 + R_0)^{-T}$ $\quad$ $C_0(P_0)$

Tax, no inflation: $\quad$ $R_1 = R_0(1 - \tau)$ $\qquad$ $P_1 = (1 + R_1)^{-T}$ $\quad$ $C_1(P_1)$

Tax and inflation: $\quad$ $R_2 = [(1 + R_0)$ $\qquad$ $P_2 = (1 + \pi)^T$

$\qquad\qquad\qquad (1 + \pi) - 1](1 - \tau) \quad (1 + R_2)^{-T} \quad C_2(P_2).$

If there is neither taxation nor inflation, with annual return R_0, saving increases by the factor $(1 + R_0)^T$ and the price of retirement consumption becomes P_0. With taxes and no inflation, the net return reduces to R_1 and the price rises to $P_1 \geq P_0$. With taxes and inflation the net return is R_2 and the price increases to $P_2 \geq P_1$. The corresponding demands for retirement consumption are $C_2(P_2) \leq C_1(P_1) \leq C_0(P_0)$. To assess the welfare consequences, consider Figure 10.2.

Without taxes and inflation consumer surplus (CS) is the sum of areas A to F. Introducing capital income taxes in an environment of price stability, equilibrium changes from (P_0, C_0) to (P_1, C_1) with less retirement

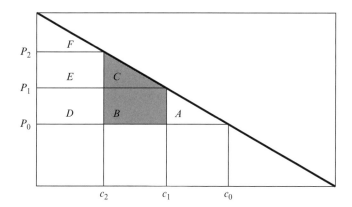

Figure 10.2 Demand for retirement consumption

Table 10.8   Welfare accounting II

Scenario	CS	TR	DWL
No tax, no inflation	A + B + C + D + E + F	–	–
Tax, no inflation	C + E + F	B + D	A
Tax and inflation	F	D + E	A + B + C

consumption at a higher price. CS is reduced to the area $C + E + F$ and capital income taxes (TR) corresponding to $B + D$ are raised. The difference, the triangle A, is a DWL of taxation; it is the reduction of CS not compensated by TR. Introducing both taxes and inflation moves the equilibrium to (P_2, C_2) with a higher price and consumption reduced further. The remaining CS is the area F, whereas TR corresponds to the rectangle $D + E$. The deadweight loss (DWL) of taxation plus inflation increases to the triangle $A + B + C$. Hence, the additional DWL of inflation is the area

$$B + C = (C_1 - C_2)\left[(P_1 - P_0) + \frac{P_2 - P_1}{2}\right]. \qquad (10.26)$$

This is no longer the traditional 'small' second-order Harberger triangle. Interaction of taxation and inflation creates a first-order welfare loss, measured by the trapezoid $B + C$ (Feldstein 1999b). Table 10.8 summarizes the welfare accounting.

If the government faces a strict budget constraint at the margin, the inflation-induced change in tax revenues $[(D + E) - (B + D) = E - B]$ (if negative) needs to be compensated by increasing other taxes. Denoting the DWL per dollar of a compensating tax by λ, the overall welfare loss is:

$$W = (B + C) - \lambda(E - B). \qquad (10.27)$$

The inefficiency of the capital income tax (DWL per dollar taxes raised) (λ_{cit}) and the inflation-induced change in capital income taxes (referred to as inflation tax for simplicity) (λ_{inf}) are measured as:

$$\lambda_{cit} = \frac{A}{B + D}; \quad \lambda_{inf} = \frac{B + C}{E - B}. \qquad (10.28)$$

With a logarithmic utility function, retirement consumption in the OLG model was given in (10.23b) as $C = [\alpha/(1 + \alpha)]Y/P$. Illustrative calculations are provided in Table 10.9.

The welfare loss of inflation is high when inflation and capital income

Table 10.9   Welfare cost of inflation in the OLG model (% of income)

Inflation (%)	1	2	3	4	5	10
Area B	0.66	1.26	1.79	2.28	2.72	4.41
Area C	0.07	0.29	0.64	1.13	1.74	6.67
Direct welfare loss	0.73	1.54	2.44	3.41	4.46	11.08
ditto by integration[1]	0.73	1.53	2.38	3.28	4.23	9.35
ditto by compensation[2]	0.75	1.59	2.51	3.51	4.58	10.68
Indirect revenue effect	−0.29	−0.56	−0.80	−1.02	−1.22	−1.97
Overall welfare loss	0.44	0.98	1.63	2.39	3.25	9.11
CIT* inefficiency (λ_{cit})	0.34	0.34	0.34	0.34	0.34	0.34
Inflation tax inefficiency (λ_{inf})	0.75	0.83	0.91	1.00	1.10	1.69

Note:
* Capital income tax; $\alpha = 0.25$, $T = 30$, $\tau = 0.3$, $\lambda = 0.3$, $R_0 = 0.06$ (with $\tau = 0.3$, $R_0 = 0.06$ is roughly consistent with $r = 0.04$ used before).
1. $B + C = [\alpha/(1 + \alpha)] Y \ln(P_2/P_1) - (C_1 - C_2) P_0$;
2. $B + C = (P_2/P_1)^{\alpha/(1 + \alpha)} - 1 - (C_1 - C_2) P_0$.

taxation interact. A low rate of 2 percent inflation induces a welfare loss equivalent to 1.54 percent of income. Calculating the welfare loss of inflation by integration (10.5) or as compensated variation (10.14) yields similar results. Indirect tax effects reduce the welfare loss. However, even at only 2 percent inflation it is still about 1 percent of income. The final two rows report measures of tax inefficiency. Every dollar raised by the capital income tax creates a welfare loss of 34 cents, in contrast to 83 cents for the inflation tax at 2 percent inflation.[24]

It may be noted that Bullard and Russell (2004) present a general equilibrium OLG life-cycle model with financial intermediation, calibrated to US post-war data, which produces a welfare cost of 10 percent inflation at 11.2 percent of output, close to the value shown in Table 10.9 for the simple OLG model.

Summing up, the welfare costs of inflation in the OLG economy are higher, the higher

- the saving preferences (α);
- the return on capital (R_0);
- the capital income tax (τ); and
- the rate of inflation (π).

Extensions   The simple OLG model considered above has been extended in several directions. Implicitly, it was assumed that a fully funded system is in place for providing old-age pensions. Tödter and Ziebarth (1999) introduce a 'pay as you go' system into the model but obtain essentially the same results. Further extensions include a more general utility function (such that the intertemporal elasticity of substitution differs from unity), endogenous labor–leisure choice, a production technology (to model the real interest rate and the capital stock), and others.

Empirical evidence   The Feldstein (1999a) report is a comprehensive empirical study of the welfare effects of inflation and the cost of disinflation. It applies a common OLG-based analytical framework, developed by Feldstein (1997), to provide empirical evidence for the US (Feldstein 1999b), Germany (Tödter and Ziebarth 1999), the UK (Bakhshi et al. 1999) and Spain (Dolado et al. 1999). The study reports welfare effects for the hypothetical policy measure of going from 2 percent inflation to price stability. Four channels are evaluated:

1. money demand and seigniorage;
2. intertemporal allocation of saving and consumption;
3. demand for owner-occupied housing; and
4. public debt service.

The money demand channel has already been discussed above (Table 10.6). The first three channels include the indirect tax revenue effects arising through the government budget constraint, which are usually ignored in welfare analyses by the assumption of lump sum taxes or transfers. The final channel accounts for the indirect welfare effects of inflation on the public debt service.

<u>Intertemporal allocation of saving and consumption</u>   In the Feldstein report, the DWL of inflation is approximated by the trapezoid (10.26) underneath the (compensated) demand for retirement consumption (10.21). The report calculates the costs of a steady, anticipated rate of 2 percent inflation. To put it differently, it estimates the benefits of going from 2 percent inflation to zero. Space limitations do not allow to review all the country specific details of the tax system included in the report.

For Germany, Tödter and Ziebarth (1999, 61) estimate the average gross yield on fixed capital at $R_0 = 10.8\%$ p.a. The average tax burden (based on 1991–95 data) amounts to 60.7 percent (compared to 41 percent for the US),[25] reducing the net yield to $R_2 = 4.24\%$. Zero inflation increases it by 63 basis points to $R_1 = 4.87\%$. The associated prices of retirement consumption ($T = 27$) imply that 2 percent inflation raises the price of a dollar spent in retirement by 4.84 cents. Turning to quantities, the

Table 10.10 *Intertemporal allocation of savings and consumption
(welfare effect of reducing inflation from 2 percent to zero as
% of GDP)*

	US	Germany	UK	Spain
Direct welfare effect	1.02	1.95	0.40	0.91
Indirect revenue effect	−0.07	−0.47	−0.12	−0.19
Overall welfare effect	0.95	1.48	0.29	0.72

Source: Feldstein (1999a, compiled from pp. 12, 73,123, and 137).

inflation-induced change in retirement consumption is approximated by $C_1 - C_2 \approx \eta_{CP} C_2 (P_2 - P_1)/P_2$, where η_{CP} is the (absolute) compensated price elasticity of consumption. The Slutsky decomposition allows us to express the unobservable elasticity as a function of the uncompensated interest elasticity of savings of the young, estimated at ($\eta_{SR} = 0.25$) as $\eta_{CP} = 1 - \sigma_y + \eta_{SR}(1 + R_2)/R_2 T$, where σ_y is the income effect. The authors obtain $\eta_{CP} = 0.854$ and calculate welfare costs of 1.95 percent of GDP. Taking into account indirect tax effects ($\lambda = 0.34$) reduces the overall loss to 1.48 percent of GDP.

Table 10.10 provides the results for the countries included in the Feldstein report. The higher welfare loss of inflation in Germany compared to the US basically rests on higher tax rates and the fact that the saving ratio (as a percentage of GDP) is almost twice as high in Germany as it was in the US in the sample period of the study.

Similar to the money demand elasticity, the interest elasticity of savings (η_{SR}) is a key parameter in the calculation of the welfare effects, but estimates in the literature vary widely. Changing it within a plausible range has a marked effect on the results. Another important parameter is the inefficiency of the tax system (λ). Except for Germany, the authors use $\lambda = 0.4$ (and alternatively $\lambda = 1.5$). For Germany, the parameter ($\lambda_{cit} = 0.34$) is estimated from the model as inefficiency of the capital income tax (10.28). In contrast, the estimated inefficiency of the inflation-induced revenue change is much higher ($\lambda_{inf} = 1.43$).

Housing demand   In many industrial countries owner-occupied housing receives preferential treatment under the personal income tax law. Mortgage interest payments and possibly maintenance and depreciation costs and local property taxes are deductible. On the other hand, the notional rental value, which represents implied investment income, is not subject to taxation. Such treatment induces excessive consumption of housing services even in the absence of inflation (Feldstein 1999b,

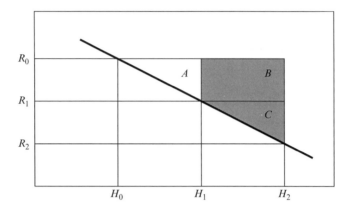

Figure 10.3   Housing demand

26; Rosen 1985). Inflation increases that loss through the deduction of nominal mortgage interest payments and raises the loss from excessive housing demand.

Let $H(R)$ ($H_R < 0$) denote the demand for owner-occupied housing and R the user cost per dollar of invested housing capital. For Germany, Tödter and Ziebarth (1999), following Feldstein (1999b), estimate the user costs in the absence of tax and inflation at $R_0 = 14.8\%$ p.a. Preferential tax treatment reduces housing cost to $R_1 = 9.09\%$ and 2 percent inflation decreases it further to $R_2 = 8.84\%$.[26]

As shown in Figure 10.3, the inflation-induced DWL of owner-occupied housing can be measured by the trapezoid:

$$B + C = (H_2 - H_1)[(R_0 - R_1) + (R_1 - R_2)/2]. \qquad (10.29)$$

The inflation-induced change in housing demand is approximated by $H_2 - H_1 \approx \varepsilon_{HR} H_2 (R_1 - R_2)/R_2$, where ε_{HR} is the compensated interest elasticity of housing demand. For Germany, ε_{HR} is estimated at 0.25. As the value of the owner-occupied housing stock is 170 percent of GDP, $H_1 - H_2 = 1.20\%$ of GDP follows. Hence, the direct (total) DWL amounts to just 0.07 (0.09) percent of GDP.

Table 10.11 reports the results. Except for Spain, the welfare losses through the housing demand channel are small compared to the savings and consumption allocation channel.[27]

Public debt service   Higher real interest rates increase the real cost of the public debt service. Inflation, if fully anticipated, leaves the real gross interest rate on public debt unchanged, whereas the inflation premium is

Table 10.11   Demand for owner-occupied housing (welfare effect of reducing inflation from 2 percent to zero as % of GDP)

	US	Germany	UK	Spain
Direct welfare effect	0.10	0.07	0.04	0.69
Indirect revenue effect	0.12	0.02	0.07	0.64
Overall welfare effect	0.22	0.09	0.11	1.33

Source: Feldstein (1999a, compiled from pp. 12, 73, 123 and 137).

Table 10.12   Public debt service (welfare effect of reducing inflation from 2 percent to zero as % of GDP)

	US	Germany	UK	Spain
Overall welfare effect	−0.10	−0.12	−0.09	−0.10

Source: Feldstein (1999a, compiled from pp. 12, 73, 123, 137).

Table 10.13   Total welfare effects (reducing inflation from 2 percent to zero as % of GDP)

	US	Germany	UK	Spain
Direct effect	1.14	2.04	0.47	1.64
Revenue change	−0.10	−0.63	−0.18	0.25
Overall welfare effect	1.04	1.41 (0.473)*	0.29	1.88

Note: * Standard deviation.

Source: Feldstein (1999a, compiled from pp. 12, 73, 123, and 137).

subject to income taxation. Reducing the rate of inflation from 2 percent to zero does not reduce the pre-tax cost of debt service; that means it does not generate a direct welfare gain. But it does reduce the tax revenue accruing from the (eligible) interest payment on the public debt, which requires a compensatory increase of other taxes (Feldstein 1999b, 72). Table 10.12 reports.

Total benefits   Table 10.13 summarizes the overall welfare benefits of eliminating 2 percent inflation, accruing from distortions of money

Table 10.14   Comparison of overall welfare effects (reducing inflation from 2 percent to zero as % of GDP)

	US		Germany		UK		Spain	
	A	B	A	B	A	B	A	B
Money demand	−0.06	−0.03	−0.12	−0.04	0.00	−0.02	−0.04	−0.07
Consumption timing	1.15	0.95	1.49	1.48	0.72	0.29	0.76	0.72
Housing demand	0.11	0.22	0.08	0.09	−0.02	0.11	−0.01	1.33
Debt service	–	−0.10	–	−0.12	–	−0.09	–	−0.10
Total	1.20	1.04	1.45	1.41	0.70	0.29	0.71	1.88

Sources: Columns A: Abel (1997) for the US and Abel (1999) for the other countries; Columns B: Feldstein (1999a).

demand, consumption timing, housing demand and the public debt service. The lowest welfare gain of price stability is estimated for the UK (0.29 percent of GDP), whereas the highest gain is reported for Spain (1.88 percent), which is largely due to the housing channel. The benefit obtained for the U.S. is 1.04 percent of GDP. At 1.41 percent of GDP, the benefit is somewhat higher for Germany.[28]

Cross-checking   The welfare gains of price stability of the Feldstein report reviewed above were obtained in a partial equilibrium, OLG-based setting. Abel (1997) used a calibrated and suitably modified version of the Sidrauski (1967) general equilibrium model to perform a robustness check for the results reported in Feldstein (1997) for the US. He introduced three modifications into the Sidrauski model: two types of capital (non-housing and housing), a government budget constraint to capture the effects of various distortionary taxes, and endogenous labor supply so that taxes on labor income are distortionary. In Abel (1999), this model was also applied to calculate welfare effects of inflation for Germany, the UK and Spain, using parameters that were calibrated to match those in the country studies. Table 10.14 reports Abel's results in comparison to those of the case studies.[29]

Despite the differences in analytic approaches, for the US and Germany the results are strikingly close to each other. Both sets of results have four features in common (Abel 1997, 164; 1999, 189): (i) benefits of price stability arising through the money demand channel are negative but tiny; (ii) benefits through the housing-demand channel are positive but relatively small; (iii) by far the largest benefits come through the reduced distortion in the effective taxation of non-housing capital; and (iv) the overall welfare gain of eliminating 2 percent inflation obtained in a general equilibrium (Sidrauski) framework and those from a partial equilibrium (OLG-based) approach in the case studies for the US and Germany exceed 1 percent of GDP.[30]

<u>User cost of capital</u> The case studies did not address the effects of inflation on the user cost of capital. Cohen et al. (1999) investigated inflation effects on the net-of-tax profitability of several kinds of business assets: equipment versus structures and short- versus long-lived assets. They find that inflation raises the user cost of capital and amplifies the distortion of the tax system, but the magnitude of the effect and its welfare consequences are rather small.

<u>Labor markets</u> With regard to the effects of inflation on labor markets there may be benefits if inflation 'greases the wheels' of the labor market and there may be costs, if inflation 'throws sand' to wage and price adjustments. Both effects can arise from nominal rigidities of wages and prices in the face of shocks. The grease effect arises from resistance to nominal wage cuts due to, for example, money illusion or fairness considerations. The sand effect derives from the impairment of the value of the price signal, it leads to misallocations, more frequent wage and price changes and higher search costs. Groshen and Schweitzer (1999) provide evidence that the grease and the sand effects roughly cancel out.

<u>Open economies</u> In open economies there are opportunities for borrowing and lending that are unavailable to closed economies. On the other hand, openness has the potential to amplify or to moderate domestic distortions such as those resulting from interactions of inflation and taxation. Desai and Hines (1999) analyzed the role of international capital flows for the burden of inflation in open economies. They found that the gain from price stability can be substantially larger than in an otherwise similar closed economy.

Inflation and growth
The preceding analysis has reported measures of several effects of inflation on the level of output and welfare. Researchers have also questioned whether inflation causes a reduction in the rate of output growth.

  Growth effects of inflation, if they are permanent, have the potential to outweigh level effects, even if they are small. Assume that price stability permanently raises welfare by w percent of baseline output Y_0. With trend growth rate g and a social discount rate $\rho > g$, the present value (PV) of the benefits is $w Y_0 (1 + \rho)/(\rho - g)$. Alternatively, assume that price stability increases the growth rate from g to $g + \omega$. The PV of that effect is $\omega Y_0 (1 + \rho)/(\rho - g)(\rho - g - \omega)$. Hence, the PVs are equal if the growth effect is:

$$\omega = (\rho - g)\frac{w}{1 + w}. \tag{10.30}$$

Let the level effect be $w = 1\%$ of GDP, $g = 2.5\%$ and $\rho = 5\%$.[31] To obtain the same PV requires an increase of the growth rate by just $\omega = 0.025$ percentage points, for example, from 2.5 to 2.525 percent. Thus, it is not surprising that it is difficult to identify statistically significant growth effects of moderate inflation.

Haslag (1997), reviewing the literature on inflation and growth, points out that theory provides little reason for expecting that a sustained rate of inflation permanently alters the real growth rate in either direction. Empirically, Lucas (1973) found no significant relation between average growth and average inflation across a sample of 18 countries. More recently, considerable empirical evidence was revealed that high inflation, exceeding 10 percent per year, has negative effects on economic growth (Fischer 1993; Barro 1995; Bruno and Easterly 1995; Sarel 1996). But those studies could not detect growth effects of inflation below 10 percent.

Using data of 21 industrial countries, Grimes (1991, 641) found that in the long run even low inflation has a negative impact on the rate of growth. In a cross-section study of 82 countries, Gomme (1993) found that inflation and output growth are negatively correlated. However, eliminating an inflation rate of 10 percent would result in a very small (less than 0.01 percentage point) increase in output growth. In contrast, Haslag (1995) reports that 10 percent inflation slows down growth by sizable 0.2 percentage points. Running regressions for each of the G7 countries, Ericsson et al. (2000) report no significant long-run effect on output growth. Andrés and Hernando (1999) found substantial level effects but no growth effect of inflation. In a study for the G7, Fountas and Karanasos (2007) report that inflation increases uncertainty about inflation, yet there is mixed evidence regarding the effect of inflation uncertainty on output growth. In the aforementioned model of Dotsey and Ireland (1996), drawing on Romer (1986), inflation can potentially influence not only the level but also the growth rate of aggregate output. They estimate the welfare cost of 10 percent inflation at 0.92 (1.73) percent of output if money is measured as currency (M1). A large part of the welfare cost of inflation is caused by the endogenous growth feature of the model, as the annual growth rate falls from 2.12 percent under zero inflation to 2.07 percent under 10 percent inflation. Summing up, there appears to be little evidence that stable single-digit inflation has a sizable impact on growth.

Cost of unanticipated inflation

So far, various channels of the costs of a steady, anticipated rate of inflation have been discussed. Quantifying the welfare costs of unanticipated changes of inflation and of inflation uncertainty is more difficult. In the former case, welfare costs essentially arise through artificial redistributions of income and wealth, which may also undermine confidence in property rights. In the latter case, welfare costs arise because most individuals are risk averse, preferring steady income and consumption flows. In this and the next subsection, the nature of inflation costs arising through these two channels is briefly discussed.

Inflation surprises emerge as a key stylized fact in Fischer et al. (2002), studying more than 200 post-war high-inflation episodes in 92 countries. Unanticipated changes in inflation are a potentially important source of inflation cost that occur through the existence of nominal contracts for goods and services, and for debts (Fischer and Modigliani 1978, 822). This results in redistributions of income and wealth, the details of which depend on the contract structure. Redistributions take place between the private and the government sector as well as within the private sector. For example, evidence suggests that wages lag behind inflation, implying a shift from wage incomes towards profit incomes.

Probably even more important are redistributions caused by unanticipated inflation from nominal creditors to nominal debtors. Since the domestic private sector is the main creditor of the government sector, an unanticipated increase in the price level lowers its outstanding real claims on the government. Within the private sector an unanticipated increase in the price level reduces the real value of outstanding corporate debt. Initially, this seems to benefit the corporate sector at the expense of the private sector. Ultimately, the lower level of corporate debt will be reflected in an increase in the value of corporate equity, leaving the net wealth of the private sector largely unaffected (ibid., 824).

Redistribution effects are not taken into account in most studies on the welfare cost of inflation employing a representative-agent framework (Doepke and Schneider 2006). Fischer and Modigliani (1978) regard welfare redistributions arising from unanticipated inflation as large, about 1 percent of GNP per 1 percent of unanticipated increase in the price level. However, it is difficult to attach a social welfare cost to such redistributions. Doing this requires a Bergson–Samuelson social welfare function that weighs the welfare of every individual appropriately (Fischer and Modigliani 1978, 827; Johansen 1991, 27). Even if a social welfare function is assumed to exist, the aggregate welfare effect of income or wealth redistributions is likely to be indetermined. Under certain conditions it can be shown that if unanticipated inflation redistributes wealth from a poorer to a richer person (or group) social wealth declines (and vice versa).

Romer and Romer (1999) and Easterly and Fischer (2001) have evidence showing that inflation affects the welfare of the poorest groups in society. Focusing on the transaction patterns of heterogeneous households, Erosa and Ventura (2002) find that inflation is effectively a regressive consumption tax. It has redistributive effects as the detrimental impact on the welfare of low-income households is larger than the impact on high-income households who find it less costly to substitute credit for money in transactions.

Doepke and Schneider (2006) formulate an OLG model of the US economy and calculate the effects of an unanticipated shock to the wealth distribution. The shock is zero sum, yet households react asymmetrically, mainly because redistribution occurs from old lenders to young borrowers. As a result, inflation decreases labor supply and increases savings. The inflation-induced redistribution has a persistent negative effect on output; however, the weighted welfare of domestic households improves. An unanticipated inflation shock of 10 percent increases aggregate welfare between 2.5 and 5.7 percent of GDP, depending on the reaction of fiscal policy. In an indexing scenario the inflation benefits still range between 1 and 2.6 percent of GDP.

Cost of inflation uncertainty
What are the implications of inflation uncertainty? Inflation is uncertain if there are (unpredictable) random fluctuations of the inflation rates about its mean.[32] Uncertainty of inflation leads agents to confuse aggregate and relative price changes and impedes disentanglement of permanent from transitory changes (Driffill et al. 1990). These arguments are stronger if the central bank adopts an inflation targeting regime than under price-level targeting as in the latter case uncertainty about the long-run price level is reduced. Except for indexed assets, inflation uncertainty reduces the safety of nominal assets and increases the relative attractiveness of real, non-reproducible assets as inflation hedges such as land, houses, gold and so on. Given the relative inelasticity of supply, the prices of such assets will tend to increase faster than the general price level. It may be that the resulting 'capital gains' increase in real wealth will result in a decline in saving and, eventually, in physical investment. Another effect of inflation uncertainty is the shortening of the length of contracts. Both effects will tend to reduce the rate of investment by firms and lead to investment in shorter-lived assets (Fischer and Modigliani 1978, 828).

Inflation uncertainty also creates uncertainty in real income and consumption. Consider an individual who consumes the certain amount C and enjoys utility $U(C)$. Alternatively, he/she is offered an uncertain consumption Z, where Z is a random variable with mean C and variance σ_C^2. Which risk premium would this individual demand to compensate him/her for uncertainty? The following condition needs to hold:

$$U(C) = E[U(Z + \psi C)], \tag{10.31}$$

where $E(\cdot)$ is the expectations operator and ψ is the relative risk premium. Applying a second-order Taylor expansion around C, (10.31) can be approximated by $U(C) = U(C) + U'\psi C + U''\sigma_C^2/2$. Solving for the risk premium yields:

$$\psi C = A\frac{\sigma_C^2}{2}, \tag{10.31'}$$

where $A = -U''/U'$ is the Arrow–Pratt measure of absolute risk aversion. A can be interpreted as the price of risk, whereas σ_C^2 measures its quantity.[33] The sign of A depends on the individuals' preferences towards risk. Risk-averse people ($A > 0$) require a positive risk premium as compensation for uncertainty. Hence, inflation uncertainty, if uncompensated, creates a welfare loss. For example, if the utility function is of the constant relative risk aversion (CRRA) type, that is, $U = C^{1-\rho}/(1 - \rho)$ for $\rho > 0$ and $\rho \neq 1$ ($U = \ln(C)$ for $\rho = 1$), the inflation risk premium falls with the level of consumption:

$$\psi C = \frac{\rho}{C}\frac{\sigma_C^2}{2}. \tag{10.31''}$$

Empirically inflation uncertainty increases with the level of inflation, such that both types of inflation costs, the level costs and the uncertainty costs, reinforce each other (Barro 1995).

Quantitatively, relatively little is known about the welfare cost of inflation uncertainty. To estimate the cost of inflation uncertainty, stochastic shocks of a realistic magnitude to productivity and money supply could be added in a general equilibrium framework. Lucas (2000, 258) conjectured: 'I am very confident that the effects of such a modification on the welfare costs . . . would be negligible'.

To check Lucas' conjecture, consider the simple OLG model discussed above. With the CRRA utility function $U = (C_y^{1-\rho} + \alpha C^{1-\rho})/(1 - \rho)$, retirement consumption becomes:

$$C = \left[\frac{a}{1 + a}\frac{Y}{P}\right], \quad a = \alpha^{1/\rho}P^{1-1/\rho}. \tag{10.32}$$

For $\rho = 1$, (10.23b) is obtained as a special case. The price of retirement consumption is $P = (1 + z)^T$, with $1 + z \equiv (1 + \pi)/(1 + R_2)$ and $R_2 = [(1 + R_0)(1 + \pi) - 1](1 - \tau)$.

Tödter (2007) estimates the coefficient of relative risk aversion from US stock return data over the period from 1926 to 2002 and obtains $\rho = 3.5$.

Table 10.15   Welfare loss of inflation uncertainty in the OLG model

	%	$
Direct welfare loss of 2% inflation	1.49	747
Std deviation of direct welfare loss	0.33	163
Std deviation of retirement consumption	1.96	613
Risk premium (inflation targeting) $\rho = 1.4$	0.072	18.73
Risk premium (inflation targeting) $\rho = 3.5$	0.068	21.08
Risk premium (inflation targeting) $\rho = 7.1$	0.089	29.53
Risk premium (price-level targeting)	0.002	0.71

Note: Own calculation, results of 10,000 Monte Carlo simulations; $\alpha = 0.25$, $R_0 = 0.06$, $\tau = 0.4$, $T = 30$; $Y = 50.000$ \$; $\hat{\pi} = 2\%$, $\sigma = 2\%$.

However, ranging from 1.4 to 7.1, the 95 percent confidence interval is fairly wide. Using the calibration ($\alpha = 0.25$, $\rho = 3.5$, $R_0 = 0.06$, $\tau = 0.4$) the trapezoid measure (10.26) yields a direct welfare loss ($B + C$) of 1.52 percent of income for 2 percent inflation, which is close to the loss shown in Table 10.9. Hence, for an individual with income $Y = \$50,000$, which is roughly the median household income in the US, the annual welfare loss of a steady inflation rate of 2 percent amounts to $758 annually ($63 monthly).

Now, let inflation be stochastic and assume that the central bank targets inflation such that $\pi_t = \hat{\pi} + \varepsilon_t$, where $\hat{\pi}$ is the inflation target and ε_t is a normal random variable with zero mean and variance σ^2.[34] The random price level of retirement consumption is $P = (1 + z_1)(1 + z_2) \ldots (1 + z_T)$. Assume that $\hat{\pi} = 2\%$ and $\sigma = 2\%$. Simulating this process 10,000 times, a mean direct welfare loss of 1.49 percent of income ($747) is obtained which is close to the deterministic loss. The simulated standard deviation of the deadweight loss is 0.33 percent of income ($163).

What is the risk premium needed to compensate for this uncertainty? The simulated standard deviation of retirement consumption is $\sigma_C = 1.96\%$. (Mean retirement consumption is $C = \$31,200$ with standard deviation of 613). The risk premium (10.31′) turns out as just $\psi C = \$21.08$.[35] Thus, Lucas was right, this is merely $\psi = 0.068\%$ of the consumption level, and indeed negligible compared to the loss created by the level of inflation.[36] Table 10.15 also shows that the risk premium is not sensitive to variation of the risk-aversion parameter.

3   Costs of reducing inflation

The theoretical and empirical evidence reviewed in Section 2 suggests that there are large costs even of low inflation and, for that matter, benefits of price stability. Does it mean that there is a 'free lunch' to be had by reducing the rate of inflation down to zero? If price stability has not yet been reached, there are likely to be disinflation costs in terms of output and employment losses, at least over the short term. Thus, an analysis of the welfare effects of inflation would be incomplete if the costs of disinflation were neglected. The hypothetical policy question raised by Feldstein (1997, 123) was: 'If the true and fully anticipated rate of inflation (i.e. the measured rate of inflation minus 2 percentage points) has stabilized at 2%, is the gain from reducing inflation to zero worth the sacrifice in output and employment that would be required to achieve it?'.

Given the benefits of achieving price stability, how large can the costs of disinflation be before reducing inflation becomes counterproductive (breakeven benefit)? The costs of reducing inflation in terms of employment and output losses are transitional, depending on:[37]

- real rigidities in the goods and labor markets;
- nominal rigidities in the formation of inflation expectations;
- the stance of monetary and fiscal policy; and
- the initial level of inflation.

Let $C(\pi)$ be the present value (as a percentage of GDP) of the cost of reducing inflation from π to zero. Applying the discount rate for a growing economy $(\rho - g)$ to obtain the annualized cost of disinflation, the breakeven value is $(\rho - g)C(\pi)$. This value is comparable to the permanent annual benefit $(W(\pi))$ of reducing inflation from 2 percent to zero. Thus, from a cost–benefit perspective, the benefit of price stability should be greater than the breakeven value:

$$W(\pi) > (\rho - g)C(\pi). \qquad (10.33)$$

One potential cost of lowering inflation rates to values close to zero which is not elaborated in more detail here but could nevertheless be potentially important is the rising probability of hitting the zero bound for nominal interest rates (zero bound problem). In that case costs would arise because monetary policy would partly forgo its power to counteract large deflationary shocks since nominal (and therefore real) interest rates could not be cut further once the zero bound is reached. In extreme cases it is even conceivable that the economy enters a deflationary spiral. In a quantitative study for the euro area, Coenen (2003) finds that distortions due to the zero bound are likely to be economically insignificant for inflation targets at or above 1 (2) percent in the case of low (high) inflation persistence. In a survey of the literature, Yates (2004, 464) concludes that the risk of hitting the zero bound seems to be 'small down to inflation rates close to

those currently pursued by central banks, but gets much larger below that'
while he judges the risk of a deflationary spiral to be very small indeed.

Output sacrifice ratio
For policy purposes the sacrifice ratio is used to quantify the transitional
costs of disinflation. The output sacrifice ratio (OSR) measures the cumulative loss of output caused by a reduction of the inflation rate by 1 percentage point.

Ball (1994) estimated the OSR by cumulating the output loss that
occurred during identified historical periods of disinflation. Another
approach estimates the OSR on the basis of a Phillips curve for inflation
dynamics. If η is the response of inflation to changes in the output gap, the
real rigidity, the OSR (σ) is often measured as $\sigma = 1/\eta$. If real rigidity is
high (small η), disinflation tends to be costly. Below it will be seen that this
measure is only valid in a special case. Performing dynamic simulations
with a structural macroeconometric model offers a third way to estimate
disinflation costs. If the model features forward-looking expectations,
anticipated and unanticipated permanent disinflations can be simulated.
Stochastic simulations yield estimates of the associated uncertainty.

Consider the following simple New Keynesian model (Tödter 2002):

$$gap_t = -\alpha(i_t - \pi_t - r) + v_t, \alpha \geq 0, \tag{10.34a}$$

$$\pi_t = \pi_t^e + \eta\,gap_t + u_t, \eta \geq 0, \tag{10.34b}$$

$$\pi_t^e = \lambda\pi_{t-1} + (1 - \lambda)\hat{\pi}, 0 \leq \lambda \leq 1, \tag{10.34c}$$

$$i_t = r + \hat{\pi} + \gamma(\pi_{t-1} - \hat{\pi}), \gamma > 1. \tag{10.34d}$$

The output gap (gap_t) depends negatively on the deviation between
the current real interest rate ($i_t - \pi_t$) and its equilibrium value (r), and
on a demand shock (v_t). The Phillips equation postulates that inflation
(π_t) exceeds inflation expectations (π_t^e) if there is a positive output gap
or a price shock (u_t); the parameter η measures real rigidity.[38] Inflation
expectations are modeled as a weighted average of lagged inflation and the
inflation target ($\hat{\pi}$), where λ measures nominal rigidity. If expectations are
forward looking and the central bank is credible, λ tends to be low.[39] The
final equation is the policy reaction function of the central bank. The interest rate is raised above its equilibrium ($r + \hat{\pi}$) if lagged inflation exceeds
the inflation target.

The following solutions (shock terms neglected) for the inflation process
and the output gap are obtained:

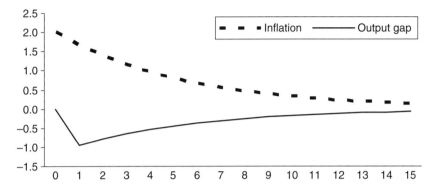

Figure 10.4   Disinflation and output adjustment

$$\pi_t - \hat{\pi} = \psi(\pi_{t-1} - \hat{\pi}) , \psi = \frac{\lambda - \alpha\eta\gamma}{1 - \alpha\eta} < 1, \qquad (10.35a)$$

$$gap_t = -\omega(\pi_{t-1} - \hat{\pi}) , \omega = \frac{\alpha(\gamma - \lambda)}{1 - \alpha\eta} > 0. \qquad (10.35b)$$

Excess inflation follows a first-order autoregressive process. Stability of the inflation process requires the mild restriction $\psi < 1$. Figure 10.4 shows the adjustment process of inflation and output following a reduction of the inflation target from 2 percent to zero, using the calibration $(\alpha = 0.7, \eta = 0.15, \lambda = 0.9, \gamma = 1.5)$.

Calculating the output loss in the New Keynesian model that results from a reduction of target inflation in $t = 1$ from $\hat{\pi}_0$ to $\hat{\pi}$ ($< \hat{\pi}_0$) yields the OSR:

$$\sigma = \frac{\sum_{t=1}^{\infty} \beta^t gap_t}{\hat{\pi} - \hat{\pi}_0} = \frac{\beta\omega}{1 - \beta\psi}, \qquad (10.36)$$

where $\beta = 1/(1 + \rho - g)$ is the discount factor. The OSR depends on all structural parameters of the model. Non-discounting and extreme nominal rigidity ($\lambda = 1$) gives $\sigma = 1/\eta$ as a special case. High real rigidity (small η) increases the OSR. Higher sensitivity of aggregate demand to the real interest rate (large α) increases the OSR as well. Finally, more aggressive monetary policy (large γ) increases the OSR in this model. Table 10.16 provides some illustrative calculations.

Empirical evidence
Estimates of the OSR in the literature vary widely, depending on the method used and the sample period. Based on euro area data from 1985:1

Table 10.16   Output sacrifice ratio in the New Keynesian model (% of GDP)

	λ	η	α	γ	σ	
					$\rho - g$ = 0	$\rho - g$ = 0.025
Benchmark	0.9	0.15	0.7	1.5	2.75	2.40
Nominal rigidity	0				1.00	0.98
	1				6.67	4.67
Real rigidity		0.50			1.53	1.44
		0			4.20	3.36
Demand elasticity			0.3		1.47	1.23
			1.5		4.24	3.88
Policy reaction				1.0	0.70	0.57
				2.0	3.76	3.39

Table 10.17   Disinflation costs of going from 2 percent to zero inflation (% of GDP)

	US	Germany	UK	Spain
Sacrifice ratio	3	4	2.8	2.6
Disinflation costs	6	11.3	5.6	5.2
Annualized disinflation cost*	0.15	0.28	0.14	0.13

Note: * Discount rate $\rho - g$ = 2.5%.

Source: Feldstein (1999a, compiled from pp. 37, 56, 126 and 138).

to 2004:4, Coffinet et al. (2007) estimate the sacrifice ratio between 1.2 and 1.4. The Feldstein (1999a) report provides empirical evidence for the four countries included. Based on Ball (1994), Feldstein (1999b) chooses σ = 3 for the US. The preferred estimate of Bakhshi et al. (1999) for the UK is σ = 2.8. For Spain, Dolado et al. (1999) estimate σ = 2.6, both very close to the US figure. For Germany, Tödter and Ziebarth (1999, 55) report estimates between 0.8 and 4.0. To avoid underestimation of disinflation costs, they use σ = 4, an estimate that was obtained by a simulation exercise with the structural macroeconometric model of the Bundesbank for Germany. Moreover, they assume that the Phillips curve is non-linear (Schelde-Andersen 1992; Huh and Jang 2007), such that disinflation costs rise more than proportionally: $C(\pi) = 4\pi^{1.5}$. Table 10.17 collects the evidence. Thus, the benefit of price stability needs to exceed between 0.13 (Spain) and 0.28 percent of GDP (Germany) to render disinflation worthwhile.

Table 10.18   Benefits and costs of going from 2 percent to zero inflation (% of GDP)

	US	Germany	UK	Spain
Benefits of price stability	1.04	1.41	0.29	1.88
Costs of disinflation (annualized)	0.15	0.28	0.14	0.13
Net welfare benefits	0.89	1.13	0.15	1.75

Source: Feldstein (1999a, compiled from pp. 37, 56, 126, 138).

A menu of choice

Table 10.18 summarizes the permanent annual welfare gain from reducing inflation from 2 percent to zero, that is, the overall welfare gain of price stability (reported in Table 10.14) minus annualized disinflation costs (from Table 10.17).

In all four countries the estimated benefit of price stability exceeds the estimated disinflation costs. The lowest gain is reported for the UK, while the highest gain is estimated for Spain. The net welfare gains reported for the US and Germany are both around 1 percent of GDP per annum.

Finally, some sensitivity considerations may be warranted. In the Feldstein report estimates of the benefits and (disinflation) costs of price stability were performed under the assumption of going from 2 percent inflation to zero. However, during the period underlying the estimates (1991–95 in the case of Germany), actual inflation was higher, 3.3 percent on average. To check the sensitivity of their results, Tödter and Ziebarth (1999, 80) calculated benefits and costs for different rates of disinflation, collected in Table 10.19.

Howitt (1990) postulated that a central bank should disinflate until the marginal gain from reducing inflation balances the marginal cost of doing so (Howitt's rule). Thus, according to this rule, reducing inflation from the (then) current level of 3.3 percent to zero would have been optimal, creating a permanent welfare gain of 1.26 percent of GDP. The benefit forgone by disinflating by only 2 percentage points would have been small (−0.13 percent of GDP).[40]

4   Conclusions

Milton Friedman's famous dictum that 'inflation is always and everywhere a monetary phenomenon' is widely accepted nowadays. There is also a broad consensus that high, volatile and unanticipated inflation

Table 10.19   *Menu of choice (Germany) (benefits and costs as % of GDP)*

Initial rate of inflation (%)	3.3	3.3	3.3	3.3	3.3	3.3
Rate of disinflation (%)	0.0	1.0	2.0	3.3	4.0	5.0
Final rate of inflation (%)	3.3	2.3	1.3	0	–0.7	–1.7
Benefits per annum	0.00	0.85	1.41	1.86	2.01	2.24
Costs of disinflation per annum	0.00	0.10	0.28	0.60	0.80	1.12
Net benefit	0.00	0.75	1.13	1.26	1.21	1.12
Loss of non-optimal disinflation	–1.26	–0.51	–0.13	0.00	–0.05	–0.14

Source: Tödter and Ziebarth (1999, 80).

induces large costs. However, it is a remarkable result of research activities in the past decade that even low, steady and anticipated inflation creates substantial welfare losses.

Theory and evidence reviewed in this chapter suggest that the benefits of price stability are large and permanent while the costs of disinflation are small in comparison and temporary. The money demand channel, though important at two-digit inflation, is of relatively minor importance at low rates of inflation. In contrast, the interaction of nominal-based tax codes and inflation creates powerful distortionary effects on the intertemporal allocation of savings and consumption. In combination with certain behavioral patterns (saving rates) and institutional facts (tax rules), even low inflation generates high welfare losses. Empirical country studies based on partial as well as general equilibrium models for the US and Germany suggest that a permanent welfare gain of about 1 percent of GDP, net of indirect tax effects and disinflation costs, can be obtained by eliminating 2 percent inflation. Expressed in present value terms, the net benefit of price stability reaches about 40 percent of GDP.[41]

Not all channels of inflation costs have yet been identified, thoroughly studied, modeled and quantified empirically. Especially costs of low inflation arising from higher probabilities of hitting the zero bound for nominal interest rates could potentially provide a justification for targeting low instead of zero or negative inflation. More work is certainly needed to complete our understanding of the benefits and costs of price stability. The welfare effects of inflation remain an important issue for future research that is likely to generate benefits for the economy that will outweigh its costs.

Notes

* The views expressed in this chapter do not necessarily reflect those of the Deutsche Bundesbank. For helpful comments we thank Ch. Gerberding, H. Herrmann and K. Wendorff. Of course, all remaining errors are ours.

1. See Chakravarty (1986, 687) on cost–benefit and Feldman (1986, 889) on welfare analysis.
2. Notwithstanding the difficulties of measuring inflation or the 'true' cost of living; see Boskin et al. (1996), Gordon (2006).
3. Surveys are provided by Driffill et al. (1990), Dowd (1994), Briault (1995), Lucas (2000) and Palenzuela et al. (2003). Advanced textbook treatments can be found in Blanchard and Fischer (1989), McCallum (1989), Heijdra and van der Ploeg (2002), and Walsh (2003) among others.
4. Fischer and Modigliani (1978, 810) describe the indexed economy as follows: Public and private institutions are fully inflation proof, current and future inflation is fully reflected in contracts inherited from the past, and future inflation is fully reflected in contracts for the future.
5. Money is said to be neutral if changes in the level of money supply have no effect on real variables in equilibrium. Money is superneutral if changes in the growth rate of money supply have no real effects on equilibrium (Blanchard and Fischer 1989, 207).
6. English (1999) provides an empirical estimate of this effect for the US.
7. Theoretical and empirical approaches to money demand are discussed by, for example, Serletis (2007).
8. The Fisher equation (10.2) will be used throughout, rather than the approximation $i \approx r + \pi$.
9. Hines (2002) traces the concept of welfare triangles back to Jules Dupuit in 1844.
10. Here, the DWL of inflation is calculated as the area between r and i. Several authors, in particular those applying general equilibrium models, calculate the DWL between zero and i; see Tower (1971) and Gillman (1995).
11. Generally, taxes create distortions due to substitution effects. For example, the substitution effect of wage taxes reduces labor supply and in a similar way capital income taxes have negative effects on investment.
12. For more on this so-called 'Hahn problem', see Hahn (1965), Bewley (1983), Heijdra and van der Ploeg (2002, ch. 12) and Walsh (2003, ch. 2).
13. See Clower (1967), McCallum (1983, 1989), Kyotaki and Wright (1989) and Dotsey and Ireland (1996).
14. See Patinkin (1965) and Sidrauski (1967). Feenstra (1986) demonstrates that there is a functional equivalence between models with money in the utility function and models with liquidity costs which show up in the budget constraint. Fischer (1974) puts money into the production function.
15. See Samuelson (1958) and Wallace (1980).
16. Walsh (2003, 91) shows that depending on 'timing' assumptions in the utility function and in the budget constraint, condition (10.12) may also appear as $U_m/U_c = i/(1 + i)$.
17. Lacker (1996) reports manufacturing and operating costs of coins and currency of approximately 0.2 percent of face value.
18. See Chari et al. (1996) and Correia and Teles (1999) on the optimality of the Friedman rule when there are distortionary taxes.
19. The concept used here differs from the seigniorage of money creation, defined as $\sigma = \Delta M/PY = \mu \, k$, where μ is the growth rate of money supply. For $\mu = g + \pi$, where g is the growth of real output, $s = \sigma + (r - g)k$. Thus, both concepts coincide at $r = g$. Empirically, seigniorage in industrial countries is about 0.5 percent of GDP.
20. See Darby (1975), Feldstein (1976), Feldstein et al. (1978), Auerbach (1981) and Gordon (1984).
21. Blanchard and Fischer (1989) and Romer (2006) include textbook treatments of the OLG model.
22. The parameter α is related to the discount factor β (≤ 1) in the following way: $\alpha = \beta^T$.

For example, $\alpha = 0.25$ corresponds to a discount factor $\beta = 0.955$ or a discount rate of 4.5 percent p.a.

23. Feldstein (1997, 150–53) discusses technical, legal, and administrative problems of indexation.
24. In this model, substituting the parameters used in Table 10.9, the optimal rate of inflation is -3.3 percent. At that rate of deflation the nominal interest would be 2.5 percent, well above the zero bound.
25. Profits of German corporations distributed to domestic individuals were subject to a variety of taxes: a trade tax (on return and capital), a corporation tax, an investment income tax, a property tax, the income tax, and the solidarity surcharge to finance German unification. Tax rules including tax rates have changed since the study was conducted.
26. Meanwhile legislation in Germany has changed considerably.
27. Dolado et al. (1999, 115) explain the exceptionally high loss for Spain by the high ratio of housing value to GDP and the enormous implicit subsidy that tax rules and inflation provide to the purchase of owner-occupied houses.
28. Tödter and Ziebarth (1999) performed a stochastic simulation exercise by simultaneously shocking all 23 parameters in their model subject to uncertainty. Repeating this exercise 10,000 times, they obtain a distribution of the overall welfare gain. The median (1.34 percent) is below the mean (1.39 percent), indicating positive skewness of the distribution. The standard deviation is 0.473 percent and with probability of 79 percent the welfare gain exceeds 1 percent of GDP.
29. Since Abel calculated the welfare effects as a percentage of steady-state consumption, his results are scaled by country-specific ratios of consumption to GDP for comparability.
30. For the United Kingdom the welfare gain through the consumption channel from the Sidrauski model is about twice the size of the country study. Concerning Spain, a large discrepancy shows up for the housing channel. The effect reported in the case study is much larger than in the Sidrauski model (and also higher than in the other country studies). Both discrepancies are difficult to explain (Abel 1999, 190; Bakhshi et al. 1999, 154; Dolado et al. 1999, 115).
31. Azar (2007) reports estimates of the US social discount rate of about 5 percent.
32. Variability or volatility of inflation is not the same as uncertainty. Inflation might be highly volatile but if the generating process is understood and predictable, uncertainty can be low.
33. Kimball (1990) discusses a third-order approximation of the utility function, which shows that the risk premium also depends on the skewness (asymmetry) of the income distribution.
34. Alternatively, a strategy of price-level targeting is assumed, where the price level is allowed to increase over time. If δ_{t-1} denotes the deviation from the price-level target in the previous period, actual inflation is corrected accordingly in the current period: $\pi_t = \hat{\pi} + \varepsilon_t - \delta_{t-1}$. Thus, uncertainty about the price level in the long run is largely eliminated.
35. Price-level targeting slashes this amount by the factor $T = 30$ to 0.71 dollars.
36. This may still be an overestimation because even simple forecasting techniques would allow us to cut inflation uncertainty in half. Lucas (2003) obtained comparably low estimates for the welfare cost of business-cycle fluctuations (DeJong and Dave 2007, 127).
37. Akerlof et al. (1996) argue that the long-run Phillips curve is not vertical but downward sloping at very low rates of inflation because of nominal wage rigidity. Feldstein (1999a, 5) points out that in sustained periods of price stability such resistance would gradually disappear.
38. See Blanchard and Gali (2007) on real wage rigidities in the New Keynesian model. Rudd and Whelan (2007) give a critical account of modeling inflation dynamics in a New Keynesian–Phillips approach.
39. Palenzuela et al. (2003) summarize the evidence on downward nominal rigidities.

Recently, based on the analysis of 13 million price records underlying the computation of the French consumer price index, Baudry et al. (2007) found that consumer prices are rather sticky (with average duration around 8 months), but they have no evidence of specific downward nominal rigidity.

40. Taking into account that substitution effects and quality changes bias the measured consumer price index upwards (Boskin et al. 1996), exceeding the true rate of inflation by probably half a percentage point in the case of Germany (Hoffmann 1998; Deutsche Bundesbank 2002), disinflating from 3.3 to 1.3 percent in the measured rate of inflation is almost consistent with price stability in the true rate of inflation and reduces the risk of hitting the zero nominal interest rate bound.

41. At a discount rate of $\rho - g = 2.5\%$.

References

Abel, A.B. (1997), 'Comment', in Romer and Romer (eds), pp. 156–66.

Abel, A.B. (1999), 'Comment on Chapters 2, 3, and 4', in Feldstein (ed.) (1999a), pp. 180–91.

Aiyagari, S.R. (1991), 'Response to a defense of zero inflation', *Federal Reserve Bank of Minneapolis Quarterly Review* (Spring), 21–4.

Akerlof, G.A. (2007), 'The missing motivation in macroeconomics', *American Economic Review*, **97** (March), 5–36.

Akerlof, G.A., W. Dickens and G. Perry (1996), 'The macroeconomics of low inflation', *Brookings Papers on Economic Activity*, No. 1, 1–59.

Andrés, J. and I. Hernando (1999), 'Does inflation harm economic growth? Evidence from the OECD', in Feldstein (ed.) (1999a), pp. 315–41.

Attanasio, O.P., L, Guiso, T. Jappelli (2002), 'The demand for money, financial innovation, and the welfare cost of inflation: an analysis with household data', *Journal of Political Economy*, **110** (2), 317–51.

Auerbach, A.J. (1981) 'Inflation and the tax treatment of firm behavior', *American Economic Review*, **71** (May), 419–23.

Azar, S.A. (2007) 'Measuring the US social discount rate aversion, *Applied Financial Economics Letters*, **3**, 63–6.

Bailey, M.J. (1956), 'The welfare costs of inflationary finance', *Journal of Political Economy*, **64** (2), 93–110.

Bakhshi, H., A. Haldane and N. Hatch (1999), 'Some costs and benefits of price stability in the United Kingdom', in Feldstein (ed.) (1999a), pp. 133–80.

Ball, L. (1994), 'What determines the sacrifice ratio?', in N.G. Mankiw (ed.), *Monetary Policy*, Chicago, IL: University of Chicago Press, pp. 155–93.

Barro, R.J. (1995), 'Inflation and economic growth', NBER Working Paper No. 5326, Cambridge, MA: National Bureau of Economic Research, October.

Baudry, L., H. Le Bihan, P. Sevestre and S. Tarrieu (2007), 'What do thirteen million price records have to say about consumer price rigidity?', *Oxford Bulletin of Economics and Statistics*, **69** (2), 139–83.

Bernholz, P. (2003), *Monetary Regimes and Inflation*, Cheltenham, UK and Northampton, MA, USA: Edward Elgar.

Bewley, T. (1983), 'A difficulty with the optimum quantity of money', *Econometrica*, **51** (5), 1485–504.

Blanchard, O. and S. Fischer (1989), *Lectures on Macroeconomics*, Cambridge MA: MIT Press.

Blanchard, O. and J. Gali (2007), 'Real wage rigidities and the New Keynesian model', *Journal of Money, Credit and Banking*, Suppl. to **39** (1), 35–65.

Boskin, M.J., E. Dulberger, R. Gordon, Z. Griliches and D. Jorgenson (1996), 'Toward a More Accurate Measure of the Cost of Living', Final Report to the Senate Finance Committee, Washington, DC, December 4.

Briault, C. (1995), 'The costs of inflation', *Bank of England Quarterly Bulletin*, February, 33–45.

Bruno, M. and W. Easterly (1995), 'Inflation crises and long-run growth', NBER Working Paper No. 5209, Cambridge, MA: National Bureau of Economic Research, October.

Bullard, J.B. and S. Russell (2004), 'How costly is sustained low inflation for the U.S. economy?,' *Federal Reserve Bank of St. Louis Review*, **86** (3), 35–67.

Cagan, P. (1956), 'The monetary dynamics of hyperinflation', in Milton Friedman (ed.), *Studies in the Quantity Theory of Money*, Chicago IL: University of Chicago Press, pp. 25–120.

Chakravarty, S. (1986), 'Cost–benefit analysis', in John Eatwell, Murray Milgate and Peter Newman (eds), *The New Palgrave: A Dictionary of Economics*, London: Macmillan, pp. 687–90.

Chari, V.V., L.K. Christiano and P. Kehoe (1996), 'Optimality of the Friedman rule in economies with distorting taxes', *Journal of Monetary Economics*, **37**, 203–23.

Chiu, J. and M. Molico (2007), 'Liquidity, redistribution, and the welfare cost of inflation', Working Paper 2007-39, Bank of Canada.

Clower, R.W. (1967), 'A reconsideration of the micro foundations of monetary theory', *Western Economic Journal*, **6** (1), 1–9.

Coenen, G. (2003), 'Zero lower bound: is it a problem in the euro area?', ECB Working Paper No. 269, European Central Bank, Frankfurt am Main.

Coffinet, J., J. Matheron and C. Poilly (2007) 'Estimating the sacrifice ratio for the euro area', *Quarterly Selection of Articles*, Banque de France, **8**, 35–48.

Cohen, D., K.A. Hasset and R.G. Hubbard (1999), 'Inflation and the user cost of capital: does inflation still matter?', in Feldstein (ed.) (1999a), pp. 199–230.

Cooley, T.F. and G.D. Hansen (1989), 'The inflation tax in a real business cycle model', *American Economic Review*, **79** (4), 733–48.

Correia, I. and P. Teles (1999), 'The optimal inflation tax', *Review of Economic Dynamics*, **2** (2), 325–46.

Craig, B. and G. Rocheteau (2005), 'Rethinking the welfare cost of inflation', *FRB Cleveland Economic Commentary*, March 1, pp. 1–4.

Craig, B. and G. Rocheteau (2007), 'Inflation and welfare: a search approach', FRB Cleveland Discussion Paper, February 16 No. 12.

Darby, M. (1975), 'The financial and tax effects of monetary policy on interest rates', *Economic Inquiry*, **13** (June), 266–76.

DeJong, D.N. and C. Dave (2007), *Structural Macroeconometrics*, Princeton, NJ and Oxford: Princeton University Press.

Desai, M.A. and J.R. Hines Jr (1999), 'Excess capital flows and the burden of inflation in open economies', in Feldstein (ed.) (1999a), pp. 235–68.

Deutsche Bundesbank (2002), 'Changes in the Official Consumer Price Statistics and their Implications for the "Measurement Bias" in the Inflation Rate', *Monthly Report*, August, 38–9.

Di Tella, R., R. MacCulloch and A. Oswald (2001), 'Preferences over inflation and unemployment: evidence from surveys of happiness', *American Economic Review*, **91** (1), 335–41.

Doepke, M. and M. Schneider (2006), 'Inflation as a redistribution shock: effects on aggregates and welfare', NBER Working Paper 12319, Cambridge, MA, June.

Dolado, J.J., J.M. González-Páramo and José Viñals (1999), 'A cost–benefit analysis of going from low inflation to price stability in Spain', in Feldstein (ed.) (1999a), pp. 95–132.

Dotsey, M. and P. Ireland (1996), 'The welfare cost of inflation in general equilibrium', *Journal of Monetary Economics*, **37**, 29–47.

Dowd, K. (1994), 'The costs of inflation and disinflation', *Cato Journal*, **14** (2), 305–31.

Driffill, J., G.E. Mizon and A. Ulph (1990), 'Costs of inflation', in B.M. Friedman and F.H. Hahn (eds), *Handbook of Monetary Economics*, Vol. II, Amsterdam: North-Holland, pp. 1014–66.

Easterly, W. and S. Fischer (2001), 'Inflation and the poor', *Journal of Money, Credit, and Banking*, **33** (2), 160–78.

Eckstein, Z. and L. Leiderman (1992), 'Seigniorage and the welfare cost of inflation:

evidence from an intertemporal model of money and consumption', *Journal of Monetary Economics*, June, 389–410.

English, W.B. (1999), 'Inflation and financial sector size', *Journal of Monetary Economics*, **44**, 379–400.

Ericsson, N.R., J.S. Irons and R.W. Tryon (2000), 'Output and inflation in the long run', FRB International Finance Discussion Paper No. 687, Washington, DC, November.

Erosa, A. and Ventura, G. (2002), 'On inflation as a regressive consumption tax', *Journal of Monetary Economics*, **49** (4), 761–95.

Feenstra, R.C. (1986), 'Functional equivalence between liquidity costs and the utility of money', *Journal of Monetary Economics*, **17**, 271–91.

Feldman, A.M. (1986), 'Welfare economics', in John Eatwell, Murray Milgate and Peter Newman (eds), *The New Palgrave: A Dictionary of Economics*, London: Macmillan, pp. 889–95.

Feldstein, M. (1976), 'Inflation, tax rules and the rate of interest: a theoretical analysis', *American Economic Review*, **66** (June), 809–20.

Feldstein, M. (1983), *Inflation, Tax Rules, and Capital Formation*, Chicago, IL: University of Chicago Press.

Feldstein, M. (1997), 'The costs and benefits of going from low inflation to price stability', in Romer and Romer (eds), pp. 123–56.

Feldstein, M. (1999a), *The Costs and Benefits of Price Stability*, Chicago, IL and London: University of Chicago Press.

Feldstein, M. (1999b), 'Capital income taxes and the benefit of price stability', in Feldstein (ed.) (1999a), pp. 1–46.

Feldstein, M., J. Green and E. Sheshinski (1978), 'Inflation and taxes in a growing economy with debt and equity finance', *Journal of Political Economy*, **86** (2), pt. 2 (April), S53–S70.

Fischer, S. (1974), 'Money and the production function', *Economic Inquiry*, **12**, 517–33.

Fischer, S. (1981), 'Towards an understanding of the costs of inflation: II', *Carnegie-Rochester Conference Series on Public Policy*, **15**, 5–41.

Fischer, S. (1993), 'The role of macroeconomic factors in growth', *Journal of Monetary Economics*, **32**, 485–512.

Fischer, S. and F. Modigliani (1978), 'Towards an understanding of the real effects and costs of inflation', *Weltwirtschaftliches Archiv*, **114** (4), 810–33.

Fischer, S., R. Sahay and C.A. Vegh (2002), 'Modern hyper- and high inflations', *Journal of Economic Literature*, **40** (3), 837–80.

Fountas, S. and M. Karanasos (2007), 'Inflation, output growth, and nominal and real uncertainty: empirical evidence for the G7', *Journal of International Money and Finance*, **26**, 229–50.

Friedman, M. (1969), 'The optimum quantity of money', in *The Optimum Quantity of Money and Other Essays*, Chicago, IL: Aldine, pp. 1–50.

Gillman, M. (1995), 'Comparing partial and general equilibrium estimates of the welfare cost of inflation', *Contemporary Economic Policy*, **13**, 60–71.

Gomme, P. (1993), 'Money and growth revisited: measuring the costs of inflation in an endogenous growth model', *Journal of Monetary Economics*, **32**, 51–77.

Gordon, R.H. (1984), 'Inflation, taxation, and corporate behavior', *Quarterly Journal of Economics*, **94** (May), 313–17.

Gordon, R.J. (2006), 'The Boskin Commission Report: a retrospective one decade later', NBER Working Paper 12311, Cambridge, MA.

Grimes, A. (1991), 'The effects of inflation on growth: some international evidence', *Weltwirtschaftliches Archiv*, **127** (4), 631–44.

Groshen, E.L. and M.E. Schweitzer (1999), 'Identifying inflation's grease and sand effects in the labor market', in Feldstein (ed.) (1999a), pp. 273–308.

Hahn, F.H. (1965), 'On some problems of proving the existence of an equilibrium in a monetary economy', in F.H. Hahn and F.P.R. Brechling (eds), *The Theory of Interest Rates*, London: Macmillan, pp. 126–35.

Harberger, A.C. (1954), 'Monopoly and resource allocation', *American Economic Review*, **44** (2) (May), 77–87.

Haslag, J.H. (1995), 'Monetary policy, banking, and growth', *Economic Inquiry*, **36** (3), 489–500.
Haslag, J.H. (1997), 'Output, growth, welfare, and inflation: a survey', Federal Reserve Bank of Dallas, *Economic Review*, 11–21.
Heijdra, B.J. and F. van der Ploeg (2002), *The Foundations of Modern Macroeconomics*, Oxford: Oxford University Press.
Hines, J.R. Jr (2002), 'Applied Public Finance Meets General Equilibrium: The Research Contributions of Arnold Harberger', University of Michigan and NBER, January.
Hoffmann, J. (1998), 'Problems of Inflation Measurement in Germany', Economic Research Group of the Deutsche Bundesbank Discussion Paper 1/98.
Howitt, P. (1990), 'Zero inflation as a long-term target for monetary policy', in R.G. Lipsey (ed.), *Zero Inflation: The Goal of Price Stability*, Toronto: C.D. Howe Institute, pp. 66–108.
Huh, H. and I. Jang (2007), 'Nonlinear Philips curve, sacrifice ratio, and the natural rate of unemployment', *Economic Modelling*, **24**, 797–813.
Ireland, P. (2007), 'On the welfare cost of inflation and the recent behavior of money demand', Boston College Working Papers in Economics, No. 662, Boston, MA.
Johansen, P.-O. (1991), *An Introduction to Modern Welfare Economics*, Cambridge: Cambridge University Press.
Kimball, M.S. (1990), 'Precautionary saving in the small and in the large', *Econometrica*, **58** (1), 53–73.
Knell, M. and H. Stix. (2005), 'The income elasticity of money demand: a meta-analysis of empirical results', *Journal of Economic Surveys*, **19** (3), 513–33.
Konieczny J.D. (1994), 'The optimal rate of inflation: competing theories and their relevance to Canada', in Bank of Canada (ed.), *Economic Behaviour and Policy Choice Under Price Stability*, Proceedings of a Conference held at the Bank of Canada, October 1993, Ottawa, pp. 1–46.
Kyotaki, N. and R. Wright (1989), 'On money as a medium of exchange', *Journal of Political Economy*, **97** (4), 927–54.
Lacker, J.M. (1996), 'Stored value card: costly private substitutes for government currency', *Federal Reserve Bank of Richmond Economic Quarterly*, **82**, 1–25.
Lagos, R. and R. Wright (2005), 'A unified framework for monetary theory and policy analysis', *Journal of Political Economy*, **113**, 463–84.
LeBlanc, F. (1690), *Traité historique des monnayes de France*, Paris; quoted by L. Einaudi (1953), 'The theory of imaginary money from Charlemagne to the French Revolution' in F.C. Lane and J.S. Riemersma (eds), *Enterprise and Secular Change*, Homewood, III: Irwin, PP. 229–61.
Lucas, R.E. Jr (1973), 'Some international evidence on output–inflation tradeoffs', *American Economic Review*, **63**, 326–34.
Lucas, R.E. Jr (1981), 'Discussion of Stanley Fischer, "Towards an Understanding of the Costs of Inflation: II"', in K. Brunner and A. Meltzer (eds), *The Cost and Consequences of Inflation*, Amsterdam: North-Holland, pp. 5–42.
Lucas, R.E. Jr (2000), 'Inflation and welfare', *Econometrica*, **68** (2), 247–74.
Lucas, R.E. Jr (2003), 'Macroeconomic priorities', *American Economic Review*, **93**, 1–14.
Marty, A.L. (1976), 'A note on the welfare cost of money creation', *Journal of Monetary Economics*, **2**, 121–4.
McCallum, B.T. (1983), 'The role of overlapping-generations models in monetary economics', *Carnegie-Rochester Conference Series on Public Policy*, New York: Macmillan.
McCallum, B.T. (1989), *Monetary Economics, Theory and Policy*, New York: Macmillan.
McCallum, B.T. and M.S. Goodfriend (1987), 'Demand for money: theoretical studies', in John Eatwell, Murray Milgate and Peter Newman (eds), *The New Palgrave: A Dictionary of Economics*, London: Macmillan, pp. 775–781.
Meltzer, A.H. (1963), 'The demand for money: the evidence from the time series', *Journal of Political Economy*, **71** (June), 219–46
Palenzuela, D.R., G. Camba-Mendez and J.A. Garcia, (2003), 'Relevant economic issues concerning the optimal rate of inflation', ECB Working Paper No. 278, European Central Bank, Frankfurt am Main.

Patinkin, D. (1965), *Money, Interest and Prices*, 2nd edn, New York: Harper & Row.
Phelps, E. (1973), 'Inflation in the theory of public finance', *Swedish Journal of Economics*, **75**, 67–82.
Romer, P.M. (1986), 'Increasing returns and long-run growth', *Journal of Political Economy*, **94** (October), 1002–37.
Romer, D. (2006), *Advanced Macroeconomics*, 3rd edn, Boston, MA: McGraw-Hill.
Romer, C.D. and D.H. Romer (1997), *Reducing Inflation: Motivation and Strategy*, Chicago, IL and London: University of Chicago Press.
Romer, C.D. and D.H. Romer (1999), 'Monetary policy and the well-being of the poor', *Federal Reserve Bank of Kansas City Economic Review*, 21–49.
Rosen, H. (1985), 'Housing subsidies: effects on housing decisions, efficiency and equity', in M. Feldstein and A. Auerbach (eds), *Handbook of Public Economics*, Vol. 1, Amsterdam: North-Holland, pp. 375–420.
Rudd, J. and K. Whelan (2007), 'Modeling inflation dynamics: a critical review of recent research', *Journal of Money, Credit and Banking*, Suppl. to **39** (1), 155–70.
Samuelson, P.A. (1958), 'An exact consumption-loan model of interest with or without the social contrivance of money', *Journal of Political Economy*, **66** (6), 467–82.
Sarel, M. (1996), 'Nonlinear effects of inflation on economic growth', *IMF Staff Papers*, 42, 199–215.
Schelde-Andersen, P. (1992), 'OECD country experiences with disinflation', in A. Blundell-Wignall (ed.), *Inflation, Disinflation and Monetary Policy*, Sydney: Ambassador Press, pp. 104–81.
Serletis, A. (2007), *The Demand for Money, Theoretical and Empirical Approaches*, 2nd edn, Boston, MA: Kluwer Academic.
Serletis, A. and K. Yavari, (2004), 'The welfare cost of inflation in Canada and the United States', *Economics Letters*, **84**, (2), 199–204.
Shiller, R.J. (1997), 'Why do people dislike inflation?', in Romer and Romer (eds), pp. 13–65.
Sidrauski, M. (1967), 'Rational choice and patterns of growth in a monetary economy', *American Economic Review*, **57**, 534–44.
Tödter, K.-H. (2002), 'Monetary policy indicators and policy rules in the P-star model', Discussion Paper 18/092, Economic Research Centre of the Deutsche Bundesbank.
Tödter, K.-H. (2007), 'Estimating the uncertainty of relative risk aversion', *Applied Financial Economics Letters*, pp. 1–30.
Tödter, K.-H., and G. Ziebarth (1999), 'Price stability versus low inflation in Germany: an analysis of costs and benefits', in Feldstein (ed.) (1999a), pp. 47–94.
Tower, E. (1971), 'More on the welfare cost of inflationary finance', *Journal of Money, Credit, and Banking*, **3**, 850–60.
Wallace, N (1980), 'The overlapping generations model of fiat money', in J. Kareken and N. Wallace (eds), *Models of Monetary Economies*, Minneapolis, MN: Federal Reserve Bank of Minneapolis, pp. 49–82.
Walsh, C.E. (2003), *Monetary Theory and Policy*, 2nd edn, Cambridge, MA: MIT Press.
Weber, A. (2007), 'A central banker's interest in Phillips curves', Symposium on The Phillips Curve and the Natural Rate of Unemployment, Kiel Institute for the World Economy, Kiel, 3 June.
Wolman, A.L. (1997), 'Zero inflation and the Friedman rule: a welfare comparison', *Federal Reserve Bank of Richmond Economic Quarterly*, **83** (4), 1–21.
Wood, J. (2005), *A History of Central Banking in Great Britain and the United States*, Cambridge: Cambridge University Press.
Yates, T. (2004), 'Monetary policy and the zero bound to interest rates: a review', *Journal of Economic Survey*, **18** (3), 427–481.
Zee, H. H. (2000), 'Welfare cost of (low) inflation: a general equilibrium perspective', *Finanzarchiv*, **57**, 376–93.

11 Cost–benefit analysis of economic globalization[1]

Clem Tisdell

1 Introduction

Wide differences of opinion exist about the costs and benefits of economic globalization. This is partly because there is disagreement about several effects of economic globalization, empirical evidence is often disputed, economic gains and costs associated with globalization are uneven between existing individuals, and also between present and future generations and between nations, and some consequences (such as reduced national ability to control economic events and changes in economic vulnerability) are difficult to quantify in monetary terms. There is lack of agreement about how interpersonal comparisons of economic benefits and costs should be made. Therefore, it is unrealistic to expect that a single monetary figure can be estimated which accurately measures the net overall benefit of economic globalization. Nevertheless, some quantitative estimates of particular features associated with globalization are available, as is illustrated in this chapter, for example, for product variety and changes in the state of the global environment. Further quantitative cost–benefit work is possible and some features for which this seems practical are identified.

The approach which I take here is to identify and critically discuss factors which seem to have a significant bearing on the estimates of costs and benefits of growing globalization. These include greater scope for gains from trading, for enhanced benefits from factor movements particularly of capital, impacts on unemployment, poverty and economic inequality, implications for economic vulnerability and for the state of the environment.

Growing economic globalization is assumed in this chapter to be a process that leads to the international extension of markets. It is reflected in the growing proportion of global economic production that is traded internationally as well as expanding international movements of capital and labour (Tisdell and Sen, 2004; Tisdell, 2005b). Financial markets have also displayed growing global integration. Let us consider these aspects.

2 Production and exchange of commodities and the international extension of markets

Using comparative statics, neoclassical economics has developed strong arguments that the extension of markets results in a potential Paretian improvement (if not a Paretian improvement) for all economic agents involved in the process. It results in greater efficiency in production by enabling greater specialization in production according to comparative advantages. It enables commodities to be exchanged more widely so that wants can be more fully satisfied. Even if perfect competition exists, the merging of submarkets (such as national markets globally) is predicted to be an effective means to reduce economic scarcity, given the absence of adverse externalities and other market failures. Within the standard neoclassical framework, the benefits of growing economic globalization outweigh any costs involved (Salvatore, 2007, ch. 3).

The traditional neoclassical argument, however, gives little attention to forms of market competition other than perfect competition and it does not consider the importance of decreasing costs of supply in some important industries.

For example, external economies of scale can be obtained by the market expansion of some competitive industries. Increased globalization enables such industries to expand in size. If the industry is fairly competitive, suppliers will earn normal profit in the long run and buyers will pay a lower price for the product. Therefore, a Kaldor–Hicks gain (a potential Paretian improvement) is likely to eventuate.

Just how much increasing globalization will alter national and regional market structures is unclear. One extreme possibility is that all such markets are transformed into perfect or near-perfect markets by greater international market competition. This, however, is probably unrealistic because some barriers to entry into national or regional markets are likely to continue to exist. Nevertheless, traditional static economic analysis would still predict the occurrence of a Kaldor–Hicks gain. For example, suppose that a monopoly exists in a regional market in a product and that the monopolist engages in limit pricing. With reduced barriers to international trade (such as a lowering of tariffs, non-tariff barriers, transport costs, and market transaction costs) even if the monopoly continues to exist in the regional market, the monopolist will be forced to reduce its limit price. Buyers within the monopolist's region benefit and employment by the monopoly rises, although other things remaining equal, the monopolist's profit falls. There is, however, a Kaldor–Hicks economic gain. There could also be some gains to the monopoly if it is exporting because it may be able to access international markets that were previously unavailable to it.

While static analysis throws some light on the economic consequences of growing economic globalization, in the long term, many of the factors held constant in static analysis change. Dynamic aspects complicate the analysis of the economic consequences of growing economic globalization but must be considered. The following questions need consideration: what consequences will economic globalization have for the evolution of market structures? What impacts is it likely to have on technological progress and innovation? This needs consideration in the light of Schumpeter's thesis (Schumpeter, 1942) and the monopoly-profit thesis of international trade. What are likely to be its consequences for the extent of product diversity?

It is probably unrealistic to expect that all markets will become less concentrated and more competitive as globalization proceeds. While many markets will become more competitive or fairly competitive in their structure, some are unlikely to show much change and others may in the long term even become less competitive as global concentration of market power increases. Some industries display such strong internal economies of scale and scope in production and marketing that natural global oligopolies or monopolies occur. In such circumstances, increased scope for international market competition may result in the elimination of smaller efficient and also less efficient suppliers and result in increased market concentration.

In such decreasing cost cases, it is usually the survival of the largest firms that are favoured because they already have a head start compared to smaller firms in terms of lower per-unit costs of production and marketing. This usually means that firms located in larger markets in developed countries or regions such as the USA and the EU are favoured when increasing scope exists for international competition. With growing globalization, their chances of globally dominating decreasing cost industries increase. This is illustrated in Figure 11.1.

In Figure 11.1, curve ABCD represents the long-run average cost experienced by a firm in producing and marketing a product X. To begin with, assume that this cost curve is the same for all firms no matter where they are located. In a country with a small market, a firm (firm one) may have annual volume of sales of X_1 and experience per-unit costs corresponding to B. On the other hand, another firm in a country with a large market (firm two) may have an annual volume of sales of X_2 and experience a level of per-unit costs corresponding to point C. Both may survive due to barriers to international trade. However, if these barriers are eliminated or become very small, the larger firm in the larger economy can be expected to drive the smaller one out of business. The comparative initial position of the firms gives a competitive advantage to the firm with the larger initial market even though both firms are equally efficient (have the

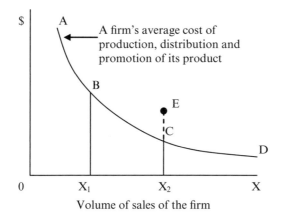

Figure 11.1   *An illustration that processes of globalization are likely to favour the survival of large firms in developed economies at the expense of smaller firms in other economies when firms experience internal decreasing average costs as a result of a larger volume of sales*

same cost curves of supply). Even if the firm with the larger initial market is less efficient than the one with the smaller marker, the larger one can have a competitive advantage. For example, if firm two has an initial level of per-unit cost corresponding to point E rather than C (because it has some X-inefficiency or is on a higher per-unit cost curve than firm one), it is likely to be able to out-compete firm one because of its initial cost advantage. This is because firm one is likely to experience significant lags as it tries to increase its market share. Firm one is subject to large losses initially in competition with firm two and therefore is likely to be driven out of business by firm two.

Note that an evolutionary process is not effective in ensuring the survival of the most-efficient firms. Competitive market evolution does not involve an efficient sorting process. Survival of firms is to some extent path-dependent and there is a chance element in whether or not the surviving firms are the most efficient. Consequently, some features of this process are analogous to the nature of biological evolution as outlined by Gould (1989, 1990, 2003) and as reinforced by empirical evidence (Gould, 2003).

Assuming decreasing costs of supply, it can also be observed that in this competitive process, surviving firms tend to become larger and may increase their market power globally. Also as a result of scale economies in production and marketing, barriers to entry to the industry can be expected to increase. This is likely to result in a long-term reduction of competition in the industry. In particular, global advertising and promotion of products can become a major entry barrier.

The media industry appears to be one that experiences substantial economies of scope and scale. With growing globalization, there is a perception that the major US media companies have been increasing their market dominance of the media globally. They have had an initial advantage because of the large size of the US market compared to other markets, as illustrated by the case shown in Figure 11.1. This increasing market domination is seen by some as a threat to local cultures, regional perspectives and social diversity. Often the extension of markets can have social consequences, the costs and benefits of which are hard to quantify. These effects are not confined to international exchange in the media industry. There is little doubt that international trade in commodities as a whole alters lifestyles and social activities.

There is a widespread belief that growing globalization stimulates economic growth. This may come about to some extent due to a more efficient allocation of resources globally. In addition there is an expectation that it will contribute positively to technological progress, innovation and diffusion of new techniques and methods. How effective growing globalization will be in the long term in promoting technical and scientific change is unclear. Application of Schumpeter's theory of technological change and innovation (Schumpeter, 1942) raises the *possibility* that on a worldwide scale, technical progress could be retarded in the long term by the changes in market structures generated by globalization. Schumpeter's theory implies that the rate of technological progress in an industry is an inverted U-shaped function of the degree of economic concentration in the industry, other things held constant (Tisdell and Hartley, 2008, ch. 9; Parker, 1974). Furthermore, Schumpeter's theory (Schumpeter, 1942) implies that the rate of technological progress displayed by firms in an industry tends to decline *eventually* in relation to their size, other things kept constant. This relationship, therefore, may have an elongated reversed-U shape. Some evidence compatible with this hypothesis was found, for example, by Scherer (1965) and more recently by Alexander et al. (1995).

Thus, Schumpeter believed that under highly competitive market conditions technical progress is retarded. In effect, this is because there is a lack of protective niches for businesses (Tisdell and Seidl, 2004). Therefore, in those industries which become much more competitive as a result of growing globalization, the rate of technological progress and innovation would be predicted to decline. Schumpeter also argued that very large firms are likely to become bureaucratic and less conducive to technical progress. As discussed above, processes of globalization will allow some firms to become very large. This will also not be favourable to technical progress. Only those industries in which firms remain of moderate size and retain some market power as globalization proceeds would maintain a high rate of technical progress and innovation. On the whole, Schumpeter's theory casts doubts on the proposition that growing globalization will have positive long-term effects on the rate of technical progress and innovation.

Another thesis that pays particular attention to the importance of imperfect competition in international trade and investment is the monopoly-profit thesis (Posner, 1961). The monopoly-profit thesis of international trade asserts that the basis of much international trade is the sale of innovative or relatively innovative commodities in which the innovating businesses have a temporary global monopoly or near monopoly. This 'temporary' monopoly may be based on legal intellectual property rights (such as patents, copyrights and trademarks) or on secrecy or a combination of both. This temporary monopoly provides innovative firms with profitable opportunities to sell their innovative commodities abroad. However, their competitive advantage may only be temporary because other businesses are likely in due course to develop competing innovations. Thus, many businesses are involved in a competitive race involving expenditure on research and development, invention and innovation and this has significant implications for the nature of international trade and investment as well as for the dynamics of change in the variety of available commodities.

The monopoly-profit thesis can be linked to the theory of the international product cycle and with new technology theories of international trade and investment generally.

The theory of the international product cycle, as presented by Vernon (1966), holds that new products are usually developed and first produced in high-income countries and initially are mainly marketed in the home market of the country where the innovation occurs. Exports to other high-income countries then commence and grow as these markets expand, innovating companies establish production plants in these countries and consequently, become multinationals.

Eventually, production of the new commodity is likely to cease in higher-income countries and gravitate to less-developed countries. Higher-income countries may then import the product from producers in less-developed countries but this may, after a time, only be in small quantities because continuing innovation in higher-income countries may make the original product obsolete in these countries. While high profits may initially and for some time be made by an innovator, eventually the profit to be made from producing and marketing the original product falls as substitutes appear. Monopoly-like advantage of innovators lasts only for a limited period of time. These processes generate marked economic and geographical life cycles for new products.

The monopoly-profit thesis (as previously pointed out) emphasizes the significance of intellectual property and knowledge for international trade and investment. Firms that have superior intellectual property and know-how have a global monopoly or near monopoly in its use. Generally, it is firms based in more developed countries which have this superiority and this provides them with advantages in international trade. Growing globalization may enable them to exploit these advantages more quickly and more widely internationally than when international trade and investment is restricted. They are likely to be net gainers from globalization. At the same time, these globalization processes enable consumers to benefit by new products being made more widely and quickly available and by lower prices if economies of scale are important.

Comparatively, larger firms (compared to smaller ones) are likely to be the main beneficiaries from this globalization process because they are more likely to find it profitable to defend their intellectual property and know-how internationally, taking into account the cost of doing so in relation to their benefits. This further adds to the argument that economic globalization is likely to strengthen market domination by some larger companies. It may also become more difficult for new firms to challenge their market domination.

In addition, economic globalization appears to be altering the nature of the international product cycle as described by Vernon (1966) and may change its duration as found, for example, by Gao and Tisdell (2005). It appears to be causing the international location of production of commodities to become more fluid, and in many cases the supply of components used for producing final products has become geographically more dispersed.

The geographical location of production of new commodities now appears to shift more quickly from developed countries to less-developed ones. Production of some commodities developed in higher income countries occurs for shorter duration than previously or, unlike in Vernon's model, may even commence offshore in less-developed regions. This is probably due to fewer restrictions on international trade and foreign direct investment. If the developers of the new products have monopoly power through intellectual property rights or can protect their knowledge by other means, these new opportunities increase their profit. On the other hand, it reduces demand for labour in more-developed countries. It fosters the rapid international transfer of skills and can contribute to the economic development of less-developed countries. For example, economic globalization is assisting the economic development of China and India. Foreign investment and technology transfer is contributing to this process.

Economic globalization also facilitates the shedding of mature industries by developed nations. For example, in recent times, global steel production has been increasingly located in China and India.

A possible negative consequence from the point of view of developers of new technology in higher-income nations is that as a result of more rapid transfer of production of new commodities to developing economies, producers in developing countries obtain the skills and know-how to become effective competitors more quickly. This globalization process reduces the duration for which the developers of the original technology are able to earn monopoly profits, even though international transfer of production may enable them to earn higher profits initially. The possibility of this occurring increases when the government of a developing country has positive industrial policies to support this process, as Japan has and as China may have.

Many modern commodities involve the combination of multiple components which may be obtained from varied geographical locations. Economic globalization facilitates the supply of these components from an increased range of locations. This flexibility in sourcing supplies usually provides suppliers of final products with scope to reduce their costs of production, taking into account the relative costs of supply of components from different locations and their quality. In such cases, the international product cycle is more complex than is indicated by Vernon's theory.

When companies are involved in production involving use of their manufactured components, they may retain production of some components involving important advances in know-how in the country where their headquarters are. These may then be shipped abroad for use in assembling the final product of the company. This may be done to retain control of the technology or it may be that the components involved require the maintenance of a high standard of quality that is not assured in the country assembling the product and manufacturing other components for it. For example, China has a high level of import of manufactured components which are used in producing final products (Tisdell, 2007c). The above-mentioned factors may help to explain the high level of China's imports of manufactured components.

Even when firms are not directly involved in international production of commodities, they have to make decisions about whether to make, buy or contract out the supply of components of their production. Growing globalization can be expected to alter their decisions in relation to these aspects. It *may* result in fewer components being made in-house and some being purchased in the marketplace or their production contracted out of the company. These decisions, however, will be constrained by strategic considerations and the possible uncertainty associated with supplies from outside the firm. These aspects have been insufficiently explored.

3   Product variety and the benefit of economic globalization

A further issue is whether economic globalization reduces or increases product variety. Furthermore, how is product variety related to human satisfaction or welfare? These issues are not fully resolved. Possibly globalization increases product standardization and reduces product variety globally. This is because it reduces the number of suppliers of products due to more widespread competitive market pressures. At the same time, in many local areas (but not all) the range of products available may increase. Globally product variety may fall, but it may rise in some local areas. Chain stores, for example, may increase the variety of products available at the local level where they operate, but tend to sell a similar range of products at all their locations. On the other hand, the growing practice of franchising may reduce the variety of commodities available both globally and in many local areas. Apart from these cross-sectional effects, another little explored aspect is the likely effect of globalization on changes in product variety with the passage of time.

Broda and Weinstein (2004, 2006) argue that the principal economic benefit from growing economic globalization is that it enables buyers in every country to have available to them a greater variety of commodities than otherwise. The set of possible choices available to buyers (and in most cases actual choices) is expanded. Neoclassical economics predicts a substantial possible increase in the economic welfare of consumers as a result of the expansion in the variety of available commodities. However, measuring the size of these benefits in monetary terms is complex and difficult. The estimates depend on the underlying theories adopted and the simplifying assumptions made in order to make estimation tractable.

Broda and Weinstein (2004, 2006) base their estimates of these economic benefits on analysis of Krugman (1980) which is related to the framework developed by Spence (1976) and Dixit and Stiglitz (1977). They find that alternative economic models of product variety of Hotelling (1929) and Lancaster (1975) cannot be easily applied to their estimation. Nevertheless, these alternative models are not theoretically irrelevant. For example, Hotelling's model implies that the global variety of products may actually fall as a result of growing globalization. This could result in reduced choice of product variety in some locations. This is a possibility not raised in the modelling by Broda and Weinstein.

Let us consider Hotelling's model briefly and then discuss the analyses of Broda and Weinstein. The Hotelling (1929) model was originally developed to predict the possible geographic location of competing businesses and is a pioneering model in location theory (Ottaviano and Thisse, 2004, p. 2573). Subsequently it was used to predict the extent to which product differentiation (variety) might occur under competitive market conditions

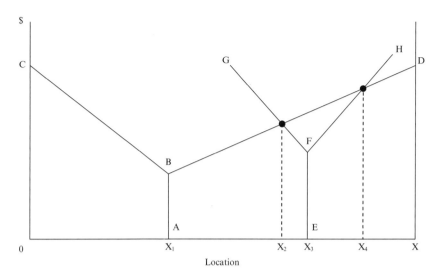

Figure 11.2 Diagram to illustrate the proposition that the forces making for globalization are likely to reduce the number of locations from which supplies are obtained. There can be less variation in sources of supply geographically as a result of globalization

and also applies to predicting the degree of differentiation in political platforms of competing political parties in democracies (Tisdell and Hartley, 2008, chs 9, 14).

The Hotelling model suggests that with growing globalization, the number of sources from which final commodities are supplied is liable to fall. This can be illustrated by Figure 11.2. There it is assumed that buyers of a product are equally located along a spectrum, X, and that suppliers of the product are initially located at two points on the spectrum; X_1 and X_3. The per-unit costs of production (inclusive of normal profit) at location X_1 is AB and at location X_3 it is EF. Production plus delivery costs per unit of the product from location X_1 and shown by the lines CB and BD and from location X_3 are GF and FH. If the product is priced at its production plus delivery cost and is relatively homogeneous, suppliers at location X_3 will supply all buyers between locations X_2 and X_4 and suppliers from location X_1 will supply the remainder of buyers. Suppose now that as a result of growing globalization, the cost of delivery falls but production cost at each location remains unaltered. As a result of this, the size of the market of supplies at location X_3 will tend to fall. In fact, it will disappear if line BD rotates sufficiently clockwise to intersect line EF. In that case, buyers located between X_2 and X_4 could have less choice of variety, if variety varies with its geographical source as assumed by Broda and Weinstein (2006, p. 548).

Nevertheless, while the Hotelling model in this static case allows the possibility that globalization will reduce product variety, it is inadequate to resolve the issue of whether on a global scale, and in the long run with technological change, globalization is likely to lower product variety, other things held equal. I have suggested above that it could do so globally but at the same time it might increase the variety of available products regionally as a result of greater ease of international trade. Broda and Weinstein (2004, 2006) have observed that between 1972 and 2001, the variety of imported goods available to American consumers increased greatly and has done likewise in many other countries. This time frame corresponds with a period of rapidly growing globalization. They estimated that American consumers would have been willing to pay the equivalent of about 2.6 per cent of GDP to have the increase in the variety of their imports available in 2001 compared to their variety in 1972 (Broda and Weinstein, 2006, p. 576). There is no doubt that greater variety of products is valued by consumers and that international trade can increase the variety of products available to them at the national level.

However, it cannot be deduced from the study by Broda and Weinstein (2004, 2006) whether globalization is increasing the variety of products available globally. It is possible for the variety available in individual countries to rise and for global variety to fall. A fall in global variety of products may, however, take some time to occur and global variety will not only be influenced by the occurrence of globalization. Furthermore, the demand for different types of imports is influenced by migration. An increased variety of sources of immigrants to a country is likely to result in a more diverse range of imports to this country from the countries of origin of immigrants.

While growing globalization increases the variety of products available in a country initially and possibly for some time, it could result in a reduction in the long term. Variety might, for example, peak after a time and then decline but not become as limited as when international trade was very restricted. Consumers might still be better off (despite the reversed-U-trend in the availability of varied products locally and eventually reduced global variety of products) than would be the case with restricted scope for international trade and investment because the latter involves even less variety locally. However, in the light of Schumpeter's theses and evolutionary considerations discussed, growing globalization may reduce the global rate of new product development and innovation. There is a strong possibility that this rate will decline in the long term. This is likely to be assessed as a negative impact.

It should be noted that Broda and Weinstein (2004, 2006) do not consider the changes in the stock of variety of commodities globally and assume that domestic variety is unaffected by an increase in the variety of imports (Broda and Weinstein, 2006, p. 580), however, it is possible that the variety of commodities produced in higher income countries, such as the USA, has declined with growing globalization because production of many commodities previously produced at home in the United States has moved offshore, for example to China. Therefore, the model of Broda and Weinstein may overstate the impact of globalization in increasing product variety in higher-income countries. Another limitation of the modelling of Broda and Weinstein is their assumption that the 'same' commodity when supplied from a different country be regarded as a different variety. For example, they regard Japanese wine as being a different product variety from French wine. However, some Australian, Californian, Chilean, Spanish and South African wines are close substitutes for some French wines. Because of data limitations and the cost of estimation using highly disaggregated models, their categorization of product varieties and products is relatively coarse. Nevertheless, they have made a useful start in providing the first estimates of the economic benefits of economic globalization arising from its impacts on the availability of a more varied basket of commodities.

Nevertheless, the cost–benefit analysis involved and the results obtained need to be assessed critically. These results depend crucially on the type of model adopted for the analysis and on the type of assumption employed to make the estimation tractable. Furthermore, the time period in which the empirical analysis is conducted should be kept in mind. For example, the effects of globalization on the growth in the available variety of commodities observed by Broda and Weinstein for the 1972–2001 period may not be sustained in future periods. In fact, they already observe a tapering off in the growth of available product varieties in the USA in the 1990s compared to the 1972–88 period and suggest that this might be because 'much of the gains from globalization arising from rise in importance of East Asian trade may have been realized prior to 1990' (Broda and Weinstein, 2006, p. 574).

4   Increased mobility of factors of production and changes in the location of development and globalization

Increasing globalization facilitates the geographical movement of factors of production and this enhanced mobility can result in substantial economic benefits. However, there appear to be few quantitative monetary estimates of these benefits. Economic benefits from increased factor mobility can include a rise in global output relative to the factors of production employed. As a result of greater mobility of factors of production, some regions may have their economic development and population increase whereas other areas may decline as economic globalization proceeds. Measurement of the benefits and costs will be heavily influenced by the type of model used to analyse the situation. Here two types of models are considered. The first is based on traditional neoclassical economics and assumes the absence of local or regional economies of agglomeration and the absence of local externalities and public goods associated with regional development. The second model takes account of economies and diseconomies of agglomeration of economic activity and local public good consequences of regional economic development along the lines highlighted by the new economic geography (see, for example, Head and Mayer, 2004). Measurements of economic benefits are more complicated in the latter case.

There is no doubt that forces involved in globalization have enhanced the international mobility of factors of production, particularly of capital. There are now fewer barriers to foreign direct investment and although international movements of labour continue to be restricted, considerable movements of labour internationally are occurring. Some of these movements of labour are illegal but many governments now woo immigrants with high levels of skill. Standard neoclassical theory implies that changes which reduce impediments to international movements of factors result in a net economic benefit, if the Kaldor–Hicks criterion is adopted. This can be illustrated by Figure 11.3. The Kaldor–Hicks criterion (also known as the potential Paretian improvement criterion) implies that there is a social economic gain from a reform if those who benefit from it could compensate any losers for their loss and be better off than before the change.

Consider a world consisting of two regions or nations, I and II, and one factor of production, X, labour or capital which can move internationally. For simplicity, suppose that only one product, Y, is produced and that the aggregate supply of the internationally mobile factor is perfectly inelastic. With restrictions on international movements of X, x_{11} if X is supplied in Region I and x_{22} if it is supplied in Region II. If ABC represents the marginal regional productivity of the mobile factor in Region I and if DEF shows its regional productivity in Region II, its marginal productivity is highest in Region I and is least in Region II. It is equal to y_3 in Region I and y_1 in Region II. This disparity would be reflected in differences in wage levels between the two regions if the factor of production is labour and in disparity or interest rates if the factor of production is capital.

Global free movement of the mobile factor of production will equalize its marginal productivity in all regions. This will raise global production when a constant aggregate amount of the factor X is employed. As

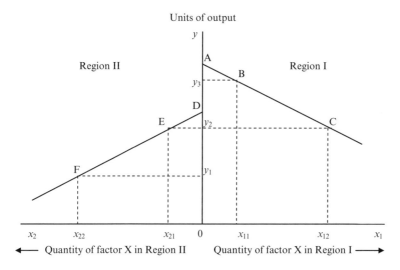

Figure 11.3   An illustration of the economic consequences of greater global mobility of factors of production based on neoclassical modelling

illustrated in Figure 11.3, the marginal productivity in each region of X equalizes at level y_2 and so does the payment for each unit of it, given competitive market conditions. If the mobile factor is labour, free movement reduces the wage rate in Region I and increases it in Region II. These regions may correspond, for example, to developed and less-developed countries, respectively. Note that the economic surplus from non-mobile factors of production rises in Region I and falls in Region II. Total production falls in the region that is naturally less productive and rises in that which is naturally more productive, and consequently differences in regional contributions to global production are magnified.

Given this neoclassical model, one could expect workers in higher-income regions to be opposed on economic grounds to immigration from lower-income regions because it reduces wages in higher-income countries. Because immigrants can generate social tensions and cultural conflict, this may also create national demands for limiting immigration. On the other hand, owners of immobile resources in higher-income countries would obtain economic benefit from such migration; for example, owners of agricultural land in the United States can increase their surplus by using low-cost labour from Mexico.

The above economic model, however, is likely to be of limited relevance for measuring the economic benefits from greater global mobility of factors of production when account is taken of secondary and tertiary industries. This is because it fails to take account of economies of agglomeration (Fujita and Thisse, 2000), substantial economies of scale and scope, and differences in sharing of economic benefits at different locations due to forms of 'open-access'. The latter benefits are quite varied and may include access to support from public welfare programmes, greater opportunities for employment choice of a wider range of jobs, improved economic prospects for offspring, and better environments, for example, in higher-income countries compared to less-developed regions. Furthermore, various types of favourable externalities may be obtained by being located in higher-income regions. Modelling these aspects in a simple way is a challenge. This is especially so when movements of different types of factors of production result in differences in external benefits.

For example, a more favourable social attitude seems to exist in higher-income countries to the immigration of skilled labour than unskilled labour. Is it because the former generates (or is believed to generate) greater positive economic externalities? Or is it because social integration of this group is believed to be easier? Or possibly there is a perception in higher-income countries that more-skilled immigrants are also likely to become less dependent on welfare benefits and therefore are not as costly to taxpayers in higher-income countries as unskilled immigrants. It is possible also that inward movement of skilled migrants and of capital to a region may accelerate technological progress and inventiveness in the region receiving these. This may provide widespread economic benefits to the region and provide momentum for its further economic growth. This economic growth may be supported by increasing returns from research and development and innovation, thereby encouraging more immigration of skilled workers and capital, including venture capital. Consequently, cumulative causation of the type suggested by Myrdal (1956) may be experienced and is also a possibility given Romer's economic growth model (Romer, 1986).

New economic geography theories of economic development stress the importance of economies of agglomeration of economic activity as contributors to regional and urban development (Neary, 2001). As outlined, for example, by Duranton and Puga (2004) and by Abdel-Rahman and Anas (2004), these economies can arise from sharing, matching and learning externalities experienced by economic agents in a locality. These theories, emphasize (unlike in the case of standard neoclassical theory) the importance of external economies of agglomeration and of other local externalities and public goods for regional development.

These theories raise the question of whether simple models based on average rather than marginal values (which are the basis of neoclassical economic theory) might throw more light on the nature of the phenomena involved in the distribution of global economic growth when increased global mobility of some factors of production occurs. If this is so, the resulting global resource allocation is unlikely to maximize global production in relation to the resources employed. Higher-income regions are likely to overdevelop in relation to lower-income regions given the theory of utilization of open-access resources (Gordon, 1954). Open-access resources are those which no-one is excluded from using. A similar proposition is that many cities are likely to exceed an optimal size because of coordination problems (Duranton and Puga, 2004, p. 2075). Nevertheless, global production is liable to be higher and incomes higher than if international mobility of factors of production is not allowed to occur or is severely restricted.

Furthermore, industrial development may not occur in ideal geographical locations due to path-dependence and myopia, as in the case of cities or central places (Tisdell, 1975). Nevertheless, even though this may be economically far from ideal, freedom of factor mobility can be expected to result in greater global production than by disallowing agglomeration.

While the above theory suggests that globalization favours the growth of higher-income countries, it does not rule out economic breakthroughs for some lower-income regions as they reform their economic systems to take advantage of their changing circumstances. Japan made such a transition and China is in the process of doing this. China and associated Asian countries have become a magnet for foreign investment, and the Asian region has strengthened as a world growth centre; a process facilitated by growing globalization. Eventually this region could become a more relatively permanent global centre of economic growth.

Some features of the new economic geography can be illustrated by a simple example. Suppose two regions, a high-income region and a low-income region, and that each contains a factor of production, P_1, which is homogeneous in inelastic supply and potentially mobile. P might be the working population in each region. Initially, however, P is restricted to its own region but subsequently with globalization it becomes perfectly mobile. Given that per capita income is initially lower in the lower-income region, P gravitates to the higher-income region as globalization proceeds. This flow will continue until per capita incomes are equalized in the regions, or a corner point solution emerges. In the latter case, all of factor P flows from the low-income region to the high-income region. What will be the benefits or costs for the higher-income region of these flows?

This can be illustrated by Figure 11.4. There curve ABCDF shows per capita income (or productivity) in the higher income region as a function of the mobile factor P. In this region, P is assumed to be initially P_1 and therefore income per capita corresponds to B. If after globalization the

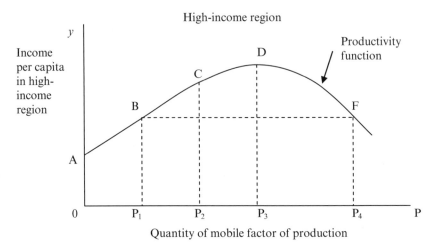

Figure 11.4   Possible economic impacts on a high-income region of inflows of a mobile factor of production from a low-income region

inflow of P to the high-income region is less than $P_4 - P_1$, all benefit. The per capita incomes of pre-existing residents of the high income region increase as well as that of immigrants, if we assume that the mobile factor is labour. On the other hand, if we assume that the interregional equilibrium is only established when migration to the high-income region exceeds $P_4 - P_1$, pre-existing residents of the high-income region suffer a reduction in their per capita income. Migrants, on the other hand, usually have higher incomes than in the absence of interregional labour mobility. Note that the maximum economic benefits for residents of the high income region would occur for inauguration of $P_3 - P_1$ persons from the low-income region.

Much cost–benefit analysis of such matters still remains to be done. Progress in this area, however, depends on estimating regional production functions which take account of agglomeration economies directly, such as has been done by Henderson (2003), or the adoption of indirect measures of their importance (Rosenthal and Strange, 2004, pp. 2128–32). The need to take account of spatial aspects of economic activity becomes more important as globalization proceeds.

5   Employment, income inequality and poverty in a globalizing world
Economic globalization has increased the extent to which the level of economic activity in many countries depends on external markets. As a result, national governments are less able than previously to regulate levels of

national employment and economic activity. Whether this rising external dependence results in greater variability of macroeconomic variables is unclear. Nevertheless, as economies become more open they may experience more frequent structural adjustment than when they are relatively closed and could experience greater job insecurity. To cope with such changes, greater adaptability of the workforce and greater mobility of labour is needed.

Views on the possible effects of globalization on inequality of income are varied. Some writers believe that differences in per capita income between nations will diverge as globalization occurs (for example, Singer, 1950; Frank, 1978) whereas others believe that convergence is more likely.

Personal income obtained from labour has become more unequal as increasing globalization has occurred in recent decades (Mishell et al., 2001; Ryscavage, 1999). Incomes of the skilled and more highly educated have increased relative to those with little skill. One explanation given for the growing inequality is that demand for skilled or more highly educated labourers has increased relative to that for unskilled due to technological change (Aghion and Williamson, 1998, pp. 42–3). Another contributing factor is that growing globalization has resulted in a higher proportion of commodities involving less-skilled labour being produced in countries that have an abundant amount of this labour. This has resulted in reduced demand for unskilled labour in higher-income countries and, as would be expected on the basis of the Samuelson–Stolper theorem, has moderated wage rises for this group (Wood, 1998). On the other hand, skilled labour is in short supply globally and the demand for it has increased strongly with global economic growth.

Economic growth and growing globalization have been associated in recent times with rising personal income inequality. The increasing divergence in incomes is mainly between the levels of income of the skilled persons and that of unskilled workers. This pattern is not consistent with that predicted by the Kuznets curve (Kuznets, 1963; Tisdell and Svizzero, 2004). Some of the economic costs associated with this growing income inequality are identified and discussed in Tisdell and Svizzero. This divergence in incomes seems to be occurring both in developed and less-developed countries. Given that skilled labour is relatively mobile internationally compared to unskilled labour, this pattern is not surprising. Furthermore, the supply of unskilled labour is still relatively elastic in many less-developed countries, but not that of skilled labour. In these circumstances, one would expect, on the basis of Lewis's theory (Lewis, 1954, 1979), that the real wages of unskilled labour in less-developed countries would remain relatively low until the level of surplus rural labour is absorbed in employment in manufacturing and tertiary industries.

While growing globalization appears to be contributing to growing inequality of personal income worldwide, it does not follow that it is a source of a growing incidence of poverty. In fact, in those developing countries that have experienced accelerated economic growth as a part of the opening up of their economies to the outside world, such as China, the incidence of poverty has fallen. China has simultaneously experienced growing income inequality and a significant fall in its incidence of poverty. However, not all countries are fortunate enough to be able to obtain significant economic growth as a result of globalization. Some are resource poor and have significant natural barriers to international trade. These include a number of small economies in the Pacific (for example, Kiribati and Tuvalu) and some land-locked countries such as, possibly, Mongolia. Natural barriers to international trade by such countries include high transport costs required to participate in such trade. Furthermore, diseconomies of scale due to their small home markets restrict their foreign trade possibilities. In some countries, social and political instability, lack of law and order, corruption, civil conflict, war and a system that is not supportive of commerce limits their ability to participate effectively in the process of economic globalization.

There is little evidence that growing economic globalization has led to the immiserization of developing countries as a whole. In fact, just the opposite has happened for several developing nations. For example, the increasing involvement of East Asian countries in economic globalization has contributed greatly to their economic growth and a reduction in their poverty rates. The result has been the opposite to that predicted by the Marxist-like theory of Frank (1978). Nevertheless, many less-developed countries have failed to exhibit economic growth and their poverty rates have risen, as is evident in Africa and to some extent in the Pacific islands. It is doubtful whether their economic misfortune can be mainly attributed to growing globalization. Yet, in many cases, political corruption has reduced their national gains from their limited participation in global trading. For example, in some cases bribes paid to local politicians and officials have reduced the royalties such nations have obtained from their exports of natural resources, such as minerals and timber.

Even countries that have reduced their incidence of poverty in step with their increased involvement in economic globalization have not always been able to reduce the incidence of poverty in all their sectors and regions. For example, the incidence of rural poverty has risen in some. This is because adjustments to changing market conditions take time and some labourers seem less mobile and less able to adjust to market change than others.

It is true that the gap between the level of per capita income in the very poorest nations and that of the richest nations has widened as economic globalization has gathered momentum in recent years. The very poorest nations have not experienced economic growth or have had very weak growth or economic decline in this period. These trends cannot be adequately explained by their involvement in the process of globalization because their involvement is limited. On the other hand, economic globalization has helped to maintain the economic growth of higher-income countries, even though at a slower rate than several of the East Asian emerging economies. Thus the widening gap between the poorest and richest nations is associated with growing globalization but not for the reason hypothesized by some Marxist writers.

Growing globalization experienced in recent decades has been associated with a decline in the global occurrence of poverty but has not been able to reduce the incidence of poverty in all developing countries and in all geographical locations (Salvatore, 2007, pp. 404–5 and references given there).

Several global indicators of trends in the incidence of poverty are available as well as its correlates, such as the number or proportion of underweight children in a population, child mortality, the proportion of children obtaining elementary education and expected length of life. For the world as a whole, these indicators have shown desirable trends as globalization has proceeded. This does not, however, mean that increasing globalization is the causal factor. Nevertheless, where economic growth has accompanied economic reforms and the opening up of economies to the outside world, as in the case of China, a significant reduction in the incidence of poverty has also occurred.

It is probably overly ambitious to attempt a cost–benefit analysis of the impact of economic globalization on reducing poverty. Nevertheless, cost–benefit analysis can be applied to many aspects of poverty-reduction policies. For example, the cost-effectiveness or productivity of public expenditure to reduce the incidence of poverty can be assessed. For example, if there is a public goal to maximize the number of persons or families escaping from poverty in relation to the public expenditure undertaken for poverty reduction, the effectiveness of public expenditure can be assessed. In some developing countries, this goal may not be achieved because some funds intended to assist the poor are obtained by the non-poor, or public administration costs incurred in distributing the funds may be higher than is necessary. While progress has been made in quantifying many of the effects of poverty alleviation programmes (see, for example, studies in Tisdell, 2007a, including Weerahewa and Prasada, 2007), actual cost–benefit analysis of these policies are very limited. There is considerable scope for applying cost–benefit analysis in this area.

Similarly, while the UN's Millennium Development Goals are of global importance, particularly those concerned with development and poverty eradication, they appear not to involve much emphasis on cost–benefit analysis (Tisdell, 2007b). These goals include halving the population with an income of less than $1 a day in 2015 compared to the situation in 1995 and reducing under-five child mortality by two-thirds between 1990 and 2015. These are definite targets. Once again, cost–benefit analysis does not appear to be emphasized. Nevertheless, given that resources for poverty alleviation are limited, a role does exist for cost–benefit analysis in designing policies for poverty alleviation.

6   Economic vulnerability, globalization and cost–benefit analysis

Economic globalization (according, for example, to the theory of comparative advantage) fosters international specialization in production. In countries possessing few resources with little variation in these, a high degree of specialization can occur with growing globalization. This lack of product diversification can make their economies very vulnerable to external changes in demand. Many developing countries are dependent on a narrow range of export commodities for their foreign exchange earnings and increasing globalization can narrow the range of commodities produced by them.

Thus, in undertaking a cost–benefit analysis of the extra trade opportunities opened up by growing globalization, account should also be taken of the extra risks of greater economic specialization. Usually, there is positive aversion to increased risk-bearing, other things remaining equal. This problem can be illustrated by Figure 11.5. Initially, a developing country is assumed to have a collection of expected income and riskiness of income possibilities as shown by the set bounded by AEDF. As a result of growing globalization, suppose that this set expands to that contained within the circular body bounded by ACDF. Given that the lines marked I_1, I_2 and I_3 represent the community's indifference curves for expected income and riskiness of income combinations (these are shown as straight lines but in practice probably increase at an increasing rate), A is initially optimal but subsequently B is optimal. Note that C gives a higher level of expected income but is not optimal because of the extra risk it entails.

Measuring risk can be quite challenging. In some cases, risks may be so uncertain that they cannot be quantified in terms of specific probability. Nevertheless, uncertainty still needs to be taken into account in cost–benefit assessment. Various criteria for decision making under uncertainty can be applied in such cases. Note also that the riskiness of increased specialization in production depends on the extent of 'lock-in' to this specialization. If it is relatively easy and low cost to switch specializations, then considerable economic flexibility exists and specialization in production poses only a minor risk. However, if this is not so, the economic risks from specialization in production can be substantial. Standard neoclassical theory assumes flexibility

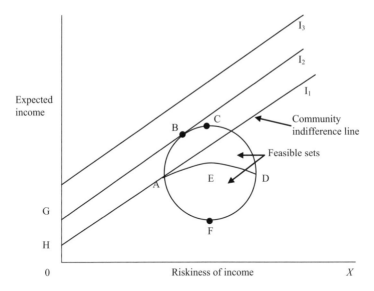

Figure 11.5 Risk and uncertainty need to be allowed for in the application of cost–benefit analysis. This creates challenges for the analysis

in resource use but New Institutional Economics (for example, of the type introduced by Williamson, 1985) does not. The background theory which an economic analyst decides is relevant influences the nature of the cost–benefit analysis undertaken and usually the results obtained. Choice of appropriate economic theories is crucial for meaningful cost–benefit analysis.

Another vulnerability concern is that increasing globalization can result in the production of commodities required for effective defence moving offshore. This reduces the self-reliance of the country experiencing this in defending itself against aggressors. It may wish to forgo some economic efficiency in such cases to secure greater security for its defence. For example, in December 2007, President George W. Bush announced that the USA would escalate its production of biofuels in order to make it less dependent on imported oil for its energy needs.

Again, it is possible that greater global competition could reduce profit margins in low levels in some decreasing cost industries, such as air travel. In such cases, the industries are economically highly vulnerable to a shock that may suddenly cause the demand for their services to drop drastically (Tisdell, 2006). This has been demonstrated, for example, by the economic impacts of terrorist attacks, such as the September 11 attacks in the USA. Furthermore, international competition and efficiency considerations may dictate the adoption of highly interdependent networks in countries such as web networks. Widespread economic disruption can occur if such networks are sabotaged. In some cases, this sabotage could make national defence more difficult. In both cases, increasing economic concentration due to economies of scale brings increased economic benefits but at the cost of greater vulnerability. Cost estimates of the measures taken to reduce this vulnerability (such as in the airline industry) could be compared with the economic benefits of industry concentration. Cost–benefit analyses would also be possible of the anti-terrorism measures adopted by governments.

To the extent that globalization results in best practices being more widely adopted in industry because of competitive pressures, it tends to make for homogeneity of productive units. This homogeneity may impede economic adjustment to changing economic conditions, and slow technical progress if diversity is favourable to such progress (ibid.). Consider the adjustment issue. Increased homogeneity tends to reduce the slope of the industry supply curve. In the simple cobweb model case, this change shows the adjustment of the market to its equilibrium after the market suffers a shock. The adjustment mechanism is therefore less beneficial than previously. However, in equilibrium and assuming static analysis there still is a net economic benefit from more widespread adoption of best practice in the industry.

This is illustrated in Figure 11.6. There, AS_1 is initially the industry supply curve but as a result of greater international competition less efficient firms in the industry become more efficient and the supply curve becomes ABS_2. Given the demand curve DD, there is an increase in economic surpluses equivalent to the area of triangle BCE. However, this benefit is offset to some extent by slower convergence to industry equilibrium if a shock occurs and if the simple cobweb model applies. Therefore, the relevant cost–benefit analysis should also be extended to take account of market adjustment mechanisms. This is in line with the view of many members of the Austrian School of Economics (for example, Hayek, 1948) that market adjustment mechanisms should be taken into account in economic assessments. There is considerable scope to expand the application of cost–benefit analysis in this area.

7   Environmental issues, particularly global warming, and cost–benefit analysis

Increasing globalization has stimulated global economic growth and has helped to bring about large increases in the level of global economic production over a long period. As a result, several transboundary and global issues have become important. For example, globalization and market extension have played a major role in the reduction of the world's genetic assets or stocks. Furthermore, the extent and the type of economic growth

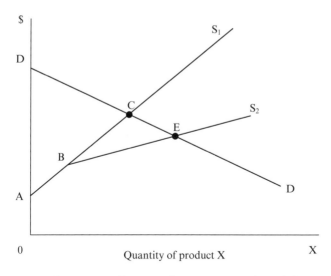

Figure 11.6 *A diagram to illustrate the proposition that while economic globalization may result in increased economic benefits in equilibrium conditions, it may add to the economic costs associated with market adjustment. Globalization may also show technical progress by reducing economic diversity*

which has occurred has, since the Industrial Revolution, been a major factor in global warming, according to most scientists.

Economic mechanisms that lead to a loss of genetic diversity of live-stock breeds as market extensions and globalization proceed are outlined in Tisdell (2003). The general arguments also apply to the genetic stock of crops and other cultivars used in agriculture. In addition, global economic growth has resulted in growing loss of genetic diversity in the wild. Several mechanisms are involved. For example, agricultural expansion and inten-sification and urban expansion eliminate the habitats of some wild species. For instance, the expansion of oil palm production in Borneo results in loss of forest habitat required for the survival of many tropical species, such as the orangutan. This conversion of forested land to agriculture is being driven by rising world demand for palm oil. Similarly, deforestation in the Amazon is occurring to make way for soya bean and cattle produc-tion, and is partly driven by world demand for these products. Not only is this reducing the stock of biodiversity in the wild but it is also adding to the amount of greenhouse gases in the atmosphere. As a result of forest loss, less carbon is sequestrated in trees.

Some cost–benefit studies have been completed of the economics of conserving biodiversity but much further work remains to be done. For example, Pearce and Moran (1994, Ch. 6) have studied the economics of conserving tropical forests taking into account the diversity of their plants and their potential for producing new pharmaceuticals. When this is taken into account as well as the other benefits for conserving these forests, such as their role in sequestrating carbon dioxide, Pearce and Moran arrive at a large net benefit per hectare for their conservation. The total economic value (both use and non-use values) from conserving such forests is shown to be high. The concept of total economic value was popularized by Pearce et al. (1989) and aims to provide estimates of tangible and intangible economic benefits from conservation (see Pearce and Moran, 1994; Tisdell, 2005a, pp. 110–13). Many of those benefits are not marketed.

Economic growth of the type experienced since the Industrial Revolution has been implicated as a major contributor to global warming. This economic growth has been based to a large extent on the utilization of fossil fuels and has been a major contributor to the build-up of greenhouse gases in the atmosphere and consequently to global warming. If economic production and consumption continue to involve the current levels of use of fossil fuels (or current trends continue), major adverse social and economic consequences are expected globally before the end of the century due to global warming.

Growing globalization by stimulating economic growth in production and consumption based on growing use of fossil fuels has accelerated the global warming problem. China and India, for example, have increased their emissions of greenhouse gases as a result of their rapid economic growth which has been facilitated by growing globalization. The hope that an environmental Kuznets relationship would solve the global warming problem has proven to be a false hope (Tisdell, 2001). That, however, is not to suggest that a return to inward-looking economies is an effective way to deal with the problem. This would merely increase the economic burden of reducing greenhouse gas emissions compared to alternative strategies such as ensuring that such emissions are efficiently reduced globally. This could in principle be achieved by ensuring that the environmental price for the emissions reflects social externality costs and is the same anywhere. This is on the basis that the emissions have common-pool consequences.

At the present time (2008), no global system of positive uniform pricing exists for greenhouse gas emissions (for example, for CO_2 emissions) although the European Union has been developing such a system for its member states. This means that while in the EU pricing has developed for greenhouse gas emissions, in many countries no such system operates and the global environmental externalities involved are unpriced. This is the case, for example, in China and India. As a consequence, industries that have a high intensity of greenhouse gas emissions tend to relocate from regions that charge for or regulate these emissions 'strictly' to regions that do not. This can be expected to stimulate foreign investment in the establishment of globally polluting industries in regions that have little or no control on their emissions, which will result in the increased production in such regions of products adding to global pollution and their increased export to countries having stricter pollution controls.

Most developing countries are reluctant to impose stricter controls on emissions of global pollutants because this is likely to slow their rate of economic growth. They also point out that their per capita level of greenhouse gas emissions are much lower than in higher-income countries. Their opposition to global pollution controls appears to be mainly based on the grounds that incomes in their countries are lower than in more-developed countries, and therefore, they should be less constrained in their growth options. Significant international political barriers exist to having uniformity or near uniformity in charges for greenhouse gas emissions in all regions. Those barriers are unlikely to be overcome soon. In these circumstances, greater economic globalization is making it more difficult to address environmental issues arising from market failures.

Apart from this, there is still (2008) continuing disagreement between nations about whether reductions in greenhouse gas emissions by nations should be mandatory, about how much individual nations should have to reduce greenhouse gas emissions and whether some (such as less-developed nations) should be required to reduce their greenhouse gas emissions at all. This disagreement is primarily about how the burden of reducing greenhouse gas emissions should be shared internationally. This conflict persists despite the finding by Nicholas Stern (H.M. Treasury, 2006, p. ii) from his in-depth cost–benefit analysis of the economics of reducing greenhouse gas emissions that 'the benefits of strong early action [to limit greenhouse gas emissions] considerably outweigh the costs'. Unfortunately, while the Stern Report indicates the collective economic wisdom of reducing greenhouse emissions, like much cost–benefit analysis it provides only a partial means for resolving social conflict.

It is impossible here to provide a detailed account of the cost–benefit analysis undertaken by Stern. He provides a range of results based on a variety of hypotheses. However, his central argument is that a realistic global target is to stabilize the atmospheric concentration of CO_2 at 550ppm by 2050 and that this will require reduction pathways to be established to lower current global greenhouse gas emissions by around 25 per cent by 2050. He estimates that about a 1 per cent reduction in GDP will be required by 2050 to achieve this result. This policy initiative will, however, avert even larger future decreases in GDP that will occur if nothing is done to reduce greenhouse gas emissions now. The net averted loss of GDP after 2050 may be of the order 4–19 per cent, that is 5–20 per cent less the 1 per cent cost of the aversion. Stern, however, recognizes that there is uncertainty in these estimates and provides a range of possible costs and benefits. He admits that his analysis involves difficult ethical and measurement issues and that 'the results have to be treated with circumspection' (ibid., p. ix). Nevertheless, his work represents a major positive contribution to the rational economic evaluation of climate change policies.

The following are some of the issues which Stern had to consider in completing his cost–benefit analysis:

1.   Estimates by national scientists of the biophysical consequences and relationships involved in climate change are imprecise. Therefore, uncertainty has to be allowed for in the cost–benefit analysis.
2.   The economic and biophysical consequences of global warming are expected to be geographically distributed in an uneven manner. For example, developing countries are likely to suffer more heavily than higher-income countries. This raises the question of how the distributional consequences of the impacts should be allowed for in the cost–benefit analysis. Stern considers the possibility of weighting the losses of low-income countries more heavily than those of higher-income countries. There may, however, be disagreement about the appropriate weights.
3.   The costs and benefits of global climate change involve a very lengthy time scale. This highlights the question of the extent to which future costs and benefits should be discounted. This matter requires consideration of philosophcal issues about the intergenerational fairness of the distribution of income and the availability of economic opportunities. One extreme possibility is not to discount at all.
4.   Gross domestic product is only a partial indicator of economic welfare. For example, it does not register the value of non-marketed commodities many of which may be lost as a result of global warming. Stern (ibid., p. x) suggests that these non-market losses would be equivalent to an extra loss in per capita consumption of about 6 per cent in this century if no action is taken to slow climate change. The accuracy of this figure is unclear but it recognizes the reality that the availability of marketed goods only partially measures economic welfare.

8   Concluding observations
According to several different measures, economic globalization has proceeded at a rapid pace in the last four decades or so. However, assessing its costs and benefits by devising a single monetary measure does not seem to be realistic. This is partly because the impacts of globalization are multidimensional, there are distributional consequences and its long-term

consequences can differ considerably from those in the medium to short term. Furthermore, there is considerable uncertainty about some of the consequences such as the long-term global environmental consequences of the type of economic growth that it has stimulated. In addition, it has stimulated the rapid economic growth of some regions (such as East Asia) which in turn is likely to alter the international balance of political power in the long run.

Economic globalization has stimulated global economic growth via changes in the international location of industries and by increasing freedom of capital movements, including foreign direct investment. However, this does not mean that it will lead to optimal location of production internationally. Nor does it mean that all industries will become more competitive nor that the potentially most efficient firms are the most likely survivors. Path-dependence is a problem in this latter case. The global market structures that emerge may not be conducive to high rates of technological progress given Schumpeter's hypotheses. Increasing inequality of personal income has been associated with growing globalization in recent decades. To a large extent, this may be due to the nature of technological progress in modern times. However, economic globalization has most likely reinforced this divergence. Also differences in per capita income (between the poorest and the richest) of nations have increased. There are many possible reasons for this. However, some nations are so poorly placed as to be unable to participate in the process of economic globalization to any significant extent. As globalization has proceeded, the incidence of global poverty has declined, especially in countries (such as China) that have experienced considerable economic growth. Nevertheless, the incidence of poverty has risen in some countries or hardly changed at all. In some cases, this is because they have little scope for international exchange. Less security of employment also appears to be a feature of growing globalization.

In addition, even in cases where growing globalization raises economic efficiency, this can be at the expense of heightened vulnerability to shocks of various kinds, such as those from terrorism and war. Furthermore, economic adjustment mechanisms can become less effective. Adjustment to shocks may be prolonged, and this also involves a cost.

Increased economic globalization and associated economic growth have brought global environmental issues to the fore. These developments, such as increased global warming, pose new global political challenges. It is likely to be difficult politically to arrive at a solution which corrects these market failures in an efficient way. It would be desirable for this problem to be resolved by strategies other than by restricting international exchange and investment. Nevertheless, an option of countries that restrict their greenhouse gas emissions would be to place international trade and investment restrictions on those nations that do not.

There appears to be a widespread belief among economists that to date growing globalization has yielded a net economic benefit. It has helped reduce the incidence of poverty globally, has contributed to a rise in incomes globally, and increased the variety of commodities available at regional levels. On the other hand, it has been associated with growing income inequality, has contributed to global environmental problems, has increased job insecurity and it is by no means clear that it will have a positive influence on technological progress in the long term.

Cost–benefit analysis of the consequences of economic globalization can be undertaken in two different ways. Quantitative conclusions can be reached by exploring the implications of economic theory for economic benefits and costs when market extension occurs. A problem with this approach is that opinions can differ about the relevant theory to apply and the cost–benefit implications of different theories are not always the same, as has been shown in this exposition. Judgement is, therefore, required to select the most relevant theory. A further problem from a policy perspective is that policy makers may not find qualitative results adequate for making a policy choice. The second approach (and one which in principle is highly desirable) is to quantify the costs and benefits involved in changes related to globalization. As shown here, Broda and Weinstein (2004, 2006) do this in relation to the growth in the available variety of commodities associated with growing globalization and Nicholas Stern (H.M. Treasury, 2006) does this in relation to policies designed to reduce the rate of global warming; a process that has been accelerated by growing globalization. Nevertheless, quantitative findings have to be interpreted cautiously because their adequacy depends on the underlying adequacy of the theory that underpins them and the assumptions employed to make the data analysis tractable.

Note

1. I wish to thank Robert Brent for his constructive comments on an earlier draft of this chapter. The usual caveat applies.

References

Abdel-Rahman, H. and Anas, H. (2004), 'Theories of systems of cities', in J.V. Henderson and J.-F. Thisse (eds), *Handbook of Regional and Urban Economics*, Vol. 4, Elsevier, Amsterdam, pp. 2293–339.

Aghion, P. and Williamson, J.G. (1998), *Growth, Inequality and Globalization*, Cambridge University Press, Cambridge.

Alexander, D.I., Hynn, J. and Linkins, I. (1995), 'Innovation and global market share in the pharmaceutical industry', *Review of Industrial Organization*, **10**, 197–207.

Broda, C. and Weinstein, D.E. (2004), 'Variety growth and world welfare', *American Economic Review*, AEA Papers and Proceedings, **94** (2), 139–44.

Broda, C. and Weinstein, D.E. (2006), 'Globalization and the gains from variety', *Quarterly Journal of Economics*, **121**, 541–85.

Dixit, A. and Stiglitz, J. (1977), 'Monopolistic competition and optimum product diversity', *American Economic Review*, 67, 297–308.

Duranton, G. and Puga, D. (2004), 'Micro-foundation of urban agglomeration economics', in J.V. Henderson and J.-F. Thisse (eds), *Handbook of Regional and Urban Economics*, Vol. 4. Elsevier, Amsterdam, pp. 2063–117.

Frank, A.G. (1978), *Dependent Accumulation and Underdevelopment*, Macmillan, London.

Fujita, M. and Thisse, J.-F. (2000), 'The formation of economic agglomerations: old problems and new perspectives', in J.-M. Huriot and J.-F. Thisse (eds), *Economics of Cities: Theoretical Perspectives*, Cambridge University Press, Cambridge, pp. 3–73.

Gao, L. and Tisdell, C. (2005), 'Foreign investment and Asia's, particularly China's, rise in the television industry. The international product life cycle reconsidered', *Journal of Asia-Pacific Business*, 6 (3), 37–61.

Gordon, H.S. (1954), 'The economic theory of common property resource: the fishery', *Journal of Political Economy*, 17, 69–77.

Gould, S.J. (1989), *Wonderful Life: The Burgess Shale and the Nature of History*, Norton, New York.

Gould, S.J. (1990), *The Individual in Darwin's World*, Edinburgh University Press, Edinburgh.

Gould, S.J. (2003), *I Have Landed. The End of a Beginning in Natural History*, Three Rivers Press, New York.

H.M. Treasury (2006), 'Stern Review on the Economics of Climate Change', www.hm-treasury.gov.uk/independent_reviews/stern_review_economics_climate_change/stern_review_report.cfm, accessed 8 December 2006.

Hayek, F.A. (1948), *Individualism and the Economic Order*, Chicago University Press, Chicago, IL.

Head, K. and Mayer, T. (2004), 'The empirics of agglomeration and trade', in J.V. Henderson and J.-F. Thisse (eds), *Handbook of Regional and Urban Economics*, Vol. 4, Elsevier, Amsterdam, pp. 2609–69.

Henderson, J.V. (2003), 'Marshall's scale economies', *Journal of Urban Economics*, 53, 1–28.

Hotelling, H. (1929), 'Stability in competition', *Economic Journal*, 39, 41–57.

Krugman, P. (1980), 'Scale economies produce differentiation and the pattern of trade', *American Economic Review*, 70, 950–59.

Kuznets, S. (1963), 'Quantitative aspects of economic growth of nations: distribution of income by size', *Economic Development and Cultural Change*, 11 (2), 1–80.

Lancaster, K. (1975), 'Socially optimal product differentiation', *American Economic Review*, 65, 567–85.

Lewis, W.A. (1954), 'Economic development with unlimited supplies of labour', *Manchester School of Economics and Social Studies*, 22, 139–91.

Lewis, W.A. (1979), 'The dual economy revisited', *Manchester School of Economics and Social Studies*, 47, 231–29.

Mishell, L., Bernstein, J. and Schmitt, J. (2001), *The State of Working America 2000–2001*, Cornell University, Ithaca, NY.

Myrdal, G. (1956), *On International Economy: Problems and Prospects*, Routledge & Kegan Paul, London.

Neary, J.P. (2001), 'Of hype and hyperboles: introducing the new economic geography', *Journal of Economic Literature*, 39, 536–64.

Ottaviano, G. and Thisse, J.-F. (2004), 'Agglomeration and economic geography', in J.V. Handerson and J.-F. Thisse (eds), *Handbook of Regional and Urban Economics*, Vol. 4, Elsevier, Amsterdam, pp. 2563–608.

Parker, J.E.S. (1974), *The Economics of Innovation*, Longmans, London.

Pearce, D., Markandya, A. and Barbier, E.B. (1989), *Blueprint for a Green Economy*, Earthscan, London.

Pearce, D. and Moran, D. (1994), *The Economic Value of Biodiversity*, Earthscan, London.

Posner, M.V. (1961), 'International trade and technical change', *Oxford Economic Papers*, 13, 232–341.

Romer, P.M. (1986), 'Increasing returns and long-run growth', *Journal of Political Economy*, **94**, 1002–37.
Rosenthal, S.S. and Strange, W.C. (2004), 'Evidence on the nature and sources of agglomeration economies', in J.V. Henderson and J-F. Thisse (eds), *Handbook of Regional and Urban Economies*, Vol. 4, Elsevier, Amsterdam, pp. 2119–71.
Ryscavage, P. (1999), *Income Inequality in America: An Analysis of Trends*, M.E. Sharpe, New York.
Salvatore, D. (2007), *International Economics*, John Wiley, Hoboken, NJ.
Schumpeter, J.A. (1942), *Capitalism, Socialism and Democracy*, 2nd edn, Harper, New York.
Scherer, F. (1965), 'Firm size market structure opportunity and the output of patented inventions', *American Economic Review*, **55**, 1110–20.
Singer, H.W. (1950), 'The distribution of gains from trade between investing and borrowing countries', *American Economic Review*, **40**, 473–85.
Spence, M. (1976), 'Product differentiation and welfare', *American Economic Review*, **47**, 407–14.
Tisdell, C.A. (1975), 'The theory of optimal city-sizes. Some elementary considerations', *Urban Studies*, **12**, 61–70.
Tisdell, C.A. (2001), 'Globalisation and sustainability: environmental Kuznets curve in the WTO', *Ecological Economics*, **39**, 185–96.
Tisdell, C.A. (2003), 'Socioeconomic causes of loss of genetic diversity: analysis and assessment', *Ecological Economics*, **45**, 365–76.
Tisdell, C.A. (2005a), *Economics of Environmental Conservation*, 2nd edn, Edward Elgar, Cheltenham, UK and Northampton, MA, USA.
Tisdell, C.A. (2005b), 'An overview of globalisation and world economic policy responses', in Tisdell (ed.), *Globalisation and World Economic Policies*, Serials Publications, New Delhi, pp. 3–16.
Tisdell, C.A. (2006), 'Can globalisation result in less efficient and more vulnerable industries?', in J.-M. Aurifeille, S. Svizzero and C. Tisdell (eds), *Leading Economic and Marginal Issues Involving Globalisation*, Nova Science, New York, pp. 168–81.
Tisdell, C.A. (2007a), *Poverty, Poverty Alleviation and Social Disadvantage*, Serials Publications, New Delhi.
Tisdell, C.A. (2007b), 'An assessment of the UN's Millennium Development Goals and its Millennium Declaration', in Tisdell (ed.) (2007a), pp. 74–87.
Tisdell, C.A. (2007c), 'Economic and business relations between China and Australia: insights into China's global economic footprint', in P.K. Basu, G. O'Neill and A. Travaglione (eds), *Engagement and Change: Exploring Management, Economic and Finance Implications of a Globalising Environment*, Australian Academic Press, Bowen Hills, Australia, pp. 11–24.
Tisdell, C.A. and Hartley, K. (2008), *Microeconomic Policy: A New Perspective*, Edward Elgar, Cheltenham, UK and Northampton, MA, USA.
Tisdell, C.A. and Seidl, I. (2004), 'Niches and economic competition: implications for economic efficiency, growth and diversity', *Structural Change and Economic Dynamics*, **15**, 119–35.
Tisdell, C.A. and Sen. R.K. (2004), 'An overview of economic globalisation: its momentum and its consequences examined', in Tisdell and Sen (eds), *Economic Globalisation, Labour and Environmental Issues*, Edward Elgar, Cheltenham, UK and Northampton, MA, USA, pp. 3–25.
Tisdell, C.A. and Svizzero, S. (2004), 'Globalization, social welfare, public policies and labor inequalities', *Singapore Economic Review*, **49**, 233–53.
Vernon, R. (1966), 'International investment and trade in the product cycle', *Quarterly Journal of Economics*, **80**, 190–207.
Weerahewa, J. and Prasada, P. (2007), 'Presence of spatial bias in the causality of child malnutrition in Sri Lanka', in Tisdell (ed.) (2007a), pp. 672–87.
Williamson, O.E. (1985), *The Economic Institutions of Capitalism*, Free Press, New York.
Wood, A. (1998), 'Globalization and the rise in labour market inequalities', *Economic Journal*, **108**, 1463–82.

12 Poverty alleviation programs and their impacts: a survey
*Jyotsna Jalan**

1 Introduction

Since the early 1980s, the Chinese economy has grown at a rapid pace with an average growth rate of well over 7–8 percent per annum. But a significant proportion of the population remains poor, vulnerable, and excluded from the growth process.[1] Similarly, the Indian economy has witnessed phenomenal growth rates since the early 1990s yet nearly a quarter of the population live below the poverty line. Other examples include Mexico where the headcount ratio was higher in 1996 compared to the 1980s despite an impressive growth rate of 9.7 percent.

Examples like those mentioned above abound. It is obvious that rapid economic growth is a necessary but not a sufficient condition to alleviate poverty at least in the short to medium term. Cost-effective social safety-net interventions by governments and/or civil society are essential to sustain the high economic growth rates, to make such growth socially inclusive and to reduce poverty simultaneously. There is an emerging consensus among policy makers that even in economies with high growth rates, government intervention is necessary to protect the poor and the vulnerable (at least in the short and medium term).

How does one assess whether the growth process and/or the social safety nets actually reach the poor and the vulnerable? Often disentangling the growth effects from program intervention impacts is challenging since one needs to determine the extent of improvements over and above that which would have happened during the course of economic growth. In evaluating a government intervention we need to assess outcomes from a specific program relative to one or more explicit counterfactuals. That is, we have to determine the net impact of the program that estimates the incremental program effects and hence provides a basis for judging the public returns on such investments.

In our survey, we analyze four programs commonly observed in developing economies that directly alleviate poverty – public works, conditional cash transfers, access to credit and poor area development programs. We comment on the characteristics of each of these programs and how each can be evaluated given their objectives. For each of the schemes we also provide a critical review of some existing case studies from different developing countries. Other policy interventions such as labor-retraining programs, school mid-day meal programs and school voucher systems also have impacts on aggregate poverty in the long term. However, we restrict our attention to poverty programs that directly benefit the poor. We also do not survey tools used in incidence analysis or examine studies that analyze the macro impacts of public policy. For an excellent survey on both these topics, see Bourguignon et al. (2002).

The chapter is organized as follows. In Section 2, we discuss the technical aspects of poverty measures and impact evaluations. However, the discussion is very brief, and interested readers should see Foster et al. (1984), Ravallion (1995), Lipton and Ravallion (1994), and Jalan and Ravallion (1998b) for further information. Also see Ravallion (2008) for details on impact evaluation techniques as used in evaluating poverty alleviation programs. Sections 3, 4, 5 and 6 examine public works, conditional cash transfers, access to credit schemes and poor area development programs, respectively. In Section 7, using case studies from different developing countries, we assess whether the projects are cost-efficient and socially useful. In the final section (Section 8), we make some general conclusions based on our survey.

2   Details on poverty measures and impact evaluation techniques: a brief survey

Poverty measurement
Poverty measures provide information on living standards, on their evolution over time, and on their distribution over households. There are different poverty measures, static and dynamic, as well as relative comparisons within the population.

Static measures include the headcount ratio or the proportion of poor in the population, and poverty indices measuring the depth and severity of poverty. The headcount ratio distinguishes the poor from the non-poor by counting the number of persons whose welfare levels are below a stipulated threshold level (poverty line). It does not identify the most vulnerable from the less vulnerable among the poor nor does it inform us about how far below the poverty line the household is located.

The poverty gap estimates the distance of a poor household's welfare levels from the poverty line. It can also be interpreted as the amount of money required by households below the poverty line to reach the poverty line.

To capture the distributional effects among the poor, measures such as the squared poverty gap or Sen's measure of poverty are used. These measures are such that they penalize losses to the poor and only the poor, penalize (or at least do not reward) inequality increases among the poor, and are continuous at the poverty line.[2]

Dynamic measures include transient poverty whereby households (or individuals) are temporarily poor often due to an unanticipated shock that causes intertemporal variability in welfare levels. Alternatively, the chronic poor are those with low welfare levels period after period. For such households, low mean consumption levels persist over time. A household that is chronically non-poor, however, could be transient poor.[3]

Transient poverty can often be attributed to imperfect credit and insurance arrangements that leave farm households highly dependent on climatic conditions exposed to income risk in underdeveloped economies. For example, using data from rural China, Jalan and Ravallion (1999) estimate that 40 percent of an exogenous shock is passed on to current consumption for the poorest wealth decile. Such a substantial proportion of uninsured risk translates into significant transient poverty. Transient poverty is also likely to be common in economies undergoing structural changes.

On the other hand, chronic poverty is often attributed to low economic growth and/or growth that is not broad based. This could be due to social exclusion of certain groups, or adverse geographical conditions, or lack of access to assets, or extreme unanticipated sequential shocks (that may affect many people) or a weak institutional environment that does not support resilience to and recovery from shocks. This is especially true in cases where access to health care is inadequate, social protection programs are lacking, where violent conflicts exist or when markets for goods and services collapse.

Typically the policies required to alleviate transient and chronic poverty are different. Long-term investments such as increasing human and physical assets of poor people, or the returns on those assets, are more appropriate to alleviate chronic poverty. Insurance and income-stabilization schemes that protect households against idiosyncratic shocks are important policy instruments when poverty is transient (Lipton and Ravallion, 1995).

Impact evaluation methods[4]

Governments are and should rightly be concerned about whether the monies they spend on projects to uplift the poor are actually reaching the poor. Does a poverty alleviation program make any difference to the status of the poor over and above what would have happened as part of the general economic progress? A simple analysis of the trend outcomes (*gross* improvements) in this framework will not give the correct impact estimate of the program. We have to determine the extent of welfare improvements beyond what would have happened in the 'natural course of events'. In other words, we have to determine the *net impact* of the program. If instead, we measure the *gross* improvements of the program, we shall in all probability seriously overestimate its impact.[5]

Net impact evaluations use either experimental or quasi-experimental design with a well-defined comparison group. Random experiments as designed in social sciences randomly assign the concerned population into treatment and control groups such that every one has an equal chance *ex ante* of receiving the program. People in the treatment group are given the treatment but behavior outcomes are observed for both treatment and control groups. With adequately large samples and well-constructed randomly assigned treatment and control groups where observable and unobservable characteristics of the two groups are not very different, differences in outcomes can be attributed to exposure to the program. Random experiments require no modeling of economic behavior or complex estimation methods to get reliable estimates of the program impacts. However, random experiments are not always politically feasible. Also, there is increasing evidence that control groups get contaminated over time, rendering the net impact estimates from a random experiment biased.

Poverty alleviation programs are typically deliberately placed – targeting specific subgroups of the population and/or particular areas that are declared to be backward, determined on the basis of certain socioeconomic criteria. In the case of quasi-experimental or non-experimental methods, non-random assignment to either the program participant group or the comparison group is corrected using statistical methods. Such methods attempt to equalize the selection bias present in treatment and comparison groups so as to yield unbiased estimates of parameters measuring program impact, such as the average treatment effect on the treated. Non-experimental methods assume exogeneity of program placement conditional on observed variates.

Methods such as propensity score matching (PSM) balance the distributions of the observed covariates between a treatment group and a control group based on similarity of their predicted probabilities of being declared a program participant. PSM uses econometric techniques to 'adjust out' the systematic differences between the non-experimental comparison group and the treatment group. Program participants are paired with observably equivalent non-participants. Once the 'matches' are made, the difference in their outcomes is interpreted as the mean effect of the program on the treated. Matching is justified on the assumption that conditioning on observed covariates, the potential selection bias in program placement is eliminated. The method does not require a parametric model linking program placement to outcomes, and thus allows estimation of mean impacts without arbitrary assumptions about functional forms and error distributions.

PSM methods are data intensive in the sense that to convincingly eliminate the bias due to non-random program placement based on observed covariates one needs to collect information on program criteria, community effects, household effects and so on. Often the questionnaires administered to the control group and the treatment group have to be the same, and preferably the two groups should be from geographically similar areas.[6]

Sometimes program design characteristics can be used to evaluate the impact of the program using regression discontinuity design (RDD) methods.[7] The basic idea underlying such methods is that impacts are estimated based on differences in outcomes and treatment between units on either side of a critical cutoff point used for determining program eligibility. Comparing a sample of individuals within a very small range around the critical point will be analogous to conducting a randomized experiment at that point. For example, proxy means test methods such as below poverty line (BPL) cards in India are, at least on paper, supposed to be issued to households whose asset score is below a predetermined critical level.[8] Households with a score to the left and to the right of the critical score may be considered as identical in the sense that in the absence of the treatment, the unconditional mean values of outcomes are the same. However, in many countries, the participation criteria is not strictly adhered to in the sense that many observed participants are ineligible to participate in a program according to the stated program criteria. This may render the RDD estimates biased. An evaluation of the *Grameen* Bank group lending scheme by Morduch (1999) discusses this problem.

In many cases, PSMs based on single cross-sections may not yield unbiased impact estimates because of the inability of the researcher to adequately control the endogeneity of program placement problem. In such cases, double difference or difference-in-difference (DD) estimators are used. DD estimators take the difference in outcomes before and after programs are implemented in project areas, minus the corresponding difference in the matched comparison areas. The DD estimator allows for temporally invariant differences (fixed effects) between participants and non-participants.

Finally, standard instrumental variable estimation (IVE) methods can also be used to control for endogeneity of program placement. However, often it is difficult to find credible instruments that can be validated by statistical tests. Using panel data of at least 4–5 periods may be recommended since lagged values of the endogenous variable can be used to instrument out the endogeneity of program placement.[9] The treatment effect estimated from such models is the local average treatment effect.

Besides the *ex post* evaluations discussed above, there are the *ex ante* evaluations, which are different from the random and quasi-experimental methods. Under the *ex ante* evaluations, program design parameters from existing programs are simulated using micro-simulation models. The advantage of these models is that they can predict the outcomes if the program design is modified.[10]

For each of the above methods we need clearly identifiable outcome indicators. Often the choice of these indicators reflects the objectives of the program that is being evaluated. For example, in programs such as the *Trabajar* workfare program in Argentina, the obvious indicators are consumption expenditure, number of days of employment and so on. But since poverty programs are typically targeted towards the poor it may be interesting to analyze the incidence of welfare impacts of the program. For public works programs, since creation and/or maintenance of public physical assets in poor areas is an important goal, it is interesting to compare infrastructure in treatment communities with those in similar non-treatment communities to assess the impact of this aspect of the program. Unfortunately few evaluations of public works programs actually assess this aspect.[11]

In the case of conditional cash transfers where transfers are made conditional on the fulfillment of some human behavior by the household members, it is useful to analyze the impact on the outcomes related to the specific conditional behavior required by the program. For example, in an evaluation of Bangladesh's Food for Education (FFE) program, the impact of the program on school attendance rate is estimated.

Similarly for self-employment programs, primary outcome indicators relate to improvements in welfare levels of participant households though it may be interesting to also analyze outcomes such as stock of livestock or earnings from livestock for beneficiary households. In some projects, many of the beneficiaries are poor women. Indicators such as empowerment of women, fertility and child malnutrition are a set of indicators that could capture the social impact of the program. In the microcredit programs, default rates, repayment rates, and incidence of loans among the poor are other relevant outcome indicators.

To capture the effectiveness of poor area programs it would be useful to estimate the impact outcomes such as welfare levels at the geographical level at which the program is being targeted. Other outcome variables could include changes in specific infrastructure stock depending on the design of the program.

3 Public works programs

Program features

Globally, whether it is in Sub-Saharan Africa, South and East Asia, Latin America or some of the transition economies such as Poland, Romania or Slovenia, public works has been and continues to be an important instrument in alleviating poverty. India's Employment Guarantee Schemes (under its various names and forms), Bangladesh's Food for Work Program, Pakistan's Income Generation Program for refugee areas, Botswana's Labor-based Relief Program, South Africa's National Public Works Program, Argentina's *Trabajar* Program, and the public works in some of the transition economies are but a few examples of workfare being used as a poverty alleviation tool.[12] To date, India's and Bangladesh's public works programs have together generated more than a billion mandays of employment (Subbarao, 1997).

A beneficiary of a public works scheme is required to provide physical labor at the public works work site in lieu of which he or she gets a wage either in kind or in cash at a predetermined rate. The 'works' that the beneficiary is employed in is typically a creation and/or maintenance of community assets that are likely to benefit the poor. It is desirable that such works be located in poorer communities so that benefits accruing to the poor are the greatest.

Public works can greatly mitigate the income risks arising from macroeconomic and agro-climatic shocks, especially for households in rural communities dependent on agriculture as a source of livelihood. In a sense, such schemes are very useful in combating transitory poverty by smoothing consumption and reducing the variability in income over time and/or across seasons. Ryan and Walker (1989) estimate that households living in drought-prone areas in India and having access to public works programs had significantly lower variability in their income streams compared to households that had no access to such schemes. This is the 'insurance' component of the public works scheme. Of course, this 'insurance' impact of the public works scheme is effective only if the scheme is introduced in a timely manner such that the timing coincides with the occurrence of the specific shock.

In Botswana, approximately one-third of income that was lost due to drought during the 1983–85 period was recovered by working in the public works scheme. Similarly, in Chile in 1983, with the recession at its peak and unemployment as high as 20 percent, the public employment program absorbed 13 percent of the labor force. As the situation improved, the scheme was gradually whittled down and finally virtually eliminated by 1989 (Deolalikar, 1995; Subbarao, 1997).

If designed properly, there is also a redistributive component to the public works scheme. If the wage rate is at par or below the prevailing minimum wage rate, the non-poor are less likely to avail themselves of the benefits of the scheme and a disproportionately larger number of poor will participate. There is thus self-selection into the program that does not necessitate substantial administrative costs to identify and target the poor.

In Argentina's *Trabajar* program, wages were set at a low rate of 200 pesos that was further revised to an even lower rate of 160 pesos, making the rate lower than the prevailing minimum wages at that time. Consequently the distribution of gains was unambiguously pro-poor, with 80 percent of program participants falling in the bottom 20 percent of the income distribution (Jalan and Ravallion, 2003). In the case of Argentina, the redistributive element was even more significant because the projects were targeted to geographically poorer areas. But there are other examples such as Bolivia's Emergency Social Fund where the wage rate was not substantially low and where fewer than half of the participants were from the poorest 40 percent of the Bolivian population (World Bank, 1990). Similarly in the Philippines, because the wage rates were set at a very high level, participants in the public works scheme were largely marginally poor or non-poor rather than being among the poorest in the population (Subbarao et al., 1997).

Impact assessments
Are public works a cost-efficient method to reach the poor while fulfilling both the distributive and insurance objectives of the scheme? There are different evaluation methods that can be used depending on the urgency of the estimates by policy makers, rigor and resource and data availability. We consider two types of evaluation methods: a rapid appraisal 'quick and dirty' method as suggested by Ravallion (1999) and a more rigorous and data-intensive method using modern impact evaluation techniques.

Using available information on poverty rates, wage rates of the unskilled, unemployment rates among the poor, labor intensity of pro-posed projects, information on benefits and costs of the schemes and to what extent projects are placed in poor areas, Ravallion (1999) proposes a rapid appraisal method that seeks to answer the following questions: 'How much impact on poverty can be expected if the current scheme was expanded? How might the existing scheme be modified to enhance its impact on poverty?'. Using two hypothetical scenarios – a middle-income country where unemployment is high due to macroeconomic crises and a low-income country facing a severe drought – Ravallion estimates that the cost of a dollar gain to the poor is approximately $2.50 in both cases. Ravallion also finds that the amount received by the poor under the program in a middle-income country is double the amount that they would get under an untargeted income transfer scheme. However, in low-income countries, lump-sum transfer would be more beneficial to the poor! Ravallion concludes that the programs could be made more cost-efficient if the labor intensity of the projects is increased, if projects are located in poor areas, or if there is greater cost-recovery from the non-poor.

Haddad and Adato (2001) use the analytical methods proposed by Ravallion to evaluate the National Public Works program implemented in South Africa in 1994. Using project-level data from the province of Western Cape that is merged with household data from magisterial districts in which the projects are based, the authors estimate the rands of public expenditure necessary to transfer one rand to the poor. Under certain assumptions, they find that 83–92 percent of public works projects outperform an untargeted transfer scheme. On average, it costs roughly 3.6 to 4.31 government rands (depending on the sensitivity of income transfers from the rich to the poor) to transfer one rand to the poor through the public works program.

However, both Ravallion, and Haddad and Adato acknowledge that there are limitations to their study and their estimates could be biased if the assumptions they make to estimate the analytical model are incorrect. While such appraisals are no substitute for rigorous impact evaluations, they do provide a benchmark to the policy-maker in making informed policy choices and better project design.

To estimate the distributional impact of public works, we need to measure the net income of the participants. That is, the income from the program net of what the participant would have anyway earned without participating in the program. We need to measure the income gains to participants conditional on pre-intervention income where the income gain is the difference in incomes with and without the program. While the income from the program is directly observable from the data, income that would have accrued to the person had he/she not participated in the program is unobserved and hence missing data. If we ignore the latter type of income in our impact estimate calculation, we would get an overestimate of the impact of the program because it is unlikely that the all labor supply to the program would have come from the pool of unemployed. Moreover, forgone income could also be in the form of household chores, search for unemployment and so on.

The typical outcome indicators used to estimate the impact of public works programs include a welfare indicator such as consumption or income to assess the impact on poverty, employment status after graduating from the program, social assets created under the program at the community level, net employment rate after the program has been in place for some time, unemployment rate, spell of unemployment, and so on.

While randomization is theoretically possible, it has rarely been used to evaluate public work schemes. Rather, non-experimental data methods such as PSM, difference in difference estimators and regression discontinuity methods have been used frequently to estimate the impact of the program.[13] Jalan and Ravallion (henceforth JR) (2003) apply recent advances in PSM to the problem of estimating the net income gains from an Argentinian *Trabajar* workfare program. They estimate that the average net income gained through program participation is about half the *Trabajar* wage. However even allowing for forgone income, the program is decidedly pro-poor with 80 percent of the participants belonging to the bottom 20 percent of the income distribution. There is little difference in the average income gains between men and women but younger workers are likely to gain more from the program. The authors also conclude that ignoring forgone income would significantly overstate the gains from the program.[14, 15]

In some countries, there have been instances where outlays on workfare programs have been reduced over time. Ravallion et al. (2005) in a follow-up of *Trabajar* participants assess the impact of a reduction in expenditure outlays on *Trabajar*. The outcome indicator is the extent of recovery of income that is lost once the participant is no longer a workfare beneficiary. Potential sources of lost income are private transfers or self-employment. The authors find that the estimated income losses to those who left the program were sizable, representing about three-quarters of the gross wage within the first six months, though falling to slightly less than half over 12 months. In regions such as Mendoza, where labor market conditions are less tight, income losses are smaller. The participants were also asked qualitative questions on whether they felt that working in a workfare site improved their chances of getting employment once they graduated from the program. A high proportion of respondents felt that the program improved their chances of getting a job; roughly half felt that it gave them a marketable skill; about one-quarter felt that it expanded their contacts. Of course, as the authors state, these qualitative impacts should be interpreted with caution because of possible biases in the responses of the participants.

Among the other evaluations of public works scheme, it is worth mentioning the public service employment (PSE) schemes implemented in transition economies where unemployed persons are employed in projects that provide services and/or support infrastructure development (public works) and are financed by the government.[16] PSE schemes are often implemented as a response to unemployment resulting from structural adjustment in these economies and on account of privatization of state-owned enterprises. Typically the participants are new entrants into the labor market or the long-term unemployed older workers. In Poland and Hungary for example, many of the participants had exhausted their unemployment insurance benefits, and the programs were seen as providing income support to families.

Also there is a fear among policy makers that participants may never exit from the program. So in these economies there are components built into the PSE schemes that should help in the longer-term employability of the participants. O'Leary et al. (1998) analyze the impact of five active labor programs including public service employment in Hungary. They use quasi-experimental methods to evaluate the programs. They find that while PSE programs, which typically involve manual unskilled labor, increase the average monthly earnings from the current job at the survey date, they do not make the participant more employable in a non-subsidized job and/or self-employment in the future.

4 Conditional cash transfers

Program features
From the above evidence it is unambiguously clear that public work schemes increase current earnings temporarily while the participant is working under the scheme. However medium- and long-term employability in non-subsidized schemes and/or self-employment opportunities are less likely to happen. So while public works schemes are viable for alleviating transitory poverty, reductions in chronic poverty that require investments in human and physical capital would need alternative public interventions. Conditional cash transfer (CCT) schemes alleviate poverty in the short and the long run while focusing on the poor in a cost-effective manner.

In recent times, with an objective to reduce chronic poverty, many developing countries, especially in Latin America, have introduced CCT interventions (see among others, Sedlacek et al., 2000; Britto, 2004; and Kakwani et al., 2005; Rawlings and Rubio, 2005 for details). *PROGRESA*, implemented by the Mexican government, is perhaps the best-known scheme in recent times, covering 5 million households (3.5 million rural households in 2004) with a budget of over $2.5 billion. Other examples include *Bolsa Escola* in urban Brazil, which covered 4.9 million families at the cost of $700 million in 2004, *PETI* in rural Brazil, the FFE program in Bangladesh, the Social Solidarity Fund in Turkey, *Programa de Asignación Familiar II (PRAF-BID II)* in Honduras, *Red de Protección Social (RPS)* in Nicaragua and *Beca Escolar* in Ecuador.[17]

Cash grants are given to the poor conditional on behavior that leads to improvements in their children's human capital. The 'good' behavior conditions vary across countries. In Honduras, children have to be enrolled in school and they can be absent from school for a maximum of 7 days during a period of 3 months. Further, pregnant women and children have to make regular visits to health clinics. While in the *PETI* program, children have to attend an after-school program regularly. In Turkey, children have to be enrolled in school with a minimum attendance of 85 percent. Further, children have to make regular health-care visits for growth monitoring and vaccinations according to a schedule set by the Ministry of Health. Similar behavioral conditions are imposed in other countries.

Targeting criteria and the benefits received by the households under these different schemes also vary. In Brazil for example, households with income per capita below 90 reais (R$) per month equivalent to half the minimum wage at the time the program was introduced, and households with children aged 6 to 15 years were eligible for the *Bolsa Escola* program. Monthly benefit is R$15 per child and up to a maximum of R$45 per household. Transfers are generally paid to the mother upon presentation of a magnetic card that greatly facilitates the monitoring of the whole program. In Honduras, the criteria are poor households with children aged 6–12 who have not yet completed grade 4, and poor households with pregnant women and/or children less than 3 years old. Under the education initiative, each child gets a voucher worth US$58 per year and average supply incentive of US$4,000 per school per year is also given. Likewise under the health initiative, each family gets US$46.3 per year and each facility gets US$6,020 per year.

CCT programs, as mentioned before, intend to raise human capital endowments among poor children so that sustainable poverty reduction in the long run can be achieved in addition to supplementing household incomes in the short run through the cash transfers. Some of these programs also provide budgetary support to schools and health centers to improve supply-side conditions.

Impact assessments
A defining feature of the CCT programs in Latin America is rigorous *ex post* evaluations of the programs. Programs such as *PROGRESA*, *RPS*, and *PRAF* use randomly selected control and treatment groups to measure changes in behavior over time. The typical outcome indicators that these studies focused on were school enrollment, preventive health checkups, vaccinations, prenatal checks, food availability, school achievements, nutritional status, anemia, child labor and so on.

The common conclusion of these random experiments is that chronic poor beneficiaries of the CCTs in these countries did not have to use their children as risk-coping instruments, thereby avoiding long-term costs on child human capital. Conditional behavior also seems to be an important instrument to improve future human capital endowments of the poor. In terms of the short-run objective of food consumption, the results from *PRAF II* and *RPS* have been very encouraging, showing a significant boost in either food purchases and/or caloric availability.

A randomized evaluation by Maluccio and Flores (2005) for *RPS* in Nicaragua shows that participant households affected by the coffee sector crisis (mainly small-scale farmers) were not only protected against lower per capita expenditures but also protected child human capital investments in terms of school enrollment rates and child labor outcomes. Households were able to maintain pre-program expenditure levels compared to a decline of 22 percent in 2001 for non-beneficiary households in the same region. Similarly, while overall enrollment rates in the coffee region increased, they increased more for households in the program (by an additional 25 and 10 percent for boys and girls, respectively). Child labor, especially for girls, decreased among program participants residing in the coffee region by 10 percent relative to their counterparts without the program.

Similarly, a recent evaluation analysis of *PRAF* in Honduras also provides evidence that welfare levels of poor households were protected in the face of the coffee crisis (Coady et al., 2004). Cash transfers given out by *PRAF* conditional on school enrollment allowed families to maintain children in school, while increasing the time dedicated by adults to coffee farming.

PROGRESA is the centerpiece of the CCT schemes implemented in developing countries. Under the program, households with children over 7 years are eligible for education transfers. Transfer amounts are progressive by age and are higher for girls in middle school. In 1999, monthly benefits started at 80 pesos in Grade 3 that increased to 265 and 305, respectively, for boys and girls in Grade 9 of middle school. Transfers were conditional on maintaining an 85 percent attendance rate and provided that children did not repeat a particular grade more than twice. On the supply side, while the program did not directly intervene, program officials coordinated with the Ministry of Education to ensure that additional resources were made available to schools to accommodate potential increases in demand for schooling. Food transfers were fixed at 125 pesos per family and were conditional on the family members having regular preventive health checkups in designated health clinics, attending nutritional and hygiene workshops. Finally, families with children under 3 years and/or pregnant women received nutritional supplements containing essential micronutrients. Households could get total transfers (education and health) up to 750 pesos, which constituted 20 percent of average household consumption in targeted areas.

Beneficiaries were identified in two stages. In the first stage, backward communities were identified using information from the national census. Communities had to have access to health and education facilities and have inhabitants in the range of 50–2,500 households. In the second stage, a community census was undertaken in the identified backward communities to construct a proxy means test score for each household and thereby classify them as poor or non-poor.

Randomized evaluation was built into the program design. From the eligible set of communities, 506 communities were chosen. Of these, 320 communities were declared the treatment group and the remaining 186 the control group. The control group did not get the project at the start of the program. Rather, program components were introduced in these communities 2 years after the start of the program. Extensive collection of baseline data and follow-up surveys were done between 1997 and 1999.

Between November 1998 and October 1999, an average transfer of 238 pesos reflecting 20 percent of consumption expenditure was made to the beneficiary families. By the end of 1999, the program covered 40 percent of all rural families in Mexico and 0.2 percent of the Mexican GDP was allocated to the project. The program was very well targeted by international standards. Some 58 percent of the benefits went to the poorest 20 percent and over 80 percent went to the bottom 20 percent of the income distribution. Administrative costs were less than 9 percent of total costs, implying that about 10 pesos were required to transfer one peso to the beneficiary household (see Handa and Davis, 2006 and Skoufias et al., 2001).

There were also significant health and nutritional impacts (Behrman and Hoddinott, 2000; Gertler, 2004; Hoddinott and Skoufias, 2004). For example, stunting among the age group 12–36 months decreased significantly. The estimated impacts of only the nutritional supplements would lead to an increase in lifetime earnings of 2.9 percent. Median food expenditures increased with more purchases of fruit, vegetables and different kinds of meat. It was estimated that the calorific value of food intake increased by 7.1 percent. Finally, prior to the program, the number of visits to health clinics by the households was less than one annually. With the introduction of the program, the number of prenatal visits by pregnant mothers increased by 8 percent. This had subsequent impacts on the health of newborns as well as the mothers during pregnancy. Incidence of illnesses among the newborns declined by 25 percent, for children in the age group 0–2 years it declined by 19 percent, and by 22 percent for children in the age group 3–5 years. Anemia among children also declined by 19 percent and adults too reported fewer workday losses on account of varying illnesses.

Impact on primary school enrollments was not significant since the rates were already high prior to the program. The major impact was observed for middle-school enrollment, with enrollment rates for girls increasing by 7.2–9.3 percent and for boys by 3.5–5.8 percent. There was a substantial reduction in incidence of child labor. Teachers reported improvements in learning achievements by children which could perhaps be explained by regular attendance, better nutrition and increased interest in academic activities. It was estimated that these educational gains could translate into an increase of 8 percent of their adult earnings *ceteris paribus* (see, Coady and Parker, 2002; Schultz, 2004; and Behrman et al., 2005 for further details).

Ex ante evaluations are required to estimate whether changes in program design of CCTs will have the desirable impacts on poverty. These evaluations should be viewed as complementary to the *ex post* randomized evaluations as reported above. Bourguignon et al. (2002) and Kakwani et al. (2005) conducted *ex ante* evaluations for *Bolsa Escola* in Brazil and CCT schemes in African countries, respectively.

Using the program design of *Bolsa Escola* in Brazil, the authors found that the program attracted out-of-school children. About one third of 10–15-year-olds not in school enrolled in response to the program. Among the poor households, one half of such children entered school. The proportion of children working and going to school would, however, increase marginally from the levels at the start of the program. Nevertheless, the impact on poverty and inequality is muted – the *Bolsa Escola* program reduced poverty incidence by one percentage point and the Gini coefficient by half a point. Impacts were greater for the ultra-poor as shown by poverty measures that are more sensitive to the bottom of the distribution. However, the effect was never significant. Both the proportion of children enrolling in school in response to program availability and the degree of reduction in current poverty turn out to be rather sensitive to transfer amounts, and rather insensitive to the level of the means test.

A similar study for 15 African countries shows that CCT programs lead to a marginal fall in headcount ratios. However, like the *Bolsa Escola* study, both the poverty gap and squared poverty indices show substantial improvements, implying that the program would have a significantly greater impact on the ultra-poor as compared with the poor.

Furthermore, simulation results show that a targeted cash transfer program would be more cost-efficient than an untargeted universal transfer scheme even though the administrative costs may be higher in the case of the former. Benefits of the program are much higher for rural than for urban children. This suggests that if identifying the poor is hard in these countries due to weak databases, it may still be worthwhile to implement an untargeted scheme in rural areas to achieve a significant impact on poverty.

As in the case of Brazil, transfers have to be large to make a significant dent in the poverty levels. However, in the case of African countries large budgetary allocations for the project may not be financially possible, which may ultimately make the program ineffective. For example, for Ethiopia, the poorest country included in the study, a program based on 40 percent of its average national poverty line would require a minimum expenditure of almost 8.31 percent of GDP. Even a country such as Côte d'Ivoire, the most affluent of the 15 countries, has to bear the burden of about 2.8 percent of its GDP if national poverty is to be reduced to the maximum level.

Finally, even if budgetary allocations are sufficient, the study shows that imposition of behavior conditions is absolutely essential if the aim is to break the vicious intergenerational cycle of poverty, since the impact on attendance is modest in the absence of such conditionalities. For example, if the budget entitlement is 40 percent of the poverty line, the headcount ratio is reduced by more than 30 percent in Ethiopia but attendance increases only marginally. This is even true for the *Bolsa Escola* program in Brazil. The Brazilian study estimates that, among poor households, there would be a decline of 58 percent among children not attending school, an increase of 7 percent for children attending school and working, and of 5 percent for children attending school and not working. By contrast, when the school enrollment condition is not imposed to receive a transfer, the pure cash transfer has a zero effect on school enrollment.

Finally, the FFE Scheme implemented in Bangladesh is conceptually similar to the CCTs except that it makes in-kind rather than cash transfers conditional on certain types of education behavior by the participant households. An FFE participant household is entitled to 15 kg of wheat or 12 kg of rice per month for one child going to school, or 20 kg of wheat or 16 kg of rice if the household sends more than one child, and *all* primary-school-age children, to school. To receive their rations, the enrolled children must attend at least 85 percent of the classes each month (see Ravallion and Wodon, 2000 and Ahmed and del Nino, 2002 for program details). These studies show that the FFE program is effectively targeted towards low-income families.

Student enrollments in FFE schools increased by 35 percent per school compared to their initial enrollment over the two-year period. Increase in enrollments was substantially more for girls than for boys. In contrast, per school enrollment in non-FFE government primary schools recorded an increase of only 2.5 percent. Significant and sizable impacts on school attendance were also estimated. Ravallion and Wodon estimate that the program led to an increase in attendance by 24 percent of the maximum feasible days of schooling. The FFE program also helped to retain children in school, reducing the number of dropouts. However, Ahmed et al. find that the quality of education may have suffered due to increased demand for schooling without any corresponding increase in supply of schools following the implementation of the program. An achievement test was designed and administered to fourth-grade students in FFE and non-FFE schools. The average test scores were lower in FFE schools when compared to the non-FFE schools and this difference was statistically significant.

The above evidence on CCTs indicates that these programs are useful in reducing uninsured exposure to risk by poor households. Often in the absence of these programs, either risk insurance cover is inadequate, leading to a running-down of assets – physical and human – and/or anticipating the risks and holding unproductive assets as a precautionary motive. In both instances, households may be driven to longer term poverty in the absence of risk-focused safety-net programs. CCTs in that sense provide some reprieve for the chronic poor by helping them accumulate assets, providing them opportunities to use their assets more productively and thus making an impact on short-term consumption needs through the cash (or in-kind) transfers. However, all CCTs target the chronic poor and exclude the vulnerable non-poor. This segment of the population is increasing steadily and could be one explanation for marginal declines in aggregate poverty even with substantial investments in programs such as the CCTs. For example, Krishna et al. (2004) estimate that while 14 percent of the poor escaped poverty, another 12 percent of the non-poor became poor, which led to only a small decline in overall poverty. The vulnerable excluded non-poor – an important growing segment of the population which also needs some cover from uninsured exposure to risk.

5 Credit schemes

Program features
Public works and CCT schemes emphasize stabilization of incomes and reduction of intertemporal variability in welfare levels. However, poverty programs can also create investment opportunities that can sustain self-employment in the short and long-term. Subsidized credit for acquiring income-generating assets, and microcredit schemes such as group lending are some examples that exist in developing countries. Also, unlike the previous interventions, microcredit schemes need not necessarily be an initiative

by the government. The best-known microcredit scheme – *Grameen* Bank – is a private endeavor with poverty alleviation as its primary objective.[18]

Traditionally, under such self-employment creation schemes, credit is often subsidized and given to the poor to purchase income-generating assets. In some instances, other forms of marketing assistance are also provided. For example, India's Integrated Rural Development Program (IRDP) creates self-employment for the poor through disbursement of subsidized credit to purchase income-generating assets. However, there is ample evidence that subsidized credit often does not reach the intended beneficiaries and is diverted to the politically powerful. It has several hidden transaction costs that make it costly for the poor to avail themselves of such loans, repayment rates are low and default rates are high. For example, Deolalikar (1995, p. 3) writes:

> A careful study by Pulley (1989) of IRDP beneficiaries observed after periods of two and four years from the time of receipt of subsidized credit found that a significant number of beneficiaries were unable to retain assets acquired with the help of the program. The lack of sustainability of assets was in large part because the subsidy element in IRDP attracted individuals with low motivation to succeed in self-employment activities. As soon as the subsidy was withdrawn, these individuals experienced business failures and defaulted on their loans.

Similarly, credit schemes that are tied to the purchase of specific assets are also found to be inadequate in targeting the poor. Often borrowers are persuaded to make asset purchases while they have no experience in either owning or maintaining that asset. For example, under the old BIMAS program in Indonesia, borrowing was tied to a package of inputs for intensified rice cultivation (Robinson and Snodgrass, 1987). Borrowers who were persuaded by bank officials to take loans for input packages that were inappropriate for their farms often did not see any reason to repay.

In contrast, there are also unsubsidized credit schemes such as the *Kupedes* and *Badan Kredit Kecamatan* (BKK) in Indonesia, Indonesia's Bank Rakyat system (*BRI*), and *Action Comunitaria* in Peru among others. For example, the BRI scheme requires individual borrowers to put up some collateral. This makes it likely that the very poorest borrowers are excluded. However, program staff members have some discretion. For example, they increase the loan size for reliable borrowers who may not be able to fully back loans with assets.

Finally, there are group lending schemes such as the *Grameen* Bank of Bangladesh – one of the most widely known self-employment creation schemes in the world with poverty alleviation as its primary objective – which serves nearly one-half of all villages in Bangladesh and has a membership of 1.8 million, of whom 94 percent are women (Khandker et al., 1994). *Fundacfon Integral Campesina (FINCA)* is another example of a group-based revolving credit fund, supervised and financed by a non-profit, non-sectarian, Costa Rican private development agency. *Bancosol* of Bolivia is another successful group-lending scheme though it differs from the *Grameen* Bank in the sense that social service is not its objective. Rather its main aim is to run a successful banking operation.

In such schemes, loans are given to groups of individuals who share the joint liability of taking the loan. Groups are formed voluntarily. This immediately addresses the problem of asymmetric information on default risk between the borrower and lender. As a consequence, loan repayment rates and expected lender profit should be better relative to credit given to individuals. Group credit schemes also solve the *monitoring or incentive* problem by inducing members of the credit group to monitor their peers. Since all members of the group will be barred from future borrowing if the group defaults, members have incentives to use moral persuasion, social ostracism, and mutual insurance to honor the external loan commitment with the distant, non-resident lender.

Impact assessments
Rigorous impact assessments on poverty alleviation of self-employment generation schemes are few and far between. Descriptive analyses of the IRDP project in India indicate that once the subsidy is withdrawn, a large number of beneficiaries default on their loans and take fresh loans to pay off the old loans. Pulley (1989) collected information on IRDP beneficiaries after two and four years from the time of receipt of subsidized credit. The author found that a significant number of beneficiaries were unable to retain assets acquired with the help of the program. This lack of sustainability was in large part because the subsidy element in IRDP attracted individuals with inadequate experience in self-employment activities. As soon as the subsidy was withdrawn, these individuals experienced business failures and defaulted on their loans. However, none of these studies used modern impact evaluation techniques.

Microcredit and microfinance have become increasingly popular worldwide. However, rigorous evaluations of the program estimating the impacts are few. As a result, most conclusions about the success (or lack thereof) of the program are based on anecdotal evidence.

An exception is Pitt and Khandker's (1998, 2002) evaluation of the *Grameen* Bank which is perhaps the first rigorous assessment of the credit programs to the poor. The authors make use of the program criterion that small loans are given to poor households who own less than half an acre of land and use regression discontinuity methods to evaluate the program. They estimate that for every 100 taka loan given to a woman (man) beneficiary, household consumption increases by 18 (11) taka. Their findings also suggest that households borrowing from the *Grameen* Bank had significant desirable effects on a variety of household and individual welfare outcomes, such as the school enrollment and nutritional status of boys and girls, asset holdings, and marginal decrease in fertility by women (Pitt et al., 1999). Furthermore, the study found that the effects on household welfare were generally stronger in the case of credit provided to women than that provided to men. Pitt and Khandker also use the seasonal component in their dataset and find that the program did help households in reducing consumption variability across seasons.

Using the same dataset, Signe-Mary McKernan (2002) estimated the non-economic impacts of the program. She found that non-credit impacts such as reduction in fertility, women's empowerment and so on increased self-employment profits by 50–80 percent.

However in a related study by Morduch (1998), the author questions the identification strategy used in Pitt and Khandker. Morduch finds that 30 percent of borrowers owned more than the threshold half acre of land, with landholdings as large as 14 acres. He writes: 'Among households labeled in the survey as 'eligible' to borrow and with access to programs, the fraction of borrowers is nearly twice as high for those holding over half an acre versus those below (63% versus 34% for the three programs combined)' (p. 6). In his analysis, Morduch estimates the impacts for only those borrowers who meet the eligibility criterion and finds that the programs did not necessarily increase consumption levels or educational enrollments for children in borrower households relative to levels in control villages. However, like Pitt and Khandker, he also finds that participation in the program led to substantially lower variation in labor supply and consumption across seasons.

Finally, microcredit schemes can also potentially have an impact on household savings. While there is no credible study on the effect on savings for the *Grameen* Bank, there is a study by Aportela (1998) for a scheme in Mexico. In 1993, the Mexican government initiated a large expansion of its savings scheme, *Pahnal*, designed for poor households. Under this scheme, households could save in post office branches with low minimum balance requirements and low user fees. Using a difference-in-difference methodology, the author finds that expansion of the program led to an increase in savings by 5 percentage points. This number increased to nearly 7 percentage points among the poorest households. The author claimed that the increase was new savings since he found no evidence of 'crowding out' by the households.

6   Poor area developmental programs

Program characteristics
The different poverty alleviation schemes discussed above can easily be geographically targeted. For example, the poor area development program in China was introduced in 1986 following concerns that certain rural areas were left behind in the development process. Under the program, 327 counties were 'national-poor counties', and substantial aid was targeted to those counties. The extra aid took the form of subsidized credit for village-level projects (provided at well-below market rates of interest), funding for public works projects (under 'food-for-work' programs), and direct budgetary support to the county government.

Areas are identified on the basis of existing socio-economic indicators such as social product per capita, grain yield, infant mortality rate and so on. While such programs may work well in economies where poverty is concentrated in specific regions, the twin problems of imperfect coverage of the poor, and leakage to the non-poor, can greatly reduce the overall impact on poverty.

Another example where credit is channeled through village communities led by village heads is the *BRI*'s *Unit Desa* (village unit) system (BKD). Many positives of the group-lending system, such as local information, constant monitoring and so on, can therefore be exploited while retaining an individual lending approach. Through the late 1990s, most BKDs have had excess capital for lending and hold balances in *BRI* accounts. The BKDs are now supervised by *BRI*, and successful BKD borrowers can graduate naturally to larger-scale lending from *BRI* units.

FINCA is another example of a group-based revolving credit fund, supervised and financed by a non-profit, non-sectarian, Costa Rican private development agency. 'Groups' in this case are the village banks that primarily tend to serve the poor predominantly female clientele. These village banks enjoy a great deal of financial autonomy in making managerial and loan decisions.

Impact assessments
In the mid-1980s, the Chinese government recognized the non-sustainability of economic reforms in the face of socio-political instability stemming from rising inequality. It therefore initiated its poor area development policy aimed at eliminating rural poverty. The objective was to provide subsidized credit, budgetary grants and public employment programs in identified backward areas.

Using data from four provinces in south-west China for the 1986–90 period, Jalan and Ravallion (1998a) find that the higher the initial household wealth, the lower the subsequent rate of growth; this is consistent with diminishing returns to own capital. By contrast, the lower the community's initial average wealth, the lower the subsequent rate of household consumption growth *ceteris paribus*, suggesting that better endowments of community capital raise the marginal returns to investment at the household level. The consumption-growth model also suggests that households living in areas targeted by the program had a higher rate of consumption growth than one would have otherwise expected. Indeed, without the program, the initial conditions in these areas appear to have been so unfavorable that we would have seen a decline in average living standards over the period. The gains were enough to prevent absolute decline. But they were not adequate to reverse the strong underlying divergent tendencies in the rural economy during our sample period. The authors use generalized method of moments to control for endogeneity of program placement.

Using county data from Shanxi, a poor province in north-west China, Rozelle et al. (1998) conclude that funds allocated directly to households for agricultural activity have a significant positive effect on growth. But investments in township and village enterprises or county state-owned enterprises do not have a discernible effect on growth. Investments in agricultural infrastructure also do not positively affect growth rates in agricultural output. The authors observe that infrastructure investments should be made on other types of basic services such as roads, schools and so on. Also, giving loans to households seemed to be more conducive in helping the poor.

7   Moving from outcome impact evaluation to a cost–benefit analysis

Evaluation of social programs may suggest that benefits of the programs are (not) reaching the intended beneficiaries and having a positive (negative or no) impact on their welfare levels. However, it could simultaneously be true that the costs incurred in transferring one unit of benefit to the intended beneficiaries may be very high. There is anecdotal evidence about high administrative costs but benefits not reaching the needy, as Caldés et al. (2006, p. 1) state: 'There is very little rigorous empirical evidence on the costs and cost structures of social safety net programs in developing countries, however, that makes proper assessment of the criticism that such programs are "expensive" difficult'.[19] Further, the costs are rarely comparable across programs even though their designs may be similar.

In Coady et al. (2004), a methodology is proposed that allows a detailed comparative analysis of three similar poverty alleviation programs in Latin America. The *cost-efficiency* of each program is computed by considering the cost of making one unit transfer to a beneficiary. That is, the cost-transfer ratio (CTR) is the ratio of non-transfer program costs to total program transfers. Several factors affect the CTR such as program characteristics about targeting and monitoring, size, type and delivery mechanism of the transfers, coverage, duration, and whether the program is expanding.[20]

However, it is often the case that programs, and especially poverty alleviation programs, are targeted towards specific areas and/or certain groups in the population. This often requires special surveys to identify the beneficiaries of the program. In programs such as the CCT schemes that are increasingly becoming popular in developing countries, transfers are conditional on certain human development behavior by the households. This requires monitoring at the community level, adding to the standard administrative costs.

While both targeting and conditioning can often lead to higher program implementation costs, there is a potential trade-off. The importance of this trade-off is noted by Grosh (1994, 46):

> The conclusion that total administrative costs are low must be somewhat tempered, however. In several of the programs, it appears that low administrative budgets have led to deficient program management. Spending more on administration with a given program framework might lead to better service quality, better incidence, or both.

It is because of this that Coady et al. (2004) refer to the CTR as 'cost-efficiency'. They use the term 'cost-effectiveness' only when they include the broader objectives (i.e. targeting and conditioning, for example) in the cost calculations.

Using data from the CCTs in Mexico (*PROGRESA*), Nicaragua (*RPS*) and Honduras (*PRAF*), Coady et al. calculate the CTRs using different sources of data for each of the programs. They estimate the CTRs for the three programs to be 0.111, 0.629 and 0.499, respectively. If we exclude the cost of external evaluation of the program these ratios change to 0.106, 0.489 and 0.325, respectively. The authors also calculate the targeting and conditioning costs for each of the three programs. They find that both these costs constitute a substantial proportion of the total cost incurred to implement the program. That is, they account for 60, 49, and 31 percent for *PROGRESA*, *PRAF* and *RPS*, respectively.

The question is whether it is worth spending vast resources to target the poor and monitor their human development behavior. If the instruments used to target the poor lead to an increase in the share of transfers reaching the poorest households, then certainly targeting is cost-effective.

In the case of each of the three programs discussed by Coady et al. (ibid.), relatively 'poor' households receive from 1.5 to 2 times their population shares. In their survey of more than 100 programs, Coady et al. (2002b) report that the median targeting performance was consistent with 50 percent of program benefits accruing to the poorest 40 percent of the population (that is, the poor receiving 1.25 times their population share).

Similarly, conditioning costs are justified if intense monitoring of the beneficiary households leads to substantial improvements in the human capital stock of the intended beneficiaries. For two of the programs, *PROGRESA* and *RPS*, human capital accumulation impacts in both education and health have been substantial. For example, in the case of *PROGRESA*, there was a substantial increase in enrollments in secondary schools. Likewise, in the case of *RPS*, substantial impacts on health and nutrition levels of the beneficiaries are observed. The percentage of children under age three who were weighed in the past six months increased substantially, which may have led to a decline by six percentage points of the prevalence of stunting for those under five. Share of food in the household budget increased and the program also had a beneficial impact on the number of different food items consumed and the nutritional quality of the diet improved, with households eating more meat, fats, and fruits (Maluccio and Flores, 2005). These estimates suggest that even though conditioning and targeting increase the implementation costs of the CCT programs in the three countries, at least the returns (that is, reaching the intended beneficiaries and improving their short- and long-term welfare levels) to those costs are large enough to justify the costs.

Using a slightly different methodology, Ravallion (1999) estimate the cost-effectiveness of public works programs in two hypothetical countries mimicking a middle-income and a low-income country, respectively.[21] Ravallion calculates the costs of transferring $1 of income to the poor in a typical middle-income country with a poverty rate of 20 percent and a typical low-income country with a poverty rate of 50 percent. If only current benefits are considered, the cost is estimated to be $5.00 for middle-income countries and $3.60 for low-income countries. However, if future gains from the assets created are factored into the benefits, the cost reduces to $2.50 for both middle- and low-income countries.

The above numbers should be interpreted with caution. For example, a well-designed public works program is self-targeted and, therefore, does not incur administrative costs for targeting. This may make the public works program more cost-efficient than other targeted programs. Specific targeted programs if not designed properly can lead to substantial leakages to the non-poor. Using data from several developing countries, Subbarao et al. (1997) estimate that the proportion of total transfer benefits to the poor range from 19 to 93 percent across countries for targeted food programs. Radhakrishna and Subbarao (1997) estimate that only 16–19 percent of the expenditure on food subsidy programs in India reach the poor. These numbers suggest that a carefully designed public works program such as Argentina's *Trabajar*, where 80 percent of the beneficiaries are from the bottom 20 percent of the population, may be more 'cost-effective' compared to other programs where administrative and leakage costs are high.

Furthermore, as Ravallion (1999, p. 4) himself claims: 'In common with other estimates of cost-effectiveness, I shall also largely ignore risk benefits. This could well be the most serious limitation of the calculations reported here, since insurance against income losses are thought to be a significant benefit from workfare programs in practice'. In particular, risk benefits may be extremely important for the poor, who lack access to risk-coping instruments or who cannot afford to insure themselves against potential risks of income/consumption shortfalls.

Finally, in the simulation methods used by Ravallion, only direct gains from the program are estimated. But does not include indirect benefits such as access to better infrastructure through the physical assets created under the program especially in poor areas and impact on rural wage-rates through a possible increase in the reservation wage could increase the actual benefits derived from the program. Using an analytical model, Gaiha (2000) estimated the indirect benefit from the Maharashtra Employment Guarantee Scheme (MEGS) in India. He analyzed the interdependence between the agricultural market wage, the MEGS wage, and non-farm wages and found substantial indirect benefits. For example, he estimated that if MEGS wages were to rise by Rs.1, rural farm wages would increase by Rs.0.17 in the short run and by Rs.0.28 in the long run.

Unlike CCTs and public works programs, there are very few detailed cost–benefit analyses for self-employment schemes. Khandker (1998) uses simple techniques to estimate the cost–benefit ratio of 0.91 with respect to improvements in household consumption via borrowing by women from the *Grameen* Bank. Similarly, he estimates a cost–benefit ratio of 1.48 for borrowing by men. However, these estimates make some simplifying assumptions that may bias the cost–benefit estimates (see Morduch, 1999 for details).

Estimating the implementation cost of programs and evaluating it against the program's stated objectives, that is, whether it reaches the intended beneficiaries or whether it raises the welfare levels of the targeted population, is important especially in the context of competing social programs for reaching the poor. In assessing the cost-effectiveness of programs it is important not only to look at project costs but also to compare the utility from the program to society as a whole.

8   Conclusions

Different programs are needed to alleviate different types of poverty. Available evidence from different impact evaluation studies suggests that while public works programs are successful in providing short-term income relief to the participants, they are unable to reduce poverty in a sustained way. They are therefore a useful tool in alleviating transitory or temporary poverty but possibly not an appropriate tool for combating persistent or more chronic poverty. This is true even in transition economies where usually a training component is built into public service employment programs.

On the other hand, conditional cash (in-kind) transfer schemes alleviate both transitory and chronic poverty. They allow for intergenerational economic mobility of households by protecting the human capital investments of children when households are hit by adverse shocks. Impacts of these schemes on actual intergenerational mobility would of course require the existence of other complementary inputs such as good macroeconomic parameters in the economy in the future. However, available *ex post* and *ex ante* evaluations suggest that current education and health investments by households increase, thereby providing a base where intergenerational economic mobility is a possibility in the future. The success of such schemes in the Latin American economies is making it an attractive option to policy makers in other developing countries where investments in human capital are always at a risk of being reduced in the face of adverse shocks to the households. The one weakness of these programs as currently implemented is that they are targeted towards the poor and therefore they exclude the vulnerable non-poor from their set of beneficiaries. In many cases, such as Mexico, it is postulated that significant declines in aggregate poverty are not observed even with the implementation of large-scale poverty reduction schemes, because while the poor may escape poverty as beneficiaries of the scheme, the non-poor may fall into poverty as they do not benefit from the programs.

Programs that provide easy credit – subsidized or otherwise – to households, so that they can invest in income-generating assets and hence create self-employment opportunities, can perhaps provide support to the vulnerable non-poor to prevent them from falling into the poverty trap. As Szekely (2001, p. 15) writes: 'in this scheme, the role of social policy is to generate income-earning *capabilities* and to create *opportunities* for using them productively' (original italics). Some of these schemes such as the *Grameen* Bank target the poor but there are others in Indonesia (*BRI's Unit Desa*) and Bolivia (*Bancosol*) where the clients are primarily non-poor. Most of these programs could also have a social impact (that is, women's empowerment, reductions in fertility, and so on). However, unlike the previous two methods of alleviating poverty there is very little rigorous evaluation available for 'credit for asset creation schemes'. Limited evidence on the *Grameen* Bank does suggest that benefits from risk reduction may be as important (or more important) than direct impacts on average levels of consumption (Pitt and Khandker, 1998, 2002; Morduch, 1999). However, it is also true that more rigorous evaluations of the different microfinance projects worldwide have to be done before one can comprehensively claim that such schemes are strongly beneficial for the poor and non-poor vulnerable population.

In all the above cases, it is extremely important to make rigorous evaluations an important component of the project. It is because randomized experiments were possible in the case of CCTs in Latin America that today we can unequivocally state that these programs work in protecting the human capital investments of the poor during periods of adverse shocks. Similarly, because of available data, one can use quasi-experimental methods to evaluate public works programs and conclude that these schemes do provide short-term income relief for the poor. Finally, it is precisely because of the lack of available data that even for a flagship microfinance program such as the *Grameen* Bank, evaluation estimates are limited. Evaluations are important in determining whether programs make cost-effective use of public funds, thereby increasing social and political accountability. Policy makers and project designers should recognize the utility of impact evaluations both in terms of concluding whether the program works and also to make modifications in project design.

Notes

*   I thank Robert Brent for his valuable suggestions. However, remaining errors are mine.

1.   In a recent paper by Ravallion and Chen (2007), the authors estimate that extreme poverty did decline between 1981 and 2001 in China. Dramatic declines in the proportion of rural poor were observed in the first few years of the 1980s. But by the late 1990s, there was a marked deceleration in reduction of poverty rates and by the end of this period there were even signs of rising rural poverty. Further, progress has been uneven over time and across provinces. Regions where initial inequality was high were able to reduce poverty at a slower rate due to both lower growth and a lower growth elasticity of poverty reduction.

2.   Details on different poverty measures are given in Ravallion (1994).

3.   See Jalan and Ravallion (1998b, 2000) for an analysis on the two types of poverty, using data from four provinces in China.

4.   For technical details of evaluation methods used in assessing poverty programs see Ravallion (2008).

5.   Heckman et al. (1997) and Dehejia and Wahba (1999) are a few papers describing the use of propensity score matching methods for non-experimental data. See Duflo and Kremer (2005) and Galasso et al. (2002) for details on random experiments.

6.   See Heckman et al. (1998) for theoretical and empirical evidence on uniformity of questionnaires and geographical areas.

7.   For an excellent paper on RDD see Van der Klaauw (2002).

8. See Jalan and Murgai (2007) for details on the BPL method.
9. See Jalan and Ravallion (1998a) for an example of the use of IVE-GMM method to assess a poverty program in China.
10. See Bourguignon and Ferreira (2003) for an excellent survey on *ex ante* evaluation methods.
11. Adato et al.'s (2000) study on the South African public works program is an exception. The report analyzes the targeting of projects across districts, the impact of the projects on communities and on persons living in the project communities in terms of access to public services.
12. For details on public works programs in countries other than the transition economies see Subbarao (1997), Haddad and Adato (2001), and Jalan and Ravallion (2003). For details on public works programs in transition economies see Betcherman et al. (2004).
13. For a survey on the different evaluations globally see Dar and Tzannatos (1998).
14. Even though the *Trabajar* evaluations 'stand out technically in demonstrating best practice empirical techniques' (Baker, 2000), there are certain limitations to the evaluation. JR uses cross-sectional datasets to estimate the impact of the program. But there could be pre-treatment income dynamics and time-invariant heterogeneity that may lead to biased estimates.
15. Ronconi (2007) evaluates the same program as that estimated by JR using panel data for the period October 2000 and May 2002. He finds the average treatment effect to be 60 pesos per month, which is substantially less compared to JR's estimate of 100 pesos. In addition, the targeting is less pro-poor than reported in JR.
16. See Wilson and Fretwell (1999) for a survey on PSEs in OECD and transition economies.
17. Nicaragua's RPS program is the smallest, covering 21,619 households with a total budget of $6.37 million. PRAF II on the other hand had a budget of $25 million covering 411,000 households (see Rawlings and Rubio, 2005; and Handa and Davis, 2006, for further details).
18. Initially Bangladesh Bank and the International Fund for Agricultural Development provided funds at an interest rate of 3 percent. By the mid-80s, funding from foreign aid agencies became an important source of funds.
19. In a survey paper, Coady et al. (2002b) find that any cost information of programs was available for only 32 of the 111 programs examined, and most of these were from programs in Latin American countries.
20. Coady et al. (2004) provide details on calculation of the CTR using project data, accounting data and household data.
21. Using similar methodology Haddad and Adato (2001) provide estimates for the public works program in South Africa.

References

Adato, M., D. Coady and M. Ruel (2000), 'An operations evaluation of *PROGRESA* from the perspective of beneficiaries, *promotoras*, school directors, and health staff', International Food Policy Research Institute (IFPRI), Washington, DC.

Ahmed A. and C. del Nino (2002), 'The Food for Education Program in Bangladesh: An Evaluation of its Impact on Educational Attainment and Food Security', International Foof Policy Research Institute (IFPRI), Washington, DC.

Aportela Fernando (1998), 'Effects of financial access on savings by low-income people', mimeo, Economics Department, MIT, Cambridge, MA.

Baker, Judy (2000), *Evaluating the Impact of Development Projects on Poverty: A Handbook for Practitioners*, Washington, DC: World Bank.

Behrman, J. and J. Hoddinott (2000), 'An evaluation of the impact of *PROGRESA* on pre-school child height', International Food Policy Research Institute (IFPRI), Washington, DC.

Behrman, Jere, Piyali Sengupta and Petra Todd (2005), 'Progressing through *PROGRESA*:

an impact assessment of a school subsidy experiment', University of Pennsylvania, *Economic Development and Cultural Change*, **54** (1), 237–75.

Betcherman, G., K. Olivas and A. Dar (2004), 'Impacts of active labor market programs: new evidence from evaluation with particular attention to developing and transition countries', Social Protection Discussion Paper Series No. 0402, World Bank: Washington, DC.

Bourguignon, François and Francisco Ferreira (2003), '*Ex-ante* evaluation of policy reforms using behavioural models', in Bourguignon, F. and L. Pereira da Silva (eds), *The Impact of Economic Policies on Poverty and Income Distribution*, New York: Oxford University Press, pp. 124–41.

Bourguignon, F., L. Pereira da Silva and N. Stern (2002), 'Evaluating the poverty impact of economic policies', mimeo, World Bank, Washington, DC.

Britto, T. (2004), 'CCT: why have they become so prominent in recent poverty reduction strategies in Latin America', Working Paper Series No. 390, Institute of Social Studies, the Hague: The Netherlands.

Caldés, N., D. Coady and J. Maluccio (2006), 'The cost of poverty alleviation transfer program: a comparative analysis of three programs in Latin America', *World Development*, **34** (5), 868–932.

Coady, D. (2000), 'Final report: The Application of Social Cost–Benefit Analysis to the Evaluation of *PROGRESA*', Report submitted to *PROGRESA*, November, Washington, DC: International Food Policy Research Institute.

Coady, D. (2001), 'Evaluation of the distributional power of *PROGRESA*'s cash transfers in Mexico', Discussion Paper No. 117, Food Consumption Nutrition Division (FCND), International Food Policy Research Institute (IFPRI), Washington, DC.

Coady, D. (2003), 'Alleviating structural poverty in developing countries: the approach of *PROGRESA* in Mexico', Background Paper for the World Development Report 2004, World Bank: Washington, DC.

Coady, D. and Susan Parker (2002), 'A cost-effectiveness analysis of demand and supply-side education interventions: the case of *PROGRESA* in Mexico', Discussion Paper No. 127, Food Consumption Nutrition Division (FCND), International Food Policy Research Institute (IFPRI), Washington, DC.

Coady, D., M. Grosh and J. Hoddinott (2002a), 'Coping with the coffee crisis in Central America: the role of social safety nets in Honduras', International Food Policy Research Institute (IFPRI), Washington, DC.

Coady, D., M. Grosh and J. Hoddinott (2002b), *The Targeting of Transfers in Developing Countries: Review of Experience and Lessons*, Social Safety Net Primer Series, Washington, DC: World Bank.

Coady, D., P. Olinto and N. Caldés (2004), 'Coping with the coffee crisis in Central America: the role of social safety nets in Honduras', International Food Policy Research Institute (IFPRI), Washington, DC.

Dar, A. and Z. Tzannatos (1998), 'Active labor market programs: a review of the evidence from evaluations', Social Protection Working Paper Series No. 9901, World Bank, Washington, DC.

Deaton, A. (1997), *The Analysis of Household Surveys: A Microeconometric Approach to Development*, Baltimore, MD: Johns Hopkins University Press.

Dehejia, Rajeev and S. Wahba (1999), 'Causal effects in non-experimental studies: re-evaluating the evaluation of training programs,' *Journal of the American Statistical Association*, **94**, 1053–62.

Deolalikar, A. (1995), 'Special employment program and poverty alleviation', *Asian Development Review*, **13** (2), 50–73.

Duflo, Esther and Michael Kremer (2005), 'Use of randomization in the evaluation of development effectiveness', in George Pitman, Osvaldo Feinstein and Gregory Ingram (eds), *Evaluating Development Effectiveness*, New Brunswick, NJ: Transaction, pp. 205–32.

Foster, J., J. Greer and E. Thorbecke (1984), 'A class of decomposable poverty measures', *Econometrica*, **52**, 761–5.

Gaiha, R. (2000), 'Rural Public Works and the Poor: A Review of the Employment

Guarantee Scheme in Maharashtra', Faculty of Management Studies, University of Delhi, India

Galasso, E., M. Ravallion and A. Salvia (2002), 'Assisting the transition from workfare to work: a randomized experiment', mimeo, Development Research Group, World Bank, Washington, DC.

Gertler, Paul (2004), 'Do conditional cash transfers improve child health? Evidence from *PROGRESA*'s control randomized experiment', *American Economic Review*, **94** (2), 336–41.

Grosh, M. (1994), *Administering Targeted Social Programs in Latin America: From Platitude To Practice*, Washington, DC: World Bank.

Haddad, L. and M. Adato (2001), 'How efficiently do public works programs transfer benefits to the poor? Evidence from South Africa', FCND Discussion Paper No. 108, Food Consumption Nutrition Division, International Food Policy Research Institute (IFPRI), Washington, DC.

Handa, S. and Benjamin Davis (2006), 'The experience of conditional cash transfers in Latin America and the Caribbean', *Development Policy Review*, **24** (5), 513–36.

Heckman, J., H. Ichimura and P. Todd (1997) 'Matching as an econometric evaluation estimator: evidence from evaluating a job-training program', *Review of Economic Studies*, **64**, 605–54.

Heckman, J., H. Ichimura, J. Smith and P. Todd (1998), 'Characterizing selection bias using experimental data', *Econometrica*, **66**, 1017–99.

Hoddinott, John and Emmanuel Skoufias (2004), 'The impact of *PROGRESA* on food consumption', *Economic Development and Cultural Change*, **53** (1), 37–62.

Hoddinott, J., E. Skoufias and R. Washburn (2000), 'The impact of *PROGRESA* on consumption', International Food Policy Research Institute (IFPRI), Washington, DC.

Jalan, J. and M. Ravallion (1998a), 'Are there dynamic gains from a poor-area development program?', *Journal of Public Economics*, **67** (1), 65–86.

Jalan, J. and M. Ravallion (1998b), 'Transient poverty in rural China', *Journal of Comparative Economics*, **26**, 338–57.

Jalan, J. and M. Ravallion (1999), 'Are the poor less insured? Evidence on vulnerability to income risk in rural China', *Journal of Development Economics*, **58**, 61–81.

Jalan, J. and M. Ravallion (2000), 'Determinants of transient and chronic poverty: evidence from rural China', *Journal of Development Studies*, **36** (6), 82–99.

Jalan, J. and M. Ravallion (2003), 'Estimating the benefit incidence of an anti-poverty program by propensity score matching', *Journal of Business and Economic Statistics*, **21** (1), 19–30.

Jalan, J. and R. Murgai (2007), 'An effective "targeting shortcut"? An assessment of the 2002 below poverty line census method', mimeo, World Bank, New Delhi.

Kakwani, N., F.V. Soares and H.H. Son (2005), 'Conditional cash transfers in African countries', UNDP Program Working Paper No. 9, Brazil.

Khandker, Shahidur (1998), *Fighting Poverty with Microcredit: Experience in Bangladesh*, New York: Oxford University Press for the World Bank.

Khandker, S., B. Khalily and Z. Khan (1994), 'Sustainability of *Grameen* Bank: what do we know?', mimeo, World Bank, Washington, DC.

Krishna, Anirudh, Patti Krist Janson, Maren Radeny, and Wilson Nindo (2004), 'Falling into poverty in villages of Andhra Pradesh: why poverty avoidance policies are needed', *Economic and Political Weekly*, July 17, pp. 3249–56.

Lipton, M. and M. Ravallion (1995), 'Poverty and policy', in Hollis Chenery and T.N. Srinivasan (eds), *Handbook of Development Economics*, Vol. 3b, New York: Elsevier, pp. 2551–657.

Maluccio J. and R. Flores (2005), 'Impact evaluation of a conditional cash transfer program: the Nicaraguan *Red de Protección Social*', International Food Policy Research Institute (IFPRI), Washington, DC.

McKernan, Signe-Mary (2002), 'The impact of micro-credit programs on self-employment profits: do non-credit program aspects matter?', *The Review of Economics and Statistics*, February, **84** (1), 93–115.

Morduch, J. (1998), 'Does microfinance really help the poor? Evidence from flagship programs in Bangladesh', mimeo, Hoover Institution, Stanford University, July.
Morduch, J (1999), 'The microfinance promise', *Journal of Economic Literature*, **XXXVII**, 1569–614.
O'Leary, Christopher J., Piotr Kolodziejczyk and Gyorgy Lazar (1998), 'The net impact of active labor programs in Hungary and Poland', *International Labor Review*, **137** (3), 321–46.
Pitt, M. and S. Khandekar (1998), 'The impact of group-based credit programs on poor households in Bangladesh: Does the gender of participants matter?', *Journal of Political Economy*, **106** (5), 958–96.
Pitt, M. and S. Khandekar (2002), 'Credit programs for the poor and seasonality in rural Bangladesh,' *Journal of Development Studies*, **39** (2), 1–24.
Pitt, M., S. Khandekar, Signe-Mary McKernan and M. Abdul Latif (1999), 'Credit programs for the poor and reproductive behavior in low-income countries: are the reported causal relationships the result of heterogeneity bias?', *Demography*, **36** (1), 1–21.
Pulley, R.V. (1989) 'Making the poor credit worthy', World Bank Discussion Papers, World Bank, Washington, DC.
Radhakrishna, R. and K. Subbarao (1997), 'India's Public Distribution System: A National and International Perspective', World Bank Discussion Paper No. 380, Washington, DC.
Ravallion, M. (1994), *Poverty Comparisons*, Chur, Switzerland: Harwood Academic Publishers.
Ravallion, M. (1999), 'Appraising workfare', *World Bank Research Observer*, **14** (1), 31–48.
Ravallion, M. (2008), 'Evaluating anti-poverty programs', in T. Paul Schultz and John Strauss (eds), *Handbook of Development Economics*, Volume 4, Amsterdam: North-Holland.
Ravallion, M. and S. Chen (2007), 'China's (uneven) growth progress', *Journal of Development Economics*, **82** (1), 1–42.
Ravallion, M., Emanuela Galasso, Teodoro Lazo and Ernesto Philipp (2005), 'What can ex-participants reveal about a program's impact?', *Journal of Human Resources*, **40** (Winter), 208–30.
Ravallion, M. and Q. Wodon (2000), 'Does child labour displace schooling? Evidence on behavioural responses to an enrollment subsidy', *Economic Journal*, **110** (462), C158–C175.
Rawlings, L. and G. Rubio (2005), 'Evaluating the impact of conditional cash transfer programs', *World Bank Research Observer*, **20** (1), 29–55.
Robinson, M. and D. Snodgrass (1987), 'The role of institutional credit in Indonesia's rice intensification program', Development Discussion Paper No. 248, Harvard Institute for International Development, Cambridge, MA.
Ronconi, L. (2007), 'Alternative estimates of the benefit incidence of workfare', Working Paper, Harvard University, Cambridge, MA.
Rozelle, S., A. Park, V. Benziger and C. Ren (1998), 'Targeted poverty investments and economic growth in China', *World Development*, **26** (12), 2137–51.
Ryan, J.G. and T. Walker (1989) *Against the Odds: Village and Household Economies in India's Semi-Arid Tropics*, Baltimore, MD: Johns Hopkins University Press.
Schultz, T. Paul (2004), 'School subsidies for the poor: evaluating the Mexican *PROGRESA* poverty program', *Journal of Development Economics*, **74** (1), 199–250.
Sedlacek Guilherme, Nadeem Ilahi and Emily Gustafsson-Wright (2000), 'Targeted conditional transfer programs in Latin America: an initial survey', mimeo, World Bank, Washington, DC.
Skoufias, E., B. Davis and S. Vega (2001), 'Targeting the poor: an evaluation of the selection of households into *PROGRESA*', *World Development*, **29** (10), 1769–84.
Subbarao, K. (1997), 'Public works as an anti-poverty program: an overview of cross-country experience', *American Journal of Agricultural Economics*, **79**, 678–83.
Subbarao, K., A. Bonerjee, J. Braithwaite, S. Carvalho, K. Ezemenari, C. Graham and A. Thompson (1997), *Safety Net Programs and Poverty Reduction: Lessons from Cross-Country Experience*, Directions in Development, Washington, DC: World Bank.

Szekely, M. (2001), 'Where to from here? Generating capabilities and creating opportunities for the poor', Research Network Working Paper No. R-431, Inter-American Development Bank (IADB), Washington, DC.

Van der Klaauw, Wilbert (2002), 'Estimating the effect of financial aid offers on college enrollment: a regression-discontinuity approach', *International Economic Review*, **43** (4) (November), 1249–87.

Wilson, S. and D.H. Fretwell (1999), 'Public service employment: a review of programs in selected OECD countries and transition economies', Special Protection Discussion Paper No. 9913, World Bank, Washington, DC.

World Bank (1990), *World Development Report 1990*, New York: Oxford University Press.

13 Too hungry to read: is an education subsidy a misguided policy for development?
*Parantap Basu**

1 Introduction

Starting from the work from Mincer (1974), economists debated whether education necessarily promotes growth. There is greater consensus among macroeconomists than microeconomists that education accelerates growth (Barro, 1997). There is considerable disagreement among microeconomists about the returns to schooling (Card, 1999). Krueger and Lindahl (2001) present a detailed survey about these alternative views. Parente and Prescott (2000) make the point that education *per se* does not necessarily promote growth. What matters for growth is not just the level of knowledge but the exploitability of knowledge which in turn depends on the incentive structure of the economy. Parente and Prescott point out that significant barriers to riches exist across the globe because business is not free to innovate. These barriers are primarily due to the presence of irrational regulatory institutions with distortionary tax structure. The policy implication is that various kinds of subsidies to promote innovation could be helpful to promote exploitability of knowledge. An education subsidy could be one of these 'incentivist' policies for growth.[1]

While this focus on incentive is quite insightful in understanding the cross-country disparity in the standard of living, the issue still remains whether a blanket policy of subsidizing education works in economies where a vast portion of the population live in poverty and chronic malnutrition. The effect of malnutrition on productivity is particularly severe due to wastage of muscular strength, illness, infections and the loss of cognitive skills.[2] The issue that I address in this short chapter is the following: is it optimal to subsidize education in economies suffering from malnutrition? In this chapter, I lay out a simple nutritional model of growth and derive the optimal policy implications to address this issue.

The chapter is organized as follows. In the following section, to motivate my theory, I present some stylized facts on malnutrition, growth and public spending on education. Section 3 lays out the model. Section 4 performs some quantitative experiments with the model to compute the output and welfare losses when education subsidy is incorrectly implemented when

355

consumption subsidy is the optimal policy. Section 5 provides a numerical illustration of the welfare gain due to timely policy intervention and welfare loss and resulting increase in cross-country inequality due to incorrect policy of subsidizing education. Section 6 concludes.

2   Some development facts

In this section, I present some cross-country development facts about malnutrition, growth and public spending on education. The malnutrition data are difficult to obtain. The World Development Indicator (WDI, April, 2007) provides two series for malnutrition: (i) malnutrition by height, which is the percentage of children under five whose height is more than two standard deviations below the median for the international reference population of ages 0 to 59 months; (ii) malnutrition by weight, which is the percentage of children under five whose weight is more than two standard deviations below the median reference standard. Given the constraint of notoriously missing data on malnutrition, I only look at the year 2000 for which the maximum number of data points are available. For 25 countries malnutrition height data are available and for 31 countries malnutrition weight data are available.[3]

Tables 13.1a and 13.1b summarize the cross-country data for malnutrition, public spending on education and growth rates over 1999–2000. The data for the last two series are also obtained from the same WDI sources. There is a negative association between malnutrition and growth. The correlation coefficients are -0.41 and -0.25 for respective malnutrition series. There is also an inverse relation between public spending on education and growth; the respective correlation coefficients are -0.42 and -0.28. The relation between public spending on education and malnutrition is also inverse; the correlations are -0.10 and -0.25. Except for height malnutrition and public education spending all these correlations are statistically significant at a level not exceeding 10 percent.

Out of these three negative correlations one of them is surprising. If public spending lowers malnutrition and malnutrition decreases growth, one expects using the chain rule that public spending should promote growth while the data tell the reverse.[4] Figure 13.1 plots the relation between public spending and growth for height malnutrition data, which is of central interest in this chapter. Although one cannot draw any causal relationship based on these correlations, based on this anomaly, one can at least question whether education is really a kingpin for growth for these economies subject to malnutrition.[5]

The questions that I pose in this chapter are the following. Is this policy emphasis on education misplaced for economies suffering from chronic malnutrition? Does education subsidy necessarily promote growth in

Table 13.1a   Malnutrition, public spending on education and growth

Country/group	Malnutrition prevalence, height for age (% of children under 5)	Public spending on education, total (% of GDP)	% GDP growth 1999–2000
Trinidad and Tobago	3.60	3.80	5.67
Dominican Republic	6.10	2.29	6.54
Russian Federation	10.60	2.94	10.00
Guyana	10.60	8.48	−1.67
Tunisia	12.30	6.84	3.52
Armenia	12.90	3.24	6.52
Colombia	13.50	4.19	1.19
Ukraine	15.90	4.17	6.97
The Gambia	19.20	2.73	2.23
Azerbaijan	19.60	3.85	10.20
Gabon	20.60	3.93	−0.21
Namibia	23.60	7.89	1.22
Mongolia	24.60	6.67	0.23
Senegal	25.40	3.38	0.49
Swaziland	30.20	6.19	−0.45
Tajikistan	30.90	2.33	7.03
Sierra Leone	33.80	4.95	0.74
Lao PDR	42.40	1.50	3.35
Rwanda	42.60	2.75	−0.95
Cambodia	44.60	1.67	6.19
Bangladesh	44.70	2.47	3.87
Lesotho	46.10	10.11	0.56
Malawi	49.00	4.14	−1.08
Ethiopia	51.50	4.02	2.88
Burundi	56.80	3.25	−2.49
Correlation malnutrition–spending education	−0.10		
Correlation malnutrition–GDP growth	−0.41*		
Correlation GDP growth–spending education	−0.42*		

Note: * Significant at about 5% level.

economies prone to malnutrition? I lay out a simple growth model in the next section to address these questions.

3 The model
Consider a simple one-sector model of growth. A single good is produced with the help of some reproducible factor (say human capital) using the following production technology:

Table 13.1b   Malnutrition, public spending on education and growth

Country/group	Malnutrition prevalence, weight for age (% of children under 5)	Public spending on education, total (% of GDP)	% GDP growth 1999–2000
Burundi	45.10	3.25	−2.49
Guyana	13.60	8.48	−1.67
Kenya	21.20	5.19	−1.62
Malawi	25.40	4.14	−1.08
Rwanda	24.30	2.75	−0.95
Equatorial Guinea	18.60	0.63	−0.90
Swaziland	10.30	6.19	−0.45
Gabon	12.00	3.93	−0.21
Guinea	32.70	1.85	−0.19
Mongolia	12.70	6.67	0.23
Senegal	22.70	3.38	0.49
Lesotho	18.00	10.11	0.56
Sierra Leone	27.20	4.95	0.74
Colombia	6.70	4.19	1.19
Namibia	24.00	7.89	1.22
Romania	3.20	2.89	2.17
The Gambia	17.20	2.73	2.23
Uganda	23.00	2.46	2.38
Ethiopia	47.20	4.02	2.88
Lao PDR	40.40	1.50	3.35
Tunisia	4.00	6.84	3.52
Indonesia	24.60	1.36	3.55
Bangladesh	47.70	2.47	3.87
Kyrgyz Republic	6.60	2.94	4.36
Trinidad & Tobago	5.90	3.80	5.67
Cambodia	45.20	1.67	6.19
Armenia	3.00	3.24	6.52
Dominican Republic	4.60	2.29	6.54
Ukraine	3.20	4.17	6.97
Russian Federation	5.50	2.94	10.00
Azerbaijan	16.80	3.85	10.20
Correlation malnutrition–spending education		−0.25**	
Correlation malnutrition–GDP growth		−0.25**	
Correlation GDP growth–spending education		−0.28**	

Note: ** Significant at the 10% level.

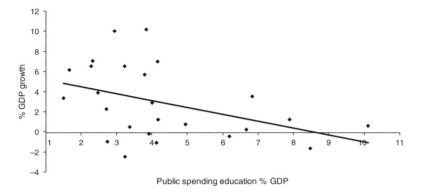

Figure 13.1 Plot of GDP growth and public spending

$$y_t = \left[\frac{c_t}{\bar{c}}\right]^{\theta} h_t \text{ when } c_t < \bar{c} \text{ with } 0 \leq \theta \leq 1, \qquad (13.1)$$

$$y_t = h_t \quad \text{when } c_t \geq \bar{c}, \qquad (13.2)$$

where y_t = level of GDP at date t, c_t is consumption at date t, $\bar{c}$ is the basic minimum nutritional level of consumption, and h_t is the level of human capital at date t.

This production function (13.1) captures the following features about the effect of malnutrition on productivity. Besides human capital, the level of nutrition measured by $(c_t/\bar{c})$ also appears as input in the production function. If the current consumption is below the basic nutritional minimum $\bar{c}$, the level of output increases until the basic nutritional minimum is reached. Once the consumption reaches the threshold nutrition level $\bar{c}$, it has no further effect on production. The production function then turns out to be a familiar Rebelo (1991) linear form.

Some clarifications about the production parameter θ is in order. θ represents the output elasticity of nutrition $(c_t/\bar{c})$. Given θ, when c_t rises towards $\bar{c}$, output rises. The rise in production is higher in economies with a higher θ. In this sense, θ represents the nutrition intensity of the technology. For θ equal to zero, nutrition has no effect on output. The larger the value of θ, the greater the adverse effect of low nutrition on output in an undernourished economy.

The single good, y_t, can be used for two purposes, consumption (c_t) and investment (i_t). This means that the economy is subject to the following resource constraint:

$$c_t + i_t = y_t. \qquad (13.3)$$

In the present context, investment basically means education which gives rise to new human capital following the education-investment technology:

$$h_{t+1} = (1 - \delta)h_t + \pi i_t \tag{13.4}$$

where $\delta \in [0, 1]$ is a parameter capturing the rate of depreciation of human capital. In other words, $1 - \delta$ is the degree of intergenerational transfer of knowledge following the tradition of Mankiw et al. (1992) and Benabou (2000).

Investment versus consumption subsidy

The parameter π represents the subsidy to investment relative to consumption which is the central policy parameter in the present context. Hereafter I shall call π the 'relative education subsidy'. I do not model the financing of these subsidies.[6] If π exceeds unity, it means that education is subsidized proportionally more than consumption and the reverse is true if π is less than unity.[7] Alternatively, the inverse of π is the relative price of investment goods in terms of consumption[8] which is the Tobin's q of human capital. A larger π due to greater subsidy to education means that an extra dose of investment is very productive which makes Tobin's q lower.[9] To prevent the Tobin's q of human capital from imploding or exploding, I assume that π stays in a compact set:

$$\underline{\pi} \leq \pi \leq \overline{\pi}. \tag{13.4a}$$

These lower and upper bounds for π are determined endogenously, which are of central interest in this chapter.

The economy consists of finitely lived altruistic agents as in Barro (1974) with a degree of intergenerational altruism parameterized by a positive fraction β. The intergenerational welfare (W_t) of the tth generation is given by:[10]

$$W_t = \sum_{s=0}^{\infty} \beta^s \ln c_{t+s}. \tag{13.5}$$

At the start of date t, the household devotes h_t units of human resources in the production process using the production technology (13.1). It then consumes c_t and invests i_t in children's education. The tth cohort thus maximizes (13.5) subject to (13.1) through (13.4), given h_0.

I shall solve the model for two scenarios: (i) an economy with no malnutrition, and (ii) an economy with malnutrition. I shall then examine the optimal education subsidy implication for each of these economies.

An economy with no malnutrition
It is easy to verify that in the case of no malnutrition (with the production function (13.2)) the economy exhibits Rebelo (1991) type endogenous growth. The growth equation takes the form:

$$\frac{c_{t+1}}{c_t} = \beta(\pi + 1 - \delta). \qquad (13.6)$$

Appendix 13A shows the details of the derivation of (13.6). A higher investment subsidy π unambiguously promotes long-run growth in an economy with no malnutrition. Thus the optimal education subsidy for an economy with no malnutrition is the maximal subsidy, $\bar{\pi}$.

An economy with malnutrition
The story is different for an economy with malnutrition. The social planner in this economy maximizes (13.5) taking into account that the production function is (13.1). The first order condition which is derived in appendix 13A (see equation 13A.2) is given by:

$$\frac{c_{t+1}}{c_t} = \beta\left[\pi\left(\frac{c_{t+1}}{\bar{c}}\right)^{\theta} + 1 - \delta\right] \cdot \left[\frac{1 - \theta h_t \bar{c}^{-\theta} c_t^{\theta-1}}{1 - \theta h_{t+1} \bar{c}^{-\theta} c_{t+1}^{\theta-1}}\right]. \qquad (13.7)$$

Appendix 13A also shows that the shadow price of the human capital (λ_t) is given by:

$$\lambda_t = \frac{\beta^t}{c_t} . [\pi - \theta \pi h_t c_t^{\theta-1} \bar{c}^{-\theta}]^{-1}. \qquad (13.7a)$$

For θ equal to zero (no nutrition effect), this shadow price is simply the discounted utility value of the Tobin's q of capital, π^{-1}. For non-zero θ, the adverse nutrition effect further raises this shadow price of capital. The reason is that a unit investment today has a higher opportunity cost because it not only entails consumption sacrifice today but also lowers total factor productivity (which is $(c_t/\bar{c})^{\theta}$) today through the nutrition channel described in (13.1).

Our central concern here is in the long-run steady state for this under-nourished economy. We have the following lemma:

Lemma 1: The undernourished economy is a stationary economy with no long-run balanced growth.

Proof: See Appendix 13A.

Since there is no long-run balanced growth in this economy, the only steady state is where both consumption and capital stock are *stationary* in levels. It is easy to verify from (13.7) that the steady state level of consumption (call it c^*) is:

$$c^* = \left[\frac{1 - \beta(1 - \delta)}{\beta\pi}\right]^{1/\theta} \bar{c}. \qquad (13.8)$$

Plugging (13.8) into the steady-state resource constraint, one obtains the following expression for the steady-state level of human capital:[11]

$$h^* = \frac{\bar{c}[1 - \beta(1 - \delta)]^{1/\theta}(\beta\pi)^{1 - (1/\theta)}}{(1 - \beta)}. \qquad (13.9)$$

For this economy to stay in a malnutrition steady state, it is both necessary and sufficient that the term in the square brackets in (13.8) must be less than unity which determines the lower bound ($\underline{\pi}$) of the relative education subsidy parameter in (13.4a) as:

$$\pi > \frac{1 - \beta(1 - \delta)}{\beta} = \underline{\pi}. \qquad (13.10)$$

The immediate implication is the following lemma.

Lemma 2: For any relative education subsidy higher than the lower bound in (13.10), an undernourished economy will stagnate.

A misguided policy of education subsidy
It is evident from (13.8) and (13.9) that in this environment, any policy to increase the relative education subsidy π above the lower bound (13.10) will depress both the steady-state consumption and the human capital further. Excessive education subsidy exacerbates poverty and stagnation. This result seems quite counterintuitive but it can be easily understood if one pays close attention to the nutrition-based production technology (13.1). An education subsidy (higher π) will provide incentive to invest more and cut back consumption. Although in the short run this may promote human capital depending on the relative strengths of substitution and wealth effects, in the long run this incentive effect on investment will be overwhelmed by the adverse malnutrition effect of lower consumption on the total factor productivity. Thus the long run effect of an education subsidy on the human capital base h^* is negative.

In summary, we have the following proposition:

Proposition 1: An economy with an initial capital stock $h_0 \leq h^*$ and initial education subsidy subject to the inequality (13.10) falls in a poverty trap of malnutrition and no growth.

Unlike the traditional Solow model, the long-run equilibrium of this economy with malnutrition is *path-dependent*. If the economy starts from a sufficiently low level of human capital, it will never grow and will remain at a low-level equilibrium trap (c^*, h^*).

Optimal education subsidy
The optimal education subsidy must facilitate the economy to transit from a regime of stagnation (13.8) to positive growth (13.6). To ensure this, the relative education subsidy parameter must be chosen such that $c^* = \bar{c}$. This requires a choice of π at the minimum possible level which means that (13.10) must hold as an equality. Once the economy makes such a transition, π should be set to its maximum level $\bar{\pi}$ which will ensure a target growth rate from the viewpoint of the policy maker.

Defining $\beta = 1/(1 + \rho)$ where ρ is the rate of time preference, the following proposition holds.

Proposition 2: The optimal relative education subsidy for the malnourished economy is :

$$\pi = \underline{\pi} = \delta + \rho \quad \text{when } c_t < \bar{c}, \quad (13.11a)$$

$$\pi = \bar{\pi} \quad \text{when } c_t \geq \bar{c}. \quad (13.11b)$$

Given that the depreciation parameter δ is a fraction, π is likely to be less than unity for a plausible value of ρ. This means that consumption should be more subsidized than investment in an undernourished economy.

4 Output and welfare consequences of an incorrect education subsidy

In this section, I pose the following question. Let the government in an undernourished economy instead of subsidizing consumption more than investment do the opposite. What are the output and welfare losses relative to a scenario where the government implements the correct policy of subsidizing consumption more?

Start off from a *baseline level* with a unit value of π, which means either no subsidy to any activity or equal proportional subsidies.[12] Focus only on the steady state, which means that we plug (13.8) into (13.5) setting $c_t = c^*$. Evaluating at π equal to unity, one obtains the following steady state welfare of such a baseline undernourished economy with no policy:[13]

$$\widetilde{W} = \frac{1}{1 - \beta} \ln \left\{ \left[\frac{1 - \beta(1 - \delta)}{\beta} \right]^{1/\theta} \bar{c} \right\}, \qquad (13.12)$$

where $\widetilde{W}$ denotes the steady-state welfare in the benchmark case of no policy, with '~' standing for no policy. Let the government now intervene at date T by tilting the subsidy wheel either to consumption or investment.[14] This means that π is switched on from unity to either less than unity or greater than unity. We analyze two policy scenarios: (i) good policy where the government correctly implements a policy of subsidizing consumption ($\pi < 1$) following proposition 2; (ii) bad policy where the government implements an incorrect policy of subsidizing investment ($\pi > 1$) when it should subsidize consumption instead.

The steady-state welfare (W^{good}) from such a good policy is given by:

$$W^{good}\ln \tilde{c}^* + \beta \ln \tilde{c}^* + \beta^2 \ln \tilde{c}^* + \ldots + \beta^{T-1} \ln \tilde{c}^* + \beta^T \ln \bar{c}$$

$$+ \beta^{T+1} \ln (\bar{c} \beta (\bar{\pi} + 1 - \delta)) + \beta^{T+2} \ln (\bar{c} \beta^2 (\bar{\pi} + 1 - \delta)^2 + \ldots \infty,$$

$$(13.13)$$

where $\tilde{c}^*$ is the steady-state consumption in a malnourished economy with no policy which is given by (13.8) evaluated at $\pi = 1$. This steady-state welfare reflects the fact that without any policy the consumption is at the malnourished steady state until the policy intervention occurs at date T. At date T, the government rightly switches π from unity to π which makes consumption exactly equal to the threshold $\bar{c}$. After date T, the consumption starts growing at the rate dictated by the growth equation (13.6).[15] Normalizing $\bar{c}$ at unity, equation (13.13) can be simplified as (proof is relegated to the appendix):

$$W^{good} = \frac{1 - \beta^T}{1 - \beta} \ln \tilde{c}^* + \frac{\beta^{T+1}}{(1 - \beta)^2} \ln \beta (\bar{\pi} + 1 - \delta). \qquad (13.14)$$

The steady-state welfare from a bad policy of excessive relative education subsidy (call it π_{bad}) reflects the fact that the malnourished economy experiences a further worsening of its consumption from $\tilde{c}^*$ to c^*_{bad} following the policy intervention at date T.[16]

$$W^{bad} = \frac{1 - \beta^T}{1 - \beta} \ln \tilde{c}^* + \frac{\beta^T}{1 - \beta} \ln c^*_{bad}, \qquad (13.15)$$

where:

$$c^*_{bad} = \left\{ \frac{1 - \beta(1 - \delta)}{\beta \pi_{bad}} \right\}^{1/\theta}. \tag{13.15a}$$

The derivation of (13.15) is outlined in the appendix.

5 Numerical application

In this section, I perform some numerical computations to illustrate the effects of various subsidy policies on output and welfare of the economy. The immediate challenge is to set the parameters at reasonable levels. The relevant structural parameters are $\beta, \delta, \theta, \bar{c}$. The threshold consumption $\bar{c}$ is normalized at the unit level. The parameter β represents the degree of intergenerational altruism. The same parameter was calibrated in Bandyopadhyay and Basu (2005) in the context of cross-country growth-inequality correlation. Following them, I set β equal to 0.83. Note that the conventional value of β in the range of 0.95 to 0.99 (as in Prescott, 1986) does not apply here because of the altruistic nature of the utility function. Each generation lives for one period which lasts for many years. Prescott's β estimate which is relevant for annual data thus will not apply in the present context.

The parameter δ is the rate of knowledge depreciation. Alternatively $1 - \delta$ is the degree of intergenerational transfer of knowledge. The same parameter again appears in Basu and Bandyopadhyay (2005) where it was calibrated to be 0.0316. We use their estimate here.

Since the nutrition elasticity parameter θ is too model specific, to the best of my knowledge there is no published estimate of it. In the absence of any information about this parameter, I fix it at the unit level. This means that output increases linearly with respect to nutrition until the threshold consumption $\bar{c}$ is reached which is a reasonable assumption.

The remaining parameters are the lower bound $\underline{\pi}$ and the upper bound $\bar{\pi}$ for the relative education subsidy. Given the chosen values of β and δ, using (13.10) one obtains $\underline{\pi}$ equal to 0.2364. As mentioned earlier, the upper bound $\bar{\pi}$ is assumed to be fixed by the policy authority to achieve a certain target growth rate. Since there is no conventional wisdom for such a target, I use the average of the annual growth rates for the sample of countries described in Tables 13.1a and 13.b. Based on the country growth rates in these two tables which were obtained from WDI sources, the average growth rate for countries with height malnutrition data is 2.43 percent and the same for countries with weight malnutrition data is 2.61 percent. I take the average of these two growth rates to arrive at an estimate of a target growth rate of 2.52 percent. Given this target growth, $\bar{\pi}$ is estimated to be 0.2667 using the growth equation (13.6).

Table 13.2   Baseline parameter values

β	0.83
δ	0.0316
$\underline{\pi}$	0.2364
$\overline{\pi}$	0.2667
θ	1
$\bar{c}$	1
T	1

The lower and upper bounds for relative education subsidies computed this way are thus 0.2364 and 0.2667. These two bounds are very close to each other, which suggests that greater consumption subsidy than education subsidy is desirable in all these countries irrespective of whether they are experiencing malnutrition stagnation or growth.[17]

The date of intervention T is chosen at 1 which means that the government promptly intervenes in the first period following the initial condition of malnutrition and poverty. We shall see later that T equal to unity is the optimal time to intervene. Table 13.2 summarizes the baseline parameter values.

Steady-state output under alternative policies
Suppose the economy starts off from a malnutrition steady state without any policy. Given the production function (13.1), the steady-state output is given by $(c^*/\bar{c})^\theta h^*$ where c^* and h^* are given by (13.8) and (13.9). In Table 13.3, I compute this steady-state output for three policy environments: (i) baseline of no policy which means that $\pi = 1$, (ii) optimal policy which means that $\pi = \underline{\pi}$ based on Proposition 2, and (iii) suboptimal policy of excessive education subsidy, which means that $\pi > 1$. There is an unambiguous loss of output compared to the baseline level if education is subsidized more than consumption. The output gain is of a quadruple order if the government rightly tilts the wheel towards consumption subsidy. This numerical exercise sheds light on the apparent empirical puzzle outlined in Section 2 that public education spending lowers growth.

Welfare gain due to timely intervention
Table 13.4 reports the comparison of the steady-state welfare from no policy ($\widetilde{W}$), good policy and bad policy for various dates of intervention T based on (13.12) and (13.14). The welfare gain is at a maximum if the intervention occurs timely at date 1. Such a welfare gain basically reveals the fact that the social benefit for policy intervention exceeds the cost. A delay in intervening is costly for society. Just a delay of one period (from $T = 1$

Table 13.3 Steady-state output from alternative policies

No Policy ($\pi = 1$)	Optimal policy ($\pi = \underline{\pi}$)	Excessive Education Subsidy ($\pi > 1$)	
0.27	1.15	$\pi = 1.1$	0.24
		$\pi = 1.2$	0.22
		$\pi = 1.3$	0.21
		$\pi = 1.4$	0.19
		$\pi = 1.5$	0.18

Table 13.4 Steady-state welfare gain due to timely intervention

T	$W^{good} - \tilde{W}$
1	76.35
2	6.33
3	5.25
4	4.36
5	3.62

to $T = 2$) in designing optimal policy leads to a 92 percent loss of societal welfare. The welfare gain from intervention asymptotically approaches zero, as is evident from (13.12) and (13.14) as T becomes larger. The same comment holds for the difference between W^{good} and W^{bad}. This difference becomes smaller as T gets larger. The lesson is that the policy intervention of any form is inconsequential if it is too late.

Implications for cross-country inequality
The model has sharp implications for cross-country disparity in output and living standards. If a correct policy of consumption subsidy is chosen right from the very outset for a malnourished economy, it will get the economy out of the poverty trap soon, and there is a chance of growth convergence. On the contrary, if a policy is misguided and becomes too obsessed with education, it could easily exacerbate cross-country inequality between poor and rich economies. The *barriers to riches* arise due to wrong choice of education subsidy instead of consumption subsidy in these malnutrition-ridden economies.

6 Conclusion
While there is a near consensus that barriers to riches arise due to lack of incentive to innovate and educate, the question that is often ignored in the

literature is whether these types of incentives are perverse in economies suffering from massive malnutrition and poverty. I start with some development facts that the public spending on education instead of promoting growth actually lowers growth for a sample of countries with malnutrition. Motivated by these stylized facts, I develop a stylized growth model of malnutrition with a nutrition-based production function. Education subsidy is a misguided policy in these economies. It exacerbates poverty and malnutrition. The optimal policy is greater consumption subsidy than education subsidy. Numerical analysis with the model reveals that the output loss due to incorrect policy of excessive education subsidy could be substantial. This explains the apparent empirical puzzle why public spending lowers growth while one expects a positive correlation between these two variables. The quantitative analysis also reveals that the welfare gain from timely policy intervention is enormous. The present analysis ignores short-run dynamics and only focuses on the long-run effects of various types of policies. A useful extension of this work is to examine the short-run dynamics of output in response to various policy interventions.

Notes

*   I thank Robert Brent for constructive comments. Mauricio Armellini is acknowledged for able research assistance. Any errors are mine.

1.   Minford et al. (2007) call these Parente–Prescott-type policies 'incentivist' and contrast this with more direct 'interventionist' policy such as public spending on R&D. Using postwar data they find evidence in favor of 'incentivist' policy.

2.   Dasgupta and Ray (1986, 1987) examine the implications of malnutrition for unemployment and argue that asset redistribution and food transfer programs can be helpful policy tools.

3.   Serbia and Montenegro and Niger are dropped from the sample because of outlying growth rates during 1999–2000.

4.   Viewed from a pure statistical perspective, correlation coefficients may not necessarily follow the rule of transitivity. The transitivity depends on the strength of bivariate correlations. For a detailed exposition on this, see Langford et al. (2001).

5.   It is also noteworthy that public spending on education includes various types of spending on public education and, therefore, it does not clearly reflect incentive-based policy advocated by Parente and Prescott (2000). However, one can also observe from the data that the public spending on education is substantially higher for many stagnating countries suffering from chronic malnutrition. For example, a near-stagnant economy such as Mongolia with a growth rate of 0.23 percent devotes 6.67 percent of its GDP to education when about 24 percent of its children suffer from height malnutrition. A similar story holds for Namibia.

6.   Think of π as a proportional education subsidy given by an external agency like the World Bank to less-developed countries.

7.   To see this, instead of π define ω_c and ω_i as proportional subsidies to consumption and investment respectively which means that the resource constraint (13.3) can be written as:

$$c_t + i_t = y_t + \omega_c c_t + \omega_i i_t$$

which can be rewritten as:

$$(1 - \omega_c)c_t + (1 - \omega_i)i_t = y_t.$$

Defining $i_t = h_{t+1} - (1 - \delta)h_t$, and noting that at date t the decision variables are c_t and h_{t+1} it is straightforward to verify that $\partial c_t/\partial h_{t+1} = -(1 - \omega_i)/(1 - \omega_c)$. Now define $\pi = (1 - \omega_c)/(1 - \omega_i)$. Thus $\pi > 1$ is equivalent to $\omega_i > \omega_c$.

8. To see this clearly employ (13.3) and (13.4) to get the following derivative $\partial c_t/\partial h_{t+1} = -1/\pi$ which means that the opportunity cost of acquiring an extra unit of human capital today (h_{t+1}) is the forgone consumption (c_t) of $1/\pi$.

9. As in Cummins and Violante (2002), Fisher (2006) and Basu and Guraiglia (2008), π can be thought of as an *investment-specific technology parameter*. Alternatively, following Gollin et al. (2004), the inverse of π can be interpreted as the barrier to investment which can be influenced by policy.

10. Think of cohorts in each generation having a one period life and they care about their offspring's welfare to the extent β. The tth generation's welfare is thus specified as: $W_t = \ln c_t + \beta W_{t+1}$. Expanding this relationship recursively forward we obtain (13.5).

11. In the steady state, the resource constraint (13.3) upon the use of (13.1) and (13.4) reduces to: $\pi c^* + \delta h^* = \pi(c^*/\bar{c})^{\theta}h^*$. Plugging (13.8) into this steady-state resource constraint, one obtains (13.9).

12. Refer to note 7 to verify that $\pi = 1$ means either $\omega_c = \omega_i = 0$ or simply $\omega_c = \omega_i$.

13. We assume here that the parameter values are such that the malnourished economy is sustainable, meaning $c^* < \bar{c}$.

14. Minford et al. (2007) distinguish between two kinds of growth-enhancing policies: (i) incentivist in the form of education subsidy; (ii) activist in the form of R&D spending.

15. The transition from no growth to a growth regime takes only one period due to the nature of the technology specified in (13.1) and (13.2).

16. I ignore here the short run impact on the welfare following this policy intervention. In principle, in (13.15) there will be a transition stage from old steady state to new steady state when consumption may rise or fall depending on the relative strengths of the substitution and wealth effects of an increase in education subsidy. I have carried out simulations with a loglinearized version of the model which suggests that the output loss also occurs in the short run in response to excessive education subsidy. The details are available from the author upon request.

17. One could, in principle, contest this result arguing that the upper bound for π was based on a very modest target growth rate of 2.52 percent. If the policy maker strives for a higher target growth rate than this, could there be a case for an education subsidy along the growth trajectory? Note that given the values of β and δ, for having a greater education subsidy than consumption subsidy ($\pi > 1$) the policy maker needs to target an implausibly high growth rate. For example even a tiny 1 percent higher education subsidy than consumption subsidy (which means that $\pi = 1.01$) requires a target growth rate of 64 percent. This result is of course dependent on the stylized nature of the model because I assume here that the education subsidy parameter π is the only vehicle of growth. Moreover, setting $\bar{\pi}$ to maximize growth alone has its costs which are not specified in the present model due to the absence of a government budget constraint. Whether growth maximization *per se* is socially desirable or not is a debatable issue. Societal welfare depends on both growth and redistributive considerations which sometimes conflict with each other. This is an issue which is beyond the scope of this chapter. See Bandyopadhyay and Basu (2001) for a model where growth and distribution jointly determine steady-state welfare. The bottom line here is that even if education subsidy could be made desirable by a policy maker with an extreme high priority for growth, the central result still holds that such a policy is not optimal in an economy cursed with malnutrition.

References

Bandyopadhyay, D. and P. Basu (2001), 'Optimal capital tax in a growth model with discrete occupational choice', *Australian Economic Papers*, **40**, 111–32.

Bandyopadhay, D and P. Basu (2005), 'What drives the cross-country growth-inequality correlation?', *Canadian Journal of Economics*, **38**, 1272–97.

Barro, R.J. (1974), 'Are government bonds net wealth?', *Journal of Political Economy*, **82**, 1095–117.

Barro, Robert J. (1997), *Determinants of Economic Growth: A Cross-Country Empirical Study*, Lionel Robbins Lectures, Cambridge, MA: MIT Press.

Basu, P. and A. Guariglia (2008), 'Does low education explain the delayed industrialization?', *Southern Economic Journal*, **75** (1), 104–27.

Benabou, R. (2000), 'Unequal societies: income distribution and the social contract', *American Economic Review*, **90**, 96–129.

Card, D. (1999), 'The causal effect of schooling on earnings', in O. Ashenfelter and D. Card (eds), *Handbook of Labor Economics*, Amsterdam: North-Holland.

Cummins, J. and G. Violante (2002), 'Investment-specific technical change in the U.S. (1947–2000): measurement and macroeconomic consequences', *Review of Economic Dynamics*, **5**, 243–84.

Dasgupta, P. and D. Ray (1986), 'Inequality as a determinant of malnutrition and unemployment: theory', *Economy Journal*, **96** (384), 1011–34.

Dasgupta, P. and D. Ray (1987), 'Inequality as a determinant of malnutrition and unemployment: policy', *Economic Journal*, **97** (385), 177–88.

Fisher, J.D.M. (2006), 'The dymanic effects of neutral and investment specific technology shocks', *Journal of Political Economy*, **114** (3), 413–50.

Gollin, D., S. Parente and R. Rogerson (2004), 'Farm work, home work and international productivity differences', *Review of Economic Dynamics*, **7** (4), 827–50.

Krueger, A.B and M. Lindahl (2001), 'Education for growth: why and for whom?', *Journal of Economic Literature*, **32**, 1101–36.

Langford E., N. Schwertman and M. Owens (2001), 'Is the property of being positively correlated transitive?', *The American Statistician*, **55** (4), 322–5.

Mankiw, G.N., D. Romer and D. Weil (1992), 'A contribution to the empirics of economic growth', *Quarterly Journal of Economics*, **107**, 407–37.

Mincer, J. (1974), *Schooling, Earnings, and Experience*, New York: Columbia University Press.

Minford, P., D. Meenagh and J. Wang (2007), 'Growth and relative living standards: testing barriers to riches using postwar panel data', Cardiff Business School Working Paper, E2007/12.

Parente, S. and E.C. Prescott (2000), *Barriers to Riches*, Cambridge, MA: MIT Press.

Prescott, E.C. (1986), 'Theory ahead of business cycle measurement', *Quarterly Review*, **10** (4), 1–15.

Rebelo, S. (1991), 'Long run policy analysis and long run growth', *Journal of Political Economy*, **99**, 500–521.

Appendix 13A

Derivation of (13.6)
The Lagrange function is:

$$L = \sum_{t=0}^{\infty} \beta^t \ln c_t + \sum_{t=0}^{\infty} \mu_t [\pi h_t + (1 - \delta) h_t - \pi c_t - h_{t+1}], \quad (13A.1)$$

where μ_t is the Lagrange multiplier associated with the flow budget constraint (13.3). The first order conditions are:

$$c_t : \mu_t \pi = \frac{\beta^t}{c_t}, \quad (13A.2)$$

$$h_{t+1} : -\mu_t + \mu_{t+1}(A\pi + 1 - \delta) = 0. \quad (13A.3)$$

Use (13A.2) and (13A.3) to eliminate the Lagrange multipliers to obtain (13.6).

Derivation of (13.7)
The Lagrange function is:

$$L = \sum_{t=0}^{\infty} \beta^t \ln c_t + \sum_{t=0}^{\infty} \lambda_t \left[\left(\frac{c_t}{\bar{c}} \right)^{\theta} \pi h_t + (1 - \delta) h_t - \pi c_t - h_{t+1} \right]. \quad (13A.4)$$

The first-order conditions are

$$c_t : \lambda_t [\pi - \theta \pi h_t c_t^{\theta-1} \bar{c}^{-\theta}] = \frac{\beta^t}{c_t}, \quad (13A.5)$$

$$h_{t+1} : -\lambda_t + \lambda_{t+1} \left[\pi \left(\frac{c_{t+1}}{\bar{c}} \right)^{\theta} + 1 - \delta \right] = 0. \quad (13A.6)$$

Using (13.A.5) and (13.A.6) one obtains (13.7).

Derivation of (13.14)

$$W^{good} = \frac{1 - \beta^T}{1 - \beta} \ln \tilde{c}^* + \beta^{T+1} [\ln(\bar{\pi} + 1 - \delta)] \cdot [1 + 2\beta + 3\beta^2 + \ldots \infty].$$

Define the terms in the Second square brackets as S. Note the following relationship:

$$(1 - \beta) S = 1 + \beta + \beta^2 + \ldots + \infty,$$

which means that

$$S = \frac{1}{(1 - \beta)^2}$$

This proves (13.14). //

Derivation of (13.15)
Note that:

$$W^{bad} = (\ln \tilde{c}* + \beta \ln \tilde{c}* + \ldots + \beta^{T-1} \ln \tilde{c}*) + (\beta^T \ln c* + \beta^{T+1} \ln c* + \ldots \infty).$$

It is now straightforward to verify (13.14). //

Proof of Lemma 1
Assume the contrary. Let there be a balanced growth path. Along such a balanced growth path, h_t/c_t (call it ω) and the growth rate (call it G) must be time invariant. We can rewrite (13.7) and the resource constraint (13.3) as follows:

$$G = \beta \left[\pi \left(\frac{Gc_t}{\bar{c}} \right)^{\theta} + 1 - \delta \right] \cdot \left[\frac{1 - \theta \omega \bar{c}^{-\theta} c_t^{\theta}}{1 - \theta \omega \bar{c}^{-\theta} c_{t+1}^{\theta}} \right], \qquad (13A.7)$$

$$\omega^{-1} + \frac{G - 1 + \delta}{\pi} = \left(\frac{c_t}{\bar{c}} \right)^{\theta}. \qquad (13A.8)$$

A simple inspection of (13.A.7) and (13.A.8) reveals that for any nonzero θ there exists no such time invariant pair of G and ω which satisfy the first-order condition and the resource constraint because of the presence of c_t in both equations. //

14 Project finance and cost–benefit analysis
Peggy B. Musgrave

1 Introduction

This chapter examines the proposition that the choice of financing public projects significantly affects the outcome of their cost–benefit evaluations. Both tax and loan finance are considered. For theoretical discussion of the essential components of cost–benefit analysis such as the appropriate discount rate, shadow pricing, the opportunity cost of real inputs and the estimation of real benefits, the reader is referred to other chapters in this volume and to Layard (1972), Drèze and Stern (1987), Layard and Glaister (1994), and Brent (2007).

The theoretical framework for cost–benefit analysis has developed through many writings that usually did not explicitly include the costs and benefits of the financial flows associated with the project but tended to concentrate on the real benefits and opportunity costs of the resource inputs. Attention was focused on the choice of discount rate to allow for ancillary welfare effects often in a second-best world.[1] Feldstein (1974), on the other hand, suggested an algorithm for project evaluation which allowed explicitly for the benefits and costs of the money flows associated with the project valued in their 'consumption equivalent' form, while proposing the private rate of time preference as the appropriate social rate of time preference, or social rate of discount, an assumption followed here.

We begin with a full employment economy with price stability, a customary assumption in the application of cost–benefit analysis. Markets are largely competitive though they may be distorted by the presence of taxes. Financial markets are of a classical, loanable funds type. The economy is closed so that all borrowing is from domestic sources. Considerations of income distribution (other than its effect on resource allocation) are disregarded. These simplifying but restrictive assumptions are left for later consideration.

2 Financial flows associated with a project

The financial flows associated with the project include the following:

1. cash expenditures for the project, (E), a financial inflow to the private sector;

2.   taxes applied to finance the project, (*T*), a financial outflow from the private sector;
3.   user fees or payments for the services of the project, (*F*), a financial outflow from the private sector;
4.   debt (*L*) incurred to finance the project or repayment of debt (*R*), a financial outflow and inflow, respectively; and
5.   interest payments (*N*) on the debt, a financial inflow.

Accepting consumption to be the appropriate criterion of economic welfare, it is not correct to assume that $1 of a financial component always corresponds to $1 added to or subtracted from private consumption, for each may generate saving as well as consumption. To obtain the full consumption equivalence of these flows, therefore, the saving component (in a fully employed economy) is assumed to be equivalent to investment, and the investment is then converted to its consumption equivalence by allowing for its rate of return, the reinvestment behavior and propensity to consume and save of its investors. This is then added to the direct consumption effects. The two streams of reinvestment and saving (= investment) are combined and accumulated over the chosen time span of the project evaluation. The present value of the consumption generated by this accumulated investment gives the shadow value or opportunity cost for each financial component. Combined with the real benefits (*B*) and real resource costs (*O*), all are presented in present value terms to give the present value of net benefits. This approach thus allows comparison of the opportunity costs of alternative methods of financing the project. For the time being it is assumed that there are no taxes in place when the project is introduced that might further affect the opportunity costs and benefits. Thus the present value of net benefits (*NB*) of a project with life of *n* years may be shown as:

$$P.V.(NB) = \sum_{t=1}^{t=n} \frac{B_t - O_t + E_t - T_t - L_t + R_t + N_t - F_t}{(1 + d)^t}, \qquad (14.1)$$

with each financial item expressed in its equivalent consumption value or opportunity cost, plus signs indicating a benefit and minus signs as a cost. The value of net benefits under this approach is then considered to be the standard by which all projects are evaluated. With an unconstrained budget, acceptance requires a positive value for net benefits, while with a constrained budget that project with the highest net benefits is chosen over alternative projects, allowing for the nature of the budgetary constraint.

Annual benefits and costs emanate from the social value of the direct output and inputs of the project (B_t and O_t) and from the indirect effects of the financial flows that are associated with the project. Theoretically, direct benefits received in year t (B_t) include aggregated consumer surpluses of the project, as well as surpluses generated by price adjustments in related markets.[2] Direct benefits should also include producer surpluses in the market for inputs. Direct resource costs (O_t) include the market costs of all material and factor inputs, shadow-priced if necessary where market prices depart from marginal social costs (see Layard, 1994, and Glaister 1994, pp. 7–14). Since this chapter is focused on the financing of the project, no further attention is given to the measurement of real benefits and resource costs.

3   Financing: effects on consumption, saving and investment

One dollar of each financial flow may have a different consumption equivalence, or opportunity cost, depending on its relative impact on consumption, saving and investment. Saving in this full employment model of the economy is assumed to equal investment, which is then assigned an opportunity cost in terms of the consumption it may be expected to generate over a prescribed time period. The combination of the immediate consumption effect and the present value of the consumption generated by the saving–investment over time equals the opportunity cost of each financial flow.

Tax finance: individual income tax

Consider first the collection of $1 of a proportional individual income tax in year 1. In consequence, disposable income of taxpayers is reduced by $1 and consumption in year 1 is reduced by m, the marginal propensity to consume. Depending on the incidence of the tax, m may differ for different classes of taxpayers but let us assume it is the average m for all taxpayers. Saving is therefore reduced by $(1 - m)$; and in a fully employed economy, it is assumed that this in turn leads to a reduction of $(1 - m)$ in investment. In year 2 this loss of $(1 - m)$ of investment would have generated $r(1 - m)$ of earnings where r is the average rate of return.[3] Of these earnings, $vr(1 - m)$ would have been reinvested, leaving $r(1 - m)(1 - v)$ as dividends of which $(1 - m_s)r (1 - m)(1 - v)$ would have been saved and invested, where m_s is now the marginal propensity to consume of capital-income recipients (assumed to be lower than m applicable to taxpayers as a whole). These two sources of investment (from reinvestment and saving) are then combined to give $r(1 - m)[v + (1 - v)(1 - m_s)]$ added to $(1 - m)$ of the first year to form the capital base for additional earnings, reinvestment, consumption and saving in the third year, and so on. To simplify the presentation, let $x = r[v + (1 - v)(1 - m_s)]$, that is, that share of the rate of return which is reinvested and saved. Then the amount of capital accumulated in year t, (K_t), may be expressed as:

$$K_t = (1 - m)(1 + x)^{t-1}. \tag{14.2}$$

The consumption generated in year $t(C_t)$ is then:

$$C_t = m_s r(1 - v)K_t = m_s r(1 - v)(1 - m)(1 + x)^{t-1}. \tag{14.3}$$

The consumption equivalence of $1 of an individual income tax, C_I, under these assumptions may be expressed as the present value of consumption over the appropriate time period that for purposes of this exercise is chosen to be 20 years. Thus:

$$P.V.(C_I) = m + m_s r(1 - v) \sum_{t=1}^{t=20} \frac{(1 - m)(1 + x)^{t-1}}{(1 + d)^t} \tag{14.4}$$

with d the chosen rate of discount.

Tax finance: corporation income tax
If the project were financed by a corporate profits tax, the process is somewhat similar. We assume that the tax of $1 falls on profits (though alternative incidence assumptions may be considered), and again that corporations retain and reinvest a proportion v of *after*-tax profits. Then corporate reinvestment will decline by v in the first year. Shareholders, in turn, will receive $(1 - v)$ less in dividends and respond by reducing their consumption by $m_s(1 - v)$ and their saving by $(1 - m_s)(1 - v)$. Thus capital in year 1, K_1, is reduced by $v + (1 - v)(1 - m_s)$ or x/r with x again equal to the share of the rate of return reinvested by the corporation and saved by dividend recipients.

In year 2, earnings are reduced by rK_1, or by x and investment (from reinvestment and saving) is reduced by $x[v + (1 - v)(1 - m_x)]$ or $x^2 r$. The sum of reduced investment for years 1 and 2 then equals $x/r + x^2/r$ or $(1 + x)x/r$. Corporate profits in year 3 decline by rK_2, that is, by $x(1 + x)$, reinvestment by $x(1 + x)v$, saving by $x(1 + x)(1 - v)(1 - m_s)$ and total investment by $(1 + x) x^2/r$. Added to K_2 it gives $(1 + x)^2 x/r$ for K_3. Repeating this process we get the present value of the accumulated foregone investment over 20 years as:

$$P.V.(K) = \sum_{t=1}^{t=20} \frac{(x/r)(1 + x)^{t-1}}{(1 + d)^t} \tag{14.5}$$

In turn, the opportunity cost, expressed as the present value of consumption attributable to the $1 of corporate income tax (C_C) is:

$$P.V.(C_C) = m_s(1 - v) + m_s r(1 - v) \sum_{t=1}^{t=20} \frac{(x/r)(1 + x)^{t-1}}{(1 + d)^t}. \quad (14.6)$$

Tax finance: sales tax and user fees
The assumption made here is that a sales tax or user fee falls on consumption and will result in an equal reduction in consumption, thus carrying an opportunity cost of $1 for each $1 of revenue, though again different incidence assumptions may be made.

Loan finance: 20-year bond
The sale of bonds to the public to finance a project draws on the supply of loanable funds in the capital market and in so doing raises the interest rate. This rise in the interest rate may result in some further adjustments in saving and investment depending on the interest elasticity of each. If the interest elasticity of saving is e and the *absolute* elasticity of investment is n, then each $1 of borrowing (withdrawal of loanable funds) raises the interest rate to increase the supply of funds by $e/(e + n)$, and to a reduction of $n/(e + n)$ in the demand for funds for investment (Harberger, 1972). The overall response to the loan in year 1 is thus a net withdrawal of loanable funds of $[1 - (e - n)/(e + n)] = 2n/(e + n)$. This loss in available loanable funds results in a loss of interest income of $i2n/(e + n)$, of consumption $im_s 2n/(e + n)$ and of saving $i(1 - m_s)2n/(e + n)$. Designating $i(1 - m_s)$ (the share of interest saved) as y, the cumulative loss of capital in year t, K_t, is $[2n/(e + n)](1 + y)^{t-1}$ and the present value of the capital accumulation foregone over the 20-year period is:

$$P.V.(K) = \sum_{t=1}^{t=20} \frac{[2n/(e + n)](1 + y)^{t-1}}{(1 + d)^t}. \quad (14.7)$$

The present value of the consumption equivalence of the loan (C_L) (before allowing for interest payments and loan repayment) is therefore:

$$P.V.(C_L) = m_s i \sum_{t=1}^{t=20} \frac{[2n/(e + n)](1 + y)^{t-1}}{(1 + d)^t}. \quad (14.8)$$

The positive value (that is, negative opportunity cost) of annual interest payments (i) and repayment of the loan (R) in year 20 must also be allowed for. Each year an interest payment of i is made, consumption increases by im_s and saving (investment) by $i(1 - m_s)$, designated here as y. The accumulated investment in year 20 out of saving each year from the annual interest payments is then:

$$K_{20} = \sum_{t=1}^{t=20} \frac{(21 - t)y(1 + y)^{t-1}}{(1 + d)}, \tag{14.9}$$

while the present value of the increased consumption (C_N) is

$$P.V.(C_N) = m_s i + m_s i \sum_{t=1}^{t=20} \frac{(21 - t)y(1 + y)}{(1 + d)^t}. \tag{14.10}$$

The loan repayment in year 20 will result in a consumption equivalence (C_R) of opposite sign to that of the original issue of the debt and discounted to its present value from the terminal year. In present value terms, therefore, it may be shown as:

$$P.V.(C_R) = [1/(1 + d)^{20}] \sum_{t=1}^{t=20} \frac{m_s i[2n/(e + n)](1 + y)^{t-1}}{(1 + d)^t}. \tag{14.11}$$

Combining equations (14.8), (14.10) and (14.11) gives the total consumption equivalence of the 20-year loan (C_B) as:

$$P.V.(C_B) = [1 - 1/(1 + d)^{20}]\left[m_s i \sum_{t=1}^{t=20} \frac{[2n/(e + n)](1 + y)^{t-1}}{(1 + d)^t}\right]$$

$$- m_s i \left[1 + \sum_{t=1}^{t=20} \frac{(21 - t)y(1 + y_t)^{t-1}}{(1 + d)^t}\right]. \tag{14.12}$$

Comparative opportunity costs and trade-offs
The foregoing mathematical expressions for the consumption equivalence, or opportunity cost, of $1 of the various means of financing a public project are shown in column (1) of Table 14.1. It is instructive to derive numerical values from these expressions by assigning reasonable values to the parameters as shown in the notes. For illustrative purposes the present values of the consumption equivalences for $100 of each type of finance are shown in columns (2) and (3). The present value consumption equivalences for the 1–20-year period are given in column (2), while column (3) shows these values for the 20–40-year time span. The accumulated capital in year 20 is given in column (4) which provides the basis for consumption beyond year 20. The reader is reminded that these figures reflect the assumptions made as to the behavior of investors and taxpayers that are embodied in the parameter values and is invited to explore their sensitivity to alternative assumptions.

However, if the background assumptions of the model are accepted, that is, of an economy operating at full capacity with all saving invested in income-earning assets, the numerical results suggest the interesting conclusion that although corporate income tax finance in the long run carries a higher opportunity cost than does financing with the individual income tax, with a shorter time horizon (20 years in our example), its consumption equivalence can be considerably lower. In fact, with the parameter values assumed here it would take nearly 40 years for corporate tax finance to reach a consumption equivalence equal to that of the individual income tax. The choice of finance between individual and corporate income tax then depends on the time perspective. It may well be that for purposes of a cost–benefit analysis the time span for all benefits and costs of the project is specified to be equal. In this case, it is not at all obvious that the income tax is always to be preferred to the corporate income tax. Much also depends on the rate of discount. The lower it is chosen to be, and the larger the spread between (r) the rate of return on corporate investment and (d) the rate of time discount, the larger will be the opportunity cost of corporate income tax finance relative to that of the individual income tax, since much of the opportunity cost of corporate tax extends over a longer time period and the present value is thus sensitive to the rate of discount. The existence of a corporate income tax in the economy to which the project is introduced may enter as a wedge between the before-tax rate of return, (r), and the private rate of time preference (i), so that $r > i$. If the latter is chosen as the social rate of discount (d), as in our model, this elevates the consumption equivalence of corporate tax financing relative to that of the individual income tax. Although a less likely assumption, corporations may retain and reinvest a proportion (v) of *pre*-tax profits. In this case, the tax will not affect reinvestment but will be reflected in a reduction of shareholders' consumption m_d and their saving of ($1 - m_d$). The difference in the consumption equivalence of the individual and corporate income taxes in this case lies simply in the differing values of m and m_s.

Financing by an individual income tax, a sales tax or user fees carry opportunity costs close to their monetary magnitudes since all may be expected largely to displace consumption rather than investment. Regarding loan finance, the consumption value of the interest paid, together with that of the discounted value of the loan repayment, exceed the opportunity cost of the withdrawal of loanable funds through the bond issue. Loan finance thus carries a negative opportunity cost or a positive benefit and, apart from other considerations, for the relatively short run would be the favored form of financing a project. However, over the longer run this advantage diminishes as displaced investment builds up. If it is the case that the project is financed out of the pool of general revenue,

Table 14.1 *Opportunity costs of project finance*

Type of finance	Present value of consumption equivalence of $1 of finance	Numerical values*		
		Present value of consumption equivalence of $100 of finance**		value of accumulated capital
	in years 1–20	years 1–20	years 20–40	in year 20
	(1)	(2)	(3)	(4)
Individual income tax	$m + m_s r(1-v) \sum\limits_{t=1}^{t=20} \dfrac{(1-m)(1+x)^{t-1}}{(1+d)^t}$	90.2	33.6	17.9
Corporation income tax	$m_s(1-v) + m_s r(1-v) \sum\limits_{t=1}^{t=20} \dfrac{(x/r)(1+x)^{t-1}}{(1+d)^t}$	49.1	92.5	93.2
Sales tax and user fees	1.0	100.0	–	–
20-year bond Bond Issue	$m_i \sum\limits_{t=1}^{t=20} \dfrac{[2n/(e+n)](1+y)^{t-1}}{(1+d)^t}$	25.8	14.2	116.5

Interest payments	$m_s i + m_s i \sum_{t=1}^{t=20} \dfrac{(21-t)\,y(1+y)^{t-1}}{(1+d)^t}$	-17.9	-7.2	-40.0***
Bond repayment	$-\,[1/(1+d)^{20}]\,m_s i \sum_{t=1}^{t=20} \dfrac{[2n/(e+n)]\,(1+x)^{t-1}}{(1+d)^t}$	-9.7	-5.4	-43.9***
Bond total		-1.8	-1.6	32.6

Notes:

* Assumed parameter values $m = -0.9$, $n = -0.2$, $i = -0.05$, $y = i(1 - m_s) = 0.02$,
$m_s = -0.6$, $e = -0.3$, $d = -0.05$, $x = r[v + (1 - v)(1 - m_s)] = 0.312$,
$v = -0.2$, $r = -0.06$.

** Negative values indicate a negative opportunity cost, i.e., a positive social benefit.

*** The negative sign here indicates an *increase* in accumulated capital in the private sector.

an opportunity cost may be obtained by weighting the various financing components according to their share in the total.

Since taxes and other distortions insert a substantial wedge between r and d, the methodology that has been outlined may put public projects to a demanding test if financing displaces private investment over a long period. However, this may overlook an asymmetry in the treatment of public and private investment. Projects in the public sector may also generate social gains that, in effect, are reinvested over a long period. Yet these reinvestments usually do not appear in the analysis, and in any case, if they are included, cover only an arbitrary useful life. While this may occur for infrastructure investments, it is also true for investments in human resources. The problem, alas, is another aspect of the difficulties of putting public and private investments into the same analytical framework.

4   Effects of the background fiscal structure

So far we have not considered the bearing on cost–benefit analysis of the country's fiscal structure which provides the background conditions into which a prospective project is introduced. There are two major effects. One is the effect on the discount rate. As was already noted, the existence of an income tax, by inserting a wedge between r, i and d, significantly affects the outcome of the analysis and the ranking of alternative sources of finance. Comparing loan finance with individual income tax finance, for instance, we expect (i) to be higher in a debt-financed general budget and therefore a higher discount rate (d). If an individual income tax is in place, the effect is to introduce a tax wedge between the gross and net rates of return on private investment, r and $(1 - t)r$, where t is the average tax rate on capital income. If the discount rate (d) is set equal to the after-tax interest rate then $r > i > d$. As the gap between r and d widens, there will be a tendency on the benefit side to favor longer-term projects but at the same time to increase the opportunity costs of those projects financed by sources that displace private investment. Thus it is not clear on balance whether a lower discount rate in relation to r and i will give greater advantage to longer-lived public projects.

Carrying the argument a step further, allowance may be made for the fact that, in the case of prevalence of public debt in the economy, the debt has to be serviced in the future, an issue that arose in considering loan finance for the project itself. If the interest payments on the debt are tax financed, the initial effect of the debt in raising the discount rate will be unwound over time. In this case, allowance should be made for a slightly falling discount rate (but rising opportunity cost of investment) over the life of the project. If interest payments were financed with a consumption tax, one would expect a smaller decline in discount rate over time and no appreciable change in the opportunity cost of private investment. However, the purpose of this chapter is not to discuss the various ramifications of the choice of discount rate but given the discount rate equal to i, the private of rate investment, to focus on the opportunity cost of the various methods of financing a project.

While the pattern of finance in the general budget can have a bearing on the discount rate and therefore the opportunity costs of financing a project, there may be more direct effects. Consider, for instance, a general expenditure tax. In this case, if the project is financed with an individual income tax, consumption equivalence will include the background expenditure tax. The question is, how should it be allowed for? Since the expenditure tax falls on consumption, it seems preferable not to make any adjustment. However, if there is a general income tax, then we can assume that the income tax to finance the project comes out of that general tax and the tax has a similar opportunity cost and again little adjustment need be made. In all, the influence of background taxes in estimating consumption equivalences appears to be of secondary importance.

5   Alternative macro models of a closed economy
So far we have considered the implications of alternative financing sources for public projects in the context of a simple neoclassical model of a full employment economy with consumption taken to be a function of income and the interest rate only. We now give brief attention to the implications of adjusting the model to allow for wealth effects, rational expectations and a neo-Keynesian system of income determination in which stabilization policy is required.

Wealth effects
Introduction of a wealth effect is unlikely to modify the opportunity cost of debt finance. Debt finance in this model involves a substitution of a claim against the government for other privately held assets with little change in total private wealth. If financed by an individual income tax, only a slight change in wealth will occur as the tax causes only a minor reduction in saving. With corporation income tax finance, there is likely to be a reduction in investment and consequently in privately held wealth. An effect of this wealth reduction may be expected to reduce the consumption parameter and thus to lower the opportunity cost of the corporate income tax finance. But this modification will be of second-order importance.

Rational expectations
We now change the assumption that the public is unaware of future tax requirements to service the debt. Rather, the public operating with perfect

foresight is aware of future tax liabilities. They will discount these liabilities (at their rate of time preference) and find the present value of future tax obligations associated with the debt to equal those of the tax that they would have had to pay in the case of tax finance. Thus, taxpayer response with regard to consumption and saving is much the same whether the project is tax or debt financed (Barro, 1974). However, if it is questionable whether the necessary degree of foresight is likely to exist, it is prudent to proceed on the assumption that it does not, even though for other reasons, private sector saving is taken to be suboptimal and for macro reasons better served by tax finance.

Neo-Keynesian model
Consider now an economy that does not equilibrate at full employment, but requires stabilization policy to achieve the proper level of aggregate demand. So far, it could be assumed that all forms of tax finance of a project leave aggregate demand and income largely unchanged, while affecting only its composition between consumption and investment, but we now consider a situation where the level of aggregate demand and employment are affected by introduction of the project. Various mixes of monetary and fiscal policy may be used to obtain the required level of aggregate demand, but depending on the mix that is chosen, the division of resource use between consumption and investment as well as the market rate of interest will differ. Assuming the economy to be at full employment before the project's introduction, the additional tax revenue needed to hold aggregate demand constant as the project is introduced will exceed the project cost via the operation of the balanced-budget multiplier. Debt finance of the project, in turn, will require some offset by tightened monetary policy. All these complications arise without proceeding to an extreme Keynesian model where private investment would be unaffected under any form of project finance.

Since cost–benefit analysis has to be conducted in a real-world economy in which aggregate demand *is* affected by choice of finance, the normative theory of project evaluation, applicable in a classical setting, becomes something of a chimera. However, rules are needed by which to evaluate projects, and the standard model may still offer valuable guidance, with any undesirable macro effects left to another branch of government to correct.

6   Choice of finance in an open economy
Returning to the earlier neoclassical assumptions, we now consider the case of the open economy where there is the further option of borrowing outside the jurisdiction. We shall consider both the case of a country borrowing abroad and the case of a local jurisdiction borrowing in the larger national economy.

Borrowing abroad

In the case of a project financed by domestic sources of finance, the methodology was to determine the effects of the diversion of funds to and from the *domestic* private sector on the level of consumption and saving (investment) in the domestic economy, expressing all in terms of their consumption equivalence and discounting to their present value at the social rate of discount. There is obviously a substantial difference in this approach when borrowing is from abroad. In the case of foreign debt, there is no withdrawal of loanable funds from the domestic economy as the debt is issued, nor is there an addition of funds when interest payments are made and the debt repaid. Thus there is a zero opportunity cost of foreign debt, except for possible adjustments in the exchange rate of the domestic currency as funds flow between the foreign lender and the project.

However, suppose the project does not generate funds sufficient to service the foreign debt and domestic taxes are required to cover interest and repayment of the loans. There will then be indirect opportunity costs associated with such taxes. Thus a 20-year, $100 foreign loan with an interest rate of i with the interest and repayment paid for with an individual income tax, and using our parameters would involve an indirect present value opportunity cost of $41. It is well to remember that this involves only the cost to the private domestic economy and does not allow for the benefit to the public project of the loan issue itself. Although a variety of estimates might be derived using alternative parameters, we may nevertheless conclude that the distinction between domestic and foreign borrowing is of considerable significance for project evaluation.

Borrowing by local jurisdictions

How is the analysis changed and how are the conditions modified in the case of a local jurisdiction the loans of which are largely raised outside that jurisdiction? To begin with, since the jurisdiction's saving and investment represent only a small fraction of the national capital market, we can assume that the supply of saving facing it is perfectly elastic at the prevailing national interest rate (i). There is no displacement effect on its own investment through the act of borrowing. Furthermore, since the loan issue, repayment and interest all involve payments to and from outside the jurisdiction in question, the opportunity cost to the private sector corresponds to that of foreign borrowing with the opportunity cost being zero. This is again modified if the interest and loan repayment are financed by taxes in which case there is an indirect opportunity cost which will again depend on the type of local tax used to service the debt.

7   Equity considerations

Under neoclassical assumptions, the choice of project finance will have little bearing on whether or not a project is accepted provided that there is no separation between r, i, and d. With respect to the discount rate, a discussion of the copious literature regarding the choice of this vital variable is not included here but see Stiglitz (1984) for coverage of the topic. In common practice, the weighted average of consumer and producer interest rates is often used as the discount rate on the assumption that this reflects the private, and in turn, social rate of time preference. This leaves aside the arguments for a rate that reflects broader social considerations. But it does not follow that the choice between alternative ways of financing the project is irrelevant. Other considerations, especially those bearing on equity, may enter and determine which financing method should be chosen. Thus costs and benefits might be given distributional weights, in which case a project will pass more readily if its financing has a more progressive incidence (Layard et al., 1980). Or, proceeding in the spirit of benefit taxation, it may be desirable for each generation to pay for the benefits it receives from the project, in which case durable projects would be debt financed while those providing current benefits would be tax financed (Ferguson, 1964). Similarly, benefits may accrue to particular groups of consumers, when there is a case to be made for user charges to finance the project. However, the outcome of the cost–benefit analysis, and in a larger sense the level, structure and time-path of public investment will be influenced by the choice of finance for the project itself, by the general setting of budget finance into which the project is introduced, as well as by public decisions on the choice of discount rate.

Notes

1. See 'Introduction' in Layard and Glaister (1994) and Feldstein's earlier critique of this approach in Layard (1972).
2. If the project is in the nature of a public good in which its services are non-rival, then the consumer surpluses should in theory be aggregated by vertical summation to give total benefits. For the relationship between public goods and cost–benefit analysis, see Musgrave (1969).
3. Feldstein (1964, p. 117), claims the social rate of return on the foregone investment to be equal to r / x where x is the 'proportion of the increased national income produced by marginal investments which the private investors receive'. This would seem to assign an unduly large value to r and is left for further discussion.

References

Barro, Robert J. (1974), 'Are government bonds net wealth?', *Journal of Political Economy*, December.
Brent, Robert J. (2007), *Applied Cost–Benefit Analysis*, 2nd edn, Cheltenham, UK and Northampton, MA, USA: Edward Elgar.
Drèze, Jean and N. Stern (1987), 'The theory of cost–benefit analysis', in A.J. Auerbach and

M. Feldstein (eds), *Handbook of Public Economics*, Vol. II, Amsterdam: North-Holland, pp. 909–89.

Feldstein, M.S. (1964), 'Net social benefit calculation and the public investment decision', *Oxford Economic Papers*, **16**, 114–31.

Feldstein, Martin S. (1972), 'The inadequacy of weighted discount rates', in Layard (ed.), pp. 311–32.

Feldstein, Martin S. (1974), 'Financing in the evaluation of public expenditures', in W.L. Smith and J.M. Culbertson (eds), *Public Finance and Stabilization Policy: Essays in Honor of R.A. Musgrave*, Amsterdam: North-Holland, pp. 13–36.

Ferguson, J.M. (ed.) (1964), *Public Debt and Future Generations*, Chapel Hill, NC: University of North Carolina Press.

Harberger, Arnold C. (1972), *Project Evaluation: Collected Papers*, London: Macmillan.

Layard, Richard (ed.) (1972), *Cost Benefit Analysis*, 1st edn, Harmonsworth: Penguin Books.

Layard, Richard and Stephen Glaister (eds) (1994), *Cost Benefit Analysis*, 2nd edn, Cambridge: Cambridge University Press.

Layard, R., L. Squire and A.C. Herberger (1980), 'On the use of distributional weights in social cost–benefit analysis comments', *Journal of Political Economy*, **88**, 1041–52.

Lind, Robert C. (ed.) (1982), *Discounting for Time and Risk in Energy Policy*, Washington, DC: Resources for the Future.

Musgrave, Richard A. (1969), 'Cost–benefit analysis and the theory of public finance', *Journal of Economic Literature*, **7** (3), 797–806.

Stiglitz, Joseph E. (1994), 'Rate of discount for cost–benefit analysis and the theory of second best', in Layard and Glaister (eds), pp. 116–59.

15 Cost–benefit analysis and the evaluation of the effects of corruption on public projects
Robert J. Brent

1 Introduction

Cost–benefit analysis (CBA) is the basis for rational economic decision making, whether it is for the government or individuals. If benefits are greater than costs, then a project or activity should be expanded. If costs are greater than the benefits, the project or activity should be contracted. And if benefits equal costs, the existing scale of operations is optimal. A social CBA obtains its measurement principles concerning the benefits and costs from applied welfare economics. Its main purpose is to incorporate considerations into public expenditure decision making that caused private market decision making to fail to produce optimally (due to the existence of externalities) or produce at all (pure public goods). However, these corrections for market failure lead only to potential gains. Once the public sector is involved there is also the potential for government failure. Public officials may have an agenda that is different from social welfare maximization. In particular, if these public officials are corrupt and try to maximize bribes which they keep for themselves, then this reality needs to be included as part of the cost–benefit evaluation.

The Executive Board of the World Bank defined corruption in 1997 as: 'The use of public office for private gain'. This definition is also the one used by Bardhan (1997) in his survey of corruption and development. Although this wrongly restricts the term 'corruption' to apply only to the public sector, since we are analyzing the effects of corruption on public projects, this definition clearly is relevant for our work. The only slight difference we make is to say that corruption is the use of public *funds* for personal gain. We narrow the focus because our analysis is directed at the consequences for evaluating projects of diverting these funds from the public sector.

Much of what can be classed as corruption behavior is illegal.[1] The literature on corruption is well aware of this. But, the fact that corruption is illegal needs to be explicitly allowed for in any CBA of the consequences of such activities. Note that CBA works within a social context. Private gain (profits) is socially acceptable in some contexts, but not all. If a person gains one million dollars from producing a vaccine for AIDS, this is a social gain of one million dollars. If a person gains one million dollars from selling child pornography, this is not a social gain at all even though the monetary consequences are identical to the health intervention. In our analysis we recognize this principle in our CBA criteria. That is, a bribe to a public official reduces the gain to the beneficiary, but the gain to the official is *not* recorded.

Whether something is a 'benefit' or a 'cost' depends on one's objectives. Our CBA models will have two social objectives: the 'size of the pie' (that is, income, or income growth, which is 'efficiency') and how the pie is distributed (whether to the rich or to the poor). Corruption adversely affects both objectives as we explain in Section 2 when we present our cost–benefit framework.

The purpose of developing this framework is to operationalize for public policy purposes a growing empirical literature by the International Monetary Fund (IMF) and World Bank that estimates the effects of corruption on the public finances of developing (and other) countries. The emphasis will be on the experience of developing countries because there is strong evidence in the literature – see, for example, Treisman (2000) – that less-developed countries have higher levels of measured corruption.[2]

To be useful for public policy it is not sufficient that studies provide separate estimates of the extent to which corruption impacts, *inter alia*, the distribution of income, the level of wages of public officials, tax revenues, and the quantity and quality of public outputs. In order to prioritize interventions these estimates need to be *combined* and included in an evaluation framework that covers the important considerations that drive normative public choices, such as measures of: benefits and costs, distributional weights, the marginal cost of public funds, and the discount rate.[3] In Section 3 we interpret the recent empirical literature on corruption in terms of the variables and parameters in the formulated comprehensive cost–benefit framework and incorporate developing-country estimates of parameter values. Having examined the estimation of individual parameter values viewed separately, we then present a complete CBA from the literature that evaluates attempts to reduce corruption which rely on all the parameter values being used together. The final section presents the summary and conclusions.

2 Cost–benefit criteria

We first form the basic cost–benefit criterion and then show how it is impacted by the existence of various forms of corruption. The final part of the analysis involves showing how to adapt the criterion to evaluate policies to combat corruption.

The cost–benefit criterion in the absence of corruption
A project involves transforming inputs into outputs. A CBA of a government project starts when it measures in monetary terms the benefits B, the maximum amount that individuals are willing to pay for the outputs, and the costs C, the minimum amount of compensation that suppliers of the inputs must receive. From there the CBA proceeds to assign weights to these benefits and costs according to the distributional characteristics of the groups receiving the benefits and incurring the costs and also for the source of compensation for the inputs. Let the distributional weight to the costs be normalized to be 1 and the weight to the beneficiaries be $1 + a$, where a is a premium assigned because the beneficiaries are assumed to be low income. We shall also assume that the financing of the costs of the project is out of tax revenues that have a marginal cost of public funds MCF, which is determined by the direct utility loss of 1 per unit of costs for giving up the tax revenue itself, and a marginal excess burden m due to the indirect utility loss from the distortion of preferences generated by the taxes. Welfare from the project in the absence of corruption W_0 in terms of the cost–benefit criterion is given as the difference between the weighted benefits and the weighted costs:

$$W_0 = (1 + a)B_0 - (1 + m)C_0.$$

This criterion is appropriate for government projects that are pure public goods where it is impossible to charge the beneficiaries fees because of the free-rider problem. For projects where charging is feasible, the repayments R play an important role. The standard welfare analysis of user fees in CBA has been carried out in Brent (1995). This analysis is where the repayments are legal such that the financers receive as tax relief what the beneficiaries pay for the outputs. Because we intend to extend the analysis to include corruption we need to record the possibility that what the beneficiaries pay R^B could be different from the sums R^C that those incurring the costs obtain as relief. Repayments by the beneficiaries reduce their gains to $B - R^B$ and repayments received by the taxpayers reduce their losses to $C - R^C$. Applying the weights to these net gains and net losses produces the cost–benefit criterion:

$$W_0 = (1 + a)(B_0 - R_0^B) - (1 + m)(C_0 - R_0^C)$$

or,

$$W_0 = (1 + a)B_0 - (1 + m)C_0 - (1 + a)R_0^B + (1 + m)R_0^C. \quad (15.1)$$

This is the complete cost–benefit criterion which we shall use as the benchmark for comparing the results with corruption. If we were to analyze repayments in the absence of corruption, it would require setting: $R_0^B = R_0^B = R$. In this situation the repayment part of the criterion would condense to: $(m - a) R$. This could be positive or negative according to the relative sizes of m and a. For the special case where $m = a$, the repayments have no welfare significance.

The cost–benefit criterion with corruption
The welfare effects of a project in the presence of corruption will be denoted by W_1. We analyze two forms types of corruption. For each type of corruption we evaluate the welfare change ΔW as: $W_1 - W_0$.

Corruption as theft with no output effects An important contribution to the literature on the effects of corruption on public projects was by Schleifer and Vishny (1993). They focus on corruption as bribing. They draw the distinction between bribing without theft, where corrupt officials turn over revenues for the project to the government, and bribing with theft, where the repayments for the project are kept by the official. We reformulate this distinction because the bribe payment itself is kept by the official in either case. So one can argue that theft is present in both situations. Because of this fact, instead of contrasting bribing without theft and bribing with theft, we analyze theft without bribing versus theft with bribing. In this framework we view bribing as affecting the net benefits of the beneficiaries and therefore altering the socially optimal output level. So in the case with which we begin our analysis of corruption, the absence of bribing means that the theft occurs without an output effect.

In the Schleifer and Vishny framework, the public official administering the project is someone different from the public decision maker deciding the outcome of the project. We interpret the role of the public official as deciding or otherwise administering the repayments for the project. For repayments not to affect output, criterion (15.1) needs to be disaggregated such that the project effect depends on: $(1 + a)B_0 - (1 + m)C_0$, while the repayment part has its impact via: $-(1 + a)R_0^B + (1 + m)R_0^C$. In this setting, the repayments that the beneficiaries make, that is, R_0^B, need not be the maximum that they are willing to pay (as given by the demand curve) for the output that has been independently decided. Call this maximum R^*. So from the beneficiaries' point of view there is a consumer surplus of: $R^* - R_0^B$. This difference provides the scope for the public official to alter repayment without affecting output.

Figure 15.1 shows the role of R^* in our cost–benefit framework on the assumption of constant costs. The project evaluator sets the quantity of the public project Q_E by equating marginal benefits (MB), as given by the demand curve and scaled up by distribution weights, with marginal costs

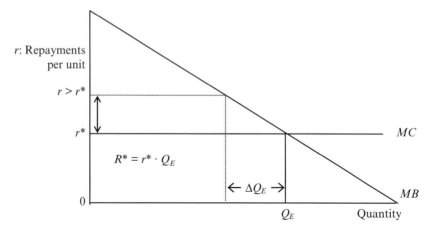

Note: Q_E is the public output level determined by equating MB with MC. Up to R^*, repayments redistribute with no effect on output. Above R^*, repayments redistribute and there is an output reduction ΔQ_E, leading to a change in benefits and costs, ΔB and ΔC.

Figure 15.1   Role of R^* on assumption of constant costs

(MC), scaled up by the marginal cost of public funds. Initially at Q_E there is no price charged and quantity is rationed by permits or waiting lists and so on. Then repayments per unit r are introduced, whether in the form of a legitimate user fee or an illegal bribe. As long as the repayment per unit was less than r^*, and hence the total repayment $R = r^*$ times Q_E was less than R^*, then repayments would just reduce the consumer surplus of the beneficiary and be transferred either to the taxpayers or to the public official personally. Output would not be affected.

We shall define as theft when a corrupt official keeps the repayments and does not transfer them so that they can be used to offset the costs of the project to the taxpayers, that is, $R_1^C 0$. Since there is no welfare significance given to the illegal gains of the official, there is no corresponding social gain from this redistribution from the taxpayers to the public official. The bribe β will be regarded as raising the repayment from their original level to R_1^B. Because this bribe, $\beta = R_1^B - R_0^B$, is treated like theft from the social welfare point of view, that is, it is simply new theft, there is again no social gain accompanying this redistribution from the beneficiaries to the public official. The with-corruption state with no output effect (that is, where benefits and costs are equal to their original levels) is:

$$W_1 = (1 + a) B_0 - (1 + m) C_0 - (1 + a) R_1^B. \qquad (15.2)$$

The resulting welfare change becomes:

$$\Delta W = -(1 + a)\beta - (1 + m) R_0^C. \tag{15.3}$$

Unlike legal repayments, bribes and theft can never be worthwhile, even with the special case where $m = a$. Because in general $m \neq a$, equation (15.3) shows that bribes and theft do not have the same social significance per dollar. If $m > a$, redistributing from beneficiaries would have a greater negative impact per dollar than redistributing from taxpayers. In either case, the welfare loss is greater than the sum of monies that have been illegally confiscated.

Corruption as theft with output effects   With outputs effects, there are changes in benefits and costs to accompany the redistributional effects of corruption already analyzed. Assuming that the bribe now raises the repayments to the beneficiaries to above R^*, beneficiaries will demand a different (lower) quantity from before. As we can see from Figure 15.1, a repayment per unit of greater than r^* intersects with the MB curve to the left of Q_E causing an output reduction. The welfare effects with corruption become:

$$W_1 = (1 + a)B_1 - (1 + m)C_1 - (1 + a)R_1^B. \tag{15.4}$$

From this we derive the welfare change as:

$$\Delta W = (1 + a)\Delta B - (1 + m)\Delta C - (1 + a)\beta - (1 + m)R_0^C. \tag{15.5}$$

The bribe and theft parts of equation (15.5) are as before. The new part is the evaluation of the quantity effect. The reduced quantity means that $\Delta B < 0$ and $\Delta C < 0$ which, in turn, implies: $(1 + a)\Delta B < 0$ and $(1 + m)\Delta C > 0$. So the output part of criterion (15.5) would be positive if: $(1 + m)\Delta C > (1 + a)\Delta B$. That is, the cost saving must exceed the loss of benefits. This could arise only if the original output were set at too high a level. However, we assume that the original output was socially optimal such that the difference $(1 + a)B_0 - (1 + m)C_0$ was maximized. In this situation, *any* output change, positive or negative, would have a negative welfare effect. In this case, $(1 + a)\Delta B - (1 + m)\Delta C < 0$ and corruption would have three adverse effects on social welfare, that is, the two unfavorable redistributional effects and the negative output effect.

The cost–benefit criterion applied to anti-corruption policies
Theft is illegal. Policies dealing with this form of corruption clearly must include analysis of how the legal system is to operate. However, for the

final part of our analysis, we shall take the legal system as given and we examine how to evaluate policies that target corruption using changes in the variables that already exist in our cost–benefit model. Following Van Rijckeghem and Weder (2001), we consider corruption to be an inverse function of the wages that the public officials receive. The analysis then relates to alternative ways of financing the higher wages.

Corruption reduction financed by taxpayers   The welfare effects of a project with policies in place to combat corruption will be denoted by W_2. The specification of the cost–benefit criterion is the same as the basic model given by equation (15.1), except that the levels of all variables may be different. So we have with the anti-corruption policies in place:

$$W_2 = (1 + a)B_2 - (1 + m)C_2 - (1 + a)R_2^B + (1 + m)R_2^C. \quad (15.6)$$

Let the rise in wages (salaries) sufficient to induce the public official to abandon corruption be equal to S. The main purpose, and effect, of paying the public official higher wages is that the original repayments by beneficiaries are not siphoned off by the official and are returned to the taxpayers. This implies that: $R_2^C = R_0^C = R_2^B = R_0^B$. In addition, output is restored to its original (optimal) level as bribing has ended. Thus: $B_2 = B_0$. But, this comes at a cost to the taxpayers who, in addition to paying for the inputs necessary for the optimal level of output, must pay the higher wages. The costs therefore are: $C_2 = C_0 + S$. With these particular outcomes, the cost–benefit criterion appears as:

$$W_2 = (1 + a)B_0 - (1 + m)(C_0 + S) - (1 + a)R_0^B + (1 + m)R_0^C. \quad (15.6a)$$

The welfare change over the corruption state (with output effects) is the difference between equations (15.6a) and (15.4) and this is equal to:

$$\Delta W = (1 + a)\Delta B - (1 + m)\Delta C - (1 + m)S + (1 + a)\beta + (1 + m)R_0^C. \quad (15.7)$$

This time $\Delta B > 0$ and $\Delta C > 0$. Returning to optimal output means: $(1 + a)\Delta B - (1 + m)\Delta C > 0$ and this is a welfare gain. In addition, there are gains from eliminating the bribes and the theft. The one cost is the additional salaries that are to be financed by the taxpayers.

Corruption reduction financed by repayments from beneficiaries   This final case is very similar to the one just analyzed provided that there are no new output effects when the beneficiaries are being charged higher prices to cover the increased salaries for the public officials. If the amount of the salaries is such that it does not make the consumer surplus $R_0 - R_0^B - S$ negative, there will be no readjustment to output other than restoring it to the no-corruption level. With beneficiaries paying for S instead of the taxpayers, equation (15.6a) is replaced by:

$$W_2 = (1 + a) B_0 - (1 + m) C_0 - (1 + a) (R_0^B + S) (1 + m) R_0^C.$$
(15.6b)

The welfare change appears as:

$$\Delta W = (1 + a)\Delta B - (1 + m)\Delta C - (1 + a)S + (1 + a)\beta + (1 + m) R_0^C.$$
(15.8)

The only difference between equations (15.8) and (15.7) is that the one new cost is $-(1 + a)S$ instead of $-(1 + m)S$. As we would expect, the welfare significance of the difference sources of financing the rise in salaries depends on the relative sizes of m and a.

With output effects caused by raising the prices to the beneficiaries to cover S, there will be an output reduction to include as part of the welfare change. The size of the output reduction depends on the relative size of S to β. As long as $S \leq \beta$, although output B_2 will not be as large as B_0, it will be still be greater than B_1. Hence $\Delta B > 0$ and $\Delta C > 0$ as in equation (15.7) and we have a positive output effect: $(1 + a) \Delta B - (1 + m) \Delta C > 0$. However, if $S \geq \beta$, paying for the higher salary is more onerous than paying for the bribe and there could be a net output loss over state 1. In terms of equation (15.8), $(1 + a) \Delta B - (1 + m) \Delta C < 0$ and there are two types of welfare loss that need to be compared with the two types of gain.

3   Empirical evidence on corruption effects from the literature

Since we developed our theoretical model with the empirical literature by the IMF and World Bank in mind, we shall focus mainly on their studies. We refer to, interpret, and adapt some of the existing macroeconomic studies to give an indication of the quantitative importance of the main variables and considerations highlighted in our cost–benefit framework. We shall supplement this experience with reference to some microeconomic studies of individual countries that enable us to delve a little deeper into the corruption transmission mechanism. The empirical work cited here just relates to individual ingredients in the cost–benefit model and does not give an overall assessment of the extent to which corruption lowers social welfare. Hence, we complete our review of the empirical work by covering a microeconomic corruption study that is the most complete attempt to date in the literature to provide a comprehensive cost–benefit analysis of anti-corruption policies.

In the macroeconomic context, we consider two kinds of empirical evidence. The first covers a wide literature that uses a corruption index, such as those constructed by Transparency International (TI) or Political Risk Services who devised the International Country Risk Guide (ICRG) index. In all the studies we cite, the corruption indices are rescaled, so that the higher the number the greater the perceived level of corruption. The TI index is on a scale of 0 to 10, while the ICRG index is on a scale of 0 to 6. When studies use both types of indices, the ICRG is also converted to a 0 to 10 scale so the results using the two indices can be compared. Most studies use the index as an independent variable, but some use it as a dependent variable. We refer always to estimates that are based on data for a cross-section of countries, except when we mention the supportive microeconomic material.

The second kind of evidence relies on behavior rather than subjective assessment. It uses government expenditure on various categories and sees whether the amount of foreign aid augments, or not, these domestic public spending levels. We use the corruption index literature to provide estimates of the effects on project outputs and revenues, and we use a foreign aid study to supply our main estimate of the extent of new theft.

Corruption and wages: estimating S
Van Rijckeghem and Weder (1997) carried out a cross-section analysis of 22 developing and low-income OECD countries, for the 1982–94 period, to estimate the effect of corruption on public official wages using the ICRG index.[4] Rijckeghem and Weder measure public sector wages by the ratio of government wages relative to manufacturing wages. They regressed relative wages (and other variables) on their measure of corruption.

Van Rijckeghem and Weder found that a one unit rise in relative wages (for example, from 100 to 200 percent) would result in a 0.81 reduction in the ICRG. This coefficient was then used to predict what the relative wage increase would have to be to eliminate corruption. For example, if a country had a corruption index of 4, then relative wages would have to rise by 224 percent (to 3.24) in order for corruption to cease. The relative wage estimates with and without corruption are presented in Table 15.1 (which is Van Rijckeghem and Weder's Table 5). We see in Table 15.1 that relative wages would have to rise greatly, somewhere in the range 2.81 to 7.37, in order to return to the no-corruption state.

Gorodnichenko and Sabrianova (2007) use the existence of differences in relative wages between the private and public sectors, as highlighted in

Table 15.1   Actual wages and wages to ensure no corruption

Country	Actual relative wage	Relative wage without corruption
Turkey	0.92	5.38
Bolivia	0.61	6.95
Colombia	0.64	4.87
Costa Rica	1.40	2.81
El Salvador	1.74	7.37
Guatemala	0.76	6.39
Mexico	0.50	5.04
Panama	0.85	6.22
Peru	0.79	5.01
Uruguay	0.92	5.15
Jordan	1.24	5.47
Egypt	0.49	6.51
Sri Lanka	0.85	5.07
Hong Kong	1.79	2.85
India	1.09	5.40
Korea	1.91	7.08
Singapore	3.49	3.49
Botswana	1.29	3.96
Ghana	0.63	6.77
Kenya	0.90	5.36
Morocco	1.01	6.04
Zimbabwe	0.97	5.13

Source: Van Rijckeghem and Weder (1997, p. 40).

the Van Rijckeghem and Weder work, to help measure the extent to which bribery takes place in Ukraine. Public sector employees were considerably underpaid, in the order of 24 to 32 percent, relative to workers in other sectors. On the assumption that labor market equilibrium would equalize monetary rewards between the public and private sectors, after allowing for non-pecuniary differences such as the number of hours worked and job security, any differences in wages between the two sectors would be matched by non-reported monetary compensation, that is, bribes. This ensures that employees in the two sectors enjoy comparable consumption levels and asset ownership as actually observed in the Ukraine context. Using their best estimate of the residual private–public wage gap, they found that bribery accounted for at least 20 percent of the total wage compensation in the public sector in Ukraine, which is equivalent to US $460–580 million or 0.9–1.2 percent of Ukraine's GDP in 2003.

It is important to note that in the context of the framework of the bribe acting as a compensating wage differential as envisaged by Gorodnichenko and Sabrianova, the public sector employee is only concerned with the total remuneration received. In this context, illegal bribes and official wage earnings are perfect substitutes. This has the implication that the amount of money received for bribes would be exactly the sum of additional wage earnings necessary to bring about no corruption, that is, no bribes. That is, this implies, $S = \beta$. In the special case where it is the beneficiaries who would finance any corruption reduction that takes place, as analyzed in Section 2, the people who pay the costs of the project get a new gain to the extent that bribes are covering costs and so what revenues are received from selling the public output to the beneficiaries can be returned to those who bear the costs. This result can be seen from equation (15.8) by substituting $S = \beta$ in it to obtain:

$$\Delta W = (1 + a)\Delta B - (1 + m)\Delta C + (1 + m) R_0^C, \qquad (15.8a)$$

where $(1 + m) R_0^C$ is the 'new' (that is, restored) gain to those who finance the costs.

More generally, when we allow for the existence of auditing and policing policies to combat corruption, which can lead to the possibility of the imposition of fines and imprisonment, bribes and wages are not perfect substitutes. In this context, as argued by Di Tella and Schargrodsky (2003), the effects of official wage increases on bribes can actually be zero. This would be the case when the probability of legal sanctions would be known to be at either extreme, either 0 or 1. If there is no chance of being caught, then increasing wages will not stop bribes taking place. When the probability of being caught is certain, bribes will not take place, so raising wages cannot lower them. It is only in the intermediate probability situations where raising wages can reduce corruption. Di Tella and Schargrodsky find empirical support for this line of reasoning in the experience of a crackdown on corruption in the city of Buenos Aires during 1996–97. In the first phase of the crackdown, when monitoring intensity was expected to be maximal, the effect of wages on the prices paid by public hospitals for resources, which include payments for bribes, was statistically insignificant. But, wages lowered input prices and bribes in the last phase of the crackdown when monitoring intensity could be expected to take intermediate values (ibid., p. 286).

Corruption and distribution: estimating β
Gupta et al. (2002) used both TI and ICRG indices to estimate the redistribution effects of corruption. The corruption indices were regressed (with

other variables) on the incomes of the poor using a cross-section analysis of 31 countries over the 1980–97 period.

In terms of the CBA framework developed in this paper, β corresponds to the bribe payments required from low-income beneficiaries. Gupta et al. specified low income as relating to the bottom 20 percent of the population. To fit in with their study, we can interpret bribe payments as being all reductions in income by the bottom 20 percent of income earners that result from corruption existing in the country.[5]

One of the main results (reported in their table 5, column 4) was that a 1 standard deviation rise in corruption (that is, a 0.78 percentage point deterioration in the growth of corruption) led to a reduction in the income growth of the bottom 20 percent of the population by 4.7 percentage points. This is a large fall in income for the low-income group considering that the average income growth for this group in the sample was 0.6 percent a year. The estimated coefficient was most statistically significant when social spending (on health, education and so on) was included in the equation. This implies that the estimate of β should be interpreted as that pertaining when output is held constant. Thus it is the redistributional and not the efficiency effects of corruption that is being revealed in this study.

Given that the bottom quintile of the income distribution was used to define low income, there is an easy way to approach the issue of what distributional weight a to apply to changes in their income. If, say, in a country the bottom 20 percent of the population earn 5 percent of the country's income, which was true of Singapore in 1998 and Uruguay in 2003,[6] then this implies that this group earns a quarter of the national average (seeing that if they had earned the average they would have had 20 percent, and not the 5 percent they actually earned, with 5%/20% being 0.25).[7] Once one knows the poor group's income relative to the mean, this is in a form to be used in Squire and van der Tak's (1975) formula for distribution weights, which in its most applied version expresses a group i's distribution weight as the inverse of the group's income y_i relative to the mean $\bar{y}$:[8]

$$a_i = \bar{y}/y_i. \qquad (15.9)$$

So, for example, if the poorest 20 percent of the population were to have an income one-quarter of the average in a particular country, their distribution weight a_i would be 5 for this quintile group. In our formulation of the CBA criterion the parameter a_i was defined as the *premium* to the beneficiary group over the average group. Thus, to use our model the weight for the lowest-income group would be:

$$1 + a_i = \bar{y}/y_i, \qquad (15.9a)$$

which makes the premium:

$$a_i = \bar{y}/y_i - 1. \qquad (15.9b)$$

Corruption and efficiency: Estimating ΔB and ΔC
In Section 2 we assumed that, if in the absence of corruption output were set optimally, then any output change, positive or negative, would be socially undesirable. We dealt with output reductions because, with bribing taking place, the effective price for beneficiaries would increase and this would lower the quantity demanded. The first study we refer to in this subsection quantifies the types of output reduction. When government expenditures rise, one does not know whether this was because output has increased, or because the costs for producing the same (or perhaps lower) level of output have risen. In the second study the authors find that both public expenditures and capital expenditures rise with corruption. For this reason we interpret this work as reporting corruption leading to an output increase. However, as we have assumed that the pre-corruption state had optimal output, there should be a welfare loss from the output expansion. In the second study this welfare loss is expressed in terms of a decrease in the quality of public investment.

Corruption leading to output reductions   Although Gupta et al.'s (2000) study does not provide evidence of *how* corruption leads to reductions in project outputs (by bribes, or otherwise), it does indicate the types of output reductions that were observed related to social expenditures (health and education). Any cost savings that accompanied the reduction in output were not estimated in the study. So ΔB was (indirectly) estimated, but not ΔC.[9] If the costs were unaffected, or less than the reduction in benefits, then $(1 + a)\Delta B - (1 + m)\Delta C < 0$ as assumed.

There were 59 countries in the sample from which the results we report were used and the period covered was 1985–97. The main results were obtained by using the ICRG index (with the TI data used to provide a sensitivity analysis). There were four social outcomes that consistently had statistically significant reductions: child mortality, infant mortality, percent of low-birthweight babies, and primary school drop-out rates. Each of these outcome variables were dependent variables in regressions with corruption and other variables as independent variables.

The regression coefficients that were estimated were for a one-unit change in the standard deviation for the corruption index. Rather than report these coefficients, we refer instead to the results that were implied by these coefficients for two sets of countries classified as low and high corruption. 'High' and 'low' corruption countries were defined relative to

Table 15.2   Corruption and social indicators

Social indicator	Units of measurement	Low corruption	High corruption
Child mortality rate	Per 1000 live births	21.2	34.1
Infant mortality rate	Per 1000 live births	16.3	30.9
Low-birthweight babies	Percent	6.0	11.0
Drop-out rates	Percent	6.2	29.2

Source: Gupta et al. (2000, p. 21).

the medium corruption level in the sample. With our cost–benefit frame-work in mind, we can treat the difference between the effects for the two sets of countries as that pertaining to changing from a no-corruption to a corruption state (or vice versa). Table 15.2 (based on Gupta et al.'s figure 5) shows that, when countries move from a low corruption state to a high corruption state, the reductions in health care and education outcomes are very large.

Golden and Picci (2005) give some insight into how corruption lowers public project output in Italy. They quantify how much physical quanti-ties of public infrastructure are obtained from a given amount of public expenditure in each of 20 regions. Corruption involves siphoning off some of the money spent so that a region is 'missing' some of the physical infra-structure that it could have otherwise been expected to obtain. The bench-mark is what infrastructure can be bought if the national average amount had been spent. In the most corrupt region, Campania, the quantity of infrastructure obtained in the mid-1990s was only 36 percent of what would have been obtained if it used resources to the same extent as the national average (after correcting for price and other regional differences).

Corruption leading to output increases   In their cross-section analysis, Tanzi and Davoodi (1997) used the ICRG index for the 1980–95 period and regressed this (and other variables) on costs and physical benefits in separate equations. The number of countries used varied by regression. Because they found that $\Delta C > 0$ and $\Delta B < 0$, it follows that $(1 + a) \Delta B - (1 + m) \Delta C < 0$ on both accounts. Again there is evidence that changing government output from no-corruption levels reduces social welfare.

Project costs were measured by public investment expenditures and expressed as a ratio of GDP. As shown in their Table 15.1, a one unit increase in the corruption index would raise the public investment ratio by 0.38 percentage points if there were no other variables in the equation;

it would raise the ratio by 0.27 if real per capita GDP was also included; and the rise would be 0.48 if both GDP and government revenue as a share of GDP were included with the corruption index. GDP was included to control for a country's level of development and government revenue was included because this is the main source of funds for public investment.

The losses of benefits due to corruption were experienced as reductions in the quality of infrastructure. The hypothesis was that new public infrastructure would come at the expense of maintaining the existing infrastructure capital stock. Consistent with the hypothesis, whenever the infrastructure quality variable was expressed by a positive attribute, that is, paved roads in good condition and railway diesels in use, the corruption index had a significant negative coefficient, and when the quality was expressed as a negative attribute, that is, power outages and telecommunication faults, the corruption index had a significant positive coefficient.

Corruption and theft: estimating R_0^C
When there is no corruption, repayments by beneficiaries go to taxpayers as relief and welfare goes up because of it – see equation (15.1). With corruption in the form of theft, this loss of relief is recorded as a cost, so R_0^C has a negative sign attached to it in equations (15.3) and (15.5). Hence evidence of any adverse effects of corruption on tax revenues is an estimate of the loss of tax relief, as it is a measure of revenues not going to the government.

The Tanzi and Davoodi study that we covered in the last subsection also supplied estimates of the effect of corruption on the loss of revenues. They found that a unit rise in the corruption index lowered tax revenues as a ratio of GDP by 1.71 percentage points when GDP was used as a control variable, and 2.51 percentage points when GDP was excluded. These are very large amounts given that developing countries have average tax ratios around 18 percent. They are only around 13 percent for developing countries with the lowest incomes (see Tanzi, 1987, Table 8.3).

Hwang (2002), like Tanzi and Davoodi, used data by Business International (BI) as well as ICRG for his corruption indices.[10] He undertook four separate cross-section analyses for the 1980–1995 period (that is, for 1980, 1985, 1990 and 1995). Tax revenues as a share of GDP were negatively related to corruption in all his estimates. The magnitude of the reduction was considerable as (using his first corruption measure which covered a sample of 51 countries) a one standard deviation increase in a country's corruption (that is, by 2.41 points) decreased the tax share ranging from about 3.35 percentage points (1990 and 1995) to 5.13 (1985). In his data he had a country that had a tax share as low as 4.04 percent (as well as one with a high of 54.52 percent).

Table 15.3 *Estimates of the marginal cost of public funds for three countries*

Country	Indirect taxes	Import taxes
Bangladesh	1.05	1.20
Cameroon	0.90	1.05
Indonesia	1.04	0.99

Source: Devarajan et al. (1999b, p.10).

Apart from confirming the Tanzi and Davoodi results for overall tax revenues, Hwang's study was interesting because it also showed that the composition of tax revenues was affected by corruption. He found that a country with a higher level of corruption imposes greater taxes on international trade as a source of revenues. This finding is particularly important in light of the recent MCF estimates that have been obtained for developing countries by Devarajan et al. (1999b). Recall that in our CBA framework, the social value of theft was given as $(1 + m) R_0^C$. So the higher the m, the greater is the social loss from the theft. If it can be shown that m is higher for trade taxes, and corruption leads to this source being more relied on, then the social loss of corruption becomes greater. Devarajan et al. provided general equilibrium estimates for $1 + m$ for three countries and these are presented in our Table 15.3 (based on their Table 2) for the case where taxes are adjusted on a uniform basis.

For Bangladesh and Cameroon the fact that corruption distorts international taxes more than domestic taxes makes the social loss of theft greater; while in Indonesia the reverse is the case.[11]

Corruption and new theft: estimating $R_0^B - R_0^C$
We defined new theft as arising whenever user fees in the form of bribes do not end up in the hands of taxpayers, such that there is a positive difference between R_0^B and R_0^C. When repayments are legal, we have: $R_0^B R_0^C$. Obviously, as bribing is illegal, there are no direct data on how much of the monies paid by beneficiaries is transferred to taxpayers and how much is siphoned off via corruption. However, there exists indirect evidence reflected in an analysis of designated foreign aid by Devarajan et al. (1999a). All of these aid payments, which we denote by R_0^{AID}, are supposed to fund new public projects. So, in the absence of corruption: $R_0^{AID} = C_0$. In so far as changes in project expenditures C_0 are equivalent in size (but opposite in sign) to changes in costs financed by taxpayers R_0^C, as in our welfare criterion (15.1), then $R_0^{AID} = C_0$ implies $R_0^{AID} = R_0^C$ and we can

Table 15.4   Sectoral expenditures as a function of concessionary loans

Sector	Proportion of a dollar of aid spent domestically (α)	Proportion of a dollar of aid spent elsewhere ($1 - \alpha$)
Agriculture	Insignificant at 5% level	1.00
Energy	Insignificant at 5% level	1.00
Industry	Insignificant at 5% level	1.00
Health	Insignificant at 5% level	1.00
Transport and communications	0.36	0.64
Other	0.65	0.35
Education (without Botswana)	0.98	0.02

Source: Devarajan et al. (1999a, p. 30).

use the relation between R_0^{AID} and C_0 as an indirect test of $R_0^B = R_0^C$. Any foreign aid that does not enhance C_0 is prima facie evidence of corruption. Although these missing funds need not be privately appropriated and could be devoted to finance other types of public expenditures, or tax relief, these other uses were not those envisaged by the aid agencies. In the words of Devarajan et al. (p. 1) quoted from a past Deputy Direct of the World Bank: 'When the World Bank thinks it is financing an electric power station, it is really financing a brothel'.

Let α be the coefficient in a regression equation between designated foreign aid R_0^{AID} (concessionary loans) as the main independent variable and domestic public expenditures (sectoral expenditures)R_0^C as the dependent variable. If there is no corruption, α should equal 1. Thus $\alpha - 1$ is the extent to which this foreign aid is being siphoned off to non-designated areas.[12] Devarajan et al. looked at panel data for 18 Sub-Saharan countries from 1971 to 1995 to estimate α. Their findings appear in our Table 15.4 (based on their Table 5).

We see in Table 15.4 that there are wide sectoral differences in the degree to which foreign aid was diverted to undesignated areas. The range is from 100 percent for agriculture, energy, industry and health, to close to zero for education. Clearly we cannot use country-wide estimates of the effects of corruption to apply to all sectors in a country when we carry out our CBAs of particular projects. Interestingly, for the 18 African countries involved in the study, the α coefficient applied to overall foreign aid in a country was 0.89, which implies that only 0.11 was siphoned off on average. Corruption was not as high as is conventionally assumed for this continent.

An overall cost–benefit analysis of anticorruption policies in Indonesia
So far we have dealt with individual ingredients of our cost–benefit framework constructed in Section 2. Now we mould the complete evaluation criterion to the cost–benefit analysis done by Olken (2007) of anticorruption policies in Indonesia. Since Olken considered output losses stemming from the bribes being paid, he is effectively doing his cost–benefit analysis within the framework discussed in Section 2. In this framework, equation (15.5) can be used to calculate the welfare changes. Since Olken does not deal with the distinction between new and old theft, his version can be interpreted to be setting old theft equal to zero ($R_0^C = 0$), in which case equation (15.5) reduces to:

$$\Delta W = (1 + a)\Delta B - (1 + m)\Delta C - (1 + a)\beta \qquad (15.5a)$$

In the formulation in Section 2, taxpayers were given a weight of unity. In Olken's version, taxpayers were considered to be above-average income earners and so costs were given a lower distribution weight (as well as applying the marginal cost of public funds m). So Olken's version was effectively:

$$\Delta W = (1 + a)\,\Delta B - (1 + m)\,(1 + a)\,\Delta C - (1 + a)\beta \qquad (15.5b)$$

Before we deal with Olken's estimates of the ingredients of equation (15.5b), we need to first explain some details of the intervention involved.

Olken evaluated both a top-down intervention, that is, a government audit paid for by taxpayers, and a grassroots community monitoring initiative related to road expenditures in 600 Indonesian villages over the 2003–04 period. As the auditing intervention was the only effective one, we shall, like Olken, focus solely on the CBA as it applied to the auditing anticorruption policy. The policy involved increasing the probability of an audit from being very unlikely, 4 percent, to being certain, 100 percent. Villages were randomly assigned to a treatment group and a control group and differences between the two groups in terms of corrupt behavior were estimated. Corruption was viewed as theft involving 'missing expenditures', being the difference between what villages reported they spent on roads and what Olken estimated they spent on roads on the basis of the materials used to build the roads and the prices that these materials cost. On average, missing expenditures amounted to 24 percent across the villages in the study. The audits led to an 8 percent point reduction in missing expenditures.

Table 15.5 (which is based on Olken's Table 13 and reconstituted to fit in with our symbols and notation) presents Olken's results. The first

Table 15.5   Cost–benefit analysis of an audit intervention for an average village

	$-\Delta C$	$-(1 + m)(1 + a)\Delta C$
Audit costs	−$335	−$389
Time costs	−$ 31	−$ 31
Total costs	−$345	−420
	$-\beta$	$-(1 + a)\beta$
Bribes	−$468	−$286
	$+\Delta B$	$+(1 + a)\Delta B$
Total benefits	+$1,238	+$1,238
	Equal-weighted net benefits	ΔW
	+$425	+$508

Source: Olken (2007, p. 240).

column of numbers shows the outcomes for costs, bribes, benefits and net benefits with equal weights (approximately, the standard efficiency outcome) and the second column of numbers shows these same outcomes with unequal weights attached.[13]

The second column was based on values for m and a based on the following considerations. Olken chose $1 + m = 1.4$ as it was within the range of values derived by Devarajan et al. (1999b) for Indonesia and Bangladesh, by Ballard et al. (1985) for the USA, and by Ahmad and Stern (1987) for India. For his distribution weights, Olken used a generalization of equation (15.9) that becomes our equation (15.10), which was the original Squire and van der Tak (1975) formulation:

$$a_i = (\bar{y}/y_i)^\eta. \tag{15.10}$$

In equation (15.10), η is a constant that is the 'inequality aversion parameter'. Equation (15.9), which we presented earlier, is the special case where $\eta = 1$. This parameter can vary between 0 (which is the standard, equal weights, efficiency-only, distribution weights methodology) and infinity (in which case one only cares about the worse-off individual or group in society). Olken chose $\eta = 2$ for his CBA.[14] This is an extreme case, as Squire and van der Tak recommended using $\eta = 1$ and this author recommends $\eta = 0.5$ (see Brent, 1998, pp. 61, 276). The choice of value for η is a value judgment. Since this has been discussed in great detail elsewhere, we do not need to repeat this here (see Brent, 1984; 1998, ch. 3; 2006, ch. 10). We just want to add a further practical point to this discussion.

Clearly, equal distribution weights are not socially optimal even though they are the implicit set of weights used in mainstream economics. A dollar to a homeless person must have a higher social value than a dollar to a multi-millionaire. The policy issue is, how much higher? The concern is that if one gives too much weight to the poor person and not enough to a rich person, the effects on the poor person will dominate so much that there is hardly any point in carrying out a formal economic evaluation. If a dollar to a poor person is valued at 1,000 times that for the rich person, what program that cares for the homeless will not be found worthwhile, and what program that (initially) greatly affects the rich, like a roads program in developing countries, would ever be found worthwhile?

The practical point is this. Not only is the η that one chooses for equation (15.10) important, the specification of the individual or group that defines i is just as vital as is the i that one selects that determines the income that is to be compared with the national average income level. If i is an individual, and almost any society has some individuals who have 1/100th of the average, then that person's weight would be 10 if $\eta = 0.5$ were selected, would be 100 for $\eta = 1$, and it would be 10,000 for Olken's choice of $\eta = 2$. All of these weights would skew public expenditure decisions greatly. However, if i is chosen as a group belonging to the lowest quintile, as we did in Section 3, and we are considering a country such as Singapore or Uruguay where the lowest quintile has an income one-quarter of the average, the weight would be 2 for $\eta = 0.5$; it would be 4 for $\eta = 1$; and 16 for $\eta = 2$. These weights would be a much more politically feasible set of alternatives.[15]

In Olken's context where his i basically relates to a village, the weights applied are very modest indeed, even though he has selected $\eta = 2$. This is because he is considering 'rich' households with incomes 18.5 percent higher than the median and 'poor' workers who get wages 13 percent below the median. The benchmark for his weights is the median household and this is set equal to 1. In Table 15.5 we see that the time costs involved with villages participating in the audits and all of the benefits have the unit weight. Households in which a government official is involved, and would involve persons who are collecting bribes to carry out the roads program, come from households 18.5 percent higher than typical households in the village, and so get a distributional weight of 0.61. Lastly, we see that the weight to the taxpayers' costs is 0.83, as $278 times 1.4 equals $469 (the audit costs times the MCF) and this times 0.83 produces the $278 figure in the table.

Overall then, including distribution weights, Olken (2007, p. 242) found that the increased chances of an audit led to social net benefits of $508 per village. Interestingly, he considered also the special case 'that in many ways better approximates the way government agencies actually make such decisions' by doing a cost-effectiveness analysis instead of a CBA. Since the cost of the audit was $335 per village and the reduction in corruption, the bribes, was $468, there was a cost saving of $133 per village from doing the audits (or $164 with the villagers' time costs). So the audits were cost-effective.

The reasoning used in the cost-effective analysis is worth highlighting as it is consistent with the main point that we have made in this chapter. Olken points out that in the cost-effectiveness analysis he 'implicitly assumes that the social value of transfers to corrupt village officials is zero' (2007, p. 242). The bribes are a transfer payment to the officials from the taxpayers. This is a cost to the taxpayers and that is recorded in the evaluation. The corresponding gain to the officials from the bribes is not considered as a social advantage as it is illegal. This is the basis of our cost–benefit framework derived earlier in this chapter. But, note that Olken did not just implicitly make this assumption in his cost-effectiveness analysis. He also implicitly made this assumption when he undertook the cost–benefit analysis that is represented in Table 15.5. His evaluation was effectively based on criteria (15.5a) or (15.5b) and these were both built on the assumption that old theft and new theft were not a social gain, but just a social cost.

4   Summary and conclusions

For a cost–benefit framework to incorporate corruption that increases or diverts money flows, it is useful to disaggregate the outcomes of a public project into an output effect, involving benefits B and costs C, and a repayments effect R, involving a transfer from beneficiaries to taxpayers. The criterion is complete when one applies weights to the output and repayments effects.[16] The weights recognize not only the social significance of the incomes of the two groups involved (receiving the benefits and financing the costs), but also the additional loss of utility from the distortionary taxes that have to be used to finance the costs.

One school of thought on corruption, identified in the survey of the literature by Aidt (2003), focuses on the potential for corruption to be efficiency enhancing. If government policies and regulations reduce efficiency, then corruption, which allows that inefficiency be reduced, would increase welfare. Aidt criticizes this theory because: the corrupt officials would have an incentive to maximize bribes and not efficiency; resources are also wasted in keeping corrupt deals secret; the efficiency-enhancing contracts that could take place cannot be enforced by courts; and, rather than the original government failure that corruption is supposed to correct be considered exogenous, it could in fact be endogenous, for it could exist precisely because of its corruption potential for officials. In this chapter we suggest an additional reason why this school of thought should be discarded. Even if those engaged in corruption *are* better off with corruption, the fact that the gains are obtained illegally means that they have no social significance. When gains are lawful, 'consumer sovereignty' requires that they be counted. But, when the gains are illegal there needs to be an asymmetry in the CBA. Payments by beneficiaries reduce their satisfaction and these need to be recorded as costs of the project. But, the payments received by the corrupt officials are not legitimate and should be ignored.

An important distinction drawn in the literature is one between bribing with theft and bribing without theft. Since bribes go to the officials and not to general taxpayers, we considered all bribing to be theft. The relevant distinction then was between old theft (diverting the resources used to finance the costs of projects) and new theft (diverting the bribe payments away from taxpayers). We treated old theft as having solely distributional consequences. New theft, on the other hand, may have output effects. This is because the bribes act like user fees and thus affect the net willingness to pay for the public projects. By assuming the explicit use of a welfare criterion, we were able to argue that any changes in output from the bribes would lower welfare. The challenge then for applied cost–benefit work is to estimate the size of the output and distributional losses from theft.

The main anti-corruption intervention that we analyzed explicitly within our cost–benefit framework was that of raising public official salaries above those that can be earned in the private sector. The evaluation of this intervention depended on who was financing the additional salaries. When taxpayers finance the salary rise, output effects relative to the corruption state are welfare improving. In addition, there are gains that accrue from removing the old and new theft. The new cost is the increased resource requirement from the taxpayers paying the higher salaries. When beneficiaries pay for the additional salaries, the main difference is that user fees have to rise and there would be an additional output loss to quantify and evaluate.

There were two main types of empirical evidence that we looked at in the recent literature by the World Bank and IMF that would make the kinds of consideration in our cost–benefit framework operational. The first type was based on corruption indices developed by non-government agencies conducting surveys of investor (and other) perceptions of the extent of corruption in a country. The drawback of these corruption indices was their subjective nature. So we employed also a second type of evidence that was more behavioral. In trying to estimate the extent to which foreign aid was convertible (fungible) into the equivalent of domestic resources, we had prima facie evidence of the existence of corruption, seeing that foreign aid was designated to be spent on public projects and not on other purposes.

We emphasized studies that were in line with our cost–benefit framework that made a discrete comparison between project outcomes with and without corruption. So we looked at estimates of public wages with and without corruption and the magnitude of changes in social indicators that corresponded with movements from high to low corruption. In these and other instances, particularly those involved with the distribution of income, the effects of corruption were seen to be large. Whether public outputs were increased or increased, and we saw evidence of both, the corruption-induced output effect lowered welfare. In addition to the adverse effects on public sector activities as a whole, we also saw that different sectors were more adversely affected by corruption than others. Existing infrastructure would be harmed more than new infrastructure, and agriculture, energy, manufacturing and health expenditures would be more diverted than those on education.

We closed our survey of the relevant empirical literature by supplementing the studies of individual ingredients in our cost–benefit framework with an evaluation that supplied estimates of all the ingredients in the criterion so that it could make an overall assessment of the net benefits of a particular anticorruption intervention, that is, increasing the chances of an audit. Bribes were shown to be more important than their dollar cost because they reduced output, so benefits were forgone and they needed to be estimated and valued. Every dollar that was stolen from the road project in Indonesia would have generated $3.41 of discounted benefits and this constituted a large part of the reason why the audit intervention was worthwhile. A cost-effectiveness would have ignored these benefits and so would have greatly undervalued the intervention. Distribution weights did not dominate the evaluation outcome because the choice of group to which the weights were to be attached meant that the weights differed only slightly from unity.

When something is being evaluated like corruption, which affects both efficiency and distribution adversely, the weights one employs for income disparities and for the excess burden of taxes will not be crucial in determining the direction (sign) of cost–benefit outcomes. But, the magnitude of these parameters becomes important when one compares alternative ways of implementing an anti-corruption strategy. This is particularly important when deciding whether to finance the cost of raising wages to eliminate corruption by raising taxes or by increasing user fees paid by beneficiaries.

Notes

1. However, Bardhan (1997) does make clear that 'corruption' and 'illegal' are not synonymous. He points out that some gratuities are deemed lawful by the US Department of Defense when they are part of 'customary exchange' motivated by extending personal relationships.

2. Treisman considers that corruption is causally related to the level of development. He uses as an instrument for development a country's latitudinal distance from the equator and finds this significantly related to corruption in 57 countries in 1998.

3. Since there do not appear to be any new conceptual issues that arise when the social discount rate is applied to the effects of corruption, and none of the empirical literature we refer to mentions discounting, we omit this from our analysis in this chapter. Note that shadow pricing is another important ingredient in carrying out a social evaluation. To avoid introducing unnecessary complications, we assume that shadow pricing is incorporated in the measurement of the benefits and costs themselves.

4. Van Rijckeghem and Weder (1997) is the full version. Van Rijckeghem and Weder (2001) is a condensed version. The wages table we report does not appear in the condensed version.

5. But, of course, not all of the beneficiaries' reduction in income actually was appropriated by the public officials. The income gain to the officials, as well as the loss to the beneficiaries, would be recorded in the Gini coefficient, which was the second measure used in the study. We focus just on the income loss to the low-income group because we want to introduce one approach to measuring distribution weights for the poor group.

6. See World Bank (2007, Table 3, p. 293).

7. This way of viewing quintile shares as shares relative to the mean was presented in Browning and Browning (1994, p. 254).

8. For a discussion of the strengths and weaknesses of the Squire and van der Tak formula, see Brent (1998, ch. 3; or 2006, ch. 10), or Chapter 6 of this volume.

9. To measure the reduction in benefits one has to estimate the willingness to pay (or the compensation that must be received) for the outputs that were diminished.

10. Both indices are assessments by informed observers; the BI had their own network of correspondents, while the ICRG used the views of foreign investors. The ICRG is more useful as it is updated annually, unlike the BI.

11. Note that when there are existing distortions in an economy, introducing an extra distortion (such as a new tax) could improve the allocation of resources, making the MCF less than 1, which appears to be the case for some of the estimates in Table 15.3. For the theory and practice of the MCF in CBA, see Brent (2006).

12. In the study itself, domestic revenues are included with foreign aid to see whether the coefficients are the same, and this is the test that is used to see whether foreign aid is 'fungible'. However, we just deal with the simple test of whether foreign aid is being siphoned off or not. Designated foreign aid, unlike domestic revenues, should never be spent on non-designated areas. In a tax reform exercise, domestic revenues from one tax could be used to replace revenues from another. In this case new domestic tax revenues would have no connection with domestic public expenditures. So by focusing only on foreign aid, we are concentrating on a less ambiguous test of corruption-like activities.

13. Note that in our 'equal-weighted' column we have both a and m set equal to unity, while Olken's equal-weighted column only sets $a = 1$ and has $m = 1.4$. So his equal-weighted net benefits are lower than ours. Since his equal-weighted estimate does allow for tax distortions, his estimates are the more standard efficiency estimates and our estimates only approximate the efficiency outcome. We both have weighted net benefits equal to $508.

14. Olken, footnote 2, states that he is assuming 'constant relative risk aversion' and it is this parameter that he is setting equal to 2. Note that he is working with an individual's utility function and not a social utility function. Yet he talks about 'social value', so his parameter is really the inequality aversion parameter. It is important to understand that it is the social marginal utility of income that is relevant for CBA and not just the

individual's marginal utility of income. The social marginal utility of income is $\partial W/\partial y_i$ and an individual's marginal utility of income is $\partial u_i/y_i$ and the two are related by the chain rule: $\partial W/\partial y_i = (\partial W/\partial u_i)(\partial u_i/\partial y_i)$.

15.   The point about the definition of i being important carries over to many different contexts. When the group involved was the state, as it was for a CBA of user fees in India, the differences among the states was so small that $\eta = 1$ was chosen, as this produced correspondingly small weight differences. Again this meant that distributional issues would not predetermine the final outcomes. See Brent (1995).

16.   Strictly, to be 'complete', the cost–benefit criterion should also include discounting and specify a social discount rate.

References

Ahmad, E. and Stern, N. (1987), 'Alternative sources of government revenue: illustrations from India, 1979–80', in D. Newbery and N. Stern (eds), *The Theory of Taxation for Developing Countries*, New York: Oxford University Press, pp. 279–332.

Aidt, T.S. (2003), 'Economic analysis of corruption: a survey', *Economic Journal*, **113**, F632–F651.

Ballard, C.L., Shoven, J.B. and Whalley, J. (1985), 'General equilibrium computations of the marginal welfare costs of taxes in the United States', *American Economic Review*, **75**, 128–38.

Bardhan, P. (1997), 'Corruption and development: a review of issues', *Journal of Economic Literature*, **35**, 1320–46.

Brent, R.J. (1984), 'On the use of distributional weights in cost–benefit analysis: a survey of schools', *Public Finance Quarterly*, **12**, 213–30.

Brent, R.J. (1995), 'Cost–benefit analysis, user prices, and state expenditures in India', *Public Finance*, **50**, 327–41.

Brent, R.J. (1998), *Cost–Benefit Analysis for Developing Countries*, Cheltenham, UK and Lyme, USA: Edward Elgar.

Brent, R.J. (2006), *Applied Cost–Benefit Analysis*, 2nd edn, Cheltenham, UK and Northampton, MA, USA: Edward Elgar.

Browning, E.K. and Browning, J.M. (1994), *Public Finance and the Price System*, 4th edn, Englewood Cliffs, NJ: Prentice Hall.

Devarajan, S., Rajkumar, A.S. and Swaroop, V. (1999a), 'What does aid to Africa finance?', Development Research Group, Washington, DC: World Bank.

Devarajan, S., Thierfelder, K.E. and Suthiwart-Narueput, S. (1999b) 'The marginal cost of public funds in developing countries', Development Research Group, Washington, DC: World Bank.

Di Tella, R. and Schargrodsky, E. (2003), 'The role of wages and auditing during a crackdown on corruption in the city of Buenos Aires', *Journal of Law and Economics*, **46**, 269–92.

Golden, M.A. and Picci, L. (2005), 'Proposal for a new measure of corruption, illustrated with Italian data', *Economics and Politics*, **17**, 37–75.

Gorodnichenko, Y. and Sabirianova, K.P. (2007), 'Public sector pay and corruption: measuring bribery from micro data', *Journal of Public Economics*, **91**, 963–91.

Gupta, S., Davoodi, H. and Alonso-Terme, R. (2002), 'Does corruption affect income inequality and poverty?', *Economics of Governance*, **3**, 23–45.

Gupta, S., Davoodi, H. and Tiongson, E. (2000), 'Corruption and the provision of health care and education services', IMF Working Paper, WP/00/116, Washington, DC: International Monetary Fund.

Hwang, J. (2002), 'A note on the relationship between corruption and government revenue', *Journal of Economic Development*, **27**, 161–77.

Olken, B.A. (2007), 'Monitoring corruption: evidence from a field experiment in Indonesia', *Journal of Political Economy*, **115**, 200–239.

Schleifer, A. and Vishny, R.W. (1993), 'Corruption', *Quarterly Journal of Economics*, **58**, 599–617.

Squire, L. and van der Tak, H. (1975), *Economic Analysis of Projects*, Baltimore, MD: Johns Hopkins University Press.

Tanzi, V. (1987), 'Quantitative characteristics of the tax systems of developing countries', Ch.8 in D. Newbery and N. Stern (eds), *The Theory of Taxation for Developing Countries*, New York: Oxford University Press.

Tanzi, V. and Davoodi, H. (1997), 'Corruption, public investment and growth', IMF Working Paper, WP/97/139, Washington, DC: International Monetary Fund.

Treisman, D. (2000), 'The causes of corruption: a cross-national study', *Journal of Public Economics*, **76**, 399–457.

Van Rijckeghem, C. and Weder, B. (1997), 'Corruption and the rate of temptation: do low wages in the civil service cause corruption?', IMF Working Paper, WP/97/73, Washington, DC: International Monetary Fund.

Van Rijckeghem, C. and Weder, B. (2001), 'Bureaucratic corruption and the rate of temptation: do wages in the civil service affect corruption, and by how much?', *Journal of Development Economics*, **65**, 307–31.

World Bank (2007), *World Development Report 2007: Development and the Next Generation*, Washington, DC: World Bank.

PART IV

DYNAMIC EVALUATIONS

16 Social security and future generations
Hans Fehr and Øystein Thøgersen[*]

1 Introduction

Design and reform of social security in the form of public pension programs have a prominent place on the policy agenda in more or less all Organisation for Economic Co-operation and Development (OECD) economies as well as in many emerging markets. According to the OECD, nearly all of their 30 member countries have implemented at least some changes to their pension programs since 1990 and 17 have had major reforms (OECD, 2007). These widespread reforms were the logical, and probably unavoidable, consequence of the general developments. The public pension programs, which essentially are financed on a pay-as-you-go (paygo) basis, matured over several decades and in most cases the generosity of the programs increased along several dimensions. It is probably fair to say that this development in many cases culminated with the implementation of quite liberal early retirement programs during the 1970s and 1980s. Then, during the last two or three decades, a growing awareness of how the financial viability of the programs is threatened by (mainly) ageing populations, ignited the current wave of reforms. Given the widely perceived seriousness of the financial problems and the intensity of the ongoing debate, a series of additional reforms in the years to come is a safe prediction.

Assessments of public pension programs must, as in the case of any other tax-transfer program, consider the trade-off between the gains caused by intended distributional effects associated with protection and income maintenance for the old and, on the other hand, the costs due to the induced distortions.[1] These trade-offs tend to be quite complex, reflecting that any program or reform proposal have both inter- and intergenerational distributional effects and distortions that must be assessed by means of an intertemporal framework. At the current stage, the typical OECD economy recognizes in particular the need for reforms in order to prevent sharply escalating tax burdens for the young and future generations.[2] This focus is reflected in the following. We consider the effects of pension reforms on the intergenerational distribution of welfare and tax burdens – and we highlight the assessments of such effects from reforms that intend to scale down unfunded pension programs in order to improve their financial viability.

Table 16.1   Old-age dependency ratios (ratio of population aged 65 and above to population aged 15–64, selected countries, %)

	2000	2015	2030	2045
France	36.4	43.9	59.3	67.7
Germany	33.3	40.2	56.6	65.3
Japan	25.3	45.4	58.8	75.9
UK	30.8	35.2	46.5	53.2
USA	21.6	24.6	36.4	40.5
OECD total	24.8	30.5	42.2	51.7

Source: OECD Factbook 2007, www.oecd.org.

Table 16.2   Escalation of early retirement (per cent of male population aged 55–64 in the workforce, selected countries)

	1980	1990	1995	2000
France	65.3	43.0	38.4	38.5
Germany	64.1	52.0	48.2	48.2
Japan	82.2	80.4	80.8	78.4
UK	62.6	62.4	56.1	59.8
USA	69.7	65.2	63.6	65.6

Sources: Fenge and Pestieau (2005, p. 6); OECD.

In order to illustrate the severity of the expected ageing, it is useful to look at some data from the OECD economies. Table 16.1 presents the dependency ratios defined as the ratio between the number of people above the age of 64 to the number of people aged 15–64. The pattern is striking and obviously critical for the financing of paygo-financed pension programs. In the average OECD economy each individual above the age of 64 was in year 2000 supported by approximately four individuals in the regular working age. In 2045 this number is expected to drop to approximately two. This development reflects a combination of strongly increased longevity and (particularly in some countries) low fertility rates.[3]

In addition, the financial burden of social security also escalates as a consequence of more early retirement over time, see Table 16.2.[4] Many OECD countries also experience an increasing number of exits from the labor force and into disability programs or equivalent schemes. These developments imply that the median real retirement age has been on a falling trend during the last decades.[5] Accordingly, the tax base for social security contribution rates deteriorates even more than suggested by the drop in dependency ratios.

Describing and comparing various public pension programs and associated reform packages, we find it useful to have in mind a three-dimensional classification inspired by Lindbeck and Persson (2003). The first dimension refers to whether contribution rates or benefit rates adjust in response to fluctuations in variables that determine the financial opportunity set of the pension program. Theory focuses on the cases of pure defined benefit (DB) or defined contribution (DC) programs. While the benefit level is exogenously given and the contribution rate adjusts accordingly in a DB program, the opposite characterizes a DC program. In reality many programs are a mixture of these strict alternatives (see Wagener, 2004). As discussed in more detail below, the DB versus DC dimension is crucial for the risk-sharing properties of the pension programs.

The second dimension relates to the degree of funding, ranging from a pure paygo program (zero funding) to a fully funded program. Paygo funding means that pensions to the old are financed by contributions from the working generation period by period. Funding, on the other hand, implies that pensions to the old are financed by previously accumulated contributions (by the same generation while participating in the labor market) plus interests.

The third dimension captures individual incentives in the sense of the strength of the tax–benefit link of the actual program, ranging from a completely flat benefit program to a perfectly actuarial program. We note that this dimension, in terms of the definitions offered by Lindbeck and Persson, focuses on the 'degree of actuarial fairness' facing each individual and influencing his/her labor supply decisions, and not 'the actuarial balance' of the program which characterizes the aggregate financial viability of the program.[6]

Figure 16.1 clarifies the relationship between the two latter dimensions. As shown by the solid arrow, many OECD economies with (almost) pure paygo programs experienced a weakening of the tax–benefit link during the 1970s and 1980s due to different types of reforms including implementation of early retirement programs.

The dotted arrows refer to three possible reform strategies. Reform A can be interpreted as basically a fiscal policy strategy. In this case the reform does not alter the rules and incentives of the pension programs facing the individuals, but the government accumulates more capital (in, say, a buffer fund), for example motivated by an intention to counteract potential increases in future contribution rates.[7] Reform B, on the other hand, maintains the pure paygo financing, but introduces improved incentives towards higher labor supply and/or a longer working career. Finally, reform C involves both more funding and an improved tax–benefit link.[8] The typical clear-cut

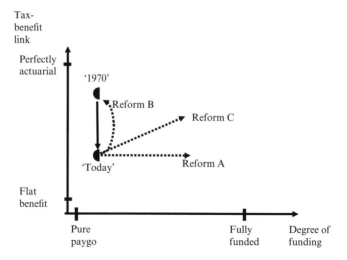

Figure 16.1   Dimensions of pension reform

example of such a reform is the introduction of real, individual (privatized) accounts as a part of the mandatory pension program. Implementation of this type of reform is well known from, for example, Chile and Sweden (see, respectively, Mesa and Mesa-Lago, 2006 and Persson, 2000).

The next section explains the main theoretical principles related to the study of intergenerational effects of pension programs and reforms. Emphasis is devoted to the clarification of the different mechanisms underlying the three dimensions of pension reform, presented above. First we consider basic key insights based on a deterministic framework. Then we move on to stochastic economies, which have received much attention recently. In Section 3 we turn to numerical assessments based on simulation models that feature several extensions necessary to provide realistic magnitudes – but still build on the same essential mechanisms as the theoretical models. Recent advances in the rich literature dealing with large-scale deterministic models in the tradition of Auerbach and Kotlikoff (1987) are given a broad treatment. Finally, the smaller, but quickly growing literature on stochastic numerical models is given ample attention. Section 4 concludes.

At the outset, we shall mention that it is obviously not possible to cover all parts of the enormous literature on intergenerational effects of social security. We shall particularly point at the fact that the highly interesting literature on political aspects of social security reform is not covered, the reason being that such a topic warrants a separate treatment.[9] Moreover, we shall only very briefly refer to the econometric literature on labor supply and retirement responses to tax-transfer policies.

2 Theoretical principles

Attempting to explain theoretical principles in a clear and transparent way, this section relies on a stylized overlapping generations framework where two generations are present in any period and the only objective of the government is to run the pension program. The young generation participates in the labor market, while the old generation is retired. The representative member of the young generation in period t (that is, generation t) supplies l_t units of labor and receives a net wage equal to $w_t(1 - \tau_t)$ per unit. Here w_t is the gross wage, and τ_t is the contribution rate of the pension program. In period $t + 1$, the representative generation t individual is old and receives a pension benefit given by p_{t+1}. Introducing θ_{t+1} as the replacement rate of the pension program, we have that $p_{t+1} = \theta_{t+1}w_t l_t$. The size of generation t is given by N_t, and n_{t+1} is population growth from period t to $t + 1$, that is, $N_{t+1} = (1 + n_{t+1})N_t$. Wage growth reflects productivity growth in our long-run setting and is given by λ_t, $w_{t+1} = (1 + \lambda_{t+1})w_t$.

The basic accounting identities of the pension programs reveal the key variables that determine their attractiveness and effects. A paygo program transfers resources between generations in the sense that total contributions from the young generation must by definition be equal to total pension benefits to the old. Thus,

$$N_{t+1}\tau_{t+1}w_{t+1}l_{t+1} = N_t\theta_{t+1}w_t l_t. \tag{16.1}$$

Substituting for N_{t+1} and w_{t+1}, we obtain:

$$\theta_{t+1} = (1 + g_{t+1})\tau_{t+1}, \quad (1 + g_{t+1}) = (1 + \lambda_{t+1})(1 + n_{t+1})\frac{l_{t+1}}{l_t}, \tag{16.2}$$

where g_{t+1} is the implicit return of the paygo program. It follows that this return is given by the growth of the aggregate wage sum which in turn is determined by three key factors: n_{t+1}, λ_{t+1} and the developments in labor supply.

In the case of a funded program, resources are transferred over the lifetime of each generation and the representative individual receives a pension which is given by own contributions plus interest earned from the fund.[10] We have that $p_{t+1} = (1 + r_{t+1})\tau_t w_t l_t = \theta_{t+1}w_t l_t$, where r_{t+1} is the relevant real interest rate. It follows that

$$\theta_{t+1} = (1 + r_{t+1})\tau_t. \tag{16.3}$$

We start out with a deterministic framework. Then the implicit return of the paygo program as well as the market return of the funded program are known for all decision makers and individuals at all points of time, and the distinction between DB and DC programs do not matter. This allows us to focus exclusively on the tax–benefit link and the choice (or mixture) between funding and paygo financing. Turning subsequently to a stochastic environment where the key variables λ_t, n_t and r_t are subject to shocks, we consider the intergenerational redistribution of risks by means of pension programs and how this depends crucially on the DB versus DC dimension.

Basic insights: deterministic framework

Effects of funding versus paygo   Consider a completely deterministic model where $n_t = n$ and $\lambda_t = \lambda$ for all t. To obtain the pure intergenerational effects of paygo financing versus funding of the pension program, we assume that the labor supply of any young generation is inelastic and equal to unity, that is, $l_t = 1$. These assumptions imply that $g_t = g$. The welfare of generation t is given by a standard utility function $U_t = u(c_{1,t}, c_{2,t+1})$, where $c_{1,t}$ is consumption in the first period of life (which takes place in period t for generation t) and $c_{2,t+1}$ is consumption in the second period of life. Both $c_{1,t}$ and $c_{2,t+1}$ are normal goods, which implies that the sign of the welfare effects are given by the effects on the net lifetime income, b_t,

$$b_t = (1 - \tau_t)w_t + \frac{1}{1 + r_{t+1}}\theta_{t+1}w_t. \tag{16.4}$$

Clearly, the case of no pension program is characterized by $\tau_t = \theta_t = 0$ and implies $b_t = w_t$.

When a paygo program is implemented, say in period $t = 1$, the initial old generation (generation 0) receives a windfall in the form of a pension benefit from the succeeding generation. This, of course, leads to an increase in this generation's consumption and welfare. All succeeding generations face both contributions while young and benefits while old. Assuming $\tau_t = \tau$ and $\theta_t = \theta$ for $t = 1, 2, 3, \ldots$, it follows from (16.2), (16.4) and the assumptions above that:

$$b_t = w_t - \frac{r_{t+1} - g}{1 + r_{t+1}}\tau w_t. \tag{16.5}$$

In the small open economy case, factor prices are given and the net effect on b_t is given by the last term on the RHS. The sign of this effect, and in turn the sign of the welfare effect, hinges on the sign of $r_{t+1} - g$.[11] The last sign is strictly positive in the empirically interesting case of dynamic efficiency, implying that the paygo program reduces b_t and welfare for all generations except the initial old generation. This reflects that the paygo program reduces the need for private saving, which in a small open economy leads to a deterioration of the net foreign asset position and correspondingly a lower steady-state net import volume.

If general equilibrium effects are taken into account (that is, the closed economy case), it follows that the reduction in private saving reduces the capital intensity of the economy and implies a lower wage level and higher real interest rates. Given dynamic efficiency, the paygo program pushes the economy further away from a golden rule growth path and welfare is reduced; see Samuelson (1975) for the original analysis or Heijdra and van der Ploeg (2002, ch. 17) for a textbook treatment.

It follows that the effects of a paygo program are essentially equivalent to the effects of public debt; see Diamond (1965) for the seminal analysis in a closed economy and Persson (1985) for open economies. This is highlighted by Auerbach and Kotlikoff (1987, pp. 149–50), who show how the implementation of a paygo program can be modeled as a type of debt policy where the future pension benefits to the young generation are an implicit social security debt.

In contrast to a paygo program, a funded pension program has no real effects in this framework. Substituting (16.3) into (16.4), we immediately see that $b_t = w_t$, just as in the case of a no pension program. This reflects that the funded program is a perfect substitute for private saving – as long as we assume that the credit market is perfect and all agents in the economy face the same interest rate. The capital accumulation in the pension fund will exactly offset lower ordinary private saving, and national saving will not be affected.

Transition from paygo to fund   Ageing and early retirement have led to a decline in the implicit return of the paygo programs and therefore a widespread ambition to implement transitions to (more) funded programs. A direct and immediate transition is obviously hard to imagine, because this implies that the old generation in the transition period would not receive any pension – or alternatively that the young generation in this period have to pay both the pension benefits to the old as well as their own contribution to the new pension fund. Neither of these brutal options seems feasible. The issue is therefore whether it is possible to implement a transition accompanied by transfers between generations in a way that leads to a Pareto-improving outcome. As shown by Breyer (1989), such a combined transition and transfer scheme does not exist.[12] This result is intuitive when we note that the transition does not lead to any aggregate income gain in the sense that income loss of the old generation in the transition period that does not receive its expected pension, is equal to the capital value of all future generations' income gain (see Sinn, 2000, and Lindbeck and Persson, 2003).

The conclusion that a Pareto-improving transition is not feasible relies on a framework that disregards distortions associated with the pension program and related behavioral responses, that is, we have considered transitions of the 'reform A' type in Figure 16.1. This conclusion is altered if the reform package consists of both a switch from paygo to fund and a tax reform that reduces the distortions caused by the contribution rate. In order to capture the latter effect, the model framework must be extended somewhat, typically by introducing endogenous labor supply in the first period of life. In this case, the utility of generation t is given by $U_t = u(c_{1,t}, c_{2,t+1}, l_t)$, and it is assumed that the contribution rates in the initial paygo program are levied as distorting payroll taxes.[13] Versions of such reform packages where distorting payroll taxes are replaced by either an actuarially relationship between contributions and benefits or by lump-sum taxes, are shown by Homburg (1990) and Breyer and Straub (1993) to yield Pareto-optimal transitions in, respectively, small open and closed economies.

The reform packages that yield Pareto-optimal transitions can be interpreted as versions of reform C in Figure 16.1. An interesting insight is that these packages can be decomposed into two separate reforms, one of type A in the figure and one efficiency-generating 'tax reform' of type C. Clearly, the latter type of reform should be implemented independent of any move to funded programs due to the obvious existence of static inefficiencies. While introductions of contributions based on lump-sum taxes seem unrealistic, moves in the direction of (more) actuarial tax–benefit links are widely observed, for example by the introduction of simulated, so-called non-financial defined contribution (NDC) schemes within paygo-financed pension programs (see Holzmann and Palmer, 2006).

The feasibility of a Pareto-optimal transition might still be problematic when intragenerational heterogeneity is taken into account. Clearly, the substitution of an actuarial tax–benefit link or lump-sum taxes for regular payroll taxes will hurt low-income individuals within the actual generation. Brunner (1996) utilizes a version of the model of Breyer and Straub (1993), which is extended to include two groups of individuals with different earning abilities within each generation. He shows that this makes it much harder (but in principle not impossible) in terms of the complexity of the necessary tax-transfer scheme to implement Pareto-optimal transitions. In Section 3 we return to the interaction between intra- and intergenerational redistribution when we look at richer simulation models.

With a view to the current reform agenda in many countries, it is clear that policy makers rarely have the luxury to implement Pareto-optimal reforms. The real issue is normally to choose between alternatives which in different ways benefit some generations (and/or subgroups within each generation) and hurt others. Comparative assessments of the various alternatives must then be based on a social welfare function. Disregarding intragenerational considerations and assuming that the utility function of the representative generation t individual is additively separable, we can introduce the social welfare function:

$$V_t = u(c_{2,t}) + \sum_{s=t}^{\infty} \frac{1}{(1 + \theta)^{s-t}} [u(c_{1,t},l_t) + \delta u(c_{2,t+1})], \qquad (16.6)$$

which weight together the utility of the current and all future generations (the first term on the RHS captures the utility of the old generation in the initial period t). We note the distinction between the individual time preference rate, δ, and the intergenerational social discount rate, θ.

The crucial issue for the assessments of reforms which impact the intergenerational distribution is obviously the specification of θ. We might imagine upfront that $\theta \geq 0$, or we can alternatively adopt a 'Benthamite' specification and weight utility by the size of each generation, that is, $(1 + \theta) = (1 + n)^{-1}$. Then the sign of θ will be the opposite of n. Generally, the specification of θ is a major topic in the social choice literature (see, for example, Portney and Weyant, 1999 for surveys of the major issues involved).

Endogenous retirement   The observed escalation of early retirement implies that the probably most important aspects of interaction between labor supply and the pension program are related to the retirement decisions of individuals. The simplest way to capture this explicitly in theoretical models is simply to assume that $l_t = 1 - x_t$, where l_t and x_t are interpreted as the fractions of the first period of life that is spent in, respectively, the labor force and as a pensioner on presumably an early retirement scheme. Alternatively, several papers specify the utility function as $U_t = u(c_{1,t}, c_{2,t+1}, \alpha_{t+1})$, where α_{t+1} is the fraction of generation t's second period of life (that is, of period $t + 1$) that is spent in the labor force (see, for example, Hu, 1979 and Andersen, 2005).

As long as the contribution rate is not levied as a lump-sum tax or the tax–benefit link is fully actuarial, the pension program distorts the retirement decision. Most paygo-financed pension programs and early retirement schemes have an ambiguous effect on labor supply because the income effect caused by the reduction in b_t in the normal case of dynamic efficiency contributes to a higher retirement age, while the substitution effect has the opposite sign. Given available evidence (see, for example, Gruber and Wise, 1999 and Fenge and Pestiau, 2005), it seems clear that the substitution effect dominates in the overwhelming majority of real-world programs, reflecting in particular very strong incentives for early retirement for low-income individuals.

Accepting the conclusion that the retirement age is lowered, individuals might choose to increase their life-cycle savings in response to more years spent in retirement. This induced retirement effect on saving was first highlighted in a well-known paper by Feldstein (1974). The existence of this effect raises the empirical question of whether, or to what extent, the first-order effect of public pensions replacing private savings (for a given retirement age, see above) is counteracted.[14] Available evidence, including Feldstein's own, indicates that this is clearly not the case, however. Calculations by Feldstein (1974, 1996), suggest that social security reduces private savings in the US by as much as 60 percent.

Intergenerational risk sharing
Turning to intergenerational risk sharing issues, we assume in this subsection that one or more of the key variables λ_t, n_t and r_t are stochastic. In a DC program ($\tau_t = \tau$), fluctuations in these variables translate into fluctuations in the replacement rate, θ_t, according to the budget constraints (16.2) and (16.3) for, respectively, paygo and funded programs. Correspondingly, in a DB paygo program $\theta_t = \theta$ and τ_t fluctuates. Focusing on risk sharing, we abstract from issues related to the potentially distorting nature of public pension schemes in most of the following theoretical analysis. Thus, unless otherwise explicitly stated, we assume that the representative individual in each generation supplies inelastically one unit of labor in the first period of life.

The potential for improved intergenerational risk sharing by means of public pension programs rests mainly on capital market imperfections, most notably the non-marketability of human capital. Because a paygo program in effect is a government-created asset that allows one generation to trade in the human capital returns of the next, such a program may serve to correct for incomplete financial markets if the correlation between the implicit return of the paygo program and other capital returns are less than perfect (see Merton, 1983; Richter, 1990; Persson, 2002; and Matsen, and Thøgersen, 2004). An additional issue is related to the fact that large fractions of the households have zero or negligible stock holdings in their portfolios, even in the US (see Poterba, 2000). This might reflect factors such as credit constraints (particularly early in life) and/or information asymmetries. Under such circumstances, a properly designed funded pension program might provide individuals with a welfare-improving stock market exposure.

Figure 16.2 is a useful tool for clarifying the various intergenerational risk-sharing effects of a paygo program and how their relevance depends

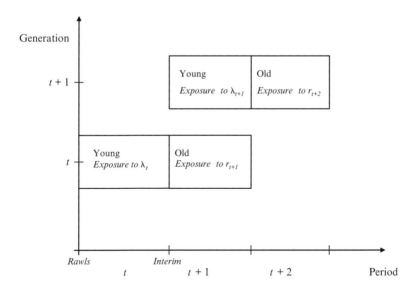

Note: Generation *t* is considered from time '*rawls*' in the case of Rawlsian risk sharing and from time '*interim*' in the case of interim risk sharing.

Figure 16.2   Shocks to labor income and stock market returns in the model economy

on the appropriate risk concept. The social security literature deals essentially with two alternative risk concepts (see Ball and Mankiw, 2001; Wagener, 2003; and Thøgersen, 2006). One is the 'Rawlsian', *ex-ante* perspective which considers individuals in a pre-birth position. The other is the 'interim' perspective which considers individuals' position contingent on realized wages in their first part of life.

At the outset, the representative generation *t* individual is exposed to a wage shock in period *t* and a capital return shock in period *t* + 1. The existence of a DC paygo program on the one hand transfers some of the wage shock to generation *t* − 1, but on the other hand provides an exposure to the wage shock of the succeeding generation *t* + 1. Thus, looking at Figure 16.2 this program pools generation *t*'s capital income risk (r_{t+1}) with the wage income risk of generation *t* + 1 (λ_{t+1}) and population risk (n_{t+1}). This effect is relevant under both risk concepts. In addition, there is an intertemporal sharing of wage income and population risks, that is, the pooling λ_t with λ_{t+1} and n_{t+1}. This effect is only relevant under Rawlsian risk sharing.

In a DB paygo program, the realization of λ_t determines both the first-period wage and the pension benefit. Consequently, the interim perspective on intergenerational risk sharing is not relevant here. In the Rawlsian case, this version of the program implies a pooling of λ_t and n_t, however.

Intergenerational income risk sharing   Early contributions to the intergenerational risk-sharing effects of paygo programs are provided by Enders and Lapan (1982, 1993) and Gordon and Varian (1988). Utilizing overlapping generations models with somewhat different features, they demonstrate that paygo programs might provide welfare gains as a consequence of intergenerational income risk-sharing corresponding to a pooling of λ_t with λ_{t+1} in the above framework. Thøgersen (1998) builds closely on Gordon and Varian's analysis and shows how the risk-sharing properties of the paygo program in the case of Rawlsian risk sharing depend crucially on whether it is a DC or a DB program.

In the stylized framework of Thøgersen, the gross wage of generation t is given by $w_t = w + \varepsilon_t$, where ε_t is a mean zero shock with a variance equal to σ^2. Both population growth and the real interest rate are constant, $r_{t+1} = r$ and $n_{t+1} = n$. Introducing a pension program with a fixed contribution rate, $\tau_t = \tau$ and $0 < \tau < 1$, we derive – consistent with (16.2), (16.4) and the fact that $(1 + \lambda_t) = (w + \varepsilon_{t+1})/(w + \varepsilon_t)$ in this specific set-up – that:

$$b_t = w - \left(\frac{r - n}{1 + r}\right)\tau w + (1 - \tau)\varepsilon_t + \frac{1 + n}{1 + r}\tau\varepsilon_{t+1}. \qquad (16.7)$$

Preferences are given by a mean-variance specification, i.e. $U_t = u[E(b_t)] - v[\mathrm{Var}(b_t)]$ where $u' > 0$ and $v' > 0$.[15] The risk-sharing properties of this program are obvious if we consider for a moment the case of $r = n$. Then $E(b_t) = w$, just as in the case of no program at all. The variance has been reduced, however. It follows from (16.7) that $\mathrm{Var}(b_t) = [(1 - \tau)^2 + \tau^2] < \sigma^2$. Thus, $\mathrm{Var}(b_t)$ is minimized for $\tau = \frac{1}{2}$, implying that $\mathrm{Var}(b_t) = \frac{1}{2}\sigma^2$. In the case of $r > n$, (16.7) implies intuitively that the gains of a lower $\mathrm{Var}(b_t)$ come at the cost of a reduced $E(b_t)$.

Looking at a DB version of the paygo program, that is the case of $\theta_t = \theta$, $0 < \theta < 1$, the conclusions are altered dramatically. Using (16.2) and (16.4), we now obtain:

$$b_t = w - \frac{r - n}{(1 + n)(1 + r)}\theta w + \left(1 + \frac{1}{1 + r}\theta\right)\varepsilon_t - \frac{1}{(1 + n)}\theta\varepsilon_{t-1}, \qquad (16.8)$$

and it follows that $\mathrm{Var}(b_t) = [(1 + \frac{1}{1 + r}\theta)^2 + (\frac{1}{1 + n}\theta)^2] > \sigma^2$. Thus, given the Rawlsian perspective, this version of the paygo program increases the variance, while $E(b_t) \le w$ in the relevant case of $r \ge n$.

A crucial issue related to the potential risk-sharing effects of paygo programs is related to the specification of the long-run wage process. As pointed out by Thøgersen (2006), a random walk assumption (that is, permanent shocks) rather than the deterministic trend assumption in the example above implies that the favorable risk-sharing effects of a DC paygo program vanish. Intuitively, this reflects that the period t wage shock is also fully reflected in the wage and DC paygo transfer in period $t + 1$. While available evidence on the stochastic properties of wage growth mainly sheds light on much more short-run developments, it still seems fair to argue that evidence is tilted towards a specification with deterministic long-run wage growth (see De Menil et al., 2006 and Thøgersen, 2006).

Comparisons between DB and DC paygo programs are also provided by Wagener (2003, 2004). Adopting an interim risk-sharing perspective, he shows that the conclusions are altered significantly as compared to Rawlsian risk sharing. In the interim case, the wage shock in the first period of life is not relevant. The key issue is whether the paygo program implies uncertain pension benefits for the old. A DC program adds an exposure to the succeeding generation's wage shock that translates into uncertain pension benefits. Intuitively, this is not the case for a DB version of the program, which therefore is favored.

A portfolio choice approach   As discussed in detail by Merton (1983) and also by Persson (2002), a paygo program can be interpreted as a 'quasi-asset'. The optimal investment in this asset, as expressed by the optimal contribution rate, will depend on its stochastic properties, notably the expected value and variance of the implicit return, g_t, and its covariance with alternative financial assets. Given a below-unity correlation between the return on alternative financial assets and g_t, the paygo asset may well be a part of individuals' optimal portfolio of pension savings.

While Persson presents some calculations based on Swedish data that suggest that a paygo program should enter the optimal total portfolio of Swedish citizens, more formalized models are provided by Dutta et al. (2000), Matsen and Thøgersen (2004) and Thøgersen (2006). Dutta et al. (2000) consider intergenerational risk sharing based on what we have defined as interim risk sharing. Employing a mean-variance specification of preferences, they derive simple closed-form solutions for the optimal paygo program, that is, the optimal portfolio share of individuals' gross wage income invested in the paygo asset. A problem related to the interpretation of these solutions is the fact that they depend on the magnitude of the realized wage in the early part of life. The wage will change over time and the solutions are time inconsistent in the sense that the optimal paygo program of generation t is not optimal for generation $t + 1$.

Adopting a somewhat extended framework that combines an overlapping generations structure with a modeling of portfolio choice based on isoelastic preferences and log-linear approximations (see Campbell and Viceira, 2002), Matsen and Thøgersen (2004) and Thøgersen (2006) derive closed-form solutions for the optimal DC paygo program under both interim and Rawlsian risk sharing – and in the latter paper also under alternative assumptions for the stochastic properties of wage income growth. As compared to a mean-variance specification, isoelastic preferences yield optimal portfolio shares that are independent of the wage realization in the first period of life. In our setting, this implies that the optimal paygo program of generation t is also optimal for succeeding generations.

Formally, the model assumes that consumption takes place in the second period, implying that the expected utility of generation t is given by $U_t = E_t(\delta \frac{1}{1-\gamma} c_{2,t+1}^{1-\gamma})$, where γ is the coefficient of relative risk aversion. Financial savings, which in this framework is the full net wage income in the first period of life, can be allocated to risk-free bonds or risky stocks. Their respective returns are r^f (which is constant) and r_{t+1}, $r^f < E_t(r_{t+1})$. It follows that:

$$c_{2,t+1} = (1 - \tau)w_t[1 + r^f + \omega(r_{t+1} - r^f)] + \theta_{t+1}w_t, \qquad (16.9)$$

where ω is the portfolio share of net wage in stocks. Substituting for θ_{t+1}, see (16.2) when τ is fixed and labor supply is exogenous and equal to unity, we can rewrite (16.9) as:

$$c_{2,t+1} = w_t[1 + r^f + \tau(g_{t+1} - r^f) + (1 - \tau)\omega(r_{t+1} - r^f)]. \qquad (16.10)$$

We observe that the effective portfolio shares in the paygo asset, stocks and bonds are, respectively, τ, $(1 - \tau)\omega$ and $1 - \tau - (1 - \tau)\omega$. Assuming perfect financial markets and no frictions, individuals choose the optimal ω given τ, while the government derives the optimal τ given knowledge about how ω will depend on τ. An alternative approach is to consider the case where the representative individual does not participate in the stock market. Then the government can optimize both ω and τ, and accordingly run a mixed paygo and funded pension program.

Utilizing log-linear approximations along the lines of Campbell and Viceira (2002), it turns out that it is possible to derive very illuminating closed-form solutions for the optimal τ and ω. Intuitively, the key factors are a measure of the trade-off between each asset's mean return and variance – in addition to the covariance between these returns, σ_{rg}. While straightforward general equilibrium models suggest that this covariance is high, reflecting a model prediction of perfect correlation between capital returns and economic growth, available numerical evidence gives another impression even for long time spans relevant for social security analyses. In particular, when stock market returns are considered rather than broader measures of capital income, this correlation tends to be low for any small or medium-sized economy and modest also for the US (see Matsen and Thøgersen, 2004 for a discussion). Given this insight, the basic message is that a low-yielding paygo program can be rationalized.

Factor price responses In closed economies, the risk-sharing effects of social security are accompanied by factor price responses. An early contribution that highlighted these responses is Smith (1982), who considered stochastic demographic changes. Building on the basic overlapping generations model of Diamond (1965), he noted that individuals who are born into large generations face disadvantages compared to individuals born into smaller generations. First, the gross wage received in the first period of life will be relatively low as a consequence of the abundance of labor (that is, a high labor–capital ratio). Second, the real interest rate earned on savings brought into the second period of life will (if the succeeding generations is relatively small) be low because of a high capital–labor ratio in this period.

Smith then considered the effects of, respectively, DB and DC types of paygo pension programs. Intuitively, a DB program will under reasonable assumptions provide welfare gains (as seen from a Rawlsian perspective as defined above). This reflects that a DB program will transfer part of the wage disturbance of the young generation to the pensioners. This will also partly offset the factor price responses to the disturbance because the DB program counteracts the effects of the disturbance on saving.

Turning to the analysis of productivity risk, which in turn leads to fluctuations in gross income and factor prices, the issue is whether, and to what extent, the gains of the direct risk-sharing effects (which we have analyzed in a partial equilibrium, small open economy framework above) are offset by the crowding-out effects of the paygo program. A meaningful analysis of this trade-off calls for numerical analyses, which will be the topic for the rest of this chapter.

3 Simulation models to assess social security policies

Since the pathbreaking work of Auerbach and Kotlikoff (1987), social security programs and policies around the world have been analyzed quantitatively with dynamic general equilibrium models that feature overlapping generations (OLG). In this section we first describe the general structure of this model and then discuss recent developments and innovations. In order to structure our presentation, we distinguish between recent innovations with deterministic and with stochastic OLG models that focus on the social security debate.

Basic set-up and implications of the Auerbach–Kotlikoff model
The Auerbach and Kotlikoff model (the AK model) builds on the discrete time OLG structure utilized in the theoretical analyses above, but extends it along several dimensions in order to obtain realism with respect to quantitative assessments. Intuitively, as soon as more than two generations are taken into account, analytical aggregation of consumer choices is not feasible and the model has to be solved by numerical simulations. The original AK model distinguishes between 55 overlapping generations (that is, ages 21 to 75), the preference structure of a 'newborn' agent who just enters the labor market is represented by a time-separable, nested constant elasticity of substitution (CES) utility function:

$$U = \frac{1}{1 - 1/\gamma}\sum_{a=1}^{55}\delta^{a-1}(c_a^{1-1/\rho} + \beta x_a^{1-1/\rho})^{\frac{1-1/\gamma}{1-1/\rho}}, \qquad (16.11)$$

where c and x denote consumption and leisure, respectively. The parameters δ, ρ, γ and β represent the time preference rate, the intra- and intertemporal elasticity of substitution, and the leisure preference, respectively. 'Newborn' agents maximize their utility function subject to the intertemporal budget constraint:

$$\sum_{a=1}^{55}[(1 - x_a)h_a w - c_a - \Gamma_a](1 + r)^{1-a} + \sum_{a=a_R}^{55}p_a(1 + r)^{1-a} = 0, \qquad (16.12)$$

where the time endowment is normalized to unity, r denotes the pre-tax return on savings, h_a defines the efficiency (or human capital) of the agent at age a and Γ_a represents the individual tax liabilities including social security contributions. Finally, p_a represent the payments from the pension program at age a after retirement at age a_R. Of course, agents are restricted in their leisure consumption by their time endowment, that is, $x_a \leq 1$.

At corner solutions, where the time constraint bites, a shadow price of labor is computed to make the corner solution satisfy the first-order condition. The utility function and the budget constraint already highlight the central assumptions of the original model. First, each agent faces a certain life span of 55 years, is endowed with an exogenous age-specific productivity profile h_a and receives retirement benefits after he/she passes a government-specified retirement age a_R. Second, the original model includes no bequest motive and abstracts from inheritances or other private intergenerational transfers. Third, agents face no liquidity constraints, that is, they might accumulate debt at a young age which they pay back later in life. Finally, individual variables are indexed only by age; there is no disaggregation within a cohort according to income class or sex. Consequently, the model cannot address distributional issues within a generation. On the other hand, the model is able to replicate the tax and social security system in some detail by the specification of individual tax payments and pension benefits. Since at the end of each period the oldest cohort alive dies, the remaining lifetime varies across cohorts living in a specific year. Consequently, fiscal reforms have a different impact on the budget constraints of the existing and future cohorts who are 'born' (that is, enter the labor market) after the reform year.

Typically, the initial long-run equilibrium is calibrated to represent the existing fiscal system. After a policy reform is announced or enacted, the model computes a transition path to the new long-run equilibrium. Given the model's solution, researchers are able to evaluate the growth effects for the macroeconomy as well as the distributional consequences of the considered reform for different current and future generations. In addition, it is also possible to quantify the aggregate efficiency consequences of a specific reform. For this purpose, Auerbach and Kotlikoff (1987) introduce the so-called 'Lump sum redistribution authority' (LSRA) which compensates existing generations after the reform with lump-sum transfers and taxes so that they end up at their pre-reform welfare. If the LSRA ends up after compensation with positive assets, the reform has improved the resource allocation of the economy. If the LSRA ends up with debt, economic efficiency has deteriorated.

In order to understand the economic implications of the model, it is useful to keep in mind that the basic effects of alternative pension financing remain as in the stylized theoretical models above. Due to the absence of bequest and liquidity constraints, individuals can perfectly provide for their old-age consumption by means of private saving. Consequently, a mandatory individualized funded pension program would only replace private savings with saving in the public pension fund but would have no real effects in the economy. On the other hand, a paygo program crowds out the capital stock and redistributes resources from young and future generations towards the elderly. Consequently, a move from a paygo to a funded program will always increase the capital stock of the economy and redistribute resources from current towards future generations. Various studies that have been carried out with the original model during the 1990s are discussed in Kotlikoff (2000). In the following we focus on the progress which has been made since then.

Recent developments with deterministic models

The demographic transition, its intra-generational consequences and its international context   Auerbach and Kotlikoff (1987) as well as Auerbach et al. (1989) have already presented initial calculations which quantify the impact of population ageing for the government and the macroeconomy in the US, Japan, Sweden and Germany. These studies clearly pointed out the dramatic increase in social security contributions and tax rates as well as a rise in wages and fall in interest rates due to ageing. However, within the structure of the original single-country model, population ageing could only be captured by an exogenously specified population vector which changes from year to year. Consequently, ageing did not change the individual consumption, saving and bequest behavior, nor did the analysis include international repercussion effects. In the following years various studies have included age-specific survival probabilities and an uncertain life span (see Broer and Lassila, 1997). However, since these studies assume perfect annuity markets, the remaining assets of those who have died are distributed to the surviving members of the respective cohort. Consequently, the economic effects of these models did not really change compared to the model with certain life span.

While the original model completely ignores intra-cohort effects of government policies, a natural idea was to distinguish various productivity (that is, human capital) profiles within a specific cohort. This innovation allows one to address new policy issues. Since agents' welfare is evaluated from an *ex post* point of view (that is, after his/her specific human capital profile has been revealed), the computed welfare changes after a policy reform capture the intragenerational distribution effects of that policy (see Fehr, 2000; Hirte, 2001; or Beetsma et al., 2003). For example, Fehr (2000) simulates an increase in the eligibility age and a partial tax financing of pension benefits, and compares the welfare and efficiency consequences of a reduction in the pension level accompanied either by a tightening or an elimination of the tax–benefit linkage. While the reduction of the pension level is in favor of future generations at the cost of current, the switch towards flat benefits clearly favors low- and burdens high-income agents and also entails dramatic efficiency losses due to the increased labor supply distortions. Consequently, these models indicate that pension policy should always keep a very tight tax–benefit linkage. Recalling Figure 16.1 above, the message is that reform types B and C are favored on efficiency grounds.

Kotlikoff et al. (2007) also allow for intracohort heterogeneity and analyze quite similar moderate and radical reform proposals for the US, as Fehr (2000) does for Germany. However, their framework features a much more detailed mapping of the demographic process. During their child-bearing years, agents give birth each year to fractions of children. This means of finessing marriage and family formation permits changes to be incorporated through time in age-specific fertility rates and the model's age-specific population shares to be closely lined up to the official population forecasts. In addition, they also assume that agents care about their children's utility when the latter are young and, as a consequence, make consumption expenditures on behalf of their children. Therefore, the model delivers the hump in the consumption profile that appears during child-rearing years in the actual data. As previous studies they include utility from leaving bequest and realistic mortality probabilities for agents. However, agents fail to annuitize their assets in old age. Consequently, agents gradually reduce their consumption in old age due to the uninsurable lifespan uncertainty and leave desired and undesired bequests to their children when they die. While agents die at different ages and have children of different ages, their heirs also inherit at different ages. Agents who were born when their parents were young receive inheritances later in their life than do their younger siblings. Kotlikoff et al. (2007) find that the burden from ageing is most evenly spread across current and future generations by a strategy of pre-funding social security with consumption taxes. However, since their model already features a lot of computational complexities, they do not compute the aggregate efficiency consequences of such a reform.

The multiple-region models of Fehr et al. (2004, 2005, 2007) build directly on Kotlikoff et al. (2007). Besides the explicit provision for immigration, the demographic transition at the national level and the household decision problem are modeled in a very similar fashion. However, the ageing processes of the US, Europe and Japan are now interlinked via the international capital market. One would expect that countries with less ageing such as the US will experience capital inflows in the future which drive up asset prices and growth. In order to isolate the quantitative impact of the open economy assumption, Table 16.3 compares the effects of ageing on asset prices in a model with closed and open economies.

Each simulation starts from a temporary equilibrium which captures the population structure of the respective countries in year 2000. Due to the diverging population dynamics and fiscal systems, the growth paths as well as the asset prices of the three regions considered differ. Table 16.3 mainly makes four points. First, the figures replicate the so-called 'asset meltdown', that is, due to ageing, asset prices increase in all countries initially and then drop afterwards. Second, the stronger is the ageing process, the lower is the level of asset prices during the next half-century. Third, due to ageing, capital will flow out of Japan and increase asset prices there.

Table 16.3   Asset prices in closed and open economies

Year	Closed economies			Open economies			Interest rate (per cent)
	USA	EU	Japan	USA	EU	Japan	
2000	1.000	1.000	1.000	1.000	1.000	1.000	9.0
2010	1.086	1.066	1.026	1.081	1.063	1.047	9.3
2020	1.109	1.095	1.012	1.114	1.074	1.064	9.3
2030	1.078	1.044	1.004	1.086	1.028	1.017	10.0
2050	1.125	1.009	0.959	1.082	1.039	1.016	12.2

Source: Fehr et al. (2005, pp. 26, 27, 28, 37, 38, 39).

In the short run, mainly Europe will benefit from capital inflows, while in the medium and long runs mainly the US will benefit. However, the effects of capital flows on asset prices are rather small. Fourth, as can be seen from the last column, ageing increases world interest rates. In particular, the last result stands in stark contrast to some other recent multicountry OLG models such as Brooks (2003), Saarenheimo (2005) or Börsch-Supan et al. (2006). These studies predict that ageing will reduce the rate of return on the international capital market during the next 50 years. In the model of Fehr et al. (2005), effective labor supply is improved by productivity growth while at the same time savings are dampened by rising tax payments and social security contributions.

Fehr et al. (2004, 2005, 2007) also account for intracohort heterogeneity. In addition to three different skill levels, they also distinguish between native and foreign individuals. Immigrants are also split into these income classes, permitting Fehr et al. to simulate the arrival of immigrants with different stocks of human and physical capital. Since especially high-skilled immigrants are known to be net taxpayers to the public system, selective immigration is often offered as a solution to the demographic transition under way in the industrialized world.[16] However, the simulations in Fehr et al. (2005) show that even a significant expansion of immigration, whether across all or among particular skill groups, will have only a minor impact on the major capital shortage and tax hikes that can be expected along the demographic transition.

While the prospects with respect to immigration seem to be quite frustrating, the model's predictions are dramatically altered when China is added to the picture. Even though china's population is ageing rapidly, its saving behavior, growth rate, and fiscal policies are currently very different from those of developed countries. As Fehr et al. (2007) demonstrate, China might eventually become the developed world's savior with respect to its long-run supply of capital and long-run general equilibrium prospects, if successive cohorts of Chinese continue to save like current cohorts, if the Chinese government can restrain growth in expenditures, and if Chinese technology and education levels ultimately catch up with those of the West and Japan.

Advances in modeling the retirement choice   Increases in the retirement ages are often seen as an alternative to tax increases or benefit cuts. Consequently, among others, Fehr (2000) as well as Kotlikoff et al. (2007) also quantify the macroeconomic and distributional consequences of an increase in the eligibility age for social security. However, the retirement choice in these models is very artificial. Given an exogenous age when they start receiving pension benefits, agents can only decide at what age they quit working. In order to achieve retirement exactly at the eligibility age for social security, either a significant drop in productivity or a dramatic increase in marginal labor income taxes is assumed at the eligibility age. This approach has mainly two disadvantages. First, the drop in individual productivity around retirement is at odds with empirical evidence, which shows only a modest decline in productivity between ages 60 and 70 (see French, 2005). Second, and even more important, since agents have no choice when to claim social security, social security rules which affect early retirement cannot be captured by these models.

Consequently, recent studies have introduced models where individuals have a labor–leisure choice in each working year, but also optimize the retirement age when they quit working and start to receive their pensions. Technically, the household optimization problem is solved in two stages. Given a price vector from the supply side of the economy, individuals first compute their optimal consumption and leisure path for alternative retirement ages. Then the retirement age which yields the highest utility level is selected in the second stage. Due to the evaluation of various alternatives and the discrete jumps in the aggregate variables, the computation is quite complicated.

Hirte (2001) was probably the first to model the retirement choice in such detail. He simulated various pension reform options for Germany which also affect the retirement choice. However, his model does not capture intragenerational heterogeneity. Therefore, the identified early retirement incentive effects are only cursory. Fehr et al. (2003) analyze early retirement incentives of the Norwegian pension system in a model that distinguishes five income classes within a generation. The Norwegian pension system is especially interesting since it consists of a flat tier and an earnings-based supplementary benefit, and includes a very generous early retirement scheme. The initial equilibrium which represents the existing

Table 16.4   Sustainable policy options and retirement age

	Initial period	Long-run equilibrium		
		Tax increase	Benefit reduction	FRA increase
Low skilled	62	65	65	71
Medium skilled	65	67	69	73
High skilled	66	69	70	74

Source: Eisensee (2005, pp. 108, 113, 115).

system is calibrated so that the retirement age increases with rising income level from age 62 to age 68. Next, various reforms of the early retirement scheme and the benefit formula are introduced and the long-run impact on the retirement behavior and the welfare of the five income classes is computed. The simulations indicate that reforms which increase the retirement age also have a positive long-run welfare impact.

Finally, Eisensee (2005) develops a framework where fiscal sustainability and the retirement decision in the US are jointly determined. The model distinguishes within a cohort between low-, medium- and high-skilled labor and extends Fehr et al. (2003) by including population ageing and the transition path, by considering differential mortality among the income classes and by simulating a closed economy. The study analyzes three policy options for the US which would all retain fiscal sustainability despite population ageing: a tax increase by 5.5 percentage points, a reduction of the replacement rate by 42 percent and an increase in the full retirement age (FRA) from 65 to 73. As shown in Table 16.4, all three alternatives increase the retirement age substantially throughout the transition.

Consequently, while tax increases only modestly increase the retirement age, the necessary adjustment of the FRA triggers a dramatic delay in retirement. The study disaggregates a direct effect and a general equilibrium effect on retirement behavior. While the direct effect measures the impact of the policy in a partial equilibrium framework, the indirect effect captures the changes in interest rates and wages. It turns out that in the first two options considered, the indirect effect increases retirement age substantially more strongly than the direct effect. While this finding explains why partial equilibrium studies often predict only a modest response of retirement behavior, it also indicates that these studies could be quite misleading.

Eisensee (2005) also computes the required policy adjustments in a traditional model where the retirement age is kept at the initial level. In this case, taxes have to be increased by 6 percentage points and replacement rates are reduced by 51 percent. Consequently, a traditional model with exogenous retirement would substantially underestimate the required adjustment. On the other hand, with exogenous retirement the FRA only has to increase to 69 years instead of 73 years. The latter might come as a surprise on first sight, but one has to remember that individuals increase their retirement age in order to receive higher pension benefits afterwards. With a fixed retirement age they have to accept dramatic reductions in pension benefits after the increase in the FRA. It is noteworthy that – in contrast to Fehr et al. (2003) – Eisensee does not compare the welfare consequences of alternative policy options with and without endogenous retirement. The study mainly indicates that it is important to include endogenous retirement in policy analysis and offers important innovations in modeling and analyzing retirement choice for future work.

Endogenous human capital and growth   Public-financed social security and education systems can both be viewed as intergenerational contracts. Each generation receives education transfers when young and social security benefits when old and has to finance these transfers at middle age via taxes and social security contributions. Due to the similar financing, human capital accumulation and the social security system are strongly linked in both directions. On the one hand, contributions to social security will in general reduce the incentive to acquire human capital, especially if pension benefits are flat and the earnings history is not taken into account. On the other hand, it is often argued that human capital investment will improve the viability of the social security system during the ongoing demographic transition. Due to the decreasing share of youth, public spending on education will fall which in turn, at least partially, compensates for higher pension outlays. In addition, investments in human capital will increase the efficiency of future workers and thus compensate their declining numbers. However, rising human capital could also undermine the viability of the pension system, if one takes into account that well-educated people live longer and have fewer children.

Consequently, it is not surprising that the interaction of the education and social security systems has become an important research area in recent years. In order to introduce human capital accumulation in the original AK model, the exogenous age-specific productivity profile h_a in equation (16.12) becomes endogenous, that is:

$$h_{a+1} = \Phi(h_a, \bar{h}, s_a),$$ (16.13)

where s_a defines the time spent for education at age a and $\bar{h}$ defines the average human capital (or state of knowledge) of the society. Of course, the time spent on education has to be subtracted from the total time endowment and cannot be used for labor. In the simplest formulation of a one-skill model there is no endogenous growth and education is simply modeled as 'on-the-job training' (see Perroni, 1995). Consequently, future (individual) productivity h_{a+1} only depends on the existing (own) productivity h_a and the time spent on on-the-job training s_a. Since in this model the initial productivity is specified exogenously as before, it is not really an innovation compared to the original model with exogenous human capital. Accordingly, more recent work has extended the human capital model in two different directions.

On the one side, Heckman et al. (1998) keep the exogenous growth assumption but introduce different skill levels and heterogeneity in endowments and the human capital production technology within cohorts. Consequently, they distinguish between schooling at the beginning of the life cycle and on-the-job training later on. However, their model does not include demographic characteristics of individuals and a social security system.[17] These features are addressed by Rojas (2004). He introduces an OLG model where individuals in each cohort have to decide in the initial period whether or not to acquire education. If they do, they receive higher wages, experience a longer lifetime and have fewer children later on. Educational subsidies that increase the educational attainment of the population therefore generate a demographic change which increases the financial pressure of the social security system. The model is calibrated in order to quantify the doubling of education subsidies in Spain during the 1990s. The simulations indicate a clear and stable intergenerational pattern of the policy reform. While elderly generations are worse off since they have to finance the higher education spending, generations that benefit directly in the initial years of the reform are the main winners. In the medium and long runs, higher social security contributions dampen the welfare increase for future generations substantially.

Whereas in Rojas (2004) education does not affect the long-run growth rate of the economy, various authors have developed human capital models with endogenous growth. Technically, this can be achieved by including a human capital externality $\bar{h}$ in the production function of either human capital (16.3) of output. On the other hand, endogenous growth models do not include a schooling choice, that is, human capital acquisition is interpreted as on-the-job training in order to keep the model dimension traceable. Endogenous and exogenous growth models sometimes come up with quite different policy conclusions. For example, an increase in life expectancy increases human capital accumulation in Rojas and, therefore, positively affects the economy. Quite the opposite happens in the endogenous growth model of Echevarria (2003, 2004). Since $\bar{h}$ captures the per

Table 16.5   Schooling, retirement, and growth

Depreciation rates	10%		0%	
Life expectancy	77	80	77	80
Schooling years	17.33	17.5	24.55	24.91
Retirement age	62.0	63.3	55.3	56.2
Growth rate (%)	2.00	1.95	4.7	4.63

Source: Echevarria (2004, Cases I &II, pp. 611, 612).

capita human capital endowment of the society, an increase in life expectancy reduces $\bar{h}$, which in turn negatively affects the economy.

Echevarria (2003) estimates that a one-year increase in life expectancy reduces the long-run growth rate by 0.02–0.05 percentage points. The opposite happens when the retirement age is increased. Since in this case returns from human capital investment rise, individuals will increase their on-the-job training, which in turn improves the long-run growth rate. For specific parameter constellations, the positive effect from a one-year increase in the retirement age dominates a simultaneous one-year increase of life expectancy. However, the retirement age is set exogenously and it is not clear how strong rising life expectancy affects the individual retirement choice. Consequently, Echevarria (2004) extends his previous model by including an endogenous retirement age. Now an increase in life expectancy also increases the retirement age. However, for all considered parameter constellations the (negative) direct effect of the reduced per capita productivity dominates the (positive) effect of the higher retirement age.

Table 16.5 is taken from Echevarria (2004) and compares the impact of an increase in life expectancy by three years on schooling, retirement and growth for depreciating and non-depreciating physical and human capital. Note that it is assumed that human capital depreciates only during schooling, not during working time! Consequently, the growth rate is lower, and people leave school earlier and retire later compared to the situation without depreciation. If both calibrations are considered, the exogenous increase in life expectancy induces agents to leave school later and retire later. Nevertheless, the growth rate still decreases by roughly 0.05 percentage points. This negative effect of higher life expectancy on economic growth rates seems to be in stark contrast with the historical observation that the rising life expectancy during the industrial revolution of the nineteenth century had a positive growth effect. However, when life expectancy is low, people do not retire, and work their whole life. Consequently, increases in life expectancy also induce an equal increase in the working periods, which in turn improves economic development.

When life expectancy passes a certain level, people start to retire before they die. This is the turning-point since from now on further increases in life expectancy have a less pronounced effect on the retirement age. As a consequence, economic growth rates will decline.

One central problem of endogenous growth models is that the specification of $\bar{h}$ is rather arbitrary but has an enormous impact on the models' dynamics. For example, Bouzahzah et al. (2002) assume that each newborn generation inherits the human capital of the previous generation. Of course, with such a specification increases in life expectancy do not have such negative consequences for economic growth! Bouzahzah et al. compare the economic effects of various policy reforms in endogenous and exogenous growth models. With respect to the pension system they simulate a switch to a funded system and an increase in the retirement age. Since the economic consequences of both reforms are very similar in both endogenous and exogenous growth models, they conclude that for pension reforms, endogenous growth does not really matter.

Recent developments with stochastic models
During the last decade, a new direction of quantitative research has extended the traditional AK model by considering various sources of idiosyncratic and aggregate economic risk (see Krueger 2006). This subsection presents the most important contributions and discusses their central findings.

Idiosyncratic risk and liquidity constraints   Hubbard and Judd (1987) have already extended the AK model by including life-span uncertainty and liquidity constraints. Since private annuity markets are missing, social security provides an insurance against longevity risk but at the same time increases welfare losses due to borrowing constraints. However, Hubbard and Judd provide only an introduction to insurance analysis. Since their model abstracts from labor income uncertainty, precautionary savings are neglected so that liquidity constraints are relevant for all young individuals. Since a meaningful analysis of the insurance and liquidity effects of social security has to include income risk, various stochastic general equilibrium models with overlapping generations have been developed recently.

İmrohoroğlu et al. (1995) were the first to examine the optimality of and the welfare effects from alternative social security arrangements in a framework with stochastic employment opportunities. Agents supply labor inelastically when they are given the opportunity to work and otherwise receive unemployment benefits. After the mandatory retirement age, individuals rely on flat-rate pension benefits. In this framework, the welfare consequences of social security reflect the trade-off between the (positive) insurance provision against income and longevity risk and the (negative) effects of stronger binding liquidity constraints. While the institutional set-up is already very favourable for social security, the calibrated initial equilibrium (without social security) lacks dynamic efficiency. When the growth rate of the economy exceeds the interest rate, it is not surprising that the introduction of social security increases the resources of all generations.

In their follow-up study, İmrohoroğlu et al. (1999) eliminate dynamic inefficiency by incorporating land as a fixed factor of production. In this setting, the introduction of social security again has positive insurance and negative liquidity effects, but it also redistributes income across generations. The simulations indicate that an economy without social security provides the highest welfare for individuals. However, this result might only reflect the negative income effects of social security for future generations. This argument also applies to a recent study by Hong and Rios-Rull (2007) who develop an OLG model with two sexes and family formation. In this set-up, marriage provides some kind of private insurance against income uncertainty, which may weaken the case for public insurance programs. However, the computed long-run welfare losses due to the introduction of social security are probably again mainly due to intergenerational redistribution.

Of course, the same critique also applies to studies that analyze the long-run consequences of gradual social security reforms. For example, Huggett and Ventura (1999) quantify the distributional consequences if the current US pension system were to be substituted by a two-tier system, where the first tier is strictly connected to former contributions and the tax-financed second tier would guarantee a minimum pension for all households with low income. Since their model allows for endogenous labor supply, the induced labor supply distortions weaken the case for social security. In addition, agents are distinguished according to ability levels within a generation, so that intragenerational distributional effects of social security arrangements could be quantified. Their simulations suggest that both high- and low-ability agents would benefit from a switch to the two-tier system while median-ability agents would lose. Since the majority of the agents in the economy is close to median, the considered reform would yield a very robust aggregate welfare loss.

Storesletten et al. (1999) consider the long-run effects when the current US pension system is either replaced by a two-tier system of personal saving accounts or completely eliminated. In contrast to Huggett and Ventura (1999), their two-tier system delivers a long-run welfare gain, which is even larger than the gain from privatization. Since their model abstracts from variable labor supply and they try to neutralize the induced intergenerational income effects by appropriate government transfers, the welfare gains are mainly due to insurance effects. Consequently, the assessment of the long-run consequences of social security may change dramatically when the implied intergenerational income effects are eliminated.

Fuster et al. (2003) present a model where individuals are linked across generations by two-sided altruism. Of course, in this framework, the intergenerational redistribution induced by public policy is (at least partly) neutralized by intervivos transfers and bequests. In addition, borrowing constraints are less binding so that social security mainly provides an insurance against uninsurable 'labor ability' shocks at birth. For this reason, Fuster et al. find that social security increases long-run welfare for most of their considered households. A final argument in favor of social security is explored by İmrohoroğlu et al. (2003). They introduce quasi-hyperbolic discounting in the framework already discussed above and show that social security may raise long-run welfare for individuals with time-inconsistent preferences if the short-term discount rate is sufficiently high. Of course, social security may always serve as a commitment device for myopic individuals who do not adequately save for their retirement.

All studies with stochastic economies discussed so far share a common deficiency which has already been mentioned above. Since they only consider the long-run effects of social security, the consequences for transitional generations are completely neglected. Therefore, the computed long-run welfare changes could be simply due to intergenerational redistribution. In order to provide a complete assessment of social security, one has to compute the transition path between steady states and separate intergenerational distribution from efficiency effects. A first study which addresses this critique is Huang et al. (1997), who compare two experiments where the existing unfunded social security system is eliminated and a private or a mandatory state-run funded system is introduced with all existing and transitional generations compensated virtually. While both experiments yield a significant aggregate efficiency gain, the government-run funding scheme is preferred to privatization due to its superior insurance properties. De Nardi et al. (1999) extend this model by including realistic US demographics and variable labor supply. The latter allows them to analyze reforms where the tax–benefit linkage of the pension system is improved, which increases welfare in their framework. Conesa and Krueger (1999) simulate an immediate, a gradual and an announced elimination of social security and compute the political support for the three proposals in the initial year. Although for all cases considered agents would prefer to be born into the final steady state, no proposal receives an initial voting majority in the closed economy case. The political support is declining when intra-cohort heterogeneity is increasing due to the rising insurance gains from flat pensions.

While Conesa and Krueger can explain why pension reforms are delayed in democratic systems, their study does not include efficiency calculations. If many individuals receive small welfare losses while the (fewer) winners receive enormous welfare gains, it might be possible that the reform receives no political support although it delivers aggregate efficiency gains. A very similar problem arises in Fuster et al. (2007), who extend their two-sided altruism model by incorporating variable labor supply and the transition paths across steady states. As before, the family insurance substitutes the missing market insurance but now the social security contributions distort the labor supply choice. The latter is reinforced by the fact that the payroll tax comes on top of personal income taxes. Consequently, they find that the majority of individuals are better off with the elimination of social security in all privatization schemes considered. However, since the resulting welfare changes are not aggregated across individuals and generations, the overall efficiency effect is not explicitly determined.

The latter is done by Nishiyama and Smetters (2007), who simulate a stylized 50 percent privatization of the US social security system. Again, the considered reform reduces the labor supply distortions but also the insurance provision of the social security system. In order to isolate the overall efficiency effects, the authors follow Auerbach and Kotlikoff (1987) by introducing an LSRA which compensates initial agents and distributes the accumulated assets (that is, efficiency gains) or debt (that is, efficiency losses) to newborn and future agents. They find efficiency gains from privatization which amount to $18.10 (in 2001 growth-adjusted dollars) per household, if wage shocks could be insured privately. Consequently, if income uncertainty is perfectly insured, the aggregate efficiency effect of social security is dominated by the distortions of the labor/leisure choice. However, if wage income shocks could not be insured, the overall efficiency effect from privatization turns into a loss of $2.40 per household.

Table 16.6 reports the welfare changes (that is, without compensation) and the efficiency effects (that is, with compensation payments for elderly) for different cohorts and income classes. In the long run, the welfare gain from privatization ranges from $76.30 for low-income households to $91.20 for top-income households. The higher gains for rich households simply indicate the redistributive features of the US social security system. Similar figures are also reported by the studies discussed above, which only compute the long-run consequences of social security reforms. However, these gains are mainly due to income redistribution, since elderly cohorts at the time of the reform realize significant welfare losses due to higher income or consumption taxes which are required to finance the existing

Table 16.6   Welfare and efficiency effects from social security privatization (in $ per household)

Age in reform year/birth year	Welfare effects for selected productivity classes				Efficiency effects
	Class 1	Class 3	Class 5	Class 8	
79	−0.2	−0.2	−0.3	−0.5	0.00
60	−22.6	−29.7	−37.5	−57.1	0.00
40	−27.6	−46.0	−75.8	−130.7	0.00
20	−5.4	−7.4	−11.2	−22.4	0.00
0	34.3	37.0	38.4	30.7	−2.4
∞	76.3	84.1	91.3	91.2	−2.4

Source: Nishiyama and Smetters (2007, Table IX, p. 1700).

pension claims. Table 16.6 shows that 60-year-olds at the time of the reform lose between $22.60 and $57.10 per household. If the LSRA is introduced and all existing generations at the time of the reform are compensated by transfers, privatization would require each future household that enters the economy in the year after the reform or later to pay $2.40 to service the debt of the LSRA.[18] In other words, the partial privatization of the US social security system does reduce economic efficiency. This clearly indicates that the (positive) insurance effects of the US social security system dominate the distortionary effects on labor supply.

Fehr and Habermann (2008) reach a similar conclusion for the German social security system. In contrast to the US system, benefits in the German system are strongly linked to former contributions. On the one hand, this institutional feature minimizes labor supply distortions but at the same time it also reduces the insurance provision against income shocks. Simulations show that a more progressive system would yield a significant aggregate efficiency again, if all initial generations are compensated by LSRA transfers.

Aggregate risk and social security   Up to now the discussion has assumed that risk is specific to the individual household. In this case *intra*generational risk-sharing arrangements such as progressive taxes or social security systems have the potential to improve the well-being of individuals. Turning to quantitative studies that consider aggregate risks, only *inter*generational risk-sharing arrangements could provide insurance, however.

The literature has looked especially at two sources of aggregate risk: demographic and productivity. As discussed above, someone who is born into a large (small) cohort, can expect lower (higher) wages during the working periods while the previous generation experiences higher (lower) interest rates during their retirement. Depending on the design of the social security system, these factor price effects are either dampened or reinforced by adjustments of contribution rates and benefits. In order to quantify such effects, various contributions in Ahlo et al. (2008) combine a detailed stochastic population model with a traditional (that is, deterministic) OLG model. This allows the pension system to be modeled in detail and distributions for all future macroeconomic and social security variables to be completed. On the other hand, this approach has a central shortcoming: when agents decide about savings, labor supply and so on, they do not take into account the demographic risk, that is, there is no precautionary behavior. Consequently, the computed welfare effects have to be interpreted with caution.

In a consistent model, the actions of individuals have to reflect the existing aggregate uncertainty. Bohn (2001) presents such an analysis, however, his framework only considers two overlapping generations. He compares the intergenerational risk-sharing implications of DB and DC pension systems when there is demographic risk. Capturing the same mechanisms as in the stylized theoretical model of Smith (1982) discussed above, Bohn shows that DB paygo pension programs are able to spread demographic risk across generations.

Sánchez-Marcos and Sánchez-Martín (2006) extend the approach of Bohn (2001) by analyzing a model with four overlapping generations and simulating the short- and long-run implications of unfunded DB systems. It turns out that now the improved intergenerational risk sharing cannot compensate the long-run crowding-out of the capital stock due to the introduction of social security. However, the simulations also show clear welfare improvements for those generations living in the short run. As before, it would be interesting to neutralize the intergenerational income redistribution in order to isolate the welfare effects from intergenerational risk sharing, but this is not done in this study.

Other recent papers capture aggregate uncertainty by productivity shocks which affect the production function of the economy. In addition, the depreciation rate is also assumed to be stochastic, in order to allow the return from capital to vary independently from the wage rate. Without social security, wage and interest rate shocks affect young and old generations separately. In accordance with the theoretical portfolio choice approach to social security design examined above, it may be optimal to have a low-yielding paygo program in an optimal portfolio. Krueger and Kubler (2006) simulated such a model with nine overlapping generations in order to analyze whether the welfare gains from improved intergenerational risk sharing dominate the welfare losses due to the long-run crowding-out of the capital stock. They are able to show that in a small open economy, social security may improve long-run welfare if individuals are very risk averse.

In a closed economy the crowding-out effect of the capital stock seems always to dominate the improved risk sharing, however. While Krueger and Kubler's model, hedging against aggregate risk was very indirect, Olovsson (2004) explores a direct mechanism to transfer aggregate risk across generations. In his three-period model, the pension benefits are indexed either to wage or to capital returns. The long-run consequences are compared to an equilibrium which reflects the existing US social security system and to a *laissez-faire* equilibrium without social security. It turns out that the economies with highly volatile pension benefits may in fact neutralize the crowding-out of the capital stock and improve long-run welfare significantly compared to the existing social security system. However, the elimination of social security would still yield the highest long-run welfare gains.

Summing up, the quantitative results of these few papers that deal with aggregate risk in OLG models indicate that in the long run the benefits from intergenerational risk sharing will not dominate the cost from intergenerational redistribution. A natural venue for future work will therefore be to design transition strategies that allow the minimization of the intergenerational redistribution and the isolation of the aggregate benefits from intergenerational risk sharing.

4   Final remarks

Surveying the intergenerational distribution effects of social security, we have attempted to cover basic theoretical insights as well as a broad selection of recent policy-relevant applications based on numerical OLG models. Given the formidable size of this literature, our survey is selective and we have not covered several issues which are important for the theoretical discussion and the social security reform process in many countries. In closing this survey, we stick to our broad focus and highlight two important issues that are likely to shape the next steps in this field.

First, the discussion in the two previous sections shows a clear distinction between the risk analysis in theoretical and numerical models. Whereas the former focuses on aggregate risk and intergenerational risk sharing, the latter concentrates on idiosyncratic risk and intragenerational risk sharing. To a large extent this reflects the fact that numerical models in the past were restricted to idiosyncratic risk mainly for technical reasons. Advances in computer technology have recently made it possible to simulate more sophisticated OLG models with aggregate risk, however.

As soon as it is possible to include a transition path in models with aggregate risk, the efficiency effects of social security could be quantified from a new perspective. This will allow the theoretical and the empirical discussions of risk and risk-sharing issues in social security to be more closely connected.

Second, despite all differences, both the theoretical and the numerical studies with aggregate and idiosyncratic uncertainties share a common characteristic. They both highlight the insurance properties of social security systems and, for this reason, social security tends to appear more favorable in terms of economic efficiency than in older studies based on deterministic models. We conjecture that future quantitative studies which include aggregate risk will strengthen this general trend.

Notes

* We appreciate valuable comments from Robert Brent. Parts of this survey were written while Hans Fehr was visiting Boston University. He thanks the Fritz Thyssen Stiftung for financial support. Øystein Thøgersen appreciates financial support from the Research Council of Norway.

1. The existence of welfare gains of a public pension system is contingent on underlying motives such as (i) an explicit desire for income redistribution, (ii) an ambition to correct market failures or (iii) paternalism (see Diamond, 1977 for a discussion).
2. This focus is well known from any OECD economy and also several emerging market economies such as some Latin American countries. It does not apply, however, to some other emerging market economies without significant social security programs (for example, China).
3. According to the UN, life expectancy is expected to rise approximately 0.2 years per year over the next 5 decades (see UN, 2004). The fertility rates vary a lot between countries, from a reasonably high 1.8–2.0 child per female in countries such as Sweden, Norway and the US to a worrying low 1.3 level in countries such as Germany and Italy.
4. To some extent the escalation of early retirement may reflect an income effect in the sense that economic growth over time increases the demand for more leisure spent in retirement. Still, it seems fair to conclude that available evidence shows that the incentive effects of generous early retirement program play a major role in most economies (see, for example, Gruber and Wise, 1999 and Fenge and Pestieau, 2005).
5. See, for example, Fenge and Pestiau (2005) for the trend in the real retirement age for Germany.
6. The actuarial balance issue is captured by the discussion of our second dimension, paygo versus funding.
7. As an example, fiscal policy in the oil-rich Norwegian economy during the last decade can be given such an interpretation. Disciplined fiscal policy has led to an accumulation of a fund that exceeds 100 percent of GDP. This fund is officially referred to as 'the State Pension Fund' despite the lack of any formalized link between the size of the fund and future pension liabilities.
8. As discussed and exemplified by Thøgersen (2001), the term 'funding' is often used in an imprecise manner in the social security literature, that is, it sometimes refers to reforms of type A in Figure 16.1 and sometimes to reforms of type C. In the literature related to the US policy debate, the terms 'funding' and 'privatization' are often used interchangeably and indicate an introduction of real, individual pension accounts (that is, a type C reform).

9.   For recent surveys of this literature, see Galasso and Profeta (2002) or De Walque (2005).
10. To what extent this holds for all individuals within each generation depends on the tax–benefit link of the program (see Figure 16.1). If, for example, the program is characterized by a weak tax–benefit link, there is an element of *intra*generational redistribution. On the other hand, if the program is fully actuarial, (16.3) holds for all individuals.
11. The importance of the sign of this expression for the effects of pension programs was first highlighted by Aaron (1966). In social security settings, the condition $r_{t+1} - g > 0$, that is, dynamic efficiency, is often referred to as the 'Aaron condition'.
12. This result also appears in Verbon (1989) and Fenge (1995).
13. Pareto-optimal transitions may also reflect the abolition of other types of distortions associated with the paygo program. This includes distortions in the labor market; see Demmel and Keuschnigg or Corneo and Marquardt (2000), and in the capital market, see Belan et al. (1998).
14. The first-order effect of public pensions replacing private saving might also be counteracted by prudent behavior in the sense that individuals perceive promised future pension benefits as risky, due, for example, to fears about the financial viability of the pension programs.
15. The specification of b_t as the argument in the utility function is equivalent to the assumption that consumption takes place in (only) the second period of life. This simplification is common in the literature on social security and intergenerational risk sharing (see, for example, Gordon and Varian, 1988 and Shiller, 1999). While this approach leads to analytical tractability, a problem related to this approach is the fact that precautionary saving issues are disregarded.
16. Storesletten (2000) has already evaluated the positive impact of immigration in the US without taking into account the demographic transition.
17. Heckman et al. (1999) apply this model in order to quantify the costs and benefits of tuition subsidies.
18. Since the LSRA accumulates debt or assets during the transition, the market interest rate is implicitly used to weight the utility of different generations during the transition. Of course, such transfers are not possible in practice, but the computed potential efficiency effects allow us to compare different policy experiments without explicitly specifying a social welfare function and social discount rates.

References

Aaron, H.J. (1966), 'The social insurance paradox', *Canadian Journal of Economics and Political Science*, **32**, 371–74.
Alho, J.M., S.E.H. Jensen and J. Lassila (eds) (2008), *Uncertain Demographics and Fiscal Sustainability*, Cambridge University Press, Cambridge.
Andersen, T.M. (2005), 'Social security and longevity', CESifo Working Paper no. 1577, CESifo, University of Munich.
Auerbach, A.J. and L.J. Kotlikoff (1987), *Dynamic Fiscal Policy*, Cambridge University Press, Cambridge.
Auerbach, A.J., R.P. Hagemann, G. Nicoletti and L.J. Kotlikoff (1989), 'The economic dynamics of an ageing population: the case of four OECD countries', *OECD Economic Studies*, **12**, 97–130.
Ball, L. and N.G. Mankiw (2001), 'Intergenerational risk sharing in the spirit of Arrow, Debreu, and Rawls, with applications to social security design', manuscript, Johns Hopkins University, Baltimore, MD.
Beetsma R., L. Bettendorf and P. Broer (2003), 'The budgeting and economic consequences of ageing in the Netherlands', *Economic Modelling*, **20**, 987–1013.
Belan, P., P. Michel and P. Pestieau (1998), 'Pareto improving social security reform', *Geneva Papers on Risk and Insurance Theory*, **23**, 119–25.
Bohn, H. (2001), 'Social security and demographic uncertainty: the risk sharing properties

of alternative policies', in J. Campbell and M. Feldstein (eds), *Risk Aspects of Investment Based Social Security Reform*, University of Chicago Press, Chicago, IL, 203–41.

Börsch-Supan, A., A. Ludwig and J. Winter (2006), 'Ageing, pension reform and capital flows: a multi-country simulation model', *Economica*, **73**, 625–58.

Bouzahzah, M., D. De la Croix and F. Docquier (2002), 'Policy reforms and growth in computable OLG economies', *Journal of Economic Dynamics and Control*, **26**, 2093–113.

Breyer, F. (1989), 'On the intergenerational Pareto efficiency of pay-as-you-go financed pension systems', *Journal of Institutional and Theoretical Economics*, **145**, 643–58.

Breyer, F. and M. Straub (1993), 'Welfare effects of unfunded pension systems when labor supply is endogenous', *Journal of Public Economics*, **50**, 77–91.

Broer, P. and J. Lassila (eds) (1997), *Pension Policies and Public Debt in Dynamic CGE Models*, Physica-Verlag, Heidelberg.

Brooks, R. (2003), 'Population aging and global capital flows in a parallel universe', *IMF Staff Papers*, **50**, 200–21.

Brunner, J.K. (1996), 'Transition from a pay-as-you-go to a fully funded pension system: the case of differing individuals and intragenerational fairness', *Journal of Public Economics*, **60**, 131–46.

Campbell, J.Y. and L.M. Viceira (2002), *Strategic Asset Allocation: Portfolio Choice for Long-Term Investors*, Oxford University Press, Oxford.

Conesa, J.C. and D. Krueger (1999), 'Social security reform with heterogeneous agents', *Review of Economic Dynamics*, **2**, 757–95.

Corneo, G. and M. Marquardt (2000), 'Public pensions, unemployment insurance, and growth', *Journal of Public Economics*, **75**, 293–311.

De Menil, G., F. Murtin and E. Sheshinsky (2006), 'Planning for the optimal mix of paygo tax and funded savings', *Journal of Pension Economics and Finance*, **5**, 1–25.

de Mesa, A.A. and C. Mesa-Lago (2006), 'The structural pension reform in Chile: effects, comparisons with other Latin American reforms, and lessons', *Oxford Review of Economics Policy*, **22**, 149–67.

de Nardi, M., S. İmrohoroğlu and T.J. Sargent (1999), 'Projected U.S. demographics and social security', *Review of Economic Dynamics*, **2**, 575–615.

De Walque, G. (2005), 'Voting on pensions: a survey', *Journal of Economic Surveys*, **19**, 181–209.

Demmel, R. and C. Keuschnigg (2000), 'Funded pensions and unemployment', *FinanzArchiv*, **57**, 22–38.

Diamond, P.A. (1965), 'National debt in a neoclassical growth model', *American Economic Review*, **55**, 1126–50.

Diamond, P.A. (1977), 'A framework for social security analysis', *Journal of Public Economics*, **8**, 275–98.

Dutta, J., S. Kapur and J.M. Orzag (2000), 'A portfolio approach to the optimal funding of pensions', *Economics Letters*, **69**, 201–06.

Echevarria, C.A. (2003) 'Life expectancy, retirement and endogenous growth', *Economic Modelling*, **21**, 147–74.

Echevarria, C.A. (2004), 'Life expectancy, schooling, retirement and growth', *Economic Inquiry*, **42**, 602–17.

Eisensee, T. (2005), 'Essays on public finance: retirement behavior and disaster relief', Institute for International Economic Studies, Stockholm University, Monograph Series no. 54, Stockholm.

Enders, W. and H.P. Lapan (1982), 'Social security taxation and intergenerational risk sharing', *International Economic Review*, **23**, 647–58.

Enders, W. and H.P. Lapan (1993), 'A model of first and second-best social security programs', *Journal of Economics*, **7** (Suppl.), 65–90.

Fehr, H. (2000), 'Pension reform during the demographic transition', *Scandinavian Journal of Economics*, **102**, 419–43.

Fehr, H. and C. Habermann (2008), 'Risk sharing and efficiency implications of progressive pension arrangements', *Scandinavian Journal of Economics*, **110**, 419–43.

Fehr, H., S. Jokisch and L.J. Kotlikoff (2004), 'The role of immigration in dealing with the developed world's demographic transition', *FinanzArchiv*, **60**, 296–324.
Fehr, H., S. Jokisch and L.J. Kotlikoff (2005), 'The developed world's demographic transition – the roles of capital flows, immigration, and policy', in R. Brooks and A. Razin (eds), *Social Security Reform*, Cambridge University Press, Cambridge, 11–43.
Fehr, H., S. Jokisch and L.J. Kotlikoff (2007), 'Will China eat our lunch or take us to dinner? Simulating the transition paths of the U.S., EU, Japan, and China', in T. Ito and A. Rose (eds), *Fiscal Policy and Management*, NBER–East Asia Seminar on Economics Vol. 16, University of Chicago Press, Chicago, IL, pp.133–98.
Fehr, H., W.I. Sterkeby, and Ø. Thøgersen (2003), 'Social security reform and early retirement', *Journal of Population Economics*, **16**, 345–61.
Feldstein, M. (1974), 'Social security, induced retirement and aggregate capital accumulation', *Journal of Political Economy*, **82**, 905–26.
Feldstein, M. (1996), 'Social security and saving: new time series evidence', *National Tax Journal*, **49**, 151–64.
Fenge, R. (1995), 'Pareto-efficiency of the pay-as-you-go pension system with intragenerational fairness', *FinanzArchiv*, **52**, 357–63.
Fenge, R. and P. Pestieau (2005), *Social Security and Early Retirement*, CESifo Book Series, MIT Press, Cambridge, MA.
French, E. (2005), 'The effect of health, wealth and wages on labor supply and retirement behavior', *Review of Economic Studies*, **72**, 395–427.
Fuster, L., A. İmrohoroğlu, and S. İmrohoroğlu (2003), 'A welfare analysis of social security in a dynastic framework', *International Economic Review*, **44**, 1247–74.
Fuster, L., A. İmrohoroğlu, and S. İmrohoroğlu (2007), 'Elimination of social security in a dynastic framework', *Review of Economic Studies*, **74**, 113–45.
Galasso. V. and P. Profeta (2002), 'The political economy of social security: a survey', *European Journal of Political Economy*, **18**, 1–29.
Gordon, R.H. and H.R. Varian (1988), 'Intergenerational risk sharing', *Journal of Public Economics*, **37**, 185–202.
Gruber, J. and D.A. Wise (1999), *Social Security and Retirement around the World*, Chicago University Press, Chicago, IL.
Heckman, J.J., L. Lochner and C. Taber (1998), 'Explaining rising wage inequality: explorations with a dynamic general equilibrium model of labor earnings with heterogeneous agents', *Review of Economic Dynamics*, **1**, 1–58.
Heckman, J.J., L. Lochner and C. Taber, (1999), 'Human capital formation and general equilibrium treatment effects: a study of tax and tuition policy', *Fiscal Studies*, **20**, 25–40.
Heijdra, B.J. and F. van der Ploeg (2002), *Foundations of Modern Macroeconomics*, Oxford University Press, Oxford.
Hirte, G. (2001), *Pension Policies for an Aging Society*, Mohr Siebeck, Tübingen.
Holzmann, R. and E. Palmer (eds) (2006), *Pension Reform – Issues and Prospects for Nonfinancial Defined Contribution (NDC) Schemes*, World Bank, Washington, DC.
Homburg, S. (1990), 'The efficiency of unfunded pension schemes', *Journal of Institutional and Theoretical Economics*, **146**, 640–47.
Hong, J.H. and J.-V. Rios-Rull (2007), 'Social security, life insurance and annuities for families', *Journal of Monetary Economics*, **54**, 118–40.
Hu, S.C. (1979), 'Social security, the supply of labour, and capital accumulation', *American Economic Review*, **69**, 274–83.
Huang, H., S. İmrohoroğlu and T.J. Sargent (1997), 'Two computations to fund social security', *Macroeconomic Dynamics*, **1**, 7–44.
Hubbard, G.R. and K.L. Judd (1987), 'Social security and individual welfare: Precautionary saving, borrowing constraints, and the payroll tax', *American Economic Review*, **77**, 630–46.
Huggett, M. and G. Ventura (1999), 'On the distributional effects of social security reform', *Review of Economic Dynamics*, **2**, 498–531.

İmrohoroğlu, A., S. İmrohoroğlu and D.H. Joines (1995), 'A life cycle analysis of social security', *Economic Theory*, **6**, 83–114.

İmrohoroğlu, A., S. İmrohoroğlu and D.H. Joines (1999), 'Social security in an overlapping generations economy with land', *Review of Economic Dynamics*, **2**, 638–65.

İmrohoroğlu, A., S. İmrohoroğlu and D.H. Joines (2003), 'Time-inconsistent preferences and social security', *Quarterly Journal of Economics*, **118**, 745–84.

Kotlikoff, L.J. (2000), 'The A-K OLG model: its past, present, and future', in G.W. Harrison, S.E.H. Jensen, L.H. Pedersen and T.F. Rutherford (eds), *Using Dynamic General Equilibrium Models for Policy Analysis*, North-Holland, Amsterdam, 13–52.

Kotlikoff, L.J., K.A. Smetters and J. Walliser (2007), 'Mitigating America's demographic dilemma by pre-funding social security', *Journal of Monetary Economics*, **54**, 247–66.

Krueger, D. (2006), 'Public insurance against idiosyncratic and aggregate risk: the case of social security and progressive income taxation', *CESifo Economic Studies*, **52**, 587–620.

Krueger, D. and F. Kubler (2006), 'Pareto improving social security reform when financial markets are incomplete?', *American Economic Review*, **96**, 737–55.

Lindbeck, A. and M. Persson (2003), 'The gains from pension reform', *Journal of Economic Literature*, **41**, 74–112.

Matsen, E. and Ø. Thøgersen (2004), 'Designing social security – a portfolio choice approach', *European Economic Review*, 883–904.

Merton, R.C. (1983), 'On the role of social security as a means for efficient risk sharing in an economy where human capital is not tradable', in Z. Bodie and J.B. Shoven (eds), *Financial Aspects of the United States Pension System*, University of Chicago Press, Chicago, IL, 325–58.

Nishiyama, S. and K. Smetters (2007), 'Does social security privatization produce efficiency gains?', *Quarterly Journal of Economics*, **122** (4), 1677–719.

OECD (2007), *Pensions at a Glance*, Organisation for Economic Co-operation and Development, Paris.

Olovsson, C. (2004), 'The welfare gains of improving risk sharing in social security', Seminar Paper no. 728, Stockholm University.

Perroni, C. (1995), 'Assessing the dynamic efficiency gains of tax reform when human capital is endogenous', *International Economic Review*, **96**, 907–25.

Persson, M. (2000), 'The reform of the Swedish pension system', in E. Balacci and F. Peracchi (eds), *Reforming Social Security: An International Perspective*, ISTAT, Rome, 213–48.

Persson, M. (2002), 'Five fallacies in the social security debate', in T. Ihori and T. Tachibanaki (eds), *Social Security Reforms in Advanced Countries*, Routledge, London, 39–51.

Persson, T. (1985), 'Deficits and intergenerational welfare in open economies', *Journal of International Economics*, **19**, 67–84.

Portney, P. and J. Weyant (1999), *Discounting and Intergenerational Equity*, Resources for the Future, Washington, DC.

Poterba, J.M. (2000), 'Stock market wealth and consumption', *Journal of Economic Perspectives*, **14**, 99–118.

Richter, W.F. (1990), 'Social security as a means of overcoming the nonmarketability of human capital', *FinanzArchiv*, **48**, 451–466.

Rojas, J.A. (2004), 'On the interaction between education and social security', *Review of Economic Dynamics*, **7**, 932–57.

Saarenheimo, T. (2005), 'Ageing, interest rates, and financial flows', Discussion Paper no. 2, Bank of Finland Research, Helsinki.

Samuelson, P.A. (1975), 'Optimal social security in a life-cycle growth model', *International Economic Review*, **16**, 539–44.

Sánchez-Marcos, V. and A.R. Sánchez-Martín (2006), 'Can social security be welfare improving when there is demographic uncertainty?', *Journal of Economic Dynamics and Control*, **30**, 1615–49.

Shiller, R.J. (1999), 'Social security and institutions for intergenerational, intragenerational and international risk sharing', *Carnegie–Rochester Series in Public Policy*, **50**, 165–204.

Sinn, H.-W. (2000), 'Why a funded pension system is useful and why it is not useful', *International Tax and Public Finance*, **7**, 389–410.

Smith, A. (1982), 'Intergenerational transfers as social insurance', *Journal of Public Economics*, **19**, 97–106.

Storesletten, K. (2000), 'Sustaining fiscal policy through immigration', *Journal of Political Economy*, **108**, 300–323.

Storesletten, K., C.I. Telmer and A. Yaron (1999), 'The risk-sharing implications of alternative social security arrangements', *Carnegie–Rochester Conference Series on Public Policy*, **50**, 213–59.

Thøgersen, Ø. (1998), 'A note on intergenerational risk sharing and the design of pay-as-you-go pension programs', *Journal of Population Economics*, **11**, 373–8.

Thøgersen, Ø. (2001), 'Reforming social security: assessing the effects of alternative funding strategies', *Applied Economics*, **33**, 1531–40.

Thøgersen, Ø. (2006), 'Intergenerational risk sharing by means of pay-as-you-go programs – an investigation of alternative mechanisms', CESifo Working Paper no. 1759, CESifo, University of Munich.

UN (2004), *World Population in 2300*, United Nations, New York.

Verbon, H.A.A. (1989), 'Conversion policies for public pension plans in a small open economy', in B.A. Gustafsson and N.A. Klevmarken (eds), *The Political Economy of Social Security*, Elsevier Science, Amsterdam, 83–95.

Wagener, A. (2003), 'Pensions as a portfolio problem: fixed contribution rates vs. fixed replacement rates reconsidered', *Journal of Population Economics*, **16**, 111–34.

Wagener, A. (2004), 'On intergenerational risk-sharing within social security schemes', *European Journal of Political Economy*, **20**, 181–206.

17 Irreversible investments: a cost–benefit perspective
Rati Ram and Rajeev K. Goel*

1 Introduction

This chapter discusses the application of cost–benefit analysis to decisions on irreversible investments. Although a wide variety of outlays might be characterized by irreversibility, we focus on investment irreversibility which has received considerable attention in recent years.[1] In general, investment irreversibility reflects the inability of the investor to recover all or most of the investment outlay either through an alternative use or by sale of the asset. This property is often stated, as by Dixit and Pindyck (1994, p. 8), hereafter D&P, and other scholars, in terms of the investment expenditure being a 'sunk cost'. The importance of considering the role of irreversibility in investment decisions arises from two related considerations. First, investment irreversibility is believed to be pervasive and not a characteristic of just a small fraction of investment outlays. Public investments are likely to be characterized by a higher degree, and wider prevalence, of irreversibility than private investments. Construction of a dam, setting up an irrigation system, building roads, bridges and other components of transport infrastructure, setting up a nuclear reactor, clearing a forest, and many other public investments are largely irreversible.[2] Second, most investment decisions are made under uncertainty, which can take many forms. Although irreversibility may sometimes modify the decision rules even for the relatively rare cases where investment costs and benefits are certain, the presence of uncertainty compounds the effect of irreversibility. The major consequence of irreversibility in the presence of uncertainty relative to a postponable investment is that the traditional net present value (NPV) rule does not apply, and often a much stricter criterion is appropriate.

The structure of the rest of the chapter is as follows. Section 2 describes briefly what might make a large part of investment expenditure a 'sunk cost'. Section 3 provides a benchmark by indicating the general cost–benefit rules for investment. In Section 4, we discuss the core point about the effect of irreversibility on cost–benefit analysis of investment decisions under uncertainty. In that section, as in most of this chapter, we draw heavily on Pindyck (1991) and D&P (1994), and also use considerable material from Brent (2006, pp. 213–22). Section 5 contains discussion of some extensions, implications, and applications and a flavor of the empirical evidence. The last section contains a few reflections and concluding observations.

2   Reasons for investments being irreversible

As noted in Section 1, the concept of irreversibility refers intuitively to the property that the investment outlay is not fully or largely 'recoverable', either through being used for another purpose (project) or through resale. In other words, the investment expenditure is a 'sunk cost'. Relative to investment by a firm, Pindyck (1991, p. 1111) and D&P (1994, p. 8) explain several factors that make most investment expenditures sunk costs. They note three types of reason that make investments irreversible. First, most capital is firm or industry specific and cannot be used productively by a different firm or in a different industry. For example, most investments in marketing and advertising are firm specific and cannot be recovered. Hence these are clearly sunk costs. Somewhat similarly, a steel plant is industry specific, and can be used only to produce steel. Although the plant could in principle be sold to another steel company, its cost should be viewed as mostly sunk, particularly if the industry is competitive. Second, even investments that are neither firm nor industry specific are often partly irreversible because of the 'lemons' problem. Buyers in markets for used machines, unable to evaluate the quality of an item, will offer a price that corresponds to the average quality in the market. Sellers, who know the quality of the item they are selling, will be reluctant to sell an above-average item. For example, office equipment, cars, trucks and computers are not industry specific, but have, even if almost new, resale values that are well below their purchase cost. Third, irreversibility can also arise because of government regulations or institutional arrangements. As an example of the former, capital controls may make it impossible for foreign (or even domestic) investors to sell assets and reallocate their funds. Relative to the latter, investments in new workers may be partly irreversible because, besides the training being 'specific' in Becker's (1975) sense, there are usually high costs of hiring, training and firing. As noted earlier, public investments may be even more irreversible than private investments. In general, since public investment is more likely to occur in areas of market failure in the presence of large positive externalities, resale value of such investments might be very low. It is difficult for the government to sell dams, irrigation systems, highways, roads and bridges, ports, airports, postal and other communication systems, and other similar structures. At an empirical level, Asplund (2000) studied the salvage values of discarded metalworking machinery, and concluded that even though such assets are expected to be non-specific, many discarded assets are scrapped rather than sold on second-hand markets, and firms can expect to get back only 20 to 50 percent of the initial price of a new machine once it is installed. Therefore, while the degree of irreversibility may vary across assets, as Drakos (2006) and other scholars have noted, one may share the view expressed by D&P (1994, p. 8) that 'most major capital investments are in large part irreversible', and Bertola's (1998, p. 3) statement that 'Investment is often irreversible: once installed, capital has little or no value unless used in production'. These statements seem even more true for public sector investments.

3   General cost–benefit rules for investments

The usual rule for judging the goodness of an investment is based on the NPV criterion. The rule is along the following lines. First, calculate the present value of the expected stream of profits (benefits) that the factory (asset) will generate. Second, calculate the present value of the stream of (expected) costs required to build the factory (asset). Finally, determine whether the excess of the former over the latter, which is the NPV, is greater than zero. If it is, the investment can be made. D&P (1994, p. 5) note that the NPV rule is also the basis for the neoclassical theory of investment, and the neoclassical rule may be expressed as: invest until the value of an incremental unit of capital is just equal to its (marginal) cost.

The NPV rule can be operationalized by considering the (expected) cost (C) and benefit (B) at each period (t) over the lifespan of the project. Let the time profile of (expected) costs be $C_0 \ldots C_n$, and of (expected) benefits $B_0 \ldots B_n$ for periods 0 through n. Also, let the discount rate be r. Then the NPV of the project at the initial period (0) can be expressed as:

$$\text{NPV}_0 = \sum_{t=0}^{n} (B_t - C_t)/(1 + r)^t. \tag{17.1}$$

The traditional rule states that so long as the NPV equals or exceeds 0, the investment may be made. In this highly simplified example, we assume that costs (Cs) and benefits (Bs) of the project are either known with certainty or one works with expected values of Bs and Cs. Also, the appropriate discount rate is known and is the same for all periods, although the expression easily permits different rates across the periods. Many questions do indeed arise in regard to the use of expression (17.1) in real-life analysis of investments or projects. However, most such questions rest on judgments about the magnitudes of Bs and Cs and the appropriate r (or rs). Relative to the neoclassical version of the NPV rule, several issues arise in determining the value of an incremental unit of capital and in the determination of its cost, and the usual approaches that deal with these questions follow either Jorgenson (1963) or Tobin (1969). Thus, in many investment-evaluation contexts, most difficulties relate not to the use of the NPV rule, but to the determination of magnitudes of Bs, Cs and rs. Relative to the public sector investments, while the NPV criterion is often considered reasonable, the difficulty of determining Cs, Bs and rs is compounded by the consideration of externalities relative to Bs, and of possible divergence between market prices and social (shadow) costs relative to Cs (and sometimes even Bs). The appropriate discount rates may also differ for private and public investments. Despite these difficulties, the NPV expression in (17.1) is usually considered as providing a reasonable basic framework for judging the goodness of an investment in both private and public sectors.

Several technical points about the NPV expression in (17.1) may be noted. First, if cost (C) is located entirely in the initial (0) period, benefit (B) is equal over all periods (starting with zero), and the number of periods is large, NPV at the initial period may be written more simply as[3]

$$NPV_0 = -C + B[1 + (1/r)] \qquad (17.1')$$

Second, Brent (2006, pp. 213–42) has explained at considerable length that one may need also to consider the investor's attitude towards risk in determining whether the investment is worthwhile even within the NPV framework. That requires a distinction between (utility of) NPV of expected benefits and expected utility of the benefits. Such a distinction is indeed important, but in the context of project (investment) evaluation, it is customary to go by the NPV of expected costs and benefits, which amounts to an assumption of risk-neutrality. Third, relative to the investor's attitude towards risk, Brent considers whether a risk 'premium' be included in the discount rate. We abstract from a direct consideration of that issue, and focus more on the role of irreversibility.

4   Irreversible investment under uncertainty

A few preliminary observations seem useful here. First, if Bs, Cs and r (or rs) are known with certainty, irreversibility of investment is not an important factor, and NPV expressions in (17.1) and (17.1') should provide an appropriate criterion in many cases.[4] The significance of irreversibility arises from the possibility that the investment may seem bad at a later point, which implies uncertainty. Second, even if the investment is irreversible, and its future value is uncertain, the NPV rule, or its neoclassical version, provides an appropriate criterion if the investment cannot be postponed. However, while, due to strategic considerations related to the competitors' behavior or other reasons, firms do not always have the opportunity to postpone investments, the delay is at least feasible for most investments. There may indeed be a cost of delay, in terms of the risk of entry by other firms or just the forgone cash flows, but such a cost does not necessarily imply that the investment cannot be postponed. In the case of public investments, postponement of investments seems even more feasible than for private firms. Thus the relevance of irreversibility to investment decisions rests on a combination of three factors. First, the investment is irreversible and to that extent the investment expenditure is a sunk cost. Second, there is uncertainty about the future value of the investment, and, third, the investment can be postponed. It is in the presence of these conditions that the traditional NPV rule or its neoclassical version warrants a major modification, and, as will be indicated later, the present value of the expected benefits may need to be substantially larger than the current-period cost (or the present value of costs in all periods) to justify investment in that period instead of postponing the decision.

A simple two-period case
To provide a simple starting-point and to fix ideas, we work with an example that is similar to the second problem in Brent (2006, pp. 242–3) and resembles the case of interest rate uncertainty considered by D&P (1994, pp. 48–50).[5] Suppose government is considering an irreversible investment that costs $3,000 in the first period and generates a perpetual annual flow of benefits valued at $300 starting in the first (0) period. Suppose also that the first-period discount rate is 10 percent, and the only uncertainty in the project is the second-period discount rate, which may be 5 percent with a probability of 0.5 (1/2) or 15 percent which also has a probability of 0.5 (1/2).

First note that if the second-period discount rate were known with certainty (at 10 percent), equation (17.1′) shows that NPV of the investment in the first period would be

$$\{-3{,}000 + 300[1 + (1/0.1)]\} = \$300. \tag{17.2}$$

Since this is positive, the traditional rule would imply that it is worthwhile for the government to make the investment (in the absence of a competing investment having a greater NPV). Three incidental observations are relevant to the foregoing scenario. First, in this case irreversibility does not matter since the project value is fully known in the first period. Second, if the investment cannot be postponed, NPV provides the correct guidance (and would do so even if there is uncertainty about the second-period discount rate). Third, even if the investment can be postponed, it would be unwise to do so. If the investment is made in the second period, NPV in the *second* period is $300, and would thus be $273 (300/1.1) in the first period, which is smaller than $300 given in equation (17.2).

Now consider the position when investment value is treated as uncertain due to uncertainty about the second-period discount rate. In that case, NPV (in the first period) of costs and expected benefits is given by: [6]

$$-3,000 + 300 + \{0.5[300 + (300/0.15)]$$

$$+ 0.5[300 + (300/0.05)]\}/1.1 = \$1,209. \tag{17.3}$$

Since this number is positive, the traditional NPV rule would suggest that the investment be made in the first period.[7] That, of course, would be correct if either the investment is reversible or the government does not have the option of waiting until the next year. If, however, the investment is irreversible (that is, the $3,000 outlay is sunk cost), and government has the ability to postpone the investment, it is not necessarily true that the positive NPV implies that the investment be made in the first period instead of waiting until the next. The major insight of much of the recent irreversible-investment literature lies in this relatively simple point. The insight is that positive NPV in the first period does not tell us whether the cost of waiting is greater or smaller than the benefit of deciding in the second period when the discount rate would become known. If the discount rate turns out to be 15 percent, NPV next year would be –$700 (–3,000 + 2,300), and the government would decide not to make the investment; the postponement avoids that potential loss. On the other hand, if the discount rate turns out to be 5 percent, the NPV in the second period would be $3,300, and government would decide to make the investment. The expected NPV in the first period of government deciding in the second period is given by weighting the NPV of investment made in the second period by its probability and discounting it to the first period, which is:

$$0.5[(-3,000/1.1) + (6,300/1.1)] = \$1,500. \tag{17.4}$$

This is higher than the NPV of $1,209 of investing in the first period given in equation (17.3). The simple example shows that the traditional rule for investment (in the first period) is wrong. The expected gain from waiting until the second period is $291 ($1,500 – $1,209), which means that the government should be willing to pay up to $291 for having the option of waiting until the second period instead of being limited to investing in the first period. Pindyck (1991) and D&P explain at length that the option to postpone the decision for an irreversible investment is much like a financial call option, and the option values in the two cases are similar.[8] They also note (D&P, pp. 30–32) that the 'value of (the) investment opportunity' (that is, of investment being made in the second period) is $1,500, which can be calculated by using standard option-pricing methods. In that terminology, the payoff from exercising the option in the first period is $1,209, but its opportunity cost in terms of the inability to invest in the second period is $1,500, and the NPV rule overlooks this opportunity cost of investment being made in the first period.

A multiperiod case
While the simple two-period case outlined above is instructive in conveying the basic point, it is restrictive in terms of the temporal dimension of investment options and characterization of the uncertainty.[9] D&P (pp. 136–46) outline a more general framework in which the number of periods is not limited and the stochastic process underlying uncertainty with regard to the investment value is specified in a more flexible form. Although mathematical treatment of the problem and the solution may seem tedious, intuition behind their procedure is relatively simple. While the project value (in terms of costs and benefits) for the first (current) period is known with certainty, its value in each future period is known only in terms of a probability distribution, and the investor can work only with the (net) expected present value. Each future period, however, reveals the true value(s) of the uncertain variable(s) in that period, and generates a new expected present value which can be discounted to the first period. The problem is to find the highest of these present values discounted to the first period, and setting that as the 'critical value' in the sense that investment is optimal if it is made when the expected present value (discounted to the first period) equals or exceeds the critical value. In general, such a critical value is larger, often by a large margin, than the investment expenditure (or its discounted present value), and thus investment based on first-period NPV is suboptimal and is worse than waiting until the critical value is attained or exceeded.

The foregoing point may be restated by noting that the traditional NPV rule judges an investment by seeing whether the (expected) net present value of benefits (V) equals or exceeds the investment cost (I), and therefore whether $V - I$ equals (or exceeds) zero. That procedure ignores the value of the option to invest later. If that value is denoted by $F(V)$, the appropriate criterion would be whether $V - I - F(V)$, and not $V - I$, equals or exceeds zero, or whether $V - I$ equals or exceeds $F(V)$. The following paragraphs indicate a formal derivation of the appropriate optimality rule and its characteristics.

D&P (pp. 136–46) start with the model developed by McDonald and

Siegel (1986) who addressed the following question: at what point is it optimal to incur a sunk cost I in return for a project whose value is V, if V evolves according to the following geometric Brownian motion?

$$dV = \alpha V dt + \sigma V dZ, \qquad (17.5)$$

where α is the 'drift' parameter and reflects the 'trend' in dV/V, σ is the variance parameter, and dZ is the increment of a Wiener process.[10] This characterization of uncertainty in the value of the investment is like a geometric random walk with a drift, and implies that the current value of the project is known, but its future values are lognormally distributed.[11] In the context of the McDonald–Siegel set-up, the problem can be viewed as one of dynamic optimization. Recalling that the value of the investment opportunity (that is, the value of the option to invest) is $F(V)$, our problem is to find a maximum for that value. In other words, we want to maximize the expected present value of $V_t - I$, or:

$$F(V) = \max E[(V_T - I)e^{-rT}], \qquad (17.6)$$

where E denotes the expectation, T is the unknown future time at which investment is made, r is the discount rate, and maximization is subject to the specification of the stochastic process for V in equation (17.5). Unlike the deterministic case in which σ is zero, the investment rule will take the form of a control variable V^* such that it is optimal to invest when $V \geq V^*$. D&P (pp. 142–3) show that the solution, giving the value of the investment opportunity $F(V)$ and the critical investment value V^*, can be expressed in the following equations, which solve the second-order differential (Bellman) equation for optimality subject to the stochastic process of equation (17.5), and three boundary conditions:

$$F(V) = A V^{\beta_1} \qquad (17.7)$$

and

$$V^* = I(\beta_1/\beta_1 - 1) \qquad (17.8)$$

where

$$A = (\beta_1 - 1)^{\beta_1 - 1}/\beta_1^{\beta_1} I^{\beta_1 - 1}. \qquad (17.9)$$

The parameter β_1 in the above equations is one of the roots of the following quadratic, in which δ is defined as $r - \alpha$ and is assumed to be positive:

$$0.5\sigma^2\beta(\beta - 1) + (r - \delta)\beta - r = 0, \qquad (17.10)$$

and is given by:

$$\beta_1 = 0.5 - (r - \delta)/\sigma^2 + \{[(r - \delta)/\sigma^2 - 0.5]^2 + 2r/\sigma^2\}^{0.5} > 1. \quad (17.11).$$

An almost identical solution is obtained by D&P (p. 152) by the options-pricing procedure (contingent claims analysis) in which the discount rate is replaced by the riskless rate of return.

D&P (pp. 142, 152–61) note the following characteristics of the critical investment value V^*.

First, since $\beta_1 > 1$, $\beta_1/(\beta_1 - 1) > 1$, and $V^* > I$, and thus the NPV rule is incorrect. Uncertainty and irreversibility drive a wedge between V^* and I, and the size of the wedge equals $\beta_1/(\beta_1 - 1)$.

Second, by way of a numerical illustration, if we set the investment cost (I) at 1 (one), and assume $r = 0.04$, $\delta = 0.04$, and $\sigma = 0.2$ (at annual rates), the following may be noted:

1. $\beta_1 = 2$, and $V^* = 2I = 2$. Thus the simple NPV rule is grossly in error. For this set of parameter values, V needs to be at least twice as large as I for the firm to invest.
2. The parameter A of equations (17.7) and (17.9) will then be 0.25, and value of the firm's investment opportunity $F(V)$ is $0.25V^2$ for $V \le 2$, and is $V - 1$ for $V > 2$, since when $V > 2$ the firm exercises the option to invest and receives the net payoff $V - 1$.
3. Thus the simple NPV rule needs to be modified to include the opportunity cost of investing now rather than waiting, which is $F(V)$. When $V < V^*$, $F(V) > V - I$ and thus $V < I + F(V)$, and the value of the project is less than its full cost, which is the direct cost I plus the opportunity cost $F(V)$.
4. $F(V)$ increases with σ, as does V^*, and thus greater uncertainty in V increases the value of the firm's investment opportunity and reduces the amount of actual investment. It can also be shown that V^* increases sharply with σ, revealing high sensitivity of investment to volatility.
5. Increase in δ ($= r - \alpha$) reduces $F(V)$ and V^* since it becomes costlier to wait due to reduced expected growth of V.
6. If r (discount rate or the risk-free rate of return) is increased, $F(V)$ increases and so does V^*. Thus higher real interest rates reduce investment, but for a reason different from that in the 'standard' model where investment is reduced due to increased cost of capital.

The main point of the foregoing discussion may be summarized simply. When an investment is (a) irreversible and (b) has an uncertain future value, and (c) the investor has the option to wait, the traditional rule that investment be made when the present value of future benefits (at least) equals present value of costs, and thus NPV $\geq$ 0, is in error. In almost all cases, the present value of the future benefits needs to exceed, perhaps substantially, the present value of costs. This is so because investment in the present period 'kills' the option to invest in a later period, and that option has a value. Equivalently, the proper rule would say that investment should be made when the NPV at least equals the value of the investment opportunity in a later period, which is like the call-option price in the finance literature. In slightly more technical language, given a simple stochastic-process representation of the uncertainty in the future value of the investment, one can obtain an analytical solution for the critical value of V (V^*), which determines when the investment is optimal, and for the value of the investment opportunity. It is shown that generally $V^* - I$ is considerably larger than zero, and also that $F(V)$ and V^* increase with (a) increase in the magnitude of the uncertainty (σ), (b) increase in the risk-free rate or discount rate (r), and (c) fall in the excess of discount rate over the trend rate ($\delta = r - \alpha$).[12]

Summary of an application

The basic model in equations (17.5) through (17.11) conveys the main theoretical point well. In the discussion following equation (17.11), we use D&P's (p. 153) illustrative parameter values for r, δ and σ to provide a quantitative flavor of the possible divergence between the standard criterion and the modified optimality rule after taking into account irreversibility and uncertainty. However, in addition to showing the implications of D&P's illustrative parameter values, an actual application should help toward a better understanding of the framework and provide some indication of procedures for estimation of the main parameters. While many applications of the basic model and its extensions are noted in the next section and listed in Table 17A.1, we summarize here one application to investment in free-stall housing by dairy producers in Texas.

   Purvis et al. (1995) noted that dairy cows outnumbered people by approximately three to one in central Texas, that manure from a 1,000-cow dairy was comparable to sewage from a city of approximately 17,000, that under the 1972 Clean Water Act units with 700 or more cows were required to operate under a national permit, and that there was thus demand for technological options for cost-effective pollution control. The predominant conventional housing technology used open corrals, and free-stall housing was an alternative that (a) involved substantial capital outlay, (b) led to increased milk production of about 10 percent, and (c) entailed a major environmental advantage in terms of water quality protection. However, the investment was largely irreversible and its benefit in terms of increased milk production (and feed costs) was uncertain. Therefore, the authors proceeded to estimate (expected) annual revenue from free-stall technology that would justify investment after taking account of irreversibility and uncertainty.

Purvis et al. (1995) noted that due to limited experience with free-stall technology, adequate time-series data were not available. Therefore, adopting an ex ante approach, they used simulations to determine the optimal investment trigger for free-stall technology. The following are the main features of their procedure.

1. The simulated annual returns from investing in free-stall technology were assumed to follow a geometric Brownian motion of the form specified in equation (17.5).
2. The parameter α (trend or drift) was taken as zero, which, as in D&P's (p. 153) numbers, meant that $\delta = r$, and implied a corresponding simplification of equation (17.11) for β_1.
3. They took r as 3 percent (0.03) because that was the estimated historical rate of return on agricultural investments.
4. Therefore, the only parameter remaining to be estimated for getting values of β_1, A and V^* of equations (17.7), (17.8), (17.9) and (17.11) was the variance σ^2.
5. For getting expected returns from free-stall technology, and for estimating the variance parameter (σ^2), the authors undertook simulations. With data from early adopters and prospective investors, a profile was developed of expected returns in a 1,000-cow free-stall facility. The expected returns were defined as the excess of expected returns from free-stall dairying over the amount being earned from open-lot technology.
6. Milk production and feed costs were modeled as stochastic. The distributions of these variables were based on expert opinion from dairy producers and researchers. A fixed milk price of $13 per hundredweight was taken.
7. Milk production was modeled as a triangular distribution. On open-lot dairy the most likely daily yield was 62 pounds per cow with expected production range from 57 to 68 pounds. The most likely free-stall yield was 68 pounds, with an expected range of 63 to 70 pounds.
8. Feed costs were modeled as a normal distribution with a standard deviation of 10 percent of average cost. The average annual cost per hundredweight of feeding cows on open-lot and free-stall modes was estimated at $5.28 and $5.19 respectively.
9. The simulations yielded an expected annual value (return) of $145,695 from installation of free-stall technology.

10. The variance parameter (σ^2) was estimated from simulations by considering the mean of N simulated log differences between investing in periods t and $t + 1$. The estimate from this discrete difference was simulated over 25,000 iterations, and the variance was calculated as:

$$(1/N) \sum_{t=1}^{N} [\{\ln(V_t) - \ln(V_{t+1})\} - \mu_r]^2$$

where μ_r denotes the simulated mean.

11. The simulations yielded the estimate of variance as 0.043, which, along with $r = 0.03$ and $\alpha = 0$ led to the estimate of β_1 from equation (17.11) as 1.7827.

Given the estimated cost of free-stall technology, the Marshallian trigger for a 3 percent discount rate (real return) was calculated as $83,448, which meant that a risk-neutral investor would adopt free-stall technology if the expected returns were at or above $83,448 in terms of the traditional NPV criterion. Since the simulated expected return from free-stall housing was estimated as $145,695, traditional analysis indicated that free-stall technology should be adopted.

However, with $\beta_1 = 1.7827$, and therefore $(\beta_1/\beta_1 - 1)$ being 2.2776, considerations of irreversibility and uncertainty require that the optimal trigger should be 2.2776 times the traditional trigger of $83,448, which implied that the expected return from free-stall housing should be at least $190,063 for the investment to be made. Since the simulated expected return was $145,695, the analysis suggested that investment in free-stall technology be not made and it would be optimal to wait. Equivalently, while the traditional analysis indicated the 'hurdle rate' to be 3 percent, the hurdle-rate (required return) with β_1 at 1.7827 needed to be 2.2776 times 3 percent (0.03) or 6.83 percent (0.0683).

Several related points may be noted about the Purvis et al. (1995) study. First, they extended the foregoing analysis by treating investment cost also as uncertain. Introduction of that uncertainty (besides the uncertainty in milk production and feed costs) raised the estimated variance to 0.048 and the optimal investment trigger from $190,063 to $198,606. Second, they made an important observation by noting (p. 548, footnote 9) that the modified optimal trigger assumes complete irreversibility of investment, and that under partial irreversibility the difference between the Marshallian trigger and the modified trigger would be smaller. They also provided an indication of how the case of a partially reversible investment could be handled. Third, their estimate of the discount (real) rate (r) was based on historical returns in agricultural investments. If adequate data were available, historical returns in dairy farming might be an alternative source of information on r. Fourth, the drift (trend) rate (α) is taken as zero. This is similar to the assumption underlying D&P's (p. 153) illustrative numbers noted in item II after equation (17.11). D&P (p. 235) assumed α to be zero for price process in the copper industry also. However, if historical data on values of dairy investments were available, the drift rate implicit in those data could be used. Fifth, in the absence of adequate empirical observations, the variance parameter was estimated by simulations. If reasonable historical data were available, σ^2 could be estimated from those. For example, to illustrate sample paths of geometric Brownian motion, D&P (p. 72) took σ as 0.20 which was approximately the standard deviation of NYSE index expressed in real terms. Relative to copper industry (p. 235) also σ was taken as 0.20. It may be interesting to note that the simulations by Purvis et al. (1995) yielded the value of standard deviation for (logarithm of) free-stall revenue as 0.207 (with σ^2 being 0.043), which is very close to D&P's number for the parameter. Relative to greenhouse construction in Greece, simulations by Tzouramani and Mattas (2004, p. 358) yielded a value of about 0.30 for σ. However, relative to the amenity value of Headwaters Forest, Conrad's (1997) regression procedure led to an estimate of 0.10 for σ (and 0.05 for α).

5   Some extensions, implications and applications, and a flavor of empirical evidence

As a starting point, it may be noted that the solution values of V^* and $F(V)$ in equations (17.7), (17.8), (17.9) and (17.11) are premised on the investment being irreversible or the entire investment expenditure I being a sunk cost. While there may certainly be cases where investment is completely irreversible, many investments are likely to be partly reversible, and thus a part of I may not be sunk cost. In all such cases, care is needed in interpreting and applying the critical values and characteristics of the solution value V^* derived in the last section. In other words, it should be understood that the solution values and the implied characteristics hold for the irreversible component of I, and the traditional rule applies to the reversible part. Some investments may resemble a mix of reversible and irreversible outlays, and that may complicate the derivation of an optimality rule. As stated in the last part of the preceding section, Purvis et al. (1995, p. 548, footnote 9) provide an indication of how the case of a partially irreversible investment can be handled.

Some extensions

The model considered in the last section depicts a relatively simple structure. It is based on (a) total irreversibility of investment, (b) uncertainty being in the project value, and (c) geometric random walk being a reasonable characterization of the project-value uncertainty. The solutions for V^* and $F(V)$ in that case do indeed nicely convey the basic consequence of investment irreversibility and uncertainty for a postponable project. However, many extensions of the paradigm of Section 4 are possible and can be useful. We summarize some of these through an extremely brief narrative.

First, recognizing that geometric Brownian motion may not be a good representation of uncertainty in some circumstances, D&P (pp. 161–73) explore alternative specifications of the stochastic process. They consider a mean-reverting specification and also a combination of Brownian motion and jump process. Second, they consider the case of output price uncertainty for a monopolist. Third, recognizing that irreversibility of investment could be softened through some 'escape routes' that firms may have, they allow temporary suspension of the project and its resumption later. This makes the project a sequence of operating options. Fourth, they allow permanent abandonment instead of suspension, and also consider an intermediate situation where both suspension and abandonment are available at different costs. Fifth, instead of focusing on a firm's investment decision, they consider equilibrium of the competitive industry that consists of many such firms. It is found that the basic results hold for uncertainty at the firm level. For industry-level uncertainty, contrary to one's first impression, while competition does destroy each firm's option to invest, that does not restore the NPV approach and caution in making an irreversible investment remains important, but for different reasons. Sixth, relative to a firm's investment decision, D&P examine investments that consist of several stages, in which case the threshold may change due to the fact that at an early stage of the sequence, 'most of the cost remains to be sunk', but as more steps are completed, less cost remains to be sunk (p. 21), and thus bygones affect later decisions. They also consider the learning curve, which reflects another effect of current decisions on the future. Seventh, they study incremental investment, the aim being to characterize optimal investment policy for capacity expansion. These extensions reinforce qualitatively the basic insight that irreversibility in uncertain investment generates an option value for postponing the decision. However, when a multistage investment generates information about the future state variables, value of that information should be considered in the decision rule. Similarly, there can be a trade-off between the plant size indicated by scale economies and the need for future flexibility.[13]

Other scholars have also extended the irreversibility models, and we note briefly some of these extensions. Abel and Eberly (1995) include fixed costs of investment, which makes investment a non-decreasing function of the shadow price of installed capital (q), and there are potentially three investment regimes that depend on the value of q. In a later work (Abel and Eberly, 1999), they note that irreversibility and uncertainty tend to reduce the capital stock due to increased user cost of capital. However, there is a 'hangover' effect in the opposite direction, which arises because irreversibility prevents the firm from selling capital even when its marginal value product is low. They note that neither effect dominates globally, and that irreversibility may increase or reduce capital accumulation. Bertola (1998) proposes, solves and characterizes somewhat more generally a model of sequential irreversible investment by a firm that faces uncertainty in technology, demand, and price of capital. Based on a closed-form solution, it is stated that the marginal revenue product of capital that induces additional investment is higher under irreversibility than the conventionally measured user cost of capital, but that in ergodic steady state, the former is on average *lower* than the latter. Vandenbroucke (1999) considers a model which allows finite values for all parameters, and shows that NPV and Dixit–Pindyck rules are nested in his more general framework. Rose (2000) and Chetty (2007) study the effects of high and low levels of interest rates on irreversible investment. Hartman and Hendrickson (2002) derive optimal investment strategy for a risk-neutral firm with partially reversible investment. Boyarchenko (2004) reports an optimal solution under any geometric Levy process for prices. Dangl and Wirl (2004) propose an algorithm when the Bellman equation cannot be solved analytically. Guo et al. (2005) propose and solve a model of investment decision in which the growth rate and volatilities of the decision variable are not constant, but shift between different states. Sabarwal (2005) considers the case when irreversible investment is financed by limited liability debt. Alvarez and Koskela (2006) consider the impacts of interest rate and revenue variability. Decamps et al. (2006) analyze the case of a decision maker who has to choose between two investment projects of different scales.

Some economic and policy implications
D&P bring out several implications of the optimality rules for irreversible investments. The first, and perhaps the most important, point is that irreversibility raises the threshold for current-period investment, generates an option value for waiting, provides an incentive to postpone the decision, and thus tends to lower investment in the short run. Second, the threshold for current-period investment rises rapidly with increased uncertainty. Third, these implications provide an explanation for the weak explanatory power of the traditional models relative to actual investment, especially in terms of the empirical observation of a relatively minor impact of interest rates and interest rate policy on investment. Fourth, the models thus imply that the degree of uncertainty is likely to have a much

stronger impact on investment than interest rates or other conventional policy choices, including antitrust action based on price–cost margin, for stimulating investment.[14] Fifth, it follows that 'Reduction or elimination of unnecessary uncertainty may be the best kind of public policy to stimulate investment' and 'the uncertainty generated by the very process of a lengthy policy debate on alternatives may be a serious deterrent to investment' (p. 14). Sixth, the result that uncertainty makes firms less eager to invest may not necessarily indicate a need for government intervention to stimulate investment. When there are complete markets for risk, and the firms are competitive price takers, a social planner would show the same degree of hesitancy (as a private firm) in making the investment decision. If markets for risk are incomplete, beneficial policy interventions exist, but need careful consideration, and the tools that are often used (for example, price floors and ceilings) can have adverse effects (p. 19). Seventh, they note (p. 20) that the competitive long-run equilibrium under uncertainty is not a static state, but a dynamic process where prices can fluctuate widely. Therefore, the microeconomics textbook picture of a firm entering an industry when prices rise to long-run average cost, and exiting when the price falls below long-run average cost, is not quite correct. For entry, price needs to be strictly above the average cost, and similarly firms will exit only when price falls sufficiently far below the average (variable) cost. Eighth, it follows (pp. 20–21) that the usual antitrust or international-trade policies, which are based on a static framework, may need substantial rethinking. For example, in industrial organization theory, excess profits suggest collusion or entry barriers, calling for antitrust action. In the dynamic perspective, based on irreversibility and uncertainty, periods of above-normal profits without new entry can occur even if all firms are small price takers and lack significant market power. In international trade, when foreign firms continue to export at a loss, there may be no predatory dumping or need for countervailing import duties; foreign firms may be simply keeping alive their option of future operations in the US market with no predatory intent.

Some applications
D&P also describe many applications of the basic model and its extensions. Some of these are indicated in the implications for firms' choices and policy interventions summarized in the preceding paragraphs, but there are several others that we state with utmost brevity. First, they apply (pp. 223–30) the model of firm entry and exit to the copper industry in a monopolistic context. They also illustrate (pp. 264–7) the case of the copper industry in the context of their discussion of the competitive industry equilibrium. Second, relative to the consideration of lay-up

(suspension) and scrapping (abandonment), they provide (pp. 237–42) an application to the oil tanker industry. Third, they discuss (pp. 396–405) an important application to offshore oil reserves to illustrate how one can value an undeveloped resource reserve and how to decide when to invest in the development and production of the resource. Fourth, they discuss (pp. 405–11) an application to electric utilities' compliance with the Clean Air Act. Fifth, they discuss (pp. 412–18) the timing of environmental policy since the design of such a policy is similar to that of an irreversible investment. They also indicated the relevance of their framework to firms' hiring and firing decisions, and noted that a new worker will not be hired until the value of the marginal product of labor is sufficiently above the wage rate, and to the extent that sunk costs are larger or uncertainty is greater, the required margin will be higher.

Besides the application of the irreversibility model to investment or hiring decisions by firms and policy intervention by government to stimulate investment and to protect the environment, D&P (pp. 23–5) indicate that the framework can have many important applications in (a) decisions by consumers on investment in durable goods, (b) decisions of workers regarding investment in education, training and other forms of human capital, (c) marriage and divorce, (d) suicide, (e) legal reforms and matters relating to constitutions, and (f) other dimensions of Becker's (1980) economic approach to social behavior. The main point in these extensions would be the inclusion of an option value of postponing the decision in the context of irreversibility and uncertainty. Although we just note such possibilities, the potential economic and social importance of these extensions might be enormous, perhaps as much as that of application of the model to firm-level investment decisions.

Many other scholars have also applied the irreversible-investment framework to a variety of economic questions, and some of these are relevant to cost–benefit analysis in the public sector. These are mentioned here with minimal details. With regard to timing of environmental policy, besides the discussion by D&P (pp. 412–18), the issue has been considered by Pindyck (2000) and Asano (2005). As summarized in Section 4, Purvis et al. (1995) studied investment in free-stall housing by dairy farmers in Texas. Conrad (1997) used a framework like that of Section 4 to evaluate whether or not the US government should preserve the Headwaters Forest wilderness area for recreational use. Similarly, while extending Conrad's work, Forsyth (2000) did a calculation of the critical amenity value in the context of the decision whether to preserve Killarney Wilderness area. Farzin et al. (1998) studied optimal timing of technology adoption by a competitive firm. Tegene et al. (1999) considered landowners' decision to convert farmland to urban use. Mahul and Gohin (1999) studied control of contagious animal disease in the context of foot-and-mouth disease in Brittany. Price and Wetzstein (1999) applied the framework to entry and exit thresholds for Georgia's commercial peach producers. Pauwels et al. (2000) report an application to emergency response decisions. Erdal (2001) examined the effect of exchange rate uncertainty on export- and import-oriented sectors. Jou (2001) studied optimal effluent fees. Maynard and Shortle (2001) apply a similar framework to adoption of cleaner technologies in US bleached pulp production. Isik et al. (2003) studied entry and exit decisions of agribusiness firms. Rob and Vettas (2003) examined the choice between foreign direct investment (FDI) and export relative to a foreign market. Bosetti et al. (2004) studied the choice between preservation, remediation and development of a partially degraded area and applied the model to Ginostra in Italy. Lee (2004) investigated the determinants of foreign equity share in international joint ventures. Parisi et al. (2004) and Parisi and Ghei (2005) applied the framework to timing of legislation. Tzouramani and Mattas (2004) studied choice of greenhouse construction type. Madlener et al. (2005) studied energy technology adoption by Turkish electric supply companies. Van Soest (2005) reported an application to the roles of environmental taxes and quotas in the timing of adoption of energy-efficient technologies. Bo (2006) provided empirical estimates of the 'hangover' effect of investment irreversibility on fixed investment and inventories. Chorn and Shokhor (2006) indicate an application to production expansion in a Central Asian gas condensate field. Eckermann and Willan (2006) did an application to the option value of delay in health technology assessment. Wong (2006) studied sequential FDI by multinational firms. Baerenklau and Knapp (2007) applied the framework to technology adoption in irrigated cotton fields in California. Milevsky and Young (2007a, b) report an interesting application to the timing of annuitization. Table 17A.1 in the appendix contains a highly abbreviated list of the foregoing applications.

Empirical evidence
The plausibility of several implications indicated in the foregoing discussion and usefulness of the applications noted above are perhaps evident. Also, there is anecdotal evidence in the observation that firms work with much higher hurdle (threshold) rates than suggested by the traditional theory. However, empirical evidence of a structured kind is not easily generated, particularly at the aggregate level. In the context of exploring aggregate investment behavior (and modification of Tobin's q) suggested by the irreversibility consideration, D&P (1994, pp. 423–5) reflect on the difficulty of incorporating irreversibility into econometric models of

aggregate investment. They note that although their models imply that irreversibility and uncertainty should raise the threshold required for a firm to invest, very little can be said about the effect of uncertainty on the firm's long-run average rate of investment or average capital stock. Moreover, there are significant aggregation problems.

Nevertheless, most microeconomic and macroeconomic evidence seems generally supportive of the irreversibility models. In an early work, Bertola and Caballero (1990) studied the demand for consumer durables and found the evidence supportive of models of irreversible investment. Caballero and Pindyck (1992) showed a positive dependence of marginal profitability of capital on volatility in US manufacturing. At an aggregate level, Pindyck and Solimano (1993) found, in a cross-country sample, that investment ratio varies negatively with the standard deviation of marginal profitability of capital. Episcopos (1995) and Bell and Campa (1997) also indicate evidence to be supportive of the basic predictions of the model. Servén (1997) reported that uncertainty and instability are important factors behind Africa's relatively poor investment record. Pattillo (1998) finds support for the framework in panel data for Ghana's manufacturing firms. Sivitanidou and Sivitanides (2000) indicate conformity of movements in office–commercial construction with the models of irreversible investment. Carnazza and Travaglini (2001) reported broad consistency of irreversible-investment theory with survey data on Italian manufacturing firms. Darku (2001) finds panel data on Ugandan firms' investments consistent with the predictions of theory of irreversible investment. Harchaoui and Lasserre (2001) find decisions by Canadian copper mines to be compatible with trigger price implied by irreversible-investment theory. Following Episcopos (1995), Sing and Patel (2001) study the UK property market and find the empirical evidence consistent with predictions of the framework. Bulan (2005) studied panel data on capital budgeting decisions of US manufacturing firms and found the evidence consistent with real-options theory. At a somewhat indirect and less structured level, Goel and Ram (1999, 2001) and Goel et al. (2004) found that, across several categories of investments that differed in the degree of irreversibility, uncertainty had a stronger negative effect when the investment was more irreversible.

Aside from testing implications of the irreversible-investment framework, some scholars have tried to judge the presence of irreversibility in investments. For example, Chun and Mun (2005) considered the structure of adjustment costs in information-technology investments in the US and reported that the estimates indicate irreversibility in such investments. Using a procedure developed by Ramsey and Rothman (1996), Speight and Thompson (2006) tested UK manufacturing investment data for time-irreversibility. They found evidence of irreversibility in (a) gross fixed capital formation and aggregate vehicle expenditure, among expenditure categories, and (b) fuels and oil refining, engineering and vehicles, and textiles and leather, among industry categories.

6 Concluding observations

Largely following Pindyck (1991) and D&P (1994), we restate the central proposition of the recent irreversible-investment literature. The main point is that the traditional NPV criterion (or its neoclassical version) is not valid for a postponable irreversible investment under uncertainty, and that a considerably stricter criterion is likely to be needed for such investment being made instead of postponing the decision to a later period. The primary logic behind that view is that ability to postpone the decision has an option value, or that the investment decision has an opportunity cost, that is overlooked in the traditional criterion. We first indicate why most investments may be largely irreversible, and state the well-known formulation for the usual NPV criterion. A simple two-period case is then discussed to bring out the main idea behind the proposition that the NPV criterion is in error. After that a multiperiod case with a more flexible specification of the stochastic process underlying the project value uncertainty is explained, and several implications of the derived optimality rule are listed. A summary of an application to investment by Texas dairy producers is included to provide an illustration of the empirical methodology and a flavor of real-life parameter values. Many extensions, implications and applications of the basic irreversibility model are stated briefly, and an indication is provided of the empirical evidence on the framework.

Despite the variations in some cases, the major implication of the theory relative to a postponable private or public investment is that, due to the combination of irreversibility and uncertainty, the usual cost–benefit analysis gets modified, and a positive NPV is not enough to justify investment. There is usually a substantial option value of waiting, which is similar to the value of a call option in the finance literature, and that explains the weak explanatory power of the traditional models of investment. Some important implications for public policy include (a) the most effective means for stimulating investment might be reduction of uncertainty, and not interest rate or tax policies, (b) several traditional policies, including price ceilings or floors, antitrust action, and international trade policies, may need substantial rethinking, and (c) hesitancy on the part of firms to invest, as suggested by the model, does not necessarily imply need for government intervention to stimulate investment, and when there is scope for beneficial intervention, its form may need considerable thought.

We noted briefly applicability of the framework to many other types of irreversible expenditures and human behavior, including (a) hiring and firing of workers by firms, (b) expenditure on consumer durables, (c) outlays by workers on education, training and other forms of human capital, (d) marriage and divorce, (e) suicide, and (f) legal reform and constitutional issues. An indication was also provided of the many empirical applications of the framework to a wide variety of investments, including several that have a bearing on various types of government policies and provision of public services. Despite the difficulty of testing the framework directly, there seems to be considerable evidence in support of its major implications.

The numerous potential applications suggest enormous potential for research in this area in terms of determining the optimality rules for comparing cost and benefits relative to specific private and public investments, and application of such rules to a wide variety of decisions by governments, firms and individuals.

Notes

*   Insightful comments were given by Professor Robert Brent on an earlier version. Helpful research assistance was provided by Jan Bauer and Utkir Kamilov. The usual disclaimer applies.

1.   Pindyck (1991) and D&P (1994) list and consider a wide variety of irreversible expenditures and behavior. Some of these are mentioned later in the text.

2.   D&P (1994, p. 4, fn 1) state that clearing a forest may be the opposite of an investment in the sense of providing immediate benefit in return for an uncertain future cost, but their methods apply to such cases also.

3.   In many cases, C is located entirely in the first (zero) period, and Bs start from period 1, in which case the NPV expression in (17.1′) becomes $-C + (B/r)$. Following, D&P's notation, we let B start in period zero itself.

4.   D&P (p. 50) show this for a simple case. The two-period example in this section also shows that one can follow the NPV rule if there is no uncertainty. In the presence of a 'drift' in the project value, however, D&P (pp. 138–9) show that it may be optimal to delay investment even in some deterministic cases.

5.   Brent (2006, pp. 223–5) provides a somewhat similar illustration that relates to the possible purchase by government of a wooded area for outdoor recreational use.

6.   The first term in the expression shows the first-period cost of $3,000, the second term is benefit in the first period, and the third term is expected present value of the stream of benefits from the second period discounted to the first period. The calculation is similar to that in Brent (2006, p. 243, item iii) and that in D&P (p. 49).

7.   Note that although expected value of the discount rate in the second period is 10 percent, expected NPV is greater with an uncertain discount rate (which has an expected value of 10) than with a certain discount rate of the same magnitude. This is because increase in the expected value for the discount rate of 0.05 (over that of 0.10) is greater than the reduction for the rate of 0.15 (over 0.10). Thus uncertainty over the discount rate makes investment in the first period more attractive than with a certain discount rate that equals the expected rate. D&P (p. 49, fn 12) indicate this result to be an implication of Jensen's inequality.

8.   Although investment in stocks is not irreversible, that in a call option may be treated as irreversible, and it is the value of that option that they compare with option value of an irreversible investment.

9.   D&P (pp. 27–54) examine, in their illustrative two- and three-period contexts, cases of uncertainty in output price, investment cost, and interest rates, and the trade-off between scale economy and flexibility. They derive rules that are similar to those indicated by the more general and flexible consideration of the case of investment-value uncertainty. When future costs are uncertain due to input-price uncertainty, the effect is similar to that of output-price uncertainty. If, however, the uncertainty pertains to total cost of investment for a multistage project, and information about it will be revealed only as the first few steps are undertaken, these steps have information value over and above the contribution to the conventional NPV calculation, and it may be desirable (optimal) to start the project even if the traditional NPV is somewhat negative. Moreover, for a project involving scale economies, investment on a smaller scale may have a value in providing future flexibility and thus offset partly the advantage of a larger investment indicated by economies of scale.

10. A Wiener process has three properties. First, it is a Markov process, and probability distributions for all future values of the process depend only on its current value. Second, it has independent increments, and third, changes in the process over any finite interval are normally distributed with a variance that increases linearly with time horizon.

11. D&P (pp. 136–7) note that this specification of the stochastic process may be an abstraction from many real projects, but provides a simple introduction to the basic ideas. They explore some alternative processes at a later point.

12. The simple two- and three-period cases considered by D&P (pp. 26–50) also indicate that, when the uncertain variable is output price, the value of the investment option increases with (a) amount of investment (I), given the output-price uncertainty, (b) initial price (given I and the price uncertainty), and (c) increase in the probability of a price increase.

13. This is indicated in note 9 in slightly greater detail.

14. Antitrust action based on price-cost margin (that is, $(P - MC)/P$, the Lerner index) may be interpreted here as intervention by the government in an imperfectly competitive industry where price is substantially higher than marginal cost and indicates considerable firm-level market power due to collusion or barriers to entry.

References

Abel, A.B. and Eberly, J.C. (1995), 'A unified model of investment under uncertainty', NBER Working Paper No. 4296, New York: NBER.

Abel, A.B. and Eberly, J.C. (1999), 'The effects of irreversibility and uncertainty on capital accumulation', *Journal of Monetary Economics*, **44**, 339–77.

Alvarez, L.H.R. and Koskela, E. (2006), 'Irreversible investment under interest rate variability: some generalizations', *Journal of Business*, **79**, 623–44.

Asano, T. (2005), 'Irreversibilities and the optimal timing of environmental policy under Knightian uncertainty', Institute of Social and Economic Research, Osaka University, Discussion Paper No. 643.

Asplund, M. (2000), 'What fraction of a capital investment is sunk costs?', *Journal of Industrial Economics*, **48**, 287–304.

Baerenklau, K.A. and Knapp, K.C. (2007), 'Dynamics of agricultural technology adoption: age structure, reversibility, and uncertainty', *American Journal of Agricultural Economics*, **89**, 190–201.

Becker, G.S. (1975), *Human Capital*, 2nd edn, New York: NBER and Columbia University Press.

Becker, G.S. (1980), *A Treatise on the Family*, Cambridge, MA: Harvard University Press.

Bell, G.K. and Campa, J.M. (1997), 'Irreversible investments and volatile markets: a study of the chemical processing industry', *Review of Economics and Statistics*, **79**, 79–87.

Bertola, G. (1998), 'Irreversible investment', *Research in Economics*, **52**, 3–37.

Bertola, G. and Caballero, R.J. (1990), 'Kinked adjustment costs and aggregate dynamics', in O. Blanchard and S. Fischer (eds), *NBER Macroeconomics Annual*, Cambridge, MA: MIT Press, pp. 237–95.

Bo, H. (2006), 'An empirical examination of the hangover effect of irreversibility on investment', *Scottish Journal of Political Economy*, **53**, 358–76.

Bosetti, V., Conrad, J.M. and Messina, E. (2004), 'The value of flexibility: preservation, remediation, or development for Ginostra?', *Environmental and Resource Economics*, **29**, 219–29.

Boyarchenko, S. (2004), 'Irreversible decisions and record-setting news principle', *American Economic Review*, **94**, 557–68.

Brent, R.J. (2006), *Applied Cost–Benefit Analysis*, 2nd edn, Cheltenham, UK and Northampton, MA, USA: Edward Elgar.

Bulan, L. (2005), 'Real options, irreversible investment and firm uncertainty: new evidence from U.S. firms', *Review of Financial Economics*, **14**, 255–79.

Caballero, R.J. and Pindyck, R.S. (1992), 'Uncertainty, investment, and industry evolution', NBER Working Paper No. 4160, New York: NBER.

Carnazza, P. and Travaglini, G. (2001), 'Impact and nature of irreversibility and uncertainty on investment decisions: a survey on Italian manufacturing firms', *Économie Appliquée*, **54**, 75–110.

Chetty, R. (2007), 'Interest rates, irreversibility, and backward-bending investment', *Review of Economic Studies*, **74**, 67–91.

Chorn, L.G. and Shokhor, S. (2006), 'Real options for risk management in petroleum development investments', *Energy Economics*, **28**, 489–505.

Chun, H. and Mun, S-B. (2005), 'The structure of adjustment costs in information technology investment', *Economics Bulletin*, **5**, 1–9.

Conrad, J.M. (1997), 'On the option value of old-growth forest', *Ecological Economics*, **22**, 97–102.

Dangl, T. and Wirl, F. (2004), 'Investment under uncertainty: calculating the value function when the Bellman equation cannot be solved analytically', *Journal of Economic Dynamics and Control*, **28**, 1437–60.

Darku, A.B. (2001), 'Private investment, uncertainty, and irreversibility in Uganda', *African Finance Journal*, **3**, 1–25.

Decamps, J.-P., Mariotti, T. and Villeneuve, S. (2006), 'Irreversible investment in alternative projects', *Economic Theory*, **28**, 425–48.

Dixit, A.K. and Pindyck, R.S. (1994), *Investment under Uncertainty*, Princeton, NJ: Princeton University Press.

Drakos, K. (2006), 'A note on uncertainty and investment across the spectrum of irreversibility', *Applied Economics Letters*, **13**, 873–6.

Eckermann, S. and Willan, A. (2006), 'The option value of delay in health technology assessment', University of New South Wales Centre for Applied Economic Research Working Paper No. 2006/06.

Episcopos. A. (1995), 'Evidence on the relationship between uncertainty and irreversible investment', *Quarterly Review of Economics and Finance*, **35**, 41–52.

Erdal, B. (2001), 'Investment decisions under real exchange rate uncertainty', *Central Bank Review*, **1**, 25–47.

Farzin, Y.H., Huisman, K.J.M. and Kort, P.M. (1998), 'Optimal timing of technology adoption', *Journal of Economic Dynamics and Control*, **22**, 779–99.

Forsyth, M. (2000), 'On estimating the option value of preserving a wilderness area', *Canadian Journal of Economics*, **33**, 413–34.

Goel, R.K. and Ram, R. (1999), 'Variations in the effect of uncertainty on different types of investment', *Australian Economic Papers*, **38**, 481–92.

Goel, R.K. and Ram, R. (2001), 'Irreversibility of R&D investment and the adverse effect of uncertainty: evidence from the OECD countries', *Economics Letters*, **71**, 287–91.

Goel, R.K., Hasan, I. and Ram, R. (2004), 'Effect of general uncertainty on venture-capital investments: a cross-country study', *Economia Internazionale/International Economics*, **57**, 305–13.

Guo, X., Miao, J. and Morellec, E. (2005), 'Irreversible investment with regime shifts', *Journal of Economic Theory*, **122**, 37–59.

Harchaoui, T. and Lasserre, P. (2001), 'Testing the option value theory of irreversible investment', *International Economic Review*, **42**, 141–66.

Hartman, R. and Hendrickson, M. (2002), 'Optimal partially reversible investment', *Journal of Economic Dynamics and Control*, **26**, 483–508.

Isik, M., Coble, K.H., Hudson, D. and House, L.O. (2003), 'A model of entry–exit decisions and capacity choice under demand uncertainty', *Agricultural Economics*, **28**, 215–24.

Jorgenson, D. (1963), 'Capital theory and investment behavior', *American Economic Review*, **53**, 247–59.

Jou, J.-B. (2001), 'Environment, asset characteristics, and optimal effluent fees', *Environmental and Resource Economics*, **20**, 27–39.

Lee, T. (2004), 'Determinants of the foreign equity share of international joint ventures', *Journal of Economic Dynamics and Control*, **28**, 2261–75.

Madlener, R., Kumbaroglu, G. and Ediger, V.S. (2005), 'Modeling technology adoption as an irreversible investment under uncertainty: the case of the Turkish electric supply industry', *Energy Economics*, **27**, 139–63.

Mahul, O. and Gohin, A. (1999), 'Irreversible decision making in contagious animal disease control under uncertainty: an illustration using FMD in Brittany', *European Review of Agricultural Economics*, **26**, 39–58.

Maynard, L.J. and Shortle, J.S. (2001), 'Determinants of cleaner technology investments in the U.S. bleached kraft pulp industry', *Land Economics*, **77**, 561–76.

McDonald, R. and Siegel, D. (1986), 'The value of waiting to invest', *Quarterly Journal of Economics*, **101**, 707–28.

Milevsky, M.A. and Young, V.R. (2007a), 'Annuitization and asset allocation', *Journal of Economic Dynamics and Control*, **31**, 3138–77.

Milevsky, M.A. and Young, V.R. (2007b), 'The timing of annuitization: investment dominance and mortality risk', *Insurance: Mathematics and Economics*, **40**, 135–44.

Parisi, F., Fon, V. and Ghei, N. (2004), 'The value of waiting in lawmaking', *European Journal of Law and Economics*, **18**, 131–48.

Parisi, F. and Ghei, N. (2005), 'Legislate today or wait until tomorrow? An investment approach to lawmaking', *Journal of Public Finance and Public Choice/Economia delle Scelte Pubbliche*, **23**, 19–41.

Pattillo, C. (1998), 'Investment, uncertainty, and irreversibility in Ghana', *IMF Staff Papers*, **45**, 522–53.

Pauwels, N., van de Walle, B., Hardeman, F. and Soudan, K. (2000), 'The implications of irreversibility in emergency response decisions', *Theory and Decision*, **49**, 25–51.

Pindyck, R.S. (1991), 'Irreversibility, uncertainty, and investment', *Journal of Economic Literature*, **39**, 1110–48.

Pindyck, R.S. (2000), 'Irreversibilities and the timing of environmental policy', *Resource and Energy Economics*, **22**, 233–59.

Pindyck, R.S. and Solimano, A. (1993), 'Economic instability and aggregate investment', *NBER Macroeconomics Annual*, New York: NBER, pp. 239–303.

Price, T.J and Wetzstein, M.E. (1999), 'Irreversible investment decisions in perennial crops with yield and price uncertainty', *Journal of Agricultural and Resource Economics*, **24**, 173–85.

Purvis, A., Boggess, W.G., Moss, C.B. and Holt, J. (1995), 'Technology adoption decisions under irreversibility and uncertainty: an ex ante approach', *American Journal of Agricultural Economics*, **77**, 541–51.

Ramsey, J.B. and Rothman, P. (1996), 'Time irreversibility and business cycle asymmetry', *Journal of Money, Credit and Banking*, **28**, 1–21.

Rob, R. and Vettas, N. (2003), 'Foreign direct investment and exports with growing demand', *Review of Economic Studies*, **70**, 629–48.

Rose, C. (2000), 'The *I–r* hump: irreversible investment under uncertainty', *Oxford Economic Papers*, **52**, 626–36.

Sabarwal, T. (2005), 'The non-neutrality of debt in investment timing: a new NPV rule', *Annals of Finance*, **1**, 433–45.

Servén, L. (1997), 'Irreversibility, uncertainty and private investment: analytical issues and some lessons for Africa', *Journal of African Economies*, **6** (supplement), 229–68.

Sing, T.-F. and Patel, K. (2001), 'Evidence of irreversibility in the UK property market', *Quarterly Review of Economics and Finance*, **41**, 313–34.

Sivitanidou, R. and Sivitanides, P. (2000), 'Does the theory of irreversible investments help explain movements in office-commercial construction?', *Real Estate Economics*, **28**, 623–61.

Speight, A.E.H. and Thompson, P. (2006), 'Is investment time irreversible? Some empirical evidence for disaggregated UK manufacturing data', *Applied Economics*, **38**, 2265–75.

Tegene, A., Wiebe, K. and Kuhn, B. (1999), 'Irreversible investment under uncertainty: conservation easements and the option to develop agricultural land', *Journal of Agricultural Economics*, **50**, 203–19.

Tobin, J. (1969) 'A general equilibrium approach to monetary theory', *Journal of Money, Credit and Banking*, **1**, 15–29.

Tzouramani, I. and Mattas, K. (2004), 'Employing real options methodology in agricultural investments: the case of greenhouse construction', *Applied Economics Letters*, **11**, 355–9.

van Soest, D.P. (2005), 'The impact of environmental policy instruments on the timing of adoption of energy-saving technologies', *Resource and Energy Economics*, **27**, 235–47.

Vandenbroucke, J. (1999), 'General trigger values of optimal investment', *Applied Economics Letters*, **6**, 287–90.

Wong, K.P. (2006), 'Foreign direct investment and forward hedging', *Journal of Multinational Financial Management*, **16**, 459–74.

Appendix 17A

Table 17A.1   Abbreviated list of selected applications of the irreversible-investments framework

	Nature of application	Citation(s)
1.	Entry and exit in US copper industry	D&P (1994, pp. 223–30)
2.	Building, mothballing and scrapping oil tankers	D&P (1994, pp. 237–42)
3.	Valuation of an oil reserve and decision on investment in development and production	D&P (1994, pp. 396–405)
4.	Using emission allowance or installing scrubbers (compliance with Clean Air Act)	D&P (1994, pp. 405–11)
5.	Homeowners' response to energy tax credits	D&P (1994, pp. 411–12)
6.	Timing of environmental policy	D&P (1994, pp. 412–18), Pindyck (2000), Asano (2005)
7.	Agricultural technology adoption (Texas dairy producers)	Purvis et al. (1995)
8.	Preservation of recreational areas	Conrad (1997), Forsyth (2000)
9.	Optimal timing of technology adoption by a competitive firm	Farzin et al. (1998)
10.	Landowners' decision to convert farmland to urban use	Tegene et al. (1999)
11.	Contagious animal disease control (foot and mouth disease in Brittany)	Mahul and Gohin (1999)
12.	Entry and exit thresholds for Georgia commercial peach producers	Price and Wetzstein (1999)
13.	Emergency response decisions	Pauwels et al. (2000)
14.	Real exchange rate uncertainty and investment in export- and import-oriented sectors	Erdal (2001)
15.	Optimal effluent fees	Jou (2001)
16.	Adoption of cleaner technologies in US bleached kraft pulp production	Maynard and Shortle (2001)
17.	Entry and exit decisions of agribusiness firms	Isik et al. (2003)
18.	FDI versus exports relative to a foreign market	Rob and Vettas (2003)
19.	Preservation, remediation or development of a partially degraded area: application to Ginostra (Italy)	Bosetti et al. (2004)
20.	Foreign equity shares in international joint ventures	Lee (2004)

Table 17A.1   (continued)

	Nature of application	Citation(s)
21.	Timing of legislation	Parisi et al. (2004), Parisi and Ghei (2005)
22.	Agricultural investment: choice of greenhouse construction	Tzouramani and Mattas (2004)
23.	Adoption of energy technology by Turkish electric supply companies	Madlener et al. (2005)
24.	Roles of environmental taxes and quotas in timing of adoption of energy-efficient technologies	van Soest (2005)
25.	Empirical estimation of the 'hangover' effect of investment irreversibility: fixed investment versus inventories	Bo (2006)
26.	Production expansion in a Central Asian gas condensate field	Chorn and Shokhor (2006)
27.	Option value of delay in health technology assessment	Eckermann and Willan (2006)
28.	Sequential FDI by multinational firms	Wong (2006)
29.	Technology adoption in irrigated cotton production in California	Baerenklau and Knapp (2007)
30.	Timing of annuitization	Milevsky and Young (2007a,b)

Note: Some of the applications include elements of an extension (or testing) of the basic framework. The distinction between implications, extensions, applications, and tests tends to become blurred in some instances.

18 Pro-growth, pro-poor: is there a trade-off?
*J. Humberto Lopez**

1 Introduction

A large number of papers have recently explored the links between growth and inequality and the resulting impact on poverty reduction. Questions arising from this debate include whether the benefits of economic growth are broadly shared by all groups of society including the poor; whether a poverty reduction strategy should mainly have a growth bias; whether there are trade-offs between pro-growth and pro-poor growth strategies; and whether pro-growth policies[1] are also the best poverty reduction policies. As a result of this debate, a few findings have emerged on which there seems to be a more or less broad consensus.

First, nobody seems to doubt the importance of growth for poverty reduction. Countries that have historically experienced the greatest reduction in poverty are those that have experienced prolonged periods of sustained economic growth. In fact, there is plenty of evidence suggesting that the poor typically do share from rising aggregate income and do suffer from economic contractions. This finding is robust to the use of a relative concept of poverty where the poor are a pre-specified proportion of the population – usually the lowest quintile of the population (Foster and Szekely, 2000; Dollar and Kraay, 2002), or an absolute definition of poverty where the poor are those with income[2] levels below a pre-specified threshold – for example purchasing power parity (PPP) adjusted US\$1 per person per day, or a country-specific poverty line computed on the basis of the cost of a country-specific subsistence package (Ravallion and Chen, 1997).

Second, progressive distributional changes are good for poverty reduction. While on the one hand it is difficult to argue that poverty reduction can be achieved through redistributive policies in the absence of economic growth, growth associated with progressive distributional changes will have a greater impact in reducing poverty than growth that leaves the distribution unchanged. For example, Ravallion (1997), Bourguignon (2003), and Son and Kakwani (2003) review the poverty–growth–inequality relationship and note that the impact of growth on poverty is reduced when inequality is high. Poverty will therefore be more responsive to growth the more equal the income distribution. Intuitively, if the poor have a low share in existing income, they will likely have a low share in newly created income.

Third, there is no strong empirical evidence suggesting a general tendency for growth as such to make income distribution more or less equal. For example, Dollar and Kraay (2002) find that, on average, the income of the poorest fifth of society rises proportionately with average incomes. Other studies concluding that changes in income and changes in inequality are unrelated include Deninger and Squire (1996), Chen and Ravallion (1997) and Easterly (1999). Growth would thus be good for the poor, or at least as good as for everybody else in society.

From a policy perspective, however, there is another issue that is likely to be more interesting than the existence of empirical regularities between growth, inequality, and poverty, namely what kind of policies a country should pursue in a successful poverty reduction strategy. Since poverty outcomes will depend on how a given policy affects growth and inequality, assessing how appropriate a particular policy is for a poverty reduction strategy will require knowledge about: (i) the links between policies and growth; (ii) the links between policies and inequality; and (iii) the relative contribution of growth and inequality in poverty reduction.

On the growth front, the literature is quite rich and there are several empirical models that offer guidance as to the expected impact that a particular policy may have on long-run growth. On the inequality front, one might take the result pointing to lack of causality from growth to inequality mentioned above at face value and select policies on the basis of their expected impact on growth. However, a number of recent papers have suggested that many pro-growth policies might be expected also to have an impact on inequality, and in some cases even conflict with the growth objective. For example, work by Barro (2000) and Lundberg and Squire (2003) suggest that greater openness to trade (something to be welcomed when one has a growth objective in mind) would go along with more inequality. Similarly, Li and Zou (2002) present empirical evidence suggesting that increases in government spending, while potentially leading to lower growth, would also reduce inequality. Thus advice based only on the expected growth impact of policies could lead to unpleasant poverty outcomes (as the anti-globalization movement has been pointing out repeatedly over the last few years).

As for the relative contribution of growth and inequality for poverty reduction a number of recent papers[3] have stressed the importance of initial conditions for poverty reduction. One message emerging from these studies is that when poverty reduction is the overriding policy objective, poorer and relatively equal countries may be willing to tolerate modest increases in income inequality in exchange for faster growth – more so than richer and highly unequal countries where any policy that leads to a deterioration in the distribution of income should be carefully analyzed.

In this chapter we provide an empirical evaluation of the impact of a number of pro-growth policies on inequality and headcount poverty. In doing so, the chapter contributes to the existing literature along two main dimensions. First, following a similar framework to that in Li and Zou (2002), and Lundberg and Squire (2003) the chapter takes into account the possibility that some policies may simultaneously influence both growth and inequality. However, unlike most of the existing empirical studies on the topic, it moves beyond the inequality analysis and infers, under plausible assumptions, the impact of the policy under consideration on poverty. In doing so, the chapter takes into account the role played by initial conditions as measured by per capita income and income inequality levels.

Second, also unlike other studies on the topic, the chapter focuses on the impact of policies on inequality changes rather than on inequality levels. In addition to being the natural choice when interest centers on the impact of policies on poverty through the growth and redistribution channels, this approach allows us to capture potential intertemporal inequality dynamics (Benabou, 1996; Ravallion, 2002) and hence potential poverty dynamics. In fact, if after implementation of a pro-growth policy that has a negative impact on inequality there are important mismatches between when the growth and inequality effects become apparent, it would be plausible to find that a policy intervention increases poverty in the short run and decreases it in the long run. This would be the case if the inequality effect were felt immediately but there were important lags before the bulk of the growth effect became noticeable. The issue is of particular interest for policy analysis because of the potential political economy risks associated with reform programs that lead to temporary increases in poverty. Further, since growth models tend to adjust very slowly (empirical estimates of the half-life of convergence found in the literature range from 20 to 40 years), it would be possible that the increases in poverty would be temporary, but still long lasting.

To anticipate some of the results below, we find that there is inequality convergence and that there is an apparent mismatch between the speeds of convergence of income and inequality, with inequality converging much faster than income. As indicated above, this could potentially lead to an increase in poverty when a policy presents a trade-off between its growth and inequality outcomes. At the policy level, on the one hand, we find that improvements in education and infrastructure and lower inflation would reduce inequality. The estimates of the coefficients for these variables always have the expected sign and are highly significant from a statistical point of view. Thus policies in these areas support both higher growth and lower inequality, and hence have a positive effect on poverty reduction.

On the other hand, we find that financial development, trade openness, and decreases in the size of government would be associated with increases in inequality. Thus, policies in these areas present some conflict with respect to growth and inequality objectives. To the extent that their positive impact on growth offsets the negative impact on inequality, these pro-growth policies would also be pro-poor (in the sense that poverty falls as a result of the implementation of the policy). Under the assumption of a log-normal income distribution, we illustrate the expected impact that progress on these areas may have on (headcount) poverty levels, and find that these policies are likely to be pro-poor in the long run (that is, the growth effect offsets the increase in inequality), but might also lead to temporary short-run increases in poverty in the absence of compensatory measures.

As for the role of initial conditions, there are two main messages that emerge from the analysis. First, in the cases where growth and inequality tend to move in different directions, the growth effect would tend to dominate in poorer and more equal countries, whereas the inequality effect would dominate in richer and more unequal economies. This implies that if the instantaneous policy impacts on growth and inequality are similar, country initial conditions will determine whether poverty increases or declines. Second, the poorer and the more unequal a country is, the lower the poverty elasticity with respect to the policy in question. This is a somewhat worrisome result because policy will be more ineffective in countries with the highest levels of poverty and therefore where one would welcome high effectiveness.

All in all, the findings of this chapter suggest that pro-growth policies, regardless of their impact on inequality, are likely to be pro-poor in the long run. In other words, the positive impact that policies have on growth should be enough to eventually offset the potential negative effects they may have on inequality. However, there is also a need to face the possibility (and its associated implications) that some reforms may lead to temporary increases in poverty, especially in high inequality countries. This is especially the case given that in this framework 'temporary' may span several years.

The rest of the chapter is structured as follows. In Section 2 we review some basic growth–inequality–poverty relationships that stress the important interrelations between growth and inequality for poverty reduction. Sections 3 to 5 provide an empirical evaluation of the impact of a number of pro-growth policies on inequality. In Section 3 we discuss the econometric models and how they can be used to infer the impact that different policies have on poverty. Section 4 addresses econometric issues, paying particular attention to the challenges involved in the estimation of a dynamic panel with country-specific effects, and reviews the data used in the empirical section. In Section 5 we present the results for the empirical inequality model, and in Section 6 we link the growth and inequality results to draw inferences about the likely impact that changes in the policy determinants under consideration may have on poverty. Section 7 closes the chapter with some conclusions.

2   Growth, inequality and poverty

If economic growth were a policy target, then evaluating whether one policy is more appropriate than another would require assessing which of the two policies provides more benefits (that is, more growth potential). Yet, as poverty has become the center of development efforts (as evidenced by, for example, the adoption of the Millennium Development Goals – MDG – framework by most international agencies) the issue has become more complex, because in this case the growth benefits of a pro-growth policy could be offset by its costs: a potential negative effect on income distribution.[4] Thus the cost–benefit analysis of policies seems critical in a poverty reduction framework.

We now review the basic elements of the poverty–growth–inequality relationship, since the understanding of those elements is a critical element to perform such cost–benefit analysis.

Formally, the degree of poverty in any given country depends upon two factors: the average income level of the country and the extent of income inequality. Formally,

$$P = P[Y, L(p)],\qquad(18.1)$$

where P is a poverty measure (which for simplicity will be assumed to belong to the Foster–Greer–Thorbecke (FGT) (1984) class[5]), Y is per capita income and $L(p)$ is the Lorenz curve measuring the relative income distribution. $L(p)$ is the percentage of income enjoyed by the bottom $100 \times p$ percent of the population.

Changes in poverty can be decomposed into a growth component that relates changes in Y to P, and an inequality component that relates poverty to changes in inequality. In general, increases in average income (growth) will reduce poverty. Thus, denoting the growth elasticity of poverty by γ one could write:

$$\gamma = \frac{\partial P}{\partial Y}\frac{Y}{P} < 0.\qquad(18.2)$$

Measuring the effect of inequality on poverty is slightly more complex because inequality can change in infinite ways. Although, intuitively, progressive distributional change is likely to reduce poverty,[6] this result cannot be generalized without additional assumptions. For example, consider the (possibly unlikely) case of a transfer from the extremely rich to the very (but not extremely) rich. This would improve inequality levels but would not affect poverty. To make the problem of the impact of inequality changes on poverty tractable, one possibility is to assume that income follows a log-normal distribution.[7] Lopez and Servén (2006) compare the theoretical quintile shares according to a log-normal distribution with their empirical counterparts using data from about 800 household surveys, and conclude that the log-normal approximation fits the empirical data extremely well. Indeed, Lopez and Servén cannot reject the null hypothesis that per capita income follows a log-normal distribution (although the same hypothesis is unambiguously rejected when applied to per capita consumption).

In turn, under this assumption it is possible to express the inequality elasticity of poverty φ as the elasticity of poverty with respect to the Gini index G:

$$\phi = \frac{\partial P}{\partial G}\frac{G}{P} > 0. \tag{18.3}$$

With these elements in mind, the elasticity of poverty with respect to change in policy X can be expressed as:

$$\frac{\partial P}{\partial X}\frac{X}{P} = \frac{\partial Y}{\partial X}\frac{X}{Y}\frac{\partial P}{\partial Y}\frac{Y}{P} + \frac{\partial G}{\partial X}\frac{X}{G}\frac{\partial P}{\partial G}\frac{G}{P}, \tag{18.4}$$

or using (18.2) and (18.3) above:

$$\frac{\partial P}{\partial X}\frac{X}{P} = \frac{\partial Y}{\partial X}\frac{X}{Y} \times \gamma + \frac{\partial G}{\partial X}\frac{X}{G} \times \phi. \tag{18.5}$$

Equation (18.5) indicates that the elasticity of poverty with respect to policy X will depend on: (i) the growth elasticity with respect to X; (ii) how growth is translated into poverty reduction; (iii) the inequality elasticity with respect to X; and finally (iv) how inequality changes are translated into poverty reduction.[8]

In principle, γ and φ could be considered to be independent of the policy in question and depend on the particular income distribution, the initial level of per capita income Y, the poverty line, and the initial

Table 18.1   Theoretical elasticities under log-normal assumption

	Growth elasticity			
PL[a] / Gini	0.3	0.4	0.5	0.6
0.16	−6.2	−3.3	−2.0	−1.2
0.33	−4.0	−2.2	−1.3	−0.9
0.50	−2.8	−1.6	−1.0	−0.7
0.66	−2.1	−1.2	−0.8	−0.5
0.90	−1.4	−0.9	−0.6	−0.4
	Inequality elasticity			
PL[a] / Gini	0.3	0.4	0.5	0.6
0.16	12.9	7.7	5.3	4.0
0.33	5.2	3.3	2.4	2.0
0.50	2.5	1.7	1.4	1.2
0.66	1.2	0.9	0.8	0.8
0.90	0.4	0.4	0.4	0.4

Note: [a] Poverty line as a share of per capita GDP.

Source: Lopez and Servén (2004, p. 23).

level of inequality *G* (see Lopez and Servén, 2006). Table 18.1 presents the theoretical elasticities of headcount poverty to growth and head-count poverty to inequality computed under the assumption that income follows a log-normal distribution. These elasticities are computed for different Gini coefficients (running from 0.3 to 0.6) and different levels of development (expressed in terms of the share of the poverty line to per capita GDP).[9]

For example, for a country where the poverty line is 33 percent of per capita income and the Gini coefficient is 0.3, the growth elasticity of poverty would be −4 (that is, growth of 1 percent of GDP would reduce poverty by 4 percent) whereas the inequality elasticity would be 5.2 (a 1 percent increase in the Gini coefficient would increase poverty by 5.2 percent). By contrast, in a country with the same income level but higher inequality, say a Gini of 0.6, the growth elasticity of poverty would be −0.9, and the inequality elasticity would be 2. Thus high initial inequality levels are likely to represent a barrier to poverty reduction, since both the impact of growth on poverty[10] and the impact of progressive distributional change on poverty will be much smaller than in countries with a more equal income distribution.

On the other hand, it is also the case that high initial poverty is also a barrier for poverty reduction. For example, consider the case of a country with a Gini of 0.4. If the country had per capita income levels that are six times the poverty line (row with the heading 0.16 in Table 18.1) the growth elasticity of poverty would be -3.3, whereas if the country had income levels that are only one and a half times the poverty line (row with the 0.66 heading in Table 18.1), this same elasticity would only be -1.2. Thus this second (and poorer) country would have to achieve a growth rate that is more than twice that of the first (and richer) country to obtain the same rate of poverty reduction. Similarly, a 1 percent decline in the Gini coefficient would lower poverty by 0.9 percent when a country has a Gini coefficient of 0.4 and the poverty line is 66 percent of per capita income levels, but would have a much higher impact (7.7 percent) when the poverty line is 16 percent of per capita income.

3 The impact of policies on growth and inequality

The previous section has reviewed the role that growth and inequality levels play for poverty reduction. It has also highlighted the fact that inferences about how a particular policy will affect poverty require knowledge about the impact of the policy on both growth and inequality. On the growth front, the literature is quite rich and there are several empirical models that offer guidance as to the expected impact that a particular policy may have on long-run growth. On the inequality front, however, not only is the literature less rich but also in most cases it is based on empirical models that relate the level (rather than the change in the level) of inequality to policies and therefore complicate the analysis of poverty.

The empirical models in this chapter are based on the following dynamic structure:

$$y_{it} - y_{it-1} = \delta y_{it-1} + \omega' x_{it} + v_i + \tau_t + \upsilon_{it}, \qquad (18.6)$$

$$g_{it} - g_{it-1} = \alpha g_{it-1} + \beta' x_{it} + \mu_i + \eta_t + \varepsilon_{it}, \qquad (18.7)$$

where y is the log of per capita income, g is the log of the Gini coefficient, x represents the set of explanatory variables (in logs) other than lagged income, v and μ are unobserved country-specific effects, τ and η are time-specific effects and υ and ε are the error terms. The subscripts i and t represent country and time period, respectively.

Beyond expressing the impact that the coefficients of the different policies may have on growth and inequality, (18.6) and (18.7) can be employed to obtain estimates of how poverty changes would be associated with a change in policy j of x. It must be noted, however, that the presence of dynamics allows us to differentiate between the immediate impact that a change in a given policy has on both income and inequality and the long-run impact that results from the dynamic feedback. For example, changes to policy j will lead in the short run to:[11]

$$\frac{dp}{dx_j} = \omega_j \times \gamma + \beta_j \times \phi, \qquad (18.8)$$

where p is the log of the poverty measure, whereas in the long run they will lead to:[12]

$$\frac{dp_{LR}}{dx_j} = -\frac{\omega_j}{\delta} \times \gamma - \frac{\beta_j}{\alpha} \times \phi. \qquad (18.9)$$

Clearly, if the dynamics in equations (18.6) and (18.7) are similar (that is, if δ is similar to α) then (18.9) reduces to (18.8) scaled up to $\delta = \alpha$. But if one of the variables adjusts much faster than the other then one should also expect to find dynamics in poverty. Figure 18.1 illustrates this point with a very simple example that assumes $\gamma = -\phi = 1$, $\delta = -0.1$, $\alpha = -0.3$, $\beta = 0.6$ and $\omega = 0.3$. This parametrization would be consistent with a policy that has a positive impact on growth and a negative impact on income distribution; in addition, the full impact on distribution is felt much faster than on growth. Inspection of Figure 18.1 would suggest an initial net adverse impact on poverty (due to the increase in inequality) that later is reversed and, as the impact of the policy on income kicks in, poverty is reduced.

The models in (18.6) and (18.7) are based on the implicit assumption that simultaneous changes in income and in inequality are motivated by the implementation of a given policy, and ignore the potential impact that growth 'as such' may have on inequality and that inequality 'as such' may have on growth. While in principle the existing empirical evidence seems to suggest that the growth process is not accompanied by changes in inequality, some authors have also found a Kuznets type of relationship between inequality and income levels. For example, Barro (2000) finds that the Gini index would rise with GDP for values of GDP of less than \$1,636 (in 1985 US dollars) and fall thereafter. Also, assuming that inequality has no impact on growth seems a bit more controversial. Alesina and Rodrik (1994), Benabou (1996) and Perotti (1996) find that inequality negatively affects growth, whereas Li and Zou (1998) and Forbes (2000) find the opposite result. To take into account potential interactions we also consider the following models:

$$y_{it} - y_{it-1} = \delta y_{it-1} + \omega' x_{it} + \xi g_{it} + v_i + \tau_t + \upsilon_{it}, \qquad (18.10)$$

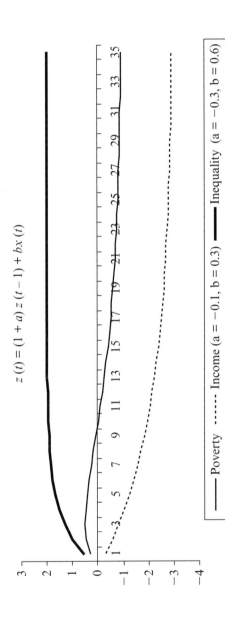

$z(t) = (1 + a) z(t - 1) + bx(t)$

Poverty ━━ Income (a = −0.1, b = 0.3) ━━ Inequality (a = −0.3, b = 0.6)

Figure 18.1   Potential for poverty dynamics

$$g_{it} - g_{it-1} = \alpha g_{it-1} + \beta' x_{it} + \chi y_{it-1} + \mu_i + \eta_t + \varepsilon_{it}. \quad (18.11')$$

Equations (18.10) and (18.11) would now result in different expressions for the changes in poverty levels, which in this case would be given by:

$$\frac{dp}{dx_j}(\omega_j + \xi\beta_j) \times \gamma + \beta_j \times \phi \quad (18.12)$$

$$\frac{dp_{LR}}{dx_j} = -\frac{1}{(\delta\alpha - \chi\xi)}(\alpha\omega_j - \xi\beta_j) \times \gamma - \frac{1}{(\delta\alpha - \chi\xi)}(\delta\beta_j - \chi\omega_j) \times \phi. \quad (18.13)$$

It is evident that for $\xi = \chi = 0$, (18.12) and (18.13) reduce to (18.8) and (18.9).

With respect to policies, we follow recent work by Loayza and Soto (2002) and Loayza et al. (2002) who propose an empirical growth model that focuses on policies that have received the most attention in academic and policy circles, and especially at the World Bank, in the context of structural adjustment operations. In addition to the lagged dependent variable, the following regressors are considered: cyclical reversion (captured by the output gap); human capital (logged rate of gross secondary enrollment); financial development (logged ratio of private domestic credit supplied by private financial institutions to GDP); government burden (logged ratio of government consumption to GDP); infrastructure (telecommunications capacity); governance/institutions (first principal component of the four indicators reported by the International Country Risk Guide – that is, prevalence of law and order, quality of bureaucracy, absence of corruption and accountability of public officials); trade openness (volume of trade adjusted by: country size – that is, area and population, whether the country is landlocked, and whether the country is an oil exporter); inflation rate; cyclical volatility (standard deviation of the output gap); real exchange rate misalignment; banking crisis (number of years that a country undergoes a banking crisis in the period under analysis) and, finally, terms of trade changes.

4 Estimation and data issues
Estimation of equations (18.6) and (18.7) (or equivalently (18.10) and (18.11)), above, poses several challenges including the presence of country-specific effects and the possible endogeneity of some of the explanatory variables with inequality. Arellano and Bond (1991) propose differencing the equations to eliminate country-specific effects. After accounting for time-specific effects (with the inclusion of period-specific dummies), equation (18.7) could be rewritten as:[13]

$$(g_{it} - g_{it-1}) - (g_{it-1} - g_{it-2}) = \alpha(g_{it-1} - g_{it-2})$$

$$+ \beta'(x_{it} - x_{it-1}) + (\varepsilon_{it} - \varepsilon_{it-1}), \qquad (18.14)$$

or

$$(g_{it} - g_{it-1}) = (1 + \alpha)(g_{it-1} - g_{it-2}) + \beta'(x_{it} - x_{it-1}) + (\varepsilon_{it} - \varepsilon_{it-1}). \qquad (18.15)$$

This differencing, however, introduces a new bias since the error term $(\varepsilon_{it} - \varepsilon_{it-1})$ is correlated with the lagged dependent variable $(g_{it-1} - g_{it-2})$. Under the assumptions that the error term ε is not serially correlated, Arellano and Bond propose a two-step generalized methods of moments (GMM) estimator using as moment conditions:

$$E[g_{it-s}(\varepsilon_{it} - \varepsilon_{it-1})] = 0 \text{ for } s \geq 2 \qquad (18.16)$$

and if the explanatory variables x are predetermined but not strictly exogenous:

$$E[x_{it-s}(\varepsilon_{it} - \varepsilon_{it-1})] = 0 \text{ for } s \geq 2. \qquad (18.17)$$

In the first step, the error terms are assumed to be independent and homoskedastic across countries and time. In the second step, the residuals obtained in the first step are used to construct a consistent estimate of the covariance matrix, and thus relax the assumptions of independence and homoskedasticity. Using the moment conditions in (18.16) and (18.17) and denoting $\theta = [\alpha \; \beta']'$, the GMM estimator of θ and corresponding covariance matrix $\Sigma\theta$ are given by:

$$\hat{\theta} = (\overline{x}'Z\hat{\Omega}^{-1}Z'\overline{x})^{-1}\overline{x}'Z\hat{\Omega}^{-1}Z'g, \qquad (18.18)$$

$$\hat{\Sigma}_{\theta} = (\overline{x}'Z\hat{\Omega}^{-1}Z'\overline{x})^{-1}, \qquad (18.19)$$

where $\overline{x} = [g_{it-1} \; x]$, Z is the matrix of instruments, and $\hat{\Omega}$ is a consistent estimate of the covariance matrix of the moment conditions constructed with the residuals of the first-step regression.

The consistency of the GMM estimator above depends on the validity of the assumption that the error terms do not exhibit serial correlation as well as on the validity of the instruments. We present two specification tests to address these issues. The first is the Sargan test of overidentifying restrictions. The second examines whether the error term ε is not serially correlated, which in turn would imply that the difference error in (18.14) does not present second-order serial correlation.

We rely on two main sources of data. Inequality data come from Dollar and Kraay's (2002) database on inequality. The growth determinants come from Loayza et al. (2002). Our regressions are then conducted using non-overlapping five-year periods spanning the years 1960–2000. Income and inequality data are taken from the latest available date within the given period. Growth and inequality determinants are averages for the five-year period in question. These transformations would reduce the sample to 291 observations for 87 countries for which we have at least two consecutive Gini coefficients. If we also eliminate countries with less than three observations (note that as implied by (18.16) and (18.17) we need a minimum of three observations per cross-section unit to run the GMM estimator outlined above), the sample is further reduced to 194 inequality observations for 61 countries.

The original sample of growth determinants is higher and includes 350 observations for 78 countries. When both databases are merged, however, the number of observations available for estimation purposes is reduced to 134 cases and 41 countries. Working with five-year averages reduces the problems associated with the original panel where 24 countries would account for more than half of the 953 observations. Further, the use of at least three observations for each country (that is, 15 years) gives a long-run perspective to the problem that is lost with the original panel, where more than 30 countries have only one observation.

Admittedly, using five-year periods also brings some complications. The reduction in the number of observations is particularly important when one considers the estimator proposed above, since we are working with a large number of variables and a small cross-section dimension (41 countries in some cases). For example, if we considered the explanatory variables as predetermined, even limiting the maximum number of lagged levels to be used as instruments to two, we would still end up with 170 instruments in some of our specifications. Not only does the problem then become too large to estimate, but also the excessive number of overidentifying restrictions relative to the sample would dramatically affect the performance of the GMM estimator. Against this background, the results presented below for the models including all the policies treat as a predetermined variable only the lagged dependent variable. Since the model is still overidentified, we can test the validity of the hypothesis that the proposed instrument set is uncorrelated with the error term, using the Sargan test for overidentifying restrictions. It must be noted in this regard that the employed specification tests generally support the econometric models. That is, Sargan and

Table 18.2   Descriptive statistics

Variable	Mean	S.D.	Max	Min
log(Gini)	−0.977	0.269	−0.296	−1.790
Δlog(Gini)	0.001	0.034	0.128	−0.164
log(GDP)	7.931	1.043	10.610	5.380
Growth	0.016	0.038	0.276	−0.229
Education	3.438	1.076	5.024	−0.518
Financial depth	−1.465	1.015	0.734	−8.205
Trade openness	0.016	0.542	2.308	−1.877
Government burden	−1.928	0.432	−0.539	−4.444
Public infrastructure	3.329	1.923	6.681	−1.608
Governance	−0.002	1.706	3.468	−3.256
Price stability	4.768	0.406	8.797	4.405
Cyclical volatility	0.025	0.021	0.316	0.002
External imbalances	4.664	0.384	7.210	3.406
Banking crisis	0.050	0.188	1.000	0.000
External conditions	−0.006	0.045	0.187	−0.212

second-order correlation tests cannot reject the hypothesis that the models are well specified and that our instrument set is valid.[14]

Table 18.2 presents some descriptive statistics for the data. The logged Gini coefficient would have a mean value of −0.977 (equivalent to a Gini of about 0.37) and show considerable dispersion (the 2 standard deviation confidence interval would range from about −0.43 to −1.51). The maximum logged Gini in the sample is −0.296 and the minimum is −1.79. There is also some evidence of a skewed distribution with a long and thin upper tail (revealing the presence of a few very unequal countries in the sample). Regarding changes in the (log) Gini, the average annual change between two five-year periods would be 0.1 percent, indicating that on average inequality changes little over time. However, there is considerable dispersion: the 2 standard deviation interval would range from about −6.8 to 6.8 percent. The changes in the Gini coefficient also present a skewed distribution but in this case it is toward the lower tail. As for the income data, average annual growth rates between two five-year periods would be about 2 percent, but dispersion is also high (very similar to that found in the changes in the Gini coefficient). The variables that aim to represent the various aspects of economic development tend to be skewed toward the lower tail, something that would reveal the presence of a few very underdeveloped countries in the sample. The inflation rate also presents a skewed distribution but in this case is likely to reflect a few instances of extreme macroeconomic mismanagement.

5   Empirical results

We start this section by presenting results for equations (18.10) and (18.11) under the restriction that $\beta = \omega = 0$. Thus equation (18.11) is basically reduced to a test of convergence for inequality considering the potential impact of income levels, whereas in equation (18.10) we explore, in addition to the speed of convergence for per capita income levels, the potential impact of inequality on growth. We estimate the equations with four different methods: ordinary least squares (OLS), fixed effects, two stage least squares (2SLS)[15], and the Arellano and Bond (1991) GMM estimator. In turn, we present the results of the Arellano and Bond estimator treating the non-lagged dependent variable regressor both as an exogenous variable and as a predetermined variable.

Inspection of Table 18.3 suggests convergence in inequality levels, with the estimators that take into account the possibility of fixed effects resulting in a faster speed of convergence. For example, while the pooled estimator suggests a half-life of about 20 years, the other estimators suggest a half-life of between 1 and 5 years. These results are consistent with the findings of Benabou (1996) and Ravallion (2002)[16] who also find inequality convergence. Further, their estimated coefficients for the speed

Table 18.3   Inequality and income levels[a]

Dependent variable Dlog(Gini)	Estimation method				
	OLS	Fixed effects	2SLS[b]	A&B[c]	A&B[d]
Lagged inequality	−0.0312	−0.175	−0.111	−0.198	−0.213
	(−4.26)	(−10.22)	(−2.16)	(−4.18)	(−4.47)
Initial income	−0.003	−0.007	−0.018	−0.009	−0.021
	(−1.27)	(−0.74)	(−0.69)	(−0.44)	(−1.02)
Summary statistics					
Number of observations	252	252	172	172	172
F (p-value)	0.00	0.00	0.37		
Sargan test (p-value)				0.40	0.68
Second-order correlation (p-value)				0.27	0.16

Notes:
a   All regressions include time dummies. *t*-statistics in parentheses.
b   Instruments are: lagged growth and lagged inequality.
c   Arellano and Bond's (1991) GMM estimator, treating initial GDP as an exogenous variable.
d   Arellano and Bond's (1991) GMM estimator, treating initial GDP as a predetermined variable.

of convergence are of a similar order of magnitude to that of our pooled estimator. Two possible interpretations behind the inequality convergence given by Ravallion are related to (i) the implications of the neoclassical growth model (which in addition to predicting income convergence across countries would also predict inequality convergence), or more pragmatically to (ii) the widespread convergence of economic policy during the 1990s. This second argument is likely to weigh less, however, when we take into account that we also find inequality convergence when we control for policy changes, and therefore for policy convergence. As for the impact of initial income on the changes in inequality, Table 18.3 does not find any significant effect, although admittedly, given how parsimonious the models are, this could be due to omitted variables bias.

Next we explore in Table 18.4 the results obtained when one regresses per capita growth on initial income and inequality. Two main messages emerge from this table. First, the speed of convergence in per capita income levels seems to be much lower than the speed of convergence for inequality, with an estimated half-life of between 8 years (Arellano and Bond estimators) and 40 years (2SLS estimator).[17] The fixed-effects estimator would

Table 18.4   Growth and inequality[a]

Dependent variable	Estimation method				
$\Delta\log(Y)$	OLS	Fixed effects	2SLS[b]	A&B[c]	A&B[d]
Initial Income	0.002	−0.035	−0.016	−0.075	−0.067
	(1.09)	(−5.38)	(−1.64)	(−3.09)	(−3.20)
Inequality	−0.008	0.011	−0.021	−0.008	−0.004
	(−1.41)	(1.03)	(−1.48)	(−0.62)	(−0.18)
Summary statistics					
No. of observations	387	387	117	222	222
F (p-value)	0.00	0.00	0.51		
Sargan test (p-value)				0.18	0.03
Second-order correlation (p-value)				0.69	0.25

Notes:
a   All regressions include time dummies. *t*-statistics in parentheses.
b   Instruments are: three lagged growth and three lagged inequality observations.
c   Arellano and Bond's (1991) GMM estimator, treating inequality as an exogenous variable.
d   Arellano and Bond's (1991) GMM estimator, treating inequality as a predetermined variable.

suggest a half-life of 18 years, and the pooled estimator cannot reject a null hypothesis of no convergence. These results would suggest that in principle, following a shock of a similar magnitude to both inequality and growth,[18] the adjustment process in inequality would be much shorter than the adjustment in per capita income levels. In turn, as noted above this could produce poverty dynamics where poverty increases initially but then subsequently decreases. The second message emerging from the table is that inequality as such does not seem to affect growth. This finding would be halfway between those of Alesina and Rodrik (1994) and Perotti (1996), who find evidence that inequality negatively affects growth, and those of Li and Zhou (1998) and Forbes (2000), who find a positive relationship between inequality and growth. It could be argued that this result is somewhat driven by the combination of countries at different levels of development. As noted by Galor (2000), it is possible to construct models where in the early stages of development inequality positively affects growth prospects, but in later stages negatively affects growth. To further explore this issue, Table 18.5 presents the results obtained when the previous growth regression is run for three different samples: low-, middle- and high-income countries. The results, however, remain virtually unchanged.

Table 18.5   Growth and inequality[a]

Dependent variable $\Delta\log(Y)$	Sample					
	Low income[b]	Middle income[b]	High income[b]	Low income[c]	Middle income[c]	High income[c]
Initial income	−0.065	−0.040	−0.028	−0.071	−0.015	−0.033
	(−5.19)	(−1.60)	(−2.15)	(−6.08)	(−0.81)	(−2.76)
Inequality	0.014	0.031	−0.027	0.017	0.022	−0.006
	(0.63)	(1.11)	(−1.57)	(0.80)	(0.68)	(−0.27)
Summary Statistics						
No. of countries	14	33	23	14	33	23
No. of observations	40	101	91	40	101	91
Sargan test (*p*-value)	0.25	0.06	0.98	0.76	0.23	0.67
Second-order correlation (*p*-value)	0.58	0.77	0.76	0.58	0.66	0.94

Notes:
a   All regressions include time dummies. *t*-statistics in parentheses.
b   Arellano and Bond's (1991) GMM estimator, treating inequality as an exogenous variable.
c   Arellano and Bond's (1991) GMM estimator, treating inequality as a predetermined variable.

Moving now to address the impact of different policies on growth and inequality, Table 18.6 reports in its first and second columns the results of two empirical growth models. The first column reports the results obtained by Loayza and Soto (2002). The second column augments that model with inequality. Two basic messages emerge from these models. First, inequality carries a negative sign (more inequality would be bad for growth) and even if it is not statistically significant at the 10 percent level, it comes quite close. However, even if one were to judge from the point estimate, our results suggest a small potential impact from inequality to growth: 1 percent deterioration in the Gini coefficient would lead to an annual growth decline of 0.007 percent. Second, not surprisingly given the lack of an apparent role for inequality in the growth specification, the point estimates of the coefficients of the different policies are very similar to those obtained by Loayza and Soto. There is, however, one improvement when one includes inequality: governance now appears to positively affect growth whereas in the Loayza and Soto specification it carried a negative sign (better governance would be associated with slower growth).[19]

As for the models for inequality, Table 18.6 presents estimates for three models. Two of them correspond to equations (18.7) and (18.11), whereas the third one is an augmented version of the model in (18.11) that takes into account possible non-linearities in the level of income (and thus tries to capture a potential Kuznets curve relationship between inequality and income levels). Overall we now find evidence suggesting that income levels may have an impact on changes in inequality. When the basic model is augmented with the initial level of GDP per capita, we obtain a negative (and significant) relationship between income levels and changes in inequality (higher income levels would be associated with lower inequality levels). When we consider initial income and its square among the explanatory variables, the last column in Table 18.6 would indicate that there appears to be an inverted-U relationship between the Gini value and income. In fact, this relationship would indicate that the Gini coefficient rises with GDP per capita values of less than US$2,940 (1985 dollars) and declines thereafter. We also find that including the initial level of GDP among the regressors does not significantly affect the estimates of the coefficients of the policy variables under consideration. We next consider these.

The results for education would indicate that countries with better education (as measured by secondary enrollment rates) would be less unequal. The estimated coefficients are very similar in the three empirical models for inequality and of a similar order of magnitude to those in the growth model. These results are in line with those of Datt and Ravallion (2002) and Lundberg and Squire (2003). Using 20 household surveys for India's 15 major states, Datt and Ravallion also conclude that poor basic

Table 18.6   Determinants of growth and distribution[a]

	Growth[b]	Growth[c]	Δlog(Gini)[d]	Δlog(Gini)[e]	Δlog(Gini)[f]
Lagged inequality			−0.242	−0.224	−0.227
(log Gini)			(−13.32)	(−11.98)	(−12.03)
Inequality		−0.007			
(log Gini)		(−1.66)			
Initial GDP per capita	−0.018	−0.125	−0.029	−0.031	0.438
(logs)	(−3.80)	(−13.44)	(−2.24)	(−2.24)	(6.23)
Initial GDP per capita squared					−0.027
(logs-squared)					(−6.93)
Initial output gap	−0.237	−0.165		0.041	
(log actual/potential GDP)	(−8.52)	(−5.84)		(0.77)	
Education	0.017	0.017	−0.022	−0.017	−0.025
(log secondary enrollment)	(6.70)	(3.99)	(−2.77)	(−1.72)	(−2.50)
Financial depth	0.006	0.011	0.014	0.013	0.012
(log private domestic credit/GDP)	(4.28)	(4.04)	(2.83)	(2.91)	(3.30)
Trade openness	0.010	0.004	0.024	0.024	0.037
(log adjusted trade volume/GDP)	(3.14)	(0.69)	(3.04)	(2.69)	(4.13)
Government burden	−0.015	−0.014	−0.018	−0.015	−0.015
(log government consumption/GDP)	(−3.18)	(−4.11)	(−2.71)	(−2.17)	(−1.75)
Public infrastructure	0.007	0.001	−0.016	−0.010	−0.025
(log per capita telephone lines)	(2.71)	(0.27)	(−3.32)	(−1.59)	(−4.67)
Governance	−0.001	0.006	0.005	0.006	0.006
(principal component ICRG)	(−0.68)	(4.63)	(1.74)	(2.02)	(2.21)
Price stability	−0.005	−0.007	0.008	0.009	0.008
(log [100 + inflation rate])	(−1.89)	(−3.08)	(2.16)	(2.87)	(2.83)
Cyclical volatility	−0.277	−0.242	0.112	0.228	0.258
(std output gap)	(−3.76)	(−4.30)	(1.41)	(2.22)	(2.48)
External imbalances	−0.006	−0.01	−0.002	−0.003	0.003
(log dollar index)	(−3.90)	(−3.36)	(−0.32)	(−0.52)	(0.50)
Banking crisis	−0.029	−0.015	−0.021	−0.022	−0.022
(frequency of years)	(−7.42)	(−4.11)	(−4.02)	(−4.23)	(−5.12)
External conditions	0.072	0.071	0.051	0.029	0.059
(growth rate of TOT)	(4.98)	(6.32)	(1.87)	(1.05)	(2.16)

Table 18.6   (continued)

	Growth[b]	Growth[c]	$\Delta\log(\text{Gini})^d$	$\Delta\log(\text{Gini})^e$	$\Delta\log(\text{Gini})^f$
Summary statistics					
Number of countries	78	48	41	41	41
Number of observations	350	165	134	133	134
Sargan (*p*-value)	0.99	0.43	0.76	0.78	0.88
Second-order correlation (*p*-value)	0.46	0.21	0.43	0.43	0.40

Notes: [a] The models are estimated with time dummies using Arellano and Bond's (1991) two-step GMM estimator. *T*-statistics are in parentheses. All regressions include time dummies. [b] Loayza and Soto (2002). [c] Model with inequality. [d] See equation (18.7). [e] See equation (18.11). [f] Augmentation of (18.11).

education is an impediment to the ability of the poor to participate in opportunities for economic growth. Lundberg and Squire also find that education is likely to be correlated with both faster growth and lower income inequality.

The estimated coefficient for financial development is always significant and suggests that progress on this front would be associated with increases in inequality. Possible explanations for this finding are: (i) the more educated (and likely richer) are able to exploit the new opportunities better; and (ii) adoption of capital-intensive technologies is likely to substitute for unskilled labor. Thus to some extent, our results would support the findings of Behrman et al. (2001a) who used household data over more than two decades for 17 Latin American countries to estimate that the financial sector liberalization reforms that took place during the 1990s negatively affected income distribution. Within a cross-country framework, Dollar and Kraay (2002) also find that financial development negatively affects inequality.

Contrary to financial development, where most of the available empirical results already suggest that more financial development implies more inequality, the available results for trade openness point toward less than unanimous conclusions. Dollar and Kraay find that trade openness positively affects income distribution. A similar result is obtained by Behrman et al. (2001a) for a set of Latin American countries. However, Sanchez and Schady (2003) find the opposite result in six Latin American countries, where trade volumes would negatively affect inequality. Spillimbergo et al. (1999) and Barro (2000) also find that trade openness would be associated with higher inequality, whereas Lundberg and Squire (2003) conclude that there seems to be a positive correlation between the Sachs–Warner index of trade liberalization and the Gini coefficient. Our results give some support to the view that trade may lead to higher inequality. The estimate of the trade coefficient is always positive and significant. Moreover, its magnitude is sizeable in the sense that it is larger than the coefficient found in the growth regressions.

As with trade openness and financial development, our results suggest that cutting the size of the government is likely to lead to faster growth, but also to increases in inequality. The estimated coefficient for this variable is always statistically significant even at the 1 percent level. Thus, there is at least some evidence that governments may be inefficient (that is, more government means less growth) but maybe with a benevolent face (that is, more government increases equality). This result is consistent with the findings of Li and Zou (2002), who also find that higher spending, while having a negative impact on growth, may positively affect inequality levels.

Public infrastructure, on the other hand, is an area that belongs to the win–win category of policies (that is, policies that both increase growth and reduce inequality). That is, not only would society as a whole be better off but also the poor would benefit more than proportionately. As noted by Ferreira (1995), productive public investment can potentially alleviate inequality even if expenditures are uniformly distributed. This would be the case if the poorest groups of society face a credit constraint that prevents them from acquiring private substitutes for infrastructure, whereas the richest class is able to complement the free public provision of these services.

The result for the governance variable may be somewhat controversial. Here we find that better governance would lead to more unequal societies. One possible reason for this finding is that once we control for policies, a country's preferred level of inequality is not related to the level of governance. However, and given the result obtained in the basic growth regression (governance would negatively affect growth), this outcome could also be due to problems with the variable we use to capture the level of governance in the different countries.

As for macroeconomic stability, the estimated coefficient of inflation indicates that inflation penalizes the poor and that countries with lower inflation would have a tendency to be more equal. Given that low inflation is also positively associated with faster growth, policies aimed at reducing inflation would also belong to the win–win category. This result would, therefore, be in line with the findings of Romer and Romer (1998), Behrman et al. (2001a), Easterly and Fisher (2001), and Lundberg and Squire (2003) who also find that high inflation and macroeconomic instability are negatively associated with the incomes of the poor.

Regarding financial crises, our results suggest that in turbulent times (at least in those countries where the turbulence is created by a financial crisis) inequality would fall. Sanchez and Schady (2003) find a similar result for a sample of six Latin American countries and explain it by noting that important downturns in the demand for tertiary educated workers are highly correlated with economic downturns. Similarly, the Asian financial crisis that started in 1997 seems to have affected more young adult urban workers working in relatively well-paid construction and financial sectors than the allegedly most vulnerable groups (Behrman et al., 2000 and 2001b) and therefore contributed to a reduction in inequality. Clearly, one has to also note that since overall per capita income is also falling, this is likely to be of little consolation for the poor who in effect will be worse off regardless of the changes in inequality.

The volatility of the business cycle is also positively related to the Gini coefficient (sharper economic fluctuations would be associated with higher inequality), although admittedly in the basic inequality specification the standard deviation of the output gap is not significant. A possible explanation for this is that poorer groups in society would likely find it more difficult to insure themselves against sharp fluctuations in output growth.

As for exchange rate management policies (that is, the degree of overvaluation), the coefficient is insignificant. This is another case where the findings of the empirical model seem to be counterintuitive: given that real exchange overvaluation would capture distortions in the allocation of resources between the tradable and the non-tradable sectors, one could a priori expect this variable to play an important role in explaining the evolution of income distribution. Finally, regarding the evolution of the terms of trade, we find this variable also to negatively affect inequality (an improvement in the terms of trade would lead to a deterioration in income inequality), a finding that would be in line with the impact of trade on inequality.

6 Poverty impact of policies

The previous section has reviewed the main results obtained when one relates inequality to a broad set of policy variables. Overall the inequality model would suggest that there are some win–win policies (education, infrastructure, and macroeconomic stability) that could be associated with growth and progressive distributional change. That is, the poor would benefit from growth more than proportionately. However, we have also found policies that present trade-offs in the sense that they push inequality and growth in different directions. Among these policies, one could mention cuts in the size of government, financial development, and trade openness.

From a policy perspective, however, the weight given to the impact that a policy has on inequality is likely to be relative and to depend on the relative importance of inequality with respect to growth. The metric we use here is given by the overall impact of the policy on poverty as discussed in Section 2, above.[20] Furthermore, the framework reviewed allows us to discriminate between the short- and long-run poverty impact of policies, something that is particularly appropriate in this context given that the estimated parameter of the lagged dependent variable in the inequality regressions is about 10 times the corresponding estimate for the income regression model (that is, given the different speeds of convergence). The presence of dynamics may eventually imply that policies that are pro-poor in the long run (in the sense that poverty falls as a result of their implementation) are not so pro-poor in the short run.

Tables 18.7 to 18.10 present the net growth elasticities associated with those policies that present growth-inequality conflicts (government size, financial development and trade openness) and also for three policies that do not present any such conflict (education, infrastructure and inflation). In Tables 18.7 and 18.8 we do not allow for any feedback effect from inequality to growth or from income levels to changes in inequality. That is, Tables 18.7 and 18.8 are based on expressions (18.8) and (18.9).[21] In Tables 18.9 and 18.10 we allow for feedback from income levels to inequality. Thus these tables are based on expressions (18.12) and (18.13) with $\xi = 0$. Tables 18.7 and 18.9 focus on short-run impacts and tables 18.8 and 18.10 on the long run. In order to deal with the country specificity of the gross elasticity of poverty to growth and the elasticity of inequality to growth, we assume that income follows a log-normal distribution and present results based on the elasticities reported in Table 18.1.

Inspection of Tables 18.7 and 18.9 suggests that (as expected) when growth and distributional change push in the same direction (that is, education, infrastructure and lower inflation) the result is a net elasticity of poverty that is always negative. In other words, progress on those fronts would lead to lower poverty. It is worth noting that the different elasticities vary significantly depending on initial conditions as given by levels of development and inequality, something that would suggest that initial conditions matter when choosing policies designed to support a poverty reduction strategy. In the cases where growth and progressive distributional change tend to move in different directions, the sign of the elasticity would be negative in most cases. The exception is government size, where the sign depends on initial country conditions, with the growth effect dominating in poorer and more equal countries, and the inequality effect dominating in richer and more unequal countries. Thus, depending on the country's income level, fiscal adjustment is likely to have a different impact on poverty.

Table 18.7   *Net short-run growth elasticities of poverty to selected policies*[b]

	Education					Finan. Development			
PL[a]/ Gini	0.3	0.4	0.5	0.6	PL[a]/ Gini	0.3	0.4	0.5	0.6
0.16	-0.39	-0.23	-0.15	-0.11	0.16	0.14	0.09	0.06	0.05
0.33	-0.18	-0.11	-0.07	-0.06	0.33	0.05	0.03	0.03	0.02
0.5	-0.1	-0.06	-0.05	-0.04	0.5	0.02	0.01	0.01	0.01
0.66	-0.06	-0.04	-0.03	-0.03	0.66	0	0.01	0.01	0.01
0.9	-0.03	-0.02	-0.02	-0.02	0.9	0	0	0	0

	Trade openness					Government burden			
PL[a]/ Gini	0.3	0.4	0.5	0.6	PL[a]/ Gini	0.3	0.4	0.5	0.6
0.16	0.25	0.15	0.11	0.08	0.16	-0.14	-0.09	-0.07	-0.05
0.33	0.08	0.06	0.04	0.04	0.33	-0.03	-0.03	-0.02	-0.02
0.5	0.03	0.02	0.02	0.02	0.5	0	-0.01	-0.01	-0.01
0.66	0.01	0.01	0.01	0.01	0.66	0.01	0	0	-0.01
0.9	0	0	0	0.01	0.9	0.01	0.01	0	0

	Infrastructure					Inflation			
PL[a]/ Gini	0.3	0.4	0.5	0.6	PL[a]/ Gini	0.3	0.4	0.5	0.6
0.16	-0.25	-0.15	-0.1	-0.07	0.16	0.13	0.08	0.05	0.04
0.33	-0.11	-0.07	-0.05	-0.04	0.33	0.06	0.04	0.03	0.02
0.5	-0.06	-0.04	-0.03	-0.02	0.5	0.03	0.02	0.02	0.01
0.66	-0.03	-0.02	-0.02	-0.02	0.66	0.02	0.01	0.01	0.01
0.9	-0.02	-0.01	-0.01	-0.01	0.9	0.01	0.01	0.01	0.01

Notes:
a   Poverty line as a share of per capita GDP.
b   Under the assumption of log-normal distribution.

When we focus on long-run elasticities (Tables 18.8 and 18.10), the first conclusion we reach is that allowing for feedback effects from income levels to inequality does not alter the main result significantly: all the pro-growth policies would lead to reductions in poverty. This is regardless of the impact that these policies may have on inequality. In other words, in the long run, a pro-growth strategy will benefit the poor. More worrisome is the fact that the elasticities of poverty with respect to the policy in question decline (in absolute value) as per capita income falls and inequality increases (that is, as headcount poverty increases). We have to admit that in some cases this is not likely to be a big problem, especially when applied

Table 18.8   Net long-run growth elasticities of poverty to selected policies[b]

	Education					Finan. Development			
PL[a]/ Gini	0.3	0.4	0.5	0.6	PL[a]/ Gini	0.3	0.4	0.5	0.6
0.16	−7.03	−3.82	−2.37	−1.5	0.16	−1.32	−0.65	−0.36	−0.17
0.33	−4.25	−2.38	−1.45	−1.03	0.33	−1.03	−0.54	−0.29	−0.18
0.5	−2.87	−1.67	−1.07	−0.77	0.5	−0.79	−.43	−0.25	−0.16
0.66	−2.09	−1.22	−0.83	−0.54	0.66	−0.63	−0.35	−0.22	−0.12
0.9	−1.36	−0.89	−0.6	−0.41	0.9	−0.44	0.28	0.18	−0.11

	Trade openness					Government burden			
PL[a]/ Gini	0.3	0.4	0.5	0.6	PL[a]/ Gini	0.3	0.4	0.5	0.6
0.16	−2.17	−1.07	−0.59	−0.27	0.16	4.21	2.18	1.27	0.7
0.33	−1.71	−0.89	−.48	−0.3	0.33	2.95	1.59	0.9	0.6
0.5	−1.31	−0.72	−0.42	−0.27	0.5	2.15	1.21	0.73	0.49
0.66	−1.05	−0.58	−0.37	−0.2	0.66	1.66	0.93	0.61	0.36
0.9	−0.74	−0.46	−0.29	−0.18	0.9	1.14	0.72	0.47	

	Infrastructure					Inflation			
PL[a]/ Gini	0.3	0.4	0.5	0.6	PL[a]/ Gini	0.3	0.4	0.5	0.6
0.16	−3.26	−1.79	−1.13	−0.73	0.16	2.15	1.17	0.73	0.47
0.33	−1.9	−1.07	−0.66	−0.48	0.33	1.28	0.72	0.44	0.32
0.5	−1.25	−0.73	−0.48	−0.35	0.5	0.86	0.5	0.32	0.23
0.66	−0.9	−0.53	−0.36	−0.25	0.66	0.62	0.36	0.25	0.17
0.9	−0.57	−0.38	−0.26	−0.18	0.9	0.4	0.26	0.18	0.12

Notes:
a   Poverty line as a share of per capita GDP.
b   Under the assumption of log-normal distribution

to policies aimed at expanding the stock of human or physical capital. For example, a given US dollar amount of investment on education or infrastructure can be expected to have a higher return in poorer countries because of the likely lower initial conditions (100 miles of new roads will double the infrastructure of a country with an initial stock of 100 miles but represent a 1 percent increase in a country with an initial stock of 10,000 miles). Similarly, expanding education coverage to 1 new child (assuming similar costs in richer and poorer countries) will represent a higher relative expansion in the poorer country where typically coverage will be lower. Thus even with a lower elasticity the same intervention (100 miles of new roads or a given expansion in education coverage) will likely have a higher

Table 18.9   Net short-run growth elasticities of poverty to selected policies[b]

	Education					Finan. Development			
PL[a]/ Gini	0.3	0.4	0.5	0.6	PL[a]/ Gini	0.3	0.4	0.5	0.6
0.16	−0.32	−0.19	−0.12	−0.09	0.16	0.13	0.08	0.06	0.04
0.33	−0.16	−0.09	−0.06	−0.05	0.33	0.04	0.03	0.02	0.02
0.5	−0.09	−0.06	−0.04	−0.03	0.5	0.02	0.01	0.01	0.01
0.66	−0.06	−0.04	−0.03	−0.02	0.66	0	0	0.01	0.01
0.9	−0.03	−0.02	−0.02	−0.01	0.9	0	0	0	0

	Trade openness					Government burden			
PL[a]/ Gini	0.3	0.4	0.5	0.6	PL[a]/ Gini	0.3	0.4	0.5	0.6
0.16	0.25	0.15	0.11	0.08	0.16	−0.1	−0.07	−0.05	−0.04
0.33	0.08	0.06	0.04	0.04	0.33	−0.02	−0.02	−0.02	−0.02
0.5	0.03	0.02	0.02	0.02	0.5	0	0	−0.01	−0.01
0.66	0.01	0.01	0.01	0.01	0.66	0.01	0	0	0
0.9	0	0	0	0.01	0.9	0.02	0.01	0	0

	Infrastructure					Inflation			
PL[a]/ Gini	0.3	0.4	0.5	0.6	PL[a]/ Gini	0.3	0.4	0.5	0.6
0.16	−0.17	−0.1	−0.07	−0.05	0.16	0.15	0.09	0.06	0.04
0.33	−0.08	−0.05	−0.03	−0.03	0.33	0.07	0.04	0.03	0.02
0.5	−0.04	−0.03	−0.02	−0.02	0.5	0.04	0.02	0.02	0.01
0.66	−0.03	−0.02	−0.01	−0.01	0.66	0.02	0.01	0.01	0.01
0.9	−0.01	−0.01	−0.01	−0.01	0.9	0.01	0.01	0.01	0.01

Notes:
a   Poverty line as a share of per capita GDP.
b   Under the assumption of log-normal distribution.

impact in the poorer country. But in many other areas (among them trade, financial sector development or macroeconomic stability) poorer countries are less likely to start from a laggard position and in these circumstances to achieve the same results (in terms of poverty reduction) of a richer country they will require a bigger policy push.

7   Conclusions
This chapter has reviewed, from a cross-country perspective, the impact of a series of pro-growth policies on inequality and headcount poverty using an approach that borrows heavily from the cost–benefit analysis literature. The main contributions of the chapter to the poverty and

Table 18.10   Net long-run growth elasticities of poverty to selected policies[b]

	Education					Finan. Development			
PL[a]/ Gini	0.3	0.4	0.5	0.6	PL[a]/ Gini	0.3	0.4	0.5	0.6
0.16	−8.52	−4.71	−2.98	−1.96	0.16	−1.91	−1.01	−0.6	−0.35
0.33	−4.85	−2.76	−1.72	−1.26	0.33	−1.27	−0.69	−0.4	−0.28
0.5	−3.16	−1.86	−1.23	−0.91	0.5	−0.9	−0.51	−0.32	−0.22
0.66	−2.23	−1.32	−0.92	−0.64	0.66	−0.69	−0.39	−0.26	−0.16
0.9	−1.4	−0.93	−0.65	−0.46	0.9	−0.46	−0.3	−0.2	−0.13

	Trade openness					Government burden			
PL[a]/ Gini	0.3	0.4	0.5	0.6	PL[a]/ Gini	0.3	0.4	0.5	0.6
0.16	−3.05	−1.6	−0.95	−0.55	0.16	5.79	3.12	1.92	1.19
0.33	−2.06	−1.12	−0.65	−0.44	0.33	3.58	1.99	1.2	0.85
0.5	−1.48	−0.84	−0.51	−0.35	0.5	2.45	1.42	0.9	0.64
0.66	−1.13	−0.64	−0.42	−0.25	0.66	1.81	1.04	0.71	0.46
0.9	−0.77	−0.49	−0.32	−0.21	0.9	1.19	0.77	0.52	0.35

	Infrastructure					Inflation			
PL[a]/ Gini	0.3	0.4	0.5	0.6	PL[a]/ Gini	0.3	0.4	0.5	0.6
0.16	−3.68	−2.04	−1.3	−0.86	0.16	2.74	1.52	0.97	0.65
0.33	−2.07	−1.18	−0.74	−0.55	0.33	1.52	0.87	0.55	0.41
0.5	−1.34	−0.79	−0.53	−0.39	0.5	0.97	0.58	0.39	0.29
0.66	−0.93	−0.56	−0.39	−0.27	0.66	0.68	0.4	0.29	0.2
0.9	−0.58	−0.39	−0.27	−0.19	0.9	0.42	0.28	0.2	0.14

Notes:
a   Poverty line as a share of per capita GDP.
b   Under the assumption of log-normal distribution.

cost–benefit analysis literature are that it: (i) explores the poverty impact of a number of policies usually considered in the growth literature through the projected interaction of growth and inequality; (ii) allows for the possibility of income and inequality dynamics which in turn allows for poverty dynamics; (iii) relies on a large database of non-overlapping five-year averages that mitigates to some extent the problems encountered when the distribution of surveys across countries is very unequal (countries with 40 surveys against others with just 1 or 2); and (iv) allows for fixed effects in a dynamic panel framework.

The findings of the chapter suggest the likelihood of inequality convergence, and that the speed of convergence for inequality is faster than the speed of convergence for per capita income levels. On the policy front, we find that improvements in education and infrastructure and lower inflation levels would lead to both growth and progressive distributional change. Financial development, trade openness and cuts in the size of the government – that is, all policies that would lead to faster growth – would be associated with increases in inequality. We also find that financial crises would be associated with reductions in inequality.

On the interaction between growth and inequality, the chapter argues that in the short run, the positive impact on growth of the identified win–lose policies would not be enough to offset the negative impact they have on inequality and therefore, in the absence of pro-poor policies that accompany those reforms or additional feedback effects from growth (such as improvements in education or infrastructure), poverty could actually increase. In the long run, however, we find that the growth impact of these policies would offset the negative impact on distribution, and therefore poverty would fall as a result of the implementation of pro-growth policies. These findings would justify the adoption of: (i) a pro-growth policy package at the center of any poverty reduction strategy; and (ii) pro-poor measures that complement such a package and avoid to the extent possible potential short-run increases in poverty (especially in high inequality countries). Finally, the chapter also highlights that the expected poverty outcome of policies may decline as poverty increases.

Notes

*   This chapter has been prepared in the context of the 'Pro-poor Growth' program sponsored by the World Bank's PREM Poverty Group. I would like to thank Veronica Alaimo, Oya Celasum, Aart Kraay, Ugo Paniza, Cico Ferreira, Tito Cordella, Ulrich Lachler and seminar participants at the World Bank, IMF, and IDB for comments received and to Peter Bocock and Patricia Macchi for editorial assistance. Views expressed in this chapter are those of the author and should not be attributed to the World Bank, its Executive Directors or the countries they represent.
1. Even though throughout the chapter we refer to 'policies' to facilitate the narrative, in many cases the specific interventions will take more the form of a 'project' than a 'policy'.
2. Strictly speaking many of the studies exploiting absolute definitions of poverty are based on per capita expenditure levels and use income levels only as a substitute on data availability grounds.
3. See, among others, Ravallion (1997, 2004), Bourguignon (2004) and Lopez and Servén (2006).
4. Clearly, not all policies will have a negative effect on income distribution.
5. The FGT class of poverty measures is given by

$$P_\alpha = \int_0^z \left[\frac{z-x}{z} \right]^\alpha f(x)\,dx$$

where α is the parameter of inequality aversion, z is the poverty line, and x is income. For $\alpha = 0$, the previous expression reduces to the familiar headcount ratio. When $\alpha = 1$ it weights each poor person by his/her distance from the poverty line (the poverty gap), and when $\alpha = 2$ the weight given to each poor person is proportional to the square of the income shortfall (squared poverty gap). Put in other words, higher values of α would give more weight to the extreme poor than to those groups closer to the poverty line z.

6. Strictly speaking, for the inequality elasticity of headcount poverty to be positive it is also required that the level of average per capita income is above the poverty line. Otherwise, there is the risk that progressive distributional changes increase poverty.

7. If the distribution of income y is log normal, then $\log(y) \sim N(\mu, \sigma)$, with $G = 2\Phi(\sigma/\sqrt{2}) - 1$ where $\Phi(\cdot)$ denotes the cumulative normal distribution (Aitchinson and Brown, 1966), and G is the Gini index.

8. Note that the poverty metric can easily be changed into a monetary metric by, for example, computing the minimum amount of cash that would be needed to achieve the same poverty reduction or avoid a poverty increase. That is, in principle it is possible to put a price tag to the different policies.

9. If one considers a typical poverty line, say US$1 per person per day, the reported elasticities would correspond to the following per capita income levels: US$2,190 (0.16), US$1,095 (0.33), US$730 (0.5), US$547 (0.66), US$405 (0.90) and US$331 (1.1).

10. This point was first made by Ravallion (1997).

11. Strictly speaking one should also consider an error term emerging from using a discrete approximation to an infinitesimal interval.

12. This assumes that $\delta \neq 0$ and $\alpha \neq 0$. If the parameter controlling the dynamics is zero, all the adjustment would take place immediately.

13. Clearly, equation (18.6) would also be subject to a similar transformation.

14. The only exception to this rule is the regression of growth on the initial value of income.

15. In equation (18.10) the instruments are three lagged growth observations and inequality with three lagged values of inequality. In equation (18.11) lagged inequality is instrumented with lagged changes in inequality and initial per capita income in equation (18.10) is instrumented with three lagged growth observations. These instruments would be valid even in the presence of fixed effects.

16. Ravallion uses a different estimation technique. Rather than relying on the relation between initial Gini and the subsequent change in the index, Ravallion (2002) measures the speed of convergence by comparing estimated trends in inequality with predicted initial levels of inequality.

17. Half-life is the time the economy needs to correct half of the initial disequilibrium. If the speed of convergence is equal to 1.6 percent per year (as in the 2SLS model in Table 18.4), then the half-life is equal to $-[\ln(2)/(1 - 0.016)] \approx 42.9$ years.

18. This would be consistent with growth and the changes in the log Gini having a similar standard deviation.

19. Loayza and Soto's (2002) results, however, are more efficient in general.

20. Admittedly, it is possible to find examples where expression (18.5) proves too general. For example, Ferreira and Leite (2003) present evidence for Brazil suggesting that the observed reductions in inequality during the 1990s were not beneficial to the bottom of the distribution.

21. Tables 18.7 to 18.10 combine the theoretical elasticities of Table 18.1 with the coefficients reported in Table 18.6. For example, the first coefficient for education in Table 18.7 uses $\gamma = 6.2$ and $\varphi = 12.9$ from Table 18.1 and, $\omega = 0.017$ and $\beta = -0.022$ from columns 1 and 3 of Table 18.6, respectively. Therefore, using equation (18.8), we have $\partial p/\partial x = 0.017*(-6.2) + (-0.022)*12.9 = -0.39$.

References

Aitchinson, J. and J. Brown (1966), *The Log-Normal Distribution*, Cambridge: Cambridge University Press.

Alesina, A. and D. Rodrik (1994), 'Distributive policies and economic growth', *Quarterly Journal of Economics*, **109**: 465–90.

Arellano, M. and S. Bond (1991), 'Some tests of specification for panel data: Monte Carlo evidence and an application to employment equations', *Review of Economic Studies*, **58**: 277–97.

Barro, R. (2000), 'Inequality and growth in a panel of countries', *Journal of Economic Growth*, **5**: 5–32.

Behrman, J., A. Deolalikar and P. Tinakron (2000), 'The effects of the Thai economic crisis and of Thai labor market policies on labor market outcomes', Thailand Development Research Institute, mimeo.

Behrman, J., N. Birdsall and M. Szekely (2001a), 'Economic reform and wage differentials in Latin America', Inter American Development Bank, mimeo.

Behrman, J., A. Deolalikar and P. Tinakron (2001b), 'What really happens to wage rates during the financial crisis?', University of Pennsylvania, mimeo.

Benabou, R. (1996), 'Inequality and growth', in B. Bernanke and J. Rotemberg (eds), *NBER Macroeconomics Annual*, Cambridge, MA: MIT Press, 11–74.

Bourguignon, F. (2003), 'The growth elasticity of poverty reduction: explaining heterogeneity across countries and time periods', in T. Eicher and S. Turnovsky (eds), *Inequality and growth: Theory and Policy Implications*, Cambridge, MA: MIT Press, pp.3–26.

Bourguignon, F. (2004), 'The poverty–growth–inequality triangle', World Bank, Washington, DC, mimeo.

Chen, S. and M. Ravallion (1997), 'What can new survey data tell us about recent changes in distribution and poverty?', *World Bank Economic Review*, **11** (2): 357–82.

Datt, G. and M. Ravallion (2002), 'Why has economic growth be more pro-poor in some states of India than others?', *Journal of Development Economics*, **68**: 381–400.

Deninger, K. and L. Squire (1996), 'A new data set measuring income inequality', *World Bank Economic Review*, **10**: 565–91.

Dollar, D. and A. Kraay (2002), 'Growth is good for the poor', *Journal of Economic Growth*, **7**: 195–225.

Easterly, W. (1999), 'Life during growth', *Journal of Economic Growth*, **4**: 239–76.

Easterly, W. and S. Fisher (2001), 'Inflation and the poor', *Journal of Money, Credit and Banking*, **33**: 160–178.

Ferreira, F. (1995), 'Roads to equality: wealth distribution dynamics with public–private capital complementarity', LSE Discussion Paper TE/95/286, London School of Economics.

Ferreira, F. and P. Leite (2003), 'Policy options for meeting the Millennium Development Goals in Brazil', Policy Research Working Paper 2975, World Bank, Washington, DC.

Forbes, K. (2000), 'A reassessment of the relationship between inequality and growth', *American Economic Review*, **90**: 869–97.

Foster, J., J. Greer and E. Thorbecke (1984), 'A class of decomposable poverty measures', *Econometrica*, **52**: 761–66.

Foster, J. and M. Szekely (2000), 'How good is growth?', *Asian Development Review*, **18**: 59–73.

Galor, O. (2000), 'Income distribution and the process of development', *European Economic Review*, **44**: 706–12.

Li, H. and H. Zou (1998), 'Income inequality is not harmful for growth: theory and evidence', *Review of Development Economics*, **2** (3): 318–34.

Li, H. and H. Zou (2002), 'Inflation, growth, and income distribution: a cross-country study', *Annals of Economics and Finance*, **3**: 85–101.

Loayza, N., P. Fajnzylber and C. Calderón (2002), 'Economic growth in Latin America and the Caribbean: stylized facts, explanations and forecasts', World Bank, Washington, DC, mimeo.

Loayza, N. and R. Soto (2002), 'The sources of economic growth: an overview', in Norman Loayza and Raimundo Soto (eds), *Economic Growth: Sources, Trends and Cycles*, Santiago: Central Bank of Chile, pp. 1–40.

Lopez, H. and L. Servén (2006), 'A normal relationship? Poverty, growth and inequality', Policy Research Working Paper 3814, World Bank, Washington, DC.

Lundberg, M. and L. Squire (2003), 'The simultaneous evolution of growth and inequality', *Economic Journal*, **113**: 326–44.

Perotti, R. (1996), 'Growth, income distribution and democracy', *Journal of Economic Growth*, **1**: 149–87.

Ravallion, M. (1997), 'Can high inequality development countries escape absolute poverty?', *Economics Letters*, **56**: 51–7.

Ravallion, M. (2002), 'Inequality convergence', World Bank, mimeo.

Ravallion, M. (2004), 'Pro-poor growth: a primer', World Bank, Policy Research Working Paper no. 3242, Washington, DC.

Ravallion M. and S. Chen (1997), 'What can new survey data tell us about recent changes in distribution and poverty?', *World Bank Economic Review*, **11**: 357–82.

Romer, C. and D. Romer (1998), 'Does economic growth reduce poverty?', NBER Working Paper no. 6793, New York.

Sanchez, C. and N. Schady (2003), 'Off and running? Technology, trade and the rising demand for skilled workers in Latin America', Policy Research Working Paper no. 3005, World Bank, Washington, DC.

Son, H. and N. Kakwani (2003), 'Poverty reduction: do initials conditions matter?', World Bank, Washington, DC, mimeo.

Spillimbergo, A.J., L. Londono and M. Szekely (1999), 'Income distribution, factor endowments, and trade openness', *Journal of Development Economics,* **59**: 77–101.

19 The value of the 1964 Surgeon General's Report

Frank Chaloupka and Richard M. Peck

1 Introduction

In this chapter we extend the framework of Murphy and Topel (2003a) and Nordhaus (2003) on the benefits of medical research. Their point of departure is the striking increase in life expectancy in the United States over the last 50 years. In 1970, average life expectancy at birth was 70.8 and it was 77.8 years in 2004, a gain of about a seven years. Attributing the increase to improvements in health knowledge, medical practice and technology, they present estimates suggesting that if the dollar value of this increase is properly taken into account, medical research has been enormously productive. Indeed, Becker (2007) argues that, given underlying willingness to pay, the increase in life expectancy may be the largest single factor in the rise of Western living standards. Because life expectancy increases are not captured by standard national income accounting, this important contribution to higher living standards is hidden or at least underestimated. The work of Murphy and Topel and Nordhaus set the record straight and they provide compelling estimates that the annual monetary value of the change in average life expectancy over the last 30 to 40 years is several trillion dollars.

The next step in this line of research is to parse out the contributions of particular innovations to the increased life expectancy in the United States. The approach of Murphy and Topel has been adapted to improvements in the treatment of cardiovascular diseases by Cutler and Kadiyala (2003). But the monetary values of a number of specific medical innovations have not been estimated. What remains is the task of determining the contribution of specific medical advancement such as improvements in the treatment of cancers, pharmaceuticals, and new diagnostic techniques, as well as changes that are not traditionally regarded as 'medical improvements' such as improved auto safety. Another type of innovation that plays a role in extending life expectancy is a greater understanding of health behaviors. Our understanding of the role of obesity, exercise, smoking, and alcohol on health outcomes has advanced significantly since 1950. This chapter examines the role that the knowledge of the health consequences of smoking and the dissemination of this knowledge has had in increasing average life expectancy over the last 40 years. We also examine the role that tobacco control measures (higher excise taxes, clean air laws, restrictions on youth access, advertising restrictions and public service ads) may have had on average life expectancy. This allows us to assign monetary values to better health knowledge and active tobacco control measures. We find an imputed value to these factors of 300 to 600 billion dollars annually.

2   The aftermath of the 1964 Surgeon General's Report

The 1964 Surgeon General's Report summarized over 7,000 scientific studies and presented evidence on the health consequences of smoking. The report had two principal findings: First, 'Cigarette smoking is associated with a 70 percent increase in the age specific death rates of males, and to a lesser extent with increased death rates of females.' The second finding was a policy conclusion: 'Cigarette smoking is a health hazard of sufficient importance in the United States to warrant appropriate remedial action.' The report made headlines when it was released. The two pieces of legislation passed in 1965 and 1969 mandated warning labels on cigarette packaging and the 1969 legislation led to a ban on cigarette advertising on television and radio. Under the Federal Communications Commission's Fairness Doctrine, anti-smoking public service advertising was broadcast from 1967 through 1970. Adult prevalence rates began to fall and, from an all-time high in 1966, per capita cigarette consumption fell almost continuously. The decline in cigarette demand during this period was principally driven by availability and dissemination of information about the health consequences of smoking. Some of this decline resulted from early state efforts to adopt tobacco control policies, including higher cigarette excise taxes in the 1960s and early restrictions on smoking in public places in the 1970s.

In the 1980s, the federal government began to take additional tobacco control measures. From 1951 to 1982, the federal cigarette excise taxes remained at 8 cents per pack; taking into account inflation, the real tax fell from 30.8 cents (1982 dollars) per pack in 1951 to 8 cents in 1982. In 1983, the tax was doubled to 16 cents per pack. In 1987, Public Law 100-202 banned smoking on domestic airlines on flights of less than two hours, which was extended to 6 hours or less in 1989. The Synar Amendment was passed in 1992 which required states to adopt and enforce laws limiting youth access to tobacco products. The Pro-Children Act of 1992 banned smoking in all facilities providing federally funded children services. By 2004, federal cigarette excise taxes had more than doubled again and were at 39 cents per pack. More importantly, average state cigarette excise taxes significantly increased and exceeded a dollar per pack by 2004. The master settlement of 1998 also increased cigarette prices substantially. In the period from 1987 to 2007, prevalence and per capita consumption continued to decline steadily, but the decline was less uniform and on average slower than in the previous 20 years.

While somewhat of an oversimplification, the overall drop in prevalence from 42.4[1] to 20.9 percent from 1966 to 2004 can be divided into two distinct periods. The first period is the announcement and more importantly the diffusion of information about the health consequences of smoking that commences with the 1964 Surgeon General's Report.[2] With relatively modest legislative initiatives (banning of cigarette advertising in the early 1970s; modest increases in state cigarette taxes in the 1960s and adoption of state restrictions on public smoking in the 1970s), prevalence went from 42.4 percent in 1966 to 32.1 percent in 1983. Presumably, since it altered behavior, this new information was valuable to its recipients. A natural question to ask is: what was the value of this information? A related research question is determining the loss generated by the lack of full information in the period before 1964.

In the mid-1989s, declines in overall smoking prevalence flattened out and the prevalence of youth smoking actually increased in the mid-1990s. The second subperiod runs from 1983 to the present. Beginning with the doubling of the federal cigarette excise tax in 1983, more aggressive tobacco control policies began to be implemented. Real state cigarette taxes have more than tripled since 1982, while state and local restrictions on smoking have become more extensive and comprehensive. With funds from earmarked excise taxes and/or settlements with the tobacco industry, states have invested considerable resources in comprehensive tobacco control programs that aim to increase cessation and prevent initiation. In 1983, nationwide adult prevalence was 33.2 percent but by 2004, adult prevalence had dropped to 20.9 percent. Though an obvious simplification, we can regard this decline as the consequence of more aggressive tobacco control measures during the period from 1983 to 2004. This allows us to provide a very rough estimate of the value of tobacco control. We also outline ways to undertake a more sophisticated analysis that takes into account other factors that may have played a role in the prevalence decline of the last 25 years.

3 The value of understanding the health consequences of smoking

Both Murphy and Topel (2003) and Nordhaus (2003a) use a framework where lifetime utility level, denoted V in the equation below, is the relevant outcome measure. Changes in medical knowledge and technology alter the function S, the probability of survival, and that in turn changes expected lifetime utility. An individual's expected discounted expected lifetime utility is:

$$V(c, S) = \int_0^\infty u(c_t)e^{-\rho t}S(t)\,dt, \tag{19.1}$$

where S is the survival function and its value at any point of time t, $S(t)$, is the probability of surviving exactly t years, c is consumption, u is the utility of consumption, and ρ is the discount factor. Within this framework, the value of an intervention is determined in the following way. Suppose that an intervention changes the survival function from S to S' and this leads to an increase in discounted expected lifetime utility, that is,

$$V(c, S') > V(c, S). \tag{19.2}$$

The annualized value of switching from S to S' is basically the equivalent variation in consumption c, that is, the increase in c required to make the person indifferent between S to S':

$$V(c, S') = V(c + \Delta c, S). \tag{19.3}$$

The annualized value of switching from the survival distribution S to S' is just Δc. Using specific functional forms and stylized parameter values that lie within the ranges estimated in other contexts and reported in the literature, Nordhaus, and Murphy and Topel estimate the annual value of the increase in life expectancy between 1970 and 1998. Both estimates fall very close to \$3.0 trillion (measured in terms of 2002 prices) annually.[3] Current estimates indicate that smokers live on average about 5.5 years less than never-smokers. The prevalence rate in 1970 was 37.4 percent and by 2004 it had declined to 20.9 percent nationally.[4] Life expectancy at birth was 70.8 years in 1970. The overall average life expectancy in 2004 was 77.8, which implies that never-smokers have an average life expectancy of about 78.9 years,[5] while smokers have an average life expectancy of 73.5 years. These numbers are calculated in the following way. Average population life expectancy is the weighted sum of the life expectancy of smokers, LE_N, and that of non-smokers, LE_S. The weights are generated by the fraction of the population that smokes, that is, the prevalence rate π. The average population life expectancy, denoted LE, is then given by the following equation.

$$\pi(LE_S) + (1 - \pi)(LE_N) = LE. \tag{19.4}$$

Our calculations also exploit the fact that the difference between LE_N and LE_S is currently 5.5 years, so that:

$$LE_N = LE_S + 5.5.$$ (19.5)

Equations (19.4) and (19.5) give us two equations in two unknowns, that is, given the smoking prevalence rate and the average life expectancy, we can back out LE_S and LE_N.

If medical technology remained at its 2004 level, then life expectancies of smokers and non-smokers would presumably remain at 2004 levels, that is, LE_S and LE_N are fixed at 73.4 and 78.9, respectively. We can then determine what average life expectancy would be if the prevalence rate were different from the actual level of 20.9. For example, under this assumption about life expectancies, a zero prevalence rate would mean that average life expectancy would rise from the actual average life expectancy of 77.8 to 78.9, the life expectancy at birth of a non-smoker. If prevalence were 100 percent, the life expectancy at birth would be 73.4 years.

Using the 1970 and 2004 prevalence rates, changes in average life expectancy imply that about 1.1 years (about 13 months), about 14.4 percent, of this 6.9 year total increase in life expectancy is due to lower smoking prevalence. Another counterfactual exercise is to suppose that prevalence rates in 2004 remained at even the higher 1966 level, 42.6 percent of the adult population smoked, which was the peak US prevalence rate, but medical technology still attained its 2004 level. Then average life expectancy would be about 76.1 instead of 77.8 years. According to a first-order approximation, if the 1966 prevalence rate continued to prevail, the increase in average life expectancy would be 17.4 percent lower. This means that from 14.4 to 17.4 percent of the $3.0 trillion gain in annual real income arises because of the drop in smoking prevalence. Accordingly, the value of the decline in prevalence, expressed as an annual willingness to accept payment, lies in the range $0.40 to $0.60 trillion.

For each additional percentage point decline in prevalence, the national average life expectancy rises by about 2.64 weeks; a 10 percentage point decline raises expected life by about 6.6 months, that is, about half a year. On the margin then, a one percentage point decline in prevalence is worth between 2.47 to 4.95 billion dollars. Presumably, this figure will rise with time as the income and the population increase. To put this in perspective, the tobacco master settlement total annual payments are about $8.1 billion in 2008, an amount that equals the value of a 1.6 to 3.2 percentage point drop in the prevalence rate. These estimates can be used for a back of the envelope cost–benefit calculation. The CDC report, *Best Practices in Tobacco Control – 2007* recommends spending annually a national total of $3.4 billion on tobacco control. By increasing life expectancy, a drop of 2 percentage points in prevalence would generate an annual amount that exceeds this recommendation. CDC argues that spending this amount for

5 years, $17.0 billion would reduce the number of smokers by 5 million. This corresponds to a prevalence rate drop of 2.4; the value of this decline in a single year ranges from $6 billion to $12.7 billion. Assuming that this decline is permanent, the total discounted value of this decline is substantial, between $200 and $423 billion, if the interest rate is 3 percent.

Another way to estimate the value of increased life expectancy is to consider how an overall change in life expectancy changes the annual probability of death at a given age. There are a number of estimates of the willingness to pay for a reduction in the annual probability of death, derived principally from wage differentials that arise when an occupation is more risky. Following Nordhaus, we assume that death is distributed exponentially. As Nordhaus observes, there are certainly more realistic probability density functions but the exponential density function is particularly tractable and provides a reasonably good approximation for the parameter values considered. Also, the link between expected length of life and the probability density function of survival is straightforward and clear. Suppose T is expected length of life, that is, the expected wait before the first negative event (death) occurs. The corresponding exponential density function is:

$$f(t|T) = \frac{1}{T}e^{-\left(\frac{t}{T}\right)} \text{ for } t \geq 0.$$

The parameter $(1/T)$ is the mean number of transitions per period, that is, deaths per year. So if $T = 50$, then the mean number of deaths per period is 0.02. In a sample of 1,000 identical individuals, the expected number of deaths per year is 20 and if T rises to 100, the expected number of deaths per year drops to 10.

With the exponential probability density, the probability at birth that a person of age 40 dies between the ages of 40 and 41 is:

$$\int_{40}^{41}\left(\frac{1}{\theta}\right)e^{-t/\theta}dt = e^{-40/T} - e^{41/T}.$$

With current (2004) prevalence rates, average expected life for the entire population is about 77.8, which indicates that the probability at birth of dying between the ages of 40 and 41 is 0.007581.[6] If 1966 prevalence rates persisted, the population expected lifetime would be 76.6, a difference of about 1.2 years. This means that the average probability that an individual selected at random dies between 40 and 41 would fall by 0.000054514. If willingness to pay for one ten-thousandth drop in the probability of death over the course of 1 year ranges between $400 and $900, with a population of 300 million, the annual value of this drop lies between 313 to 704 billion dollars, which is quite close to earlier estimates. These amounts are between 7 and 16 percent of measured GDP, which in 2004 was $4.4 trillion.

In addition to the value to the current population, value can also be calculated for individuals born in the present and future. In any one year the total discounted value of extending life by L years is approximately V. If the total cohort size is C_0 then the total present value to the cohort of extending life by L years is VC_0. If the rate of population increase is g, then the value of extended life to the cohort t at time t is $VC_0(1 + g)^t$. The present discounted value of this is:

$$\frac{VC_0(1 + g)^t}{(1 + r)^t} = VC_0\left(\frac{1 + g}{1 + r}\right)^t.$$

Adding over time and taking the present value gives:

$$\sum_{t=0}^{\infty} VC_0\left(\frac{1 + g}{1 + r}\right)^t \approx VC_0\frac{1}{r - g}.$$

Using the Nordhaus figure that an increase in life expectancy of 1 year has an annual value of $900, the addition to income that arises from the increase in life expectancy of 1.2 years was $1,080. Using an interest rate of r equal to 3 percent, the present value of this annual increase in income is $36,000. The current number of live births in the United States is about 4,000,000 and this increases about 1.7 percent per year. Using the formula above, the total discounted value is therefore $11.1 trillion but the annualized amount is about $0.33 trillion. This annualized amount is in line with the estimates for the current population.

4   The value of tobacco control

In 1983, smoking prevalence was 32.1 percent and in 2004 prevalence was 20.9. Starting in the 1980s, tobacco control was much more vigorously pursued.[7] More than half of the total decline in prevalence between 1965 and 2004 occurs after 1983, suggesting that perhaps more than half of the total decline in prevalence over 40 years is attributable to tobacco control measures. If we assume that this is so, then 47 percent of the decline between 1966 and 2004 arises primarily from the informational content of the 1964 Surgeon General's Report and similar documents, and 53 percent arises from more vigorous tobacco control. This means that the annual value of the information revealed by researchers on the health consequences of smoking is roughly 0.18 to 0.28 trillion dollars with the balance, 0.21 to 0.32 trillion dollars arising from tobacco control measures.

5   Limitations and scope for further research

These estimates are obviously back of the envelope, crude calculations with many shortcomings. The research challenge is to correct for these various shortcomings and compute a more refined, defensible estimate of value of the decline in smoking prevalence. Some of these adjustments involve more refined epidemiological calculation which takes into account the more complicated effects of smoking cessation on length of life. Other adjustments should be made for longstanding socioeconomic trends that tend, on net, to reduce smoking. There are large-scale models (SIMSMOKE comes to mind) that allow for the impact of various tobacco control measures on prevalence and life expectancy to be simulated. These simulations presumably control for underlying trends and allow for the interaction of policies, allowing more careful calculation of the impact of tobacco control measures on prevalence. There are also interesting and subtle endogeneity issues that should be accounted for in a thorough analysis. We discuss briefly each of these issues in turn before concluding.

We have assumed that all current non-smokers have the life expectancy profile of never-smokers, but some of the current non-smokers are in fact ex-smokers. In fact in 2006 there were 45.3 million adult smokers but 45.7 million ex-smokers; the remaining 127.8 million adults were never-smokers. It takes some time, however, after cessation before an ex-smoker's expected lifetime becomes similar to that of a never-smoker; and in the case of older smokers who quit, life expectancy always remains lower than never-smokers. This means that using current prevalence rates will overstate the gains in life expectancy attributable to lower prevalence to the current population. The gains from a particular intervention also depend on the age distribution of the population and our estimates are not age adjusted. On the other hand, the median population is about 37 years, which is the age when the health consequences of smoking begin to appear, which suggests that age adjustment may not have a large affect on the monetary value of lower smoking prevalence.

Occasionally, there are references to the notion that economic consequences of smoking are generated not solely because of the change in mean expected lifetime but because smoking increases the variance of lifetime (this is also said of cancers). While much of the research on the value of medical advances has focused on expected life, an interesting question is the role that changes in standard deviation is playing in the value of health advances. Research would focus on determining the value of a reduction in the variance of lifetime, holding expected lifetime constant, that is, to evaluate the value of mean preserving spreads of the survival function S. Changes in the survival function (S in Section 3) typically imply changes in expected life, but also alter higher moments and more generally the

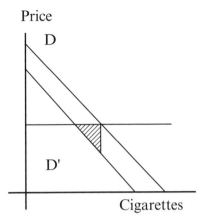

Figure 19.1   Traditional deadweight loss calculation

age distribution of death. Currently, the standard deviation of lifetime is about 16.5 years, which means that 84 percent of deaths occur after the age of 63; Murphy and Topel (2003b) note that in 1900, 18 percent of all deaths occurred before the age of one.

The conventional approach to measuring benefits and the change in benefits is to calculate consumer surplus along with changes in consumer surplus. While this approach is sensible for measuring the impact of price changes when a partial equilibrium approach is warranted, it is not clear how it captures the value of changes in information. One approach is that suggested by Dixit and Norman (1978). Their work was originally motivated by the problem of measuring the welfare impact of advertising. Advertising can be viewed as activity that alters consumers' information about the product and its attributes. We briefly outline the way their approach could measure the value of new health information concerning a particular consumer good.

Traditional benefit analysis would typically use the full information demand curve to determine the deadweight loss from the failure to be fully informed (Figure 19.1). Individuals who underestimate the health consequences of smoking have demand curve D; when they are fully informed their demand curve shifts down to D′. The downward shift of the demand for cigarettes reflects that the perceived benefits of smoking are lower when accurate information about the health consequences of smoking is obtained. Without this information, cigarettes are regarded as benign and the quantity consumed is higher. The deadweight loss from overconsumption is the hatched area in Figure 19.1.

The optimal amount of smoking (assuming consumer sovereignty)

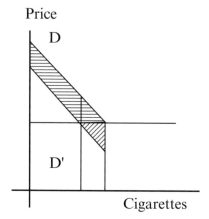

Figure 19.2   Alternative deadweight loss calculation

is where the supply curve (which is also the average and marginal cost curve) intersects the demand curve D'. The area under the demand curve is the consumer surplus generated when health consequences are correctly perceived by consumers. The original consumption level determined by the demand curve D is higher than the full information and presumably efficient level determined by D', indicating that in the absence of information about the bad effects of smoking, too many cigarettes are consumed. The loss that arises from this overconsumption is the amount given by the hatched rhombus in Figure 19.2.

It can be argued that this estimate may not fully reflect the value of additional information, that is, willingness to pay for information about the true health consequences of smoking. A method of dealing with this issue is suggested by the Dixit and Norman (1978) approach to the welfare analysis of advertising. Their analysis suggests looking at the change in consumer surplus using both the demand curve for cigarettes before the information is available and the demand curve for tobacco when information about the health consequences of smoking is released. Using the initial demand curve the change in consumer surplus is the two hatched regions in Figure 19.2.

These are upper and lower estimates which is standard for the Dixit–Norman approach. If the cost of tobacco control is below the lower range, then tobacco control and tobacco research have made a net contribution to social welfare. If these costs are higher than the upper limit, then tobacco control costs do not pass a standard cost–benefit test. The third possibility is that costs lie between the lower and upper limit so that the approach is inconclusive.

An interesting and unexplored issue is the relationship between this framework and the approach used by Murphy and Topel (2003) and Nordhaus (2003). Presumably the value of the changes calculated in a partial equilibrium demand and supply framework should roughly match up with the estimated computed with the life-cycle approach of Murphy and Topel, and Nordhaus. The actual analytical links between the two frameworks are not immediately obvious so further theoretical research is required to fill in the gaps that connect the value of changes in life expectancy and changes in the demand for cigarettes, as consumer information about smoking health consequences becomes known. If set out in sufficient detail, this framework would allow a comparison of the value of information derived from changes in the demand for cigarettes and the value of changes in life expectancy that arise from acquiring information about the health consequences of tobacco. If the estimates are dissimilar, it may signal that one or both approaches are flawed; for example, the consumer surplus approach is a partial equilibrium approach that may not allow for important feedback effects.

Prevalence and education levels are closely correlated: prevalence falls with more education. The prevalence rate for those with a general equivalency diploma degree is 46.0 percent, 23.8 for those with a only a high school diploma but 9.6 percent for those with a BA and 6.9 for those with graduate training.[8] The standard human capital interpretation is that there are complementarities between the stock of educational human capital and health human capital. Educational attainment has been rising throughout the twentieth century and presumably will continue to rise in the current century. For example, in 1965, only 12.5 percent of the population had a college degree while in 2006, 28.4 percent had a college degree or more education. More relevantly, 22.4 percent had at least a college degree in 1983 so that the college educated rose by 6 percentage points over the last 20 years. This demographic change alone will tend to reduce prevalence rates. There are other demographic factors to take into account. Prevalence rates tend to fall with age, so that changes in the age composition will affect overall prevalence. The age composition in turn reflects fertility rates but also immigration levels (immigrants tend to be below the median population age).

Major tobacco control policies widely used in the US include higher excise tax rates, clean indoor air laws and state funding for comprehensive tobacco control programs. Tobacco control policies also include advertising restrictions, as well as counter advertising, education and cessation services. The impact of these policy tools varies. For example, because of smuggling and cross-border shopping, the efficacy of any one state's excise taxes depends on the excise taxes imposed by neighboring jurisdictions.

There are interactions between tobacco control policies; cessation services are more effective if stricter clean air laws are implemented. In addition, the efficacy of policies depends on the demographic features of the population and how they are changing over time. To take into account all of these second-order and feedback effects requires complicated modeling and large-scale simulations. The tools to do this are available and this is a logical next step in this sort of analysis.

The 'new' health economics emphasizes health as an investment in human capital. More recent approaches also stress that health behaviors and expenditures are part of an evolving dynamic system in which there are a large number of feedback effects. Feedback effects arise because of complementarities between the inputs that affect health outcomes. Advancement in the treatment of any one health problem may change the rate of return to improvements in some other health problem; thus an initial change may induce changes in research directions that give rise to additional improvements. For example, the eradication of infectious diseases has increased length of life; it has also shifted the production function that relates inputs to health outcomes. As the length of life becomes longer, morbidity and mortality outcomes are more closely linked with health behaviors such as amount of exercise, controlling weight, correct diet and limiting substance abuse. An implication of this framework is that health behaviors in general and smoking prevalence in particular may be endogenously determined by length of life and medical technology. In 1920, life expectancy at birth was under 60 years, so that expected life years lost due to smoking were limited. As life expectancy has increased, the expected life years lost due to smoking has increased, so that the opportunity cost of smoking has gone up, which should lead to a reduction in smoking prevalence, all else equal. This indeed happened.

Nordhaus (2003) has broken up change in the overall increase of average life expectancy and attributed portions of the change to various health and medical innovations. Eliminating malnutrition and upgrading hygiene, essentially providing clean safe water and modern sewer systems, plays the largest role in expanding life expectancy from 1890 to 1940. The availability of antibiotics and other medical advances has also significantly lengthened life expectancy since the Second World War. Changes in life expectancy attributable to these changes, however, have increased the return to never smoking as measured by increased life expectancy. When life expectancy is 50 years, lifetime smoking reduces life expectancy by a modest amount primarily because smoking-related illnesses are particularly evident after age 50. When life expectancy for never-smokers is 80, smoking lowers life expectancy by 5.5 years, about 7 percent.

Higher incomes also raise the value of this life extension that accrues to never-smokers. Taken together, these changes raise the return to never-smoking, so reductions in prevalence will be larger in societies where the never-smoker's life expectancy is greater. This suggests that prevalence rates in less-developed countries will, all else equal, be higher because the life expectancy in general is lower. Addressing problems of nutrition and hygiene and ensuring access to antibiotics will have an unintended impact on prevalence, leading to its reduction.

Models of rational addiction suggest that higher discount rates increase the propensity to acquire addictive and dangerous habits. The reasoning is quite clear. Since the negative consequences of addictive behavior lie in the future, individuals who heavily discount the future consequences will view the cost of addictive behavior as lower than a person who weighs the present and future costs more equally. Typically, most of the benefits are in the present and near term, so if costs are lower, the net benefit, benefits minus costs, is more likely to be positive. If this is so, the individual will begin or continue smoking. As average lifetime increases, personal discount rates may also be affected. Becker and Mulligan (1997) have argued that time preference is endogenous; a low life expectancy leads to higher rates of time preference. Hence other changes in health infrastructure will lower time preference rates. This in turn leads to lower initiation and prevalence rates – standard rational addiction models predict that those with high rates of time preference are more likely, all else equal, to smoke.

6 Conclusion

Our rough results indicate that understanding the health consequences of cigarette smoking had a significant impact on national health outcomes and on average life expectancy. The increase in life expectancy due to the drop in prevalence has an annual value that lies between $300 and $700 billion per year, numbers that seem fairly robust to the exact method of calculation. As we pointed out, however, these estimates have considerable scope for refinement, which would be a major undertaking. The endogeneity mechanisms proposed by Becker and others are certainly plausible, but their empirical importance is unproven. Attempting to gauge the actual importance of these endogenous effects remains a major challenge.

Notes

1. Measured prevalence rates differ across surveys. The 1966 rate of 42.2 is from the Adult Use of Tobacco Survey (AUTS). Though both studies used in-person interviews, the 1966 National Health Interview Survey (NHIS) gives a slightly lower prevalence rate of 40.2 for 1966. Using this lower prevalence will of course change our estimates, making them somewhat lower, but the basic conclusions remain. These figures were taken from 1989 Surgeon General's Report *Reducing the Health Consequences of Smoking:*

25 Years of Progress. Finally, published prevalence tables are usually age adjusted so that the reported rate corresponds to constant age distribution of some particular year (year 2000, for example). So on the Centre for Disease Control and Preventions (CDC) website, the NHIS 1965 prevalence rate is reported at 42.4; see www.cdc.gov/tobacco/data_statistics/tables/adult/table_2.htm, accessed 10 February 2008.

2. Information about the adverse health consequences of smoking had been dribbling out throughout the 1950s and was widely speculated upon well before the Surgeon General's Report. There were articles in the Readers Digest in the early 1950s that anticipated the conclusions of the 1964 Surgeon General's Report.

3. Nordhaus provides growth rate estimates while Murphy and Topel state an explicit amount; we use the Nordhaus growth rate estimates of 'health income' (1.7 percent annually) to extend the Murphy–Topel estimates to the year 2004. Using these same growth rate estimates, the total increase in health income can be inferred, and doing so gives a figure of $3.0 trillion annually.

4. Prevalence rates are from the CDC website, www.cdc.gov/tobacco/data_statistics/tables/adult/table_2.htm, accessed 1 February 2008.

5. Life expectancy data come from United States Life Tables, National Vital Statistic Reports, Volume 55, Number 17 (August 21, 2007) and the CDC website.

6. The United States Life Tables for 2003 indicate that this probability is 0.002308, so the level estimate is the right order of magnitude but off by a factor of 3.

7. During the period from 1966 to 1983, prevalence fell 0.62 percentage points per year while during the period from 1983 to 2004, prevalence fell 0.53 percentage points annually.

8. These figures come from the CDC's Morbidity and Mortality Weekly Report, 'Cigarette Smoking Among Adults – United States 2006' **56**(44), 1157–61 (November 9, 2007)

References

Becker, G.S., (2007), 'Health as human capital: synthesis and extensions', *Oxford Economic Papers*, **59**, 379–410.

Becker, G.S. and Mulligan, C.B. (1997), 'The endogenous determination of time preference', *Quarterly Journal of Economics*, **112**, 729–58.

Cutler, D.M., and Kadiyala, S. (2003), 'The return to biomedical research: treatment and behavioral effects', in Murphy and Topel (eds) (2003a), pp. 110–62.

Dixit, A. and Norman, V., (1978), 'Advertising and welfare', *Bell Journal of Economics*, **9** (1) (Spring), 1–17.

Murphy, K.M. and Topel, R.H. (eds) (2003a), *Measuring the Gains From Medical Research*, Chicago: University of Chicago Press.

Murphy, K.M. and Topel, R.H. (2003b), 'Introduction', in Murphy and Topel (eds) (2003a), pp. 1–80.

Murphy, K.M. and R. Topel (2003c), 'The economic value of medical research', in Murphy and Topel (eds) (2003a), pp. 41–73.

Nordhaus, W.D. (2003), 'The health of nations: the contribution of improved health to living standards', in Murphy and Topel (eds) (2003a), pp. 9–40.

Index